Microsoft® Outlook
365 Complete

IN PRACTICE

2019

©Chris Ryan/Getty Images

Microsoft® Outlook
365 Complete

IN PRACTICE

2019

Michael-Brian
Ogawa
UNIVERSITY OF HAWAII

Randy Nordell
AMERICAN RIVER COLLEGE

Mc
Graw
Hill

©Chris Ryan/Getty Images

MICROSOFT OUTLOOK 365 COMPLETE: IN PRACTICE, 2019

Published by McGraw-Hill Education, 2 Penn Plaza, New York, NY 10121. Copyright © 2020 by McGraw-Hill
Education. All rights reserved. Printed in the United States of America. Previous editions © 2017. No part
of this publication may be reproduced or distributed in any form or by any means, or stored in a database or
retrieval system, without the prior written consent of McGraw-Hill Education, including, but not limited to, in
any network or other electronic storage or transmission, or broadcast for distance learning.

Some ancillaries, including electronic and print components, may not be available to customers outside the
United States.

This book is printed on acid-free paper.

3 4 5 6 7 8 9 QVS 26 25 24 23 22

ISBN 978-1-260-81869-7 (bound edition)
MHID 1-260-81869-1 (bound edition)
ISBN 978-1-260-81830-7 (loose-leaf edition)
MHID 1-260-81830-6 (loose-leaf edition)

Managing Director: *Terry Schiesl*
Portfolio Manager: *Wyatt Morris*
Product Developers: *Alan Palmer*
Marketing Manager: *Corban Quigg*
Content Project Manager: *Harvey Yep*
Buyer: *Susan K. Culbertson*
Design: *Egzon Shaqiri*
Content Licensing Specialist: *Shawntel Schmitt*
Cover Image: *©Deklofenak/Getty Images*
Compositor: *SPi Global*

Library of Congress Control Number: 2019945006

dedication

To Nicole, I owe my deepest gratitude to you for encouraging me throughout this endeavor. Your love and support made this project successful, as you were always there to keep me moving forward regardless of what you had on your plate. I can hardly wait to spend more time with you!

—M.B. Ogawa

Bob and Lanita, thank you for generously allowing me to use the cabin where I completed much of the work on this project. Don and Jennie, thank you for teaching me the value of hard work and encouraging me throughout the years. Kelsey and Taylor, thank you for keeping me young at heart. Kelly, thank you for your daily love, support, and encouragement. I could not have done this without you. I'm looking forward to spending more time together on our tandem!

—Randy Nordell

brief contents

contents

about the authors

MICHAEL-BRIAN OGAWA, Ph.D.

UNIVERSITY OF HAWAII

Michael-Brian Ogawa, "M.B.," is a faculty member in the Information and Computer Sciences Department at the University of Hawaii at Manoa. He has been an educator for over a decade and worked with students ranging from elementary school through graduate school. M.B. holds a bachelor's degree in Business Administration, master's degrees in Library and Information Science and Educational Technology, and a doctor of philosophy in education from the University of Hawaii at Manoa. M.B. co-authored *Microsoft Outlook 2007: A Professional Approach, Microsoft Office Outlook 2013 Complete: In Practice, Microsoft Office Outlook 2016 Complete: In Practice*, published articles on student academic success and school librarianship, and speaks at a variety of conferences. In his spare time, he enjoys his family, baseball, running, and reading.

RANDY NORDELL, Ed.D.

AMERICAN RIVER COLLEGE

Dr. Randy Nordell is a professor of business technology at American River College in Sacramento, California. He has been an educator for over 25 years and has taught at the high school, community college, and university levels. He holds a bachelor's degree in business administration from California State University, Stanislaus, a single subject teaching credential from Fresno State University, a master's degree in education from Fresno Pacific University, and a doctorate in education from Argosy University. Randy is the lead author of the *Microsoft Office 365: In Practice, Microsoft Office 2016: In Practice,* and *Microsoft Office 2013: In Practice* series of texts. He is also the author of *101 Tips for Online Course Success* and *Microsoft Outlook 2010.* Randy speaks regularly at conferences on the integration of technology into the curriculum. When not teaching and writing, he enjoys spending time with his family, cycling, skiing, swimming, backpacking, and enjoying the California weather and terrain.

preface

What We're About

We wrote *Microsoft Outlook 365 Complete: In Practice, 2019 Edition* to meet the diverse needs of both students and instructors. Our approach focuses on presenting Outlook topics in a logical and structured manner, teaching concepts in a way that reinforces learning with practice projects that are transferrable, relevant, and engaging. Our pedagogy and content are based on the following beliefs.

Students Need to Learn and Practice Transferable Skills

Students must be able to transfer the concepts and skills learned in the text to a variety of projects, not simply follow steps in a textbook. Our material goes beyond the instruction of many texts. In our content, students practice the concepts in a variety of current and relevant projects *and* are able to transfer skills and concepts learned to different projects in the real world. To further increase the transferability of skills learned, this text is integrated with SIMnet so students also practice skills and complete projects in an online environment.

Your Curriculum Drives the Content

The curriculum in the classroom should drive the content of the text, not the other way around. This book is designed to allow instructors and students to cover all the material they need to in order to meet the curriculum requirements of their courses no matter how the courses are structured. *Microsoft Outlook 365 Complete: In Practice, 2019 Edition* teaches the marketable skills that are key to student success. McGraw-Hill's Custom Publishing site, Create, can further tailor the content material to meet the unique educational needs of any school.

Integrated with Technology

Our text provides a fresh and new approach to an Outlook applications course. Topics integrate seamlessly with SIMnet with 1:1 content to help students practice and master concepts and skills using SIMnet's interactive learning philosophy. Projects in SIMnet allow students to practice their skills and receive immediate feedback. This integration with SIMnet meets the diverse needs of students and accommodates individual learning styles. Additional textbook resources found in SIMnet (Resources and Library sections) integrate with the learning management systems that are widely used in many online and onsite courses.

Reference Text

In addition to providing students with an abundance of real-life examples and practice projects, we designed this text to be used as a Microsoft Outlook 365 reference source. The core material, uncluttered with exercises, focuses on real-world use and application. Our text provides clear step-by-step instructions on how readers can apply the various features available in Microsoft Outlook in a variety of contexts. At the same time, users have access to a variety of both online (SIMnet) and textbook practice projects to reinforce skills and concepts. Both SIMnet and this text are updated with the most current Outlook 365 features. For the most current updates, please refer first to SIMnet.

instructor walkthrough

Textbook Learning Approach

Microsoft Outlook 365 Complete: In Practice, 2019 Edition uses the *T.I.P. approach*:

- **T**opic
- **I**nstruction
- **P**ractice

Topic

- Each Office application section begins with foundational skills and builds to more complex topics as the text progresses.
- Topics are logically sequenced and grouped by topics.
- Student Learning Outcomes (SLOs) are thoroughly integrated with and mapped to chapter content, projects, end-of-chapter review, and test banks.
- Reports are available within SIMnet for displaying how students have met these Student Learning Outcomes.

Instruction (How To)

- *How To* guided instructions about chapter topics provide transferable and adaptable instructions.
- Because *How To* instructions are not locked into single projects, this textbook functions as a reference text, not just a point-and-click textbook.
- Chapter content is aligned 1:1 with SIMnet.

Practice (Pause & Practice and End-of-Chapter Projects)

- Within each chapter, integrated Pause & Practice projects (three to five per chapter) reinforce learning and provide hands-on guided practice.
- In addition to Pause & Practice projects, each chapter has nine comprehensive and practical practice projects: Guided Projects (three per chapter), Independent Projects (three per chapter), and Challenge Projects (three per chapter). Additional projects can also be found in the Library or Resources section of SIMnet.
- Pause & Practice and end-of-chapter projects are complete content-rich projects, not small examples lacking context.
- Select auto-graded projects are available in SIMnet.

Chapter Features

All chapters follow a consistent theme and instructional methodology. Below is an example of chapter structure.

Main headings are organized according to the *Student Learning Outcomes (SLOs).*

SLO 1.1 **Working with Outlook**

One of the main features in Outlook is handling email, but personal management software that contains the following fea

- *Email*
- *Calendar*

---

account to send and receive email.

Outlook enables you to create and send email, reply to received e other recipients, save and manage email, and flag and categorize email. sending pictures and other types of computer files to others. Email is an i and business activities, and it is hard to imagine a day without the use of

STUDENT LEARNING OUTCOMES (SLOs)

After completing this chapter, you will be able to:

SLO 1.1 Identify the basic components of Microsoft Outlook (p. O1-

SLO 1.2 Navigate throughout the Outlook environment and identify panes in the Outlook window (p. O1-7).

SLO 1.3 Distinguish between Outlook being used as a stand-alone a Microsoft Exchange environment (p. O1-14).

SLO 1.4 Distinguish between the different types of email accounts email account in Outlook (p. O1-15).

SLO 1.5 Use Outlook to create, send, and receive email (p. O1-17).

SLO 1.6 Use attachments in email (p. O1-29).

SLO 1.7 Differentiate email arrangements and icons (p. O1-34).

SLO 1.8 Explain the importance and process of cleaning up an Inb

A list of Student Learning Outcomes begins each chapter. All chapter content, examples, and practice projects are organized according to the chapter SLOs.

CASE STUDY

Throughout this book you have the opportunity to put into practice the application features that you are learning. Each chapter begins with a case study that introduces you to the Pause & Practice projects in the chapter. These Pause & Practice projects give you a chance to apply and practice key skills. Each chapter contains three to five Pause & Practice projects.

Central Sierra Insurance (CSI) is a multi-office insurance company that handles all lines of commercial and personal insurance policies. As a thriving and growing insurance agency,

CSI encourages its employees to be active in community organizations and events.

Pause & Practice 1-1: You set up an email account using Microsoft Outlook. You will need an email account that is provided by your school or a free email service such as Gmail.com or Outlook.com.

Pause & Practice 1-2: You send an email message to your instructor and use the Cc function to send a copy to yourself. You also read the message, reply to it, and print it for your records.

Pause & Practice 1-3: You reply to a message with an email attachment. You also forward the message to your instructor as an attachm

The *Case Study* for each chapter is a scenario that establishes the theme for the entire chapter. Chapter content, examples, figures, Pause & Practice projects, SIMnet skills, and projects throughout the chapter are closely related to this case study content. The three to five Pause & Practice projects in each chapter build upon one another and address key case study themes.

How To instructions enhance transferability of skills with concise steps and screen shots.

type of email account the recipient has, text formatting might not be visible to the recipient.

Send an Email

Once you select your recipients and type the subject and body of the email, you are ready to send the email message. Click the **Send** button to the left of the *To* and *Cc* buttons and your email message will be sent. A copy of it will be automatically saved in the *Sent Items* folder in your *Folder* list.

▶ **HOW TO: Send an Email Message**

1. Click the **New Email** button [*Home* tab, *New* group]. A new email message opens in a new window.
2. Click the **To** button and select the names or email addresses from the *Select Names* dialog box.
   - You can also add recipients to the *Cc* and *Bcc* fields.
3. Click **OK**. The email addresses will appear in the *To, Cc,* and/or *Bcc* fields.
4. Type a brief subject in the *Subject* field.
5. Type a brief message in the body of the message. Remember to always include your name in the body of the email.

How To instructions are easy-to-follow concise steps. Screen shots and other figures fully illustrate How To topics.

Students can complete hands-on exercises in either the Office application or in SIMnet.

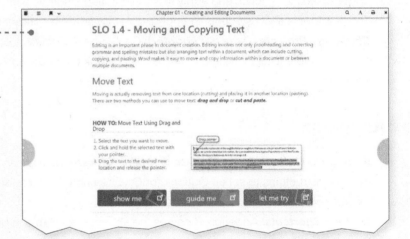

a chance to apply and practice key skills. *Each chapter contains three to five Pause & Practice projects.*

Central Sierra Insurance (CSI) is a multi-office insurance company that handles all lines of commercial and personal insurance policies. As a thriving and growing insurance agency,

Pause & Practice 1-2: You send an email message to your instructor and use the *Cc* function to send a copy to yourself. You also read the message, reply to it, and print it for your records.

Pause & Practice 1-3: You reply to a message with an email attachment. You also forward the

Pause & Practice projects, which each cover two to three of the student learning outcomes in the chapter, provide students with the opportunity to review and practice skills and concepts. Every chapter contains three to five Pause & Practice projects.

▶ MORE INFO

Chapter 2 covers the special email features available in Outlook. Chapter 6 discusses the use of rules for handling both incoming and outgoing email, and chapter 7 provides the reader with information about setting up the different types of email accounts.

More Info provides readers with additional information about chapter content.

Another Way notations teach alternative methods of accomplishing the same task or feature, such as keyboard shortcuts.

ANOTHER WAY

In a new email message, click the **Options** tab and then click the **Bcc** button in the *Show Fields* group. *Bcc* recipients can now be selected by clicking the **Bcc** button (Figure 1-31).

Marginal notations present additional information and alternative methods.

End-of-Chapter Projects

Nine learning projects at the end of each chapter provide additional reinforcement and practice for students. Many of these projects are available in SIMnet for completion and automatic grading.

- **Guided Projects (three per chapter):** Guided Projects provide guided step-by-step instructions to apply Outlook features, skills, and concepts from the chapter. Screen shots guide students through the more challenging tasks. End-of-project screen shots provide a visual of the completed project.
- **Independent Projects (three per chapter):** Independent Projects provide students further opportunities to practice and apply skills, instructing students what to do, but not how to do it. These projects allow students to apply previously learned content in a different context.
- **Challenge Projects (three per chapter):** Challenge Projects are open-ended projects that encourage creativity and critical thinking by integrating Outlook concepts and features into relevant and engaging projects.

Appendix

- **Setting Up Outlook for an On-Site or Online Classroom Environment:** Appendix A includes step-by-step instructions to set up Outlook for On-Site and Online classroom environments using an Exchange server or Microsoft 365 Admin Center.
- **Outlook Shortcuts:** Appendix B covers the shortcuts available in Microsoft Outlook. Information is in a table format for easy access and reference.
- **Outlook Quick Reference Guide:** Appendix C covers actions, alternative methods, and keyboard shortcuts for tasks in Outlook.
- **Exchange Server versus Stand-Alone Usage:** Appendix D includes a detailed description of differences between using Outlook with and Exchange Server and as a Stand-Alone application.
- **Quick Tips and Troubleshooting:** Appendix E covers tips to improve user efficiency and troubleshooting instructions when features do not work as expected.

Additional Resources
in SIMnet

Students and instructors can find the following resources in the Library or Resources sections in SIMnet.

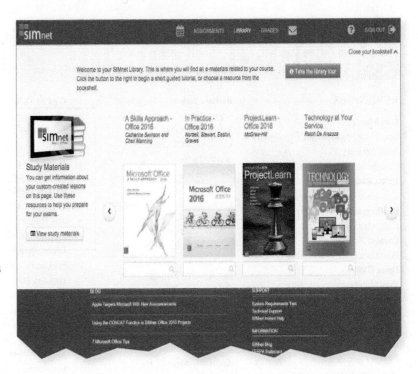

Student Resources

- **Data Files:** Files contain start files for all Pause & Practice, Capstone, and end-of-chapter projects.
- **SIMnet Resources:** Resources provide getting started and informational handouts for instructors and students.
- **Check for Understanding:** A combination of multiple choice, fill-in, matching, and short answer questions are available at the end of each SIMbook chapter in SIMnet to assist students in their review of the skills and concepts covered in the chapter.

Capstone Projects

- **Integrating Applications:** Projects provide students with the opportunity to learn, practice, and transfer skills using multiple Office applications.
- **Integrating Skills:** Projects provide students with a comprehensive and integrated review of all of the topics covered in each application (Word, Excel, Access, PowerPoint and Outlook). Available in individual application texts.

Appendices

- The appendices include details about the differences between the use of an Exchange server and stand-alone use of Outlook. Instructions for setting up user accounts in an Exchange server or the Microsoft Admin center are included. Two reference guides are included in table format to quickly reference actions, alternative methods, and keyboard shortcuts to tasks. A troubleshooting guide is included to help resolve common errors.

Instructor Resources

- **Instructor's Manual:** An Instructor's Manual provides teaching tips and lecture notes aligned with the PowerPoint presentations for each chapter.
- **Test Bank:** The extensive test bank integrates with learning management systems (LMSs) such as Blackboard, WebCT, Desire2Learn, and Moodle.
- **PowerPoint Presentations:** PowerPoint presentations for each chapter can be used in onsite course formats for lectures or can be uploaded to LMSs.
- **SIMnet Resources:** These resources provide getting started and informational handouts for instructors.
- **Solution Files:** Files contain solutions for all Pause & Practice, Capstone, Check for Understanding, and end-of-chapter projects.

acknowledgments

REVIEWERS

Lori Mueller
Southeast Missouri State University

Scott Straub
College of Western Idaho

Philip Reaves
University of Western Georgia

B. Bhagyavati
Columbus State

Carolyn E. Johnson
Northern Oklahoma College

Dona Gibbons
Troy University

Denise Sullivan
Westchester Community College

Suzanne Marks
Bellevue College

Phyllis Fleming
Middlesex County College

Salli DiBartolo
Eastern Florida State College

Teresa Roberson
Northwest-Shoals Community
College

Amy Chataginer
Mississippi Gulf Coast Community
College

Dr. Lucinda Stanley
Wor-Wic Community College

Bill Dorin
Indiana University Northwest

Anita Laird
Schoolcraft College

Sue Bajt
Harper College

Ralph Argiento
Guilford Technical Community
College

Annette D. Rakowski
Bergen Community College

Beth Deinert
Southeast Community College

Jo Stephens
University of Arkansas Community
College Batesville

Terry Beachy
Garrett College

Vincent Kayes
Mount Saint Mary College,
Newburgh

Kimberly Madsen
Kellogg Community College

Nicolas Rouse
Phoenix College

Barbara Hearn
Community College of Philadelphia

Terribeth Gordon
University of Toledo

Stacy Martin
Southwestern Illinois College

Dr. Hamid Nemati
University of North Carolina at
Greensboro

Beverly Amer
Northern Arizona University

Michael L. Matuszek
San Antonio College

Sandra Metcalf
Grayson College

David Cook
Stephen F. Austin State University

Donnie W. Collins
Andrew College

Frank Whittle
Dutchess Community College

Robert LaRocca
Keiser University

Adnan Turkey
DeVry University

Sheryl S. Bulloch
Columbia Southern University

Richard Flores
Citrus College

Dmitriy Chulkov
Indiana University Kokomo

Mary Locke
Greenville Technical College

Sherrie Drye
North Carolina A&T State
University

Andrew Smith
Marian University Indianapolis

Crystal Theaker
Chandler-Gilbert Community
College

Pam Cummings
Minnesota State Community and
Technical Colleg

Tina LePage
Chandler-Gilbert Community
College

Darenda Kersey
Black River Technical College

Amy Rutledge
Oakland University

Brian Fox
Santa Fe College

Trey Cherry
Edgecombe Community College

Gigi N. Delk
The University of Texas at Tyler

Dr. Richard A. Warren
Vernon College

Debra Morgan
Eastern Washington University.

Pamela Bilodeau
Olympic College

Jim Hughes
Northern Kentucky University

Diane Shingledecker
Portland Community College

Hyo-Joo Han
Georgia Southern University

Becky McAfee
Hillsborough Community College
Home

Karen Donham
University of Arkansas at
Monticello

Craig Bradley
Shawnee Community College

Elodie Billionniere
Miami Dade College

Joan Rogers
Hillsborough Community College

Genalin F. Umstetter
Delta College

Michael Kato
University of Hawaii

Ann Konarski
St. Clair County Community
College

Dr. Mark W. Huber
University of Georgia

Kathleen Morris
The University of Alabama

Rebecca Leveille
American River College

Dory Eddy
Colorado Christian University

Masoud Naghedolfeizi
Fort Valley State University

Joe Vargas
Santa Barbara Business College

Donna Kamen
Truckee Meadows Community
College

David Sanford
Northwood University Home

Ken Werner
Alaska Vocational Technical Center

Gigi Simonsen
Northeast Community College

Paula Gregory
Yavapai College

Mordechai Adelman
Touro College

Ron Oler
Ivy Tech Community College of
Indiana

Sandra LaFevers
Joliet Junior College

Sherilyn Reynolds
San Jacinto College

Melissa Nemeth
Indiana University

Barbara Garrell
Delaware County Community
College

Astrid Todd
Guilford Technical Community
College

Deedee Flax
Dodge City Community College

Elizabeth P. Sigman
Georgetown University

Preston Clark
Cornell University

Sara Rutledge
Mount Aloysius College

Robyn Barrett
St. Louis Community College

William Neiheisel
Gwinnett College

Sheila Gionfriddo
Luzerne County Community
College

Teodoro Llallire
Fairleigh Dickinson University

Tracy Driscoll
Bishop State Community College

Sam McCall
St. Philip's College

Joyce King
Bay College

John Schrage
Southern Illinois University
Edwardsville

John Maloney
Miami Dade College

Lisa Friesen
Southwestern Oklahoma State
University

Shelley Ota
University of Hawaii

Heidi Eaton
Elgin Community College

LaVaughn Hart
Las Positas College

Sandy Keeter
Seminole State College

Kathy J. Schaefer
Southwest Minnesota State University

Edward Hall
Seward County Community College

Saiid Ganjalizadeh
The Catholic University of America

Melinda Norris
Coker College

Phillip Dickson
Black River Technical College

Kathy Powell-Case
Colorado Northwestern Community College

Marianne Daugharthy
College of Western Idaho

Ann Taff
Tulsa Community College

Lydia Slater
Rock Valley College

Seyed Roosta
Albany State University

Pamela Silvers
Asheville-Buncombe Technical Community College

Phillip Davis
Del Mar College

Logan Phillips
Tulsa Community College

Dianne Hill
Jackson College

Jeff Harper
Indiana State University

Carla K. Draffen
West Kentucky Community & Technical College

Colin Onita
San Jose State University

N. T. Izuchi
Quinsigamond Community College

Camille Rogers
Georgia Southern University

Luy Parker
California State University, Northridge

Homer Sharafi
Prince George's Community College

Bill Courter
Jackson College

Robert Wardzala
University of Findlay

Lindsey Huber
Northern State University

David Rosenthal
Seton Hall University

Sandro Marchegiani
University of Pittsburgh

Linda Johnsonius
Murray State University

Barbara Bracken
Wilkes University

Marie Hassinger
Susquehanna University

Rich Cacace
Pensacola State College

Arcola Sullivan
Copiah-Lincoln Community College

Angela Mott
Northeast Mississippi Community College

Tony Hunnicutt
College of the Ouachitas

Stephen D. Ross
Mississippi Delta Community College

Alex Morgan
De Anza College

Aaron Ferguson
University of Maryland University College

Patricia White
University of Maryland University College

Anne Acker
Jacksonville University

Pam Shields
Mt. Hood Community College

Nancy Lilly
Central Alabama Community College

Mandy Reininger
Chemeketa Community College

Alison Rampersad
Lynn University

Jeanine Preuss
South Puget Sound Community College

Timothy J. Lloyd
University of Maryland University College

Betsy Boardwine
Virginia Western Community College

Meg Murray
Kennesaw State University

Lynne Lyon
Durham College

Peter Meggison
Massasoit Community College

Sujing Wang
Lamar University

Alla Zakharova
University of South Alabama

Rachel E. Hinton
SUNY Broome Community College

Rhoda A. M. James
Citrus College

Gena Casas
Florida State College at Jacksonville

James D. Powell
College of the Desert

Sue Joiner
Tarleton State University

Dawn Nelson
University of Dubuque

Carlos Jimenez
El Paso Community College

Diane Smith
Henry Ford College

Steven Brennan
Jackson College

Mehran Basiratmand
Florida Atlantic University

Sharolyn Sayers
Milwaukee Area Technical College

Charles Wunker
Webber International University

Doreen Palucci
Wilmington University

Kristy McAuliffe
San Jacinto College

Rob Lemelin
Eastern Washington University

Nancy Severe
Northern Virginia Community College

Julie Becker
Three Rivers Community College

David Childress
Kentucky Community & Technical College System

Carolyn Kuehne
Utah Valley University

Carolyn Carvalho
Kent State University

Irene Joos
La Roche College

Dr. Shayan Mirabi
American InterContinental University

Zhizhang Shen
Plymouth State University

Kirk Atkinson
Western Kentucky University: WKU

Nisheeth Agrawal
Calhoun Community College

Dr. Bernard Ku
Austin Community College

Jennifer Michaels
Lenoir-Rhyne University

William Barrett
Iowa Western Community College

Naomi Johnson
Dickinson State University

Gilliean Lee
Lander University

Clem Lundie
San Jose City College

Cynthia C. Nitsch
MiraCosta College

Beth Cantrell
Central Baptist College

Bernice Eng
Brookdale Community College

Paul Weaver
Bossier Parish Community College

William Penfold
Jamestown Community College

Kathrynn Hollis-Buchanan
University of Alaska

Carmen Morrison
North Central State College

Marie Campbell
Idaho State University

Jpann G. Becento
Navajo Technical University

Annette Yauney
Herkimer College

Judy Jernigan
Tyler Junior College

Elise Marshall
University of North Florida

Karen Waddell
Butler Community College

Allison Bryant
Howard University

William Spangler
Duquesne University

Henry Bradford
Massasoit Community College

Julie Haar
Alexandria Technical & Community College

Martha Balachandran
Middle Tennessee State University

Cheryl Jordan
San Juan College

Mary Kennedy
College of DuPage

Pengtao Li
California State University Stanislaus

Odemaris Valdivia
Santa Monica College

Joyce Quade
Saddleback College

Pam Houston
Oglala Lakota College

Marc Isaacson
Augsburg University

Penny Cypert
Tarrant County College

Manuel T. Uy
Peralta Colleges

Bonnie Smith
Fresno City College

Brenda Killingsworth
East Carolina University

Ember Mitchell
Dixie State University

Emily Holliday
Campbell University

Holly Bales
International Business College in Indianapolis

Elizabeth Sykes
Golden West College

TECHNICAL EDITORS

Karen May
Blinn College

Andrea Nevill
College of Western Idaho

Richard Finn
Moraine Valley Community College

Chris Anderson
North Central Michigan College

Gena Casas
Florida State College

Leon Blue
Pensacola State College

Amie Mayhall
Olney Central College

Patrick Doran
University of Wisconsin Milwaukeex

Thank you to the wonderful team at McGraw-Hill for your confidence in us and support throughout this project. Alan, Wyatt, Tiffany, Corban, Debbie, Harvey, and Julianna, we thoroughly enjoy working with you all! A special thanks to Debbie Hinkle for her thorough and insightful review of the series. Thank you to all of the reviewers and technical editors for your expertise and invaluable insight, which helped shape this book.

—Randy, Kathleen, Annette, Pat, and M.B.

Windows 10, Office 365/2019, and File Management

CHAPTER OVERVIEW

Microsoft Office 2019 and Windows 10 introduce many new and enhanced features. Office 2019 includes the Office features added to Office 365 since the release of Office 2016. The integration of Office 2019 and Windows 10 improves file portability and accessibility when you use *OneDrive*, Microsoft's free online cloud storage. Office 2019, Office 365, Office Online, Office mobile apps, and Windows 10 enable you to work on tablet computers and smartphones in a consistent working environment that resembles your desktop or laptop computer.

STUDENT LEARNING OUTCOMES (SLOs)

After completing this chapter, you will be able to:

SLO Intro. 1   Explore select features of Windows 10 (p. Intro-2).

SLO Intro. 2   Use basic features of Microsoft Office and navigate the Office working environment (p. Intro-12).

SLO Intro. 3   Create, save, close, and open Office files (p. Intro-19).

SLO Intro. 4   Customize the view and display size in Office applications and work with multiple Office files (p. Intro-28).

SLO Intro. 5   Print, share, and customize Office files (p. Intro-32).

SLO Intro. 6   Use the *Ribbon*, tabs, groups, dialog boxes, task panes, galleries, and the *Quick Access* toolbar (p. Intro-37).

SLO Intro. 7   Use context menus, mini toolbar, keyboard shortcuts, and function keys in Office applications (p. Intro-41).

SLO Intro. 8   Organize and customize Windows folders and Office files (p. Intro-46).

CASE STUDY

Throughout this book, you have the opportunity to practice the application features presented in the text. Each chapter begins with a case study that introduces you to the Pause & Practice projects in the chapter. These Pause & Practice projects give you a chance to apply and practice key skills in a realistic and practical context. Each chapter contains three to five Pause & Practice projects.

American River Cycling Club (ARCC) is a community cycling club that promotes fitness. ARCC members include recreational cyclists who enjoy the exercise and camaraderie as well as competitive cyclists who compete in road, mountain, and cyclocross races throughout the cycling season. In the Pause & Practice projects, you incorporate many of the topics covered in the chapter to create, save, customize, manage, and share Office files.

Pause & Practice Intro-1: Customize the Windows *Start* menu and *Taskbar*, create and save a PowerPoint presentation, create a folder, open and rename an Excel workbook, and use Windows 10 features.

Pause & Practice Intro-2: Modify an existing document, add document properties, customize the *Quick Access* toolbar, export the document as a PDF file, and share the document.

Pause & Practice Intro-3: Copy and rename files, create a folder, move files, create a zipped folder, and rename a zipped folder.

SLO INTRO. 1

Using Windows 10

Windows 10 is an *operating system* that controls computer functions and the working environment. Windows 10 uses the familiar *Windows desktop*, *Taskbar*, and *Start menu*. The Windows operating system enables you to customize the working environment and to install applications (apps), such as Microsoft Office. Visit the *Microsoft Store* to download additional apps similar to how you would add an app to your smartphone. Your *Microsoft account* stores your Microsoft settings, enabling you to download apps from the Microsoft Store, and to connect to Microsoft Office, *OneDrive*, and *Office Online*.

Windows 10

The Windows 10 operating system controls interaction with computer hardware and software applications (apps; also referred to as programs). *Windows 10* utilizes a *Start menu* where you select and open an app. Alternatively, you can open apps using the *Taskbar*, the horizontal bar that displays at the bottom of the Windows desktop. When you log in to Windows 10 using your Microsoft account, your Microsoft account synchronizes your Windows, Office, and *OneDrive* cloud storage among computers.

Microsoft Account

In Windows 10 and Office 365/2019, your files and account settings are portable. In other words, your Office settings and files travel with you and are accessible from different computers. You are not restricted to using a single computer. When you sign in to Windows 10 using your Microsoft account (user name and password), Microsoft uses this information to transfer your Windows and Office 2019 settings to the computer you are using. Different types of Microsoft accounts exist: Personal, Education, and Business.

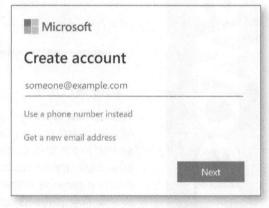

Figure Intro-1 Create a Microsoft account

Your Microsoft account not only signs in to Windows and Office but also to other free Microsoft online services, such as *OneDrive* and *Office Online*. As a student, you can get a free education Microsoft account at https://products.office.com/en-us/student/office-in-education. Also, you can create a free personal Microsoft account at https://signup.live.com (Figure Intro-1).

Windows Desktop and Taskbar

The Windows desktop is the working area of Windows. When you log in to Windows, the desktop displays (Figure Intro-2). The *Taskbar* displays horizontally at the bottom of the desktop. Click an icon on the *Taskbar* to open apps and folders (see Figure Intro-2). Pinning is used to add shortcuts to the *Taskbar* or the *Start* menu. You can pin the *Settings, File Explorer,* and other frequently used apps to the *Taskbar* (see "Customize the Taskbar" later in this section).

Figure Intro-2 Window desktop and *Taskbar*

Start Menu

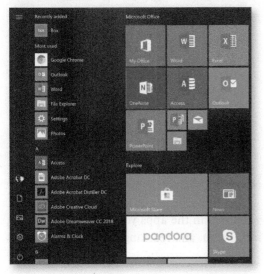

Windows 10 utilizes a redesigned *Start* menu (Figure Intro-3) that you open by clicking the **Start button** located in the bottom left of the *Taskbar.* From the *Start* menu, you open apps, files, folders, or other Windows resources. The *Start* menu is divided into two main sections. The left side of the *Start* menu displays the *Account, Documents, Pictures, Settings,* and *Power* buttons. This section also displays *Recently added* and *Most used* items, as well as an alphabetical listing of all apps installed on your computer. The right side of the *Start* menu displays tiles (large and small buttons) you click to open an application or window.

Figure Intro-3 Windows *Start* menu

You can customize which apps and items appear on either side of the *Start* menu, arrange and group apps on the *Start* menu, resize the *Start* menu, and display the *Start* menu as a **Start page** when you log in to Windows. See "Customize the Start Menu" later in this section for information about customizing the *Start* menu.

Add Apps

Windows 10 uses the term **apps** generically to refer to applications and programs. Apps include the Windows 10 Weather app, Microsoft Excel program, Control Panel, Google Chrome, or *File Explorer.* Many apps are preinstalled on a Windows 10 computer, and additional apps can be installed on your computer. Install an app, such as Office 2019 or Quicken, by downloading it from a web site. These apps are referred to as **desktop apps** or **traditional apps**.

The *Microsoft Store* app is preinstalled on Windows 10 computers. Install apps such as Netflix, Yelp, and Spotify from the Microsoft Store. These apps are referred to as **modern apps** and look and function similar to apps you install on your smartphone. Many apps in the Microsoft Store are free, and others are available for purchase.

▶**HOW TO:** Add an App from the Microsoft Store

1. Click the **Start** button to open the *Start* menu.
2. Click the **Microsoft Store** button (tile) to open the Microsoft Store app (Figure Intro-4) and click the **Apps** tab.
   - If the *Microsoft Store* tile is not available on the *Start* menu, locate the *Microsoft Store* button in the alphabetic listing of all apps.
3. Search for and select an app in the Microsoft Store (Figure Intro-5).
   - The Microsoft Store includes different categories of apps.
   - You can search for apps by typing keywords in the *Search* box in the upper-right corner.
   - When you select an app, information about the app displays.
4. Click the **Get**, **Buy**, or **Free trial** button to install the app.
   - You must have a payment method stored in your Microsoft account to purchase apps from the Microsoft Store.
5. Click **Launch** to open the installed app.
   - When you install an app, the app displays in the *Recently added* area on the *Start* menu and *All apps* list of applications.

Figure Intro-4 *Microsoft Store* app on the *Start* menu

Figure Intro-5 Install an app from the Microsoft Store

Customize the Start Menu

When you start using Windows 10 or after you have installed apps, you can customize what appears on your *Start* menu. When you **pin** an app to the *Start* menu, the corresponding app tile remains on the right side of the *Start* menu. Pin the apps you most regularly use, unpin the apps you don't want displayed on the *Start* menu, and rearrange and resize app tiles to your preference.

▶ HOW TO: Customize the Start Menu

1. Click the **Start** button to open the *Start* menu.

2. Move an app tile on the *Start* menu by clicking and dragging the app tile to a new location. The other app tiles shuffle to accommodate the placement of the moved app tile.

3. Remove an app tile from the *Start* menu by right-clicking the app tile and selecting **Unpin from Start** from the context menu (Figure Intro-6).

   • The app tile is removed from the right side of the *Start* menu, but the program or task is not removed from your computer.

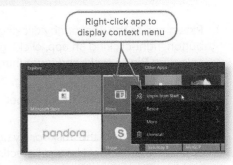

Figure Intro-6 Unpin an app from the *Start* menu

4. Pin an app tile to the *Start* menu by right-clicking the app in the alphabetic listing of apps in the *Start* menu and selecting **Pin to Start** (Figure Intro-7).

   • Drag the newly added app tile to the desired location on the *Start* menu.

Figure Intro-7 Pin an app to the *Start* menu

5. Resize an app tile by right-clicking the app tile, selecting **Resize**, and selecting **Small**, **Medium**, **Wide**, or **Large**.

   • Some apps only have *Small*, *Medium*, and *Wide* size options.

6. Turn on or off the live tile option by right-clicking the app tile, selecting **More**, and selecting **Turn Live Tile on** or **Turn Live Tile off**.

   • Live tile displays rotating graphics and options on the app tile. When this option is turned off, the name of the app displays on the tile.

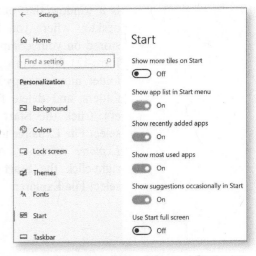

Figure Intro-8 *Settings* button on the *Start* menu

7. Uninstall an app by right-clicking the app you want to uninstall and selecting **Uninstall**.

   • Unlike the unpin option, this option uninstalls the program from your computer, not just your *Start* menu.
   • The *Uninstall* option is not available for some pre-installed Microsoft Windows apps.

8. Resize the *Start* menu by clicking and dragging the top or right edge of the *Start* menu.

9. Customize *Start* menu settings by clicking the **Start** button, selecting **Settings** button (Figure Intro-8) to open the *Settings* window, clicking the **Personalization** button, and clicking the **Start** option at the left (Figure Intro-9).

   • Click the **X** in the upper-right corner to close the *Settings* window.

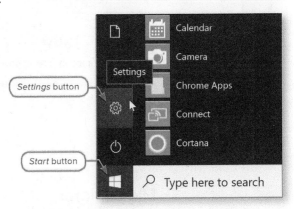

Figure Intro-9 Use full screen *Start* menu

Customize the Taskbar

The *Taskbar* is the horizontal bar located at the bottom of the Windows desktop, and you can quickly open an app by clicking an icon on the *Taskbar* rather than opening it from the *Start* menu. You can customize the *Taskbar* by pinning, unpinning, and rearranging apps. The right side of the *Taskbar* is the *System Tray,* which displays smaller icons of system applications that automatically run in the background of the Windows operating system.

▶ HOW TO: Customize the Taskbar

1. Pin an app to the *Taskbar* by clicking the **Start** button, right-clicking an app, clicking **More**, and selecting **Pin to taskbar** (Figure Intro-10).
   - You can also pin an app to the *Taskbar* by right-clicking an app from the alphabetic listing of apps in the *Start* menu.

2. Unpin an app from the *Taskbar* by right-clicking an app icon on the *Taskbar* and selecting **Unpin from taskbar** (Figure Intro-11).
   - You can also unpin apps from the *Taskbar* by right-clicking an app in the *Start* menu, clicking **More**, and selecting **Unpin from taskbar**.

3. Rearrange apps on the *Taskbar* by clicking and dragging the app to the desired location on the *Taskbar* and releasing.

Figure Intro-10 Pin an app to the *Taskbar*

Figure Intro-11 Unpin an app from the *Taskbar*

▶ MORE INFO

If using a touch screen, press and hold an app on the *Start* menu or *Taskbar* to display the app options.

File Explorer

The *File Explorer* in Windows 10 is a window that opens on your desktop where you browse files stored on your computer (Figure Intro-12). You can open a file or folder, move or copy items, create folders, and delete files or folders. Click the **Start** button and select **File Explorer** to open a *File Explorer* window. Alternatively, right-click the **Start** button and select **File Explorer**.

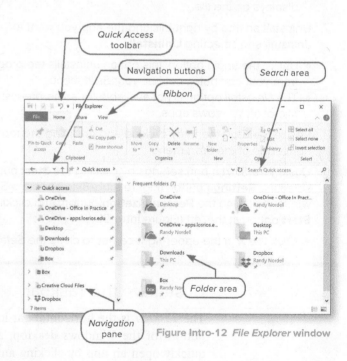

Figure Intro-12 *File Explorer* window

▶ MORE INFO

You can pin the *File Explorer* to the *Taskbar* for easy access to this window.

The *File Explorer* has different areas:

- *Navigation pane*: The *Navigation* pane displays folders on the left. The **Quick access** area at the top of the *Navigation* pane displays shortcuts to favorite folders. You can pin or unpin folders in the *Quick access* area of the *Navigation* pane.
- *Navigation buttons*: The navigation buttons (*Back, Forward, Recent location,* and *Up*) are located directly above the *Navigation* pane and below the *Ribbon.* Use these buttons to navigate a File Explorer window.
- *Folder pane*: When you select a folder in the *Navigation* pane, the contents of the folder display in the *Folder* pane to the right of the *Navigation* pane. Double-click a folder or file in the *Folder* pane to open it.
- *Ribbon*: The *Ribbon* is located near the top of *File Explorer* and includes the *File, Home, Share,* and *View* tabs. When you click a tab on the *Ribbon,* the *Ribbon* displays the options for the selected tab. Other contextual tabs display when you select certain types of files. For example, the *Picture Tool Manage* tab opens when you select a picture file in the *Folder* pane.
- *Quick Access toolbar*: The *Quick Access* toolbar is above the *Ribbon.* From the *Quick Access* toolbar, click the **New Folder** button to create a new folder or click **Properties** to display the properties of a selected file or folder. You can add buttons, such as *Undo, Redo,* and *Rename,* to the *Quick Access* toolbar.
- *Search*: The *Search* text box is located on the right of the *File Explorer* window below the *Ribbon.* Type key words in the *Search* text box to find files or folders.

OneDrive

OneDrive is a cloud storage area where you store files in a private and secure online location that you access from any computer. With Windows 10, the *OneDrive folder* is one of your storage location folder options, similar to your *Documents* or *Pictures* folders (Figure Intro-13). You can save, open, and edit your *OneDrive* files from a *File Explorer* folder. Your *OneDrive* folder looks and functions similar to other Windows folders. *OneDrive* synchronizes your files so when you change a file stored in *OneDrive* it is automatically updated on the *OneDrive* cloud.

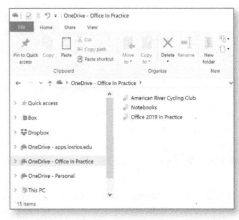

Figure Intro-13 *OneDrive* folder in a *File Explorer* window

When you store your files in *OneDrive,* you have the option of storing the files on *OneDrive* only (in the cloud) or syncing the files to your computer so they are saved on both your computer and on the cloud. You can customize which *OneDrive* folders and files are cloud only (not stored on your computer) and which folders and files are synced to your computer.

▶**HOW TO:** Customize OneDrive Settings

1. Open a *File Explorer* window using one of the following methods:
   - Click the **Start** button and select the **File Explorer** button.
   - Click the **File Explorer** button on the *Taskbar* (if available).
   - Right-click the **Start** button and select **File Explorer**.

2. Right-click the **OneDrive** folder in the *Navigation* pane of the *File Explorer* window and select **Settings** to open the *Microsoft OneDrive* dialog box.

   - Alternatively, right-click the **OneDrive** icon (if available) in the *System Tray* (right side of the *Taskbar*) and select **Settings**.

3. Click the **Account** tab and click the **Choose folders** button to open the *Sync your OneDrive files to this PC* dialog box (Figure Intro-14).

   - Check the **Sync all files and folders in OneDrive** box to sync all files and folders to your computer.
   - You can also select only those folders to sync in the *Or sync only these folders* area by selecting or deselecting the check boxes. Use this option to save storage space on your computer.

4. Click **OK** to close the *Sync your OneDrive files to this PC* dialog box and click **OK** to close the *Microsoft OneDrive* dialog box.

Figure Intro-14 Customize *OneDrive* folders to sync to your computer

OneDrive Online

In addition to the *OneDrive* folder on your computer, you can also access your *OneDrive* files online using an internet browser such as Microsoft Edge, Google Chrome, or Mozilla Firefox. When you access *OneDrive* online using a web browser, you can upload files, create folders, move and copy files and folders, and create Office files using *Office Online* (*Office Online* is discussed in *SLO Intro.2: Using Microsoft Office 2019*).

 MORE INFO

OneDrive online may display differently and include different features depending on the type of Microsoft account you have: personal, education, or business.

▶ **HOW TO:** Use OneDrive Online

1. Open an internet browser window and navigate to the *OneDrive* web site (www.onedrive.live.com), which takes you to the *OneDrive* sign-in page.

   - Use any internet browser to access *OneDrive* (Microsoft Edge, Google Chrome, Mozilla Firefox).

2. Click the **Sign in** button in the upper-right corner of the browser window.

3. Type your Microsoft account email address and click **Next** (Figure Intro-15).

4. Type your Microsoft account password and click **Sign in**. The *OneDrive* page displays.

   - If you are on your own computer, check the **Keep me signed in** box to stay signed in to *OneDrive* when you return to the page.
   - The different areas of *OneDrive* are listed under the *OneDrive* heading on the left (Figure Intro-16).
   - Click **Files** to display your folders and files in the folder area.
   - At the top of the page, buttons and drop-down menus list the different actions you can perform on selected files and folders.

Figure Intro-15 Log in to *OneDrive* online

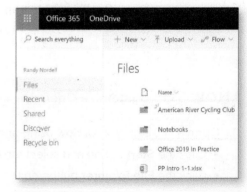

Figure Intro-16 *OneDrive* online environment

Cortana

In addition to using the search tools in *File Explorer,* you can also use **Cortana**, which is the Windows search feature. While the search feature in *File Explorer* searches only for content on your computer, *Cortana* searches for content on your computer, on the internet, and in the Microsoft Store. You can either type keywords for a search or use voice commands to search for content.

When you open *Cortana,* other content, such as weather, upcoming appointments, and popular news stories, displays in the *Cortana* pane.

▶HOW TO: Search Using Cortana

1. Click the **Cortana** search area on the *Taskbar* to open the *Cortana* pane (Figure Intro-17).
   - If the *Cortana* search area is not on the *Taskbar,* click the **Start** button, right-click **Cortana** in the list of apps, and select **Pin to taskbar**.
2. Type keywords for your search in the **Type here to search** area at the bottom of the *Cortana* pane.
   - You can also click the microphone icon and speak to enter keywords as the search.
   - Content from your computer, the internet, and the Microsoft Store displays in the *Cortana* pane (Figure Intro-18).
   - The search results are grouped into categories such as *Best match, Photos, Search suggestions, Store,* and *Places.* These categories vary depending on the search results.
3. Click a result in the *Cortana* pane to view a file, search the internet, or view apps in the Microsoft Store.
   - The buttons at the top of the *Cortana* pane filter your search by *Apps, Documents, Email,* and *web.*
   - The *More* button displays a drop-down list of additional filter options.
4. Click the **Menu** button at the top left to display other content options in the *Cortana* pane (see Figure Intro-18).
   - The other content options are *Home, Notebook,* and *Devices.*

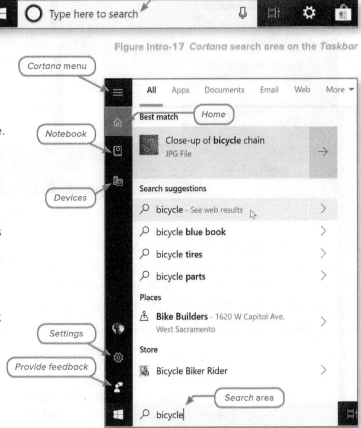

Figure Intro-17 *Cortana* search area on the *Taskbar*

Figure Intro-18 Use *Cortana* to search your computer, the internet, and the Microsoft Store

Task View

Task View displays all open apps and windows as tiles on your desktop, and you can choose which item to display or close. This feature is very helpful when you have multiple items open and need to select or close one. Additionally, *Task View* displays a timeline of tasks you've worked on in Windows. Scroll down in *Task View* to display previous days.

▶HOW TO: Use Task View

1. Click the **Task View** button on the *Taskbar* (Figure Intro-19).

   - All open apps and windows display on the desktop (Figure Intro-20).

Figure Intro-19 *Task View* button on the *Taskbar*

Figure Intro-20 *Task View* with open apps and windows displayed on the desktop

2. Select the app or window to open or close.

   - Click a tile to open an app. The app opens and *Task View* closes.
   - Click the **X** in the upper-right corner of an app to close an app. *Task View* remains open when you close an app.

3. Scroll down to view tasks from previous days.

Settings

In Windows 10, the ***Settings*** window is where you change global Windows settings, customize the Windows environment, add devices, and manage your Microsoft account. Click the **Settings** button (Figure Intro-21) on the *Taskbar* or *Start* menu to open the *Settings* window (Figure Intro-22). The following categories are typically available in the *Settings* window. *Settings* categories and options may vary depending on the version of Windows you are using and updates to Windows.

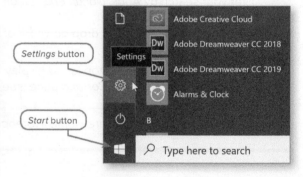

Figure Intro-21 *Settings* button on the Start menu

- ***System***: Display, notifications, and power
- ***Devices***: Bluetooth, printers, and mouse

- *Phone*: Link your Android and iPhone
- *Network & internet*: Wi-Fi, airplane mode, and VPN
- *Personalization*: Background, lock screen, and colors
- *Apps*: Uninstall, defaults, and optional features
- *Accounts*: Your account, email, sync, work, and family
- *Time & Language*: Speech, region, and date
- *Gaming*: Game bar, DVR, broadcasting, and Game Mode
- *Ease of Access*: Narrator, magnifier, and high contrast
- *Cortana*: Cortana languages, permissions, and notifications
- *Privacy*: Location and camera
- *Update & Security*: Windows Update, recovery, and backup

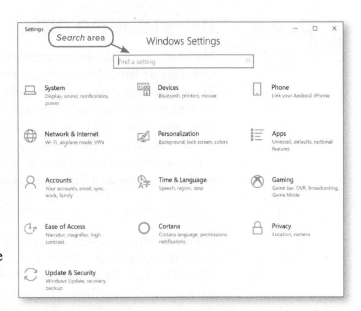

Figure Intro-22 *Settings* window

> **MORE INFO**
>
> If you can't find an item in *Settings*, use the *Search* dialog box (*Find a setting*) to type keywords. If *Settings* is not available on the *Taskbar*, you can find it in the list of apps on the *Start* menu.

Action Center

The ***Action Center*** in Windows 10 provides a quick glance of notifications and buttons to open other commonly used settings and features in Windows. The *Action Center* displays notifications such as emails and Windows notifications. Click an action button to turn on or off features or open other windows or apps such as the *Settings* menu (*All Settings* button) or OneNote (*Note* button). Click the **Action Center** button on the right side of the *Taskbar* (last button in the *System Tray*) to open the *Action Center* pane, which displays on the right side of your screen (Figure Intro-23).

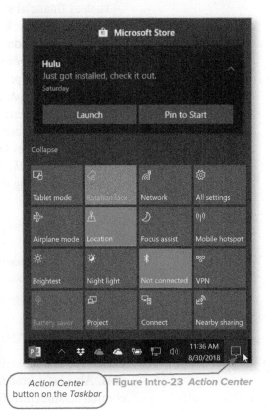

Action Center button on the *Taskbar*

Figure Intro-23 *Action Center*

> **ANOTHER WAY**
>
> **Windows+A** opens the *Action Center*. The *Windows* key is typically located near the bottom-left corner of the keyboard.

Using Microsoft Office

Microsoft Office includes common software applications such as Word, Excel, Access, and PowerPoint. These applications give you the ability to work with word processing documents, spreadsheets, presentations, and databases in your personal and business projects. Microsoft offers a variety of Office products and gives users the ability to work with these productivity apps on different technology devices.

Figure Intro-24 Microsoft Office application tiles on the *Start* menu

Office 2019 and Office 365

Microsoft Office is a suite of personal and business software applications (Figure Intro-24). *Microsoft Office 2019* and *Microsoft Office 365* are similar software products; the difference is how you purchase the software. Office 2019 is the traditional model of purchasing the software, and you own that software for as long as you want to use it. Office 365 is a subscription that you pay monthly or yearly, similar to how you purchase Netflix or Spotify. If you subscribe to Office 365, you automatically receive updated versions of the applications when they are released.

The common applications typically included in Microsoft Office 2019 and 365 are described in the following list:

- *Microsoft Word*: Word processing software used to create, format, and edit documents such as reports, letters, brochures, and resumes
- *Microsoft Excel*: Spreadsheet software used to perform calculations on numerical data such as financial statements, budgets, and expense reports
- *Microsoft Access*: Database software used to store, organize, compile, and report information such as product information, sales data, client information, and employee records
- *Microsoft PowerPoint*: Presentation software used to graphically present information in slides such as a presentation on a new product or sales trends
- *Microsoft Outlook*: Email and personal management software used to create and send email and to create and store calendar items, contacts, and tasks
- *Microsoft OneNote*: Note-taking software used to take and organize notes, which can be shared with other Office applications
- *Microsoft Publisher*: Desktop publishing software used to create professional-looking documents containing text, pictures, and graphics such as catalogs, brochures, and flyers

> **MORE INFO**
>
> Office 365 includes regular updates that include new and enhanced features, while Office 2019 does not include these regular updates. So, differences in features may exist between the Office 2019 and Office 365.

Office 365 Products, Versions, and Update Channels

Office 365 is a subscription to the Office applications and can be purchased for home or business. Also, as a student, you can get Office 365 for education free (https://products.office.com/en-us/student/office-in-education). The Office applications that come with an Office 365 subscription can vary depending on the Office 365 product subscription you have. With an Office 365 subscription, you can install the Office applications (both PC and Mac) on multiple computers and mobile devices.

Another advantage of an Office 365 subscription is regular updates that enhance the functionality of the apps. The version and build of your Office 365 is determined by the update channel, which is the frequency of updates. This is typically set by your school or business. If you have Office 365 Home or Personal, you determine the update channel. If you have an Office 365 for education or business, the college or business determines the update channel. The following are common update channels:

- *Semi-annual Channel*: Receives updates two times a year in January and July
- *Semi-annual Channel (Targeted)*: Receives new feature updates earlier than the Semi-annual Channel. These semi-annual updates are rolled out in March and September.
- *Monthly Channel*: Receives new feature updates as soon as they are available, which is typically every month

▶ HOW TO: View Your Office 365 Product Information

1. Open an Office application and open a blank or existing file if necessary.
2. Click the **File** tab to open the *Backstage* view.
3. Click **Account** at the left to display *User Information* and *Product Information*.
   - The *Product Information* area displays the Office 365 product installed on your computer (Figure Intro-25).
   - The *About [Application]* area displays the version, build, and update channel.
   - The *Version* number indicates the year and month of the most recent update. For example, "Version 1808" means 2018 and the eighth month (August).
4. Click the **Update Options** button to select an update option: *Update Now, Disable Updates, View Updates,* or *About Updates.*
   - Click the **Update Now** button to manually check for Office 365 updates.
5. Click the **What's New** button to view the new features included in the most recent Office 365 updates for your update channel.
6. Close the **Back** arrow to close the *Backstage* view and return to the file.

Figure Intro-25 *Product Information* displayed in the *Account* area on the *Backstage* view

Office Desktop Apps, Office Mobile Apps, and Office Online

Office desktop apps are the full-function Office 2019 or 365 programs installed on your computer (PC or Mac). Both Office 2019 and Office 365 are considered Office desktop apps. Because of the increased popularity and capabilities of tablets and mobile devices, Office software is also available for both tablets and smartphones. *Office mobile apps* are the Office 365 programs that can be installed on tablets or other mobile devices. Office mobile apps do not have the full range of advanced features available in Office desktop applications, but Office mobile apps provide users the ability to create, edit, save, and share Office files using many of the most common features in the Office suite of programs.

The *Office Online* apps are free online apps from Microsoft that work in conjunction with your Microsoft account and *OneDrive* (Figure Intro-26). With *Office Online,* you can work with Office files online through a web browser, even on computers that do not have Office 2019 or 365 installed. Click the **App** launcher in the upper-left corner of *OneDrive* to display the *Office Online* applications. This list of *Office Online* apps may display differently depending on the type of Microsoft account you are using.

You can access *Office Online* from your *OneDrive* web page to create and edit Word documents, Excel workbooks, PowerPoint presentations, and OneNote notebooks. *Office Online* is a scaled-down version of Office and not as robust in terms of features, but you can use it to create, edit, print, share, and collaborate on files. If you need more advanced features, you can open *Office Online* files in the desktop version of Office.

Figure Intro-26 *Office Online*

▶ HOW TO: Create an Office Online File

1. Open an internet browser Window, navigate to the *OneDrive* web site (www.onedrive.live.com), and log in to *OneDrive.* If you are not already logged in to *OneDrive,* use the following steps.

   - Click the **Sign in** button, type your Microsoft account email address, and click **Next**.
   - Type your Microsoft account password and click **Sign in** to open your *OneDrive* page.

2. Click the **New** button and select the type of *Office Online* file to create (Figure Intro-27).

   - A new file opens in the *Office Online* program.
   - The new file is saved in your *OneDrive* folder (both online and on your computer).

3. Rename the file by clicking the file name at the top of the file, typing a new file name, and pressing **Enter** (Figure Intro-28).

   - You can also click the **File** tab to open the *Backstage* view, select **Save As**, and choose **Save As** or **Rename**.
   - Click the **Open in *[Office application]*** button (for example, **Open in Excel**) to open the file in the Office desktop application (see Figure Intro-28).

4. Close the browser tab or window to close the file.

   - *Office Online* automatically saves the file as you make changes.

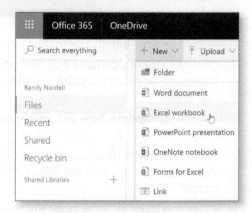

Figure Intro-27 Create an *Office Online* file from your online *OneDrive* page

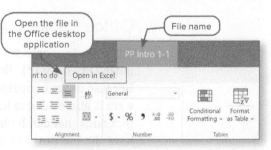

Figure Intro-28 Rename an *Office Online* file

Open an Office Desktop Application

When using Windows 10, you open an Office desktop application by clicking the application tile on the *Start* menu or the application icon on the *Taskbar.* If your *Start* menu and *Taskbar* do not display the Office applications, click the **Start** button and select **Word**, **Excel**, **Access**, or **PowerPoint** from the alphabetic list of apps to launch the application (Figure Intro-29).

You can also use *Cortana* to quickly locate an Office desktop app (Figure Intro-30).

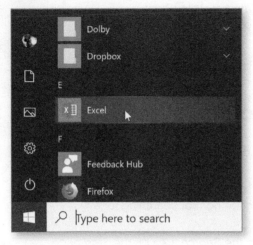

Figure Intro-29 Open an Office desktop app from the *All apps* area on the *Start* menu

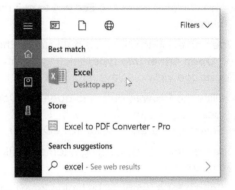

Figure Intro-30 Use *Cortana* to find and open an app

> **MORE INFO**
>
> Add commonly used apps to your Windows *Start* menu and/or *Taskbar* to save time. See the "Customize the *Start* Menu" and "Customize the *Taskbar*" sections in *SLO Intro.1: Using Windows 10.*

Office Start Page

Most of the Office applications (except Outlook and OneNote) display a ***Start page*** when you launch the application (Figure Intro-31). From this *Start* page, you can create a new blank file (for example, a Word document, an Excel workbook, an Access database, or a PowerPoint presentation), create a file from an online template, search for an online template, open a recently used file, or open another file. These options vary depending on the Office application.

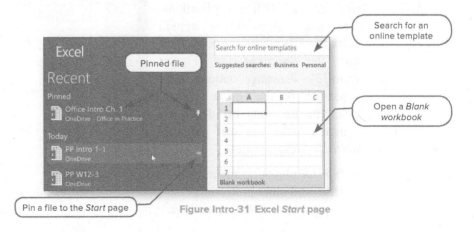

Figure Intro-31 Excel *Start* page

1. Open an Office application from the *Start* page or *Taskbar.*
2. Open a file listed in the *Recent* area on the left side of the *Start* menu by clicking the file name. The file opens in the working area of the Office application.
   - The *Recent* area on the left side of the *Start* page displays recently used and pinned files.
3. Open a new blank file by clicking the **Blank [file type]** tile (*Blank workbook, Blank document,* etc.) to the right of the *Recent* area (see Figure Intro-31).
   - You can also press the **Esc** key to exit the *Start* page and open a new blank file.
4. Open an existing file that is not listed in the *Recent* area by clicking the **Open Other [file type]** link (Figure Intro-32). The *Open* area on the *Backstage* view displays.
   - Click the **Browse** button to open the *Open* dialog box where you can locate and open a file.
   - Select a different location (*OneDrive* or *This PC*) and select a file to open.
5. Open a template by clicking a template file on the right or searching for a template.
   - Search for a template by typing keywords in the *Search* area on the *Start* page.
   - Click a link to one of the categories below the *Search* area to display templates in that category.
6. Pin a frequently used file to the *Start* page by clicking the **pin** icon (see Figure Intro-31).
   - The pin icon is on the right side of items listed in the *Recent* area and at the bottom right of templates displayed in the *Templates* area (to the right of the *Recent* area).
   - Pinned files display at the top of the *Recent* area.

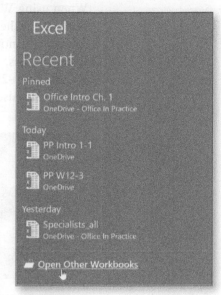

Figure Intro-32 *Open Other Workbooks link on the Start page*

▶ **MORE INFO**

In Access, you have to open an existing database or create a new one to enter the program.

Backstage View

Office incorporates the *Backstage view* into all Office applications (including *Office Online* apps). Click the **File** tab on the *Ribbon* to open the *Backstage* view (Figure Intro-33). *Backstage* options vary depending on the Office application. The following list describes common tasks you can perform from the *Backstage* view:

- *Info*: Displays document properties and other protection, inspection, and version options.

Figure Intro-33 *Backstage view in Excel*

- *New*: Creates a new blank file or a new file from a template or theme.
- *Open*: Opens an existing file from a designated location or a recently opened file.
- *Save*: Saves a file. If the file has not been named, the *Save As* dialog box opens when you select this option.
- *Save As*: Opens the *Save As* dialog box.
- *Print*: Prints a file, displays a preview of the file, or displays print options.
- *Share*: Invites people to share a file or email a file.
- *Export*: Creates a PDF file from a file or saves it as a different file type.
- *Close*: Closes an open file.
- *Account*: Displays your Microsoft account information.
- *Options*: Opens the *[Application] Options* dialog box (for example, *Excel Options*).

▶ MORE INFO

Options on the *Backstage* view vary depending on the Office application you are using.

Office Help—Tell Me

In all the Office 2019/365 applications, ***Tell Me*** is the help feature (Figure Intro-34). This feature displays the commands in the Office application related to your search. The *Help* fea-
ture in older versions of Office displayed articles describing the feature and how to use it. The *Tell Me* feature provides command options that take you directly to a command or dialog box. For example, if you type *PivotTable* in the *Tell Me* search box in Excel, the results include the option to open the *Create PivotTable* dialog box, as well as other options such as *Recommended PivotTables* and *Summarize with PivotTable*.

Figure Intro-34 *Tell Me* search box

▶ **HOW TO: Use Tell Me**

1. Place the insertion point in the **Tell me what you want to do** search box at the top of the *Ribbon* (see Figure Intro-34).
2. Type keywords for the command or feature for which you are searching.
3. Select an option from the search results list (Figure Intro-35).
   - When you select a search result, it may apply a command, open a dialog box, or display a gallery of command choices.

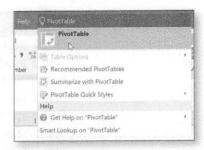

Figure Intro-35 *Tell Me* search results

▶ ANOTHER WAY

Alt+Q places the insertion point in the *Tell Me* dialog box.
The previous *Help* feature is still available in Office. Press **F1** to open the *Help* pane on the right.

Mouse and Pointers

If you are using Office on a desktop or laptop computer, use your mouse (or touchpad) to navigate around files, click tabs and buttons, select text and objects, move text and objects, and resize objects. Table Intro-1 lists mouse and pointer terminology used in Office.

Table Intro-1: Mouse and Pointer Terminology

Term	Description
Pointer	Move your mouse to move the pointer on your screen. A variety of pointers are used in different contexts in Office applications. The following pointers are available in most of the Office applications (the appearance of these pointers varies depending on the application and the context used): • *Selection pointer:* Select text or an object. • *Move pointer:* Move text or an object. • *Copy pointer:* Copy text or an object. • *Resize pointer:* Resize objects or table columns or rows. • *Crosshair:* Draw a shape.
Insertion point	The vertical flashing line indicating where you type text in a file or text box. Click the left mouse button to position the insertion point.
Click	Click the left mouse button. Used to select an object or button or to place the insertion point in the selected location.
Double-click	Click the left mouse button twice. Used to select text.
Right-click	Click the right mouse button. Used to display the context menu and the mini toolbar.
Scroll	Use the scroll wheel on the mouse to scroll up and down through your file. You can also use the horizontal or vertical scroll bars at the bottom and right of an Office file window to move around in a file.

Touch Mode and Touch-Screen Gestures

The user interface in Windows 10 and Office 2019 has improved touch features to facilitate the use of Windows and the Office applications on a tablet computer or smartphone. On tablets and smartphones, you can use a touch screen rather than using a mouse, so the process of selecting text and objects and navigating around a file is different from a computer without a touch screen.

In Office 2019/365, *Touch mode* optimizes the Office working environment when using a computer with a touch screen to provide more space between buttons and commands. Click the **Touch/Mouse Mode** button on the *Quick Access* toolbar (upper left of the Office app window) and select **Touch** from the drop-down list to enable *Touch* mode (Figure Intro-36). To turn off *Touch* mode, select **Mouse** from the *Touch/Mouse Mode* drop-down list.

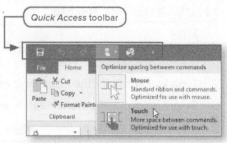

Figure Intro-36 Turn on *Touch* mode

> ## MORE INFO
>
> The *Touch/Mouse Mode* button displays on the *Quick Access* toolbar when using a touch-screen computer.

Table Intro-2 lists common gestures used when working on a tablet or smartphone (these gestures vary depending on the application used and the context).

Table Intro-2: Touch-Screen Gestures

Gesture	Used To	How To
Tap	Select text or an object or position the insertion point. Double tap to edit text in an object or cell.	
Pinch	Zoom in or resize an object.	
Stretch	Zoom out or resize an object.	
Slide	Move an object or selected text.	
Swipe	Select text or multiple objects.	

> **MORE INFO**
>
> Window 10 has a ***Tablet mode*** that optimizes all of Windows and apps for touch screens. When you turn on the *Tablet mode* feature in Windows, the *Touch mode* in Office apps turns on automatically. Click the **Action Center** button on the Windows *Taskbar* and click the **Tablet mode** button to turn on this feature in Windows.

Creating, Saving, Closing, and Opening Office Files

Creating, saving, opening, and closing files is primarily done from the *Start* page or *Backstage* view of the active Office application. Both the *Start* page and the *Backstage* view provide many options and a central location to perform these tasks. You can also use shortcut commands to create, save, and open files.

Create a New File

When you create a new file in an Office application, you can create a new blank file or a new file based on a template (in PowerPoint, you can also create a presentation based on a theme). On the *Start* page, click **Blank *[file type]*** to create a new blank file in the application you are using (in Word, you begin with a blank document; in Excel, a blank workbook; in Access, a blank desktop database; and in PowerPoint, a blank presentation).

1. Open an Office application. The *Start* page displays when the application opens (Figure Intro-37).

2. Click **Blank *[file type]*** to open a new file.

   - The new file displays a generic file name (for example, *Document1*, *Book1*, or *Presentation1*). You can rename and save this file later.
   - When creating a new Access database, you are prompted to name the new file when you create it.
   - A variety of templates (and themes in PowerPoint only) display on the *Start* page, and you can search for additional online templates and themes using the *Search* text box at the top of the *Start* page.

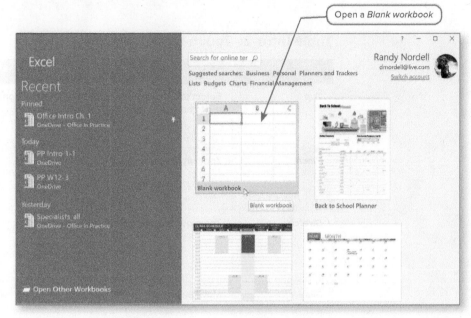

Open a *Blank workbook*

Figure Intro-37 *Start* page in Excel

► MORE INFO

Esc closes the *Start* page opens a blank file in the Office application (except in Access).

If you have been using an application already and want to create a new file, you create it from the *Backstage* view. From the *Backstage* view, the new file options are available in the *New* area.

1. Click the **File** tab to display the *Backstage* view.

2. Select **New** on the left to display the *New* area (Figure Intro-38).

3. Click **Blank *[file type]*** to open a new blank file or select a template or theme to use.

   - The new file displays a generic file name (*Document1*, *Book1*, or *Presentation1*). You can name and save this file later.
   - When you are creating a new Access database, you are prompted to name the new file when you create it.

Figure Intro-38 *New* area on the *Backstage* view in Excel

Save a File

In Access, you name a file as you create it, but in Word, Excel, and PowerPoint, you name a file after you have created it. When you save a file, you type a name for the file and select the location to save the file. You can save a file on your computer, an online storage location such as *OneDrive,* or portable device, such as a USB drive.

▶ HOW TO: Save a File

1. Click the **File** tab to display the *Backstage* view.
2. Select **Save** or **Save As** on the left to display the *Save As* area (Figure Intro-39).
   - If the file has not already been saved, clicking *Save* or *Save As* takes you to the *Save As* area on the *Backstage* view.
3. Click the **Browse** button to open the *Save As* dialog box (Figure Intro-40).
   - Alternatively, type the file name in the *Enter file name here* text box and click **Save**. To change the save location, click the **More options** link to open the *Save As* dialog box or select a save location at the left (*OneDrive* or *This PC*) and select a folder from the list of folders (see Figure Intro-39).
4. Select a location to save the file in the *Folder* list on the left.
5. Type a name for the file in the *File name* area.
   - By default, Office selects the file type, but you can change the file type from the *Save as type* drop-down list.
6. Click **Save** to close the dialog box and save the file.

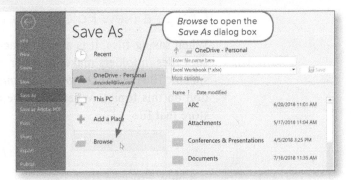

Figure Intro-39 *Save As* area on the *Backstage* view in Excel

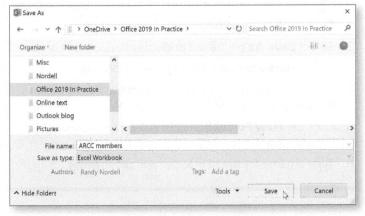

Figure Intro-40 *Save As* dialog box

AutoSave

AutoSave is a new feature that automatically saves a file that is stored on *OneDrive,* Microsoft's cloud storage area. The *AutoSave* feature turns on by default when you save a file to *OneDrive,* and changes made to the file are automatically saved as you work on a file.

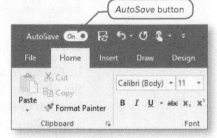

Office 2019 Note: The *AutoSave* feature is not available in Office 2019.

This feature displays in the upper-left corner of the file (Figure Intro-41). Click the **AutoSave** button to turn it on or off. When *AutoSave* is on, the save options on the *Backstage* view change from *Save* and *Save As* to *Save a Copy.*

Figure Intro-41 *AutoSave* feature

Create a New Folder When Saving a File

When saving files, it is a good practice to create folders to organize your files. Organizing your files in folders makes it easier to find files and saves time when you are searching for a specific file (see *SLO Intro.8: Organizing and Customizing Folders and Files* for more information on this topic). When you save an Office file, you can also create a folder in which to store that file.

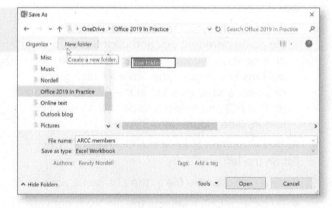

> ▶ **HOW TO:** Create a New Folder When Saving a File

1. Click the **File** tab to display the *Backstage* view.
2. Select **Save As** on the left to display the *Save As* area.
3. Click **Browse** to open the *Save As* dialog box.
4. Select a location to save the file from the *Folder* list on the left.
5. Click the **New Folder** button to create a new folder (Figure Intro-42).
6. Type a name for the new folder and press **Enter**.

Figure Intro-42 Create a new folder

> ▶ **ANOTHER WAY**
>
> **F12** opens the *Save As* dialog box (except in Access). On a laptop, you might have to press **Fn+F12**. See more about the *Fn* (Function) key in *SLO Intro. 7: Using Context Menus, the Mini Toolbar, and Keyboard Shortcuts.*

Save As a Different File Name

After you have saved a file, you can save it again with a different file name. If you do this, you preserve the original file, and you can continue to revise the second file for a different purpose.

▶HOW TO: Save As a Different File Name

1. Click the **File** tab to display the *Backstage* view.
2. Select **Save As** on the left to display the *Save As* area.
3. Click the **Browse** button to open the *Save As* dialog box (see Figure Intro-42).
4. Select a location to save the file from the *Folder* list on the left.
5. Type a new name for the file in the *File name* area.
6. Click **Save** to close the dialog box and save the file.

> ▶ MORE INFO
>
> If *AutoSave* is turned on, **Save a Copy** is the save option on the *Backstage* view rather than *Save* and *Save As.*

Office File Types

By default, Office saves a file in the most current file format for that application. You also have the option of saving files in older versions of the Office application. For example, you can save a Word document as an older version to share with or send to someone who uses an older version of Word. Each file has an extension at the end of the file name that determines the file type. The *file name extension* is automatically added to a file when you save it. Table Intro-3 table lists common file types used in the different Office applications.

Table Intro-3: Office File Types

File Type	Extension	File Type	Extension
Word Document	.docx	Access Database	.accdb
Word Template	.dotx	Access Template	.accdt
Word 97-2003 Document	.doc	Access Database (2000-2003 format)	.mdb
Rich Text Format	.rtf	PowerPoint Presentation	.pptx
Excel Workbook	.xlsx	PowerPoint Template	.potx
Excel Template	.xltx	PowerPoint 97-2003 Presentation	.ppt
Excel 97-2003 Workbook	.xls	Portable Document Format (PDF)	.pdf
Comma Separated Values (CSV)	.csv		

Close a File

You can close a file using the following different methods:

- Click the **File** tab and select **Close** on the left.
- Press **Ctrl+W**.
- Click the **X** in the upper-right corner of the file window. This method closes the file and the program if only one file is open in the application.

When you close a file, you are prompted to save the file if it has not been named or if changes were made after the file was last saved (Figure Intro-43). Click **Save** to save and close the file or click **Don't Save** to close the file without saving. Click **Cancel** to return to the file.

Open an Existing File

You can open an existing file from the *Start* page when you open an Office application or while you are working on another Office file.

▶ **HOW TO: Open a File from the Start Page**

1. Open an Office application to display the *Start* page.

2. Select a file to open in the *Recent* area on the left (Figure Intro-44).

   - If you select a file in the *Recent* area that has been renamed, moved, or is on a storage device not connected to the computer, you receive an error message.

3. Alternatively, click **Open Other** *[file type]* (for example, *Open Other Presentations*) to display the *Open* area of the *Backstage* view (see Figure Intro-44).

   - Click the **Browse** button to open the *Open* dialog box (Figure Intro-45).
   - Select a location from the *Folder* list on the left.
   - Select the file to open and click the **Open** button.
   - If the file opens in *Protected View,* click the **Enable Editing** button to enable you to edit the file.

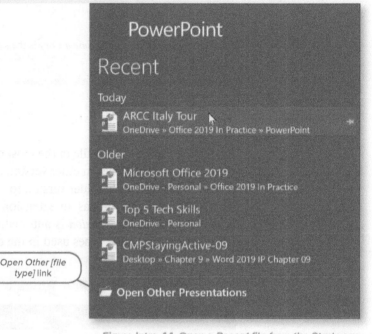

Figure Intro-44 Open a *Recent* file from the *Start* page

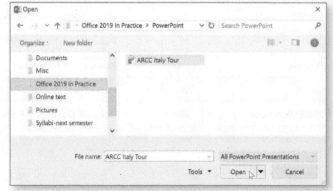

Figure Intro-45 *Open* dialog box

When working on a file in an Office application, you might want to open another file. You can open an existing file from within an Office application using the *Open* area on the *Backstage* view.

> ▶ **HOW TO:** Open a File from the Backstage View

1. Click the **File** tab from within an open Office application to display the *Backstage* view.
2. Click **Open** on the left to display the *Open* area on the *Backstage* view (Figure Intro-46).
3. Click the **Browse** button to open the *Open* dialog box.
   - Alternatively, select a file to open from the list of *Recent* files on the right of the *Open* area on the *Backstage* view.
4. Select a location from the *Folder* list on the left.
5. Select the file to open and click the **Open** button.
   - If the file opens in *Protected View*, click the **Enable Editing** button to enable you to edit the file.

Figure Intro-46 *Open* area on the *Backstage* view

You can also open a file from a *File Explorer* folder. When you double-click a file in a *File Explorer* folder, the file opens in the appropriate Office application. Windows recognizes the file name extension and launches the correct Office application.

PAUSE & PRACTICE: INTRO-1

For this project, you log in to Windows using your Microsoft account, customize the Windows *Start* menu and *Taskbar,* create and save a PowerPoint presentation, create a folder, open and rename an Excel workbook, and use Windows 10 features.

File Needed: ***ARCC2020Budget-Intro.xlsx*** *(Student data files are available in the* Library *of your SIMnet account.)*
Completed Project File Names: ***[your initials] PP Intro-1a.pptx** and **[your initials] PP Intro-1b.xlsx***

1. Log in to Windows using your Microsoft account if you are not already logged in.
   a. If you don't have a Microsoft account, you can create a free account at https://signup.live.com.
   b. If you are using a computer on your college campus, you may be required to log in to the computer using your college user name and password.

2. Pin the Office apps to the *Start* menu. If these apps tiles are already on the *Start* menu, skip steps 2a–e. You can pin other apps of your choice to the *Start* menu.
   a. Click the **Start** button at the bottom left of your screen to open the *Start* menu.
   b. Locate *Access* in the alphabetic list of apps, right-click the **Access** app, and select **Pin to Start** (Figure Intro-47). The app displays as a tile on the right side of the *Start* menu.
   c. Repeat step 2b to pin **Excel**, **PowerPoint**, and **Word** apps to the *Start* menu.
   d. Display the *Start* menu and drag these Office app tiles so they are close to each other.
   e. Click the **Start** button (or press the **Esc** key) to close the *Start* menu.

Figure Intro-47 Pin *Access* to the *Start* menu

3. Use *Cortana* and the *Start* menu to pin Office apps to the *Taskbar*.
   a. Click the **Cortana** button (to the right of the *Start* button) on the *Taskbar* and type *Access*. *Cortana* displays content matching your search.
   b. Right-click the **Access** option near the top of the *Cortana* pane and select **Pin to taskbar** (Figure Intro-48). The app pins to the *Taskbar*.
   c. Click the **Start** button to open the *Start* menu.
   d. Right-click the **Excel** tile on the right side of the *Start* menu, click **More**, and select **Pin to taskbar**. The app pins to the *Taskbar*.
   e. Use either of the methods described above to pin the **PowerPoint** and **Word** apps to the *Taskbar*.
   f. Drag the Office apps on the *Taskbar* to rearrange them to your preference.

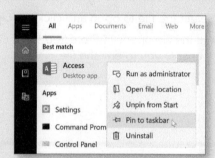

Figure Intro-48 Use *Cortana* to find an Office app and pin it to the *Taskbar*

4. Create a PowerPoint presentation and save the presentation in a new folder.
   a. Click the **PowerPoint** app tile on your *Start* menu to open the application.
   b. Click **Blank Presentation** on the PowerPoint *Start* page to create a new blank presentation.
   c. Click the **Click to add title** placeholder and type American River Cycling Club to replace the placeholder text.
   d. Click the **File** tab to open the *Backstage* view and click **Save As** on the left to display the *Save As* area.
   e. Click **Browse** to open the *Save As* dialog box (Figure Intro-49).
   f. Select a location to save the file from the *Folder* list on the left. If the *OneDrive* folder is an option, select **OneDrive**. If it is not, select the **Documents** folder in the *This PC* folder. You can also save to a portable storage device if you have one.
   g. Click the **New Folder** button to create a new folder.

Figure Intro-49 *Save As* area on the *Backstage* view in PowerPoint

h. Type American River Cycling Club as the name of the new folder and press **Enter** (Figure Intro-50).

i. Double-click the **American River Cycling Club** folder to open it.

j. Type [your initials] PP Intro-1a in the *File name* area.

k. Click **Save** to close the dialog box and save the presentation. Leave the file and PowerPoint open. If you saved your file to OneDrive, you may receive a notification about automatic saving.

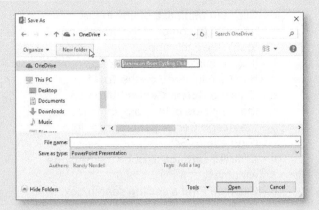

Figure Intro-50 Create a new folder from the *Save As* dialog box

5. Open an Excel file and save as a different file name.

a. Click the **Excel 2019** app button on the *Taskbar* to open the *Start* page in Excel.

b. Click the **Open Other Workbooks** link on the bottom left of the Excel *Start* page to display the *Open* area of the *Backstage* view.

c. Click **Browse** to open the *Open* dialog box (Figure Intro-51).

d. Browse to your student data files and select the **ARCC2020Budget-Intro** file.

e. Click **Open** to open the workbook. If the file opens in *Protected View,* click the **Enable Editing** button.

f. Click the **File** tab to open the *Backstage* view.

g. Click **Save As** on the left to display the *Save As* area and click **Browse** to open the *Save As* dialog box. If this file is stored on OneDrive, click **Save a Copy** rather than *Save As.*

h. Locate the **American River Cycling Club** folder (created in step 4h) in the *Folder* list on the left and double-click the folder to open it.

i. Type [your initials] PP Intro-1b in the *File name* area.

j. Click **Save** to close the dialog box and save the workbook. Leave the file and Excel open.

Figure Intro-51 *Open* area on the *Backstage* view

6. Use the *Tell Me* feature in Excel to find a command.

a. Click the **Tell Me** search box on the *Ribbon* of the Excel window and type PivotTable (Figure Intro-52).

b. Click **PivotTable** to open the *Create PivotTable* dialog box.

c. Click the **X** in the upper-right corner of the *Create PivotTable* dialog box to close it.

7. Open the *Microsoft Store* app, the *Action Center*, and the *Settings* window.

a. Click the **Cortana** search area and type Microsoft Store.

b. Click **Microsoft Store** at the top of the *Cortana* pane to open the *Microsoft Store* app.

c. Click the **Apps** tab in the top left and browse the available apps in the Microsoft Store.

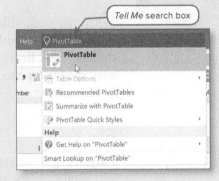

Figure Intro-52 Use the *Tell Me* feature to find a command

d. Click the **Minimize** button in the upper-right corner of the *Store* window to minimize this app (Figure Intro-53). The app is still open, but it is minimized on the *Taskbar.*

e. Click the **Action Center** button on the right side of the *Taskbar* to display the *Action Center* pane on the right (Figure Intro-54).

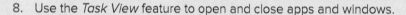

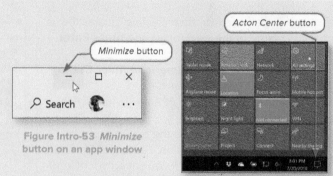

Figure Intro-53 *Minimize button on an app window*

f. Click **All settings** to open the *Settings* window.

g. Click the **Find a setting** search box, type Printer, and view the search results.

Figure Intro-54 Windows 10 *Action Center*

h. Click the **Minimize** button to minimize the *Settings* windows to the *Taskbar.*

8. Use the *Task View* feature to open and close apps and windows.

a. Click the **Task View** button on the left side of the *Taskbar* (Figure Intro-55). All open apps and windows display tiled on the Windows desktop.

b. Click the **Store** app to open it. *Task View* closes and the *Store* app displays on your Windows desktop.

c. Click the **Task View** button again.

d. Click the **X** in the upper-right corner to close each open app and window. You may be prompted to save changes to a file.

Figure Intro-55 *Task View* button on the *Taskbar*

e. Click the **Task View** button again or press **Esc** to return to the desktop.

<img id="SLO INTRO. 4" />

Working with Files

When you work with Office files, a variety of display views are available. You can change how a file displays, adjust the display size, work with multiple files, and arrange windows to view multiple files. Because most people work with multiple files at the same time, Office makes it easy and intuitive to move from one file to another or to display multiple document windows at the same time.

File Views

Each of the different Office applications provides you with a variety of ways to view your document. In Word, Excel, and PowerPoint, the different views are available on the *View tab* (Figure Intro-56). You can also change views using the buttons on the right side of the *Status bar* at the bottom of the file window (Figure Intro-57). In Access, the different views for each object are available in the *Views* group on the *Home* tab.

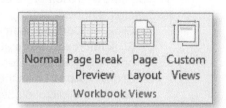

Figure Intro-56 *Workbook Views* group on the *View* tab in Excel

Figure Intro-57 PowerPoint views on the *Status* bar

Table Intro-4 lists the views that are available in each of the different Office applications.

Table Intro-4: File Views

Office Application	Views	Office Application	Views
Word	Read Mode Print Layout web Layout Outline Draft	**Access** (Access views vary depending on active object)	Layout View Design View Datasheet View Form View SQL View Report View Print Preview
Excel	Normal Page Break Preview Page Layout Custom Views	**PowerPoint**	Normal Outline View Slide Sorter Notes Page Reading View Presenter View

Change Display Size

Use the *Zoom* feature to increase or decrease the display size of your file. Using *Zoom* to change the display size does not change the actual size of text or objects in your file; it only changes the size of your display. For example, if you change the *Zoom* level to 120%, you increase the display of your file to 120% of its normal size (100%), but changing the display size does not affect the actual size of text and objects in your file. Decrease the *Zoom* level to 80% to display more of your file on the screen.

You can increase or decrease the *Zoom* level several different ways. Your *Zoom* options vary depending on the Office application.

- *Zoom level on the Status* bar (Figure Intro-58): Click the + or − button to increase or decrease *Zoom* level in 10% increments.
- *Zoom group on the View tab* (Figure Intro-59): The *Zoom* group includes a variety of *Zoom* options. The options vary depending on the Office application.
- *Zoom dialog box* (Figure Intro-60): Click the **Zoom** button in the *Zoom* group on the *View* tab or click the **Zoom level** on the *Status* bar to open the *Zoom* dialog box.

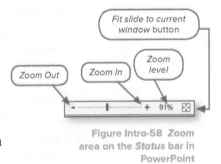

Figure Intro-58 *Zoom* area on the *Status* bar in PowerPoint

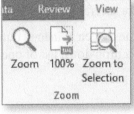

Figure Intro-59 *Zoom* group in Excel

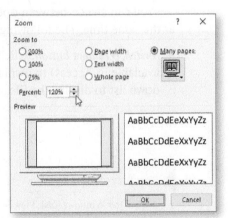

Figure Intro-60 *Zoom* dialog box in Word

Manage Multiple Open Files and Windows

When you are working on multiple files in an Office application, each file is opened in a new window. *Minimize* an open window to place the file on the Windows *Taskbar* (the bar at the bottom of the Windows desktop), *restore down* an open window so it does not fill the entire computer screen, or *maximize* a window so it fills the entire computer screen. The *Minimize*, *Restore Down/Maximize*, and *Close* buttons are in the upper-right corner of a file window (Figure Intro-61).

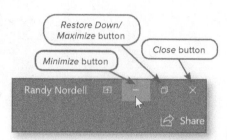

Figure Intro-61 Window options buttons

- *Minimize*: Click the **Minimize** button (see Figure Intro-61) to hide the active window. When a document is minimized, it is not closed. It is reduced to a button on the *Taskbar* and the window does not display. Place your pointer on the application icon on the Windows *Taskbar* to display thumbnails of open files. Click an open file thumbnail to display the file (Figure Intro-62).

- *Restore Down/Maximize*: Click the **Restore Down/ Maximize** button (see Figure Intro-61) to decrease the size of an open window or to maximize the window to fill the entire screen. This button toggles between *Restore Down* and *Maximize*. When a window is restored down, change the size of a window by clicking and dragging a border of the window. You can also move the window by clicking and dragging the title bar at the top of the window.

Figure Intro-62 Display minimized file on the *Taskbar*

- *Close*: Click the **Close** button (see Figure Intro-61) to close the window. If there is only one open file, the Office application also closes when you click the *Close* button on the file.

You can switch between open files or arrange open files to display more than one window at the same time. The following are several methods to do this:

- *Switch Windows button*: Click the **Switch Windows** button [*View* tab, *Window* group] (not available in Access) to display a drop-down list of open files. Click a file from the drop-down list to display the file.

- **Windows Taskbar.** Place your pointer on an Office application icon on the Windows *Taskbar* to display the open files in that application. Click a file thumbnail to display it (see Figure Intro-62).
- **Arrange All button**: Click the **Arrange All** button [*View* tab, *Window* group] to display all windows in an application. You can resize or move the open file windows.

Snap Assist

The **Snap Assist** feature in Windows provides the ability to position an open window to the left or right side of your computer screen and fill half the screen. When you snap an open window to the left or right side of the screen, the other open windows tile on the opposite side where you can select another window to fill the opposite side of the computer screen (Figure Intro-63).

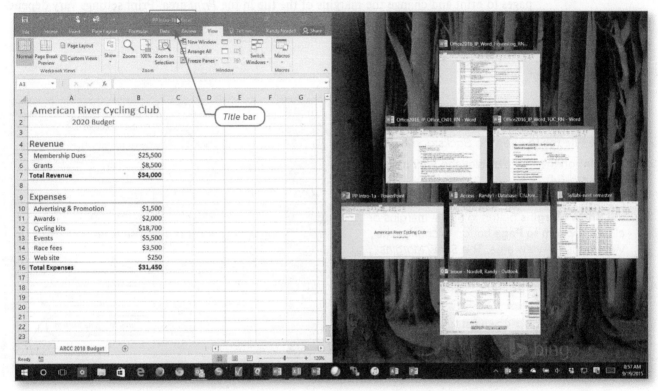

Figure Intro-63 Windows *Snap Assist* feature

▶HOW TO: Use Snap Assist

1. Click the **title bar** of an open window.
2. Drag it to the left or right edge of the computer screen and release the pointer.
   - The window snaps to the side of the screen and fills half of the computer screen (see Figure Intro-63).
   - The other open windows and apps display as tiles on the opposite side.
   - If you use a touch-screen computer, press and hold the title bar of an open window and drag to either side of the computer screen.
3. Select a tile of an open window or app to fill the other half of the screen.

> **MORE INFO**
>
> *Snap Assist* also enables you to snap a window to a quadrant (quarter rather than half) of your screen. Drag the **title bar** of an open window to one of the four corners of your computer screen.

Printing, Sharing, and Customizing Files

Use *Backstage* view in any of the Office applications, to print a file and to customize how a file is printed. You can also export an Office file as a PDF file in most of the Office applications. In addition, you can add and customize document properties for an Office file and share a file in a variety of formats.

Print a File

Print an Office file if you need a hard copy. The *Print* area on the *Backstage* view displays a preview of the open file and many print options. For example, you can choose which page or pages to print and change the margins of the file in the *Print* area. Print settings vary depending on the Office application you are using and what you are printing.

▶ HOW TO: Print a File

1. Open the file you want to print from a Windows folder or within an Office program.
2. Click the **File** tab to open the *Backstage* view.
3. Click **Print** on the left to display the *Print* area (Figure Intro-64).
   - A preview of the file displays on the right. Click the **Show Margins** button to adjust margins or click the **Zoom to Page** button to change the view in the *Preview* area. The *Show Margins* button is only available in Excel.
4. Change the number of copies to print in the *Copies* area.
5. Click the **Printer** drop-down list to choose from available printers.
6. Customize what is printed and how it is printed in the *Settings* area.
   - The *Settings* options vary depending on the Office application and what you print.
   - In the *Pages* area (*Slides* area in PowerPoint), select a page or range of pages (slides) to print.
   - By default, all pages (slides) are printed when you print a file.
7. Click the **Print** button to print your file.

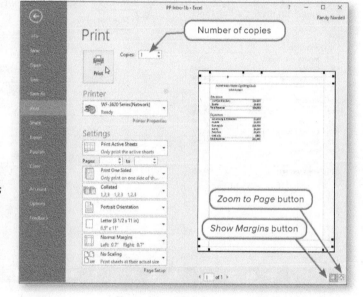

Figure Intro-64 *Print* area on the *Backstage* view

▶ ANOTHER WAY

Press **Ctrl+P** to open the *Print* area on the *Backstage* view.

Export as a PDF File

Portable document format, or **PDF**, is a specific file format that is often used to share files that are not to be changed, or to post files on a web site. When you create a PDF file from an Office application file, you are actually exporting a static image of the original file, similar to taking a picture of the file.

The advantage of working with a PDF file is that the format of the file is retained no matter who opens the file. PDF files open in the Windows Reader app or Adobe Reader, which is free software that is installed on most computers. Because a PDF file is a static image of a file, it is not easy for other people to edit your files. When you want people to be able to view a file but not change it, PDF files are a good choice.

▶ HOW TO: Export a File as a PDF File

1. Open the file you want to export as a PDF file.
2. Click the **File** tab and click **Export** to display the *Export* area on the Backstage view (Figure Intro-65).
3. Select **Create PDF/XPS Document** and click the **Create PDF/ XPS** button. The *Publish as PDF or XPS* dialog box opens.
   - XPS (XML Paper Specification) format is an alternative to a PDF file. XPS is a Microsoft format and is not widely used.
4. Select a location to save the file.
5. Type a name for the file in the *File name* area.
6. Click **Publish** to close the dialog box and save the PDF file.

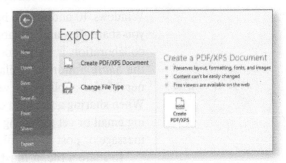

Figure Intro-65 *Export* a file as a PDF file

> ▶ **MORE INFO**
>
> Microsoft Word can open PDF files, and you can edit and save the file as a Word document.
>
> If Adobe Acrobat is installed on your computer, *Save as Adobe PDF* displays as an option on the *Backstage* view.

Document Properties

Document properties are hidden codes in a file that store identifying information about that file. Each piece of document property information is called a ***field***. You can view and modify document properties in the *Info* area of the *Backstage* view.

Some document properties fields are automatically generated when you work on a file, such as *Size, Total Editing Time, Created,* and *Last Modified.* Other document properties fields, such as *Title, Comments, Subject, Company,* and *Author,* can be modified. You can use document property fields in different ways such as inserting the *Company* field in a document footer.

▶ HOW TO: View and Modify Document Properties

1. Click the **File** tab and click **Info** (if not already selected). The document properties display on the right (Figure Intro-66).
2. Click the text box area of a field that can be edited and type your custom document property information.

Figure Intro-66 Document properties

3. Click the **Show All Properties** link at the bottom to display additional document properties.
   - Click **Show Fewer Properties** to collapse the list and display fewer properties.
   - This link toggles between *Show All Properties* and *Show Fewer Properties*.
4. Click the **Back** arrow to return to the file.

Share a File

Windows 10 and Office have been enhanced to help you share files and collaborate with others. Because collaboration is so important and commonly used, the *Share* button is available in the upper-right corner of the application window, except on Access. When sharing a file with others, you can send a sharing email or get a sharing link to paste into an email message or post in an online location.

To share a file, it must first be saved in *OneDrive*. If you try to share a file that is not saved in *OneDrive*, Word prompts you to save your document to *OneDrive* before sharing it. Depending on the type of Microsoft account you're using, the sharing options display in a *Send Link* window (education and business Microsoft accounts) (Figure Intro-67) or the *Share* pane (personal Microsoft account). The *Send Link* window or *Share* pane displays a variety of sharing options.

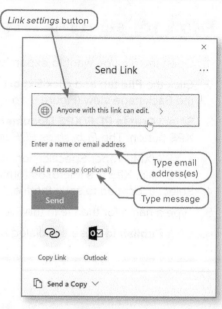

Figure Intro-67 *Send Link* window

▶ HOW TO: Share an Online File (Education and Business Microsoft Accounts)

Figure Intro-68 *Share* button

1. Open the file to share.
   - If the file is not saved in *OneDrive*, save the file to *OneDrive*.
2. Click the **Share** button (Figure Intro-68) in the upper-right corner of the Word window to open the *Send Link* window (see Figure Intro-67). The *Share* button icon may display differently in Office 2019.
3. Click the **Link settings** button (see Figure Intro-67) to open the *Link settings* window (Figure Intro-69).
   - Select who can use the sharing link.
   - Check the **Allow editing** box to enable recipients to edit the shared file. Deselect the **Allow editing** box to enable recipients to open and view the shared file, but restrict them from editing it.
   - Set an expiration date for the sharing link if desired (optional).
4. Click **Apply** to set the sharing link options and to return to the *Send Link* window (see Figure Intro-67).
5. Type the email address of the person with whom you are sharing the file in the *Enter a name or email address* area.
   - If typing multiple email addresses, separate each with a semicolon.
6. Type a message to recipient(s) in the *Add a message* area. This is optional.
7. Click the **Send** button. An email is sent to people you invited.
8. Click the **X** to close the confirmation window.

Figure Intro-69 *Link settings* window

If you're using a personal Microsoft account, the *Share* pane opens at the right after you click the *Share* button.

▶ **HOW TO:** Share an Online File (Personal Microsoft Account)

1. Open the file to share.
   - If the file is not saved in *OneDrive,* save the file to *OneDrive.*
2. Click the **Share** button in the upper-right corner of the Word window to open the *Share* pane to the right of the Word window (Figure Intro-70). The *Share* button icon may display differently in Office 2019.
3. Type or select the email address of the person with whom you are sharing the file in the *Invite people* area.
4. Select **Can edit** or **Can view** from the *Permission* drop-down list.
   - *Can edit* enables users to edit a shared document.
   - *Can view* enables users to open and view a shared document but restricts users from editing the document.
5. Type a message to recipient(s) in the *Message* area.
6. Click the **Share** button. An email is sent to people you invited.
7. Click the **X** to close the *Share* pane.

Figure Intro-70 Share a *OneDrive* file

Creating a sharing link (hyperlink) is another way to share a file with others rather than sending an email through Word. You can create and copy a sharing link and email the sharing link to others. You have the option of creating an *Edit link* or a *View-only link.*

▶ **HOW TO:** Create a Sharing Link (Education and Business Microsoft Accounts)

1. Open the file to share.
   - If the file is not saved in *OneDrive*, you are prompted to save the file to *OneDrive.*
2. Click the **Share** button in the upper right of the Word window to open the *Send Link* window.
3. Click the **Link settings** button to open the *Link settings* window (see Figure Intro-69).
   - Select who can use the sharing link.
   - Check the **Allow editing** box to enable recipients to edit the shared file. Deselect the **Allow editing** box to enable recipients to open and view the shared file, but restrict them from editing it.
   - Set an expiration date for the sharing link if desired (optional).
4. Click **Apply** to set the sharing link options and to return to the *Send Link* window.
5. Click the **Copy Link** button to open the window that displays the sharing link (Figure Intro-71).
6. Click the **Copy** button to copy the sharing link.
7. Click the **X** to close the confirmation window.
8. Paste the copied sharing link in an email, Word document, or other online location.

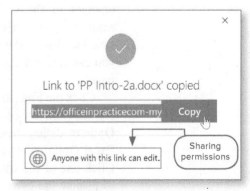

Figure Intro-71 Copy sharing link

If you're using a personal Microsoft account, the *Share* pane opens at the right after you after you click the *Share* button.

▶ **HOW TO:** Create a Sharing Link (Personal Microsoft Account)

1. Open the file to share.
   - If the file is not saved in *OneDrive*, you are prompted to save the file to *OneDrive*.
2. Click the **Share** button in the upper right of the Word window to open the *Share* pane to the right of the Word window.
3. Click **Get a sharing link** at the bottom of the *Share* pane (see Figure Intro-70).
4. Click the **Create an edit link** or **Create a view-only link** button (Figure Intro-72) to create a sharing link.
   - *Can edit* enables users to open, view, and edit a shared document.
   - *Can view* enables users to open and view a shared document but restricts users from editing the document.
5. Click the **Copy** button to copy the sharing link (Figure Intro-73).
6. Click the **Back** arrow to the left of *Get a sharing link* at the top of the *Share* pane to return to the main *Share* pane, or click the **X** to close the *Share* pane.
7. Paste the copied sharing link in an email, Word document, or other online location.

Figure Intro-72 Create a sharing link

Figure Intro-73 Copy a sharing link

▶ **ANOTHER WAY**

You can also share a file through email by clicking the **Send as attachment** link at the bottom of the *Share* pane. The email share options require the use of Microsoft Outlook (email and personal management Office application) to share the selected file through email.

Program Options

Use program options to apply global changes to the Office program. For example, you can change the default save location to the *OneDrive* folder or you can turn off the opening of a *Start* page.

Click the **File** tab and select **Options** on the left to open the *[Program]* **Options** dialog box (Word Options, Excel Options, etc.) (Figure Intro-74). Click one of the categories on the left to display the category options on the right. The categories and options vary depending on the Office application.

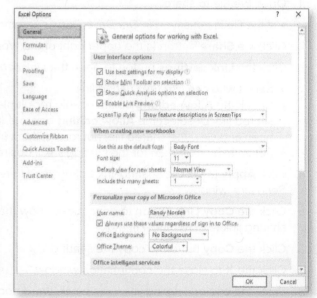

Figure Intro-74 *Excel Options* dialog box

Using the Ribbon, Tabs, and Quick Access Toolbar

Use the *Ribbon*, tabs, groups, buttons, drop-down lists, dialog boxes, task panes, galleries, and the *Quick Access* toolbar to modify your Office files. This section describes different tools used to customize your files.

The Ribbon, Tabs, and Groups

The ***Ribbon***, which appears at the top of an Office file window, displays the many features available. The *Ribbon* is a collection of ***tabs***. Each tab includes ***groups*** of commands. The tabs and groups available vary for each Office application. Click a tab to display the groups and commands available on that tab.

Some tabs always display on the *Ribbon* (for example, the *File* tab and *Home* tabs). Other tabs are contextual, which means that they only appear on the *Ribbon* when you select a specific object. Figure Intro-75 displays the contextual *Table Tools Fields* tab that displays in Access when you open a table.

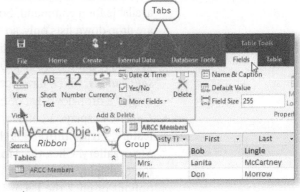
Figure Intro-75 Contextual *Table Tools Fields* tab displayed

 MORE INFO

The *Ribbon* may appear slightly different depending on the version of Office you are using.

Ribbon Display Options

The *Ribbon* displays by default in Office applications, and you can customize the appearance of the *Ribbon*. The ***Ribbon Display Options*** button is in the upper-right corner of an Office application window (Figure Intro-76). Click the **Ribbon Display Options** button to select one of the three options:

- ***Auto-Hide Ribbon***: Hides the *Ribbon*. Click at the top of the application to display the *Ribbon*.
- ***Show Tabs***: Displays *Ribbon* tabs only. Click a tab to open the *Ribbon* and display the tab.
- ***Show Tabs and Commands***: Displays the *Ribbon* and tabs, which is the default setting in Office applications.

Figure Intro-76 *Ribbon Display Options*

 MORE INFO

Ctrl+F1 collapses or expands the *Ribbon*. Also, double-click a tab name on the *Ribbon* to collapse or expand it.

Buttons, Drop-Down Lists, and Galleries

Groups on each of the tabs contain a variety of *buttons*, *drop-down lists*, and *galleries*. The following list describes each of these features and how they are used:

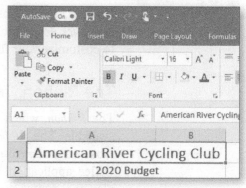

- **Button**: Applies a feature to selected text or an object. Click a button to apply the feature (Figure Intro-77).
- **Drop-down list**: Displays the various options available for a command. Some buttons are drop-down lists only, so when you click these buttons a drop-down list of options appears (Figure Intro-78). Other buttons are *split buttons*, which have both a button you click to apply a feature and an arrow you click to display a drop-down list of options (Figure Intro-79).

Figure Intro-77 Bold button in the Font group on the Home tab

- **Gallery**: Displays a collection of option buttons. Click an option in a gallery to apply the feature. Figure Intro-80 is the *Styles* gallery. Click the **More** button to display the entire gallery of options or click the **Up** or **Down** arrow to display a different row of options.

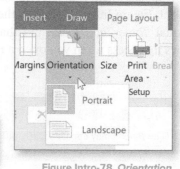

Figure Intro-80 Styles gallery in Word

Figure Intro-78 Orientation drop-down list

Figure Intro-79 Merge & Center split button—button and drop-down list

Click the arrow on a split button to display the drop-down list

Dialog Boxes, Task Panes, and Launchers

Office application features are also available in a *dialog box* or *task pane*. A *launcher*, which is a small square that displays in the bottom right of some groups, opens a dialog box or displays a task pane when clicked (see Figure Intro-82).

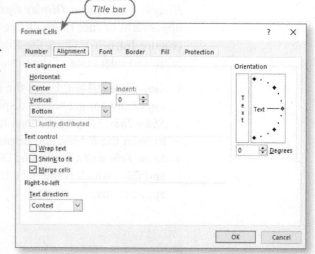

- **Dialog box**: A new window that opens to display additional features. Move a dialog box by clicking and dragging the title bar. The title bar appears at the top of the dialog box and displays the title. Figure Intro-81 shows the *Format Cells* dialog box that opens after you click the *Alignment* launcher in Excel.

Figure Intro-81 Format Cells dialog box

- **Task pane**: Opens on the left or right of an Office application window. Figure Intro-82 shows the *Clipboard* pane, which is available in all Office applications. Task panes are named according to their purpose (for example, *Clipboard* pane or *Navigation* pane). You can resize a task pane by clicking and dragging its left or right border. Click the **X** in the upper-right corner to close a task pane.

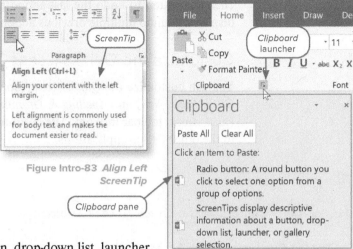

Figure Intro-83 *Align Left ScreenTip*

ScreenTips

ScreenTips display descriptive information about a button, drop-down list, launcher, or gallery selection. When you place your pointer on an item on the *Ribbon*, a *ScreenTip* displays information about the selection (Figure Intro-83). The *ScreenTip* appears temporarily and displays the command name, keyboard shortcut (if available), and a description of the command.

Figure Intro-82 *Clipboard* pane

Radio Buttons, Check Boxes, and Text Boxes

Dialog boxes and task panes contain a variety of options you can apply using ***radio buttons***, ***check boxes***, ***text boxes***, ***drop-down lists***, and other buttons (Figure Intro-84).

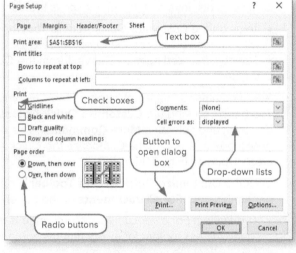

Figure Intro-84 *Page Setup* dialog box in Excel

- ***Radio button***: A round button you click to select one option from a group of options. A selected radio button displays a solid dot inside the round button. Radio buttons are mutually exclusive.
- ***Check box***: A square button you click to select one or more options. A check appears in a selected check box.
- ***Text box***: An area where you type text.

A task pane or dialog box may also include drop-down lists or other buttons that open additional dialog boxes. Figure Intro-84 shows the *Page Setup* dialog box in Excel, which includes a variety of radio buttons, check boxes, text boxes, drop-down lists, and command buttons that open additional dialog boxes (for example, the *Print* and *Options* buttons).

Quick Access Toolbar

The ***Quick Access toolbar*** is located above the *Ribbon* on the upper left of each Office application window. It contains buttons to apply commonly used commands such as *Save, Undo, Redo,* and *Open.* The *Undo* button is a split button (Figure Intro-85). You can

Figure Intro-85 *Quick Access* toolbar

click the button to undo the last action performed, or you can click the drop-down arrow to display and undo multiple previous actions.

Customize the Quick Access Toolbar

You can customize the *Quick Access* toolbar to include commands you regularly use, such as *Quick Print*, *New*, and *Spelling & Grammar*. The following steps show how to customize the *Quick Access* toolbar in Word. The customization process is similar for the *Quick Access* toolbar in the other Office applications.

▶**HOW TO:** Customize the Quick Access Toolbar

1. Click the **Customize Quick Access Toolbar** drop-down list on the right edge of the *Quick Access* toolbar (Figure Intro-86).

2. Select a command to add to the *Quick Access* toolbar. The command displays on the *Quick Access* toolbar.
   - Items on the *Customize Quick Access Toolbar* drop-down list with a check display on the *Quick Access* toolbar.
   - Select a checked item to remove it from the *Quick Access* toolbar.

3. Add a command that is not listed on the *Customize Quick Access Toolbar* by clicking the **Customize Quick Access Toolbar** drop-down list and selecting **More Commands**. The *Word Options* dialog box opens with the *Customize the Quick Access Toolbar* area displayed (Figure Intro-87).

4. Click the **Customize Quick Access Toolbar** drop-down list on the right and select **For all documents** or the current document.
   - If you select *For all documents*, the change is made to the *Quick Access* toolbar for all documents you open in Word.
   - If you select the current document, the change is made to the *Quick Access* toolbar in that document only.

5. Select the command to add from the alphabetic list of commands on the left and click the **Add** button.
   - If you can't find a command, click the **Choose commands from** drop-down list and select **All Commands**.
   - The list on the right contains the commands that display on the *Quick Access* toolbar.

6. Rearrange commands on the *Quick Access* toolbar by selecting a command in the list on the right and clicking the **Move Up** or **Move Down** button.

7. Click **OK** to close the *Word Options* dialog box.

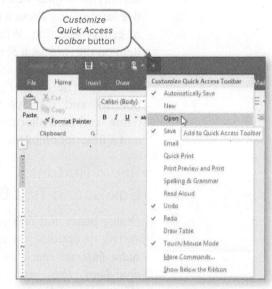

Figure Intro-86 Add a command to the *Quick Access* toolbar

Figure Intro-87 Customize the *Quick Access* toolbar in the *Word Options* dialog box

SLO INTRO. 7

Using Context Menus, the Mini Toolbar, and Keyboard Shortcuts

Most of the commands used for formatting and editing your files display in groups on the tabs. But many of these features are also available using context menus, the mini toolbar, and keyboard shortcuts. Use these tools to quickly apply formatting or other options to text or objects.

Context Menu

A *context menu* displays when you right-click text, a cell, or an object such as a picture, drawing object, chart, or *SmartArt* (Figure Intro-88). The context menu is a vertical list of options, and the options are contextual, which means they vary depending on what you right-click. Context menus include options that perform an action (*Cut* or *Copy*), open a dialog box or task pane (*Format Cells* or *Insert*), or display a drop-down list of selections (*Filter* or *Sort*).

Mini Toolbar

The *mini toolbar* is another context menu that displays when you right-click or select text, a cell, or an object in your file (see Figure Intro-88). The mini toolbar is a horizontal rectangular menu that lists a variety of formatting options. These options vary

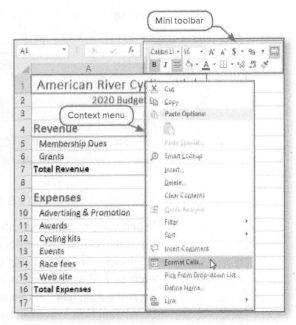

Figure Intro-88 Context menu and mini toolbar

depending on what you select or right-click. The mini toolbar contains a variety of buttons and drop-down lists. The mini toolbar typically displays above the context menu, and it automatically displays when you select text or an object, such as when you select a row of a table in Word or PowerPoint.

Keyboard Shortcuts

You can also use a *keyboard shortcut* to quickly apply formatting or perform commands. A keyboard shortcut is a combination of keyboard keys that you press at the same time. These can include the **Ctrl**, **Shift**, **Alt**, letter, number, and function keys (for example, **F1** or **F7**). Table Intro-5 lists common Office keyboard shortcuts.

Table.Intro-5: Common Office Keyboard Shortcuts

Keyboard Shortcut	Action or Displays	Keyboard Shortcut	Action or Displays
Ctrl+S	Save	Ctrl+Z	Undo
F12	*Save As* dialog box	Ctrl+Y	Redo or Repeat
Ctrl+O	*Open* area on the *Backstage* view	Ctrl+1	Single space
Shift+F12	*Open* dialog box	Ctrl+2	Double space
Ctrl+N	New blank file	Ctrl+L	Align left
Ctrl+P	*Print* area on the *Backstage* view	Ctrl+E	Align center
Ctrl+C	Copy	Ctrl+R	Align right
Ctrl+X	Cut	F1	*Help* pane
Ctrl+V	Paste	F7	*Spelling* pane
Ctrl+B	Bold	Ctrl+A	Select All
Ctrl+I	Italic	Ctrl+Home	Move to the beginning
Ctrl+U	Underline	Ctrl+End	Move to the end

> **MORE INFO**
>
> See *Appendix A: Microsoft Office Shortcuts* (online resource) for additional Office keyboard shortcuts.

Function Keys on a Laptop

When using a laptop computer, function keys perform specific Windows actions on your laptop, such as increase or decrease speaker volume, open Windows *Settings*, or adjust the screen brightness. So, when using a numbered function key in an Office application, such as *F12* as a shortcut to open the *Save As* dialog box, you may need to press the **Function key** (**Fn** or **fn**) on your keyboard in conjunction with a numbered function key to activate the Office command (Figure Intro-89). The *Function key* is typically located near the bottom left of your laptop keyboard next to the *Ctrl* key.

Figure Intro-89
Function key

PAUSE & PRACTICE: INTRO-2

For this project, you work with a document for the American River Cycling Club. You modify the existing document, add document properties, customize the *Quick Access* toolbar, export the document as a PDF file, and share the document.

File Needed: ***ARCCTraining-Intro.docx*** *(Student data files are available in the* Library *of your SIMnet account.)*
Completed Project File Names: ***[your initials] PP Intro-2a.docx*** and ***[your initials] PP Intro-2b.pdf***

1. Open Word and open the ***ARCCTraining-Intro*** file from your student data files. If the file opens in *Protected View*, click the **Enable Editing** button.

2. Save this document as [your initials] PP Intro-2a in the *American River Cycling Club* folder in your *OneDrive* folder.
   a. In *Pause & Practice Intro-1*, you created the *American River Cycling Club* folder in *OneDrive* or other storage area. Save this file in the same location.
   b. If you don't save this file in *OneDrive*, you will not be able to complete steps 7 and 9 in this project.

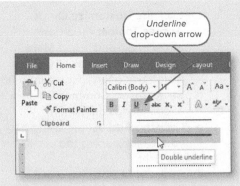

Figure Intro-90 Apply *Double underline* to selected text

3. Use a button, drop-down list, and dialog box to modify the document.
   a. Select the first heading, "**What is Maximum Heart Rate?**"
   b. Click the **Bold** button [*Home* tab, *Font* group].
   c. Click the **Underline** drop-down arrow and select **Double underline** (Figure Intro-90).
   d. Click the **launcher** in the *Font* group [*Home* tab] to open the *Font* dialog box (Figure Intro-91).
   e. Select **12** from the *Size* area list or type 12 in the text box.
   f. Click the **Small caps** check box in the *Effects* area to select it.
   g. Click **OK** to close the dialog box and apply the formatting changes.
   h. Select the next heading, "**What is Target Heart Rate?**"
   i. Repeat steps 3b–g to apply formatting to selected text.

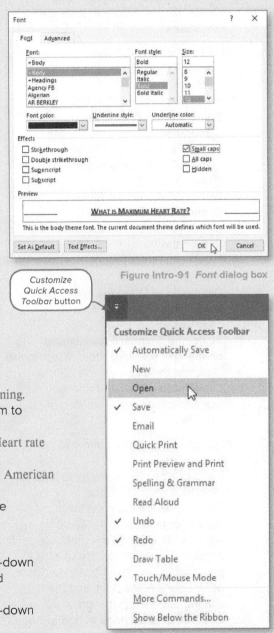

Figure Intro-91 *Font* dialog box

4. Add document properties.
   a. Click the **File** tab to display the *Backstage* view.
   b. Select **Info** on the left (if not already selected). The document properties display on the right.
   c. Click the **Add a title** text box and type ARCC Training.
   d. Click the **Show All Properties** link near the bottom to display additional document properties.
   e. Click the **Specify the subject** text box and type Heart rate training.
   f. Click the **Specify the company** text box and type American River Cycling Club.
   g. Click the **Back** arrow on the upper left to close the *Backstage* view and return to the document.

5. Customize the *Quick Access* toolbar.
   a. Click the **Customize Quick Access Toolbar** drop-down arrow and select **Open** if it is not already selected (Figure Intro-92).
   b. Click the **Customize Quick Access Toolbar** drop-down arrow again and select **Spelling & Grammar**.

Figure Intro-92 *Customize Quick Access Toolbar* drop-down list

c. Click the **Customize Quick Access Toolbar** drop-down arrow again and select **More Commands**. The *Word Options* dialog box opens (Figure Intro-93).

d. Select **Insert Comment** in the list of commands on the left.

e. Click the **Add** button to add it to your *Quick Access* toolbar list on the right.

f. Click **OK** to close the *Word Options* dialog box.

g. Click the **Save** button on the *Quick Access* toolbar to save the document.

Figure Intro-93 Customize the *Quick Access* toolbar in the *Word Options* dialog box

6. Export the file as a PDF file.

a. Click the **File** tab to go to the *Backstage* view.

b. Select **Export** on the left.

c. Select **Create PDF/XPS Document** and click the **Create PDF/XPS** button. The *Publish as PDF or XPS* dialog box opens (Figure Intro-94).

d. Select the **American River Cycling Club** folder in your *OneDrive* folder as the location to save the file.

e. Type [your initials] PP Intro-2b in the *File name* area.

f. Deselect the **Open file after publishing** check box if it is checked.

g. Select the **Standard (publishing online and printing)** radio button in the *Optimize for* area.

h. Click **Publish** to close the dialog box and create a PDF version of your file.

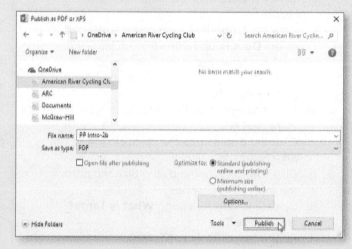

Figure Intro-94 *Publish as PDF or XPS* dialog box

7. Create a sharing link to share this file with your instructor.

a. If you don't have the ability to save to *OneDrive*, skip all of step 7.

b. Click the **Share** button in the upper-right corner of the Word window. The *Send Link* window opens (Figure Intro-95). If you are using a personal Microsoft account, the *Share* pane opens at the right, and the sharing options differ slightly.

c. Click the **Link settings** button to open the *Link settings* window.

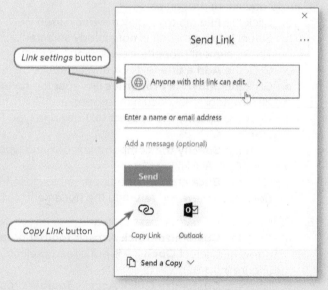

Figure Intro-95 *Send Link* window

d. Click the **Anyone** button and check the **Allow editing** box (if necessary) (Figure Intro-96).

e. Click **Apply** to return to the *Send Link* window.

f. Click the **Copy Link** button to create a sharing link.

g. Click **Copy** to copy the sharing link and click the **X** in the upper-right corner to close the sharing link window (Figure Intro-97).

h. Use your email account to create a new email to your instructor. Include an appropriate subject line and a brief message in the body.

i. Press **Ctrl+V** to paste the sharing link to your document in the body of the email and send the email message.

8. Save and close the document (Figure Intro-98).

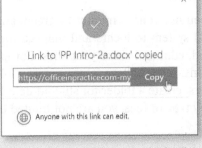

Figure Intro-97 Copy a sharing link

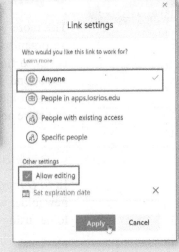

Figure Intro-96 *Link settings* window

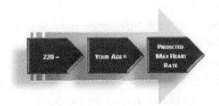

Figure Intro-98 PP Intro-2a completed

American River Cycling Club

www.arcc.org Cycling...a way of life info@arcc.org

WHAT IS MAXIMUM HEART RATE?

The maximum heart rate is the highest your pulse rate can get. To calculate your **predicted maximum heart rate**, use this formula:

(Example: a 40-year-old's predicted maximum heart rate is 180.)

Your actual maximum heart rate can be determined by a graded exercise test. Please note that some medicines and medical conditions might affect your maximum heart rate. If you are taking medicines or have a medical condition (such as heart disease, high blood pressure, or diabetes), always ask your doctor if your maximum heart rate/target heart rate will be affected.

WHAT IS TARGET HEART RATE?

You gain the most benefits and decrease the risk of injury when you exercise in your target heart rate zone. Usually this is when your exercise heart rate (pulse) is 60 percent to 85 percent of your maximum heart rate. Do not exercise above 85 percent of your maximum heart rate. This increases both cardiovascular and orthopedic risk and does not add any extra benefit.

When beginning an exercise program, you might need to gradually build up to a level that is within your target heart rate zone, especially if you have not exercised regularly before. If the exercise feels too hard, slow down. You will reduce your risk of injury and enjoy the exercise more if you don't try to over-do it.

To find out if you are exercising in your target zone (between 60 percent and 85 percent of your maximum heart rate), use your heart rate monitor to track your heart rate. If your pulse is below your target zone (see the chart below), increase your rate of exercise. If your pulse is above your target zone, decrease your rate of exercise.

MAX AND TARGET HEART RATES

Age	Predicted Max Heart Rate	Target Heart Rate (60-85% of Max)
20	✓ 200	120-170
25	✓ 195	117-166
30	✓ 190	114-162
35	✓ 185	111-157
40	✓ 180	108-153
45	✓ 175	105-149
50	✓ 170	102-145
55	✓ 165	99-140
60	✓ 160	96-136
65	✓ 155	93-132
70	✓ 150	90-128

Organizing and Customizing Folders and Files

The more you use your computer to create and edit files, the more important it is to create an organized system to locate and manage files. Use *folders* to store related files to make it easier to find, edit, and share your files. For example, you can create a folder for the college you attend. Inside the college folder, create a folder for each of your courses. Inside each of the course folders, create a folder for student data files, solution files, and group projects. Folders can store any type of files; you are not limited to Office files.

Create a Folder

In *SLO Intro. 3: Creating, Saving, Closing, and Opening Office Files*, you learned how to create a new folder when saving an Office file in the *Save As* dialog box. You can also create a Windows folder using *File Explorer*. You can create folders inside other folders.

▶HOW TO: Create a Windows Folder

1. Click the **File Explorer** on the *Taskbar* or click the **Start** button and select **File Explorer** to open a *File Explorer* window.
   - Your folders and computer locations display on the left in the *Navigation* pane.
2. Select the location in the *Navigation* pane where you want to create a new folder.
3. Click the **Home** tab and click the **New folder** button [*New* group]. A new folder is created (Figure Intro-99).
   - The *New Folder* button is also on the *Quick Access* toolbar in the *File Explorer* window.
4. Type the name of the new folder and press **Enter**.

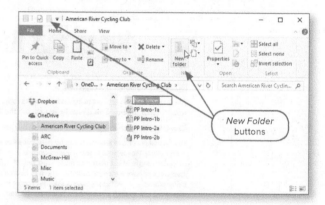

Figure Intro-99 Create a new Windows folder

> **ANOTHER WAY**
>
> **Ctrl+Shift+N** creates a new folder in a Windows folder.

Move and Copy Files and Folders

Moving a file or folder is cutting it from one location and pasting it in another location. Copying a file or folder creates a copy, and you can paste in another location so the file or folder is in two or more locations. If you move or copy a folder, the files in the folder are moved or copied with the folder. Move or copy files and folders using the *Move to* or *Copy to* buttons on the *Home* tab of *File Explorer*, keyboard shortcuts (**Ctrl+X, Ctrl+C, Ctrl+V**), or the drag-and-drop method.

To move or copy multiple folders or files at the same time, press the **Ctrl** key and select multiple items to move or copy. Use the **Ctrl** key to select or deselect multiple non-adjacent files or folders. Use the **Shift** key to select a range of files or folders. Click the first file or folder in a range, press the **Shift** key, and select the last file or folder in the range to select all of the items in the range.

▶ HOW TO: Move or Copy a File or Folder

1. Click the **File Explorer** on the *Taskbar* or click the **Start** button and select **File Explorer** to open a *File Explorer* window.

2. Select a file or folder to move or copy.
   - Press the **Ctrl** key or the **Shift** key to select multiple files or folders.

3. Click the **Home** tab in the *File Explorer* window.

4. Click the **Move to** or **Copy to** button [*Organize* group] and select the location where you want to move or copy the file or folder (Figure Intro-100).

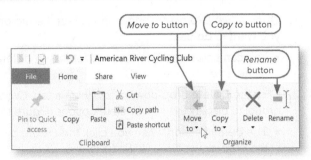

Figure Intro-100 Move or copy a selected file or folder

   - If the folder is not available, select **Choose location** to open the *Move Items* or *Copy Items* dialog box.
   - To use keyboard shortcuts, press **Ctrl+X** to cut the file or folder or **Ctrl+C** to copy the file or folder from its original location, go to the desired new location, and press **Ctrl+V** to paste it.
   - To use the drag-and-drop method to move a file or folder, select the file or folder and drag and drop to the new location.
   - To use the drag-and-drop method to copy a file or folder, press the **Ctrl** key, select the file or folder, and drag and drop to the new location.

> **ANOTHER WAY**
>
> Right-click a file or folder to display the context menu and select **Cut**, **Copy**, or **Paste**.

Rename Files and Folders

You can rename a file or folder in a *File Explorer* window. When you rename a file or folder, only the file or folder name changes. The contents of the file or folder do not change.

▶ HOW TO: Rename a File or Folder

1. Click the **File Explorer** on the *Taskbar* or click the **Start** button and select **File Explorer** to open a *File Explorer* window.

2. Select the file or folder you want to rename.

3. Click the **Rename** button [*Home* tab, *Organize* group] (see Figure Intro-100).

4. Type the new name of the file or folder and press **Enter**.

> **ANOTHER WAY**
>
> Select a file or folder to rename, press **F2**, type the new name, and press **Enter**. You can also right-click a file or folder and select **Rename** from the context menu.

Delete Files and Folders

You can easily delete files and folders. When you delete a file or folder, it is moved from its current location to the *Recycle Bin* on your computer. The *Recycle Bin* stores deleted items. If a file or folder is in the *Recycle Bin*, you can restore it to its original location or move it to a different location. You also have the option to permanently delete a file or folder. If an item is permanently deleted, you do not have the restore option.

▶ HOW TO: Delete Files and Folders

1. Open a *File Explorer* window and select the file or folder you want to delete.
   - You can select multiple files and folders to delete at the same time.

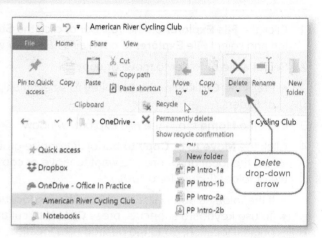

2. Click the **Delete** drop-down arrow [*Home* tab, *Organize* group] to display the list of delete options (Figure Intro-101).
   - The default action when you click the *Delete* button (not the drop-down arrow) is *Recycle*.

3. Delete a file by selecting **Recycle**, which moves it to the *Recycle Bin*.
   - *Recycle* deletes the item(s) and moves it (them) to the *Recycle Bin*.
   - When you *Recycle* an item, you are not prompted to confirm the deletion. To change the default setting, select **Show recycle confirmation** from the *Delete* drop-down list. A confirmation dialog box displays each time you delete or recycle an item.

Figure Intro-101 Delete selected folder

4. Delete a file permanently by clicking the **Delete** drop-down arrow and selecting **Permanently delete**. A confirmation dialog box opens. Click **Yes** to confirm the deletion.
   - *Permanently delete* deletes the item(s) from your computer.

▶ **ANOTHER WAY**

Press **Ctrl+D** or the **Delete** key on your keyboard to recycle selected item(s).
Press **Shift+Delete** to permanently delete selected item(s).

Create a Zipped (Compressed) Folder

If you want to share multiple files or a folder of files with classmates, coworkers, friends, or family, you can *zip* the files into a *zipped folder* (also called a *compressed folder*). For example, you can't attach an entire folder to an email message, but you can attach a zipped folder to an email message. Compressing files and folders decreases their size. You can zip a group of selected files, a folder, or a combination of files and folders, and then share the zipped folder with others through email or in a cloud storage location such as *OneDrive*.

▶ HOW TO: Create a Zipped (Compressed) Folder

1. Open a *File Explorer* window.

2. Select the file(s) and/or folder(s) you want to zip (compress).

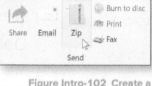

3. Click the **Zip** button [*Share* tab, *Send* group] (Figure Intro-102). A zipped folder is created.
   - The default name of the zipped folder is the name of the first item you selected to zip.

4. Type a name for the zipped folder and press **Enter**. Alternatively, press **Enter** to accept the default name.
   - The icon for a zipped folder looks similar to the icon for a folder except it has a vertical zipper down the middle of the folder.

Figure Intro-102 Create a zipped folder

Extract a Zipped (Compressed) Folder

If you receive a zipped folder via email or download a zipped folder, save the zipped folder to your computer and then *extract* its contents. Extracting a zipped folder creates a regular Windows folder from the zipped folder.

▶ HOW TO: Extract a Zipped (Compressed) Folder

1. Select the zipped folder to extract.
2. Click the **Compressed Folder Tools** tab.
3. Click the **Extract all** button (Figure Intro-103). The *Extract Compressed (Zipped) Folders* dialog box opens (Figure Intro-104).
4. Click **Extract** to extract the folder.
   - Both the extracted folder and the zipped folder display.
   - If you check the **Show extracted files when complete** check box, the extracted folder will open after extracting.

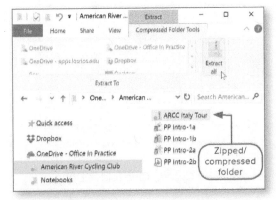

Figure Intro-103 Extract files from a zipped folder

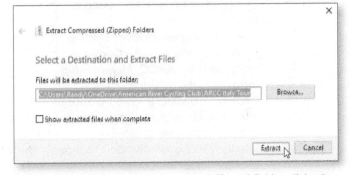

Figure Intro-104 *Extract Compressed (Zipped) Folders* dialog box

For this project, you copy and rename files in your *OneDrive* folder on your computer, create a folder, move files, create a zipped folder, and rename a zipped folder.

Files Needed: *[your initials] PP Intro-1a.pptx*, *[your initials] PP Intro-1b.xlsx*, *[your initials] PP Intro-2a.docx*, *[your initials] PP Intro-2b.docx*, and **ARCC_Membership-Intro.accdb** *(Student data files are available in the Library of your SIMnet account.)*
Completed Project File Names: *[your initials] PP Intro-1a.pptx*, *[your initials] PP Intro-1b.xlsx*, *[your initials] PP Intro-2a.docx*, *[your initials] PP Intro-2b.docx*, *[your initials] PP Intro-3.accdb*, and **ARCC Italy Tour-2020** (zipped folder)

---

1. Copy and rename a file.
   a. Click the **File Explorer** on the *Taskbar* or click the **Start** button and select **File Explorer** to open a *File Explorer* window. If *File Explorer* is not available on the *Taskbar* or *Start* menu, use *Cortana* to find and open a *File Explorer* window.
   b. Browse the *File Explorer* window to locate your student data files.
   c. Select the **ARCC_Membership-Intro** file.
   d. Click the **Copy to** button [*Home* tab, *Organize* group] and select **Choose location** from the drop-down list to open the *Copy Items* dialog box.
   e. Browse to locate the *American River Cycling Club* folder you created in *Pause & Practice: Intro-1*.
   f. Select the **American River Cycling Club** folder and click the **Copy** button to copy the **ARCC_Membership-Intro** file to the *American River Cycling Club* folder (Figure Intro-105). The *Copy Items* dialog box closes and the copied file displays.

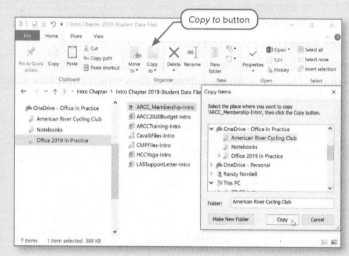

Figure Intro-105 *Copy Items* dialog box

   g. Use the *File Explorer* window to browse and locate the *American River Cycling Club* folder. Double-click the folder to open it.
   h. Click the **ARCC_Membership-Intro** file in the *American River Cycling Club* folder to select it.
   i. Click the **Rename** button [*Home* tab, *Organize* group], type [your initials] PP Intro-3 as the new file name, and press **Enter** (Figure Intro-106).

2. Create a new folder and move files.
   a. With the *American River Cycling Club* folder still open, click the **New folder** button [*Home* tab, *New* group] (see Figure Intro-106).
   b. Type ARCC Italy Tour as the name of the new folder and press **Enter**.
   c. Select the *[your initials] PP Intro-1a* file.

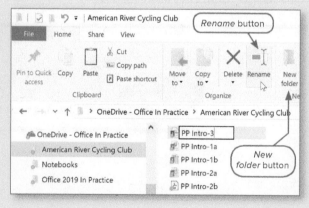

Figure Intro-106 Rename a file

d. Press the **Ctrl** key, select the *[your initials] PP Intro-1b*, *[your initials] PP Intro-2a*, *[your initials] PP Intro-2b*, and *[your initials] PP Intro-3* files, and release the **Ctrl** key. All five files should be selected.

e. Click the **Move to** button [*Home* tab, *Organize* group] and select **Choose location** to open the *Move Items* dialog box (Figure Intro-107).

f. Browse to locate the *ARCC Italy Tour* folder in the *Move Items* dialog box.

g. Select the **ARCC Italy Tour** folder and click the **Move** button to move the selected files to the *ARCC Italy Tour* folder.

h. Double-click the **ARCC Italy Tour** folder to open it and confirm the five files are moved.

i. Click the **Up** or **Back** arrow above the *Navigation* pane to return to the *American River Cycling Club* folder (see Figure Intro-107).

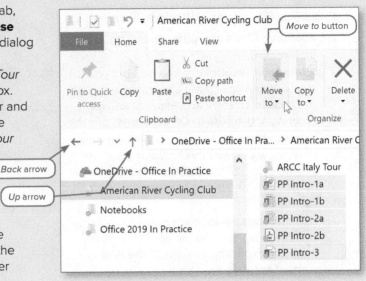

Figure Intro-107 Move selected files to a different folder

3. Create a zipped folder.
   a. Select the **ARCC Italy Tour** folder.
   b. Click the **Zip** button [*Share* tab, *Send* group]. A zipped (compressed) folder is created.
   c. Place the insertion point at the end of the zipped folder name, type *–2020*, and press **Enter** (Figure Intro-108).

4. Email the zipped folder to your instructor.
   a. Use your email account to create a new email to send to your instructor.
   b. Include an appropriate subject line and a brief message in the body.
   c. Attach the **ARCC Italy Tour-2020** zipped folder to the email message and send the email message.

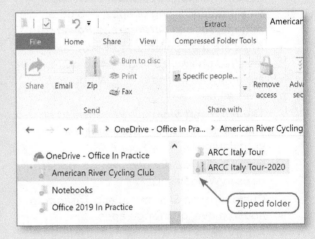

Figure Intro-108 Create a zipped folder

Chapter Summary

Intro. 1 Explore select features of Windows 10 (p. Intro-2).

- **Windows 10** is a computer operating system.
- A **Microsoft account** is a free account you create. When you create a Microsoft account, you receive an email address, a **OneDrive** account, and access to **Office Online**.
- The **Windows desktop** is the working area of Windows 10, and the **Taskbar** displays at the bottom of the desktop. You can rearrange icons and pin applications to the *Taskbar.*
- Use the **Start menu** in Windows 10 to select a task. You can pin applications to the *Start* menu and customize the arrangement of apps.
- The left side of the **Start menu** displays **Recently added** apps, **Most used** apps, an alphabetic listing of apps, and other buttons, such as **Settings** and **Power**.
- **Apps** are the applications or programs installed on your computer. App buttons are arranged in tiles on the Windows 10 *Start* menu.
- The **Microsoft Store** is a Windows 10 app you use to search for and install apps on your computer.
- Install both **traditional apps** and **modern apps** in Windows 10.
- Customize the *Start* menu and *Taskbar* to add, remove, or arrange apps.
- *File Explorer* is a window that displays files and folders on your computer.
- *OneDrive* is the cloud storage area where you can store files in a private and secure online location.
- The **OneDrive folder** in Windows 10 is one of your file storage location options.
- Access *OneDrive* folders and files using an internet browser window.
- **Cortana** is a search tool in Windows 10 used to locate information on your computer and the internet.
- **Task View** displays all open apps and windows as tiles on your desktop. Select an app or window to display or close.
- Use the **Settings** window to customize the Windows environment.

- The **Action Center** displays notifications and buttons to open many common Windows settings and features.

Intro. 2 Use basic features of Microsoft Office and navigate the Office working environment (p. Intro-12).

- **Office 2019/365** is application software that includes **Word, Excel, Access, PowerPoint, Outlook, OneNote**, and **Publisher**.
- **Office 2019** and **Office 365** include the same application products, but they differ in how you purchase them. Office 365 includes features that may not be available in Office 2019.
- **Office desktop apps** are the full-function Office 2019 or 365 products you install on your laptop or desktop computer.
- **Office universal apps** are a scaled-down version of Office applications installed on a tablet or mobile device.
- **Office Online** is free online software that works in conjunction with your online *Microsoft* account.
- A **Start page** displays when you open each of the Office applications. You can open an existing file or create a new file.
- The **Backstage view** in each of the Office applications performs many common tasks such as saving, opening an existing file, creating a new file, printing, and sharing.
- **Tell Me** is the Office help feature that displays Office commands related to specific topics.
- Use the mouse (or touchpad) on your computer to navigate the pointer on your computer screen. Use the pointer or click buttons to select text or objects.
- When using Office 2019/365 on a touch-screen computer, use the touch screen to perform actions. You can choose between **Touch Mode** and **Mouse Mode** in Office applications.

Intro. 3 Create, save, close, and open Office files (p. Intro-19).

- Create a new Office file from the *Start* page or *Backstage* view of the Office application.

- Assign a file name when you save a file for the first time.
- *AutoSave* is a new feature that automatically saves a file stored in *OneDrive*.
- Create folders to organize saved files, and you can save a file as a different file name.
- Office applications use a variety of different file types.
- Close an Office file when finished working on it. If the file has not been saved or changes have been made to the file, you are prompted to save the file before closing.
- Open an existing file from the *Start* page or from the *Open* area on *Backstage* view in each of the Office applications.

Intro. 4 Customize the view and display size in Office applications and work with multiple Office files (p. Intro-28).

- Each Office application has a variety of display views.
- Select an application view from the options on the *View tab* or the view buttons on the *Status bar*.
- The *Zoom* feature changes the display size of your file.
- *Minimize*, *restore down*, or *maximize* an open Office application window.
- Work with multiple Office files at the same time and switch between open files.
- *Snap Assist* enables you to arrange an open window on one side of your computer screen and select another window to fill the other side of the screen.

Intro. 5 Print, share, and customize Office files (p. Intro-32).

- Print a file in a variety of formats. The *Print* area on the *Backstage* view lists print options and displays a preview of your file.
- Export a file as a *PDF (portable document format)* file and save the PDF file to post to a web site or share with others.
- *Document properties* store information about a file.
- Share Office files in a variety of ways and enable others to view or edit shared files. To share a file with others, save the file in *OneDrive*.

- Program options are available on the *Backstage* view. Use program options to apply global changes to an Office application.

Intro. 6 Use the *Ribbon*, tabs, groups, dialog boxes, task panes, galleries, and the *Quick Access* toolbar (p. Intro-37).

- The *Ribbon* appears at the top of an Office window. It contains *tabs* and *groups* with commands to format and edit files.
- The *Ribbon Display Options* provides different ways to display the *Ribbon* in Office applications.
- A variety of *buttons*, *drop-down lists*, and *galleries* display within groups on each tab.
- *Dialog boxes* contain additional features not always displayed on the *Ribbon*.
- Click the *launcher* in the bottom-right corner of selected groups to open a dialog box.
- A *ScreenTip* displays information about commands on the *Ribbon*.
- Dialog boxes contain *radio buttons*, *check boxes*, *drop-down lists*, and *text boxes*.
- The *Quick Access toolbar* contains buttons that enable you to perform commands and displays in all Office applications. It is located in the upper left.
- Add or remove commands on the *Quick Access* toolbar.

Intro. 7 Use context menus, mini toolbar, keyboard shortcuts, and function keys in Office applications (p. Intro-41).

- A *context menu* displays when you right-click text or an object. A context menu contains different features depending on what you right-click.
- A *mini toolbar* is another context menu that displays formatting options.
- Use *keyboard shortcuts* to apply features or initiate commands.
- Numbered *function keys* perform commands in Office applications. On laptops, you may have to press the **Function key** (**Fn** or **fn**) to activate the numbered function keys.

Intro. 8 Organize and customize Windows folders and Office files (p. Intro-46).

- *Folders* store and organize files.
- Create, move, or copy files and folders. Files stored in a folder are moved or copied with that folder.
- Rename a file to change the file name.
- A deleted file or folder moves to the *Recycle Bin* on your computer by default. Alternatively, you can permanently delete files and folders.
- *Zip* files and/or folders into a *zipped (compressed) folder* to email or to share multiple files as a single file.
- *Extract* a zipped folder to create a regular Windows folder and to access its contents.

Check for Understanding

The SIMbook for this text (within your SIMnet account) provides the following resources for concept review:

- Multiple-choice questions
- Short answer questions
- Matching exercises

For these projects, you use your *OneDrive* to store files. If you don't already have a Microsoft account, see *SLO Intro.1: Using Windows 10* for information about creating a free personal Microsoft account.

Guided Project Intro-1

For this project, you organize and edit files for Emma Cavalli at Placer Hills Real Estate. You extract a zipped folder, rename files, manage multiple documents, apply formatting, and export as a PDF file. [Student Learning Outcomes Intro.1, Intro.2, Intro.3, Intro.4, Intro.5, Intro.6, Intro.7, Intro.8]

Files Needed: ***CavalliFiles-Intro*** (zipped folder) *(Student data files are available in the* Library *of your* SIMnet *account.)*
Completed Project File Names: ***PHRE*** folder containing the following files: ***BuyerEscrowChecklist-Intro***, ***CavalliProspectingLetter-Intro***, *[your initials]* ***Intro-1a.accdb***, *[your initials]* ***Intro-1b.xlsx***, *[your initials]* ***Intro-1c.docx***, *[your initials]* ***Intro-1d.docx***, and *[your initials]* ***Intro-1e.pdf***.

Skills Covered in This Project

- Copy and paste a zipped folder.
- Create a new folder in your *OneDrive* folder.
- Extract a zipped folder.
- Move a file.
- Rename a file.
- Open a Word document.

- Use *Task View* to switch between two open Word documents.
- Turn off *AutoSave*.
- Save a Word document with a different file name.
- Change display size.
- Use a mini toolbar, keyboard shortcut, context menu, and dialog box to apply formatting to selected text.
- Export a document as a PDF file.

---

1. Copy a zipped folder and create a new *OneDrive* folder.
   a. Click the Windows **Start** button and click **File Explorer** to open the *File Explorer* window. If *File Explorer* is not available on the *Start* menu, use *Cortana* to find and open the *File Explorer* window.
   b. Browse in the *File Explorer* window to locate your student data files.
   c. Select the ***CavalliFiles-Intro*** zipped folder from your student data files and press **Ctrl+C** or click the **Copy** button [*Home* tab, *Clipboard* group] to copy the folder.
   d. Select your ***OneDrive*** folder on the left of the *File Explorer* window, and click the **New folder** button [*Home* tab, *New* group] to create a new folder. If you don't have *OneDrive* available, create the new folder in a location where you store your files.
   e. Type PHRE and press **Enter**.
   f. Press **Enter** again to open the *PHRE* folder or double-click the folder to open it.
   g. Press **Ctrl+V** or click the **Paste** button [*Home* tab, *Clipboard* group] to paste the copied ***CavalliFiles-Intro*** zipped folder in the *PHRE* folder.

2. Extract a zipped folder.
   a. Select the ***CavalliFiles-Intro*** zipped folder.
   b. Click the **Compressed Folder Tools Extract** tab and click the **Extract all** button (Figure Intro-109). The *Extract Compressed (Zipped) Folders* dialog box opens.
   c. Uncheck the **Show extracted files when complete** box if it is checked.
   d. Click the **Extract** button. The zipped folder is extracted, and the *PHRE* folder now contains two *CavalliFiles-Intro* folders. One folder is zipped and the other is a regular folder.

e. Select the zipped **CavalliFiles-Intro** folder and click the **Delete** button [*Home* tab, *Organize* group] to delete the zipped folder.

3. Move and rename files.
   a. Double-click the **CavalliFiles-Intro** folder to open it.
   b. Click the first file, press and hold the **Shift** key, and click the last file to select all four files.
   c. Press **Ctrl+X** or click the **Cut** button [*Home* tab, *Clipboard* group] to cut the files from the current location (Figure Intro-110).
   d. Click the **Up** arrow to move up to the *PHRE* folder.
   e. Press **Ctrl+V** or click the **Paste** button [*Home* tab, *Clipboard* group] to paste and move the files.
   f. Select the **Cavalli files-Intro** folder and press **Delete** to delete the folder.
   g. Select the **CavalliPHRE-Intro** file and click the **Rename** button [*Home* tab, *Organize* group].
   h. Type [your initials] Intro-1a and press **Enter**.
   i. Right-click the **FixedMortgageRates-Intro** file and select **Rename** from the context menu.
   j. Type [your initials] Intro-1b and press **Enter**.

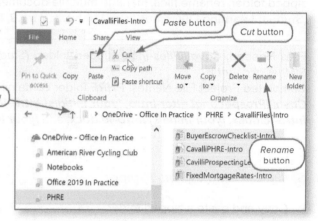

Figure Intro-109 Extract a zipped folder

Figure Intro-110 *Cut* files to move from a folder

4. Open two Word documents and rename a Word document.
   a. Click the **BuyerEscrowChecklist-Intro** file, press the **Ctrl** key, and click the **CavalliProspectingLetter-Intro** file to select both files.
   b. Press the **Enter** key to open both files in Word. If the files open in *Protected View*, click the **Enable Editing** button.
   c. Click the **Task View** button on your *Taskbar* (Figure Intro-111). All open windows display as tiles on your desktop.
   d. Select the **BuyerEscrowChecklist-Intro** document.
   e. Click the **AutoSave** button [*Quick Access* toolbar] to turn *AutoSave* off (if *AutoSave* is on).
   f. Click the **File** tab to open the *Backstage* view and select **Save As** on the left.
   g. Click the **Browse** button to open the *Save As* dialog box.
   h. Type [your initials] Intro-1c in the *File name* text box and click **Save**. The file is saved in the *PHRE* folder.
   i. Click the **X** in the upper-right corner of the Word window to close the document. The *CavalliProspectingLetter-Intro* document remains open.

Figure Intro-111 *Task View* button on the *Taskbar*

5. Change display size and edit and rename a Word document.
   a. Press the **Task View** button on your *Taskbar* and select the **CavalliProspectingLetter-Intro** document.

b. Click the **Zoom In** or **Zoom Out** button in the bottom right of the document window to change the display size to **120%** (Figure Intro-112).

c. Select "**Placer Hills Real Estate**" in the first body paragraph of the letter. The mini toolbar displays (Figure Intro-113).

d. Click the **Bold** button on the mini toolbar to apply bold formatting to the selected text.

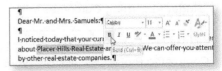

e. Select "**Whitney Hills resident**" in the first sentence in the second body paragraph and press **Ctrl+I** to apply italic formatting to the selected text.

f. Select the text that reads "**Emma Cavalli**," below "Best regards,".

Figure Intro-113 Use the mini toolbar to apply formatting

g. Right-click the selected text and select **Font** from the context menu to open the *Font* dialog box.

h. Check the **Small Caps** box in the *Effects* area and click **OK** to close the *Font* dialog box.

i. Select "**Emma Cavalli**" (if necessary) and click the **Bold** button [*Home* tab, *Font* group].

j. Click the **File** tab and select **Save As** on the left. If the file is saved in *OneDrive* and *AutoSave* is turned on, select **Save a Copy**.

Figure Intro-114 *Save* area on the *Backstage* view.

k. Type [your initials] Intro-1d in the *File name* text box and click **Save** (Figure Intro-114).

6. Export a Word document as a PDF file.

a. With the *[your initials] Intro-1d* still open, click the **File** tab to open the *Backstage* view.

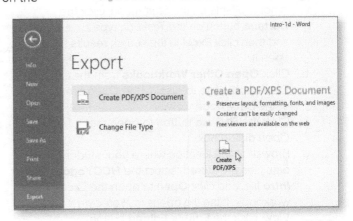

b. Select **Export** on the left, select **Create PDF/XPS Document** in the *Export* area, and click the **Create PDF/XPS** button (Figure Intro-115). The *Publish as PDF or XPS* dialog box opens.

Figure Intro-115 Export as a PDF file

c. Deselect the **Open file after publishing** check box if it is checked.

d. Select the **Standard (publishing online and printing)** radio button in the *Optimize for* area.

e. Type [your initials] Intro-1e in the *File name* text box, select a location to save the file, and click **Publish**.

f. Click the **Save** button on the *Quick Access* toolbar or press **Ctrl+S** to save the document.

g. Click the **X** in the upper-right corner of the Word window to close the document and Word.

7. Your *PHRE* folder should contain the files shown in Figure Intro-116.

Figure Intro-116 Intro-1 completed

Guided Project Intro-2

For this project, you modify an Excel file for Hamilton Civic Center. You create a folder, rename a file, add document properties, use *Tell Me* to search for a topic, share the file, and export a file as a PDF file. [Student Learning Outcomes Intro.1, Intro.2, Intro.3, Intro.5, Intro.6, Intro.7, Intro.8]

File Needed: *HCCYoga-Intro.xlsx (Student data files are available in the Library of your SIMnet account.)*
Completed Project File Names: *[your initials] Intro-2a.xlsx* and *[your initials] Intro-2b.pdf*

Skills Covered in This Project

- Open Excel and an Excel workbook.
- Create a new folder.
- Save an Excel workbook with a different file name.

- Add document properties to a file.
- Use *Tell Me* to search for a topic.
- Open a Word document.
- Share a file.
- Export a file as a PDF file.

---

1. Open Excel and open an Excel workbook.
   a. Click the Windows **Start** button and click **Excel** to open this application. If Excel 2019 is not available on the *Start* menu, click the **Cortana** button on the *Taskbar*, type Excel, and then click **Excel** in the search results to open it.
   b. Click **Open Other Workbooks** from the Excel *Start* page to display the *Open* area of the *Backstage* view.
   c. Click the **Browse** button to open the *Open* dialog box.
   d. Browse to the location where your student data files are stored, select the **HCCYoga-Intro** file, and click **Open** to open the Excel workbook. If the file opens in *Protected View,* click the **Enable Editing** button.

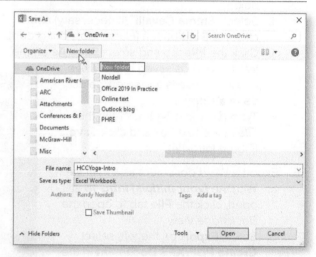

Figure Intro-117 Create a new folder from the *Save As* dialog box

2. Save a file as a different file name in your *OneDrive* folder.
   a. Click the **File** tab to open the *Backstage* view and select **Save As** (or **Save a Copy**) on the left.
   b. Click the **Browse** button to open the *Save As* dialog box.
   c. Select the **OneDrive** folder on the left and click the **New folder** button to create a new folder (Figure Intro-117). If *OneDrive* is not a storage option, select another location to create the new folder.
   d. Type HCC and press **Enter**.
   e. Double-click the **HCC** folder to open it.
   f. Type [your initials] Intro-2a in the *File name* area and click **Save** to close the dialog box and save the file.

3. Add document properties to the Excel workbook.
   a. Click the **File** button to open the *Backstage* view and select **Info** on the left if it is not already selected. The document properties display on the right.
   b. Place your insertion point in the *Title* text box ("Add a title") and type Yoga Classes as the worksheet title.
   c. Click the **Show All Properties** link at the bottom of the list of properties to display more properties (Figure Intro-118).

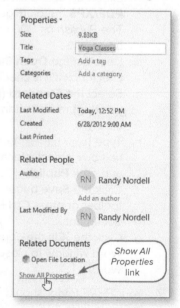

Figure Intro-118 Add document properties

d. Place your insertion point in the *Company* text box and type Hamilton Civic Center as the company name.

e. Click the **Back** arrow in the upper left of the *Backstage* window to return to the Excel workbook.

4. Use *Tell Me* to search for a topic.

a. Click the **Tell Me** search box at the top of the *Ribbon* and type Cell formatting (Figure Intro-119).

b. Select **Get Help on "Cell formatting"** and click **More Results for "Cell formatting"** to open the *Help* pane at the right.

c. Click the first result link to display information about the topic.

d. Click the **Back** arrow to return to the search list.

e. Click the **X** in the upper-right corner to close the *Help* pane.

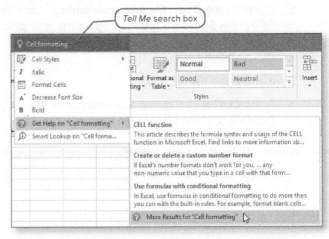

Tell Me search box

Figure Intro-119 Use *Tell Me* to search for a topic

5. Share an Excel workbook with your instructor. If your file is not saved on *OneDrive*, skip step 5.

a. Click the **Share** button in the upper-right corner of the Word window to open the *Send Link* window (Figure Intro-120). If you're using a personal Microsoft account, the *Share* pane displays at the right, and the sharing options differ slightly.

b. Click the **Link settings** button to open the *Link settings* window (Figure Intro-121).

c. Click the **Anyone** button and check the **Allow editing** box (if necessary).

d. Click **Apply** to close the *Link settings* window and return to the *Send Link* window.

e. Type your instructor's email address in the *Enter a name or email address* area (see Figure Intro-120).

f. Type a brief message to your instructor and click the **Send** button.

g. Click the **X** in the upper-right corner of the confirmation window to close it.

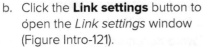

Link settings button

Figure Intro-120 *Send Link* window

Figure Intro-121 *Link settings* window

6. Export an Excel file as a PDF file.

a. Click the **File** tab to open the *Backstage* view.

b. Select **Export** on the left, select **Create PDF/XPS Document** in the *Export* area, and click the **Create PDF/XPS** button (Figure Intro-122). The *Publish as PDF or XPS* dialog box opens.

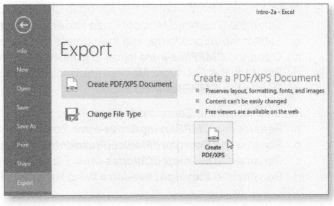

Figure Intro-122 Export as a PDF file

c. Deselect the **Open file after publishing** check box if it is checked.

d. Select the **Standard (publishing online and printing)** radio button in the *Optimize for* area.

e. Type [your initials] Intro-2b in the *File name* text box, select a location to save the file, and click **Publish**.

7. Save and close the Excel file.

a. Press **Ctrl+S** or click the **Save** button on the *Quick Access* toolbar to save the worksheet.

b. Click the **X** in the upper-right corner of the Excel window to close the file and Excel.

Independent Project Intro-3

For this project, you organize and edit files for Courtyard Medical Plaza. You extract a zipped folder, delete a folder, move files, rename files, export a file as a PDF file, and share a file.
[Student Learning Outcomes Intro.1, Intro.2, Intro.3, Intro.5, Intro.8]

File Needed: ***CMPFiles-Intro*** (zipped folder) *(Student data files are available in the* Library *of your SIMnet account.)*

Completed Project File Names: ***[your initials] Intro-3a.pptx***, ***[your initials] Intro-3a-pdf.pdf***, ***[your initials] Intro-3b.accdb***, ***[your initials] Intro-3c.xlsx***, and ***[your initials] Intro-3d.docx***

Skills Covered in This Project

- Copy and paste a zipped folder.
- Create a new folder in your *OneDrive* folder.
- Extract a zipped folder.
- Delete a folder.

- Move a file.
- Rename a file.
- Open a PowerPoint presentation.
- Export a file as a PDF file.
- Open a Word document.
- Share a file.

1. Copy a zipped folder and create a new *OneDrive* folder.
   a. Open a *File Explorer* window, browse to locate the ***CMPFiles-Intro*** zipped folder in your student data files and **Copy** the zipped folder.
   b. Go to your *OneDrive* folder and create a new folder named Courtyard Medical Plaza within the *OneDrive* folder. If *OneDrive* is not a storage option, select another location to create the new folder.

2. Paste a copied folder, extract the zipped folder, and move files.
   a. Open the *Courtyard Medical Plaza* folder and **Paste** the zipped folder.
   b. Extract the zipped folder and then delete the zipped folder.
   c. Open the ***CMPFiles-Intro*** folder and move all of the files to the *Courtyard Medical Plaza* folder.
   d. Return to the *Courtyard Medical Plaza* folder to confirm the four files were moved.
   e. Delete the ***CMPFiles-Intro*** folder.

3. Rename files in the *Courtyard Medical Plaza* folder.
   a. Rename the ***CMPStayingActive-Intro*** PowerPoint file as [your initials] Intro-3a.
   b. Rename the ***CourtyardMedicalPlaza-Intro*** Access file as [your initials] Intro-3b.
   c. Rename the ***EstimatedCalories-Intro*** Excel file as [your initials] Intro-3c.
   d. Rename the ***StayingActive-Intro*** Word file as [your initials] Intro-3d.

4. Export a PowerPoint file as a PDF file.
   a. Open the ***[your initials] Intro-3a*** file from the *Courtyard Medical Plaza* folder. The file opens in PowerPoint. If the file opens in *Protected View,* click the **Enable Editing** button.
   b. Export this file as a PDF file. Don't have the PDF file open after publishing and optimize for **Standard** format.
   c. Save the file as [your initials] Intro-3a-pdf and save in the *Courtyard Medical Plaza* folder.
   d. Close the PowerPoint file and exit PowerPoint.

5. Share a file with your instructor. If your files are not saved in *OneDrive*, skip step 5.
   a. Return to your *Courtyard Medical Plaza* folder and open the ***Intro-3d*** file. The file opens in Word. If the file opens in *Protected View*, click the **Enable Editing** button.
   b. Click the **Share** button in the upper-right corner of the Word window to open the *Send Link* window. If you're using a personal Microsoft account, the *Share* pane displays at the right, and the sharing options differ slightly.
   c. Click the **Link settings** button to open the *Link settings* window, click the **Anyone** button, check the **Allow editing** box (if necessary), and click **Apply** to close the *Link settings* window and return to the *Send Link* window.
   d. Type your instructor's email address in the *Enter a name or email address* area.
   e. Type a brief message to your instructor and click the **Send** button.
   f. Click the **X** in the upper-right corner of the confirmation window to close it.

6. Save and close the document and exit Word.

7. Close the *File Explorer* window containing the files for this project (Figure Intro-123).

Figure Intro-123 Intro-3 completed

Independent Project Intro-4

Independent Project Intro-4

For this project, you modify a Word file for Life's Animal Shelter. You create a folder, rename a document, add document properties, modify a document, create a sharing link, export a document as a PDF file, and create a zipped folder.
[Student Learning Outcomes Intro.1, Intro.2, Intro.3, Intro.5, Intro.6, Intro.7, Intro.8]

File Needed: ***LASSupportLetter-Intro.docx*** *(Student data files are available in the* Library *of your SIMnet account.)*
Completed Project File Names: ***[your initials] Intro-4a.docx***, ***[your initials] Intro-4b.pdf***, and **LAS files** (zipped folder)

Skills Covered in This Project

- Open a Word document.
- Create a new folder.
- Save a file with a different file name.
- Apply formatting to selected text.
- Add document properties to the file.
- Create a sharing link.
- Export a file as a PDF file.
- Create a zipped folder.

1. Open a Word document, create a new folder, and save the document with a different file name.
   a. Open Word.
   b. Open the ***LASSupportLetter-Intro*** Word document from your student data files. If the file opens in *Protected View*, click the **Enable Editing** button.
   c. Open the **Save As** dialog box and create a new folder named LAS in your *OneDrive* folder. If *OneDrive* is not a storage option, select another location to create the new folder.
   d. Save this document in the *LAS* folder and use [your initials] Intro-4a as the file name.

2. Apply formatting changes to the document using a dialog box, keyboard shortcut, and mini toolbar.
   a. Select "**To:**" in the memo heading and use the launcher to open the *Font* dialog box.
   b. Apply **Bold** and **All caps** to the selected text.
   c. Repeat the formatting on the other three memo guide words "**From:**", "**Date:**", and "**Subject:**".
   d. Select "**Life's Animal Shelter**" in the first sentence of the first body paragraph and press **Ctrl+B** to apply bold formatting.
   e. Select the first sentence in the second body paragraph ("**Would you again consider . . .** ") and use the mini toolbar to apply *italic* formatting.

3. Add the following document properties to the document:
   Title: Support Letter
   Company: Life's Animal Shelter

4. Get a link to share this document with your instructor and email your instructor the sharing link. If your file is not saved on *OneDrive*, skip step 5.
   a. Click the **Share** button in the upper-right corner of the Word window. The *Send Link* window opens. If you are using a personal Microsoft account, the *Share* pane opens at the right, and the sharing options differ slightly.
   b. Click the **Link settings** button to open the *Link settings* window, click the **Anyone** button, check the **Allow editing** box (if necessary), and click **Apply** to return to the *Send Link* window.
   c. Click the **Copy Link** button to create sharing link.
   d. Click **Copy** to copy the sharing link and click the **X** in the upper-right corner to close the sharing link window.
   e. Use your email account to create a new email to your instructor. Include an appropriate subject line and a brief message in the body.
   f. Press **Ctrl+V** to paste the sharing link to your document in the body of the email and send the email message.
   g. Click the **Task View** button on the Windows *Taskbar* and select the ***Intro-4a*** document to display this document.
   h. Use the **Save** command on the *Quick Access* toolbar to save the file before continuing.

5. Export this document as a PDF file.
   a. Export this file as a PDF file. Don't have the PDF file open after publishing and optimize for **Standard** format.
   b. Save the file as [your initials] Intro-4b and save in the *LAS* folder.
   c. Save and close the document and exit Word.

6. Create a zipped folder.
   a. Use *File Explorer* to open the ***LAS*** folder in your *OneDrive* folder.
   b. Select the two files and create a zipped folder.
   c. Name the zipped folder LAS files.

7. Close the open *File Explorer* window (Figure Intro-124).

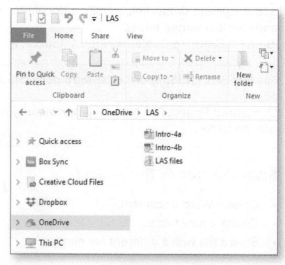

Figure Intro-124 Intro-4 completed

Challenge Project Intro-5

For this project, you create folders to organize your files for this class and share a file with your instructor.
[Student Learning Outcomes Intro.1, Intro.5, Intro.8]

Files Needed: Student data files for this course
Completed Project File Name: Share a file with your instructor

Using *File Explorer*, create *OneDrive* folders to contain all of the student data files for this class. Organize your files and folders according to the following guidelines:

- Create a *OneDrive* folder for this class.
- Create a *Student data files* folder inside the class folder.
- Copy and paste the student data files in the *Student data files* folder.
- Extract student data files and delete the zipped folder.
- Create a *Solution files* folder inside the class folder.
- Inside the *Solution files* folder, create a folder for each chapter.
- Create a folder to store miscellaneous class files such as the syllabus and other course handouts.
- Open one of the student data files and share the file with your instructor.

Challenge Project Intro-6

For this project, you save a file as a different file name, customize the *Quick Access* toolbar, share a file with your instructor, export a file as a PDF file, and create a zipped folder.
[Student Learning Outcomes Intro.1, Intro.2, Intro.3, Intro.5, Intro.6, Intro.8]

File Needed: Use an existing Office file
Completed Project File Names: *[your initials] Intro-6a* and *[your initials] Intro-6b*

Open an existing Word, Excel, or PowerPoint file. Save this file in a *OneDrive* folder and name it [your initials] Intro-6a. If you don't have any of these files, use one from your Pause & Practice projects or select a file from your student data files.

With your file open, perform the following actions:

- Create a new folder on *OneDrive* and save the file to this folder using a different file name.
- Customize the *Quick Access* toolbar to add command buttons. Add commands such as *New*, *Open*, *Quick Print*, and *Spelling* that you use regularly in the Office application.
- Share your file with your instructor. Enable your instructor to edit the file.
- Export the document as a PDF file. Save the file as [your initials] Intro-6b and save it in the same *OneDrive* folder as your open file.
- Zip the files in the folder.

Microsoft® Office

IN PRACTICE

outlook

©Chris Ryan/Getty Images

Outlook Overview and Email Basics

CHAPTER OVERVIEW

Microsoft Outlook (usually referred to as **Outlook**) is the most widely used email and personal management software today. It is used in both the business environment and personal and home environment. Outlook is part of the Microsoft Office 365 suite of application software. This book covers the different aspects of Outlook and how this software is used to help manage your electronic communication, schedule your appointments and meetings, organize your personal and business contacts, and arrange your list of to-do items.

This first half of this book (chapters 1–5) introduces you to the main features of Outlook. Once you complete the first half of the book, you will be proficient using the main features in Outlook. The remaining chapters cover each of these areas in depth and introduce you to the advanced aspects of Outlook. As you read each chapter and complete the projects, you will become an Outlook expert at home and at work.

Today, most people equate Microsoft Outlook with email, and these two terms have become almost synonymous in their use. Email is an integral part of Outlook, but Outlook is much more than just email, which you will discover as you study each chapter. Almost everyone uses email on a daily basis, and Outlook is widely used in both the business and home environment to manage email accounts. It is important to remember that Outlook is not email but rather a computer software program that handles email accounts. Just as your mail carrier is not the mail itself but rather the person who delivers your mail to your home mailbox, Outlook delivers email received through your existing email account(s). Outlook requires you to create an email account to send and receive email.

Outlook enables you to create and send email, reply to received email, forward email to other recipients, save and manage email, and flag and categorize email. Email is one method of sending pictures and other types of computer files to others. Email is an integral part of personal and business activities, and it is hard to imagine a day without the use of an email program.

STUDENT LEARNING OUTCOMES (SLOs)

After completing this chapter, you will be able to:

SLO 1.1   Identify the basic components of Microsoft Outlook (p. O1-3).

SLO 1.2   Navigate throughout the Outlook environment and identify the different panes in the Outlook window (p. O1-7).

SLO 1.3   Distinguish between Outlook being used as a stand-alone program and in a Microsoft Exchange environment (p. O1-14).

SLO 1.4   Distinguish between the different types of email accounts and set up an email account in Outlook (p. O1-15).

SLO 1.5   Use Outlook to create, send, and receive email (p. O1-17).

SLO 1.6   Use attachments in email (p. O1-29).

SLO 1.7   Differentiate email arrangements and icons (p. O1-34).

SLO 1.8   Explain the importance and process of cleaning up an Inbox (p. O1-37).

OUTLOOK

CASE STUDY

Throughout this book you have the opportunity to put into practice the application features that you are learning. Each chapter begins with a case study that introduces you to the Pause & Practice projects in the chapter. These Pause & Practice projects give you a chance to apply and practice key skills. Each chapter contains three to five Pause & Practice projects.

Central Sierra Insurance (CSI) is a multi-office insurance company that handles all lines of commercial and personal insurance policies. As a thriving and growing insurance agency, Central Sierra regularly hires qualified personnel to enhance their sales and support staff.

CSI encourages its employees to be active in community organizations and events.

Pause & Practice 1-1: You set up an email account using Microsoft Outlook. You will need an email account that is provided by your school or a free email service such as Gmail.com or Outlook.com.

Pause & Practice 1-2: You send an email message to your instructor and use the *Cc* function to send a copy to yourself. You also read the message, reply to it, and print it for your records.

Pause & Practice 1-3: You reply to a message with an email attachment. You also forward the message to your instructor as an attachment and delete a message.

SLO 1.1

Working with Outlook

One of the main features in Outlook is handling email, but Outlook is so much more! It is personal management software that contains the following features:

- *Email*
- *Calendar*
- *Contacts*
- *Tasks*
- *Notes*
- *Journal*

Microsoft Outlook combines the email, calendar, contacts, tasks, notes, and journal features into personal management software (Figure 1-1). Each of the Outlook features operate independently; yet they integrate seamlessly. Outlook also integrates with Microsoft Word, Excel, Access, and other Microsoft products.

Email

Email is the commonly used term for electronic mail (Figure 1-2). Outlook provides users the capability of creating, sending, and receiving email. Outlook manages a single email account or multiple email accounts. In Outlook, email is activated by clicking the **Mail** button.

> **MORE INFO**
>
> Chapter 2 covers the special email features available in Outlook. Chapter 6 discusses the use of rules for handling both incoming and outgoing email, and chapter 7 provides the reader with information about setting up the different types of email accounts.

Figure 1-1 Outlook interface

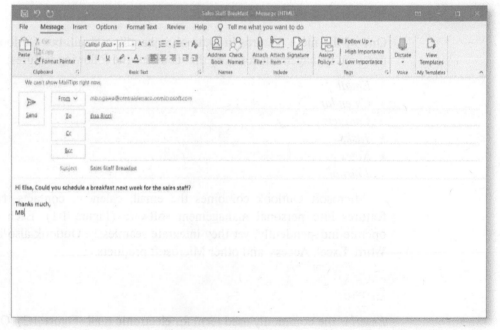

Figure 1-2 Email message

Calendar

Calendars organize daily, weekly, and monthly schedules. You may use a daily planner, a calendar that hangs on your wall at home or at work, or a smartphone to manage your daily activities. Outlook *Calendar* (Figure 1-3) is an electronic calendar for scheduling appointments or events. Outlook Calendar also replicates calendar entries, records electronic reminders, sends meeting requests, and shares calendar entries with other Outlook users or other devices.

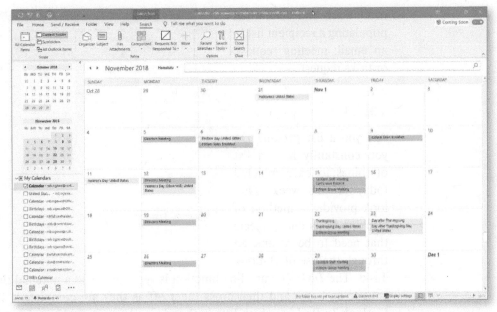

Figure 1-3 Outlook Calendar

Another advantage of an Outlook calendar is that you can synchronize your work and home calendars. As the popularity of multifunction (smart) cell phones increases, the potential to have your Outlook calendar synchronized between your work, home, and cell phone is not only a reality but also commonplace for working professionals.

MORE INFO

Outlook Calendar is covered in chapters 4 and 9 of this text.
Outlook Contacts is thoroughly covered in chapters 3 and 8.

Contacts

Outlook also provides an area to manage names, email addresses, phone numbers, and other information about business contacts, coworkers, friends, and family. Similar to the way the Outlook calendar replaces the old paper calendar, Outlook *Contacts* (Figure 1-4) allows you to electronically store personal information. It functions as a database, which is a collection of information. One of the many benefits of Outlook Contacts is creating, deleting, and managing contacts without being required to understand the structure and components of the database.

Use Contacts to save personal and company information

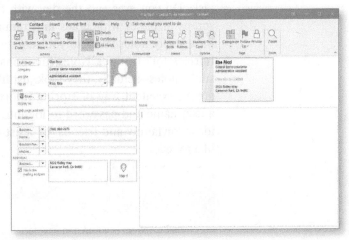

Figure 1-4 Outlook Contact

in Outlook and also when populating a recipient list in an email, meeting request, or tasks request.

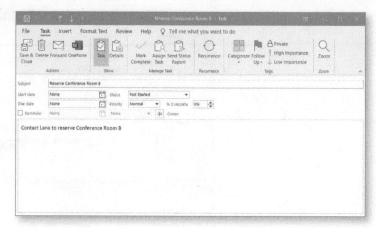
Figure 1-5 Outlook Task

Tasks

Are you a list person? Do you constantly have a list of things to be completed today or this week? Outlook provides a method of tracking tasks and projects that need to be completed through the use of Outlook Tasks. The *Tasks* (Figure 1-5) function is very similar to a notepad that you use to write down your to-do items and then cross them off as they are completed. Tasks are included in the Outlook *To-Do List*, which lists both tasks and emails that have been flagged for action.

Four advantages of using Outlook Tasks are listed here:

- Tasks are electronic and are shared between computers and cell phones.
- Many details, which are not typically written down on a piece of paper, can be added to a task.
- Create reminders to alert you to an upcoming due date and time for a task.
- Assign Tasks to another Outlook user.

> **MORE INFO**
>
> Outlook tasks and to-do items are covered in chapter 5.

Notes

Outlook *Notes* (Figure 1-6) are used to keep track of information that does not necessarily or neatly fall into the category of a calendar item, contact, or task. Do you ever end the day with a pocket full of scraps of paper with notes and reminders? Do you have sticky notes stuck to your computer monitor or refrigerator? Outlook Notes functions like electronic sticky notes—actually, they look just like them. Notes are an excellent way of storing information such as a user name and password to log into a web site, gift ideas for family and friends, or a list of books you'd like to read.

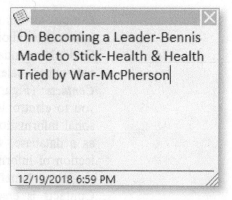

On Becoming a Leader-Bennis Made to Stick-Health & Health Tried by War-McPherson

12/19/2018 6:59 PM

Figure 1-6 Outlook Note

> **MORE INFO**
>
> Outlook Notes is covered in chapter 10.

Journal

Outlook *Journal* (Figure 1-7) tracks the amount of time spent working on a particular document or project. The journal is primarily used in the business environment and enables you to associate specific Microsoft Office documents to a journal entry.

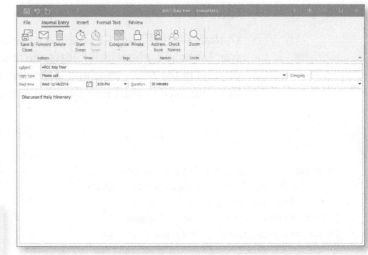

Figure 1-7 Outlook Journal

SLO 1.2

Navigating Outlook

The Outlook working environment (Figure 1-8) has a much different look and feel than that of Microsoft Word, Excel, PowerPoint, and Access. The Outlook user interface is divided into multiple sections, called *panes*. When working with different items such as email messages in Outlook, you select them by clicking each item. Selected items are typically highlighted in blue.

Figure 1-8 Outlook environment

As you work through this book and use Outlook, you will become familiar with the Outlook user interface and the different panes available. Outlook provides consistency throughout this program to allow you to quickly become comfortable navigating through its working environment.

Outlook Today

Outlook Today (Figure 1-9) is an introductory screen that provides you with information about your Inbox and other email folders, current calendar items, and upcoming tasks. *Outlook Today* displays in the *Folder* pane and is the default view when you open Outlook. *Outlook Today* can be customized to meet your personal needs.

> **MORE INFO**
>
> By default, the *Navigation* bar displays four icons and a *Navigation Options* button (...). To switch the display from icons to text, follow these steps: Click the **Navigation Options** button, and select **Navigation Options** to display the *Navigation Options* dialog box. Deselect the **Compact Navigation** check box and click **OK**. The *Navigation* bar changes to a text display. Chapter 5 provides more information about customizing *Outlook Today*.

Figure 1-9 *Outlook Today*

Outlook Panes

The Outlook program window is divided into panes. The number and type of panes displayed varies for each Outlook view.

The *Folder pane* (Figure 1-10) is located on the left side of the Outlook window, and it contains folders for organizing your Outlook items. The contents of the *Folder* pane change based on the selected view. The main features of Outlook—Mail, Calendar, People, and Tasks—are represented by icons in the *Navigation* bar located at the bottom of the *Folder* pane. Click an icon to change views quickly and easily. Click the **Navigation Options** button (...) to display a list of navigation options including *Notes* and *Folders*. You can use the keyboard shortcuts listed in "Another Way" to quickly navigate the Outlook window.

> **ANOTHER WAY**
>
> *Mail*: **Ctrl+1**
> *Calendar*: **Ctrl+2**
> *Contacts*: **Ctrl+3**
> *Tasks*: **Ctrl+4**
> *Notes*: **Ctrl+5**
> *Folder list*: **Ctrl+6**
> *Shortcuts*: **Ctrl+7**
> *Journal*: **Ctrl+8**

⊿ Favorites
mb.ogawa@centralsierraco.onmic...
▷ mb.ogawa@OfficeInPractice.c...
⊿ mb.ogawa@centralsierraco.on...
Inbox
Drafts
Sent Items
Deleted Items 1
Archive
▷ Conversation History
Junk Email
Outbox
RSS Feeds
Search Folders
▷ Groups

Figure 1-10 *Folder* pane

You control the appearance of the Outlook window by selecting a view to display in the *Folder* pane. Click an icon in the *Navigation* bar to change the *Outlook* view. Adjust the width of the *Folder* pane to increase or decrease the size of the selected view. Click the **Minimize the Folder Pane** button to increase the working area of the Outlook window.

▶ **HOW TO: Adjust the Width of the Folder Pane**

1. Click and hold the right border of the *Navigation* pane (Figure 1-11).
2. Drag the border to the left or right as desired.

The *Reading pane* (Figure 1-12) is an optional pane that is available in most of the main features in Outlook, although it is primarily used with the *Mail* feature. The *Reading* pane displays the contents of the item selected in the *Folder* pane or content area. The *Reading* pane can be set to appear below or to the right of the *Folder* pane, or it can be turned off from the *View* tab. The *Reading* pane will vary depending on the task (for example, Mail, Calendar, or Contacts) selected in the *Folder* pane.

Figure 1-11 Resize the *Navigation* pane

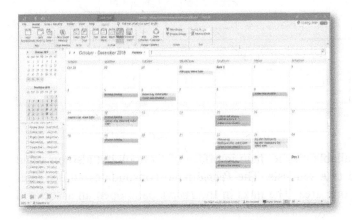

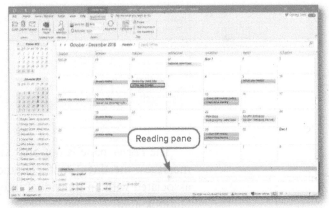

Figure 1-12 *Reading* pane displayed in the Calendar

▶ **HOW TO: Change the Location of the Reading Pane**

1. Click the **Mail** button in the *Navigation* bar.
2. Click the **View** tab.
3. Click the **Reading Pane** button in the *Layout* group.
4. Choose the desired location: *Right*, *Bottom*, or *Off* (Figure 1-13).

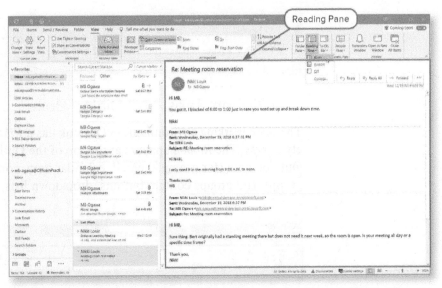

Figure 1-13 *Reading* pane

The *Reading* pane can also be resized in the same manner as the *Folder* pane. Move the boundary to the desired height or width by clicking and holding the top edge (when the *Reading* pane displays at the bottom) or the left edge (when the *Reading* pane displays on the right).

The **People pane** (Figure 1-14) provides a collection of information associated with the sender including communication history, meeting requests, and attachments. Expand or collapse the *People* pane by clicking the **Minimize the Folder** button in the upper-right corner of the *Folder* pane.

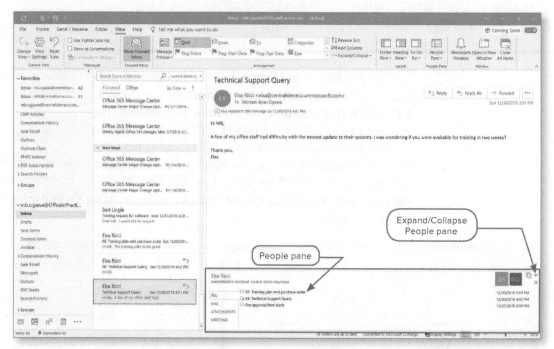

Figure 1-14 *People* pane

The *People* pane is not only available on the main interface of Outlook but also on email messages, meetings, contacts, and task requests. The *People* pane consolidates all activities associated with an individual into one area. The links in the *People* pane open an associated Outlook item.

> **MORE INFO**
>
> The *People* pane is covered in chapters 2 and 3.

The Ribbon, Tabs, and Dialog Boxes

The main working environment in Outlook has a **Ribbon** (Figure 1-15), which includes a variety of *tabs*. The *Ribbon* appears at the top of the Outlook window and at the top of any open Outlook item (for example, email, calendar item, contact, or task). Each tab has a variety of groups, and groups contain buttons, drop-down lists, and galleries.

Figure 1-15 Outlook *Ribbon*

Some versions of Office 365 include a *Simplified Ribbon* (Figure 1-16). The simplified Ribbon includes commonly used features on its interface. Less commonly used features are

Figure 1-16 Outlook Simplified *Ribbon*

available by clicking the **More** (. . .) button. The full Ribbon is used throughout the text due to the in-depth exploration of the tools and features in Outlook. You can switch between the full Ribbon and simplified Ribbon by clicking the **Switch Ribbon** button on the lower right corner of the Ribbon (Figure 1-17).

Figure 1-17 *Switch Ribbons* button

> **MORE INFO**
>
> Collapse the *Ribbon* by pressing **Ctrl+F1** or click the small **up arrow** in the upper-right corner of the Outlook window. When the *Ribbon* is minimized, you can restore it by pressing **Ctrl+F1** or by clicking the small **up arrow** in the upper-right corner of the Outlook window and selecting **Show Tabs and Commands**.

As you move your pointer over a button on the *Ribbon*, *ScreenTips* (Figure 1-18) appear that tell you what that button represents and provide a shortcut key combination if available.

Figure 1-18 *ScreenTip*

Tabs are *context sensitive*, which means that the choices of tabs and the content of the tabs change based on the Outlook item or Folder you select. Each tab is divided into *groups* where the size of the buttons in each group will vary depending on the size of the open window.

A few groups on each tab have a *launcher* button at the bottom-right corner of the group. When you click the launcher button, a *dialog box* (Figure 1-19) opens. The opened dialog box contains additional options for the selected group.

> **MORE INFO**
>
> The name of the dialog box is not always the same as the name of the group that was expanded. Some dialog boxes contain features that are distributed between a few groups.

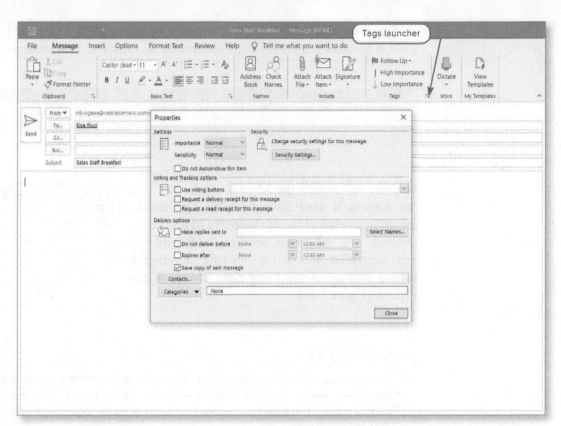

Figure 1-19 Dialog box

Views

Each of the features in Outlook (Mail, Calendar, Contacts, Tasks, Notes, and Journal) has preset views. The selected view controls how the folder selected in the *Folder* pane displays in the Outlook window. You can also create custom views.

> **MORE INFO**
>
> Many of the dialog boxes that you will use in Outlook are the same as or very similar to the dialog boxes used in previous versions of Outlook.

▶**HOW TO: Change to a Different View**

1. Click the **View** tab.
2. Click the **Change View** button [*Current View* group] (Figure 1-20).

Figure 1-20 *Change View* button

3. Select the view you want. Notice the different views available; the different views are context sensitive.

Folder List

The *Folder list* (Figure 1-21) displays all the folders available in Outlook in the *Folder* pane. To display the *Folder* list, click the **Navigation Options** button [. . .] in the *Navigation bar*, and click **Folders**. The benefit of viewing the *Folder* list is that you can see all folders available in the folder hierarchy in which they reside, rather than viewing just one set of folders at a time. Use this view to move folders up or down a level or to drag specific items into a folder.

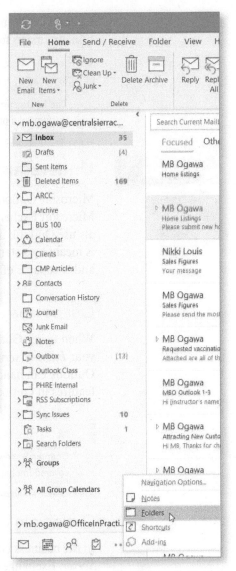

Figure 1-21 *Folder* list

> **ANOTHER WAY**
>
> **Ctrl+6** displays the *Folder* list in the *Folder* pane. Additionally, you can press **Ctrl+Y** to select any folder.

> **MORE INFO**
>
> The *Folder* list is covered more thoroughly in chapter 6 where we start using multiple folders for email, contacts, and tasks.

Tell me what you want to do. . .

The *Tell me what you want to do*. . . (Figure 1-22) feature displays results as you type keywords related to your search and you can choose options available in Outlook, Help, or Smart Lookup. Each character you type further refines your search. The options in Outlook perform functions. *Outlook Help* provides additional information about your search. Smart

Figure 1-22 *Tell me what you want to do. . . feature*

Lookup performs an internet search for your query, which can include background information, an image search, and a web search.

SLO 1.3

Understanding Outlook Environments

Microsoft Outlook can be configured as either a *stand-alone program* or in conjunction with a Microsoft Exchange Server (also referred to as an *Exchange server* or *Exchange*). Many individuals use Outlook on their home computer without connecting to an *Exchange server*; this is what is meant by a stand-alone program. Outlook is still part of the Microsoft Office suite of software and is capable of performing all the main functions of this personal management software.

Outlook as a Stand-Alone Program

When using Outlook in the home or personal environment, Outlook connects directly with your *internet service provider* (*ISP*) and manages your email through the accounts you set up. Outlook can handle a single email account or multiple email accounts. Advanced and specialty features in Outlook are available only when Outlook is used in conjunction with Exchange.

Outlook in an Exchange Environment

In the business environment, Microsoft Outlook is typically connected to a *Microsoft Exchange Server*. Exchange on a business network handles all the incoming and outgoing mail. Each individual user of Exchange is actually a client of the Exchange network, and the network administrator sets up an account for each individual user. In addition to handling email, Exchange also stores all the data associated with calendars, contacts, tasks, notes, and journals.

Outlook in an Exchange environment has the same user interface as in a stand-alone environment, but Outlook with an Exchange server does allow you more functionality. An Exchange server will enable you to perform enhanced features such as:

- Using voting buttons and tracking responses
- Sending meeting requests and tracking responses
- Recalling messages
- Sharing your calendar, contacts, tasks, and email with others
- Using *MailTips*
- Using a common global contact list

Adding an Email Account in Outlook

Multiple email accounts can be configured in Outlook. In previous versions of Outlook, only one Exchange account could be connected, but Outlook enables you to set up multiple Exchange accounts. Four types of email accounts can be configured in Outlook, and Outlook provides you with the *Simplified Account Creation* feature to walk you through the process of adding an email account to Outlook.

Types of Email Accounts

Microsoft Exchange accounts are used primarily in medium- to large-business settings. These email accounts are set up through the company network or email administrator. An Exchange account has an individual mailbox assigned to each user and resides on an Exchange file server. Outlook connects to the Exchange server to retrieve your email. Exchange accounts use Messaging Application Programming Interface (MAPI) and provide enhanced functionality when used with Outlook. Recalling messages, tracking voting responses, and sharing Outlook with others on your Exchange system are features that are associated with Exchange accounts and Outlook.

POP3 accounts are internet email accounts that are associated with your internet service provider (ISP). If you have an ISP such as Comcast or AT&T, you have an email account (or multiple email accounts) through your provider. This POP3 account can be configured in Outlook to send and receive email. When using Outlook with this type of account, your email messages are downloaded to Outlook.

IMAP accounts are also internet accounts but are not always associated with an ISP. IMAP accounts create folders on a server to store and organize messages for retrieval by other computers and give you the options to read message headers only and to select which messages to download. These types of accounts are becoming increasingly popular as personal email accounts. Gmail is an example of an IMAP email account.

HTTP accounts use the hypertext transfer protocol used on the web to create, view, send, and receive messages.

Add an Email Account

To create, send, and receive email, Outlook must be set up to recognize your email account. In the past, it has been a challenge to get all the specific information needed to set up an email account, but new to Outlook is the Simplified Account Creation (Figure 1-23) feature which was added to automatically detect the incoming and outgoing server.

To set up your account, you will need to supply your email address and password to access the account. This gives Outlook the location of your Exchange or internet mailbox, and your password provides access to the account. An account needs to be set up only once, and it will be stored in Outlook for future use.

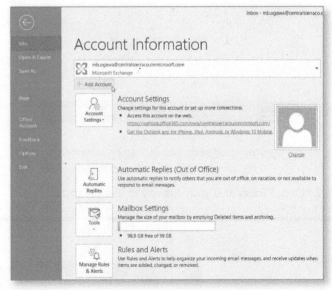

Figure 1-23 Account set up

MORE INFO

The first time you open Outlook, you will be prompted to set up an account. The *Simplified Account Creation* dialog box automatically opens for you.

Outlook will automatically detect the type of email account being configured.

HOW TO: Set Up an Email Account

1. Click the **File** tab. The *Backstage* view opens.
2. Click the **Add Account** button. The *Simplified Account Creation* dialog box opens (Figure 1-24).
3. Type your email address in the **Email address** field.
4. Click the **Connect** button.
5. Type your password into the **Password** field.
6. Click the **Connect** button. Outlook will automatically detect your email account and validate it with your password. Three green check marks display when your account has been configured properly (Figure 1-25).

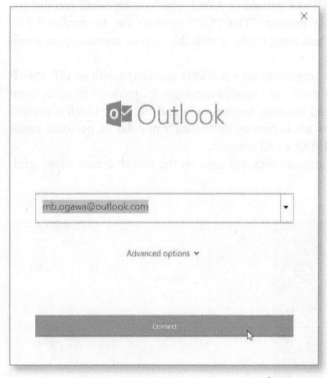

Figure 1-24 *Simplified Account Creation* dialog box

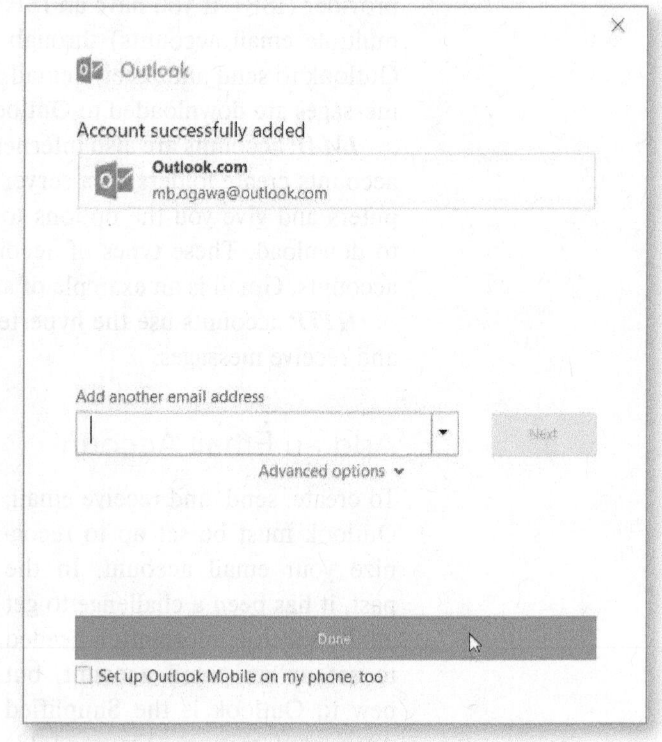

Figure 1-25 Successful configuration of an account

7. Click **Finish** and you're ready to use Outlook.

MORE INFO

You may need to speak with your instructor or system administrator for details when adding your account.

MORE INFO

Chapter 7 provides additional information on setting up multiple email accounts.

PAUSE & PRACTICE: OUTLOOK 1-1

For this project, you set up an email account using Microsoft Outlook. If you do not have an email account, you can set one up using a free service, such as Outlook (outlook.com) or Gmail (gmail.com).

Files Needed: None
Completed Project File Name: None

1. Launch Outlook.

2. Open the *Add Account* dialog box.
   a. Click the **File** tab to open the *Backstage* view.
   b. Click the **Add Account** button.
   c. Type your email address in the **Email address** field and click **Connect**.
   d. Type your password in the **Password** field and click **Connect**.
   e. Click **Next**. If you are using a school email account, you may need to contact your system administrator for the manual setup information.

SLO 1.5

Creating, Sending, and Receiving Email

Creating and sending an email message is very similar to sending a letter—just much easier and quicker! You select recipients, type the subject of the message, type the message, and send—no stamp or going to the post office.

> **ANOTHER WAY**
>
> **Ctrl+N** opens a new email message when you are in Outlook *Mail*.

> **MORE INFO**
>
> When you press **Ctrl+N**, Outlook creates a new item of the task selected in Outlook. For example, if you select *Calendar* in the *Navigation* bar and click **New**, you get a new calendar appointment.

Figure 1-26 *New Email* button

Create New Email

To create a new email message, make sure the *Mail* button (Figure 1-26) is selected in the *Navigation* bar and then click the **New Email** button in the *New* group on the *Home* tab. Outlook opens a new email message (Figure 1-27).

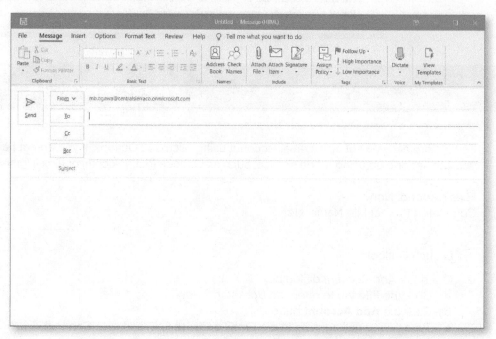

Figure 1-27 New email message

Select Recipients

An email message can be addressed to one recipient or multiple recipients. Type the email address into the *To* field or click the **To** button and select from your *Contact* list. If you are typing the email addresses, separate each email address with a semicolon (;).

When you click the *To* button (Figure 1-28), Outlook opens your *Contacts.* Choose a single recipient or select multiple recipients.

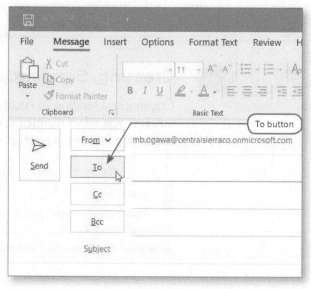

Figure 1-28 Select the *To* button

▶HOW TO: Select Recipients

1. Click the **Mail** button in the *Navigation* bar.
2. Click the **New Email** button to open a new email message.
3. Click the **To** button on the new email message. The *Select Names* dialog box opens.
   - You can also type an email address in the *To* field.

4. Select recipient(s) (Figure 1-29).

5. Click the **To** button below the names.

6. Click **OK** to close the *Select Names* dialog box.

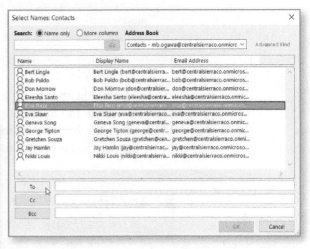

Figure 1-29 Select recipients from contacts list

Cc and Bcc

Two other options that are available when selecting recipients for your email message: *Carbon copy (Cc)* and *Blind carbon copy (Bcc)* (Figure 1-30). *Cc* is used when someone is not the main recipient of the message, but they need to be kept informed of the contents of the message or ongoing email discussion.

Bcc is used when you do not want those receiving the email message to see other recipients' email addresses or names. When a recipient receives an email, he or she will be able to see other recipients' names and email addresses in both the *To* and *Cc* fields, but the *Bcc* field is hidden.

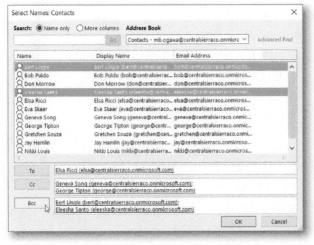
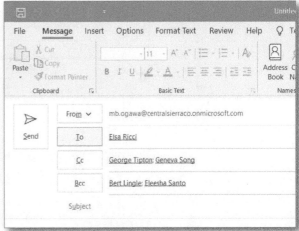

Figure 1-30 Select recipients in the Cc and Bcc fields

The *Cc* button appears on a new message and can be used like the *To* button to select recipients. By default, the *Bcc* button or field is not available when you open a new email message. Click either the *To* or *Cc* button to open the *Select Names* dialog box. Once this dialog box is open, the *Bcc* field is available.

Subject Line and Body

The *Subject line* alerts recipients to the subject of the email, and the *body* contains the contents of the email (Figure 1-31). When a new email message is created, the email is untitled (top center), but once a subject is typed, it becomes the message title. When typing text in the subject and body of the message, you have the option of selecting **Dictate** [*Message* tab, *Voice* group] to voice your message instead of typing it.

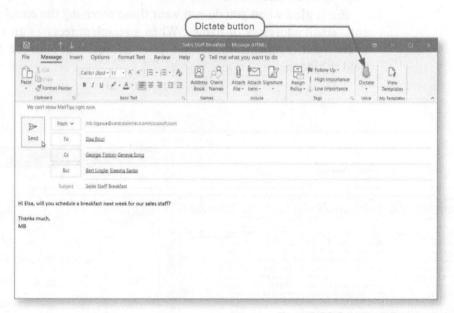

Figure 1-31 Enter text in an email

Format Text

Outlook provides users with many of the same formatting features that are available in Microsoft Word. These text formatting features can be used in the body of the email message. Many of the commonly used formatting features are available on the *Message*

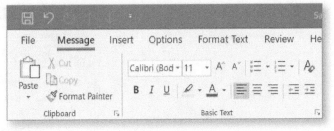

Figure 1-32 Formatting options

tab in the *Basic Text* group (Figure 1-32). Expand the *Basic Text* group by clicking the launcher in the bottom-right corner of the group. The *Font* dialog box opens.

More formatting options are available by clicking the *Format Text* tab, which opens this tab for additional formatting features (Figure 1-33).

Figure 1-33 Additional formatting options

> ### MORE INFO
>
> Be careful to not overdo it with text formatting in the body of an email message. Depending on the type of email account the recipient has, text formatting might not be visible to the recipient.

Send an Email

Once you select your recipients and type the subject and body of the email, you are ready to send the email message. Click the **Send** button to the left of the *To* and *Cc* buttons and your email message will be sent. A copy of it will be automatically saved in the **Sent Items** folder in your *Folder* list.

▶ HOW TO: Send an Email Message

1. Click the **New Email** button [*Home* tab, *New* group]. A new email message opens in a new window.
2. Click the **To** button and select the names or email addresses from the *Select Names* dialog box.
   - You can also add recipients to the *Cc* and *Bcc* fields.
3. Click **OK**. The email addresses will appear in the *To*, *Cc*, and/or *Bcc* fields.
4. Type a brief subject in the *Subject* field.
5. Type a brief message in the body of the message. Remember to always include your name in the body of the email.

6. Click **Send** (Figure 1-34).

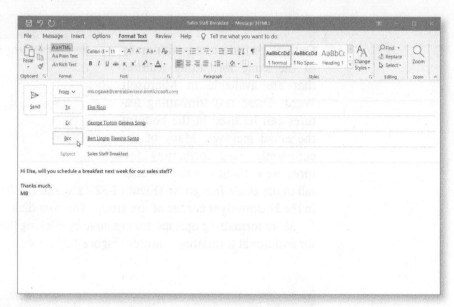

Figure 1-34 Sample email message

> **MORE INFO**
>
> Be careful about the information you include in an email message. An email can easily be forwarded to others, which can have ethical and confidentiality implications.

Save an Email Draft

If you are working on an email and do not have time to finish it or would like to look it over later before sending it, you can save and close the message. When you save a message in Outlook, it is stored in the *Drafts* folder in the *Folder* list.

> **MORE INFO**
>
> Changing the default time interval for saving drafts is covered in chapter 8.

To save an unfinished message, click the **Save** button on the *Quick Access* toolbar or press **Ctrl+S**. Microsoft Office Outlook automatically saves all unfinished messages for you. By default, unfinished messages are saved to your *Drafts* folder every three minutes (Figure 1-35). You can, however, change this time interval or location.

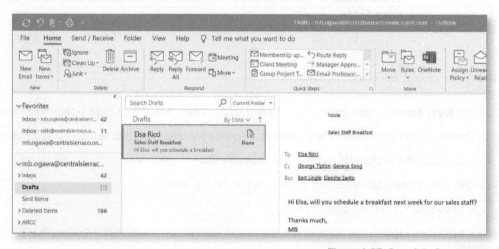

Figure 1-35 Saved draft message

Open an Email

To open an email in your Inbox, double-click the message. The message opens in a new window. Outlook provides users with a *Reading* pane, which allows the message to be read without opening it in a new window. To view the message in the *Reading* pane, click once on the message in the *Folder* pane and the contents of the message displays in the *Reading* pane (either to the right or at the bottom). In addition to reading the message, you can also click the *Read Aloud* button [*Home* tab, *Speech* group] to have the message read to you.

> **ANOTHER WAY**
>
> **Ctrl+O** opens a selected email from the *Folder* or *Reading* pane in a new window.

> **MORE INFO**
>
> Throughout this text when you are asked to open an email, use a new window; do not just view it in the *Reading* pane. Double-click an email in the *Folder* pane to open it.

Reply, Reply All, and Forward

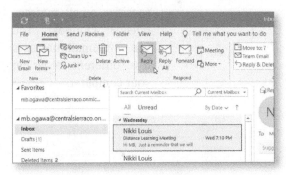

Figure 1-36 Reply to a message

When responding to an email, you have three main options: *Reply*, *Reply All*, and *Forward*. Use **Reply** to send a message to the original sender (Figure 1-36). **Reply All** sends a response to the sender and the other email recipients (those in the *To* and *Cc* lines). **Forward** enables you to send the email message you received to recipients of your choice.

Unlike previous versions, Outlook creates replies and forwarded messages within the Outlook window. If you prefer to write replies in a new window, click the **Pop Out** button in the reply message.

Both *Reply* and *Reply All* keep the same body and subject line. The body text moves down to make room for your message, and the subject is preceded by "RE:" to indicate this email is a reply. Either the original sender (*Reply*) or the sender and other recipients (*Reply All*) will automatically be in the *To* or *Cc* lines. The difference when using *Forward* is the *To* field will be empty and the subject includes "FW:" in front of the subject (Figure 1-37).

To use any of the response options, open the email and choose either *Reply*, *Reply All*, or *Forward*. *Another Way* includes keyboard shortcuts to help you quickly manage email.

> **ANOTHER WAY**
>
> *Reply*: **Ctrl+R**
> *Reply All*: **Ctrl+Shift+R**
> *Forward*: **Ctrl+F**

> **MORE INFO**
>
> When viewing a message in the *Folder* or *Reading* panes, the *Reply*, *Reply All*, and *Forward* buttons are located in the *Respond* group on the *Home* tab. Clicking any of these buttons opens the message.

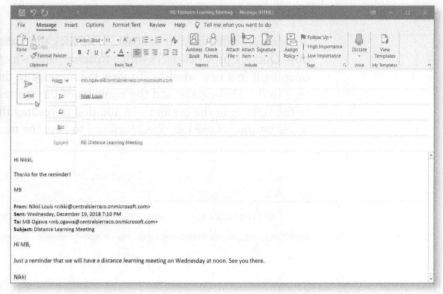

Figure 1-37 Sample reply message

Save an Email in a Windows Folder

When an email message is sent, the original message remains in your Inbox and a copy of
the message is automatically saved in the *Sent Items* folder. There are times when you want
to save an important or
sensitive email message
outside Outlook. You
can save email messages
to a different folder on
your computer.

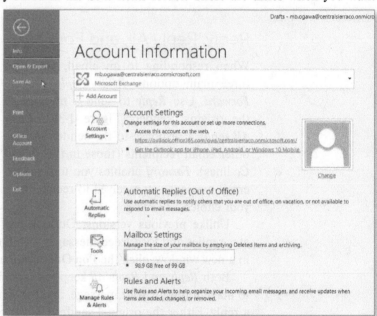

▶ **HOW TO: Save an Email in a
Windows Folder**

1. Click the message to be saved in the
   Folder pane or open the message in a new window.
2. Click the **File** tab. The *Backstage* view opens.
3. Click the **Save As** button to open the *Save As* dialog box
   (Figure 1-38).
4. Browse to the desired location to save the file.
   - By default, the *File name* will be the subject line of the
     email. You can change this as desired.
5. Click the **Save** button.

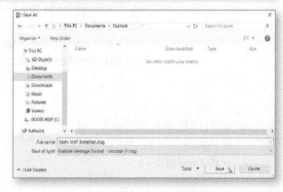

Figure 1-38 Save a message dialog box

Print an Email

If you are on your way to a meeting and need additional information from an email in your Inbox, you might want to print the email to take with you. Also, you might want to print the contents of one of your Inbox folders. The *Print* option in Outlook prints either an individual email in *Memo Style* or the contents of a folder in *Table Style*.

> ▶ **HOW TO:** Print an Email

1. Select the email or folder to be printed.
2. Click the **File** tab to open the *Backstage* view.
3. Click the **Print** button (Figure 1-39).

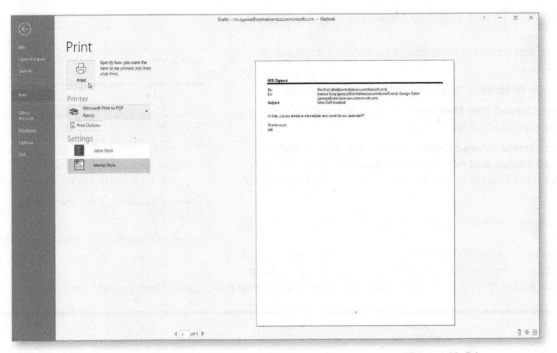

Figure 1-39 Print a message

4. Select the type of printout you would like in the *Print What* area.
5. Click the **Print** button.

Recall an Email Message

Have you ever sent a message and realized, after you pressed the *Send* button, that you omitted information, included incorrect information, or forgot to include an attachment? Outlook provides us with a ***Recall*** feature (Figure 1-40) that allows you to recall a message and gives you the option of replacing it with a new message.

The *Recall* feature works only in conjunction with an Exchange server. Assuming the original message has not been read, the original message is deleted, and the recipient is informed that you, the sender, deleted the message from his or her mailbox. If you are replacing the original message with a new one, the original message will be deleted when the *Recall* message is opened. The recall will fail if the recipient opens the original message before it is deleted or opened before the recall message. If you have selected the *Tell me if recall succeeds or fails for each recipient* check box, you will receive an email notification in your Inbox informing you of the recall status.

Figure 1-40 *Recall This Message*

▶**HOW TO:** Recall an Email Message

1. Locate and open the message to be recalled in your *Sent Items* folder.
2. Click the **Actions** button [*Message* tab, *Move* group].
3. Choose **Recall This Message**. The *Recall This Message* dialog box opens (Figure 1-41).
4. Select **Delete unread copies of this message** or **Delete unread copies and replace with a new message**. Outlook tracks this action to let you know if the recall was successful.
5. Click **OK**.
   - If you are just deleting unread copies, Outlook performs the recall.
   - If you are replacing the email message with a new one, the original message opens so you can modify it. Press **Send** after editing the message to perform the recall and replace the original message with the new one.

Figure 1-41 *Recall This Message* dialog box

> ▶ MORE INFO
>
> If you are recalling a message that was sent to a large number of recipients, you will not want to select the *Tell me if recall succeeds or fails for each recipient* check box. If you do select it, your Inbox will be filled with recall success/failure notifications.

Resend an Email Message

Resending a message is useful if you want to resend a previously sent message. If someone did not receive your original message or if you want to send the same message to new recipients, you can resend a previously sent message rather than creating and sending a new message. The process to resend a message is similar to recalling a message.

▶ HOW TO: Resend an Email Message

1. Locate and open the message to be resent in your *Sent Items* folder.
2. Click the **Actions** button [*Message* tab, *Move* group].
3. Choose **Resend This Message** (Figure 1-42).
4. Select recipients to receive the message.
5. Click **OK**.

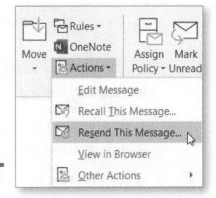

Figure 1-42 *Resend This Message*

▶ ANOTHER WAY

Recall or resend an email message by opening the message and clicking the **File** tab where both the recall and resend options are available on the *Backstage* view.

PAUSE & PRACTICE: OUTLOOK 1-2

For this project, you send an email message to your instructor and use the *Cc* function to send a copy to yourself. You also read the message, reply to it, and print it for your records.

Files Needed: None
Completed Project File Name: None

1. Click the **Mail** button in the *Navigation* bar.

2. Create a new email message by clicking the **New Email** button [*Home* tab, *New* group].

3. Enter the following information in the email message fields:

   To: [your instructor's email address]
   Cc: [your email address]
   Subject: Central Sierra Information Request
   Body: Hi Don, could you please email me the latest employee information sheet when you have a chance?
       Thank you,
       [your name]

4. Click the **Send** button to send the message.

5. View the message you sent in your *Sent Items* folder using the *Reading* pane.
   a. Click the **Sent Items** folder.
   b. Select the message.
   c. Select the **Right** or **Bottom Reading** pane option based on your preference [*View* tab, *Layout* group, *Reading Pane* button].

6. Reply to the message.
   a. Click the **Reply** button [*Home* tab, *Respond* group].

b. Click the body section of the message and type the following:
I will look it up and send it to you as soon as I retrieve it.
[your name]
c. Click the **Send** button.

7. Print the reply message.
a. Select the reply message in your Inbox.
b. Click the **Print** button [*File* tab, *Backstage* view].

8. Print the reply message.
a. Select the reply message in *Sent Items* folder.
b. Click the **Print** button [*File* tab, *Backstage* view].

9. Submit the printed copy to your instructor (Figure 1-43).

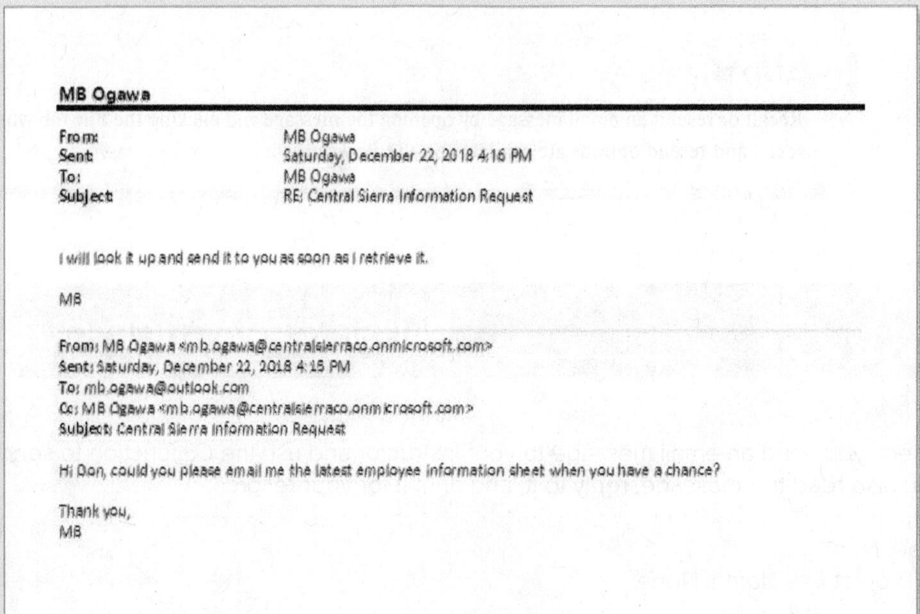

MB Ogawa

From:	MB Ogawa
Sent:	Saturday, December 22, 2018 4:16 PM
To:	MB Ogawa
Subject:	RE: Central Sierra Information Request

I will look it up and send it to you as soon as I retrieve it.

MB

From: MB Ogawa <mb.ogawa@centralsierraco.onmicrosoft.com>
Sent: Saturday, December 22, 2018 4:15 PM
To: mb.ogawa@outlook.com
Cc: MB Ogawa <mb.ogawa@centralsierraco.onmicrosoft.com>
Subject: Central Sierra Information Request

Hi Don, could you please email me the latest employee information sheet when you have a chance?

Thank you,
MB

Figure 1-43 Pause & Practice 1-2 completed

Handling Attachments

One of the many benefits of email is that a file or multiple files can easily be attached to and sent with an email. Pictures, Word documents, and Excel spreadsheets are examples of files to attach to an email.

Attach a File

Outlook integrates with *OneDrive*, Microsoft's cloud storage system. You can attach a file from *OneDrive* or your local computer to an email message by clicking the **Attach File** button (Figure 1-44) on the *Message* tab in the *Include* group. Options include selecting a *Recent Item*, *Browse web Locations*, or *Browse This PC*.

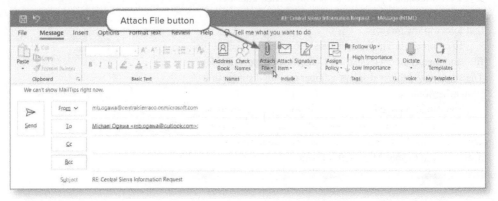

Figure 1-44 *Attach File* button

Certain file types and objects cannot be attached to email. Microsoft Access database files and entire folders cannot be attached to an email message. One way to get around this limitation is to *compress* or *zip* the files or folders and then attach the compressed (zipped) file. Compressed (zip) files can take the take multiple files and store them as a single file. Compressed files make it possible to send multiple files as a single attachment by placing multiple files into a single file. It also compresses the file to reduce its size and increase its portability.

You might have sent email messages asking your recipients to refer to an attachment, but you might not have always remembered to attach the referenced document to your message. If you forget to attach a file and reference an attachment in your email message, the *Attachment Reminder* feature warns you. An *Attachment Reminder* warning displays with two options *Don't Send* and *Send Anyway*. This ensures you attach files to email messages. Selecting *Don't Send* will return you to your message, while selecting *Send Anyway* will send your message as is (Figure 1-45).

Figure 1-45 *Attachment Reminder*

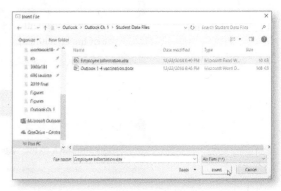

Figure 1-46 *Insert File* dialog box

▶ HOW TO: Attach a File

1. Click the **Attach File** button [*Message* tab, *Include* group]. A list of recently used files is displayed.
2. Click **Browse This PC. . .**
3. Browse through the files on your computer (Figure 1-46).

4. Select the files. Use the **Ctrl** and **Shift** keys to select multiple files.

5. Click **Insert**.
   - The attached files will appear below the subject line (Figure 1-47).

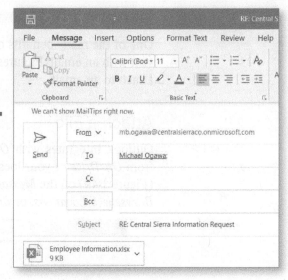

Figure 1-47 Attached file

> **MORE INFO**
>
> If you are attaching more than three or four files, consider grouping them in one compressed (zipped) folder and attach that folder to the message.
>
> To compress or zip multiple files into one folder, select the files and then right-click **Send To, Compressed (zipped) Folder**. The compressed folder displays a zipper on it to distinguish it from other folders.
>
> You can also attach files located in your *OneDrive* storage by selecting **Browse web Locations** and clicking your *OneDrive* account. If you do not see your *OneDrive* account, you may need to log in to your Microsoft account.

Preview an Attachment

Outlook enables you to preview most types of attachments received in email messages without opening them. When you click the attachment as shown in Figure 1-45, the attachment displays in the body of the message (Figure 1-48). Return to the email message by clicking the **Show Message** button in the *Message* group on the *Attachments* tab.

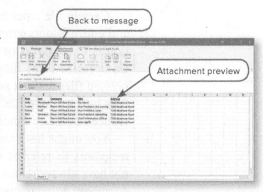

Figure 1-48 Preview an attachment

> **MORE INFO**
>
> When an attachment is being previewed, the area above the attachment displays the file name and the size of the attachment.

> **ANOTHER WAY**
>
> Click the **Back to message** text above the attachment to return to the message.

Open and Save Attachments

Usually when an attachment is received via email, you will want to open and/or save the attachment. The attachment displays below the subject line in the email.

Outlook made attachment handling much easier with the new drop-down arrow next to attachments. The drop-down list includes open, save, print, copy, or remove.

> ### MORE INFO
> Attachments are usually associated with specific software. For example, if you receive a compressed Excel worksheet, you need Excel on your computer to be able to open the file.

▶ HOW TO: Open an Attachment

1. Open an email message, click the drop-down arrow on the right of the attachment to display attachment handling options.
2. Click **Open**. It opens in a new window (Figure 1-49).

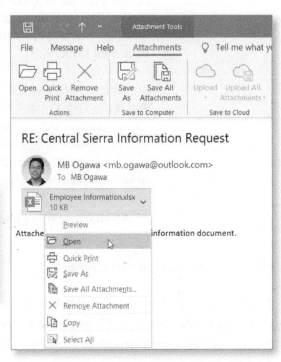

> ### MORE INFO
> It is important to have virus protection software installed and up to date on your computer. Attachments and links in email messages are main ways viruses are spread between computers. Virus protection software could be the best investment you make each year.

Figure 1-49 Opened attachment

> ### ANOTHER WAY
> Open an attachment by double-clicking the attachment, right-clicking the attachment and choosing **Open**, or clicking the **Open** button in the *Actions* group of the *Attachments* tab.

Outlook has the ability to save attachments to your *OneDrive* account. If you are logged into your *OneDrive* account, you can save attachments directly to your *OneDrive* folder. Having attachments saved in your *OneDrive* folder allows you easy access to these saved files from anywhere.

▶HOW TO: Save an Attachment to OneDrive

1. Click the drop-down arrow next to the attachment.
2. Select **Upload** (Figure 1-50).
3. Click your **OneDrive** account. You will see a cloud with the text *Saved* next to the attachment.

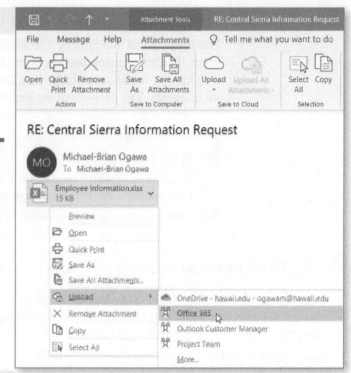

If an attachment is opened, it can be saved the same way you save any other open document. Typically, you can save an open document by pressing **Ctrl+S** or clicking the **Save** icon located on the *File* tab or *Quick Access* toolbar. Be sure to specify the location where you want the document saved.

> **ANOTHER WAY**
>
> Select an attachment and click the **Upload** button on the *Save to Cloud* group in the *Attachments* tab.

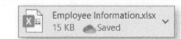

Figure 1-50 Upload attachments to *OneDrive*.

An attachment can also be saved without opening it from the email.

▶HOW TO: Save an Attachment

1. Click the drop-down arrow next to the attachment.
2. Click **Save As**. The *Save As* dialog box opens.
3. Choose the desired location to save the file and specify a file name.
4. Click **Save**.

> **MORE INFO**
>
> If an email has multiple attachments, Outlook has a *Save All Attachments* option. Pressing it will allow you to save multiple attachments all at once rather than saving each one individually.

Forward an Email as an Attachment

When you forward an email with an attachment, the attachment is automatically included in the email to be forwarded. There might be times when you want to forward an entire email as an attachment rather than forwarding only the contents of the email.

▶ HOW TO: Forward an Email as an Attachment

1. Open the message to be forwarded.
2. On the *Message* tab, click the **More** button in the *Respond* group.
3. Select **Forward as Attachment** (Figure 1-51). A new email opens with the selected email as an attachment. The subject line is the same as the original message with *FW:* in front indicating that the message is being forwarded (Figure 1-52).

Figure 1-51 *Forward as Attachment* button

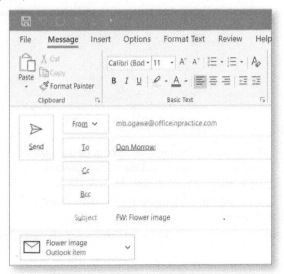

Figure 1-52 *Forward as Attachment* message

4. Select recipients and add any necessary information in the body of the message.
5. Press **Send**.

> ### ANOTHER WAY
> Press **Ctrl+Alt+F** to forward an open email or one selected in the *Folder* pane.

Attach Other Outlook Items

Other Outlook items such as contacts, tasks, calendar items, and Outlook business cards can be attached to an email and sent. These items can be sent either as an attachment or as text in the body of the email.

▶ HOW TO: Attach Other Outlook Items

1. Start a **New** email message.
2. Click the **Insert** tab.
3. Click the **Attach Item** button (Figure 1-53) [*Message* tab, *Include* group].
4. Select the **Outlook Item**. The *Insert Item* dialog box opens.
5. Select a **Business Card**, **Calendar**, or **Outlook Item** from the drop-down list.
6. Select the items to be attached. Use the **Ctrl** key to select nonadjacent items or the **Shift** key to select a range of items.

Figure 1-53 *Attach Item* button

7. Choose whether to insert the items as *Text only* or as an *Attachment* (Figure 1-54).
8. Click **OK**. The Outlook item will be attached to the email message.

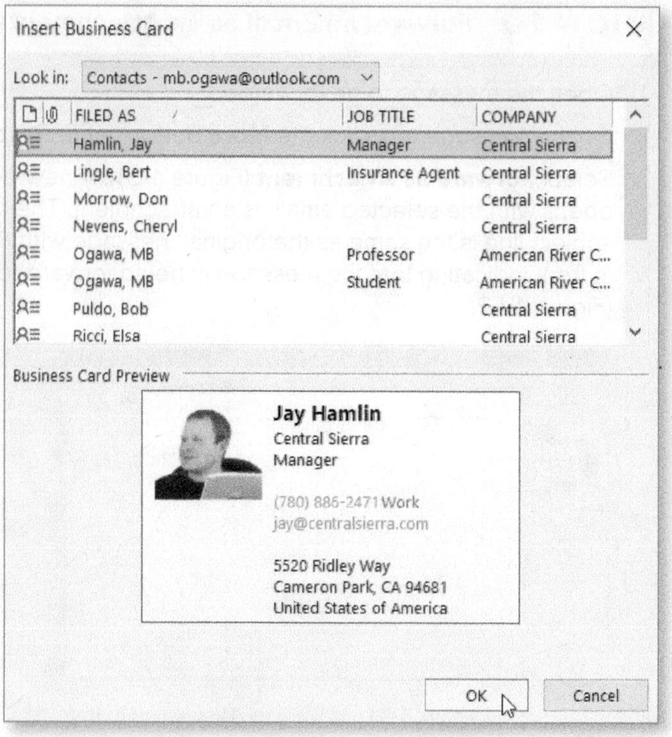

Figure 1-54 Insert an Outlook item as an attachment

> **MORE INFO**
>
> The *Attach Item* button is available in the *Include* group on *Message* tab, and the *Outlook Item* button is available in the *Include* group on the *Insert* tab. Both of these buttons open the *Insert Items* dialog box.

SLO 1.7

Understanding Arrangement and Icons

As mentioned in *SLO 1.2: Navigating Outlook*, the working environment in Outlook is divided into panes. There are typically three panes in Outlook: ***Folder***, ***Reading***, and ***People***. There is also the ***To-Do bar*** that can be open or collapsed.

In the *Folder* pane, you arrange emails in numerous different ways to meet your needs and preferences. Outlook also provides users with many ***icons*** to help easily and quickly identify different aspects of an email displayed in the *Folder* pane. The icons on each email in the *Folder* pane can tell you if a message has been read, if it has been replied to or forwarded, if there is an attachment, if it is marked ***important***, if it is ***flagged*** for action, or if it is assigned to a ***category***.

The *Reading* pane includes additional details about a selected Outlook item such as the content of an email message. The *People* pane displays Outlook content related to a person including email, attachments, and meetings.

> **MORE INFO**
>
> ***Message options*** are covered in chapter 3, which describes how to use the different features associated with Inbox icons. Chapter 5 covers how to customize the user interface.

Email Arrangement

Arrangement controls the order in which email messages display in the *Folder* pane. Typically email messages are arranged or sorted with the most recently received email at the top of the list (arranged by date and time in descending order). The *View* tab provides different *View* and

Arrangement options. Outlook has upgraded the arrangement options so it is easier to quickly change the arrangement of emails.

Conversation arrangement (Figure 1-55) groups all emails related to a particular email conversation (by subject), which is intended to greatly reduce the number of redundant emails displayed in the *Folder* list (Figure 1-56). The *Conversation* arrangement groups emails together to occupy less space in your list of emails and gives you the ability to expand the conversation to see all related messages, including those in the *Sent Items* folder.

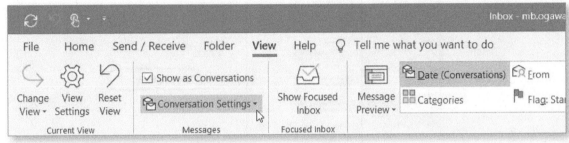

Figure 1-55 *Conversation Settings* button

When multiple emails exist within a conversation, clicking the small triangle to the left of an email will expand the conversation. Collapse the conversation by clicking the small triangle to the left of the conversation subject in the *Folder* pane.

Outlook includes many preset arrangement options. These options appear in the *Arrangement* group on the *View* tab.

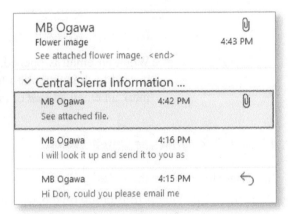

Figure 1-56 *Conversation* arrangement

> **MORE INFO**
>
> When you click the small triangle next to a conversation, the message expands to show the related messages in the current folder. When you click the triangle again, the conversation expands to include related messages in other folders.

Read/Unread Email

When the Inbox (or any other folder) is selected in the *Folder* pane, the contents of that folder display in the *Folder* pane. The vertical blue line to the left of the email shows whether or not the email has been read. When an email has not been read, the email is bold. Once the email has been opened and read, the email will no longer appear bold (Figure 1-57).

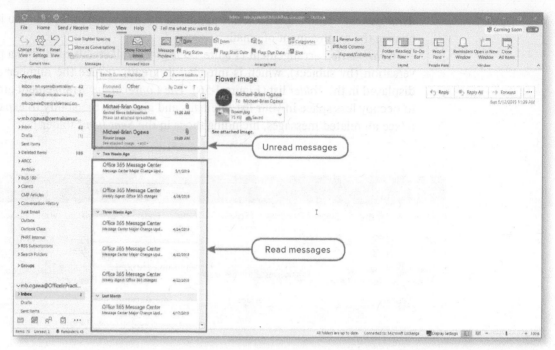

Figure 1-57 Read and unread messages

Mark as Read/Unread

When an email is opened, Outlook marks it as read. You might want to mark a message as unread to draw attention to it in the folder or *Folder* pane. Use the *Home* tab, *Tags* group to mark an email as *read* or *unread*.

▶ **HOW TO:** Mark as Unread/Read

1. Select the email in the message list to be marked as read or unread.
2. In the *Home* tab *on Tags* group on the, click the **Unread/Read** button (Figure 1-58).

Figure 1-58 *Unread/ Read* button

▶ **ANOTHER WAY**

Right-click the email and choose **Mark as Read** or **Mark as Unread**.

▶ **MORE INFO**

The entire contents of a folder can be marked as read by either right-clicking the folder and choosing **Mark All as Read** or by clicking the **Mark All as Read** button in the *Clean Up* group on the *Folder* tab.

Replied to and Forwarded

By scanning your email in the message list, you easily see the response action for each email. Messages that have been replied to have an envelope icon with an arrow pointing to the left, and those that have been forwarded have an envelope icon with an arrow pointing to the right.

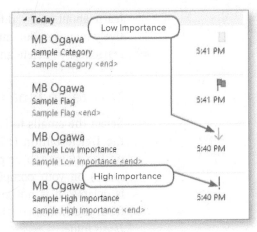

Figure 1-59 Sample Inbox

Attachment

Outlook uses a *paper clip* icon to indicate that an email has an attachment.

Flag

When a message is flagged for follow up or has a flag for recipients, the *flag* icon is used. This flag appears in different shades of red depending on the action of the flag (*Today, Tomorrow, This Week*) (see Figure 1-59).

Importance

Importance can be set for each email to one of three levels: **high**, **low**, and **normal**. High importance is indicated by a red exclamation point, low importance uses a blue arrow pointed down, and normal importance uses no special icon (see Figure 1-59). (Normal importance is the default on all new email messages.)

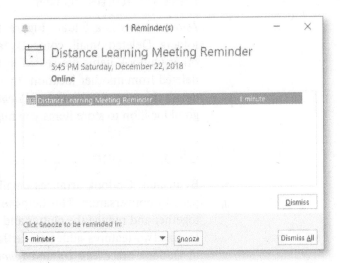

Figure 1-60 *Reminder(s) window*

Reminder

When an email is received that includes a reminder, it is marked with a small *bell* icon. An electronic reminder displays on your computer on the reminder day and time (Figure 1-60). You have the options of opening the email, dismissing the reminder, or choosing snooze to be reminded again later.

Category

Categories are used to group Inbox items. Colors are used to distinguish categories, and the category names can be customized to meet your individual needs. Categories are not limited to email messages; they can also be advantageous for grouping contacts, tasks, and calendar items (see Figure 1-57).

Cleaning Up Your Inbox

It is important to manage your Inbox effectively. When you receive mail (postal mail) at home or work, you read it and then determine what action needs to be taken. Bills need to be paid, information needs to be filed and saved, junk mail discarded, and other mail is thrown away after you've responded to it. Your email Inbox is very similar. Throughout this text, you will learn about many different tools to help you effectively manage your Inbox. For now, it is important to learn how to delete an email you no longer need.

Delete an Email

Select the emails to be deleted, and then either click the **Delete** button (Figure 1-61) in the *Delete* group on the *Home* tab or press the **Delete** key (not *Backspace*) on your computer keyboard. When an email is deleted, it is not gone forever. It has been moved from your *Inbox* (or the folder it is in) to your *Deleted Items* folder.

Figure 1-61 *Delete* button

> **ANOTHER WAY**
>
> Outlook items can also be deleted by right-clicking the item and choosing **Delete**, or selecting an email message in the *Folder* pane and pressing **Ctrl+D**.

Deleted Items Folder

Deleted Items is a folder (Figure 1-62) in your list of *Mail* folders. Deleted email, contacts, tasks, calendar items, and other Outlook items are stored in this folder when they are deleted from another location. By default, Outlook does not delete the items in the *Deleted Items* folder, but this is not a good location to store items you might need.

Clean Up and Ignore

By default, Outlook arranges emails displayed in the *Folder* pane by conversation. This helps to both group related items together and reduce the clutter and redundant emails in your Inbox. Two features added to further manage conversations in Outlook are ***Clean Up*** and ***Ignore***. *Clean Up* will remove redundant messages in an email conversation. *Clean Up* can also be used on an entire folder and subfolders (Figure 1-63).

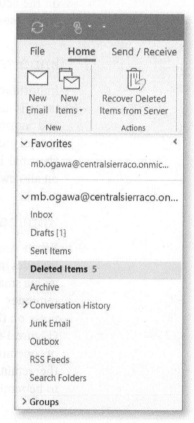

Figure 1-62 *Deleted Items* folder

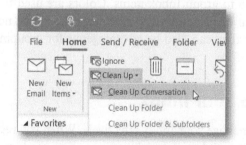

Figure 1-63 *Clean Up Conversation* button and dialog box

Ignore deletes all emails related to a specific conversation and any new received email that is related to that conversation.

Both *Clean Up* and *Ignore* are handy features to help manage the volume of emails you receive. By default, when you *Clean Up* or *Ignore* a conversation, the deleted emails are moved to the *Deleted Items* folder.

Empty Deleted Items

It is a good idea to regularly empty your *Deleted Items* folder. The items in this folder can be manually deleted.

▶ **HOW TO:** Empty Deleted Items

1. Click the **Deleted Items** folder in the *Folder* pane.

2. Click the **Folder** tab.

3. Click the **Delete All** button (Figure 1-64) in the *Clean Up* group. A dialog box opens confirming that you want to empty the *Deleted Items* folder.

4. Choose **Yes** to delete items in the *Deleted Items* folder.

Figure 1-64 *Delete All* button

▶ **ANOTHER WAY**

Right-click the **Deleted Items** folder and choose **Empty Folder**.

It is a good idea to have Outlook automatically empty the *Deleted Items* folder each time you exit Outlook. The default settings in Outlook can easily be changed to do this.

▶ **HOW TO:** Change the Default Setting to Automatically Empty Deleted Items Each Time You Exit Outlook

1. Click the **File** tab to open the *Backstage* view.

2. Click the **Options** button on the left. The *Outlook Options* dialog box opens.

3. Click the **Advanced** button on the left.

4. Select the **Empty Deleted Items folder when exiting Outlook** check box (Figure 1-65).

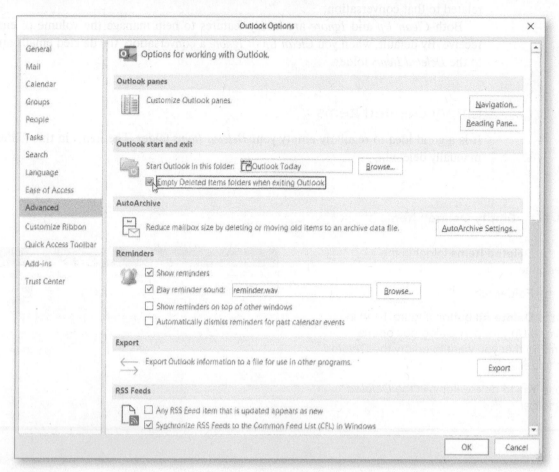

Figure 1-65 *Empty Deleted Items* folder when exiting Outlook option

5. Click **OK** to close the *Outlook Options* dialog box.

> **MORE INFO**
>
> The *Outlook Options* dialog box will be referenced throughout this text. This area allows you to custom-
> ize settings in Outlook. *Outlook Options* and other Outlook features are located on the *Backstage* view,
> which is accessed by clicking the **File** tab. *Outlook Options* is covered in chapter 7.

Even when Outlook items have been deleted and the *Deleted Items* folder has been emptied, Outlook still provides you with the ability to recover deleted items if you are using an Exchange server. The ***Recover Deleted Items*** button (Figure 1-66) in the *Clean Up* group on the *Folder* tab allows you to select previously deleted items to recover. These recovered items will be placed in your *Deleted Items* folder.

Figure 1-66 *Recover Deleted Items* button

For this project, you reply to a message with an email attachment. You also forward the message to your instructor as an attachment and delete a message.

File Needed: ***Employee Information.xlsx***
Completed Project File Name: None

1. Reply to the message with the subject ***Central Sierra Information Request***.
   a. Select the message in your Inbox.
   b. Click the **Reply** button in the message.

2. Add the following text to the body of the message:
   I just found the employee data sheet and attached it to this message.
   [your name]

3. Attach the ***Employee Information.xlsx*** file to the message.
   a. Click the **Attach File** button on the *Message* tab, *Include* group.
   b. Select **Browse This PC** from the drop-down list.
   c. Select the **Employee Information.xlsx** file.
   d. Click **Open**.

4. Click the **Send** button to send the message. The message appears in your Inbox.

5. Select the message and forward it to your instructor as an attachment.
   a. Click the message to select it.
   b. Click the **Forward as Attachment** option [*Home* tab, *Respond* group, *More* button].
   c. Enter your instructor's email address in the *To* field.
   d. Enter the following text in the body of the message:
      Attached is the requested verification email for the employee data.
      [your name]
   e. Click the **Send** button.

6. Delete the initial reply message that indicated that you would send the message as soon as you retrieved it.
   a. Select the initial reply message in your Inbox.
   b. Click the **Delete** button [*Home* tab, *Delete* group].

7. Empty the *Deleted Items* folder.
   a. Click the **Deleted Items** folder.
   b. Click the **Empty Folder** button [*Folder* tab, *Clean Up* group].
   c. Click **Yes** to confirm the deletion of messages in the *Deleted Items* folder (Figure 1-67).

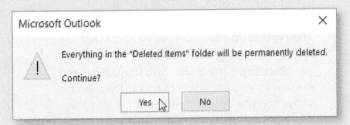

Figure 1-67 Confirmation for deleting items

Chapter Summary

1.1 Identify the basic components of Microsoft Outlook (p. O1-3).

- Outlook includes six major features: *Email, Calendar, Contacts, Tasks, Notes,* and *Journal.*
- ***Email***: Use to create, send, and receive email; manage a single email account or multiple email accounts
- ***Calendar***: An electronic calendar used to create appointments or events, edit these items, replicate calendar items, set electronic reminders, create meeting requests, and share calendar items with other Outlook users or other devices
- ***Contacts***: An area to record names, email, phone numbers, and other information about business contacts, coworkers, friends, and family
- ***Tasks***: An electronic notepad used to write down your ***To-Do List*** and then cross them off as they are completed
- ***Notes***: Electronic sticky notes that are an excellent way of storing information such as a user name and password to log into a web site, gift ideas for family and friends, or a list of books you'd like to read
- ***Journal***: Primarily used in the business environment and enables you track time spent on a project or document

1.2 Navigate throughout the Outlook environment and identify the different panes in the Outlook window (p. O1-7).

- Outlook is divided into sections called ***panes***. Each pane includes features specific to its section.
- ***Outlook Today*** is the welcome screen for Outlook which provides you with information about your mailbox, calendar items, and task list.
- The ***Navigation bar*** allows you to quickly switch between different features in Outlook.
- The ***Reading*** pane allows you to quickly read messages or see details in tasks. This can be shown on the bottom or right of the window.
- The ***Ribbon*** appears at the top of the Outlook window and includes a variety of ***tabs***. Each tab displays ***groups***; groups contain buttons, drop-down lists, and galleries.

- You can choose from a variety of preset views to personalize your experience.
- The ***Folder list*** displays all of the folders in the *Folder* pane.
- The ***Outlook Help*** button allows you to quickly search for topics on which you might have a question or need additional information.

1.3 Distinguish between Outlook being used as a stand-alone program and in a Microsoft Exchange environment (p. O1-14).

- Outlook as a ***stand-alone program*** connects directly to your internet service provider and can manage multiple email accounts.
- Outlook is typically connected to an ***Exchange server*** in business environments and has the following features:

  - Using voting buttons and tracking responses
  - Sending meeting requests and tracking responses
  - Recalling messages
  - Sharing your calendar, contacts, tasks, and email with others
  - Using *MailTips*
  - Using a common global contact list

1.4 Distinguish between the different types of email accounts and set up an email account in Outlook (p.O1-15).

- ***Microsoft Exchange*** accounts are used primarily in medium- to large-business settings. These email accounts are set up through the company network or email administrator. An Exchange account has an individual mailbox assigned to each user and resides on an Exchange file server.
- ***POP3*** accounts are internet email accounts that are associated with your internet service provider (ISP). When using this type of account, Outlook downloads the messages.
- ***IMAP*** accounts are also internet accounts but are not always associated with an ISP. IMAP accounts create folders on a server to store and organize messages for retrieval by other computers and gives you the option to read message headers only and select which messages to download.

- **HTTP** accounts use the hypertext transfer protocol used on the web to create, view, send, and receive messages. This type of account is not automatically supported by Outlook but can be configured by installing an add-in.
- You can set up an email account by clicking the **Add Account** button [*File* tab].

1.5 Use Outlook to create, send, and receive email (p. O1-17).

- Select recipients, type the subject of the message, type the message, and send email messages.
- The **To** field indicates whom a message is addressed, while the **Cc** field is used to send a *carbon copy* of a message to another person. The **Bcc** field is used to send a *blind carbon copy* of a message to a recipient. *Bcc* is used when you do not want those receiving the email message to see other recipients' email addresses or names.
- Sent messages are automatically copied to the **Sent Items** folder.
- If you are not ready to send an email message, save it as a draft to the **Drafts** folder.
- You can **Reply**, **Reply All**, or **Forward** a message.
- Save email messages as .msg files to a location on your computer.

1.6 Use attachments in email (p. O1-29).

- Attach files from your computer or *OneDrive* to email messages.
- You cannot attach a Microsoft Access file or a folder to an email message.
- Most common attachments, such as images, can be previewed by clicking them within a message.
- Attachments can be saved to your computer.
- Email messages can be forwarded to recipients as attachments.
- Attach Outlook items, such as business cards, to email messages.

1.7 Differentiate email arrangements and icons (p. O1-34).

- Email messages can be grouped in **Conversation**, which groups all emails related

to a particular email conversation. This ensures your email is less cluttered, as only the newest message in a conversation displays.

- **Unread** messages are bolded, while **read** messages are not. Outlook allows you to mark messages that are read as unread or unread as read. Marking messages as unread ensures they maintain the bold appearance and are easy to identify.
- A **paper clip** icon is used to indicate that a message has an attachment.
- A **flag** is used to indicate that follow-up on a message is needed.
- Set the importance of an email messages as high, normal, or low to indicate the priority one should place on the message.
- Add reminders to email messages that require an action.
- Categories can be used to group emails by similar subjects.

1.8 Explain the importance and process of cleaning up an Inbox (p. O1-37).

- When you delete an email message, it is sent to the **Deleted Items** folder, as opposed to being deleted from your account.
- Emptying your *Deleted Items* folder will delete any messages that were moved to that location.
- **Clean Up** removes redundant messages in an email conversation. *Clean Up* can also be used on an entire folder and subfolders.
- **Ignore** deletes all emails related to a specific conversation and deletes any new received email that is related to that conversation.
- **Recover Deleted Items** allows you to restore previously deleted items.

Check for Understanding

The SIMbook for this text (within your SIMnet account), provides the following resources for concept review:

- Multiple-choice questions
- Short answer questions
- Matching exercises

Guided Project 1-1

For this project, you request a meeting with Jay Hamlin of Central Sierra Insurance to discuss ways of attracting new customers. You send an email message to request a meeting and include a Cc to yourself so that you can keep this message at the top of your message list.
[Student Learning Outcomes 1.1, 1.2, 1.5, 1.7]

Files Needed: None
Completed Project File Name: None

Skills Covered in This Project

- Create a new message.
- Select *To* recipient.
- Select *Cc* recipient.
- Add a subject to a message.
- Add a body to a message.
- Mark a message as low importance.
- Flag a message for follow up.
- Send a message.

1. Create a new email message to Jay Hamlin.
   a. Click the **New Email** button [*Home* tab, *New* group].
   b. In the *To* field, type your instructor's email address.
   c. In the *Cc* field, type your email address.
   d. In the *Subject* field, type Attracting New Customers Meeting Request.

2. In the body of the message, type the following text:

   Hi Jay, I was wondering if you are available to meet next week to discuss our strategies to attract new customers. I am available on Monday from 2:00 P.M. to 3:00 P.M. or Tuesday from 3:00 P.M. to 4:00 P.M. Please let me know if either of these days work for your schedule. If not, please send me alternative times that you are available.

   Thanks,
   [your name]

3. Mark the message as *Low Importance* and flag the message for follow up.
   a. Click the **Low Importance** button [*Message* tab, *Tags* group].
   b. Click **Follow Up** [*Message* tab, *Tags* group] and select **Tomorrow**.

4. Click the **Send** button to send the message (Figure 1-68).

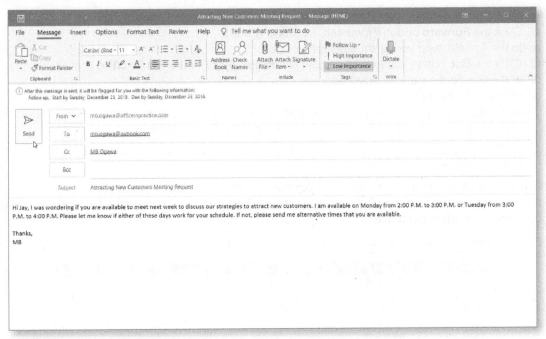

Figure 1-68 Guided Project 1-1 completed

Guided Project 1-2

For this project, you follow up with Jay since he was unable to respond to your first message. You forward your original message to him and ask if he is available to meet.
[Student Learning Outcomes 1.1, 1.2, 1.5, 1.7]

Files Needed: None
Completed Project File Name: None

Skills Covered in This Project

- Identify an unread message.
- Open a message.
- Identify a message as low importance.
- Forward a message.
- Select *To* recipient.

- Add a *Bcc* to a message.
- Select *Bcc* recipient.
- Modify the body of a message.
- Remove *Low Importance* tag.
- Mark a message as high importance.
- Send a message.

1. Open the message sent in *Guided Practice 1-1*.
   a. Click the **Mail** button to confirm you are in your Inbox.
   b. Click the message with the subject **Attracting New Customers Meeting Request**. The message should have the *Low Importance* tag (downward pointing arrow) on the message.

2. Forward the message to Jay Hamlin and modify the body of the message.
   a. Click the **Forward** button [*Home* tab, *Respond* group].
   b. In the *To* field, type your instructor's email address.
   c. Click the **Bcc** button [*Options* tab, *Show Fields* group] to ensure the *Bcc* field is available.
   d. In the *Bcc* field, type your email address.
   e. In body of the message, type:

   Hi Jay, I just wanted to follow up with you regarding our meeting to attract new customers. Are you available next week to meet? Please let me know at your earliest convenience.

   Thank you,
   [your name]

3. Change the importance of the message from low importance to high importance.
   a. Click the **Low Importance** button [*Message* tab, *Tags* group] to remove *the Low Importance* tag.
   b. Click the **High Importance** button [*Message* tab, *Tags* group].

4. Click the **Send** button to send the message (Figure 1-69).

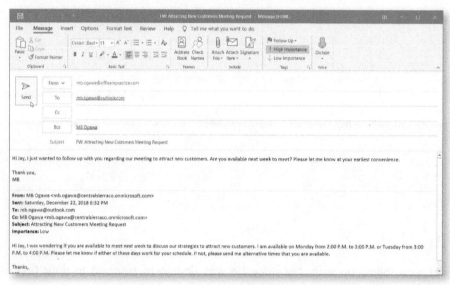

Figure 1-69 Guided Project 1-2 completed

Guided Project 1-3

For this project, you reply to the message as Jay Hamlin. You save a draft of your message, save a copy of your message as a .msg file, and print a copy of the message.
[Student Learning Outcomes 1.1, 1.2, 1.5, 1.7]

Files Needed: None
Completed Project File Name: ***[your initials] Outlook 1-3.msg***

Skills Covered in This Project

- Open a message.
- Identify a message as high importance.
- Reply to a message.
- Select a *Cc* recipient.
- Edit the body of a message.
- Save a message as a file.
- Send a message.
- Create a new message.
- Add an attachment to a message.

1. Open the message sent in *Guided Practice 1-2*.
   a. Click the **Mail** button to confirm you are in your Inbox.
   b. Click the message with the subject ***FW: Attracting New Customers Meeting Request***. The message should have the *High Importance* tag (red exclamation point) on the message.

2. Forward the message to Jay Hamlin and modify the body of the message.
   a. Click the **Forward** button [*Home* tab, *Respond* group].
   b. Ensure the *To* field has your email address.
   c. In the *Cc* field, type your instructor's email address.
   d. In the body of the message, type:
      Hi [your name], Thanks for checking in with me regarding the meeting about new customers. I accidentally missed your first message. I am available to meet on Tuesday at 2:00 P.M.

      Elsa, could you please schedule the conference room for us next week Tuesday from 2:00 P.M. to 3:00 P.M.

      Jay

3. Save the message to your computer.
   a. Click **Save As** [*File* tab].
   b. Locate the driver and folder where the file is to be stored.
   c. Change the file name to be ***[your initials] Outlook 1-3*** in the *File Name* area.
   d. Click the **Save** button.

4. Click the **Send** button to send the message.

5. Create a new email message to your instructor.
   a. Click the **New Email** button [*Home* tab, *New* group].
   b. In the *To* field, type your instructor's email address.
   c. In the *Cc* field, type your email address.
   d. In the *Subject* field, type [your initials] Outlook 1-3.

6. In the body of the message, type:

   Hi [instructor's name]. Attached are my three guided practice assignments from Outlook Chapter 1.
   Thanks,
   [your name]

7. Attach the message you saved to your computer to the email message.
   a. Click the **Attach File** button.
   b. Locate the message you saved in step 3.
   c. Select the message and click the **Insert** button (Figure 1-70).

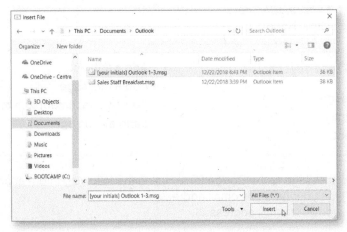

Figure 1-70 Attach a saved message

8. Click the **Send** button to send the message (Figure 1-71).

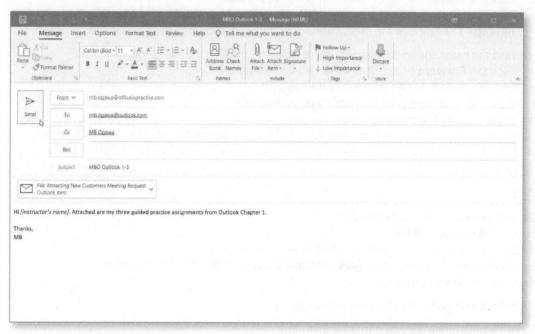

Independent Project 1-4

You received a request from Mr. and Mrs. Dodge over the phone requesting a vaccination schedule for their newborn child. For this project, you send them an email message with a vaccination schedule. [Student Learning Outcomes 1.1, 1.2, 1.5, 1.6, 1.7]

File Needed: ***Outlook 1-4 vaccination.docx***
Completed Project File Name: None

Skills Covered in This Project

- Create a new message.
- Select a *To* recipient.
- Select a *Cc* recipient.

- Add a subject.
- Add a message.
- Add an attachment to a message.
- Send a message.

1. Create a new email message to the Dodge family using the following information:
   a. In the *To* field, type your partner's email address.
   b. In the *Cc* field, type your email address.

2. In the *Subject* field, type Requested vaccination information for your newborn.

3. Type a short message to the Dodge family indicating that you attached the requested vaccination schedule.

4. Attach the file **Outlook 1-4 vaccination.docx** to the message.

5. Send the message (Figure 1-72).

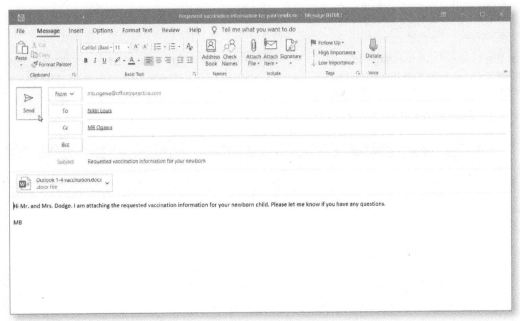

Figure 1-72 Independent Project 1-4 completed

Independent Project 1-5

You received a request from Dr. Lee at Courtyard Medical Plaza to verify the message to the Dodge family was sent. For this project, you send him the message that you sent and print a copy for the patient's records.

[Student Learning Outcomes 1.1, 1.2, 1.5, 1.6, 1.7, 1.8]

Files Needed: None
Completed Project File Name: None

Skills Covered in This Project

- Open a message.
- Print a message.
- Forward a message as an attachment.
- Select a *To* recipient.
- Select a *Bcc* recipient.
- Add a message.
- Send a message.

1. Locate and open the message sent in *Independent Project 1-4* with the subject **Requested vaccination information for your newborn**. The message has a paper clip icon next to it to indicate that it has an attachment.

2. Print the message in a memo format (Figure 1-73).

3. Forward the message as an attachment to the following recipients:
   a. In the *To* field, type your partner's email address.
   b. In the *Cc* field, type your email address.

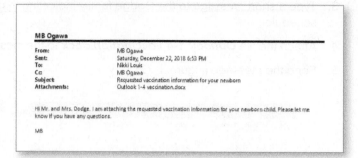

4. Edit the body of the message to indicate to Dr. Lee that the attached message was sent to the Dodge family.

Figure 1-73 Printed message in memo format

5. Send the message (Figure 1-74).

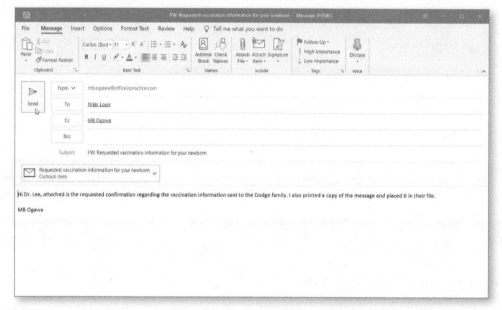

Figure 1-74 Independent Project 1-5 completed

Independent Project 1-6

You noticed that your Inbox is becoming cluttered because you included yourself as a *Cc* or *Bcc* on all of your previous messages to the Dodge family and Dr. Lee. For this project, you forward the messages as an attachment to yourself and your instructor to keep it as one message. Next, you clean your Inbox by deleting all previous messages regarding the Dodge family and Dr. Lee.
[Student Learning Outcomes 1.1, 1.2, 1.5, 1.6, 1.7, 1.8]

Files Needed: None
Completed Project File Name: None

Skills Covered in This Project

- Open a message.
- Forward a message as an attachment.
- Select a *To* recipient.
- Select a *Cc* recipient.
- Edit the subject.
- Edit the message.
- Send a message.
- Delete messages.

1. Locate and open the message sent in *Independent Project 1-5* with the subject **FW: Requested vaccination information for your newborn**. The message has a paper clip icon next to it to indicate that it has an attachment.

2. Forward the message as an attachment to the following recipients:
   a. In the *To* field, type your email address.
   b. In the *Bcc* field, type your instructor's email address.

3. Edit the subject of the message to indicate that the message contains all of the Dodge family messages.

4. Edit the body of the message to indicate that the message is a summary of all messages related to the Dodge family.

5. Send the message (Figure 1-75).

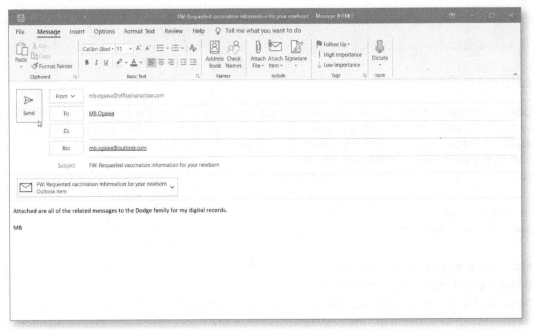

Figure 1-75 Message sent for Independent Project 1-6

6. Locate the following messages sent regarding the Dodge family:
   Requested vaccination information for your newborn
   FW: Requested vaccination information for your newborn

7. Delete the two messages listed in step 6 (Figure 1-76).

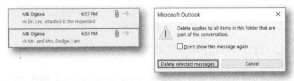

Figure 1-76 Deleting messages for Independent Project 1-6

Challenge Project 1-7

Search for an image online that is representative of you. Compose a message to your instructor with the image as an attachment that explains briefly why and how the image represents you.

Note: Use images that are legal under copyright. You many need to use a search engine such as http://search.creativecommons.org/ to find licensed content.

Files Needed: None
Completed Project File Name: None

[Student Learning Outcomes 1.1, 1.2, 1.5, 1.6, 1.8]

- Send the message to your instructor.
- Add your email address to the Cc field.
- The subject of the message should be Challenge 1-7: Visually Representing [your name].
- Include the image as an attachment.
- Explain how the image represents you in three to five sentences.
- Add a citation for the image at the bottom of your message.

Challenge Project 1-8

Compose a message that includes a list of five activities you would like to try in the next five years. For each of the activities you list, compose a short paragraph about that activity and why you find it interesting. Research each of the activities you choose on the internet. Use your own words when composing the paragraphs about each place.
[Student Learning Outcomes 1.1, 1.2, 1.5, 1.8]

Files Needed: None
Completed Project File Name: None

- Send the message to your instructor.
- Add your email address to the Cc field.
- The subject of the message should be Challenge 1-8: [your name]'s Activities.
- Use formatting to differentiate the activity names from their description and explanation for wanting to participate in each.

Challenge Project 1-9

Search for a job online that you would like to have. Compose an application letter to the employer highlighting a few reasons why you would be qualified for the position. The application letter should be short and concise. Attach your resume to the email message.
[Student Learning Outcomes 1.1, 1.2, 1.5, 1.6, 1.8]

Files Needed: None
Completed Project File Name: None

- Send the message to your instructor.
- Add your email address to the *Cc* field.
- The subject of the message should be Challenge 1-9: [your name]'s application for [job name].
- Include your resume as an attachment.
- Address the body of the email message to your instructor.
- Include a few reasons why you would be qualified for the position in the body of the message.

Source of screenshots Microsoft Office 365 (2019): Word, Excel, Access, Powerpoint, Outlook.

Email Special Features

OUTLOOK

CHAPTER OVERVIEW

One of the benefits of using Outlook to handle your email accounts is the vast array of features available to customize your messages and the Outlook environment. As your understanding of Outlook increases, you will want to customize email messages and change some of the default settings in Outlook to more fully meet your needs and preferences.

This chapter prepares you to customize email by using the different email options available in Outlook. These include marking an email as important, using delivery and read receipts, delaying the delivery of an email, flagging an email for recipients, and many more. You will also learn how to use voting buttons and change the look of your email by using stationery, themes, and signatures. After completing chapter 1 and this chapter, you will be able to customize Outlook and use email options to meet your personal and professional needs.

STUDENT LEARNING OUTCOMES (SLOs)

After completing this chapter, you will be able to:

SLO 2.1 Differentiate between the types of email formats (p. O2-55).

SLO 2.2 Customize email using the different types of message options available in Outlook (p. O2-56).

SLO 2.3 Use categories to organize email messages into different groups (p. O2-66).

SLO 2.4 Add *Follow Up* flags to email messages to add reminders to messages (p. O2-69).

SLO 2.5 Use email voting buttons to get responses from recipients and to automatically track responses (p. O2-74).

SLO 2.6 Customize your emails by using signatures, themes, templates, and desktop alerts (p. O2-78).

CASE STUDY

For the Pause & Practice projects, you work with a partner on a business project. You use email to identify meeting dates and locations. You send and reply to email messages with a partner and use Outlook's email special features.

Pause & Practice 2-1: You send a plain text formatted message to a peer to request information about your peer's availability to meet about a business project.

Pause & Practice 2-2: You organize your email messages using categories. You also create a custom follow up flag for your message.

Pause & Practice 2-3: You use voting buttons to determine a good location for your lunch meeting.

Pause & Practice 2-4: You create a signature and insert it in an email message to your partner. You also forward the stream of messages to your instructor.

Understanding Email Formats

Not all email accounts operate on the same mail format. Outlook provides flexibility in the type of email messages that are available for different situations. The message format you choose determines the types of formatting features you can use, such as fonts, formatted text, colors, styles, bullets, numbering, line spacing, and indents. It is important to note that just because you can and do use advanced formatting features in the body of your email it does not mean that the recipient of your email will be able to see them.

There are three different types of mail formats available in Outlook: plain text, Hypertext Markup Language, and Rich Text Format.

Plain Text

All email applications support plain text mail format because it does not include most text formatting features. *Plain text* format does not support bold, italic, or any of the other advanced text formatting features. Pictures cannot be displayed in the body of the message when using plain text format; although, pictures can be attached to the message and sent.

Hypertext Markup Language

Hypertext Markup Language (HTML) message format is the default format in Outlook. HTML format lets you format the body of your email message similar to a Microsoft Word document. HTML is the most commonly used message format and allows your recipients to receive a message in the same format as you sent it unless the recipient's email application supports only plain text formatting.

Outlook Rich Text Format

Rich Text Format (RTF) is unique to Outlook users and is supported in an Exchange environment. This format allows users to use the different formatting features available in Outlook. When using RTF, Outlook automatically converts these messages to Hypertext Markup Language (HTML) by default, when you send them to an internet recipient so that the message formatting is maintained and attachments are received. It is probably best to use HTML format if you are sending messages outside an Exchange environment.

Set Default and Change Message Format

As mentioned previously, HTML message format is the default setting in Outlook. The default message format can be changed, and the message format for an individual email can also be modified.

If you change the default message setting, then all new emails will have the new default message format.

▶HOW TO: Set Default Message Format

1. Click the **File** tab. The *Backstage* view opens.
2. Click the **Options** button on the left. The *Outlook Options* dialog box opens (Figure 2-1).
3. Click the **Mail** button. The mail options display.

Figure 2-1 *Outlook Options* dialog box

4. Select the default message format desired in the *Compose messages* area.

5. Click **OK** to close the *Outlook Options* dialog box.

If you are sending a message to recipients whose email application supports only plain text format, you can change the setting on an individual email rather than changing the default setting.

▶ HOW TO: Change Message Format

1. Start a new email message.

2. Click the **Format Text** tab.

3. In the *Format* group, choose the desired message format (Figure 2-2).

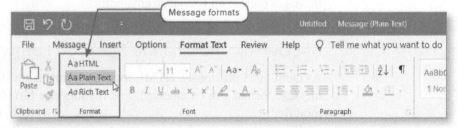

Figure 2-2 Select message format

SLO 2.2

Using Message Options

Outlook provides users with a wide variety of message options to enhance an individual email message. The most common message options are available on the *Message* tab. The Clipboard, Basic Text, and Tags groups include a ***dialog box launcher*** (Figure 2-3). Clicking the **dialog box launcher** opens a dialog box. Clicking on the **expand button** opens a dialog box that includes additional options related to the group. Not all groups have an expand button.

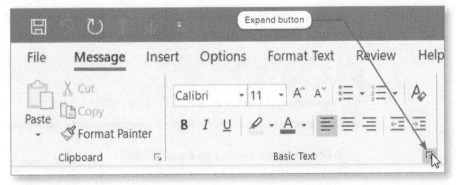

Figure 2-3 Expand button

Note that the new email window includes an *Options tab* (Figure 2-4) on the ribbon. Use the groups on the *Options* tab to change themes, select fields to display, and track email.

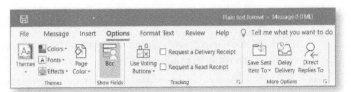

Figure 2-4 *Options* tab

Properties Dialog Box

Open the *Properties dialog box* (Figure 2-5) to change Importance and Sensitivity default settings, to change message security settings, to select vote and track options, and to select delivery options. To open the *Properties dialog box*, display the *Message* tab and click the **dialog box launcher** on the *Tags* group or select the **Options** tab, and click the **dialog box launcher** on the *Tracking* group.

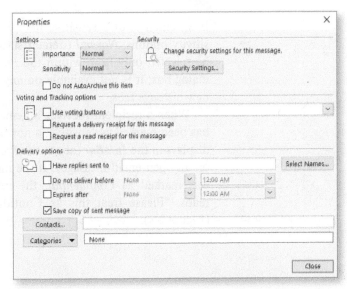

Figure 2-5 *Properties* dialog box

> ### MORE INFO
>
> In all the Microsoft Office products, the dialog box launcher button in the bottom-right corner of a group on a tab can be used to open a dialog box.

Importance

Outlook gives you the option of marking an email at one of three levels of importance: normal, high, and low. *Normal* importance is the default setting for all new email messages.

An email message can be marked as *High Importance* to notify your recipients that it is important (Figure 2-6). The *High Importance* button

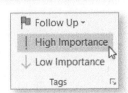

Figure 2-6 *High Importance* tag

is the red exclamation point in the *Tags* group on the *Message* tab. A message can be marked as **Low Importance** by clicking on the **Low Importance** (blue down arrow) button.

When recipients receive an email marked as *High Importance* or *Low Importance*, the email will be marked with the corresponding Inbox icon (Figure 2-7), which alerts them to the importance of the email.

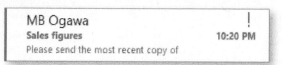

Figure 2-7 Message with high importance

Sensitivity

If an email is of a sensitive nature, mark it to alert recipients. Outlook offers several sensitivity options: **Normal** (default setting), **Personal**, **Private**, and **Confidential**. Sensitivity can be selected only from within the *Properties* dialog box; it is not available on any of the new message tabs.

When a recipient receives an email that has been marked as sensitive, a notification displays in the **InfoBar** (above the *From* line on an open email message). If the message was marked as *Confidential*, the message reads, "Please treat this as Confidential" (Figure 2-8).

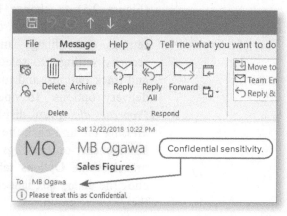

Figure 2-8 Confidential message

Security

The **Security Settings** button (Figure 2-9) in the *Properties* dialog box provides users with the options of encrypting a message and attachment and including a digital signature. Digital signatures and encryption are available in the *Security Properties* dialog

Figure 2-9 *Security Settings* button

box (Figure 2-10). A *digital signature* is a way of authenticating your email to assure recipients you are who you say you are. The process of *encrypting* a message and attachment scrambles both the message itself and the attached file, which adds a layer of security. The sender uses a *public key* to encrypt a message, and the recipient of an encrypted message must have a *private key* to view the contents of the message and attachment.

Figure 2-10 *Security Properties* dialog box

▶ MORE INFO

A *Do not AutoArchive this item* check box is located in the *Properties* dialog box. Archiving will be covered in chapter 10.

Digital signatures and encrypting will be covered in chapter 10.

Delivery and Read Receipts

Have you ever sent an email and wondered if the recipients received or read the email? When using Outlook in conjunction with Exchange, *delivery* and *read receipts* can be used to provide you, the sender, with an electronic receipt that an email has been delivered to or opened by its intended recipients. When a delivery or read receipt has been requested (Figure 2-11), the sender receives an email confirmation that the email has been delivered and/or opened by each recipient.

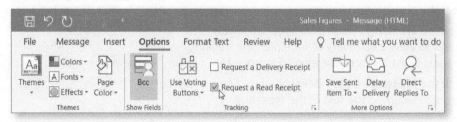

Figure 2-11 *Request a Read Receipt*

When a recipient receives a message that has a delivery receipt, Outlook automatically generates a receipt that is sent to the sender. If an email has a read receipt request, the recipient receives a notification that a read receipt has been requested (Figure 2-12). The recipient is given the option of sending or declining to send a read receipt.

Figure 2-12 *Request a Read Receipt notification*

▶ MORE INFO

When a sender requests a read receipt, it is good email etiquette to send a receipt, even though Outlook provides you with an option to not send a receipt.

Requesting a delivery or read receipt can be done from the *Tracking* group on the *Options* tab or from the *Properties* dialog box (Figure 2-13).

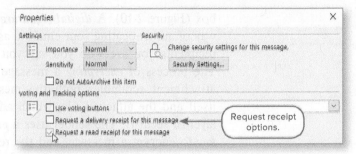

Figure 2-13 *Request a read receipt for a message* in the *Properties dialog box*

> **MORE INFO**
>
> Don't solely rely on these receipts because read and delivery receipts work only with Microsoft Exchange. This means that you will not receive these notifications from users not using Exchange. Also, just because a recipient opens an email does not necessarily ensure that he or she will read the email.

Outlook uses *tracking* to record this information. Tracking is unique to Exchange and provides the sender with a summary of the receipts received. Once a delivery or read receipt has been received, a *Tracking* button will be available on the original email (usually in the *Sent Items* folder). The message will include tracking information the *InfoBar*.

▶ **HOW TO:** View Tracking Results

1. Click the **Sent Items** folder in the *Navigation* pane.
2. Open the sent email with a delivery or read receipt.
3. Click the **Tracking** button [*Message* tab, *Show* group] to view a summary of receipts. The tracking displays in the body of the email (Figure 2-14).
4. Click the **Message** button [*Message* tab, *Show* group] to return to the text of the message.

Figure 2-14 Tracking a message

> **MORE INFO**
>
> Depending on the size of the email window (or Outlook window) that is open, the buttons and groups might appear differently on the tabs.

Delivery Options

Suppose you are leaving town tomorrow but need to send an email on Friday, and, since you'll be gone, you want to have replies sent to a coworker in your office. Outlook provides users with customized delivery options. The delivery options include having replies sent to other users, delaying delivery, setting an expiration date and time, and saving the sent email in a different location.

Sent email messages are by default saved in the *Sent Items* folder. This location can be changed for an individual email by clicking the **Save Sent Item To** button in the *More Options* group on the *Options* tab (Figure 2-15). You can choose a folder from the *Folder* list as the location to save this email, use the default folder, or choose to not save the message. This option applies only to the current message.

Figure 2-15 *Save Sent Item To* button

Figure 2-16 *Delay Delivery* button

The ***Delay Delivery*** (Figure 2-16) option available on standalone and Exchange servers allow you to specify the date and time when an email is to be sent. When this feature is used, an email can be created and sent, and it will stay in your *Outbox* folder until the scheduled delivery date and time. When you click the **Delay Delivery** button, the *Properties* dialog box opens.

▶**HOW TO:** Set the Delay Delivery Option

1. Start a new email message and click the **Options** tab.
2. Click the **Delay Delivery** button. The *Properties* dialog box opens.
3. Select the **Do not deliver before** check box (Figure 2-17).
4. Set the day and time for delivery.
5. Click **Close** to close the *Properties* dialog box.
6. Click **Send**. The message is stored in your *Outbox* folder until the specified time to be delivered.

Figure 2-17 Delivery options

> **MORE INFO**
>
> A rule can also be created to delay the delivery of all emails you send. Rules will be covered in chapter 6.

Having other users reply to an email can be beneficial and is available on standalone and Exchange servers. When the ***Direct Replies To*** option is selected (Figure 2-18), you can select individuals from your contacts to receive replies from an email you've sent.

Figure 2-18 *Direct Replies To* button

▶**HOW TO:** Use the Direct Replies To Feature

1. In a new email message, click the **Options** tab.
2. Click the **Direct Replies To** button. The *Properties* dialog box opens.
3. Click the **Select Names** button (Figure 2-19). The *Have Replies Sent To* dialog box opens.
4. Select recipients from the contact list and press **OK** to close the *Have Replies Sent To* dialog box.
5. Click **Close** to close the *Properties* dialog box.

Figure 2-19 *Direct Replies To* options

Certain emails are time sensitive and are no longer relevant to the recipient after a duration time. The ***Expires after*** feature, available for Exchange users, lets you set a time for when an email expires. When an email expires, it still remains visible and can be opened from the recipient's Inbox, but it is marked with a strikethrough (Figure 2-20).

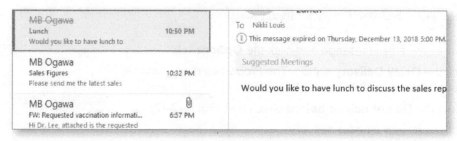

Figure 2-20 Expired message

▶HOW TO: Set an Expiration Day and Time

1. Start a new message and click the **expand button** at the bottom right of the *Tags* group on the *Message* tab (Figure 2-21). The *Properties* dialog box opens.

Figure 2-21 Expand button

2. Check **Expires after**.

3. Set the date and time the email is to expire (Figure 2-22).

4. Click **Close** to close the *Properties* dialog box.

Figure 2-22 Set expiration date and time

Follow Up Flag

Flagging an item for *Follow Up* marks an email with a flag and automatically lists this email as a *To-Do* item. This is typically done on an email you have received in your Inbox and serves as a reminder that you have to follow up with some action on this email.

An email can be marked for follow-up by clicking the **Follow Up** button in the *Tags* group on the *Message* tab and choosing a flag (Figure 2-23). Email messages marked with a flag will display a flag icon in the *Folder* pane.

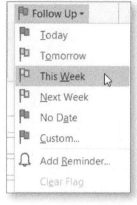

Figure 2-23 Flag a message for follow-up

Flag for Recipients

A ***Custom flag*** (Figure 2-24) can be used to create a ***Flag for Recipients***. *Flag for Recipients* attaches a flag and message to an email and gives you the option of including a reminder date and time. Outlook provides preset ***Flag to*** messages from which to choose, or you can create your own custom message. If a reminder is set (optional), recipients receive an Outlook reminder that opens on their computer screen at the designated date and time.

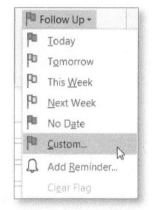

Figure 2-24 Flag a message for follow-up

> **MORE INFO**
>
> The specific follow-up options (*Today, This Week, Custom*) are available only when using an Exchange server. If you are not using an Exchange server, you can still add a flag to messages.

▶ HOW TO: Flag an Email for the Recipient

1. Start a new message and click the **Follow Up** button [*Message* tab, *Tags* group].
2. Select **Custom**. The *Custom* dialog box opens (Figure 2-25).
3. Deselect the **Flag for Me** check box.
4. Select the **Flag for Recipients** check box.
5. Select a **Flag to** message, or type in your own custom message.
6. Select the **Reminder** check box and set a date and time.
7. Click **OK** to close the *Custom* dialog box.

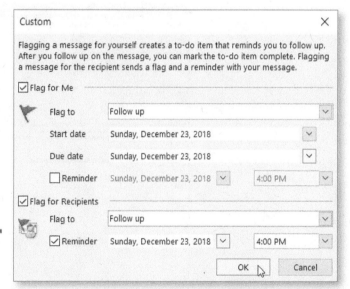

Figure 2-25 *Custom* dialog box

When an email includes a *Flag for Recipients*, a notification displays in the *InfoBar* (above the *From* line on an open email message) visible to both the sender and receiver of the message (Figure 2-26).

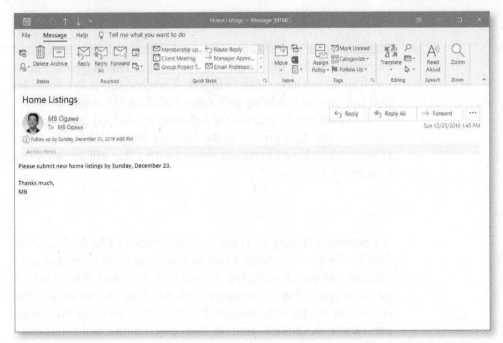

Figure 2-26 Follow-up message

Permission

The **Permission** option in the *Permission* group on the *Options* tab ensures sensitive information is not forwarded, printed, or copied. For the permission feature to function properly, your company must enable the **Information Rights Management (IRM)**. If IRM is not enabled for your company, you will not see any options in the *Permission* group.

If the IRM is enabled, the permission can be set to **Do Not Forward** or a custom configuration such as only allowing users on the same Exchange server to view and edit content. When the *Do Not Forward* permission is selected, recipients will receive a notification in the *InfoBar* informing them of the restrictions (Figure 2-27).

Figure 2-27 *Do Not Forward* Permission in *InfoBar*

For this Pause & Practice project, you send a plain text formatted message to a peer. The message will request information about your peer's availability to meet about a business project. The message is very important and requires follow-up.

1. Create a new email message.
   a. Click the **Mail** button in the *Navigation* bar.
   b. Click the **New Email** button [*Home* tab, *New* group].

2. Click the **Plain Text** button [*Format Text* tab, *Format* group].

3. Enter the following information in the email message fields.

   > *To*: your partner's email address
   > *Cc*: your e-mail address
   > *Subject*: Business Project Meeting
   > *Body*: Hi [partner name], are you available to meet next week Monday for our business project?
   >   Thank you,
   >   [your name]

4. Click the **High Importance** button [*Message* tab, *Tags* group].

5. Click the **Send** button.

6. Open the message your partner sent to you with the subject ***Business Project Meeting***.

7. Reply to the email with the following message in the body:

   > Monday sounds great! Let's meet for lunch.
   > [your name]

8. Click the **Request a Read Receipt** option [*Options* tab, *Tracking* group].

9. Click the **Send** button (Figure 2-28).

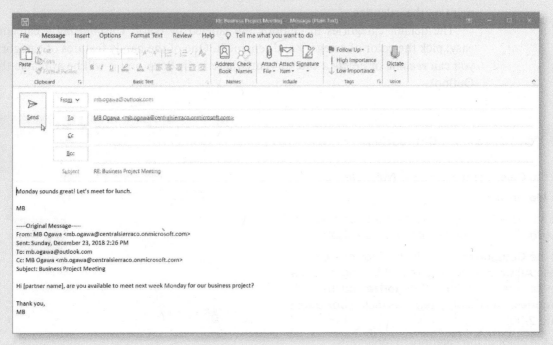

Figure 2-28 PP Outlook 2-1 completed

Using Categories

You may want to group together related emails, tasks, calendar items, or contacts, but you do not want to create a separate folder in which to store these related items. For example, you might want to group all your cycling buddies' contact information together so they are easy to find or group together tasks and emails related to the upcoming fundraiser at work.

The *Category* feature can be used to mark Outlook items as part of a particular group. One of the useful and unique aspects of categories is that they are global; they can be used throughout Outlook (emails, calendars, contacts, tasks, notes, and journals) to mark different types of Outlook items. Whereas folders are useful for grouping specific items together, they store only one type of Outlook item. Categories are yet another method provided by Outlook to help you organize information. Each of the different areas of Outlook displays these Outlook items by category.

> **MORE INFO**
>
> Categories were introduced in chapter 1.

Customize a Category

Outlook is set up with default categories for your use. These categories are really not all that useful until you customize them to meet your individual needs. Each category has a color, and the default name is the name of the color.

Use categories both for work and personal use. An instructor can set up categories for each of his or her courses so these categories can be used to mark emails from students, students' contact records, and calendar items and tasks associated with each course. At home, you could have a different category for each member of the family and one for vacation, church, school, birthdays, anniversaries, and others. When calendar items are marked with a category, it is very easy to visually distinguish by color the category of the event or appointment on the calendar.

The default categories in Outlook are labeled by color. *Customizing* a category is very easy; pick the color of category and rename it. One of the handy features of categories is that you can *rename* or *create* a category anywhere in Outlook and it will be available throughout Outlook.

▶ HOW TO: Customize Categories

1. Click the **Calendar** button in the *Navigation* bar.
2. Click **Month** view.
3. Click any appointment or event on your calendar. The *Calendar Tools Appointment* tab will be displayed.
4. Click the **Categorize** button in the *Tags* group and choose **All Categories** (Figure 2-29), or right-click the calendar item and choose **Categorize** and then **All Categories**. The *Color Categories* dialog box opens (Figure 2-30).
5. Click the color of the category to rename.
6. Click the **Rename** button.

Figure 2-29 All categories

7. Type the new name of the category on the left and press **Enter** (you can also click another category).

8. Continue to rename categories as desired.

9. Press **OK** when finished. Your categories are now set up and ready to use.

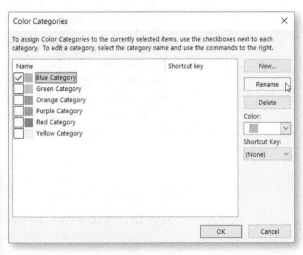

Figure 2-30 Rename a category

> **MORE INFO**
>
> The *Color Categories* dialog box can be accessed throughout Outlook. Simply click an email, calendar item, contact, or task and follow the preceding steps.

> **MORE INFO**
>
> When using multiple calendars, you will need to open an appointment to apply a category.

New categories can also be created following a similar process and can be done throughout Outlook. Once your categories are renamed or created, you are able to assign a category to any Outlook item. You can select or open the item to be categorized. For example, click the **Calendar** button on the *Navigation* bar and select an appointment to be categorized, then click the **Categorize** button in the *Tags* group [*Calendar Tools Appointment* tab], and select the category.

▶ HOW TO: Create a New Category

1. Click the **Mail** button in the *Navigation* bar.

2. Select any email message in your Inbox.

3. Click the **Categorize** button in the *Tags* group on the *Home* tab and choose **All Categories**, or right-click the mail item and choose **Categorize** and then **All Categories**. The *Color Categories* dialog box opens.

4. Click the **New** button. The *Add New Category* dialog box opens (Figure 2-31).

5. Type the name of the category in the *Name* text box.

6. Click the **Color** drop-down arrow and select a color.

   - You can also add a shortcut key to the category by clicking the **Shortcut Key** drop-down arrow and selecting an option from the drop-down list.
   - You can apply a category that has a shortcut key assigned by selecting an Outlook item and pressing the shortcut key (for example, **Ctrl+2**)

7. Click **OK**. The new category is added to your list of categories.

8. Click **OK** to close the *Color Categories* dialog box.

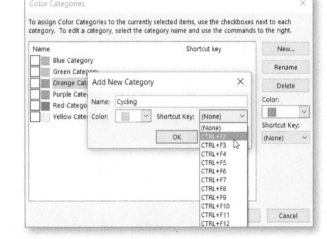

Figure 2-31 New category color and shortcut key

Assign a Category

Once your categories are renamed or created, you can assign a category to any Outlook item. You can select or open the item to be categorized. Click the **Categorize** button, and then select the category. You can also right-click the item in the *Content area*, choose **Categorize**, and then select the category.

Remove a category from an Outlook item by following this same process and selecting **Clear All Categories**.

> ### MORE INFO
>
> Outlook items can be assigned to more than one category. When viewing items by category, an item that is assigned to multiple categories appears in both or multiple category sections; although, it is still only one Outlook item.

View by Categories

When categories have been assigned to Outlook items, you usually see the color and category when viewing the items in the *Content area* (Figure 2-32).

Figure 2-32 Outlook calendar *Content Area*

Within most of the areas in Outlook, you have the option of viewing items by category. This is a filter accessed by selecting the **View Settings** button [*View* tab, *Current View* group] (Figure 2-33). The *Advanced View Settings: Calendar* dialog box opens. Select the **Filter. . .** button to open the *Filter* dialog box and select the **More Choices** tab. Click the **Categories. . .** button to select the categories that you would like to be visible (Figure 2-34).

Figure 2-33 *View Settings* button

Figure 2-34 Categories filter

Set a Quick Click Category

A category you use regularly can be defined as the *Quick Click* category. Setting a *Quick Click* category enables you to add any type of related Outlook item. You can assign a *Quick Click* category to an email message, a calendar appointment, or a contact record. To add an item to the *Quick Click* category, click the **Categories** field in the *Folder* pane. The *Quick Click* category effectively becomes the default category rather than having to choose a category from the list.

▶ **HOW TO:** Set a Quick Click Category

1. Click an Outlook item such as a calendar appointment in the *Content area*.
2. Click **Categorize** in the *Tags* group and choose **Set Quick Click**. You can also right-click the item in the *Folder* pane, choose **Categorize**, and then select **Set Quick Click**. The *Set Quick Click* dialog box opens.
3. Choose the category to be used as the *Quick Click* category.
4. Press **OK** (Figure 2-35).

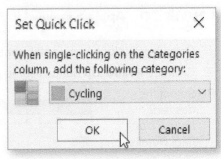

Figure 2-35 *Set Quick Click* dialog box

SLO 2.4

Using Follow Up Flags

Most of you have a stack of to-do items in your office or a pile of papers and bills by your computer at home. At some point you intend to take action on each of these items. Outlook provides you with *Follow Up flags* (Figure 2-36) to mark items for further attention. When an Outlook item is marked with a *Follow Up* flag, it becomes a *To-Do* item.

Numerous flags are available for you to mark items depending on their priority. The types of *Follow Up* flags available in Outlook are:

- *Today*
- *Tomorrow*
- *This Week*

Figure 2-36 *Follow Up flag*

- *Next Week*
- *No Date*
- *Custom*

> **ANOTHER WAY**
>
> You can also mark an Outlook item with a *Follow Up* flag by right-clicking the item, choosing **Follow Up**, and then clicking on the desired **Follow Up flag**.

> **MORE INFO**
>
> *Follow Up* flags become a darker shade of red as the marked item approaches its due date. Outlook items marked with a *No Date Follow Up* flag display as dark red, which is the same color as a *Today Follow Up* flag. An Outlook item turns red when it is past its due date.

Apply a Follow Up Flag

Follow Up flags can be used on email messages and contacts. Tasks are automatically marked with a *Follow Up* flag based on the due date of the task, but these flags can also be changed.

▶**HOW TO:** Apply a Follow Up Flag

1. Open the Outlook item (email, contact, or task).
2. Click the **Follow Up** button [*Home* tab, *Tags* group] (Figure 2-37).
3. Select the desired *Follow Up* flag. Details of the follow-up status are included in the *InfoBar* of the Outlook item.
4. Close the Outlook item. This marked item is now included in the list of *To-Do* items.

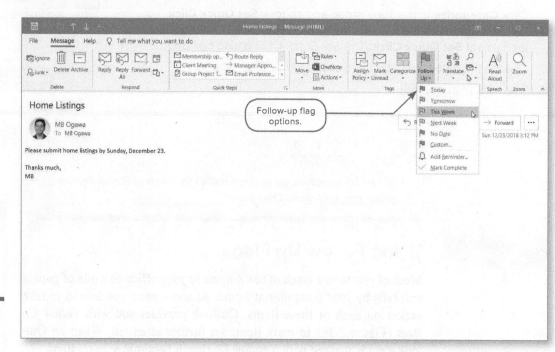

Figure 2-37 Apply a *This Week Follow Up* flag

Create a Custom Follow Up Flag

A reminder and/or custom *Follow Up* flag can be added to an Outlook item. If a reminder is set, an electronic reminder opens on your computer screen providing you with details about the marked item.

A custom *Follow Up* flag can be set to give more specific follow-up details on an Outlook item. These include a custom message, start date, due date, and reminder. Outlook provides a few default messages for custom flags, or you can type your own custom flag message.

▶ **HOW TO:** Create a Custom Follow Up Flag

1. Open an Outlook item (email, contact, or task).
2. Click the **Follow Up** button [*Home* tab, *Tags* group].
3. Select **Custom** or **Add Reminder**. The *Custom* dialog box opens (Figure 2-38).
4. Enter the desired details in the *Custom* dialog box.
5. Click **OK** to close the dialog box. Details of the follow-up status appear in the *InfoBar* of the Outlook item.

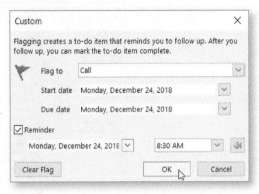

Figure 2-38 *Custom Follow Up* flag

▶ MORE INFO

If you are using a smartphone to sync to Outlook, these reminders will appear on your phone as the item comes due.

Set a Quick Click Follow Up Flag

On the right side of the email message list, an area in the upper-right corner displays *Follow Up* flags. A flag can be added by clicking this area of the email message without having to select a specific flag.

The ***Quick Click flag*** can be customized to flag the Outlook item with the flag you use most regularly.

▶ **HOW TO:** Set a Quick Click Follow Up Flag

1. Click the **Follow Up** button [*Home* tab, *Tags* group].
2. Choose **Set Quick Click**. The *Set Quick Click* dialog box opens (Figure 2-39).
3. Choose the desired *Follow Up* flag for *Quick Click* from the list of flag options.
4. Press **OK**.

Figure 2-39 *Quick Click Follow Up* flag

To apply the *Quick Click* flag to a selected item, simply click the **Follow Up flag** area of the Outlook item and the *Quick Click* flag will be set on that item.

View To-Do Items

Outlook items marked with a *Follow Up* flag will remain in their location in Outlook (Inbox, Contacts, or Tasks), but they are also consolidated in the To-Do List (Figure 2-40).

As mentioned previously, To-Do items are all Outlook items marked with a *Follow Up* flag and can include email, tasks, and contacts. The To-Do items are also listed in the *To-Do* bar.

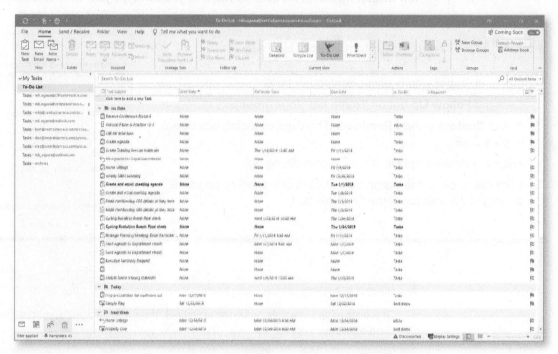

Figure 2-40 To-Do List

> **MORE INFO**
>
> In addition to the To-Do List and the *To-Do* bar, rules and search folders can be used to group items that have been flagged for follow up.
>
> Rules and search folders are covered in chapter 6.

Mark a Flagged Item as Complete

When an Outlook item marked with a *Follow Up* flag has been completed, you can use *Mark Complete* to indicate the item has been completed, and the flag will be replaced with a check mark. Or, if the To-Do List displays, the item will be crossed out indicating that it has been marked as complete.

The following list explains the ways to use *Mark Complete* for an item that has been flagged:

- Click the **flag** icon and the *Mark Complete* check replaces the flag.
- Right-click the item, choose **Follow Up**, and click **Mark Complete**.
- Click the **Complete** check box in the To-Do List to mark an item as completed.
- Open the item, click the **Follow Up** button in the *Tags* group, and choose **Mark Complete**.

> **MORE INFO**
>
> You can remove a flag (different than marking it as completed) by selecting the Outlook item, opening the **Follow Up** menu, and choosing **Clear Flag**.

For this Pause & Practice project, you organize your email messages using categories. You also create a custom *Follow Up* flag for your message and mark an item as complete.

1. Open the email message you received in *Pause & Practice Outlook 2-1*. The subject is **Re: Business Project Meeting**.

2. Create a new category.
   a. Click the **Categorize** button [*Message* tab, *Tags* group] and select **All Categories. . .**.
   b. Click the **New** button. The *Add New Category* dialog box displays.
   c. Type the category name Business Project.
   d. Change the color to red (first row, first column).
   e. Click the **OK** button.
   f. Click **OK** to close the *Color Categories* dialog box.

3. Add a custom *Follow Up* flag to the message.
   a. Click the **Follow Up** button [*Message* tab, *Tags* group] and select **Custom. . .**.
   b. Click the **Start date** drop-down arrow and select **Today**.
   c. Click the **Due date** drop-down arrow and select tomorrow's date.
   d. Click the **Reminder** option.
   e. Click the **OK** button.

4. Click the **Reply** button [*Message* tab, *Respond* group].

5. Reply to the message with following message in the body:

   Sure, are there any foods you like to eat?
   [your name]

6. Click the **Send** button.

7. Open the message your partner sent to you and reply with the following message:

   I like to eat Italian and Japanese cuisine. How about you?

8. Change the subject to My lunch preferences.

9. Click the **Send** button.

10. Click the **Tasks** button on the *Navigation* bar.
    a. Click the **To-Do List** under *My Tasks*.
    b. Double-click the email in your To-Do List.
    c. Click the **Follow Up** button in the *Tags* group and choose **Mark Complete**.

11. See Figure 2-41 for the completed *Pause & Practice 2-2* project.

Figure 2-41 PP Outlook 2-2 completed

Using Voting Buttons

Voting buttons are a useful way of gathering responses to a question sent via email. The advantage of using voting buttons rather than having respondents reply to an emailed question is that you can specify the response choices and Outlook automatically tracks and tallies the voting responses received. The tracking feature also lets you, the sender of the message, see who has and hasn't voted. You can also export the voting results to Excel.

> ## MORE INFO
>
> Voting buttons and tracking responses will work only in an Exchange environment.

Preset Voting Buttons

A question can be typed into the body of an email or in the subject line. The *Use Voting Buttons* feature is located on the *Options* tab of a new message. Outlook provides you with preset voting buttons. The preset voting buttons are *Approve;Reject*, *Yes;No*, and *Yes;No;Maybe*.

▶HOW TO: Use Preset Voting Buttons

1. Start a new email message and click the **Options** tab.
2. Click the **Use Voting Buttons** button.
3. Choose from one of the three preset options (Figure 2-42).
4. Type and send the email.

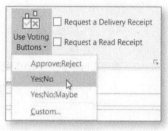

Figure 2-42 Preset voting options

> ## MORE INFO
>
> When voting buttons are used, you will see a message in the *InfoBar* stating, "You have added voting buttons to this message."

Custom Voting Buttons

What if you wanted to use the voting buttons to determine your coworkers' preferences for lunch on Friday? The preset buttons would not be effective in this case. Outlook provides you the option of creating custom voting buttons (Figure 2-43). Custom voting buttons could be used to find the day of the week that works best for a team meeting or the choice of restaurant for a Friday lunch. As the sender of the message and question, you can create your own custom voting buttons in the *Properties* dialog box by typing each voting option separated by a semicolon.

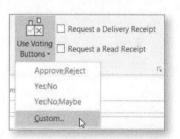

Figure 2-43 Custom voting options

▶ HOW TO: Create Custom Voting Buttons

1. Start a new email message and click the **Options** tab.
2. Click the **Use Voting Buttons** button.
3. Choose **Custom**. The *Properties* dialog box opens.
4. Select the **Use voting buttons** check box.
5. Select and delete the preset voting buttons (*Accept;Reject*).
6. Type your voting choices. Separate each choice with a semicolon (Figure 2-44).
7. Click **Close** to close the *Properties* dialog box. The *InfoBar* informs you that you are using voting buttons on this message.
8. Type and send the email.

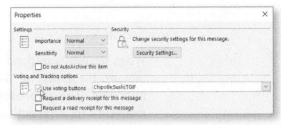

Figure 2-44 Custom voting buttons

Respond Using Voting Buttons

When a recipient receives an email with voting buttons, a *Vote* button displays to the left of the *Reply* button in the *Respond* group. Also, a message displays in the *InfoBar* alerting the recipient to vote by using the *Vote* button.

When the *Vote* button is clicked, the voting choices appear in a list below the button. The recipient makes his or her selection from the list of choices.

After the selection is made, the recipient chooses one of the following two options: *Send the response now* or *Edit the response before sending*. If *Send the response now* is selected, Outlook automatically replies to the email and includes the recipient's voting selection.

If *Edit the response before sending* is selected, a reply email opens allowing the recipient to include an email response in addition to his or her voting selection. After typing a response in the body, the recipient must send the response.

▶ HOW TO: Reply Using Voting Buttons

1. Open the email message that has voting buttons.
2. Click the **Vote** button and make a selection (Figure 2-45).
3. Choose either *Send the response now* or *Edit the response before sending*.
   - If you choose *Send the response now*, click **OK** and you are finished and your voting selection has been sent.

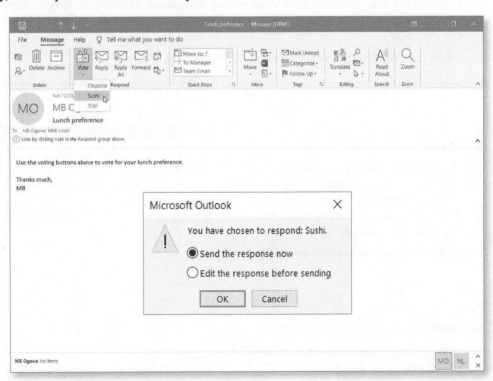

Figure 2-45 Voting response

- If you chose *Edit the response before sending* and click **OK**, a reply email automatically opens.
- Type additional information you would like to include in the body of the email.
- Click **Send**.

4. Close the original email.

Track Voting Responses

When recipients respond to an email with voting buttons, the sender of the message receives the responses. The responses received include the recipient's voting selection in front of the original subject (Figure 2-46). Also, Outlook uses tracking to record the responses received.

Figure 2-46 View voting responses option

▶ HOW TO: Track Voting Responses

1. Open a voting response you received. The voting response displays in both the subject line and the *InfoBar*.

2. Click the **InfoBar**, and then click **View voting responses**. The original email message opens. A summary of the voting responses displays in the *InfoBar*, and the individual voting response displays in the body of the message.

3. Close both of the open email messages after you are finished.

 ANOTHER WAY

Voting responses can also be viewed by opening the original message from your *Sent Items* folder. Any sent message that has tracking will be marked with a tracking icon rather than a message icon (Figure 2-47).

MORE INFO

Results of the voting can be copied and pasted into Excel.

Figure 2-47 Voting responses

O2-76

For this Pause & Practice project, you use voting buttons to determine a good location for your lunch meeting.

1. Open the message with the subject **My lunch preferences**.

2. Reply to the message using voting options to determine your partner's top choice.
   a. Click the **Reply** button [*Message* tab, *Respond* group].
   b. Click the **Use Voting Buttons** button [*Options* tab, *Tracking* group] and select **Custom**.
   c. Ensure the **Use voting buttons** option is checked. Delete the text in the text field and type French Cuisine;Italian Cuisine;Japanese Cuisine. Be sure to include a semicolon (;) between each choice.
   d. Click the **Close** button.
   e. Add the following text to the body of the message:

   Use the voting options above to select your preference. I do not have a preference, so I would like you to choose.

   [your name]

   f. Click the **Send** button.

3. Open your partner's message to you and select *Italian Cuisine*.
   a. Click the **Vote** button [*Message* tab, *Response* group] and select **Italian Cuisine**.
   b. Click the **Send Response Now** radio button and click **OK**.

4. Check your Inbox for the latest message with the voting response (Figure 2-48).

Figure 2-48 PP Outlook 2-3 completed

Customizing Your Email

Have you ever received an email where the body of the message had decorative fonts, colors, and background graphics? Most likely, the sender did not spend a huge amount of time customizing the design of the email specifically for you.

As covered in chapter 1, users have control over how to format the body of an email message. But Outlook also provides users with many features to customize the look of emails by using signatures, stationery, themes, and templates. The default settings can be changed so that each new email created will have a consistent and customized look.

Create a Signature

A *signature* is a saved group of information that can be inserted into the body of an email. Typically, a signature can include the sender's name, title, company, address, and contact information. Signatures can also include logos and graphics. Signatures save time by storing this information so you don't have to type the full text each time you create an email. Signatures can be manually or automatically inserted at the bottom of each new email you create. You can create and save multiple signatures.

▶ HOW TO: Create a Signature

1. Click the **File** tab to open the *Backstage* view.

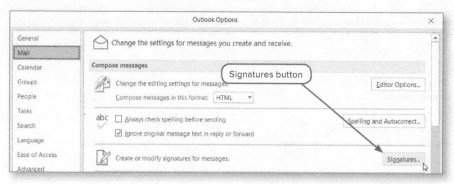

Figure 2-49 *Outlook Options* dialog box

2. Click **Options** on the left. The *Outlook Options* dialog box opens (Figure 2-49).

3. Click the **Mail** button on the left.

4. Click **Signatures**. The *Signatures and Stationery* dialog box opens.

5. Click **New**. The *New Signature* dialog box opens (Figure 2-50).

6. Type the name for your signature and press **OK** to close the *New Signature* dialog box.

7. Type your signature information in the *Edit signature* section of the dialog box. You can use different fonts, sizes, styles, colors, and alignments to customize your signature.

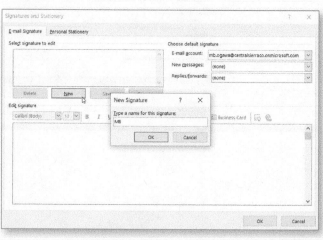

Figure 2-50 *Signatures and Stationery* dialog box

8. Press **Save** when you are satisfied with your signature (Figure 2-51).

9. Click **OK** to close the *Signatures and Stationery* dialog box.

10. Click **OK** to close the *Outlook Options* dialog box.

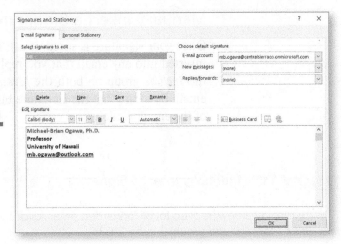

Figure 2-51 Sample signature

> **ANOTHER WAY**
>
> The *Signatures and Stationery* dialog box can be opened from a new email message, replies, or forwards by clicking the **Signature** button on the *Message* tab and selecting **Signatures**.

> **MORE INFO**
>
> Signatures are not limited to names and contact information. Any information that is commonly inserted into the body of an email can be saved as a signature including paragraphs of text. You can create and save multiple signatures.
>
> Signatures are stored on your computer, not on the Exchange server.

Set a Default Signature

The default settings on signatures can be changed to automatically insert your signature on all new emails, on all replies and forwards, or on all new emails, replies, and forwards. Or the default settings can be set to *(none)*.

▶ HOW TO: Set a Default Signature

1. Start a new email message and click the **Signature** button [*Message* tab, *Include* group].

2. Choose **Signatures**. The *Signatures and Stationery* dialog box opens. (This dialog box can also be opened from the *Backstage* view by choosing **Options**, **Mail**, and then **Signatures**.)

3. Set your desired signature defaults in the *Choose default signature* area (Figure 2-52).

4. Click **OK** to close the *Signatures and Stationery* dialog box.

Figure 2-52 Default signature

> **MORE INFO**
>
> Be careful to not use your signature as the default on all emails as it might appear pretentious. When sending emails or replying to coworkers, friends, or family, a signature is usually not necessary.

> **MORE INFO**
>
> If you have multiple email accounts in Outlook, you can set up different default signatures for each account.

Manually Insert a Signature

Once your signature is saved, it can be inserted into any new message you create, or it can be inserted into any email that you reply to or forward. The *Signature* button will be available in the *Include* group on both the *Message* and *Insert* tabs on any new, replied to, or forwarded email. Be aware that the signature button icon might appear differently depending on the size of the email window.

▶ HOW TO: Manually Insert a Signature

1. To display a new, replied to, or forwarded email, click the **Signature** button [*Message* tab, *Include* group] or [*Insert* tab, *Include* group] (Figure 2-53).

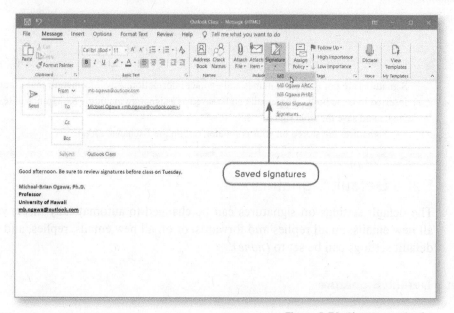

Figure 2-53 Signature selection

2. Choose the signature to insert into the body of the email. The signature is inserted into the body of the email with a couple of blank lines left above it for the email text.

▶ MORE INFO

Only one signature can be inserted in the body of an email. If you insert a second signature, it replaces the first one.

Themes

Themes are a set of fonts, colors, backgrounds, and fill effects in the body of an email. All emails include a theme. The default setting is the *Office Theme*, which includes a white background with dark and subtle colors. A theme can be selected and customized for each email you create.

The *Themes* group is on the *Options* tab of an email message (Figure 2-54). You can change the theme, color set, font set, effects, and page color to customize the look of your email. **Page color** is the background of the body of an email and is not limited to solid colors; you can change the page color to include a **gradient**, **texture**, **pattern**, or **picture**.

> **MORE INFO**
>
> Be careful about making your email message look too fancy and colorful. If you're using email in a business setting, you want your email to look professional. Using a picture as a background also increases the file size of your email. Sometimes less is more!

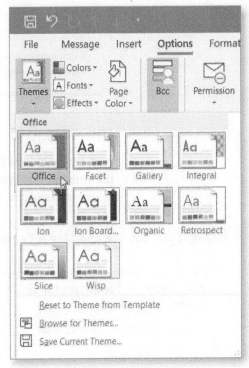

Figure 2-54 Themes

Set the Default Theme and Font

To add consistency to your email documents, you might want to change the default settings to control the look of all emails you create. The default settings can be changed to include a theme, consisting of fonts, colors, and background graphics. If you are not using a theme, you can change the default settings for the font, size, style, and color used on all new emails, replies and forwards.

▶ HOW TO: Set the Default Theme and Font

1. Click the **File** tab to open the *Backstage* view.
2. Click the **Options** button on the left. The *Outlook Options* dialog box opens.
3. Click the **Mail** button.
4. Click the **Stationery and Fonts** button. The *Signatures and Stationery* dialog box opens.
5. Click the **Personal Stationery** tab if it is not already displayed (Figure 2-55).
6. Set your default preferences for **Theme**, **New mail messages**, and/ or **Replying or forwarding messages**.

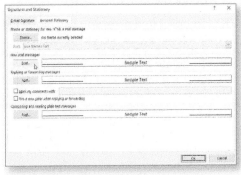

Figure 2-55 Personal stationery

   - Click the **Font** button under *New mail messages* to modify fonts for new email messages.
   - Click the **Font** button under *Replying or forwarding messages* to modify fonts for replies or forwarded messages.
7. Click **OK** to close the *Signatures and Stationery* dialog box.
8. Click **OK** to close the *Outlook Options* dialog box.

Create and Use Templates

New to Outlook is the *Templates* feature. *Templates* allow you to create preset messages with information that you commonly send to recipients. Once you create a template, you can reuse it for messages that require the same response.

▶ HOW TO: Create and Use a Template

1. Start a new message or reply to a message and select the **View Templates** button [*Message* tab, *My Templates* group].

2. The *My Templates* pane opens.

3. Click the **Mail** button.

4. Click the **+ Template** link.

5. Click the **Personal Stationery** tab if it is not already displayed (Figure 2-56).

6. Type a title into the title field and the message in the message field.

7. Click **Save**.

8. Your new template will be available in the *My Templates* pane.

9. When typing a message in the body, you can click one of your templates to enter the pre-defined text (Figure 2-57).

10. To edit a template, you can move the cursor over the template and click the edit icon.

11. To delete a template, you can move the cursor over a template and click the delete icon.

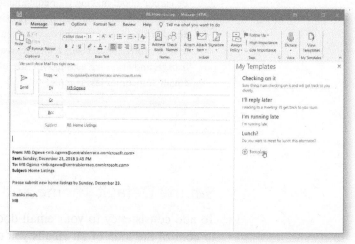

Figure 2-56 Create a template

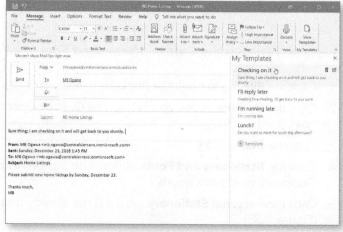

Figure 2-57 Select a template

Desktop Alerts

A *desktop alert* is a notification you receive when a new email arrives in your Inbox (Figure 2-58). The desktop alert appears in a corner of your computer screen and remains open for a few seconds. By default, desktop alerts are turned on. They also appear when you receive a meeting request or task request.

Figure 2-58 Desktop alert

The desktop alert notifies you of the name of the sender, the subject, and a portion of the body of the message. Outlook allows you to perform actions on an email when a desktop alert displays. When a desktop alert appears, open the email message by clicking the desktop alert. You can also flag or delete the message from the desktop alert.

People Pane

The *People pane* appears at the bottom of an email message (Figure 2-59) and consolidates other Outlook items associated with an individual. The *People* pane displays email messages, meetings, task requests, and attachments as links. Clicking a link displayed in the *People* pane opens that Outlook item. The *People* pane can also be collapsed or expanded by clicking the small arrow in the upper-right corner of the pane.

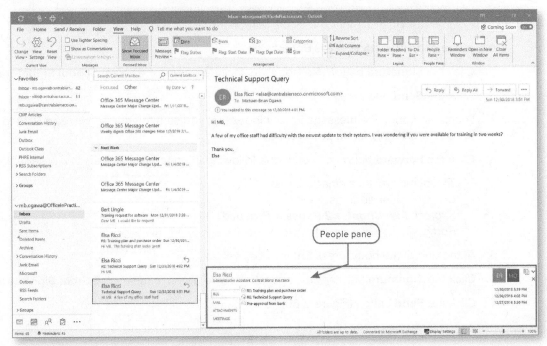

Figure 2-59 *People* pane

PAUSE & PRACTICE: OUTLOOK 2-4

For this Pause & Practice project, you create a signature and insert it in an email message to your peer. You also forward the stream of messages to your instructor.

1. Create a new signature.
   a. Click the **File** tab to open the *Backstage* view and select **Options**. The *Outlook Options* dialog box opens.

b. Select the **Mail** option.

c. Click the **Signatures** button. The *Signatures and Stationery* dialog box opens.

d. Click the **New** button.

e. Type School Signature and click **OK**.

f. In the *Edit signature* text area, type:

[Your Name]
Student, [Institution Name]
[your email address]

g. Select your name and click **Bold** and **Italicize**.

h. Select the second and third lines of your signature and click **Bold**.

i. Click the **Save** button.

j. Click the **OK** button.

k. Click the **OK** button in the *Outlook Options* dialog box to close it.

2. Select the message from your partner indicating his or her choice, *Italian Cuisine*. The subject should be **Italian Cuisine: My lunch preferences**.

3. Click the **Reply** button to reply to the message including the following information in the email message fields.

Cc: Your email address
Body: Thanks, [partner name]. Let's meet at the Italian restaurant on campus for the business project meeting on Monday at noon. See you there!

4. At the end of the body, press **Enter** twice.

5. Click the **Signature** button [*Message* tab, *Include* group] and select **School Signature**.

6. Click the **Send** button.

7. Locate and open the message in your Inbox that you sent to your partner and Cc'd to yourself with the subject *RE: My lunch preferences*.

8. Click the **Forward** button and enter the following information in the email message fields:

To: your instructor's email address
Cc: your email address
Subject: **FW: Chapter 2 Pause & Practice**
Body: Hi [instructor name], these are the Pause and Practice assignments for chapter 2.

9. At the end of the body, press **Enter** twice.

10. Click the **Signature** button [*Message* tab, *Include* group] and select **School Signature**.

11. Click the **Send** button (Figure 2-60).

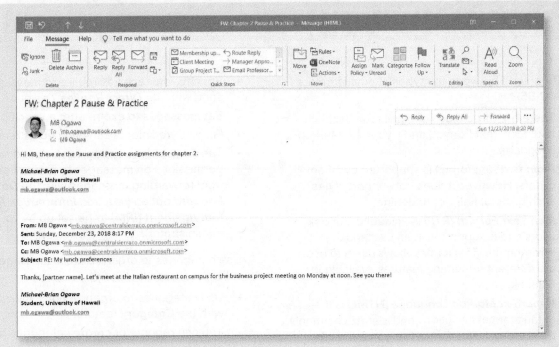

Chapter Summary

2.1 Differentiate between the types of email formats (p. O2-55).

- There are three types of email formats: plain text, Rich Text Format, and Hypertext Markup Language.
- *Plain text* font format is supported by all email clients. However, it does not support styles such as bold, italic, or underline.
- *Rich Text Format (RTF)* is unique to Outlook users and is supported in an Exchange environment. This format allows users to use the different formatting features available in Outlook.
- *Hypertext Markup Language (HTML)* is the default format in Outlook and is most commonly used today. HTML format lets you format the body of your email message similar to a Microsoft Word document.
- It is probably best to use HTML format if you are sending messages outside an Exchange environment.

2.2 Customize email using the different types of message options available in Outlook (p. O2-56).

- The *dialog box launcher* opens additional options for each group.
- The *Options tab* includes additional options for each Outlook item.
- The *Properties dialog box* includes additional message properties.
- There are three levels of importance that can be placed on messages: *High*, *Normal*, and *Low*. The default level of importance is *Normal*.
- Messages can be marked with different levels of sensitivity. They are *Normal* (default setting), *Personal*, *Private*, and *Confidential*.
- Outlook allows you to apply *Security Settings*, such as *digital signatures* and *encrypting* messages using a *public key*. A *private key* is used by the receiver to decrypt the message.
- You can request *delivery* and or *read receipts* when sending messages.
- By using delivery options, you can change where sent items are saved and delay the delivery of messages.
- *Tracking* allows a sender to identify when a message is read by a recipient and is available on Exchange servers.

- Specify who receives replies to messages you send with the *Direct Replies To* option.
- Set messages to expire after a specific date.
- Flags for recipients can be used as reminders.
- The *Permissions* option can be used to set permissions on messages to prevent others from forwarding messages with the *Do Not Forward* option (requires *Information Rights Management (IRM)* to be set up by your administrator).

2.3 Use categories to organize email messages into different groups (p. O2-66).

- Use categories to organize email messages with the *Category* feature.
- You can *rename* or *create* categories based on your needs.
- Create *Quick Click* categories for commonly used categories across email messages, calendar appointments, and contact records.
- View items within a specific category using the view settings.

2.4 Add *Follow Up* flags to email messages to add reminders to messages (p. O2-69).

- *Follow Up flags* can be used as reminders.
- *Follow Up* flags create To-Do items.
- The *Quick Click flag* can be customized to your preference.
- When a To-do item is completed, use the *Mark Complete* button to place a check mark next to the item.

2.5 Use email voting buttons to get responses from recipients and to automatically track responses (p. O2-74).

- *Voting buttons* allow you to quickly gather replies from other users.
- Voting buttons have the following presets: *Approve;Reject, Yes;No,* and *Yes;No;Maybe.*
- You can customize the voting buttons to include any choices.
- Voting buttons allow you to automatically track replies, as opposed to manually counting.

2.6 Customize your emails by using signatures, themes, templates, and desktop alerts (p. O2-78).

- *Signatures* allow you to quickly add a group of information to your emails.

- You can create multiple signatures to choose from.
- Signatures can be automatically added to your messages or you can manually add them.
- **Themes** can be used to quickly improve the aesthetics of your messages by adjusting the **page color**, **gradient**, **texture**, **pattern**, or **picture**.
- **Templates** can used to quickly respond to messages where a consistent response is needed.
- **Desktop alerts** appear in a corner of the screen and give you an overview of a message received, meeting request, or task request.

Check for Understanding

The SIMbook for this text (within your SIMnet account), provides the following resources for concept review:

- Multiple-choice questions
- Short answer questions
- Matching exercises

Guided Project 2-1

For this project, you work as a Real Estate Agent for Placer Hills Real Estate (PHRE). You recently spoke with a client that is looking to purchase her first home. Create an email message to follow up with the conversation.

[Student Learning Outcomes 2.1, 2.2, 2.6]

Skills Covered in This Project

- Select message format.
- Apply a theme.
- Create a signature.
- Add a signature to a message.

1. Create a new email message to Katie Binstead.
   a. Click the **New Email** button [*Home* tab, *New* group].
   b. In the *To* field, type your instructor's email address.
   c. In the *Cc* field, type your email address.
   d. In the *Subject* field, type Home of your dreams follow-up.

2. Click the **Rich Text** button [*Format Text* tab, *Format* group].

3. Click the **Themes** button [*Options* tab, *Themes* group] and select **Organic**.

4. Create a new signature.
   a. Click the **File** tab and select **Options**.
   b. Click the **Mail** button on the left.
   c. Click **Signatures**. The *Signatures and Stationery* dialog box opens.
   d. Click **New**. The *New Signature* dialog box opens.
   e. Type [your name] PHRE for your signature and press **OK** to close the *New Signature* dialog box.

5. Edit the signature.
   a. In the *Edit signature* section of the dialog box, type the following information:

   [your name], Real Estate Agent
   Placer Hills Real Estate

   b. Click the **Save** button. Then click **OK**.
   c. Click **OK** to close the *Outlook Options* dialog box.

6. In the body of the message, type the following text:

   Hi Katie, It was great speaking with you about your ideas for a new home for your family. It is definitely an exciting endeavor. I am looking forward to helping you find the home of your family's dreams.

   Thanks,

7. Press **Enter** after the "Thanks" line.

8. Click the **Signature** button [*Message* tab, *Include* group] and select **[your name] PHRE** to insert your signature.

9. Click the **Send** button to send the message (Figure 2-61).

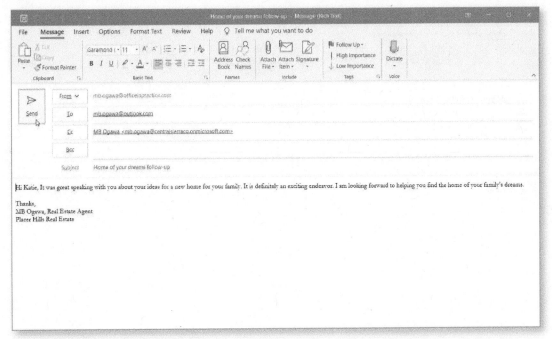

Figure 2-61 Guided Project 2-1 completed

Guided Project 2-2

For this project, you follow up with Katie regarding her family's dream home. You ask her to decide on the number of bedrooms her family wants to help you search for possible options. Since Katie's family is serious about purchasing a home, you create a category for her email messages.
[Student Learning Outcomes 2.1, 2.2, 2.3, 2.5, 2.6]

Skills Covered in This Project

- Create a category.
- Set a *Quick Click* category.

- Select a message format.
- Apply a theme.
- Add a signature to a message.
- Add custom voting buttons to a message.

1. Open the email message you sent in *Guided Project 2-1* from the *Sent Items* folder.

2. Create a new category called "Katie" (Figure 2-62).
   a. Click the **Categorize** button [*Message* tab, *Tags* group] and select **All Categories**.
   b. Click the **New** button and type Katie in the *Name* text field.
   c. Click the **drop-down arrow** next to color and select **yellow**.
   d. Click the **OK** button to close the *Add New Category* dialog box.
   e. Ensure the **Katie** check box is selected and click **OK**.

3. Create a new email message to Katie.
   a. Click the **New Email** button [*Home* tab, *New* group].
   b. In the *To* field, type your instructor's email address.
   c. In the *Cc* field, type your email address.
   d. In the *Subject* field, type Number of bedrooms for property.

Figure 2-62 "Katie" category

4. Click the **Rich Text** button [*Format Text* tab, *Format* group].

5. Click the **Themes** button [*Options* tab, *Themes* group] and select **Organic**.

6. In the body of the message, type the following text:

   Hi Katie, To help me find as many homes as possible for us to check out, could you please use the voting button above to select the number of bedrooms your dream home should have?

   Thanks,

7. Press **Enter** after the "Thanks" line.

8. Click the **Signature** button [*Message* tab, *Include* group] and select **[your name] PHRE** to insert your signature.

9. Add voting buttons for two bedrooms, three bedrooms, or four bedrooms to the message.
   a. Click the **Use Voting Buttons** button [*Options* tab, *Tracking* group] and select **Custom**.
   b. Ensure the **Use voting buttons** option is checked and replace the text *Approve;Reject* with 2 bedrooms;3 bedrooms;4 bedrooms.
   c. Click **Close**.

10. Click the **Send** button to send the message (Figure 2-63).

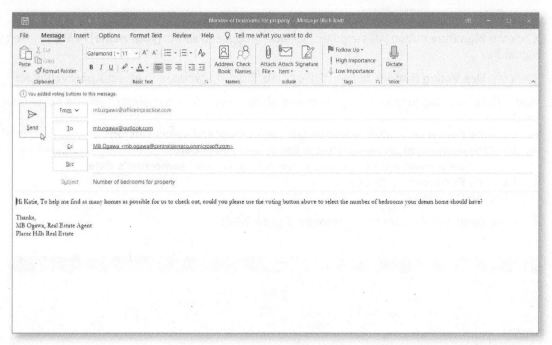

Figure 2-63 Guided Practice 2-2 completed

Guided Project 2-3

For this project, you send one final message to Katie to confirm a full day of house tours next week on Thursday.
[Student Learning Outcomes 2.1, 2.2, 2.3, 2.4, 2.5, 2.6]

Skills Covered in This Project

- Apply a category to a message.
- Select a message format.

- Apply a theme.
- Add a signature to a message.
- Add preset voting buttons to a message.
- Add a custom *Follow Up* flag.

1. Open the email message you sent in *Guided Project 2-2* from the *Sent Items* folder.

2. Click the **Categorize** button [*Message* tab, *Tags* group] and select **Katie**.

3. Create a new email message to Katie.
   a. Click the **New Email** button [*Home* tab, *New* group].
   b. In the *To* field, type your instructor's email address.
   c. In the *Cc* field, type your email address.
   d. In the *Subject* field, type Property Tour.

4. Click the **Rich Text** button [*Format Text* tab, *Format* group].

5. Click the **Themes** button [*Options* tab, *Themes* group] and select **Organic**.

6. In the body of the message, type the following text:

   Hi Katie, I would like to confirm that you are available next week Thursday for the property tour. I found 6 homes that meet your needs. Please use the voting button above to approve or reject this date.

   Thanks,

7. Press **Enter** after the "Thanks" line.

8. Click the **Signature** button [*Message* tab, *Include* group] and select **[your name] PHRE** to insert your signature.

9. Click the **Use Voting Buttons** button [*Options* tab, *Tracking* group] and select **Approve;Reject**.

10. Add a *Follow Up* flag to the message with a reminder to call Katie tomorrow if you do not receive a response.
    a. Click the **Follow Up** button [*Message* tab, *Tags* group] and select **Custom**.
    b. Click the **drop-down arrow** next to the flag to and select **Call**.
    c. Click the **drop-down arrow** next to the due date and select **tomorrow's date**.
    d. Click the **Reminder** check box.
    e. Click the **OK** button.

11. Click the **Send** button to send the message (Figure 2-64).

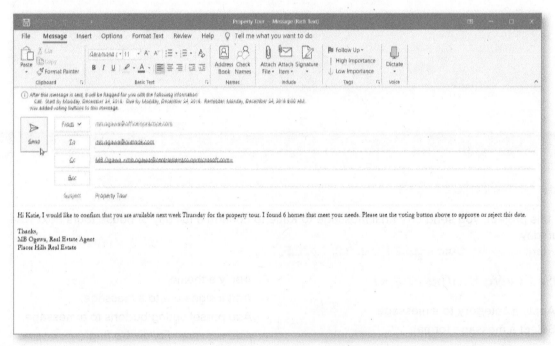

Figure 2-64 Guided Practice 2-3 completed

Independent Project 2-4

For this project, you are an organizer for the American River Cycling Club (ARCC). You decide to develop a training cycle for the upcoming season. Therefore, you email your members and ask them to vote on a variety of cycling activities to determine priorities for each.
[Student Learning Outcomes 2.1, 2.2, 2.4, 2.5, 2.6]

Skills Covered in This Project

- Select a message format.
- Apply a theme.
- Create a signature.
- Add a signature.
- Add a custom voting button.
- Add a *Follow Up* flag

1. Create a new message to the ARCC.
   a. In the *To* field, type your instructor's email address.
   b. In the *Cc* field, type your email address.

2. Type ARCC Training Poll in the subject line.

3. Change the message format to **Rich Text Format**.

4. Apply the **Integral** theme to the message.

5. In the body of the message, type the following text:

   > Hi everyone. As we prepare for the upcoming training season, I would like to know which type of training you prefer. If you would like to recommend another type of training, please send me a message listing the type of training. Based on the results of the poll, I will set up a training schedule to accommodate our needs as best as possible.

   > Thanks,

6. Create a signature named *[your name] ARCC*. The signature should have the following format:

   [your name]
   Organizer, ARCC

7. Add the *[your name] ARCC* signature to the message after the "Thanks" line.

8. Add a custom voting button with the following options: **Road;Mountain;Cyclocross**.

9. Add a *Follow Up* flag with a reminder for next week.

10. Click the **Send** button to send the message (Figure 2-65).

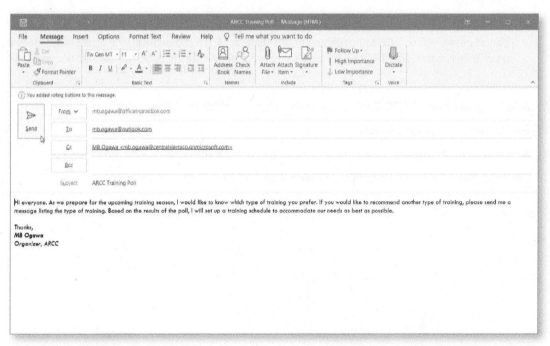

Figure 2-65 Independent Project 2-4 completed

Independent Project 2-5

For this project, you categorize the message sent in *Independent Project 2-4*. You also share the results of the poll from with the ARCC members.

[Student Learning Outcomes 2.1, 2.2, 2.3, 2.4, 2.6]

Skills Covered in This Project

- Create a category.
- Apply a category to a message.
- Select a message format.
- Apply a theme.
- Add a signature.
- Set the message priority.
- Add a *Follow Up* flag.

1. Create a new category called "Cycle Training" using red as the category color and apply it to the message you sent in *Independent Project 2-4*.

2. Create a new message to the ARCC.
   a. In the *To* field, type your instructor's email address.
   b. In the *Cc* field, type your email address.

3. Add the subject Results: ARCC Training Poll.

4. Change the message format to **Rich Text Format**.

5. Apply the **Integral** theme to the message.

6. In the body of the message, type the following text:

   Hi everyone. Based on the poll, we have the following results:

   50% Mountain
   25% Road
   25% Cyclocross

   Therefore, we will schedule our training in this manner. A few members also sent me other ideas for training sessions, which I will do my best to incorporate. Please check your email for our schedule.

   Thanks,

7. Add the *[your name] ARCC* signature to the message after the "Thanks" line.

8. Set the message priority to **low**.

9. Add a *Follow Up* flag with a reminder in three days and a due date in one week.

10. Click the **Send** button to send the message (Figure 2-66).

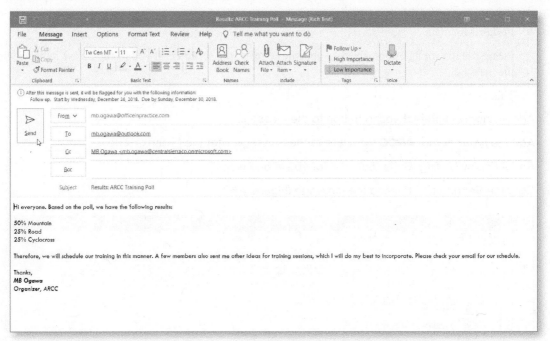

Figure 2-66 Independent Project 2-5 completed

Independent Project 2-6

For this project, you familiarize yourself with the basic components of Outlook.
[Student Learning Outcomes 2.1, 2.2, 2.3, 2.4, 2.6]

Skills Covered in This Project

- Apply a category to a message.
- Select a message format.
- Apply a theme.
- Add a preset voting button.
- Add a signature.
- Add a *Follow Up* flag with a reminder.

1. Apply the **Cycle Training** category to the message you sent in *Independent Project 2-5*.

2. Create a new message to the ARCC.
   a. In the *To* field, type your instructor's email address.
   b. In the *Cc* field, type your email address.

3. Add the subject Training Schedule.

4. Change the message format to **Rich Text Format**.

5. Apply the **Integral** theme to the message.

6. In the body of the message, type the following text:

   Hi everyone. Listed below is our training schedule for the upcoming quarter.

   Monday: Mountain
   Tuesday: Road
   Wednesday: Off

Thursday: Cyclocross
Friday: Mountain

Please use the voting button above to approve or reject the schedule. If you reject, please indicate why in the message.

Thanks,

7. Add an **Approve;Reject** voting button to the message.

8. Add the *[your name] ARCC* signature to the message after the "Thanks" line.

9. Add a *Follow Up* flag with a reminder for you in one week.

10. Click the **Send** button to send the message (Figure 2-67).

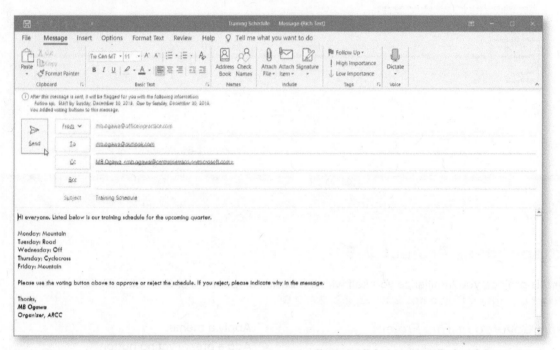

Figure 2-67 Independent Project 2-6 completed

Challenge Project 2-7

Compose a message to your instructor to request a meeting regarding your upcoming term paper. This message is of high importance to you. Be sure to use voting options to allow your instructor to quickly select a meeting day.
[Student Learning Outcomes 2.1, 2.2, 2.4, 2.6]

*   Send the message to your instructor.
*   Add your email address to the *Cc* field.
*   The subject of the message should be "Challenge 2-7: Term Paper for ENG 100 Meeting Request."
*   Change the message format to Rich Text Format.
*   Use voting buttons and the five days of the week to request a day to meet with your instructor.
*   Add a *Follow Up* flag to the message and set a reminder for yourself for a week from today.
*   Add your signature to the email message.

Challenge Project 2-8

Consider the types of email messages you received throughout your life. Develop three to five *Template* responses you could create to respond to common queries. Compose a message to your instructor and include the title and *Template* response.
[Student Learning Outcomes 2.1, 2.2, 2.3, 2.4, 2.6]

- Send the message to your instructor.
- Add your email address to the *Cc* field.
- The subject of the message should be "Challenge 2-8: Templates to improve my productivity."
- Change the message format to HTML format.
- Request a delivery receipt.
- Create a category named "School" using a color that you have not assigned to a category and apply it to the message after you receive it in your Inbox.
- Add a *Follow Up* flag to the message and set a reminder for yourself for one week from today.
- Apply a theme to your email message. The theme should have a professional appearance.

Challenge Project 2-9

Search online for a job that you would like to have in the future (you may use the position you found in *Challenge Project 1-9*). Compose an email to several coworkers as if you had the job. Include a request using the voting buttons so that you can compile your coworkers' responses. The content of your message and request should be within the scope of your job duties, so it will be important to review the job duties for your selected position.
[Student Learning Outcomes 2.1, 2.2, 2.3, 2.4, 2.5, 2.6]

- Send the message to your instructor.
- Add your email address to the *Cc* field.
- The subject of the message should be "Challenge 2-9: Coworkers Inquiry."
- Change the message format to Rich Text Format.
- Add a *Follow Up* flag to the message and set a reminder for yourself for a week from today.
- Categorize your copy of the message using an appropriate category.
- Use voting buttons to automatically track responses based on your inquiry.
- Create and use a signature for your job.
- Apply a theme that is appropriate to the content of the email message.

Contacts

OUTLOOK

CHAPTER OVERVIEW

The Outlook *Contacts* feature stores information about family members, neighbors, friends, coworkers, and businesses. Outlook Contacts include fields for full name, company, job title, email address, web page address, business, home, fax, and mobile telephone numbers, and home and business addresses. Contacts are stored electronically and integrate seamlessly with other Microsoft Office products. Outlook contacts synchronize with cell phones and other electronic devices.

STUDENT LEARNING OUTCOMES (SLOs)

After completing this chapter, you will be able to:

SLO 3.1   Differentiate between the *Contacts* folder and the *Global Address List* (p. O3-99).
SLO 3.2   Create a contact record from different sources (p. O3-100).
SLO 3.3   Update contact records by editing contact information and fields (p. O3-105).
SLO 3.4   Use and modify the different contact views (p. O3-110).
SLO 3.5   Create a contact group and produce email from a contact or contact group (p. O3-113).
SLO 3.6   Create a group and produce shared Outlook items (p. O3-121).

CASE STUDY

For the Pause & Practice projects, you work with partners in class to create contacts and a contact group. You also add pictures to contacts to help you match names to faces.

Pause & Practice 3-1: You create a contact with your personal information. You also send it to a partner and create a contact from a business card attached to an email.

Pause & Practice 3-2: Modify a contact to include a picture and a mailing address. You also add a secondary email address.

Pause & Practice 3-3: Create a contact group, update contact information, and send the contact group to your instructor.

Pause & Practice 3-4: Create a group, modify the group settings, add group members, and create a conversation.

Understanding Contacts

A *contact* is a set of related information about an individual or organization. A contact may include a name and email address or a complete listing of name, address, email, telephone numbers, photograph, and miscellaneous information.

Contacts are viewed in the *People* module (Figure 3-1). The *Folder* pane includes the different *Contact* folders and groups, while the content area includes the contacts and reading pane with details for each record.

Database Terminology

The *Contacts* folder in Outlook is similar to a database. Remember, a database is a collection of related data, and you will use the Outlook *Contacts* folder to add, delete, update, sort, and retrieve information. Each individual piece of information in a contact is a *field*, and a *record* is a group of related data fields. For

Figure 3-1 *Contacts* folder

example, a name, address, and email address are all fields within a *contact record*. In Outlook, a group of related records are saved in a *Contact* folder.

Contacts versus Global Address List

If you are using Outlook in a home environment (as a stand-alone program rather than on an Exchange server), your contacts will, by default, be saved in the *Contacts* folder (see Figure 3-1). You can choose email recipients from a list of contacts (Figure 3-2). You can also create, edit, and delete records. When you click the **To** button on a new email, your **Contacts address book** opens. This address book lists the names and email addresses of your contacts.

If you are using Outlook in an Exchange environment, in addition to your *Contacts* address book, you will also have a **Global Address List**. This address book contains the contacts for all the individuals in your organization. Your

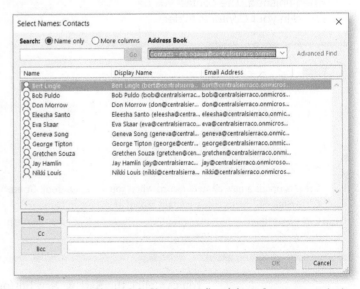

Figure 3-2 Choose email recipients from your contacts

Exchange server administrator maintains the *Global Address List*. You cannot add contacts to this folder, but you can save contacts from the *Global Address List* to your *Contacts* folder.

SLO 3.2 — Creating Contacts

Adding contact records to your *Contacts* folder can be accomplished in a number of ways. You can create a new contact from scratch, from the same company, from an email you received, from an electronic business card you received, or from the *Global Address List*.

Create a New Contact

To create a new contact, select the *People* button in the *Navigation* bar. When you click the **New Contact** button on the *Home* tab, a new contact record opens with the General page displayed. The *General* page is the default page, and it displays name, address, phone numbers, and internet information. The buttons in the *Show* group [*Home* tab] determine the number and type of fields displayed.

HOW TO: Create a New Contact

1. Click the **People** button in the *Navigation* bar.
2. Click the **New Contact** button on the *Home* tab. A new contact record opens (Figure 3-3).
3. Type in the desired contact information.
4. Click the **Save & Close** button in the *Actions* group on the *Contact* tab when finished. The contact will be saved in your *Contacts* folder.

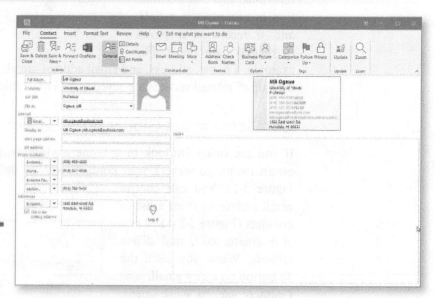

Figure 3-3 *New Contact dialog box*

You can click the **Save & New** button in the *Actions* group on the *Contact* tab (Figure 3-4) to save the current contact in the *Contacts* folder and to open a new blank contact record.

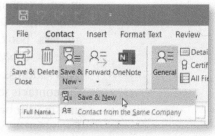

Figure 3-4 *Save & New contact option*

Create a New Contact from the Same Company

When adding contacts for individuals from the same company, you do not have to retype some of the common information such as company name, web page address, and business address. You can utilize Outlook's **Contact from the Same Company** feature (Figure 3-5) which preserves existing company information on a new contact record while providing blank fields for the new contact's personal information.

When the **Contact from the Same Company** option is selected, a new contact record opens that contains company information in select fields and provides blank fields for *Full Name*, *Job title*, *Email*, and other fields that are specific to the individual being added to your contacts. The name of the contact (in the *Title* bar at the top center of the contact) will be the company name until an individual's name is typed in the *Full Name* field.

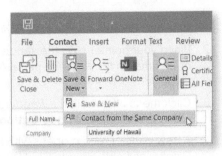

Figure 3-5 *Save & New Contact from the Same Company* option

▶ **HOW TO:** Create a New Contact from the Same Company

1. With an existing contact record open, click the drop-down arrow on the **Save & New** button in the *Actions* group on the *Contact* tab.

2. Click the **Contact from the Same Company** option. A new contact record opens with blank fields for the individual's information (Figure 3-6).

3. Type the desired information.

4. Click **Save & Close** when done.

Figure 3-6 *New Contact from the Same Company*

> **MORE INFO**
>
> Entering contact record information can be a time-consuming process if you have numerous contacts to add. See *SLO 8.3: Importing and Exporting Contact Information* for details on import contact records from other files such as a database, spreadsheet, or comma separated values (CSV) file.

Create a Contact from a Received Email

Are there times when you receive an email and want to add the sender to your contact list? In Outlook you can easily create a contact using the sender's email information.

▶ HOW TO: Create a Contact from a Received Email

1. Click the **Email** button in the *Navigation* bar.

2. Place your pointer over the sender's name in an open email or an email in the *Reading* pane. A communications window displays.

3. Click the **. . .** button in the *Reading Pane* (Figure 3-7) and then click **. . .** and select **Add to Outlook Contacts** (Figure 3-8).

4. A new contact record opens with the *Full Name, Email,* and *Display as* fields already filled in with the new contact's information.

5. You can edit existing information or add any additional information (Figure 3-9).

6. Click **Save & Close** when done.

Figure 3-7 *Open Contact Card*

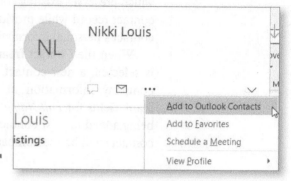

Figure 3-8 Add a contact

> ▶ **ANOTHER WAY**
>
> With an email open, you can right-click the sender's name and choose **Add to Outlook Contacts**.

Create a Contact from an Electronic Business Card

One of the advantages of using Outlook is being able to send and receive contact records between Outlook users. A very effective and easy method of adding contacts to your *Contacts* folder is by having another Outlook user send you a contact as a business card.

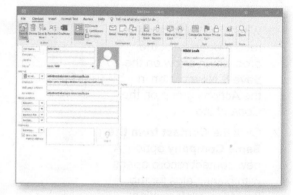

Figure 3-9 New contact from email

▶ HOW TO: Create a Contact from an Electronic Business Card

1. In an open email or an email in the *Reading* pane, click the attached electronic business card (in the attachment area). The *Attachments* tab opens and the attachment displays in the body of the email (Figure 3-10).

2. Click the **Open** button in the *Actions* group. The contact record opens (Figure 3-11).

3. Edit the contact and click **Save & Close**.

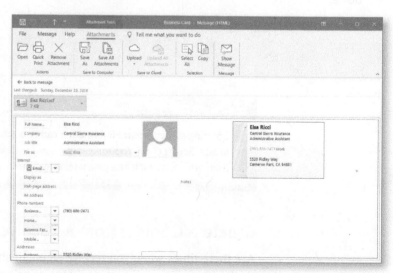

Figure 3-10 Business card in the attachments

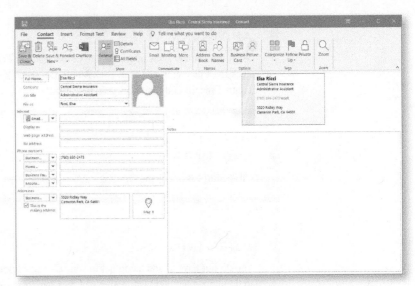

Figure 3-11 Business card opened as a contact

Add a Contact from the Global Address List

If you are using Outlook in a business environment with an Exchange server, most likely you will have a *Global Address List* populated with contacts from within your organization. This global list is created and maintained by the network administrator.

The *Global Address List* contains the contact records for all employees in the organization and usually contains **contact groups**. You can add a contact or contact group from the *Global Address List* to your *Contacts* folder.

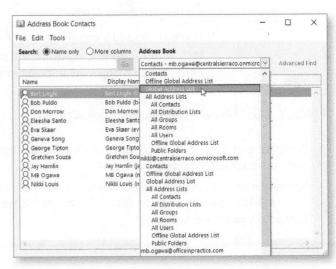

Figure 3-12 *Global Address List* option

▶ **HOW TO:** Add a Contact from the Global Address List

1. Select the *Contacts* folder and click the **Address Book** button in the *Find* group on the *Home* tab. The *Address Book* dialog box opens.

2. Click the **down arrow** on the right side of the *Address Book* drop-down menu (Figure 3-12).

3. Choose **Global Address List**. The list of contacts and contact groups displays.

4. Right-click the contact you want to add to your *Contacts* folder and click **Add to Contacts** (Figure 3-13). The contact record opens in a new window.

5. Click **Save & Close** to save it to your *Contacts* folder.

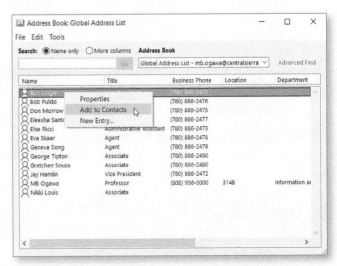

Figure 3-13 Add *Global Address* contact to personal contacts

Duplicate Contacts

If you try to add a contact to your *Contacts* folder and it has the same name as an existing contact, Outlook adds a duplicate entry. Outlook allows you to link contacts together into a single entry, which merges the information in each of the records.

▶ HOW TO: Manage Duplicate Contacts

1. Select one of the duplicate contacts and click the **...** button and select **Link Contacts** (Figure 3-14).

2. Select the contact that you would like to link to and click **OK** (Figure 3-15). You may need to search for the duplicate contact if you do not see it.

Figure 3-14 Link contacts

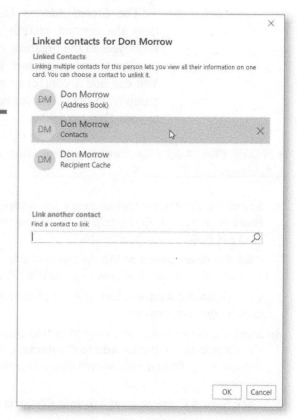

Figure 3-15 Select contacts to link

For this Pause & Practice project, you create a contact with your personal information. You also send it to a partner and create a contact from a business card attached to an email.

1. Click the **People** button in the *Navigation* bar.
2. Create a contact for yourself.
   a. Click the **New Contact** button [*Home* tab, *New* group].
   b. Enter your full name, company (school name), job title (student), and email address in the appropriate fields.
   c. Click the **Save & Close** button [*Contact* tab, *Actions* group].
3. Create a contact for your instructor.
   a. Click the **New Contact** button [*Home* tab, *New* group].
   b. Enter your instructor's full name, company (school name), job title (professor), and email address in the appropriate fields.
   c. Click the **Save & Close** button [*Contact* tab, *Actions* group].
4. Forward your contact record to a partner.
   a. Select your contact.
   b. Click the **As a Business Card** option [*Home* tab, *Share* group, *Forward Contact* button].
   c. Type your partner's email address in the *To* field.
   d. Click the **Send** button (Figure 3-16).
5. Save your partner's business card to your contacts.
   a. Open the email message that your partner sent with his or her business card.
   b. Double-click the attached business card to open it.
   c. Click the **Save & Close** button [*Contact* tab, *Actions* group].

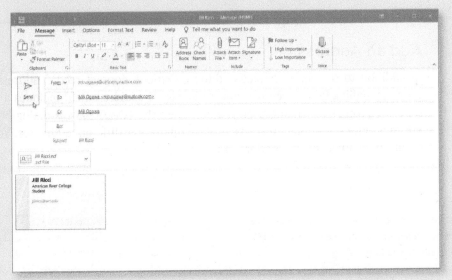

Figure 3-16 PP Outlook 3-1 completed

Editing a Contact Record

Outlook provides you with many fields in a contact record to store information. Not all the information in a contact record has to be completed to save a record. In addition to providing fields to store standard information, Outlook allows you to change the names of the fields, add multiple email addresses, include a picture, and open a map to the contact's address.

Change a Field Name

You can customize many of the fields of a contact record to better meet your needs. Any field with a drop-down menu to the right of the field name is a field name that can be changed. For example, if you would like the mobile (cell) phone number to be listed as the primary phone number, you can change the field from *Mobile* to *Primary*.

▶ **HOW TO:** Change a Field Name in a Contact Record

1. Change the view to *Business Card* view [*Home* tab, *Current View* group, *Business Card* button].
2. Open the contact record where you want to change a field name.
3. Click the **drop-down arrow** to the right of the field name you want to change (Figure 3-17).
   - A list of available field names displays.
   - Those with a check mark are already being used.
4. Click the desired field in the list of available field names.

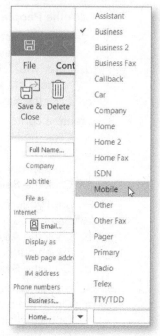

Figure 3-17 Change field name

Add an Address

In addition to storing a contact's address, Outlook contact record addresses can be used to generate mailing lists, envelopes, and/or labels. The address field includes a text box where you type the address information, or you can open the *Check Address* dialog box to type the field information. Each contact record can store up to three different addresses. You have the options of business, home, or other addresses.

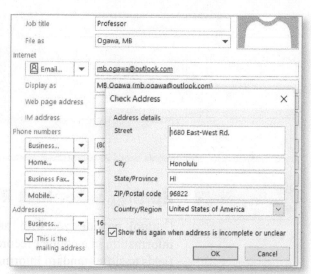

Figure 3-18 *Check Address* dialog box

Add Multiple Email Addresses

Do you have more than one email account? Outlook lets you store up to three email addresses per contact record. Each email address is added to the Outlook *Address Book*. The main email address is labeled *Email*, and the additional email address fields are labeled *Email 2* and *Email 3* (Figure 3-19).

Figure 3-19 Add multiple email addresses

Insert a Picture

To further customize a contact record, you can add a contact's picture. Figure 3-20 is the default image before you customize it. The picture appears on the contact record when it is open. Also, if you have a picture saved in a contact record and you receive an email from that contact, his or her picture appears on the email message.

Figure 3-20 Default contact picture

▶ HOW TO: Insert a Picture in a Contact Record

1. Open a contact record and click the **picture icon**. The *Add Contact Picture* dialog box opens.
2. Find and select the picture you want to appear on the contact record.
3. Click **OK** to close the dialog box.
4. Click **Save & Close** to close the contact record (Figure 3-21).

Figure 3-21 Contact with a picture

If you decide that you do not want the picture on the contact record or that you would like a different picture, you can easily change or delete it.

▶ HOW TO: Change or Remove a Picture

1. Open the contact record.
2. Click the **Picture** button in the *Options* group on the *Contacts* tab.
3. Click either **Change Picture** or **Remove Picture**.
   - If you select *Change Picture*, the *Add Contact Picture* dialog box opens and you can select a new picture.
   - If you select *Remove Picture* (Figure 3-22), the picture will be removed from the contact record. The picture will only be deleted from the contact record, not from your computer.

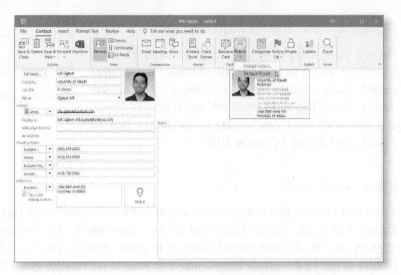

Figure 3-22 *Remove Picture* option

> ANOTHER WAY
>
> Right-click the picture on the contact record and choose either **Change Picture** or **Remove Picture**.

> MORE INFO
>
> If you use your smartphone to sync with Outlook (not all smartphones will do this), you will have the option of syncing your Outlook contacts. If you receive a phone call from a recipient whose contact record has a picture, the picture displays on the smartphone screen during the incoming call.

Use the Map It Feature

How many times have you used the internet to get a map or driving directions to a location? You had to go to the web site and type the address to find the desired information. Microsoft Outlook provides users with a map feature (Figure 3-23) called *Map It* that links an address from a contact record to an interactive internet map. So, rather than you having to go to a different web site and type an address, Outlook opens Bing *Maps* from an address in a contact record with the click of a button (Figure 3-24).

Figure 3-23 *Map It* button

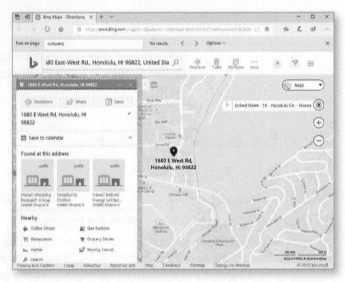

Figure 3-24 Bing map

1. Open an existing contact record that has an address.
2. Click the **Map It** button next to the address in the contact. An internet window opens with the contact record address mapped.

▶ ANOTHER WAY

Click the **More** button in the *Communicate* group on the *Contact* tab and choose **Map**.

People Pane

The ***People pane***, which is available in the main Outlook interface and on email messages, is also available on contact records (Figure 3-25). This feature provides a list of related Outlook activity associated with a contact.

This pane is located at the bottom of the contact record. Clicking one of the links displayed in the *People* pane opens the selected Outlook item. You can choose how to display or group the information in the *People* pane by clicking **All**, **Mail**, **Attachments**, or **Meetings**. Collapse or expand the *People* pane by clicking the small arrow in the upper-right corner of the pane.

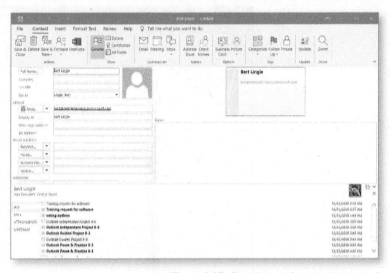

Figure 3-25 *People* pane in a contact record

▶ ANOTHER WAY

Display the *People* pane by clicking the **People Pane** button on the *View* tab in the *People Pane* group.

Delete a Contact

To delete an existing contact, simply select the contact and press **Delete**. When a contact record is deleted, it is moved to the *Deleted Items* folder where it stays until it is permanently deleted. If you delete a contact by mistake, use the *Undo* button to restore the contact, or open the *Deleted Items* folder and drag the contact back to the *Contacts* folder (drag and drop the deleted contact on the *People* button).

▶ ANOTHER WAY

Ctrl+D deletes a selected Outlook item.

You can also select the contact and click the **Delete** button on the *Contact* tab or right-click the contact and choose **Delete**.

SLO 3.4

Using and Modifying Views in Contacts

Outlook provides you with preset views in which to display your contacts. These different views display different contact information and varying amounts of information. Change the view by clicking on one of the views in the *Current View* group on the *Home* tab (Figure 3-26).

Figure 3-26 Contact views

Contact Views

By default, there are five different preset contact views. There are mixed, list, and card views.

- *People* (*People Card* view)
- *Business Card* (*Card* view)
- *Card* (*Card* view)
- *Phone* (*List* view)
- *List* (*List* view)

You can change views by selecting a view in the *Current View* group on the *Home* tab. Click the **More** button to display all available views in the *Current View* gallery.

The *Arrangement* group on the *View* tab includes options to arrange and sort your contacts. The three preset arrangements are *Categories*, *Company*, and *Location*.

Sort Contacts

When viewing contacts in a *List* view, the easiest way to sort or arrange records is to click the column heading. The column by which the records are sorted will be shaded, and the sorting order will be indicated by a small triangle pointing up (ascending order) or down (descending order) (Figure 3-27). Toggle between ascending and descending order by clicking the column header.

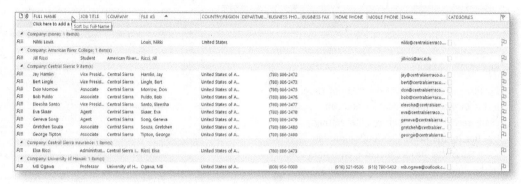

Figure 3-27 Sort contacts in a *List* view

ANOTHER WAY

Click **Reverse Sort** button on the *View* tab in the *Arrangement* group to switch between ascending and descending order.

Modify a View

As the number of contacts you have stored in Outlook increases, you may want to utilize customized views provided by Outlook to help you quickly find a contact. By default, contacts are sorted by last name, but you can group contact records by company or sort them by full name.

In addition, each of the existing contact views can be modified to assist you with finding a contact. You can customize the fields displayed, sort criteria, fonts, font sizes, and styles.

Click the **View Settings** button on the *View* tab to customize the current view. Listed below are descriptions for each of the view settings.

- *Columns*: Column headers available in list view
- *Group By*: Groups records together by field
- *Sort*: Orders records by a field
- *Filter*: Searches for records by criteria
- *Other settings*: Options for visual modifications for the records such as font size
- *Conditional Formatting*: Allows formatting to records meeting selected criteria
- *Format Columns*: Specify formatting for columns
- *Reset Current View*: Reset to default options

▶**HOW TO: Modify View Settings**

1. Click the **People** button in the *Navigation* bar.
2. Select the desired contacts view in the *Current View* group on the *Home* tab.
3. Click the **View** tab.

4. Click the **View Settings** button. The *Advanced View Settings* dialog box for the current view opens (Figure 3-28).

5. Make any desired changes. Each of the buttons on the left opens an additional dialog box.

6. Click **OK** to close the *Advanced View Settings* dialog box.

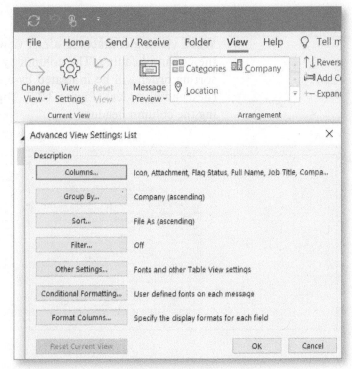

Figure 3-28 *Advanced View Settings: List* dialog box

> **MORE INFO**
>
> Feel free to experiment with different views in the *Contacts* folder because you can easily reset views to their original settings by clicking the **Reset View** button on the *View* tab or the **Reset Current View** button in the *Advanced View Settings* dialog box.

PAUSE & PRACTICE: OUTLOOK 3-2

For this Pause & Practice project, you modify your contact to include your picture and a mailing address. You also add a secondary email address.

File Needed: A picture of yourself (If you do not have a picture, general picture files are available **johnsanchez.jpg** and **jillricci.jpg**.)
Completed Project File Name: None

1. Edit your contact.
   a. Select the **People** button in the *Navigation* bar.
   b. Click **Business Card** view [*Home* tab, *Current View* group].
   c. Double-click your contact.
   d. Select the **Add Picture** option [*Contact* tab, *Options* group, *Picture* button].
   e. Locate your picture and click **OK**. If you do not have a picture, you can use one of the provided images (**johnsanchez.jpg** or **jillricci.jpg**) and change it to your image later.
   f. Click the **E-mail** drop-down arrow and select **E-mail 2**.
   g. Type a secondary email address if you have one.
   h. Click the **Business** drop-down arrow under the *Address* section and select **Other**. Click the **This is a mailing address** check box.
   i. Type your school's address.
   j. Click the **Save & Close** button.

2. Forward your updated contact as a business card to a different partner from *Pause & Practice 3-1*.
   a. Select your contact.
   b. Click the **As a Business Card** option [*Home* tab, *Share* group, *Forward Contact* button].

c. Type your partner's email address in the *To* field.
   d. Click the **Send** button.

3. Save your partner's business card to your
   contacts (Figure 3-29).
   a. Open the email message that your
      partner sent with his or her business
      card.
   b. Double-click the attached business
      card to open it.
   c. Click the **Save & Close** button
      [*Contact* tab, *Actions* group].

Figure 3-29 PP Outlook 3-2 completed

Using Contacts and Contact Groups

One of the most beneficial aspects of the *Contacts* folder is the ability to use this stored information to send emails. An email can be sent to one or more contacts in your *Contacts* folder or the *Global Address List*. You also have the ability to create contact groups, which are saved groups of contacts, and send an email to the entire contact group.

Send an Email to a Contact

You can send an email to contacts in your *Contacts* folder from any Outlook module. When you click the **New Email** button or the **Forward** button on the *Home* tab of the *Mail* module, an insertion point displays in the *To* text box. Click the **To** button to open the *Select Names* dialog box. If you have more than one address book, use the *Address Book* drop-down arrow to select the appropriate address book. Scroll through the list of names to locate the contact. To insert the name in the *To* text box, you can double-click the name, or click the name and then click the **To** button, or press **Enter**. Click **OK** after all contacts have been selected. The *Select Names* dialog box closes and you return to the email composition window.

You can send an email to contacts that are stored in your *Contacts* folder in several ways. When you have an email message open, you can click the **To** button and select the contacts from the *Select Names* dialog box. You can also choose contacts from different address books by selecting from the list in the *Address Book* drop-down menu.

▶ **HOW TO:** Send an Email to a Contact

1. Click the **To** button on an email message (new, reply, or forward). The *Select Names* dialog box opens.

2. Use the *Address Book* drop-down list to select an address book.

3. Select the desired contacts (Figure 3-30).
   • Use **Ctrl** to select nonadjacent contacts.
   • Use **Shift** to select a range of adjacent contacts.

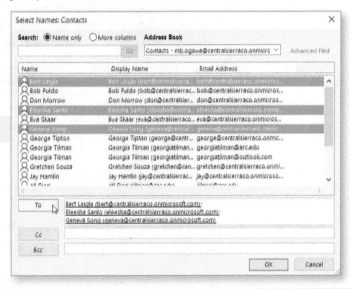

Figure 3-30 Select multiple contacts to send an email to

4. Click the **To** button (you can also put contacts in the *Cc* or *Bcc* fields).
   - Double-click a name to insert it into a recipient field.
   - Alternatively, typing the first few letters of recently used email addresses will present a list of possible autofill names.
5. Click **OK**. Your email recipient list (*To* field) is populated with these contacts.

When you click the **People** button on the *Navigation* bar, the *Folder* pane displays a list of your address books. Click an address book to display your contacts. You may see the contacts in a list or a card format. The *Current View* group [*Home* tab] controls the appearance of your contacts (*People, Business Card, Card, Phone,* or *List*). Use the *View* tab, *Layout* group to select the *Reading Pane* option. To create an email message, click the **New Items** button [*Home* tab, *New* group] and select **Email Message**.

> **HOW TO:** Create an Email to a Selected Contact

1. Click the **People** button in the *Navigation* bar.
2. Select the desired contacts.
3. Click the **Email** button in the *Communicate* group on the *Home* tab (Figure 3-31). A new email message opens with the selected contacts in the *To* field.

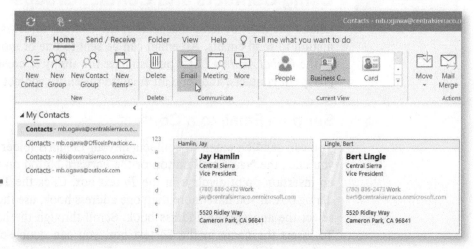

Figure 3-31 Create new email message to selected contacts

> **ANOTHER WAY**
>
> With a record selected in the *People* view, click the **Email** button in the contact (Figure 3-32). The *Email* button is not available in the *Communicate* group when in *People* view as it is located within each contact.

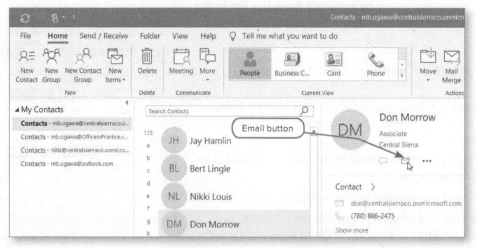

Figure 3-32 Create new email message to a contact from the *People* view

Forward a Contact as a Business Card

When you want to send your contact record or another contact record to others via email, you can send this information as an electronic business card attached to an email and the recipient can easily add the contact record to his/her *Contacts* folder.

> **HOW TO: Forward a Contact as a Business Card**

Figure 3-33 *Forward Contact As a Business Card*

1. Click the **People** button in the *Navigation* bar.
2. Select the contacts to be forwarded in the *Content area*.
3. Click the **Forward Contact** button in the *Share* group on the *Home* tab.
4. Choose **As a Business Card** (Figure 3-33). A new email opens with the business card attached, and a graphic of the business card displays in the body of the email (Figure 3-34). This graphic can be deleted.

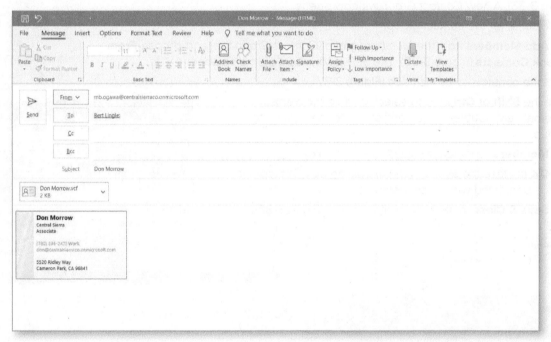

Figure 3-34 Attached business card

5. Populate the recipient list and click **Send**.

> **ANOTHER WAY**
>
> With the contact record open, click the **Forward** button in the *Actions* group on the *Contact* tab.

> **MORE INFO**
>
> Contact records can be forwarded as a business card (internet format), in Outlook format, or as a text message. Business card format is a more generic format that can be used with other email software programs.

Create a Contact Group

Contact groups (also known as distribution lists) are commonly used when regularly sending emails to a group of contacts. A contact group is a collection of contact records. The contact group can include just a few contacts or numerous contacts.

Contact groups are useful to quickly send email to a department, team, or committee. Also, they help to ensure that all members of a group are included in an email and no one is inadvertently left off the recipient list.

Contact groups are named and stored in your *Contacts* folder (or another folder created as a *Contacts* folder). Most *Global Address Lists* include numerous contact groups that have been created by the Exchange administrator.

▶ HOW TO: Create a Contact Group

1. Click the **People** button in the *Navigation* pane.
2. Click the **New Contact Group** button in the *New* group on the *Home* tab (Figure 3-35). A new *Contact Group* window opens.
3. Type a name for the contact group.
4. Click **Add Members** from the *Members* group [*Contact Group* tab] and choose **From Outlook Contacts** (Figure 3-36). The *Select Members* dialog box opens.
5. Select the contacts to be included (Figure 3-37).
   - Use the **Shift** or **Ctrl** keys to select multiple recipients.
   - Alternatively, double-click a contact to add the contact to a group.
6. Click **Members**. Contacts display in the text box.
7. Click **OK** to close the *Select Members* dialog box. The contact group is populated with these members.
8. Click **Save & Close** to save the contact group (Figure 3-38).

Figure 3-35 *New Contact Group* button

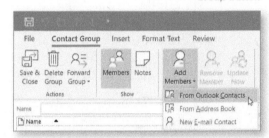

Figure 3-36 Select members from *Outlook Contacts* button

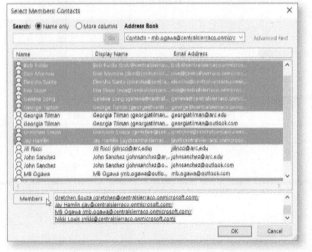

Figure 3-37 Select members from *Outlook Contacts*

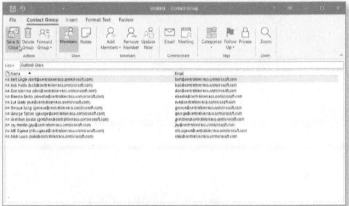

Figure 3-38 Contact group members

▶ ANOTHER WAY

Ctrl+Shift+L opens a new contact group.

Send an Email to a Contact Group

Insert a contact group to an email in the same way you insert a contact record. Start a new email, reply, or forward a message. Click the **To** button and select the contact group from the *Select Names* dialog box. The email message will be sent to all those who are members of the contact group.

▶HOW TO: Send an Email to a Contact Group

1. Click the **People** button in the *Navigation* bar.
2. Select the desired contact group in the *Content area*.
3. Click the **Email** button in the *Reading* pane (Figure 3-39). A new email opens with the contact group as the recipient.
4. Add a subject and type an email message (Figure 3-40).

Figure 3-39 *Email* button when a contact group is selected

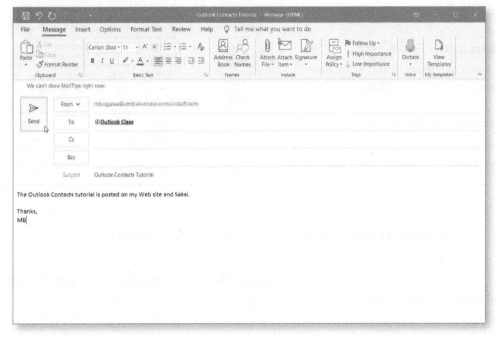

Figure 3-40 Email message to a contact group

5. Click **Send**.

Modify a Contact Group

After you create a group, you may need to add new members, delete members, or update contact information. To modify a contact group, open the contact group window, select the *Contact Group* tab, and select a button in the *Members* group.

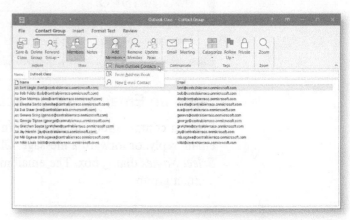

Figure 3-41 Add additional members to a contact group

▶ **HOW TO:** Add Members to a Contact Group

1. Click the **People** button in the *Navigation* bar.
2. Open the contact group to be modified.
3. Click the **Add Members** button in the *Members* group and choose **From Outlook Contacts** (Figure 3-41). The *Select Names* dialog box opens.
4. Select the contacts to add to your contact group from your *Contacts* folder or the *Global Address List*.
5. Click the **Members** button (Figure 3-42).
6. Click **OK**. The *Select Members* dialog box closes and the new members are now included in your contact group.
7. Click **Save & Close** to save the updated contact group.

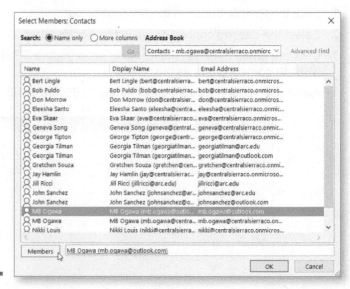

Figure 3-42 Select members to add to a contact group

Members can also be easily removed from your contact group.

▶ **HOW TO:** Remove Members from a Contact Group

1. Click the **People** button in the *Navigation* bar.
2. Open the contact group to be modified.
3. Select the members to be removed in the list of group members.
4. Click the **Remove Member** button in the *Members* group (Figure 3-43).
5. Click **Save & Close** to save the updated contact group.

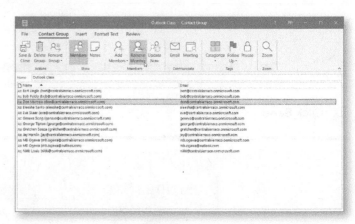

Figure 3-43 Remove a member from a contact group

The *New Email Contact* option is used to add a member to the contact group who is not currently in your *Contacts* folder.

▶ HOW TO: Add a New Email Contact to a Contact Group

1. Click the **People** button in the *Navigation* bar.
2. Open the contact group to be modified.
3. Click the **Add Members** button in the *Members* group and choose **New Email Contact**. The *Add New Member* dialog box opens.
4. Type the contact information. Select the **Add to Contacts** check box, and Outlook will add this contact to your *Contacts* folder.
5. Click **OK** to add the new member to the contact group and to close the *Add New Member* dialog box (Figure 3-44).
6. Click **Save & Close** to save the updated contact group.

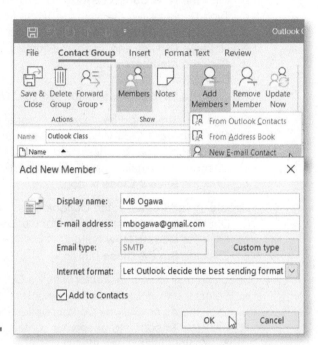

Figure 3-44 Add a new contact group member that is not in your contacts list

Update a Contact Group

When you edit a contact record in your *Contacts* folder and the contact record is included in a group, the change made to the contact does not automatically update the contact record within a group. You will need to open the contact group and update the contact (Figure 3-45).

Figure 3-45 Update contact group when you modify contact records

For this Pause & Practice project, you create a contact group, update contact information, and send the contact group to your instructor.

1. Create an Outlook contact group using your two partners from *Pause & Practice 3-1* and *Pause & Practice 3-2*.
   a. Click the **People** button in the *Navigation* bar.
   b. Click the **New Contact Group** button [*Home* tab, *New* group].
   c. Type Outlook Class Group in the *Name* field.
   d. Select **From Outlook Contacts** [*Contact Group* tab, *Members* group, *Add Members* button].
   e. Hold the **Ctrl** key and select the contact information for your two partners and yourself.
   f. Click the **Members** button.
   g. Click **OK**.
   h. Click the **Save & Close** button [*Contact Group* tab, *Actions* group].

2. Change your email address to your personal email address.
   a. Click **Business Card** view [*Home* tab, *Current View* group].
   b. Double-click your business card.
   c. Change your email address to your personal email address.
   d. Click the **Save & Close** button.

3. Update the addresses in the *Outlook Class Group*.
   a. Double-click the business card for *Outlook Class Group*.
   b. Click the **Update Now** button.
   c. Click the **Save & Close** button.

4. Send an email to your instructor with the *Outlook Class Group* contact as an attachment (Figure 3-46).
   a. Select the *Outlook Class Group* contact.
   b. Click the *As an Outlook Contact* option [*Home* tab, *Share* group, *Forward Contact* button].
   c. Click the **To** button to open your contacts.
   d. Select your instructor and click the **To** button.
   e. Click **OK**.
   f. Add your email address in the *Cc* field.
   g. Change the subject to Outlook Pause & Practice 3-3.
   h. Type a short message to your instructor indicating that you attached the completed Pause & Practice exercises.
   i. Click the **Send** button.

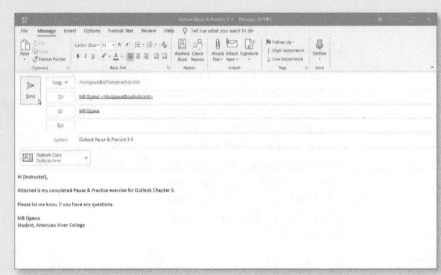

Figure 3-46 PP Outlook 3-3 completed

Using Groups

The *Groups* feature is used with an Exchange server. *Groups* are similar to Contact Groups because they let you manage its members and send email messages to several people at once. *Groups* include a shared location for conversation history, meetings, files, and notebook. In Outlook, you will work with conversations and meetings, while files and notebooks are managed in Sharepoint. *Groups* are more useful than Contact Groups when users want to keep a record of conversations, maintain a shared calendar, share files, and share notebooks. Group items can be set to appear within *Groups* and not in other areas of Outlook. This allows you to separate group work from other tasks.

Create a Group

Groups are commonly used when you regularly work with the same people on a project. A group is a saved group of contact records, conversation history, and shared meetings. It can include just a few contacts or numerous contacts.

Groups are useful to quickly send email, track conversations, and create meetings. They can be set to be public (visible) to anyone in your organization or private (selected people can view its contents). Groups are named and stored in your *Contacts* folder.

▶ **HOW TO:** Create a Group

1. Click the **People** button in the *Navigation* bar.
2. Click the **Group** button in the *New* group on the *Home* tab (Figure 3-47). A *Create Group* dialogue box opens (Figure 3-48).
3. Type a name for the group. Outlook will automatically create an email address linked to your group.
4. Type a description for your group.
5. You can select a classification if they are defined on the Exchange server.
6. Select **Public** in the *Privacy* section. You can select **Private** to allow only group members to access the content of the group.
7. Check **Send all group email and events to members' inboxes**. **They can change this setting later**. This option ensures group members also receive email messages in their inbox.
8. Click **Create**. The *Add Members* window opens.

Figure 3-47 *Group button*

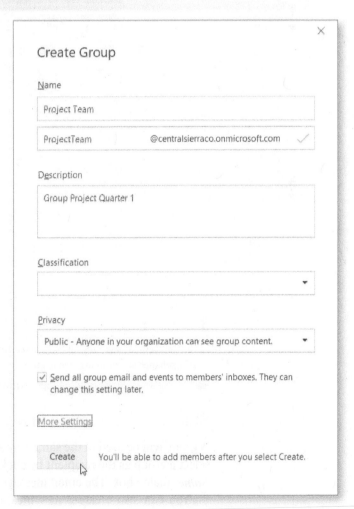

Figure 3-48 *Create Group window*

9. Search for people in your organization to add them to the group. (Figure 3-49). Click on the name of each person you search for to add them.

10. Click the **Add Members** button to close the *Add Members* dialogue box. The group is populated with selected members.

11. Click **Edit Group** [*Home* Tab, *Project Team* group, *Group Settings* button]. The *Edit Group* dialogue box.

12. Click the **Edit** button (Figure 3-50). Your project team opens in *Outlook Web Access*.

13. Click the **Edit button**.

14. Select an image from your computer and click **Open**.

15. Click the **Save** button and close your browser window. A *Groups* section is created in your *Folder* pane (Figure 3-51).

Figure 3-50 Change your photo from *Outlook Web* Access

Figure 3-49 Add members of your organization

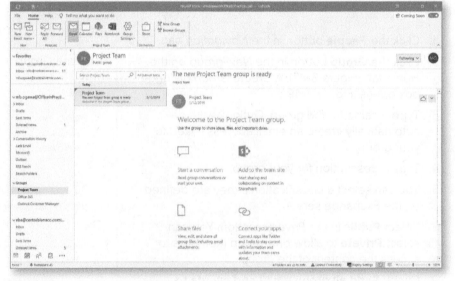

Figure 3-51 *Groups* section

> ## MORE INFO
>
> Members for a group can be selected from within your organization. You will need to be on an Exchange server to use this feature.

Start a Conversation in a Group

A group can be used in the same way a contact group is used. On a new email, reply, or forward, select a group as the recipient by clicking the **To** button and choosing the group from the *Select Names* dialog box. The email message will be sent to all those who are members of the group.

You can also create a new message to a group by clicking the **New Conversation** button when your group is selected.

▶HOW TO: Start a Conversation in a Group

1. Click the **Mail** button in the *Navigation* bar.
2. Click your group (Figure 3-52).
3. Click the **New Email** button in the *New* group on the *Home* tab. A new email opens with the group as the recipient.
4. Add a subject and type the email message (Figure 3-53).

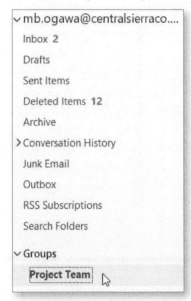

Figure 3-52 Select a group

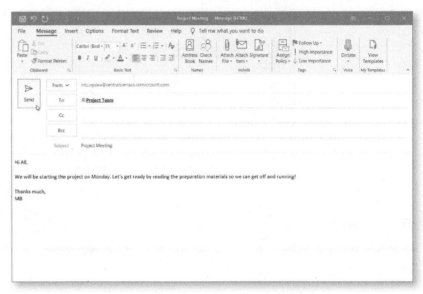

Figure 3-53 Email message to a group

5. Click **Send**.

> ### ANOTHER WAY
>
> With a group selected in the *People* view, click **Ctrl+N**.

> ### MORE INFO
>
> As with *Reply All*, only use groups when it is important that all members of the group receive the email.

> ### MORE INFO
>
> You cannot delete messages in your *Group* folder because a conversation history is maintained for all members. If you receive copies of messages to your Inbox, you can delete them there.

Replying to a Group

The *Group* folder allows you to send replies to the group, which helps to keep all members apprised of the most up-to-date information. You reply within the message itself or click the **Reply All** button.

▶ HOW TO: Reply to an Email to a Group

1. Click the **Mail** button in the *Navigation* bar.
2. Click the group name.
3. Click a conversation.
4. Click the **Add a message . . .** button and type your message to the group (Figure 3-54).

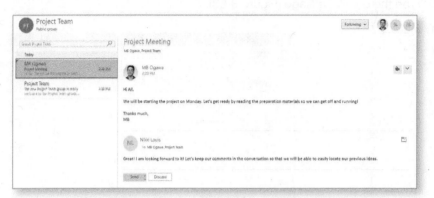

Figure 3-54 Reply to a group

5. Click **Send**.

Edit a Group

You can edit a group by removing people, adding new people, setting individuals as administrators of the group, allowing people outside your organization to email the group, or deleting the group.

▶ HOW TO: Add Members to a Group

1. Click the **Mail** button in the *Navigation* bar.
2. Click the group name.
3. Click **Add Members** [*Home* tab, *Group Name* group, *Group Settings* button] (Figure 3-55). The *Add Members* dialogue box opens.
4. Search for names of contacts to add to your group and click their names as they appear (Figure 3-56).
5. Click **OK**. The *Add Members* dialog box closes and the new members are now included in your group.

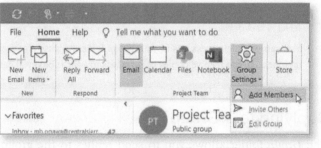

Figure 3-55 *Add Members*

Figure 3-56 Select members to add to a group

▶ **ANOTHER WAY**

If you are looking for volunteers from your organization, you can invite people to join a group with a
URL. Click **Invite Others** [*Home* tab, *Group Name* group, *Group Settings* button] and copy the URL or
send a message directly to other members of your organization.

Members can also be easily removed from your contact group.

▶ **HOW TO:** Remove Members from a Group

1. Click the **Mail** button in the *Navigation* bar.

2. Click the group name.

3. Click **Edit Group** [*Home* tab, *Group Name* group, *Group Settings* button]. The *Edit Group* dialogue box opens.

4. Move the pointer over the name of an individual that you want to remove from the group. An **X** appears near their name.

5. Click the **X** to remove the person from the group (Figure 3-57).

6. Click **OK**. The *Edit group* dialog box closes and the member is removed from the group.

▶ **MORE INFO**

When removing members from a group, any messages sent to their Inbox will not be deleted. However, they will not have access to the conversation history, as the group disappears from their *Groups* folder in their *Folder* pane.

Figure 3-57 Remove a person from a group

You can give owner status to other people in the group. This allows them to edit the group such as adding and removing members by using the *Edit group* dialog box.

▶ **HOW TO:** Give Owner Status to a Group Member

1. Click the **Mail** button in the *Navigation* bar.

2. Click the group name.

3. Click **Edit Group** [*Home* tab, *Group Name* group, *Group Settings* button]. The *Edit Group* dialogue box opens.

4. Move the pointer over the name of an individual that you want to have as the owner.

5. Click the **Make owner** link (Figure 3-58).

6. Click **OK**. The *Edit group* dialog box closes and the user will be an owner of the group.

Figure 3-58 Make another group member an owner of the group

It is especially useful if multiple people are responsible for the group or if you are leaving the group. By default, groups can only receive email messages from within the organization. The group owner can change this setting to allow messages from outside the organization.

▶ HOW TO: Allow Email from Outside the Organization

1. Click the **Mail** button in the *Navigation* bar.
2. Click the group name.
3. Click **Edit Group** [*Home* tab, *Group Name* group, *Group Settings* button]. The *Edit Group* dialogue box opens.
4. Click the *Let people outside the organization email the group* check box (Figure 3-59).
5. Click **OK**.

Figure 3-59 Allow email from people outside the organization

> **MORE INFO**
>
> You can remove administrator privileges by clicking the **Remove admin status** link.

When a project is completed, you may want to delete the group so that it does not clutter each member's *Folder* pane. Once a group is deleted, you cannot recover its contents.

▶ HOW TO: Delete a Group

1. Click the **Mail** button in the *Navigation* bar.
2. Click the group name.
3. Click the **Edit Group** button [*Group Name* group]. The *Edit group* dialog box opens.
4. Click the **Delete group** button (Figure 3-60).
5. Click the **I understand that the group will be permanently deleted** check box (Figure 3-61).

Figure 3-61 Confirm group removal

Figure 3-60 Delete group

6. Click **OK**.

For this Pause & Practice project, you create a group, add members, and send an email to the group. You will need to be on an Exchange server to complete this project.

1. Create an Outlook group including your two partners from *Pause & Practice 3-1* and *Pause & Practice 3-2*.
   a. Click the **Group** button [*Home* tab, *New* group].
   b. Type Outlook Class Team in the *Name* field.
   c. Type Pause & Practice 3-4 in the *Description* field.
   d. Ensure the *Privacy* is set to **Public - Anyone in your organization can see what's inside**.
   e. Click the **Send all group email and events to members' inboxes. They can change this setting later.** check box.
   f. Click **Create**.
   g. Search for your two team members and add them to the group.
   h. Click **OK**.

2. Add your instructor to your *Outlook Class Team* group.
   a. Click the **Mail** button in the *Navigation* bar.
   b. Click the *Outlook Class Team* group.
   c. Click the **Add Members** [*Home* tab, *Outlook Class Team* group, *Group Settings* button].
   d. Search for your instructor's name and click it to add.
   e. Click **OK**.

3. Send an email to the *Outlook Class Team* group.
   a. Click the **Mail** button in the *Navigation* bar.
   b. Click the *Outlook Class Team* group.
   c. Click the **New Email** button [*Home* tab, *New* group].
   d. Change the subject to Outlook Pause & Practice 3-4.
   e. Type a short message to your instructor indicating that you created an Outlook group (Figure 3-62).
   f. Click the **Send** button.

Figure 3-62 PP Outlook 3-4 completed

Chapter Summary

3.1 Differentiate between the *Contacts* folder and the *Global Address List* (p. O3-99).

- An Outlook **contact** is referred to as a **record** or **contact record**.
- A record includes a group of related information about a person such as name, phone number, email address, address, company, and job title.
- Each individual piece of information such as an email address or a phone number is called a **field**.
- Each record is saved to the *Contacts* folder.
- The **Contacts Address book** contains all of your contacts in a single location, which is searchable.
- When using Outlook in an Exchange environment, a **Global Address List** includes all the members of the organization.

3.2 Create a contact record from different sources (p. O3-100).

- Create a new contact from using the default template by clicking the **New Contact** button.
- When creating multiple contacts from the same organization, use the **Contact from the Same Company** option on the *Save & New* button.
- You can create a contact based on an email you receive.
- A business card can be used to create a contact.
- Contacts in the *Global Address List* (Exchange environments only) can be saved to your personal contacts list.
- The *Global Address List* includes **contact groups** including your defined groups and ones your organization predefines.
- Linking duplicate accounts merges information.

3.3 Update contact records by editing contact information and fields (p. O3-105).

- Field names for specific records can be modified within a record.
- Records can contain multiple email addresses such as **Email**, **Email 2**, and **Email 3**.
- Each record can contain multiple addresses such as business and home.

- Outlook helps you format addresses when it does not recognize the format.
- Each record can contain multiple email addresses.
- You can add pictures to records, which will show up when you receive an email from the contact.
- **Map It** allows you to check Bing *Maps* from a contact record.
- You can receive updates from individuals in the **People pane**.

3.4 Use and modify the different contact views (p. O3-110).

- There are five contact views: *People*, *Business Card*, *Card*, *Phone*, and *List*.
- The *People* view includes all of the contacts' information as *People Cards*. Actions, such as sending an email message, are listed within the *People Card*.
- The *Business Card* view displays each contact as a business card.
- The *Card* view displays information as cards and is more condensed than the *Business Card* view.
- The *Phone* view displays contacts as a list based on phone numbers.
- The *List* view displays contacts as a list and includes different company groups.
- You can sort your contacts in list view by clicking the column header (field name).
- The *Advanced View Settings: List* dialog box can be used to customize the sorting of contacts.

3.5 Create a contact group and produce email from a contact or contact group (p. O3-113).

- You can create a contact group, which contains multiple contacts, to send email messages to members.
- When you click the **To** button in a new email message, you can select a contact or contact group instead of manually typing email addresses.
- When selecting multiple email addresses, hold the **Ctrl** key to select nonadjacent contacts and the **Shift** key to select adjacent contacts.

- When selecting a contact or **contact group** in card or list view, click the **Email** button in the *Communicate* group to create a new message.
- The *People Card* view includes the email button within the *People Card*.
- You can forward contacts to others as business cards.
- Add or remove members from a contact group at any time.
- You can use the **New Email Contact** option to add a member to a contact group when they are not listed in your *Contacts* folder.
- When you update contact fields, you need to update a contact group to ensure it has the most up-to-date fields.

3.6 Create a group and produce shared Outlook items (p. O3-121).

- You can create a **Group**, which contains multiple contacts, to send email messages to members.
- The **Groups** feature allows you to maintain a conversation history, shared calendar, shared files, and shared notebooks with members.
- You can create an email message to the Group by selecting the Group name in the *People* view and click the **New Conversation** button. Alternatively, when you click the **To** button in a

new email message, you can select the group from your address list.
- Replies will be sent to all group members.
- Messages are available only in the group folder unless you modify the group to also deliver messages to group members' Inboxes.
- Messages in the group folder cannot be deleted.
- You can add or remove group members when editing a group.
- Groups can receive email from outside the organization if the option is selected when the group is created or edited.
- When groups are deleted, all of the data associated with the group is also removed.
- When you click the **To** button in a new email message, you can select a contact or contact group instead.

Check for Understanding

The SIMbook for this text (within your SIMnet account), provides the following resources for concept review:

- Multiple-choice questions
- Short answer questions
- Matching exercises

Guided Project 3-1

For this project, you work as an insurance agent for Central Sierra Insurance. As a new member to the team, you begin setting up your Outlook contacts to make it easy to contact your associates. You will need to work with two partners for this guided project.
[Student Learning Outcomes 3.1, 3.2, 3.5]

Files Needed: None
Completed Project File Name: None

Skills Covered in This Project

- Create a new contact.
- Add information in fields.
- Create contacts from the same company.
- Select contacts within the *To* and *Cc* fields of an email.
- Email contacts as a business card.

1. Click the **People** button in the *Navigation* bar.
2. Create a contact for your manager (either one of your partners, but be sure each person creates a unique contact).
   a. Click the **New Contact** button [*Home* tab, *New* group].
   b. Partner with another student and enter his or her full name, company (Central Sierra), job title (manager), business phone number, and email address in the appropriate fields.
   c. Click the **Contact from the Same Company** option [*Contact* tab, *Actions* group, *Save & New* button].
   d. Create another contact for your other partner. Include his or her full name, company (Central Sierra), job title (insurance agent), business phone number, and email address in the appropriate fields.
   e. Click **Save & Close** both contact records.
3. Create a new message to your instructor.
   a. Click the **Mail** button in the *Navigation* bar.
   b. Click **New Email** [*Home* tab, *New* group].
   c. In the *To* field, enter your instructor's email address.
   d. In the *Cc* field, enter your email address.
   e. In the *Subject* field, type Outlook Guided Project 3-1.
   f. In the message area, type:

   Dear [instructor name],

   Attached is my Outlook Guided Project 3-1.

   Thank you,
   [your name]

   g. Click the **Business Card** option [*Message* tab, *Include* group, *Attach Item*] and select **Other Business Cards**.
   h. Select the two cards you created and click **OK**.
   i. Your email message should look similar to Figure 3-63.
   j. Click the **Send** button.

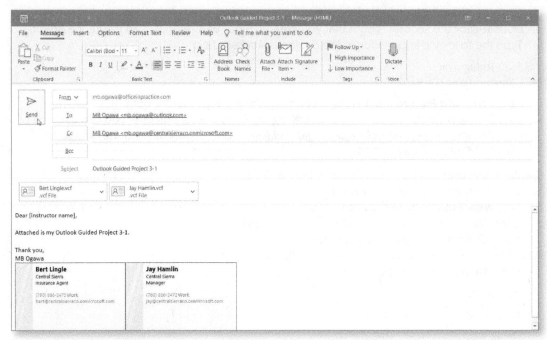

Figure 3-63 Guided Project 3-1 completed

Guided Project 3-2

For this project, you edit contacts to add additional information. You also add a picture to each of the contacts so that you can easily match your coworkers' faces and names when receiving email.
[Student Learning Outcomes 3.1, 3.3, 3.4, 3.5]

Files Needed: ***johnsanchez.jpg*** and ***jillricci.jpg***
Completed Project File Name: None

Skills Covered in This Project

- Edit contacts.

- Include an address in contacts.

- Include a photo in contacts.

- Select contacts within the *To* and *Cc* fields of an email.

- Email contacts as a business card.

1. Edit the two contacts you created in *Guided Project 3-1* to include their addresses and pictures.
   a. Click the **People** button in the *Navigation* bar.
   b. Click the **Business Card** button [*Home* tab, *Current View* group].
   c. Double-click the first record that you created (your partner that is a manager).
   d. Type the following information in the *Business Address* field:

      5520 Ridley Way
      Cameron Park, CA 94681

   e. Select the **Add Picture** option [*Contact* tab, *Options* group, *Picture* button].
   f. Locate your partner's picture and click **OK**. If you do not have a picture, you can use one of the provided images (***johnsanchez.jpg*** or ***jillricci.jpg***) and change it to his or her image later.

g. Click the **Save & Close** button.

h. Double-click the second record that you created (your partner that is an insurance agent).

i. Type the following information in the *Business Address* field:

   5520 Ridley Way
   Cameron Park, CA 94681

j. Select the **Add Picture** option [*Contact* tab, *Options* group, *Picture* button].

k. Locate your partner's picture and click **OK**. If you do not have a picture, you can use one of the provided images (***johnsanchez.jpg*** or ***jillricci.jpg***) and change it to his or her image later.

l. Click the **Save & Close** button.

2. Create a new message to your instructor (Figure 3-64).

   a. Click the **Mail** button in the *Navigation* bar.
   b. Click **New Email** [*Home* tab, *New* group].
   c. In the *To* field, enter your instructor's email address.
   d. In the *Cc* field, enter your email address.
   e. In the *Subject* field, enter Outlook Guided Project 3-2.
   f. In the message area, type:

      Dear [instructor name],

      Attached is my Outlook Guided Project 3-2.

      Thank you,
      [your name]

   g. Click the **Business Card** option [*Message* tab, *Include* group, *Attach Item*] and select **Other Business Cards**.
   h. Select the two cards you edited above and click **OK**.
   i. Click the **Send** button.

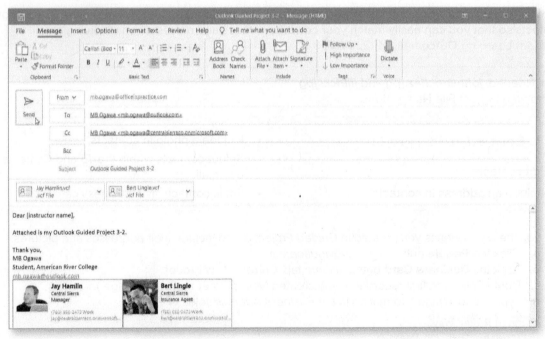

Figure 3-64 Guided Project 3-2 completed

Guided Project 3-3

For this project, you create a contact group for your coworker and manager. You also include yourself in the contact group.
[Student Learning Outcomes 3.1, 3.5]

Files Needed: None
Completed Project File Name: None

Skills Covered in This Project

- Create a contact group.
- Select contacts within the *To* and *Cc* fields of an email.
- Email a contact group as an Outlook item.

1. Create an Outlook contact group using your two coworkers from *Guided Project 3-2*.
   a. Click the **People** button in the *Navigation* bar.
   b. Click the **New Contact Group** button [*Home* tab, *New* group].
   c. Type Central Sierra Team in the *Name* field.
   d. Select **From Outlook Contacts** [*Contact Group* tab, *Members* group, *Add Members* button].
   e. Hold the **Ctrl** key and select the contact information for your two partners and yourself.
   f. Click the **Members** button.
   g. Click **OK**.
   h. Click the **Save & Close** button [*Contact Group* tab, *Actions* group].

2. Send an email to your instructor with the *Central Sierra Team* contact as an attachment (Figure 3-65).
   a. Select the **Central Sierra Team** contact.
   b. Click the **As an Outlook Contact** option [*Home* tab, *Share* group, *Forward Contact* button].
   c. Click the **To** button to open your contacts.
   d. Select your instructor and click the **To** button.
   e. Click **OK**.
   f. Add your email address in the *Cc* field.
   g. Change the subject to Outlook Guided Project 3-3.
   h. In the message area, type:

   Dear [instructor name],

   Attached is my Outlook Guided Project 3-3.

   Thank you,
   [your name]

   i. Click the **Send** button.

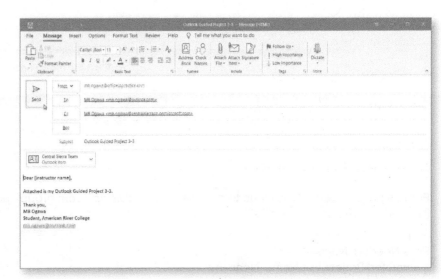

Figure 3-65 Guided Project 3-3 completed

Independent Project 3-4

For this project, you work as an academic advisor for Sierra Pacific Community College District (SPCCD), a community college district made up of four individual community colleges. Due to the decentralized nature of the multiple campuses, you realize that it is important that you keep in touch with advisors on the other campuses and communicate with each other as a group. You will work with two other group members for this independent project.
[Student Learning Outcome 3.6]

Files Needed: None
Completed Project File Name: None

Skills Covered in This Project

- Create a group.
- Add members to a group.
- Modify the description of a group.
- Subscribe group members to receive messages to their Inbox.
- Set the permission of the group to public.

1. Create a group named **SPCC Advising Team**.

2. Ensure the group is *Public* and all group members receive conversations to their inbox.

3. Add your two partners to the group.

4. Add following the text SPCC Academic Advisors to the Description (Figure 3-66).

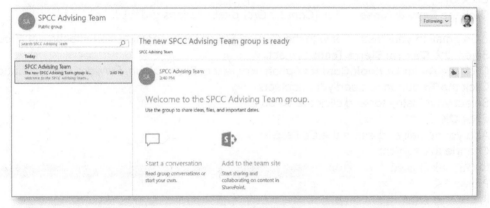

Figure 3-66 Independent Project 3-4 completed

Independent Project 3-5

For this project, you will continue to edit the *SPCC Advising Team* group and send an email to the team.
[Student Learning Outcome 3.6]

Files Needed: None
Completed Project File Name: None

- Give admininistrator privileges to group members.
- Add a new group member.
- Send email to a group.

1. Add your instructor as a new group member.
2. Give your instructor administrator privileges.
3. Create a new conversation to the *SPCC Advising Team* group.
4. Add the subject Independent Project 3-5.
5. In the body of the message, type the following text:

    Hi everyone. Welcome to the SPCC Advising Team Group. Let's use this Group to keep everyone apprised of the happenings at our school in terms of advising issues. (Figure 3-67).

Figure 3-67 Independent Project 3-5 completed

Independent Project 3-6

In this project, you continue to work with your group by replying to conversations and editing permissions.
[Student Learning Outcome 3.6]

Files Needed: None
Completed Project File Name: None

Skills Covered in This Project

- Give permission to people outside the organization to send messages to a group.
- Reply to a conversation.
- Delete a group member.
- Use email features in a conversation.

1. Reply to the *Independent Project 3-5* conversation with the following text.

    Thank you for creating this group. We just started required advising for all students. It is quite busy!

2. Create a new conversation to the *SPCC Advising Team* group.
3. Add the subject Independent Project 3-6.

4. In the body of the message, add the following text:

    Hi everyone. I noted in the previous conversation that my campus has required advising. I was wondering if other campuses have this requirement. If so, how is it working for you?

5. Give permission to people outside the organization to email the group.

6. Delete one of your group members (not the instructor) (Figure 3-68).

Figure 3-68 Independent Project 3-6 completed

Challenge Project 3-7

Create a contact group for your family and friends to use to send group updates. Include as much information as possible. If you are concerned about privacy, you can create information for fields that are sensitive.
[Student Learning Outcomes 3.1, 3.2, 3.3, 3.5]

- Create at least five new contacts for friends and family members.
- Use as many fields as possible. At minimum, each record should have the full name, email address, phone number, and mailing address completed.
- Include a picture for each contact.
- Create a contact group for the members.
- Use a descriptive name for the group.
- Email the contact group to your instructor as an email attachment.
- Change the subject of your message to Outlook Challenge Project 3-7.
- Include a short message indicating why the contact group name is appropriate.

Challenge Project 3-8

Write an email message to an organization that you belong to describing an upcoming event. Create contacts and a group for the organization. Add your instructor to the group. If you are not on an Exchange server, describe the group and how the feature will help you manage the organizational content.
[Student Learning Outcomes 3.1, 3.2, 3.3, 3.6]

- Create at least five new contacts for your organization.
- Use as many fields as possible.
- At minimum, each record should have the full name and email address of each member.
- Create a group for the members.
- Use a descriptive name for the group.
- Write an email message to the organization describing an upcoming event.
- Save the message as a draft.
- Save the draft as a file.
- Email the draft message as an attachment to your instructor.
- Change the subject of your message to Outlook Challenge Project 3-8.

Challenge Project 3-9

Write an email to your instructor comparing the use of *Contact Groups* and *Groups*. Include a brief description of each and possible reasons to use one over the other.
[Student Learning Outcomes 3.1, 3.2, 3.3, 3.5, 3.6]

- Describe *Contact Groups*.
- Describe *Groups*.
- Identify the benefits and drawbacks of *Contact Groups*.
- Identify the benefits and drawbacks of *Groups*.
- Describe at least one situation where *Contact Groups* would be better than *Groups*.
- Describe at least one situation where *Groups* would be better than *Contact Groups*.
- Change the subject of your message to Outlook Challenge Project 3-9.

Source of screenshots Microsoft Office 365 (2019): Outlook, Word, Excel, Access, PowerPoint, Outlook.

Calendar

CHAPTER OVERVIEW

Years ago, we used daily planners or a calendar that hung on a wall or refrigerator to manage appointments (many of us still do!). Today, we use Outlook Calendar to integrate mail, appointments, and contacts. One of the many advantages to using Microsoft Outlook is that it integrates different Outlook tasks. As personal management software, Outlook not only handles your emails (and multiple email accounts) and contacts but also provides an electronic calendar to be used in conjunction with your email.

In this chapter, you'll learn about many of the features of **Outlook Calendar** and how it integrates with both email and contacts. In future chapters, you will see how calendar items can be used with Tasks, Categories, and the *To-Do* bar. As you progress through this text and continue to utilize Outlook in your daily life for both business and personal use, you will find that Outlook Calendar not only surpasses your expectations but it is an invaluable organizational tool.

STUDENT LEARNING OUTCOMES (SLOs)

After completing this chapter, you will be able to:

SLO 4.1   Understand the different types of calendar items (p. O4-139).
SLO 4.2   Navigate between different calendar views (p. O4-140).
SLO 4.3   Create and edit calendar items (p. O4-143).
SLO 4.4   Create and use meeting requests (p. O4-149).
SLO 4.5   Work with group calendars (p. O4-157).

CASE STUDY

For the Pause & Practice projects, you begin building your personal calendar by adding a meeting with your instructor and your friend's birthday. You use the features of Outlook to create, modify, and request meetings with others.

Pause & Practice 4-1: For this Pause & Practice project, you create calendar items for an upcoming meeting with your instructor regarding an assignment. You also create a recurring event for your friend's birthday with a reminder set a week in advance to ensure you have time to purchase a gift.

Pause & Practice 4-2: You follow up with the two calendar items you created in *Pause & Practice 4-1*. You had an emergency at home, so you decide to send a meeting request to your instructor to apologize for not being able to attend the meeting and reschedule. You also send a meeting request to have lunch with your friend Lynne to give her the gift you purchased.

Pause & Practice 4-3: You realize that the emergency at home is going to take more time than expected. You decide to create a group to include all your instructors to ensure they are aware of your situation and the time that you will be out of class.

Understanding Calendar Items

People who use a calendar to help organize their lives can only imagine having a calendar hanging on their wall or refrigerator instead of keeping all of their appointments on an electronic calendar. But most people who have converted to Outlook Calendar cannot imagine going back to a paper calendar.

An Outlook calendar has many advantages over a paper calendar.

- An Outlook calendar can be viewed in monthly, weekly, daily, or other formats, unlike a paper calendar that has a fixed view.
- Reminders can be set to alert you on your computer or phone about upcoming appointments or events.
- Calendar items can easily be moved, copied, deleted, or scheduled to recur at specific intervals.
- Categories group calendar items and color them for visual recognition.
- Additional information and details can be included in the body, and items such as contacts and Word documents can be attached to a calendar item.
- Calendar items can be set to recur on a specific interval (daily, weekly, monthly, or yearly).
- Create Meeting requests in the calendar to invite others to the meeting, and track responses of those attending the meeting.
- Calendars can be synchronized with many cell phones and tablets that have a calendar feature.

The three main types of calendar items are appointments, events, and meeting requests. Each of these items has a distinct purpose and use, but all are created in a similar fashion. You may use the same new calendar item to create each of these different calendar items. For example, an appointment can easily be changed to an event by changing the duration of the calendar item. This consistency makes it easy to learn how to use Outlook Calendar.

Appointments

An *appointment* (Figure 4-1) is a calendar item that has a duration of less than 24 hours, such as a sales meeting, your child's water polo game, or a date with your significant other. This is

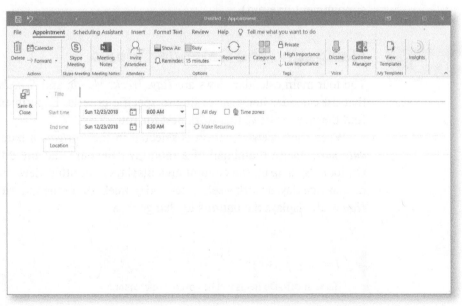

Figure 4-1 New appointment

the most common type of calendar item and can be used for storing all types of appointments or for scheduling blocks of time that are less than a day in length.

Events

Events (Figure 4-2) are those calendar items that last for 24 hours or more, like vacations, conferences, birthdays, or long holidays.

When a new appointment is open, it can easily be converted

Figure 4-2 Event

to an event by clicking the **All day** check box to the right of the *Start time* and *End time*. Conversely, an event can be converted to an appointment by deselecting the **All day** check box and setting the specific time of the appointment.

Meeting Requests

A *meeting request* (Figure 4-3) is used to create a calendar item and to invite others to this meeting. It looks similar to both an appointment and an event, but the meeting request includes a *To* line used to invite attendees and a *Send* button. A meeting request looks like a combination of a calendar item and a new email and can be either an appointment or event. If you are using

an Exchange server, you can select from available rooms if your administrator enabled this feature.

An appointment or event can easily be converted to a meeting request by clicking the **Invite Attendees** button in the *Attendees* group on the *Appointment* or *Events* tab (the tab name will vary depending on whether the calendar item is an appointment or event).

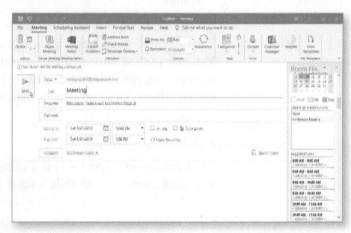

Figure 4-3 Meeting request

SLO 4.2

Navigating the Calendar Views

The four main calendar views are *Day*, *Week*, *Month*, and *Schedule*. Other views are available that list calendar items according to specific criteria. Experiment with the different views to find the view or views that work best for you.

When the **Calendar** button is selected in the *Navigation* bar, the *Folder* pane displays the *date navigator* (a thumbnail of a monthly calendar) and the different calendars available to Outlook. By default, the content area displays a monthly view, but you can change the view to display one day, a work week, a seven-day week, or a schedule view. The *Arrange* group on the *Home* tab displays the buttons to change views.

> ### MORE INFO
> Tasks and To-Do items will be covered in chapter 5.

Day View

Day view (Figure 4-4) displays the calendar one day at a time with the calendar divided into half-hour segments. Events display at the top of the daily calendar, while appointments appear on the calendar at their scheduled times.

The date appears at the top of the calendar, and you have the option to move backward or forward one day at a time on the calendar by clicking the left or right arrow to the left of the date. You are able to move to a specific date on the calendar by clicking the date in the thumbnail calendar provided at the top of the *Folder* pane.

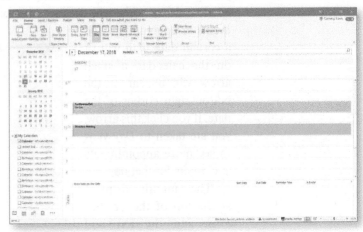

Figure 4-4 *Day* view

Week View

Week view has two different display options: *Work Week* (Figure 4-5) or *Week*. *Work Week* view shows a Monday through Friday work week, while *Week* view presents a Sunday through Saturday week.

As with *Day* view, *Week* view displays events at the top of the calendar and appointments appear at their set times. The *Daily Task List* is located at the bottom of the *Content area* and can either be minimized or turned off.

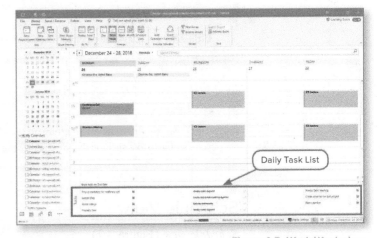

Daily Task List

Figure 4-5 *Work Week* view

The date displays at the top of the calendar in the *Content area* showing the date range for the week. The left and right arrows to the left of the date will move you backward or forward one week at a time.

Month View

Month view (Figure 4-6) displays an entire month. Both events and appointments display on the dates on which they occur. Events appear at the top of the date cell, and appointments appear below the events. Additional details about items on the calendar can be made visible by moving your pointer over the item. Depending on the size of your computer monitor and the Outlook window, *Month* view will display three or four calendar items on each day. If there are more events or appointments on a certain date than will fit on the calendar, a small arrow will appear at the bottom-right corner of the date. If you click this arrow, you are taken to *Day* view to see more appointments and events for that day.

The month displays at the top of the *Content area*, and the left and right arrows to the left of the month will move you backward or forward one month at a time.

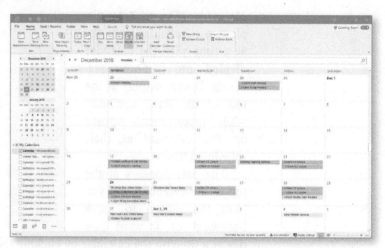

Figure 4-6 *Month* view

▶ **ANOTHER WAY**

Ctrl+Alt+4 displays the calendar in *Month* view.

▶ **MORE INFO**

The *Today* button in the *Go To* group on the *Home* tab will always take you to the current day. Also, you can move to a specific day by clicking the date navigator in the *Folder* pane.

Schedule View

Schedule view (Figure 4-7) displays your calendar in timeline view in the *Content area*. The timeline displays horizontally rather than vertically (*Day* and *Week* views). In *Schedule* view, you are able to type a new appointment directly on the calendar, double-click a time slot to open a new appointment, or click the *New Appointment* button on the *Home* tab.

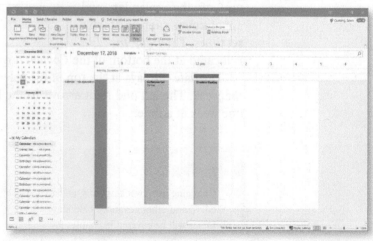

Figure 4-7 *Schedule* view

One of the distinct advantages of using the *Schedule* view is the ability to view multiple calendars in the *Content area*. When using Outlook in an Exchange environment, it is common to share your calendar with others in your organization. When others have shared their calendars with you, you can select one or more of these shared calendars to display in *Schedule* view, which helps facilitate scheduling meetings, appointments, and events.

Other Views

In addition to the four main calendar views, Outlook also has other preset views available. These different views show calendar items in a list rather than *Day*, *Week*, or *Month* view (Figure 4-8). The different preset views are:

- *Calendar* (*Calendar* view)
- *Preview* (*Calendar* view)
- *List* (*List* view)
- *Active* (*List* view)

To access these other views, click **Change View** on the *View* tab and choose the view you want. Return to *Calendar* view by following the same steps and choosing **Calendar**.

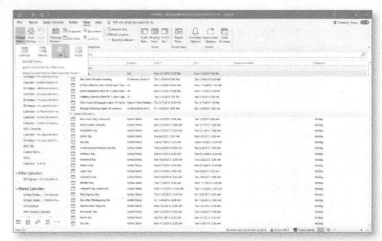

Figure 4-8 Additional views

SLO 4.3

Creating and Editing Calendar Items

Creating a calendar item varies depending on the calendar view. In all the calendar views, you can type an appointment directly on the calendar. In *Day* and *Week* views, the duration of an appointment can be adjusted by clicking and dragging the top or bottom edge of the appointment.

Usually, the best way to create a calendar item is to open a new calendar item window. The *New Appointment* window provides title and location fields to enter detailed information about the appointment or event.

Create an Appointment

When you are in the Outlook Calendar, create a new appointment by clicking the **New Appointment** button on the *Home* tab. The *New Appointment* window opens with an insertion point in the *Title* box. Change the date by clicking the calendar button to the right of the *Start time* and *End time* boxes.

▶ **HOW TO:** Create an Appointment

1. Click the **Calendar** button in the *Navigation* bar.

2. Click the **New Appointment** button on the *Home* tab. A new appointment window opens (Figure 4-9).

3. Type the *Title* and *Location* of the appointment. After you enter a subject, the title appears in the *Title* bar at the top of the open calendar item.

4. Set the *Start time* and *End time* dates and times for this appointment.

5. Enter additional information about this appointment in the body of the new appointment.

6. Click **Save & Close**. The appointment appears on your calendar.

Figure 4-9 New appointment

Create an Event

Creating a new event will vary depending on the calendar view. When you are in *Day* or *Week* view, create a new event by double-clicking the event area at the top of the calendar in the *Content area*. In *Month* view, create a new event by double-clicking the date of the event (or the first day of the event).

An appointment can always be converted to an event by clicking the **All day** check box to the right of the date and time.

▶ **HOW TO: Create an Event**

1. Click the **New Appointment** button on the *Home* tab or press **Ctrl+N**. A new appointment window opens.

2. Type the *Title* and *Location* of the event.

3. Click the **All day** check box.
   - The calendar item changes from an appointment to an event (Figure 4-10).
   - In the *Title* bar after the title, the type of calendar item displays (*Appointment*, *Event*, or *Meeting*).

4. Set the *Start time* and *End time* dates for this event.

5. Enter additional information about this event in the body of the new appointment.

6. Click **Save & Close**. The event appears on your calendar.

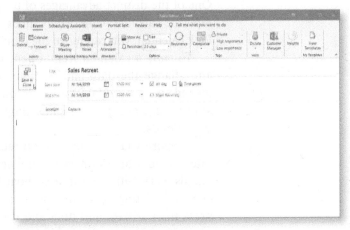

Figure 4-10 Event

Reminders

A *reminder* can be set on all calendar items. This reminder opens on your computer screen to remind you of an upcoming appointment, event, or meeting.

By default, a reminder window displays 15 minutes before appointments and 0.5 days (12 hours) before an event. To change the reminder default settings, click the **File** tab, and select **Options**. The *Outlook Options* dialog box opens. Click **Calendar** on the left to change the default reminder time. Click **Advanced** on the left of the *Outlook Options* dialog box to change the default setting for displaying reminders and to play a reminder sound. You can easily change the reminder time by clicking the **Reminder** drop-down menu (Figure 4-11). You can customize the sound for reminders or choose to change the reminder setting to none.

When it is time for an appointment or event reminder, a *Reminder* window displays on your computer (Figure 4-12). The *Reminder* window includes the title of the calendar item, the start date and time, and the location. The *Reminder* dialog box options include *Open Item*, *Dismiss*, *Dismiss All*, and *Snooze*. If you choose *Snooze*, you will be reminded again in a specified amount of time. Click the drop-down menu to select a time.

Figure 4-11 *Reminder* drop-down menu

Figure 4-12 *Reminder* window

▶ MORE INFO

To display the *Reminder(s)* window, click the **View** tab, **Reminders Window** button [*Window* group].

Move and Copy Calendar Items

One of the distinct advantages of using an Outlook calendar is the ability to easily move and replicate calendar items. Many times, an appointment is rescheduled, and, when using an Outlook calendar, you can move the item to a new date or time.

To *move* a calendar item, open the item from the calendar by double-clicking the item and change the date and/or time of the item. When you save and close the item, it is moved to its new date and time on the calendar. If an appointment has been moved to another day and has the same time, drag and drop the calendar item to the new date on the calendar.

Suppose you have jury duty three days in a row and you don't want to create three separate calendar appointments. Similar to other Office applications, the *Cut* and *Copy* commands work with the same keyboard shortcuts (**Ctrl+X** for cut and **Ctrl+C** for copy). To *copy* an existing appointment to another date, select the appointment on the calendar, press the **Ctrl** key, and drag and drop the appointment on the new date. As you are dragging the calendar item, you will see a small plus sign by the pointer to indicate that you are copying a calendar item rather than moving it (Figure 4-13). The appointment is copied to the new date.

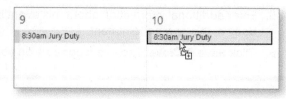

Figure 4-13 Copy appointment using **Ctrl** and drag and drop

> **ANOTHER WAY**
>
> **Ctrl+C** copies a selected calendar item.
> **Ctrl+X** cuts a selected calendar item.
> **Ctrl+V** pastes a copied or cut calendar item to a new location.

Recurring Appointments and Events

When a calendar item has a recurring pattern, set up the item as a *recurring appointment* or *event* rather than just copying the item to another location. A recurring appointment or event is typically used for appointments or events that occur on a regular basis such as weekly sales meetings, monthly lunch socials, birthdays, or anniversaries.

A calendar item can be set to recur daily, weekly, monthly, or yearly. *Recurrence* pattern options include daily, weekly, monthly, or yearly. Select a range of recurrence option to end after a certain number of occurrences, end on a certain date, or have no end date.

▶ HOW TO: Create a Recurring Appointment or Event

1. Create a new calendar appointment.
2. Fill in the *Title*, *Location*, *Start time*, *End time*, and any other needed details in the body.
3. Click the **Recurrence** button in the *Options* group (Figure 4-14). The *Appointment Recurrence* dialog box opens (Figure 4-15).

Figure 4-14 *Recurrence* button

4. Confirm the correct start and end times in the *Appointment time* section.

5. Set the desired *Recurrence pattern*.

6. Select the *Range of recurrence* for *Start* and *End*.

7. Click **OK** to close the dialog box.

8. Click **Save & Close** to close the recurring appointment. A circling arrow icon appears on the appointment or event.

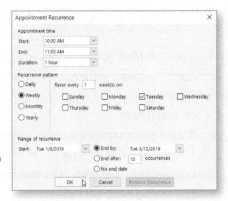

Figure 4-15 *Appointment Recurrence* dialog box

> ### ANOTHER WAY
>
> When a calendar item is open, **Ctrl+G** opens the *Appointment Recurrence* dialog box.

Recurring items can be edited. When you open a recurring calendar item, Outlook will give you two options. *Just this one* edits that specific calendar item without changing all the recurring items or recurrence pattern. *The entire series* edits the entire series of recurring calendar items (Figure 4-16).

Figure 4-16 *Open Recurring Item* dialog box

Delete a Calendar Item

You can delete calendar items by selecting the items to be removed from the calendar and either pressing the **Delete** key on your keyboard, clicking the **Delete** button on the *Appointment* tab, or right-clicking the calendar item and selecting **Delete**. A single click on a calendar item selects a calendar item and outlines it, while double-clicking a calendar item opens the item for editing.

When deleting a recurring item, you are given the options to either *Delete Occurrence* or *Delete Series*.

Deleted calendar items are stored in the *Deleted Items* folder in the *Mail* module and remain there until this folder is permanently emptied. If you delete a calendar item by mistake, open the *Deleted Items* folder and drag the calendar item from the *Deleted Items* folder to the *Calendar* button in the *Navigation* bar. The calendar item is restored to its correct location on the calendar.

> ### ANOTHER WAY
>
> **Ctrl+D** deletes a selected calendar item.

Create a Calendar Item from an Email

There may be times when you receive an email and would like to create a calendar item based on the information in that email. Rather than retyping all the information in the email, you can easily convert it to a calendar item.

▶HOW TO: Create a Calendar Item from an Email

1. Click the **Mail** button in the *Navigation* bar.
2. Click the email to be converted to a calendar item (do not open the email).
3. Drag and drop the email on the *Calendar* button in the *Navigation* bar. A plus sign displays while dragging the calendar item.
4. A new calendar appointment opens. The title is the same as the email subject, and the date is the current date. The body of the new calendar item will contain the information from the body of the email.
5. Edit the calendar item *Start* and *End* dates and times.
6. Edit the body of the calendar item.
7. Click **Save & Close**.

▶ **ANOTHER WAY**

Select or open an email, click the **Move** button in the *Move* group, and choose **Calendar**. A new calendar appointment opens. When you save and close the appointment window, the original email message will be moved to your *Deleted Items* folder.

PAUSE & PRACTICE: OUTLOOK 4-1

For this Pause & Practice project, you create calendar items for an upcoming meeting with your instructor regarding an assignment. You also create a recurring event for your friend's birthday with a reminder set a week in advance to ensure you have time to purchase a gift.

1. Create a new appointment.
   a. Click the **Calendar** button in the *Navigation* bar.
   b. Click the **New Appointment** button [*Home* tab, *New* group].
   c. Enter the following information for the new appointment:

   Title: Meeting for ENG 100 Paper
   Location: Hamilton Hall 303A
   Start time: Next week Monday's date, 9:00 AM
   End time: Next week Monday's day, 10:00 AM
   Body: Email copy of paper to the instructor by Friday.

   d. Click the **Reminder** drop-down arrow [*Appointment* tab, *Options* group].
   e. Select **3 days**.
   f. Click the **Save & Close** button (Figure 4-17).

2. Create a new appointment.
   a. Click the **New Appointment** button [*Home* tab, *New* group].
   b. Enter the following information for the new appointment:

   Title: Lynne's Birthday
   Location: None
   Start time: July 17 of the current year
   End time: July 17 of the current year

Click the **All day** check box.

Body: Buy Lynne a present. She likes sports and tech gadgets.

  c. Click the **Reminder** drop-down arrow [*Appointment* tab, *Options* group].

  d. Select **1 week**.

  e. Click the **Recurrence** button [*Event* tab, *Options* group].

  f. Click the **Yearly** radio button under *Recurrence pattern* and click **OK**.

  g. Click the **Save & Close** button (Figure 4-17).

3. Email the two calendar items to your instructor as Outlook items.

  a. Click the **Mail** button in the *Navigation* bar.

  b. Click the **New Email** button [*Home* tab, *New* group].

  c. Enter the following information in your message:

To: instructor's email address
Cc: your email address
Subject: Outlook Pause & Practice 4-1
Body: Hi [instructor name],

Attached are my calendar items for the Pause & Practice 4-1 exercise.

Sincerely,
[student name]

  d. Click the **Attach Item** button [*Message* tab, *Include* group] and select **Outlook Item**.

  e. Select the **Calendar** option and locate the two calendar items you created.

  f. Press the **Ctrl** key and select the two calendar items and click **OK**.

  g. Click **Send**.

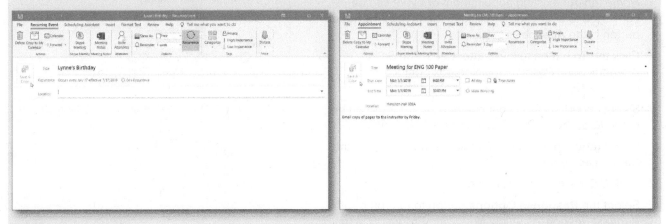

Figure 4-17 PP Outlook 4-1 completed

SLO 4.4   Creating and Using Meeting Requests

Suppose you are organizing a meeting within your company and you want to keep track of those who will be attending and those who are not able to attend the meeting. Outlook provides you with a calendar feature that not only creates a calendar appointment but also sends this appointment to others via email and tracks whether or not the recipients will attend the meeting.

Meeting requests are used to invite others to a meeting. It can be either an appointment or event. The advantage of using a meeting request over an email to invite attendees to a meeting is that the recipients receive a meeting invitation and are given the options to *Accept*, *Tentative*, *Decline*, or *Propose New Time*. When the recipient accepts the meeting request, the meeting is automatically added to the recipient's Outlook calendar and a response is sent to the sender of the meeting request. The meeting request will automatically track the attendees' responses.

> **MORE INFO**
>
> Tracking responses for meeting requests works only when used in an Exchange environment.

Create and Send a Meeting Request

Create a meeting request by clicking the **New Meeting** button on the *Home* tab or by selecting or opening an existing calendar item and clicking the **Invite Attendees** button in the *Attendees* group (Figure 4-18).

Figure 4-18 *Invite Attendees* button

> **MORE INFO**
>
> When sending a meeting request, provide a brief message and your name in the body.

▶ HOW TO: Create and Send a Meeting Request

1. Click the **New Meeting** button in the *New* group on the *Home* tab. An existing appointment or event can be converted to a meeting by clicking the **Invite Attendees** button in the *Attendees* group.

2. Click the **To** button to invite attendees. The *Select Attendees and Resources* dialog box opens (Figure 4-19).

3. Select attendees from your contacts. Attendees can be either *Required* or *Optional* to attend the meeting.

4. Select required resources for the meeting and click the **Resources** button.

5. Click **OK** to close the dialog box.

6. Select the **Response Options** button to turn on or off *Request Responses*, *Allow New Time Proposals*, and *Allow Forwarding*. By default, all options are turned on.

7. Fill in the *Title*, *Location*, *Start* and *End* times (date and time), and any additional information needed in the body (Figure 4-20).

8. Click **Send** to send the meeting request.

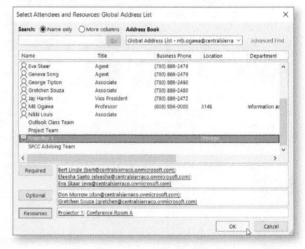

Figure 4-19 Select attendees

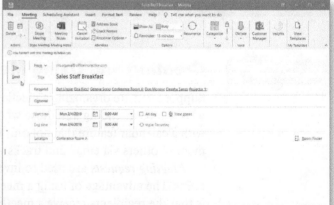

Figure 4-20 Filled meeting request

> **MORE INFO**
>
> When you open a new meeting request, it will always be an appointment. The meeting request can be changed to an event by clicking the **All day** check box.

> **MORE INFO**
>
> Resources and available rooms are set up by the Exchange administrator. If you do not see these options, your organization may not have set up resources on the server.

> **ANOTHER WAY**
>
> **Ctrl+Shift+Q** opens a new meeting request.

A meeting can also be created directly from a received email. When you receive an email and need to create a meeting based upon the information in that email, you do not have to go to your calendar to create a new meeting. Create a new meeting from this email by clicking the **Meeting** button in the *Respond* group on the *Message* tab (Figure 4-21). The contents of the email message display in the body of the new meeting window. You have the option to add attendees and make any other necessary changes before sending the meeting request.

Figure 4-21 Create a meeting request from an email message

> **ANOTHER WAY**
>
> **Ctrl+Alt+R** creates a new meeting from an existing email message.

> **MORE INFO**
>
> When creating a meeting from an email message, it is a good idea to edit and format the body of the meeting to enhance the appearance of this calendar item.

Respond to a Meeting Request

When you receive a meeting request, it arrives in your Inbox like other emails you receive. The Inbox icon for a meeting request will look different than an email icon by including a calendar with avatar icon.

When you open the meeting request, it will look similar to an email, but the *Respond* group includes four additional options: *Accept*, *Tentative*, *Decline*, or *Propose New Time*. When a response is selected, a dialog box opens with the following options: *Edit the Response Before Sending*, *Send the Response Now*, or *Do Not Send a Response*.

If you choose *Accept*, *Tentative*, or *Propose New Time*, the meeting request is removed from your Inbox and added to your calendar, and a response email is sent to the meeting organizer. If you choose *Decline*, the meeting request is moved from your Inbox to the *Deleted Items* folder, and a response is sent to the meeting organizer.

Calendar Preview inserts a snapshot of your calendar in the body of the meeting request which enables you to view existing calendar items on the day of the new meeting request. Double-clicking the calendar preview will take you to your calendar.

▶ HOW TO: Respond to a Meeting Request

1. Click the **Mail** button on the *Navigation* bar.
2. Open the meeting request from your Inbox.
3. Click one of the response buttons in the *Respond* group: **Accept**, **Decline**, or **Tentative**.
4. Choose **Edit the Response Before Sending** or **Send the Response Now** (Figure 4-22).
   - If you choose *Edit the Response Before Sending*, the email opens and you are able to enter a response in the body of the email before sending.
   - If you choose *Send the Response Now*, the response is automatically sent to the meeting organizer.
5. Click **OK** to close the dialog box.
6. Click **Send** if necessary. If you chose *Accept* or *Tentative*, the response is sent and the meeting request is removed from your Inbox and placed on your calendar.

Figure 4-22 Respond to a meeting request

▶ MORE INFO

It is probably best not to use the *Don't Send a Response* option. If you use this option, the meeting organizer will not know if you will attend the meeting.

Propose a New Time for a Meeting Request

If you are unable to attend a requested meeting at a particular date and time, you have the option of proposing a new time. When you click *Propose New Time* in the *Respond* group, you are given two options: *Tentative and Propose New Time* and *Decline and Propose New Time* (Figure 4-23). The *Propose New Time* dialog box opens. You can propose a new time by either dragging the meeting to a new time slot on the date and time timeline or entering a new date and time in the *Meeting start time* and *Meeting end time* boxes.

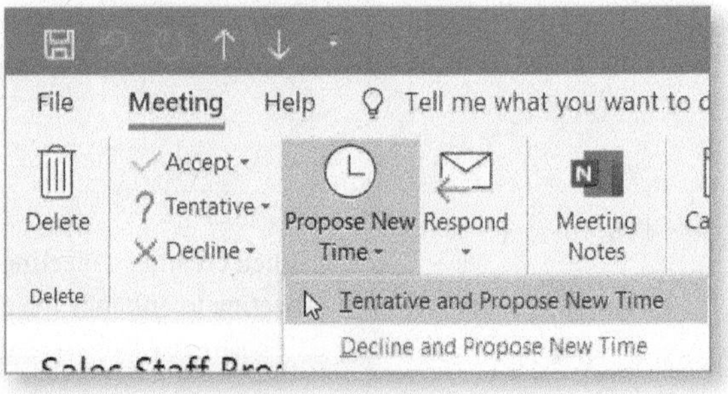

Figure 4-23 Propose a new meeting time

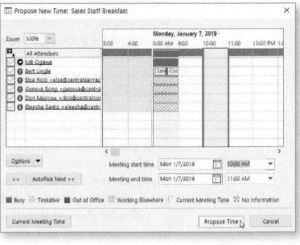

▶ HOW TO: Propose a New Time for a Meeting

1. Open the meeting request from your Inbox.
2. Click the **Propose New Time** button.
   - Choose either **Tentative and Propose New Time** or **Decline and Propose New Time**.
   - The *Propose New Time* dialog box opens (Figure 4-24).

Figure 4-24 *Propose New Time* dialog box

3. Edit the date and/or time.

4. Click **Propose Time**. A *New Time Proposed* Meeting request window opens. Notice the proposed changes below the subject line (Figure 4-25).

5. Type a brief message in the body.

6. Click **Send**. The response is sent, and the meeting request is removed from your Inbox and placed on your calendar.

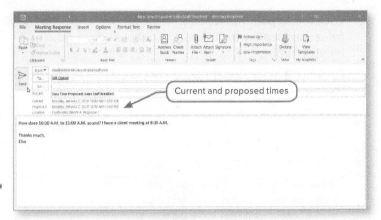

Figure 4-25 Proposed meeting time changes

> **MORE INFO**
>
> Outlook can automatically pick a new meeting time that accommodates your schedule and the other attendees' schedules. Using the *Scheduling Assistant* will be covered in chapter 9.

Track Meeting Request Respondents

When you organize a meeting and send a meeting request, you will receive meeting request responses in your Inbox (Figure 4-26). The responses will tell you the attendance status for each individual.

Outlook tracks the responses of those individuals who respond to a meeting request. When you open the meeting request from the calendar, Outlook displays a summary of responses in the *Info* bar above the *To* button. When using Outlook with an Exchange server, obtain more detailed tracking information by clicking the **Tracking** tab.

Figure 4-26 Meeting request acceptance in the Inbox

▶ **HOW TO: Track Meeting Request Respondents**

1. Select the *Calendar* module.

2. Open the meeting request you created (Figure 4-27).

3. The summary of responses received displays in the *Info* bar (Exchange users).

4. Click the **Tracking** tab. The body of the meeting request displays the names of those invited to the meeting, the attendance status (*Meeting Organizer, Required Attendance,* or *Optional Attendance*), and the response of each individual (Figure 4-28).

Figure 4-27 Open calendar item with meeting responses

5. Click the **Appointment** button in the *Show* group to close the tracking and return to the meeting request.

6. Click the **X** in the upper-right corner to close the meeting request.

Figure 4-28 Tracking status

> **ANOTHER WAY**
>
> When you open any of the meeting request responses you received in your Inbox, a summary of responses display above the body of the message.

> **MORE INFO**
>
> New in Outlook is the ability for all meeting invitees to track responses. You do not need to depend on the meeting creator to see the current status.

> **MORE INFO**
>
> When viewing the tracking of a meeting request, you can copy the tracking status to the clipboard and paste it into Excel.

Change and Update a Meeting Request

It is not uncommon for a meeting to have to be rescheduled to a different day, time, or location. Also, you might need to invite additional attendees to a previously scheduled meeting. The meeting organizer can make changes to the meeting and add attendees. When this is done, a *meeting update* must be sent to attendees. Attendees will again be given the option of accepting or declining the changes to the meeting.

> **HOW TO: Change and Update a Meeting Request**

1. Select the *Calendar* module and open the meeting request you created.

2. Change the meeting date and time or location if necessary (Figure 4-29).

3. Click the **Contact Attendees** button in the *Attendees* group on the *Meeting* tab. Add or remove attendees, send a new email message, or send a reply message.

4. Click **Send Update** after making any necessary changes. Changes are saved to the meeting on your calendar.

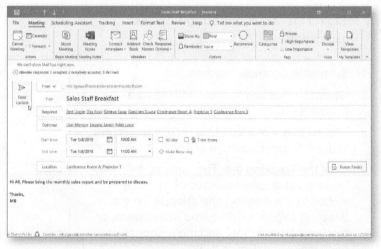

Figure 4-29 Updated meeting location and time

> **MORE INFO**
>
> If attendees are added to or deleted from an existing meeting, you will be given the options of *Send updates to only added or deleted attendees* or *Send update to all attendees*.

Cancel a Scheduled Meeting

Only the meeting organizer can cancel a meeting. When a meeting is canceled, all the attendees will receive a meeting cancellation email. The meeting is removed from your calendar, and the attendees will have the option of removing the meeting from their calendars.

> **MORE INFO**
>
> When you are the meeting organizer (creator), Outlook will not allow you to delete a meeting without sending a meeting cancellation email.

▶ HOW TO: Cancel a Meeting

1. Select the *Calendar* module and open the meeting request.
2. Click the **Cancel Meeting** button in the *Actions* group (Figure 4-30). The *Send Update* button becomes a *Send Cancellation* button, and a message displays in the *Info* bar.
3. Click the **Send Cancellation** button. The meeting request is removed from your calendar, and all those invited to the meeting will receive an email notifying them of the meeting cancellation.

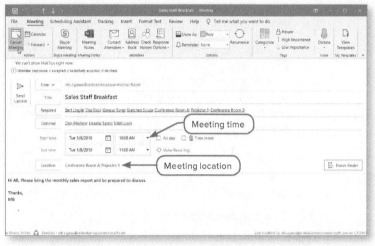

Figure 4-30 *Cancel Meeting* button

PAUSE & PRACTICE: OUTLOOK 4-2

For this Pause & Practice project, you follow up with the two calendar items you created in Pause & Practice 4-1. You had an emergency at home, so you decide to cancel the initial meeting and send a new meeting request to your instructor to apologize for not being able to make the meeting and to reschedule. You also send a meeting request to have lunch with your friend Lynne to give her the gift you purchased.

1. Click the **Calendar** button in the *Navigation* bar.
2. Delete the initial appointment with your instructor regarding the ENG 100 paper.
   a. Double-click the original meeting.
   b. Click the **Delete** button [*Appointment* tab, *Actions* group].
3. Create and send a meeting request to your instructor regarding the ENG 100 paper.
   a. Click the **New Meeting** button [*Home* tab, *New* group].
   b. Enter the following information for the new meeting request:

   To: Instructor's email address
   Title: Reschedule meeting for ENG 100 paper
   Location: Hamilton Hall 303A

Start time: One day after your initial meeting, 9:00 AM
End time: One day after your initial meeting, 10:00 AM
Body: Hi [instructor name],

My apologies; an emergency occurred at home and I need to reschedule our meeting. Are you available on Tuesday at the same time? Please use the meeting request response so that it can automatically be added to our calendars.

Thanks much,
[your name]

   c. Click the **Send** button.

4. Create and send a meeting request to Lynne regarding her birthday.
   a. Click the **New Meeting** button [*Home* tab, *New* group].
   b. Enter the following information for the new meeting request:

     To: A partner's email address
     Title: Birthday Lunch
     Location: ARC Student Center Cafe
     Start time: July 17 of the current year at noon
     End time: July 17 of the current year at 1:00 PM
     Body: Hi Lynne,

Are you available for lunch on your birthday? My treat; let's eat at the ARC Student Center Cafe. Use the meeting request response so that it can automatically be added to our calendars.

[your name]

   c. Click the **Send** button.

5. Open the meeting request to Lynne that you received from your partner.

6. Propose a new meeting time.
   a. Click the **Propose New Time** button [*Meeting* tab, *Respond* group] and select **Tentative and Propose New Time**.
   b. Select **2:00 PM** as the meeting start time and **3:00 PM** as the meeting end time.
   c. Click the **Propose Time** button.
   d. In the body, type: Hi [partner name],

Sorry, I have lunch plans with my mother. How about coffee at the ARC Student Center Café at 2:00 PM?

Lynne

   e. Click the **Send** button.

7. Locate the message from your partner and open it.

8. Forward the message proposed time message from your partner to your instructor.
   a. Click the **Forward** button [*Meeting Request* tab, *Respond* group].
   b. Enter the following information in the message:

     To: Instructor's email address
     Cc: Your email address
     Subject: Outlook Pause & Practice 4-2
     Body: A short message indicating that you submitted your Pause & Practice project

c. Click the **Send** button (Figure 4-31).

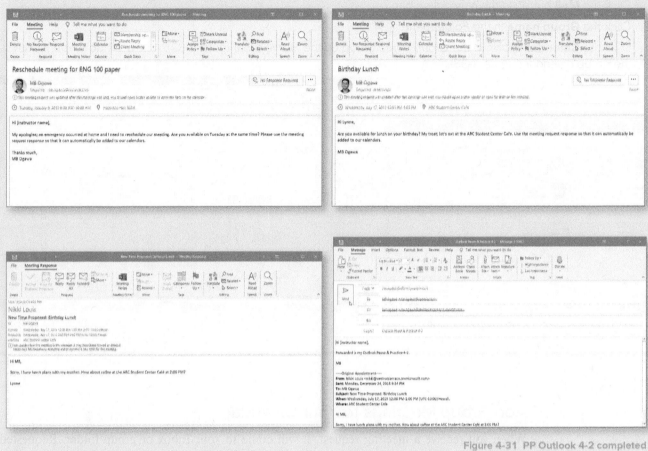

Figure 4-31 PP Outlook 4-2 completed

Working with Group Calendars

Calendars also work with the *Group* feature on Exchange servers. A *group calendar* is shared with all group members and is separate from each individual's calendar. Therefore, those working in groups should be sure to check both the group calendar and their personal calendar for appointments and meetings.

The group calendar works similarly to the calendar, where you create meeting requests, respond to meeting requests, propose new times, track meeting requests, and update meeting requests. One important difference is that the group calendar does not include individual appointments, as a group calendar is shared among multiple users. If you create a new appointment in a group calendar, Outlook will create it as a meeting request for the group.

Accessing the Group Calendar

Since all of the features of the group calendar are similar to the calendar, this section will focus on accessing the group calendar and adding group meetings to your personal calendar.

▶HOW TO: Access the Group Calendar

1. Click the **Mail** button in the *Navigation* bar.
2. Click the **Group name** in the *Folder* pane.
3. Click the **Calendar** button in the *Group name* group on the *Home* tab (Figure 4-32). A new window opens with the group calendar (Figure 4-33).

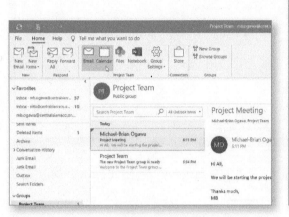

Figure 4-32 Select group

Figure 4-33 Group calendar

Add Group Meetings to Your Calendar

When you receive a meeting request, it will come to your Inbox or group folder. Requested meetings appear in your calendar slightly transparent, as they have not been added to your calendar (Figure 4-34). You can accept the meeting request from your Inbox or the calendar item (Figure 4-35).

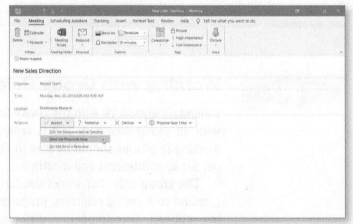

Figure 4-35 Accept group meeting

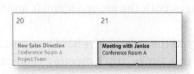

Figure 4-34 Tentative calendar item on the left

> **MORE INFO**
>
> You can display your calendar next to the group calendar by clicking the check box next to the group calendar in the *Folder* pane. This makes it easier to compare your schedule when creating or responding to meeting requests (Figure 4-36).

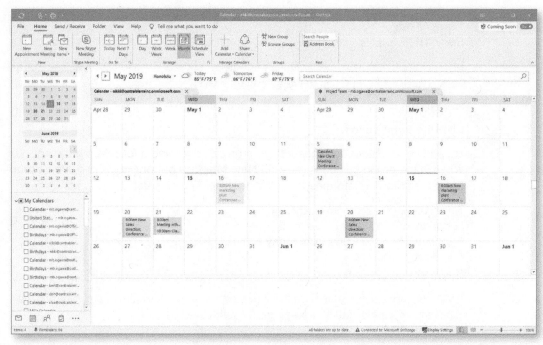

Figure 4-36 Side-by-side calendar display

PAUSE & PRACTICE: OUTLOOK 4-3

For this Pause & Practice project, you follow up by creating a group and a group calendar item. You had an emergency at home, so you decide to create a group with all of your instructors for the semester and create a group calendar item for the dates that you will be unavailable. You send a meeting request to your instructors to apologize for missing class and would like to set up a meeting with everyone. This Pause & Practice project works only with Exchange servers.

1. Click the **People** button in the *Navigation* bar.

2. Create a Group named **Course Instructors**.
   a. Click the **New Group** button. The *Create Group* dialog box opens.
   b. Type Course Instructors in the *Name* field.
   c. Type Current Semester in the *Description* field.
   d. Select **Private - Only approved members can see what's inside**.
   e. Click the option **Send all group email and events to members' inboxes. They can change this setting later**.
   f. Click **Create**.
   g. Add your instructor and a partner to the *Group*.

3. Create and send a meeting request to your group regarding the emergency.
   a. Click the **Calendar** button on the *Navigation* bar.
   b. Click the **Course Instructors calendar** check box in the *Folder* pane.
   c. Uncheck your calendar. Only the *Course Instructors* calendar is displayed.
   d. Click the **New Meeting** button [*Home* tab, *New* group].
   e. Enter the following information for the new meeting request:

   Title: Home Emergency
   Location: none
   Start time: Next week Monday
   End time: Next week Friday

Time: All day
Body: Hi [instructor names],

My apologies; the emergency at home was much more serious than expected. I will be absent for the entire week. I have created a group to ensure everyone receives updates.

[your name]

   f. Click the **Send** button.

4. Create and send a meeting request to your group regarding a follow-up meeting.
   a. While in the group calendar, click the **New Meeting** button [*Home* tab, *New* group].
   b. Enter the following information for the new meeting request:

Title: Follow-up meeting to emergency
Location: ARC Student Center Cafe
Start time: Two Mondays from today at 10:00 AM
End time: 11:00 AM
Body: Hi [instructor names],

I was wondering if everyone is available to meet on the date listed in the group calendar? I would like to explain my situation and discuss options for your classes.

Thank you,
[your name]

   c. Click the **Send** button.

5. Accept the second meeting request from a partner for two Mondays from today.
   a. Click the **Calendar** button in *Navigation* bar.
   b. Double-click the transparent meeting request.
   c. Click **Accept** and **Send the Response Now**. The group calendar should look similar to Figure 4-37.

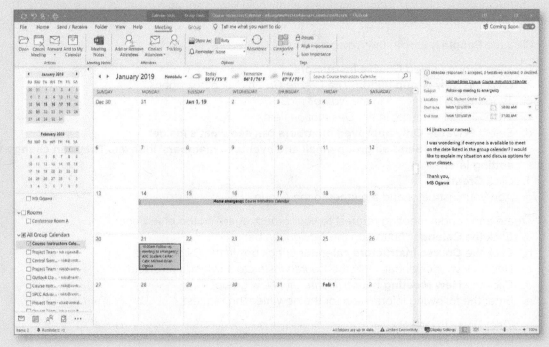

Figure 4-37 PP Outlook 4-3 completed

Chapter Summary

4.1 Understand the different types of calendar items (p. O4-139).

- An Outlook calendar can be viewed by day, week, month, or other formats unlike paper-based calendars.
- The *date navigator* is a thumbnail display of the monthly calendar in the *Folder* pane.
- You can receive reminders for appointments or events on your computer or mobile device.
- Calendar items can recur at regular intervals.
- Meeting requests can be used to invite others and track their responses.
- Calendars can be synchronized with phones and other mobile devices.
- There are three main types of calendar items: appointments, events, and meeting requests.
- An *appointment* is a calendar item that has a duration of less than 24 hours.
- *Events* are those calendar items that last for 24 hours or more.
- A *meeting request* is used to create a calendar item and to invite others to this meeting.

4.2 Navigate between different calendar views (p. O4-140).

- Calendars can be displayed in *Day*, *Week*, *Month*, or *Schedule* views.
- *Day view* displays the calendar one day at a time with the calendar divided into half-hour segments.
- *Week view* displays the calendar as a *Work Week* or *Week* and divides the calendar into half-hour segments. The work week is Monday through Friday, while the week is Sunday through Saturday.
- *Month view* displays an entire month of the calendar.
- *Schedule view* displays your calendar horizontally in timeline view in the *Content area*.

4.3 Create and edit calendar items (p. O4-143).

- Appointments and events can include a *Title*, *Location*, *Start time*, *End time*, and additional information in the body.
- Appointments can be converted to events by clicking the **All day** check box.

- You can add *reminders* to appointments and events to alert you prior to their start times.
- Calendar items can be *moved* or *copied*.
- *Recurring appointments* or *events* can be used for items that occur on a regular schedule such as a weekly meeting or a birthday.
- You can drag and drop an email message to the *Calendar* button to create a new calendar item from an email message.

4.4 Create and use meeting requests (p. O4-149).

- *Meeting requests* are used to invite others to a meeting (appointment or event).
- Recipients of meeting requests can respond in the following ways: *Accept, Tentative, Decline,* or *Propose New Time*.
- The *Calendar Preview* inserts a snapshot of your calendar into the meeting request and enables you to view appointments and events on the day and time of the meeting request.
- You can reply to an email message with a meeting request.
- Selecting *Accept, Tentative,* and *Propose New Time* places the meeting time in your calendar.
- Outlook tracks your invitees' responses to your meeting request.
- You can update a meeting and automatically send a *meeting update* message to all recipients. This will give all attendees the option of accepting or declining the meeting.
- Canceling a meeting will delete it from your calendar.
- When you receive a meeting cancellation, the meeting is marked as canceled in your calendar. You can manually delete the meeting from your calendar since it is not automatically removed with the cancellation.

4.5 Work with group calendars (p. O4-157).

- *Group calendars* are a shared calendar for groups.
- Group meetings are partially transparent in your calendar until they are accepted.
- Group appointments are created as meetings because they are shared among the group members.

- Group calendars work similarly to calendars with meeting requests and include the following responses to requests: *Accept*, *Tentative*, *Decline*, or *Propose New Time*.
- You can reply to group meeting requests from your Inbox or from the calendar item.

Check for Understanding

The SIMbook for this text (within your SIMnet account), provides the following resources for concept review:

- Multiple-choice questions
- Short answer questions
- Matching exercises

Guided Project 4-1

For this project, you are an administrative assistant at Courtyard Medical Plaza. You manage calendars for several doctors and make appointments on the phone throughout the day. You use Outlook's calendar feature to keep the appointments organized. Today, you received two appointment requests from patients and recorded them on the calendar.
[Student Learning Outcomes 4.1, 4.2, 4.3]

Skills Covered in This Project

- Create a new appointment.
- Select start and end times.
- Edit the body of an appointment.
- Set a reminder.

1. Create a new appointment.
   a. Click the **Calendar** button in the *Navigation* bar.
   b. Click the check box next to your calendar in the *Folder* pane.
   c. Uncheck all other calendars to ensure only your personal calendar is displayed.
   d. Select the next day on the calendar.
   e. Click the **New Appointment** button [*Home* tab, *New* group].
   f. Enter the following information for the new appointment:

   Title: Jim Heely (Dr. Greg Lam)
   Location: Exam Room 1
   Start time: Tomorrow at 8:00 AM
   End time: Tomorrow at 9:00 AM
   Body: Sore throat, cough, fever, nausea

   g. Click the **Reminder** drop-down menu [*Appointment* tab, *Options* group].
   h. Select **5 minutes**.
   i. Click the **Save & Close** button.

2. Create a new appointment.
   a. Click the **New Appointment** button [*Home* tab, *New* group].
   b. Enter the following information for the new appointment:

   Title: Janice Yoro (Dr. Shirley Louis)
   Location: Exam Room 3
   Start time: Next week Tuesday at 1:00 PM
   End time: Next week Tuesday at 2:00 PM
   Body: Annual check up

   c. Click the **Reminder** drop-down menu [*Appointment* tab, *Options* group].
   d. Select **5 minutes**.
   e. Click the **Save & Close** button.

3. Email the two calendar items to your instructor as Outlook items.
   a. Click the **Mail** button in the *Navigation* bar.
   b. Click the **New Email** button [*Home* tab, *New* group].
   c. Enter the following information in your message:

   To: instructor's email address
   Cc: your email address

Subject: Outlook Guided Project 4-1
Body: Hi [instructor name],

Attached are my calendar items for the Guided Project 4-1 exercise.

Sincerely,
[your name]

 d. Click the **Attach Item** button [*Message* tab, *Include* group] and select **Outlook Item**.
 e. Select the **Calendar** option and locate the two calendar items you created.
 f. Press the **Ctrl** key, select the two calendar items, and click **OK**.
 g. Click **Send** (Figure 4-38).

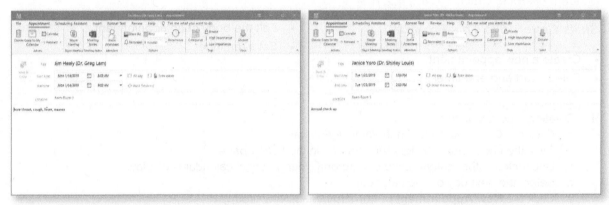

Figure 4-38 Guided Project 4-1 completed

Guided Project 4-2

For this project, you send meeting requests to two doctors to ensure they know when they are seeing their patients. Drs. Lam and Louis also indicated that they want to set up weekly meetings, so you create a recurring calendar item for the weekly meeting and send the request to both of them.
[Student Learning Outcomes 4.1, 4.2, 4.3, 4.4]

Skills Covered in This Project

- Create a new appointment.
- Select start and end times.
- Edit the body of an appointment.
- Set a reminder.
- Set recurrence.
- Send a meeting request.

1. Send a meeting request to Dr. Lam for the upcoming appointment.
   a. Open the appointment with the Title "***Jim Heely (Dr. Greg Lam)***."
   b. Click the **Invite Attendees** button [*Appointment* tab, *Attendees* group].
   c. Type a partner's email address in the *To* field.
   d. Click the **Send** button.

2. Send a meeting request to Dr. Louis for the upcoming appointment.
   a. Open the appointment with the Title "***Janice Yoro (Dr. Shirley Louis)***."
   b. Click the **Invite Attendees** button [*Appointment* tab, *Attendees* group].
   c. Type a partner's email address in the *To* field.
   d. Click the **Send** button.

3. Create a new appointment.
   a. Click the **Calendar** button in the *Navigation* bar.
   b. Click the **New Appointment** button [*Home* tab, *New* group].
   c. Enter the following information for the new appointment:

   Title: Weekly Doctors' Meeting
   Location: Conference Room
   Start time: Mondays at 3:00 PM
   End time: Mondays at 4:00 PM
   Body: See agenda sent by administrative assistant.

   d. Click the **Reminder** drop-down menu [*Appointment* tab, *Options* group].
   e. Select **30 minutes**.
   f. Click **Recurrence** to open the *Appointment Recurrence* dialog box.
      - Select **Weekly** on **Monday** under *Recurrence pattern*.
      - Click **OK**.
   g. Click the **Invite Attendees** button [*Appointment* tab, *Attendees* group].
   h. Type a partner's email address in the *To* field.
   i. Click the **Send** button.

4. Email the three meeting requests to your instructor as Outlook items.
   a. Click the **Mail** button in the *Navigation* bar.
   b. Click the **New Email** button [*Home* tab, *New* group].
   c. Enter the following information in your message:

   To: Instructor's email address
   Cc: Your email address
   Subject: Outlook Guided Project 4-2
   Body: Hi [instructor name],

   Attached are my meeting requests for the Guided Project 4-2 exercise.

   Sincerely,
   [your name]

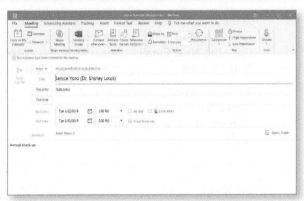

   d. Click the **Attach Item** button [*Message* tab, *Include* group] and select **Outlook Item**.
   e. Select the **Sent Items** option and locate the three meeting requests you sent.
   f. Press the **Ctrl** key and select the three sent mail items and click **OK**.
   g. Click the **Send** button (Figure 4-39).

Figure 4-39 Guided Project 4-2 completed

Guided Project 4-3

For this project, you must cancel an appointment for Jim, who stated that he was not feeling well enough to come to his appointment. You must also reschedule Janice's annual appointment for the next day, as she just found out that she is in charge of snacks for her son's baseball game.
[Student Learning Outcomes 4.1, 4.2, 4.3, 4.4]

Skills Covered in This Project

- Cancel a meeting request.
- Respond to a meeting request.
- Update a meeting request.
- Accept a meeting request.
- Track meeting request responses.

1. Cancel Jim Heely's appointment and send the cancellation to Dr. Lam.
   a. Open the appointment with the title "*Jim Heely (Dr. Greg Lam)*."
   b. Click the **Cancel Meeting** button [*Meeting* tab, *Actions* group].
   c. Click the **Send Cancellation** button.

2. Update Janice Yoro's appointment date.
   a. Open the appointment with the title "*Janice Yoro (Dr. Shirley Louis)*."
   b. Change the start and end time to be Wednesday (keep the same time).
   c. Click the **Send Update** button.

3. Accept the *Weekly Doctors'* meeting request you received.
   a. Open the email with the title "*Weekly Doctors' Meeting*."
   b. Click the **Accept** button [*Meeting* tab, *Respond* group] and select **Send the Response Now**.

4. Click your initial message to ensure you received a response from your partner.

5. Email the three meeting requests to your instructor as Outlook items.
   a. Click the **Mail** button in the *Navigation* bar.
   b. Click the **New Email** button [*Home* tab, *New* group].
   c. Enter the following information in your message:

   To: instructor's email address
   Cc: your email address
   Subject: Outlook Guided Project 4-3
   Body: Hi [instructor name],

   Attached are my meeting requests for the Guided Project 4-3 exercise.

   Sincerely,
   [your name]

   d. Click the **Attach Item** button [*Message* tab, *Include* group] and select **Outlook Item**.
   e. Select the **Sent Items** option and locate the meeting cancellation, updated time, and acceptance you sent.
   f. Press the **Ctrl** key and select the three sent mail items and click **OK**.
   g. Click the **Send** button (Figure 4-40).

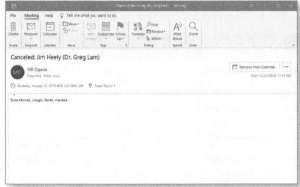

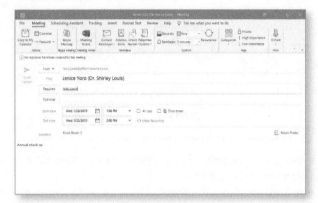

Figure 4-40 Guided Project 4-3 completed

Independent Project 4-4

For this project, you work as a dispatcher for Central Sierra Insurance (CSI). As a dispatcher, you make and receive many calls to and from clients and arrange meetings. You collaborate with a team of insurance agents. You use Outlook's group calendar to help you better organize CSI's schedule. This Independent Project is completed using an Exchange server.
[Student Learning Outcomes 4.1, 4.2, 4.5]

Skills Covered in This Project

- Create a group.
- Create a new appointment.

- Create a new event.
- Select start and end times.
- Edit the body of an appointment.
- Set a reminder.

1. Create a group named *Central Sierra Insurance Agents*. Set the privacy to public and subscribe members to receive messages in their Inbox.

2. Add your instructor and two partners to the group.

3. Create the following meetings in the *Central Sierra Insurance Agents* group calendar:

Title	Location	Start time	End time	Body	Reminder
Strategic Planning Agent: All members	Conference Room A	Next week Friday, All day	Next week Friday, All day	Prepare slides	1 Day
Dorilyn Sharuma (New Client) Agent: Shawn	3A	Next week Monday, 9:00 AM	Next week Monday, 11:00 AM	New customer packet	15 Minutes
Matthew Schmidt (client for 5 years) Agent: Jane	3A	Next week Tuesday, 1:00 PM	Next week Tuesday, 2:00 PM	Client just got married. New insurance options.	30 Minutes
Janine Shephard (client for 3 years) Agent: Shawn	3A	Next week Monday, 2:00 PM	Next week Monday, 3:00 PM	Review current policy to see where she can lower payments.	30 Minute
Clint Howard (Manager) Agent: All members	Mario's Italian Restaurant	Next week Thursday, 12:00 PM	Next week Thursday, 1:30 PM	Lunch meeting about current clients	2 Hours

4. Email the five calendar items you created to your instructor as email attachments.
   a. Include your email address in the *Cc* field.
   b. Add a short message indicating that the five Outlook calendar items are attached in the message.
   c. Change the subject of your message to Outlook Independent Project 4-4 (Figure 4-41).

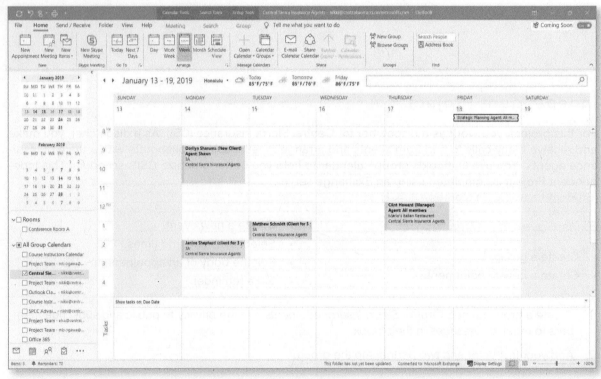

Figure 4-41 Independent Project 4-4 completed

Independent Project 4-5

For this project, you categorize all of the calendar items for CSI. You also send out meeting requests to others to ensure everyone is in agreement. You request that your colleague take one of your appointments, as you forgot that you had a doctor's appointment when you decided to meet with Janine because you did not centralize all of your personal and work appointments on one calendar. Since this is completed on a group calendar, an Exchange server is required for this project.
[Student Learning Outcomes 4.1, 4.2, 4.4, 4.5]

Skills Covered in This Project

- Create a category.
- Apply categories to calendar items.
- Accept meeting requests.
- Modify messages for meeting requests.
- Update a meeting request.

1. Create a new category called Central Sierra Insurance.

2. Apply the category to the five appointments you created in *Independent Project 4-4*.

3. Accept the strategic planning meeting request from your partners.

4. Accept the *Clint Howard (Manager)* request from your partners.

5. Modify the *Janine Shephard* meeting by updating the agent to Jane in the title field and request that he or she take the meeting. Shawn forgot that he had a doctor's appointment at that time. Be sure to include a message indicating why you would like Jane to meet with Shawn's client.

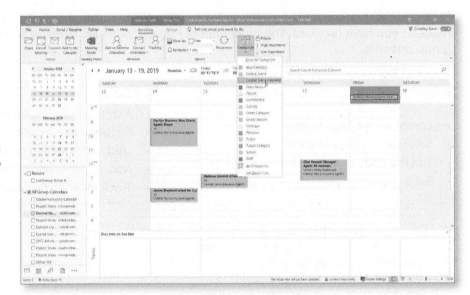

6. Email your instructor with your five calendar items as attachments.
    a. Include your email address in the Cc field.
    b. Add a short message indicating that the five Outlook calendar items are attached in the message.
    c. Change the subject of your message to Outlook Independent Project 4-5 (Figure 4-42).

Figure 4-42 Independent Project 4-5 completed

Independent Project 4-6

For this project, you add your weekly sales meeting to your calendar. You also respond to the meeting requests you have received. This Independent Project continues to utilize an Exchange server with the group calendar.

[Student Learning Outcomes 4.1, 4.2, 4.3, 4.4, 4.5]

Skills Covered in This Project

- Create a new appointment.
- Select start and end times.
- Edit the body of an appointment.
- Set a reminder.

- Set recurrence.
- Apply categories to calendar items.
- Respond to a meeting request.
- Update a meeting request.
- Accept a meeting request.
- Track meeting request responses.

1. Create a new meeting with the following information:
   Title: Weekly Sales Meeting Agent: All members
   Location: Conference Room B
   Start time: Next week Thursday, 4:00 PM
   End time: Next week Thursday, 5:00 PM
   Reminder: 15 minutes
   Recurrence: Weekly with no end date
   Category: Central Sierra Insurance

2. Open the "Dorilyn Sharuma" meeting request and tentatively accept and propose a new time 8:30 AM to 11:00 AM. Indicate that Shawn should arrive 30 minutes early to review the New Customer Packet for Home Owners, as opposed to car insurance.

3. Email your instructor with the "Weekly Sales Meeting" and updated "Dorilyn Sharuma" calendar items as attachments.
   a. Include your email address in the *Cc* field.
   b. Add a short message indicating that the five Outlook calendar items are attached in the message.
   c. Change the subject of your message to Outlook Independent Project 4-6 (Figure 4-43).

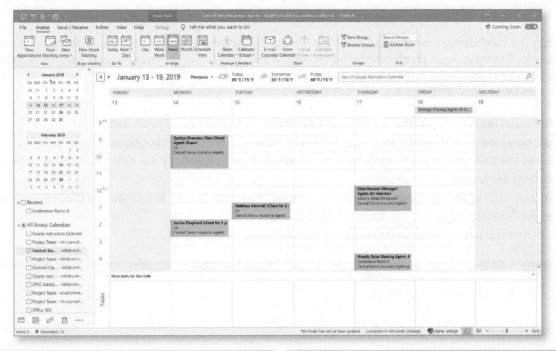

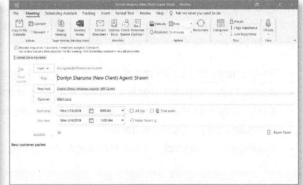

Figure 4-43 Independent Project 4-6 completed

Challenge Project 4-7

Create a personal calendar for your current school, work, and personal schedules for the semester. Be sure to include items such as classes, work, appointments, and events such as birthdays or anniversaries. [Student Learning Outcomes 4.1, 4.2, 4.3]

- Include your class schedule for the semester.
- Include your work schedule if applicable.
- Include events such as birthdays or anniversaries.
- Use *Recurrence pattern* options when applicable.
- Email the calendar to your instructor as an email attachment. Specify the dates to include within the current semester.
- Change the subject of your message to Outlook Challenge Project 4-7.

Challenge Project 4-8

Modify the calendar you created in *Challenge Project 4-7* by adding categories and sending out meeting requests. Create at least three categories (school, work, personal). You may include additional categories, such as clubs. Send at least three meeting requests to a partner in class.
[Student Learning Outcomes 4.1, 4.2, 4.3, 4.4]

- Create at least three categories for your calendar and apply them to each item.
- Set up at least three meetings with a partner in class and send the meeting requests.
- Email the calendar to your instructor as an email attachment. Specify the dates to include within the current semester.
- Attach each of the meeting requests to your email message (attach each meeting request message as an Outlook item).
- Change the subject of your message to Outlook Challenge Project 4-8.

Challenge Project 4-9

Modify the calendar you created in *Challenge Project 4-8* by responding to meeting requests. For the three meeting requests you received, accept one, decline one, and propose a new time for the third one.
[Student Learning Outcomes 4.1, 4.2, 4.4]

- Respond to the three meeting requests you received in *Challenge Project 4-8*.
- Accept one request, decline a request, and propose a new time for the final request.
- Attach each of the meeting request responses to your email message (attach each meeting request message as an Outlook item).
- Change the subject of your message to Outlook Challenge Project 4-9.

Source of screenshots Microsoft Office 365 (2019): Word, Excel, Access, PowerPoint, Outlook.

Tasks, To-Do Items, and User Interface

OUTLOOK

CHAPTER OVERVIEW

So far in this text, we have covered the Outlook working environment and three of the four major components of Outlook: Email, Contacts, and Calendar. The fourth major component of Outlook is Tasks.

Many people have a list of tasks to accomplish on any given day or week and enjoy the satisfaction of crossing off tasks that they have completed. Outlook provides a tool that can be used to keep track of your daily tasks. The Tasks feature maintains a running list of tasks to be completed. As with calendar items and contacts, Outlook Tasks provides users with many electronic benefits not available on a paper list of tasks, such as electronic reminders, categories, and recurrence. Outlook also allows you to customize the user interface to better meet your needs and preferences.

STUDENT LEARNING OUTCOMES (SLOs)

After completing this chapter, you will be able to:

SLO 5.1   Distinguish between tasks and To-Do items (p. O5-174).

SLO 5.2   Create and use tasks in Outlook (p. O5-175).

SLO 5.3   Understand and customize the *Tasks* views and the *To-Do* bar (p. O5-184).

SLO 5.4   Assign tasks to and accept tasks from other Outlook users (p. O5-186).

SLO 5.5   Customize the user interface in Outlook (p. O5-192).

CASE STUDY

For the Pause & Practice projects, you are in the early stages of working on a group project for a class in which you are enrolled. You take the lead and create tasks for yourself to complete to prepare the group to work together. However, you forgot about a doctor's appointment and need to assign a task to a colleague to help you complete it before its due date.

Pause & Practice 5-1: You create assignments based on a class project. You initially set up a few tasks to prepare for group work.

With a partner, you exchange email and create a task from an email message.

Pause & Practice 5-2: You forgot about a doctor's appointment and assign a task to a group member. You also accept tasks, send updates, and complete a task.

Pause & Practice 5-3: You customize Outlook by selecting *Outlook Today* as your default start screen, add your Inbox to your *Favorites*, and add the *Print* button to the *Quick Access* toolbar.

Understanding Tasks and To-Do Items

Tasks and *To-Do items* are closely related, yet there are distinct differences. Tasks are those individual items that are kept in the *Tasks* area of Outlook and also appear in the list of To-Do items.

To-Do items are a much broader category of Outlook items. Any email or contact that has a *Flag for Recipient* or includes a *Follow Up* flag will also appear in the *To-Do List* and *To-Do* bar. So, To-Do items are the broader umbrella category under which tasks are included.

View the *Task List* by clicking the **Task** button in the *Navigation* bar. Click **To-Do List** or **Tasks** to display the tasks.

Tasks

A task in Outlook can be created to remind you to make a follow-up phone call for an upcoming fundraiser event or to order theater tickets when they go on sale Wednesday. When a task is created,

Figure 5-1 *Task List*

Outlook automatically marks the task with a *Follow Up* flag and the task appears in both the *Task List* (Figure 5-1) and the *To-Do List*.

Task List

The *Task List* is a list of the tasks you have created in Outlook. This list appears in the *Content area* when you click the **Tasks** button on the *Navigation* bar and select **Tasks** in the *My Tasks* area of the *Folder* pane. The *Task List* includes only tasks and does not include other flagged items in Outlook.

Flagged Items

You may need to take additional action on an email you received or with a client in your *Contacts*. In addition to a task, which is automatically flagged in Outlook, emails and contacts can also be flagged for follow up. This feature in Outlook provides you with the option of flagging these Outlook items as an additional reminder. When an item is flagged, it appears as a To-Do item.

> **MORE INFO**
>
> Depending on the types of email accounts you have set up, you might have more than one *Task List* in the *My Tasks* area of the *Folder* pane. Also, you can create additional task folders.

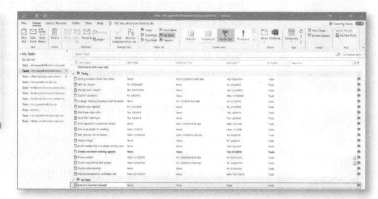

Figure 5-2 *To-Do List*

To-Do List

As mentioned previously, the *To-Do List* (Figure 5-2) is a more comprehensive list of items than the *Task List*. The *To-Do List* includes all Outlook items that have been marked with a flag, which includes tasks, emails, and contacts. The *To-Do List* is available in the

My Tasks area in the *Folder* pane of *Tasks*. When the *To-Do List* is selected, the list of To-Do items appears at the right in the *Content area*.

> ▶ **MORE INFO**
>
> The icon for each item in the *To-Do List* identifies the type of Outlook item.

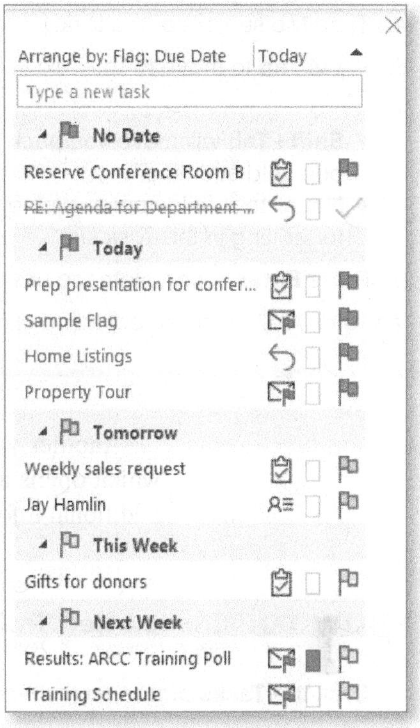

To-Do Bar

The **To-Do bar** (Figure 5-3) is located to the right of the *Content area* in Outlook and can be displayed in all the Outlook modules (*Mail*, *Calendar*, *Contacts*, *Tasks*, *Notes*, and *Journal*). The *To-Do* bar includes a date navigator (calendar thumbnail), upcoming calendar items, and To-Do items. The *To-Do* bar can be customized to show different amounts of information and can be turned on or off [*View* tab, *Layout* group, *To-Do Bar* button, *Tasks*].

Arrange by: Flag: Due Date | Today ▲

Type a new task

◢ ⚑ **No Date**
Reserve Conference Room B
~~RE: Agenda for Department ...~~

◢ ⚑ **Today**
Prep presentation for confer...
Sample Flag
Home Listings
Property Tour

◢ ⚑ **Tomorrow**
Weekly sales request
Jay Hamlin

◢ ⚑ **This Week**
Gifts for donors

◢ ⚑ **Next Week**
Results: ARCC Training Poll
Training Schedule

Figure 5-3 *To-Do* bar

SLO 5.2

Creating and Using Tasks

Creating a task is similar to creating a new email or calendar item and is accomplished in a couple of different ways. The benefits of Outlook tasks, compared to a paper list of tasks, are the ability to include additional details with the task, start and due dates, reminders, and recurrence.

Tasks can also be created from existing information in Outlook. If you receive an email about an upcoming fundraiser for which you are involved, you are able to create a task from the information included in the email. This can also be done from a calendar item.

> ▶ **MORE INFO**
>
> When you click the **Tasks** button on the *Navigation* bar, by default the *To-Do List* is selected in the *My Tasks* area of the *Folder* pane and this list appears in the *Content area*. To access *Tasks*, click the **Tasks** folder in the *My Tasks* area of the *Folder* pane.

Create a New Task

The quickest way to create a new task is to simply type the subject of the task in the *Click here to add a new Task* area above the list of tasks in the *Content area*.

▶**HOW TO:** Create a New Task in the Content area

1. Click the **Tasks** button on the *Navigation* bar.
2. Click the **Tasks** folder in the *My Tasks* area of the *Folder* pane.

3. Click the **Click here to add a new Task** area above the *Task List* in the *Content area* (Figure 5-4).

4. Type the subject of the task.

5. Press **Tab** to move to the next field.

   - **Shift+Tab** will move you back one field at a time.
   - Not all task fields are available for editing in the *Task List*.

6. Press **Enter** to complete the new task. The task appears in the *Task List* in the *Content area*.

7. To cancel a task, select it and click the **Remove from List** button on the *Home* tab [*Manage Task* group].

Figure 5-4 Create a new task in the *Content area*

Another way to create a new task is by clicking the **New Task** button on the *Home* tab, which opens a new task in a new window. When the new task opens, type a subject and any additional information you desire.

▶ HOW TO: Create a New Task

1. Click the **Tasks** button on the *Navigation* bar.

2. Click the **Tasks** folder in the *My Tasks* area of the *Folder* pane.

3. Click the **New Task** button in the *New* group on the *Home* tab. The *New Task* window displays.

4. Type the subject of the task.

5. Press **Tab** to move to the next field to add the *Start* and *Due* dates and additional information as desired.

6. Click **Save & Close** on the *Task* tab to complete the new task (Figure 5-5). The task appears in the *Task List* in the *Content area*.

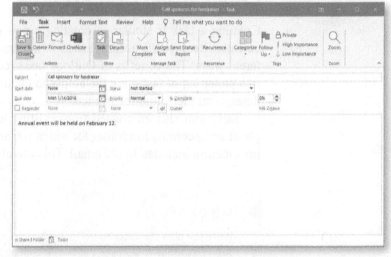

Figure 5-5 New *Task* window

▶ ANOTHER WAY

Press **Ctrl+N** to create a new task while in the *Tasks* area. A new task can also be created anywhere in Outlook by pressing **Ctrl+Shift+K**. A new task can also be created in the *To-Do* bar by clicking the **Type a new task** area.

Edit a Task

You can edit a task when you create it, or open an existing task to add or delete information. To open an existing task, double-click the task in the *Task List* in the *Content area*.

A task can include a start date and due date. These dates can be typed or you can click the drop-down arrow (Figure 5-6) to the right of *Start date* or *Due date* and select from the calendar thumbnail.

The **Status** of the task can be set to *Not Started*, *In Progress*, *Completed*, *Waiting on someone else*, or *Deferred* (Figure 5-7). By default a new task status is set at *Not Started*.

The **Priority** of a task can be set to *High*, *Normal*, or *Low* (Figure 5-8). The priority setting in a task is similar to the **Importance** settings in an email or a calendar item. The default priority setting on a new task is *Normal*.

Set an electronic **Reminder** (see Figure 5-8) for a task by clicking the **Reminder** check box in the *New Task* window. The reminder date can be either typed or selected from the thumbnail calendar when you click the drop-down arrow to the right of the date field. A specific time can also be set.

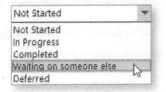

Figure 5-6 Select Task *Start Date*

Figure 5-7 Task *Status*

When it is time to complete a task, a *Reminder* window (Figure 5-9) displays on your computer. The *Reminder* window includes the *Subject*, *Start Time*, and *Start Date*. The *Reminder* window options include *Open Item*, *Dismiss*, *Dismiss All*, and *Snooze*. If you choose *Snooze*, you will be reminded again in a specified amount of time. Click the drop-down menu to select a time.

Figure 5-8 Reminder and high priority set for task

MORE INFO

It is not necessary to include a reminder on all items. Include reminders on only those for which you feel a reminder is really important. Reminders can become annoying if they are constantly popping up on your computer screen.

Figure 5-9 Reminder window

Also, within a task there are other task options available in the *Tags* group on the *Task* tab.

By default, a **Follow Up flag** is assigned to each new task created based upon the due date of the task. This flag can be changed to a different flag selected from the preset flags, or a custom flag can be created (Figure 5-10). These custom flags are similar to those used for emails and are found on the *Task* tab in the *Tags* group.

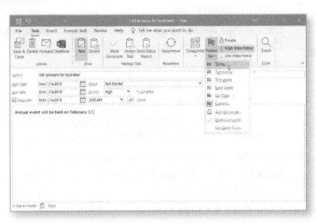

Figure 5-10 *Follow Up* flag options

Categories can be used to group tasks (or other Outlook items) by a common category. If you have a list of tasks to be completed for an upcoming fundraiser, a "Fundraiser" category can be created and all tasks pertaining to this fundraiser can be assigned to this category. Tasks can then be viewed by category to show all the tasks grouped and listed by their category. Add a category by clicking the **Categorize** button on the *Tasks* tab in the *Tags* group.

> **MORE INFO**
>
> Categories were briefly introduced in chapter 2 and will be covered more thoroughly in chapters 8, 9, and 10.
>
> Delegates will be covered in chapter 9.

A task can also be marked as *Private*. This marking does not change any aspect of this task for the owner, but rather this feature is important when using delegates in Outlook. *Delegates* are those individuals with whom you share or give permission to certain areas of your Outlook, such as Calendar or Tasks.

Attach a File or an Outlook Item

Another distinct advantage of Outlook Tasks compared to a paper list of tasks is the ability to attach or include additional resources with a task. If you were creating a task for an upcoming fundraising event, you might want to attach a contact record, an Excel spreadsheet, or an email as a reference and additional information for this task that is to be completed.

Attachments include Word or Excel documents, pictures, or almost any other type of file. An *Outlook Item* (Figure 5-11) such as a contact record, email, calendar item, or a business card can also be attached.

Figure 5-11 Attach *Outlook Item* button

▶**HOW TO:** Attach a File or an Outlook Item to a Task

1. Open an existing task.

2. Click the **Insert** tab.

3. Click either **Attach File**, **Outlook Item**, or **Business Card** in the *Include* group. The *Insert* dialog box opens.

4. Browse to the file or Outlook item to be attached or included in the task.

5. Select the files or Outlook items (Figure 5-12). Use the **Shift** or **Ctrl** keys to select multiple items.

6. Click **OK** (for *Outlook Item* or *Business Card*) or **Insert** (for *Attach File*). The files or items will be attached to the task.

7. Click **Save & Close** to save and close the task.

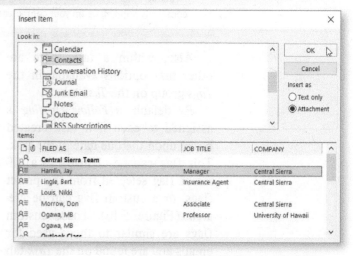

Figure 5-12 Select an Outlook item

Mark a Task as Complete

Outlook gives you the satisfaction of being able to cross off items on your *Task List* when they are marked as complete. When a task is marked as complete, it remains in your *Task List*, but a line is drawn through it and it is grayed out.

An item can be marked as complete in a number of different ways. When a task is open, it can be marked as completed in the following ways:

- Click the **Mark Complete** button (Figure 5-13) in the *Manage Task* group on the *Task* tab. The task will automatically close, and it will be marked as complete in the *Task List*.
- Click **Completed** in the *Status* drop-down menu, and then click **Save & Close**.
- In the *% Complete* box, type 100 and click **Save & Close**.

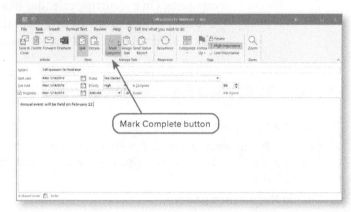

Figure 5-13 Mark a task as complete

From the *Task List* in the *Content area*, a task can be marked as complete in the following ways:

- In the *Task List*, click the **Completed** check box to the left of the task subject.
- Right-click the task in the *Task List* and choose **Mark Complete**.
- Select the task in the *Task List* in the *Content area*, and click the **Mark Complete** button in the *Manage Tasks* group on the *Home* tab (Figure 5-14).

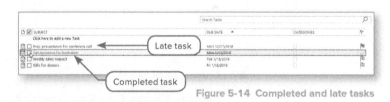

Figure 5-14 Completed and late tasks

Recurring Task

When you have a task that needs to be completed on a regular basis, create a recurring task. It could be taking out the trash every Monday night or making a weekly sales deposit at the bank.

Recurring tasks are similar to recurring calendar items. The unique aspect of a recurring task is that the task will regenerate itself (create a new recurring task) once the task is marked as complete. On a recurring calendar item, the recurring item displays on the calendar every time it recurs, while a recurring task item shows only the current task. The task icon for a recurring task is different than for a regular task.

Figure 5-15 *Recurrence* button

▶ HOW TO: Create a Recurring Task

1. Create a new task or open an existing task.
2. Click the **Recurrence** button in the *Recurrence* group on the *Task* tab (Figure 5-15). The *Task Recurrence* dialog box opens (Figure 5-16).
3. Set the **Recurrence pattern**.
4. Set the **Range of recurrence**.
5. Click **OK**.

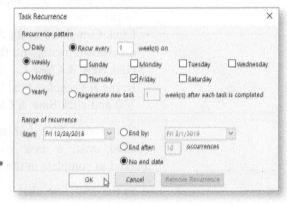

Figure 5-16 *Task Recurrence* dialog box

> ### ANOTHER WAY
> When a task is open, **Ctrl+G** opens the *Task Recurrence* dialog box.

To regenerate a recurring task, mark the existing recurring task as complete and the recurring task will automatically regenerate itself.

▶ HOW TO: Mark a Recurring Task as Complete

1. Open the recurring task.
2. Click the **Mark Complete** button in the *Manage Task* group on the *Task* tab. The open task will automatically close and regenerate itself in the *Task List* in the *Content area* (Figure 5-17).

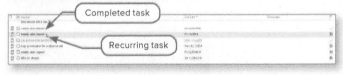

Figure 5-17 Completed recurring tasks

> **ANOTHER WAY**
>
> A task can be marked as complete by either clicking the **Completed** check box for the task in the *Content area* or by opening the task and choosing **Completed** in the *Status* drop-down menu.

Create a Task from an Email

Email can have information upon which you must take action. An email can easily be converted to a task by dragging the email from the list of emails in the *Content area* to the *Tasks* button in the *Navigation* bar. The original email will remain in your Inbox.

When this is done, a new task window is opened. The subject of the task is the same as the subject of the email, and the body of the email is included in the body of the task. The task window also includes the header information (*From*, *Sent*, *To*, etc.).

The body of the email can be edited to include only the pertinent information; you can also edit the task to include any additional options such as *Start date*, *Due date*, or *Reminder*.

HOW TO: Create a Task from an Email

1. Click the **Mail** button on the *Navigation* bar.
2. Click the email to be converted to a task.
3. Drag it to the *Tasks* button in the *Navigation* bar (a small box will appear below the pointer when dragging the email to the *Tasks* button) and release the pointer (Figure 5-18). A new task opens (Figure 5-19).
4. Edit the new task.
5. Click **Save & Close**.

Figure 5-18 Drag an email to the *Tasks* button to create a new task

> **ANOTHER WAY**
>
> You can also select an email, click the **Move** button in the *Move* group, and choose **Tasks**. When you do this, a new task window opens and the entire email message will be an attachment to the task.
>
> Remember when using this method that the email message will no longer be in your list of email messages but will be moved to your *Deleted Items* folder.

Figure 5-19 New task from email

Create a Task from a Calendar Item

When you need to complete a task prior to an upcoming appointment or event on your calendar, create a task from an existing calendar. This is similar to creating a task from an email message.

When you drag a calendar item to the *Tasks* button in the *Navigation* bar, the date of the calendar item becomes the due date of the task. The body of the task includes information from the calendar item.

▶**HOW TO:** Create a Task from a Calendar Item

1. Click the **Calendar** button on the *Navigation* bar.

2. Click the appointment or event to be converted to a task.

3. Drag it to the *Tasks* button in the *Navigation* bar (a small box will appear below the pointer when dragging the email to the *Tasks* button) and release the pointer. A new task opens (Figure 5-20).

4. Edit the new task.

5. Click **Save & Close**.

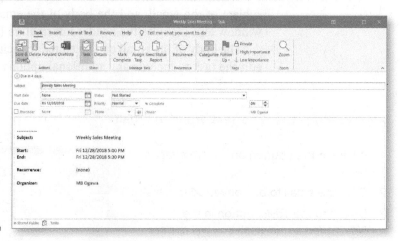

Figure 5-20 New task from calendar item

PAUSE & PRACTICE: OUTLOOK 5-1

For this Pause & Practice project, you create tasks based on a class project. You initially set up a handful of tasks to prepare for group work. With a partner, you email each other and create a task from an email message.

1. Create a new task.
   a. Click the **Tasks** button on the *Navigation* bar.
   b. Click the **Tasks** folder in the *My Tasks* area of the *Folder* pane.
   c. Click the **New Task** button in the *New* group on the *Home* tab.
   d. Enter the following information for the new task:

   Subject: Create email list for BUS project
   Start date: Today's date
   Due date: Tomorrow's date
   Reminder: Tomorrow's date at 9:30 AM
   Priority: High
   Message: Collect group email addresses

   e. Click the **Save & Close** button.

2. Email a partner in class to request his or her phone number.

3. Create a new task based on the email message you received regarding the phone number request.
   a. Select the email message your partner sent you regarding the phone number request.
   b. Click and drag the message to the *Tasks* button on the *Navigation* bar. A new task window opens.
   c. Edit the task in the following way:

   Subject: Do not change
   Start date: Today's date
   Due date: Two days from today
   Reminder: Two days from today's date at 9:00 A.M
   Priority: High
   Message: Edit contacts to include phone numbers

   d. Click the **Save & Close** button.

4. Edit the task with the subject *Create email list for BUS project* to be 50 percent complete.
   a. Click the **Task** button on the *Navigation* bar.
   b. Double-click the task to open it.
   c. Type 50% in the *% Complete* text box.
   d. Click the **Save & Close** button.

5. Create a new task to email a meeting agenda the day before each meeting.
   a. Click the **New Task** button in the *New* group on the *Home* tab.
   b. Enter the following information for the new task:

   Subject: Create and email meeting agenda
   Start date: None
   Due date: The upcoming Tuesday
   Message: Develop agenda based on previous meeting

   c. Click the **Recurrence** button [*Task* tab, *Recurrence* group].
   d. Set the recurrence to be every Tuesday with no end date.
   e. Click the **OK** button.
   f. Click the **Save & Close** button.

6. Email the three tasks to your instructor as Outlook items.
   a. Click the **Mail** button on the *Navigation bar*.
   b. Click the **New Email** button [*Home* tab, *New* group].
   c. Enter the following information in your message:

   To: Instructor's email address
   Cc: Your email address
   Subject: Outlook Pause & Practice 5-1
   Body: Hi [instructor name],

   Attached are my Outlook items for the Pause & Practice 5-1 exercise.

   [your name]

   d. Click the **Outlook Item** button [*Message* tab, *Include* group].
   e. Select the **Tasks** option and locate the three tasks you created.
   f. Press the **Ctrl** key and select the three tasks and click **OK**.
   g. Click **Send** (Figure 5-21).

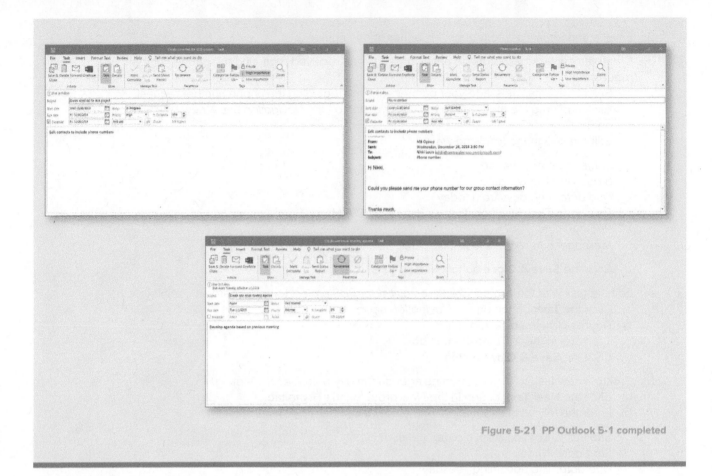

Figure 5-21 PP Outlook 5-1 completed

SLO 5.3

Viewing Tasks and To-Do Items

Another advantage to using Outlook Tasks as opposed to using a paper list of to-do items is that tasks can be grouped and viewed in a variety of ways. Outlook provides you with many different preset views for grouping and viewing tasks in the *Content area*.

Task Views

The different task views are available on both the *Home* and *View* tabs, and you easily change from one view to another by selecting the drop-down arrow in the *Current View* group on the *Home* tab

Figure 5-22 Change how you view tasks

(Figure 5-22) or clicking the **Change View** button in the *Current View* group on the *View* tab. The preset task views include:

- *Detailed*
- *Simple List*

- *To-Do List*
- *Prioritized*
- *Active*
- *Completed*
- *Today*
- *Next 7 Days*
- *Overdue*
- *Assigned*
- *Server Tasks*

> MORE INFO
>
> Preset views throughout Outlook can be customized, and new views can be created. This topic will be covered in chapters 8, 9, and 10.

Reading Pane

Just as for email, Outlook provides a *Reading* pane for tasks, which displays the contents of the selected task. The *Reading* pane can be shown to the right or at the bottom of the *Content area*, or it can be turned off (Figure 5-23).

Figure 5-23 *Reading* pane options

The size of the *Reading* pane can be adjusted by clicking and dragging the right or left edge of the pane when it displays on the right. When the *Reading* pane displays at the bottom, the size can be adjusted by dragging the top edge up or down.

Tasks in Calendar Views

One of the many advantages of using Outlook is the integration of the different components in Outlook. An example of this is how tasks are connected to the calendar. When you are using your calendar in Outlook, the current tasks display at the bottom of the *Day* and *Week* views in the **Daily Task List** (Figure 5-24), but not in *Month* view. You can turn this feature on or off by selecting an option from the *Daily Task List* button [*View* tab, *Layout* group].

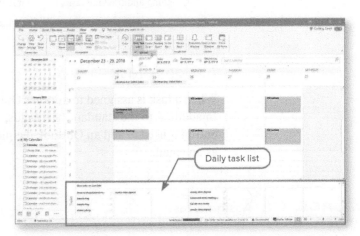

Daily task list

Figure 5-24 *Daily Task List*

Customize the To-Do Bar

The *To-Do* bar (Figure 5-25) provides you with a summary of both your calendar and flagged items in Outlook. It displays to the right of the Outlook working environment. The *To-Do* bar has four components: **Date Navigator**, **Appointments**, **Task List**, and **People**. The *Task List* includes tasks and flagged items but does not include completed items.

In the *Layout* group on the *View* tab, you are given options for the items to be displayed in the *To-Do* bar: *Calendar, People, Tasks*, and *Off*. Drag the left edge of the *To-Do* bar to the right or left to adjust its width. You can customize the *To-Do* bar by removing any of the existing components or adjusting the amount of content to be shown.

Figure 5-25 *To-Do bar*

▶ HOW TO: View Items in the To-Do Bar

1. Select **Tasks** in the *Navigation* bar and click the **View** tab.
2. Click the **To-Do Bar** button in the *Layout* group.
3. Choose the desired items to view (Figure 5-26).

Figure 5-26 *To-Do Bar options*

SLO 5.4 Managing Tasks

Another advantage of Outlook Tasks is its ability to assign tasks to others and to track the progress and completion of these tasks. For example, if you were planning an upcoming event, many tasks would have to be completed prior to the event. Each of these assignments could be saved as a task, and you could delegate selected tasks to individuals.

▶ MORE INFO

Assigning and tracking tasks is available only when using Outlook in an Exchange environment.

Assign a Task

When a task is assigned to another Outlook user, the task request becomes similar to an email. In addition to the standard task fields, *To* and *Send* buttons appear on the task request. The *To* button is used to add an Outlook recipient, and the *Send* button is used to send the task request as an email.

▶ HOW TO: Assign a Task

1. Create a new task or open an existing task.
2. Click the **Assign Task** button (Figure 5-27) in the *Manage Task* group on the *Task* tab. A task request email opens.

Figure 5-27 *Assign Task* button

Figure 5-28 Assign task to a recipient

3. Click the **To** button and choose a recipient.
4. Include a brief message in the body of the task request.
5. Click **Send** (Figure 5-28).

> **MORE INFO**
>
> Assign a task request to only one recipient to ensure that a task is completed. If multiple individuals are to be assigned a task, think about how to break the task into smaller parts to assign individually. Also, always include a brief message in the body of the task request.

Accept a Task Request

When a task is assigned to another Outlook user, it is received in the user's Inbox and looks similar to an email. When the recipient opens the task request, he or she has the option to either accept or decline the task request.

When the task request is either accepted or declined, the recipient again has two options: *Edit the response before sending* or *Send the response now*. If *Edit the response before sending* is chosen, the task request recipient will be able to type a message to the task originator before sending the response. If *Send the response now* is chosen, the response to the task request is automatically sent.

When the task request has been accepted and the response has been sent, the task request is removed from the recipient's Inbox and placed in his or her *Task List*. The person accepting the task request is now the owner of this task.

▶ **HOW TO: Accept a Task Request**

1. Click the **Mail** button in the *Navigation* bar.
2. Open the task request message in your inbox.
3. Choose **Accept** (Figure 5-29). An *Accepting Task* dialog box opens.
4. Select **Edit the response before sending** (Figure 5-30).
5. Click **OK** to close the dialog box. The task request response opens, and you type a response in the body.

Figure 5-29 *Accept* task button

Figure 5-30 *Accepting Task* dialog box

6. Click **Send** (Figure 5-31). The task request is removed from your Inbox and moved to your *Task List*. The originator of the task will receive a *Task Accepted* message from you.

Figure 5-31 Completed task response

Task Icons

Different icons are used to help you distinguish between tasks requested, tasks accepted, and tasks declined. These icons display on your task request emails in your Inbox.

Task Icons

Icon	Icon Name and Description
	Task Request. The task request appears in the recipient's Inbox and displays the task icon with a hand at the bottom, indicating that the task is being handed off or assigned, and an envelope icon at the top.
	Task Accepted. When a task recipient accepts a task, you receive a *Task Accepted* message in your Inbox. The icon has the task with a hand at the bottom and a check at the top.
	Task Declined. When a task recipient declines a task, you receive a *Task Declined* message in your Inbox. The icon has the task with a hand at the bottom and a red **X** at the top.

Update a Task and Send a Status Report

A status report can be sent to the originator of the task and others to give an update on the progress of this task. The *Status* and *% Complete* on the task can be specified to give the originator a status update.

The *Details* section of the task is used to provide a more detailed task status to the originator of the task. The *Details* section of the task is available by clicking the **Details** button in the *Show* group on the *Task* tab.

▶ **HOW TO:** Update a Task and Send a Status Report

1. Click the **Tasks** button on the *Navigation* bar.

2. Open the accepted task in your *Task List*.

Figure 5-32 Task details

Figure 5-33 *Send Status Report* button

3. Click the **Details** button (Figure 5-32) in the *Show* group on the *Task* tab.

4. Fill in details for this task.

5. Click the **Task** button in the *Show* group.

6. Fill in the **Status** and **% Complete**.

7. Click the **Send Status Report** button (Figure 5-33) in the *Manage Task* group on the *Task* tab. A *Task Status Report* email window is opened. This message contains detailed status report information for the recipients.

8. Include a brief message in the body (Figure 5-34).

9. Select other recipients if necessary. The originator of the task will automatically be a recipient.

10. Click **Send**. The recipients will receive a *Task Status Report* email in their Inboxes.

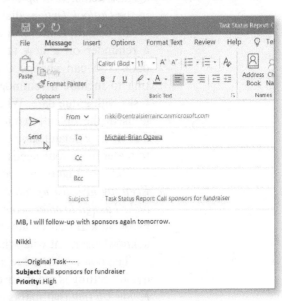

Figure 5-34 Status report

Complete a Task

As mentioned previously in this chapter, tasks can be marked as completed in many ways. When a task is marked as completed, the originator of the task automatically receives an email informing him or her that the task is complete. In the *Task List* of both the originator and the owner of the task, the task has a line through it to indicate it is a completed task.

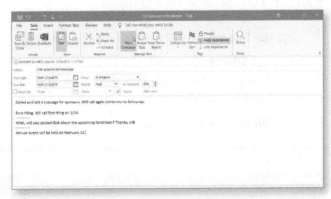

Figure 5-35 Mark a task as complete

> **ANOTHER WAY**
>
> A task can also be marked as complete by selecting the task in the *Content area*, clicking the check box before the task, and then clicking the **Mark Complete** button in the *Manage Task* group (Figure 5-35) or by right-clicking the task and choosing **Mark Complete**.

Task Options

Outlook provides you with the flexibility of customizing the default settings for all task items. *Task options* are available in the *Outlook Options* dialog box.

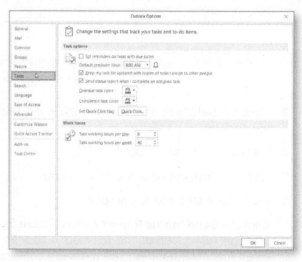

By default, Outlook does not include a reminder on a new task with a due date. You can change the default setting to include a reminder on all new tasks with a due date. When a reminder is used, the default reminder setting is 8 AM. This default time can be changed to better meet your needs.

Refer to Figure 5-36 and notice that *Keep my task list updated with copies of*

Figure 5-36 Outlook *Task* options

tasks I assign to other people and *Send status report when I complete an assigned task* are selected by default. If you create a task and assign it to someone else, it is important to receive an acknowledgement when the task is completed.

The color of overdue and completed tasks can be changed in the *Task Options* area. The default setting is red for overdue tasks and gray for completed tasks. You can set a *Quick Click Follow Up* flag that marks a task with the specified flag when it is clicked.

▶ **HOW TO:** Modify Task Options

1. Click the **File** tab. The *Backstage* window displays.
2. Choose **Options** on the left. The *Outlook Options* dialog box opens.
3. Click **Tasks** to change task default settings. The *Task Options* window displays.
4. Change the default settings.
5. Click **OK** to close the *Outlook Options* dialog box.

PAUSE & PRACTICE: OUTLOOK 5-2

For this Pause & Practice project, you assign a task to a group member because you forgot about a doctor's appointment. You also accept tasks, send updates, and complete a task.

1. Assign the task with the subject *Create and email meeting agenda* to your partner.
   a. Click the **Tasks** button on the *Navigation* bar.
   b. Open the task with the subject *Create and email meeting agenda*.

    c. Click the **Assign Task** button [*Task* tab, *Manage Task* group].

    d. In the *To* text area, type your partner's email address (or select it if it is in your contacts).

    e. In the message area, type:

> Hi [partner's name], I have a doctor's appointment this week and will be unable to type the meeting agenda. Could you please type and send it to the group?
>
> Thanks,
> [your name]

    f. Click the **Send** button.

2. Accept the task request from your partner.
    a. Click the **Mail** button on the *Navigation* bar.
    b. Open the email message from your partner.
    c. Click the **Accept** button [*Task* tab, *Respond* group].
    d. Select the **Edit the response before sending** radio button and click **OK**.
    e. In the message, type:

> Hi [partner's name], Sure! I will type and send the agenda to the group. I hope all is well with you.
>
> [your name]

    f. Click the **Send** button.

3. Send an update that the task is 25 percent complete.
    a. Click the **Tasks** button on the *Navigation* bar.
    b. Open the task that you accepted.
    c. Change the *% Complete* to **25%**.
    d. Click the **Send Status Report** button [*Task* tab, *Manage Task* group].
    e. In the email status report, add the following text to the message:

> Hi [partner's name], Just wanted to let you know that I started the agenda and am about 25% through it. Should be finished by the end of the day.
>
> [your name]

    f. Click the **Send** button.
    g. Click the **Save & Close** button.

4. Complete the task.
    a. Open the task from step 3.
    b. Click the **Mark Complete** button [*Task* tab, *Manage Task* group].

5. Email the task request email, task accepted email, task status report email, and the completed task to your instructor as Outlook items.
    a. Click the **Mail** button on the *Navigation* bar.
    b. Click the **New Email** button [*Home* tab, *New* group].
    c. Enter the following information in your message:

> *To*: Instructor's email address
> *Cc*: Your email address
> *Subject*: Outlook Pause & Practice 5-2
> *Body*: Hi [instructor name],
>
> Attached are my Outlook items for the Pause & Practice 5-2 exercise.
>
> [your name]

    d. Click the **Attach Item** button [*Message* tab, *Include* group] and select **Outlook Item**.
    e. Select the **Inbox** option and select the three email messages.
    f. Select the **Tasks** option and locate the completed task.
    g. Press the **Ctrl** key and select the three tasks and click **OK**.
    h. Click **Send** (Figure 5-37).

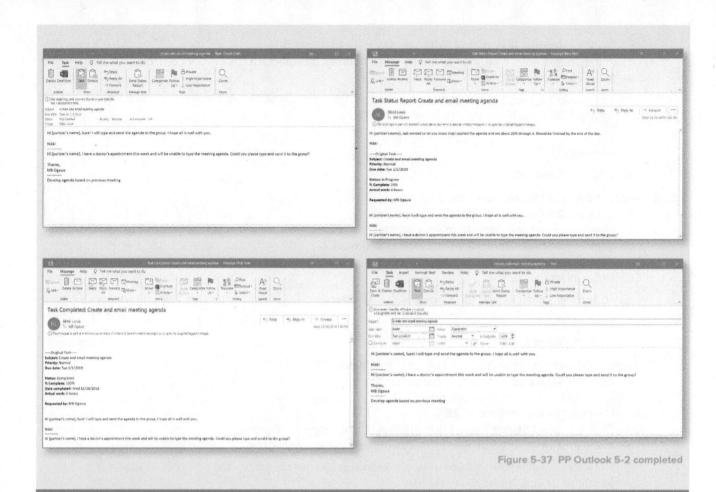

Figure 5-37 PP Outlook 5-2 completed

Customize the User Interface in Outlook

Now that you are an advanced Outlook user and regularly use the different tasks and special features offered by Outlook, you might want to customize the user interface. You are able to customize the look and content of *Outlook Today*, the *Navigation* bar, *Favorites*, and the *Quick Access* toolbar. Customize how information displays in the *Content area* by selecting the fields to display and how information is sorted and grouped.

Outlook Today

Outlook Today displays a snapshot of your upcoming calendar, tasks, and message items. To display *Outlook Today*, click the **Mail** button in the *Navigation* bar. Then click the email account at the top of the *Folder* pane. Click an item in *Outlook Today* to move to that item.

Customize *Outlook Today* to show *Outlook Today* at startup, select folders to display, select the number of days to display in the Calendar, and select the number of tasks to display.

▶ **HOW TO:** Customize Outlook Today

1. Click the **Customize Outlook Today** button above the *Messages* heading in the *Content area*. The *Customize Outlook Today* screen displays (Figure 5-38).
2. Click the **Startup** check box to automatically display *Outlook Today* each time you open Outlook.
3. In the *Messages* area, choose the folders to display in *Outlook Today*.

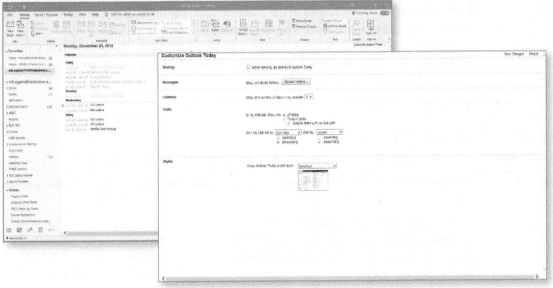

Figure 5-38 Customize *Outlook Today*

4. In the *Calendar* area, select the number of days to display.

5. In the *Tasks* area, customize the tasks to display.

6. In the *Styles* area, select the style of *Outlook Today*.

7. Click **Save Changes**.

Navigation Bar Options

On the *Navigation bar*, you can choose which buttons are displayed, the order of buttons displayed, and whether a button is large or small. Click the . . . (ellipsis) button at the bottom of the *Navigation* bar and select **Navigation Options . . .** to open the *Navigation Options* dialog box (Figure 5-39).

The *Maximum number of visible items* refers to the number of buttons available on the *Navigation* bar without clicking the . . . button to reveal more options. *Compact Navigation* uses icons instead of words for each of the *Navigation* bar items and is the default view in Outlook. Unchecking the *Compact Navigation* option will display large text for each of the navigation items, such as *Mail*. You are able to modify the order of the buttons displayed in the *Navigation* bar by selecting an item and clicking the *Move Up* or *Move Down* button. The *Reset* button resets the *Navigation* bar to the original Outlook default settings.

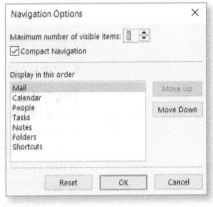

Figure 5-39 *Navigation Options* dialog box

Favorites Folders

At the top of the *Folder* pane above your mail folders is an area called *Favorites* (Figure 5-40). Folders that you regularly use can be added to this area for easy access to the

Figure 5-40 *Favorites*

folders. When a folder is placed in the *Favorites* area, the folder is not actually moved to a different location, but rather a link to the folder is created in the *Favorites* area.

Mail, *Search*, and *RSS Feeds* folders can be added to the *Favorites* area. Clicking a folder in the *Favorites* area displays the contents of that folder in the *Content area*.

▶ HOW TO: Add a Folder to Favorites

1. Click the folder to be added to *Favorites*.
2. Click the **Folder** tab on the *Ribbon* and then click the **Add to Favorites** button in the *Favorites* group.

Folders can be removed from the *Favorites* area by selecting the folder to be removed and clicking the **Add to Favorites** button (Figure 5-41).

Figure 5-41 *Add to Favorites* button

▶ ANOTHER WAY

A folder can also be added to *Favorites* by right-clicking the folder and choosing **Add to Favorites**. A *Favorites* folder can also be removed by right-clicking the folder and choosing **Remove from Favorites**.

▶ MORE INFO

Customizing the *Quick Access* toolbar can be done in any of the Microsoft Office applications.

Customize the Quick Access Toolbar

The ***Quick Access toolbar***, by default, displays above the *File* tab on the *Ribbon*. If you prefer, you can change the location of the *Quick Access* toolbar to appear below the *Ribbon*. When you start Outlook, the *Send/Receive All Folders* button and the *Undo* button appear on the *Quick Access* toolbar. You can easily add frequently used buttons to the *Quick Access* toolbar.

Other commands can be added to this toolbar by clicking the **Customize Quick Access Toolbar** button to the right of the toolbar and selecting the command to be added to the toolbar. More command options are available by clicking **More Commands** in the drop-down menu (Figure 5-42). When you click **More Commands**, the *Outlook Options* window opens with a list of commands you can copy to the toolbar. Commands can be removed from this toolbar by deselecting the item in the *Customize Quick Access Toolbar* list.

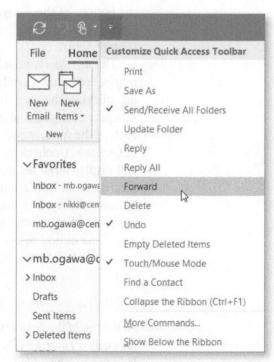

Figure 5-42 Add *Forward* to the *Quick Access* toolbar

Optimize Space for Touch Displays

Many devices are equipped with touch displays. Based on Outlook's default view, it may be difficult to tap buttons on the *Ribbon*. You can optimize the button layout for touch displays which creates more space between icons by selecting the **Touch** option [*Touch/Mouse Mode* on the *Title* bar] (Figure 5-43). A comparison of the two modes is displayed in Figure 5-44.

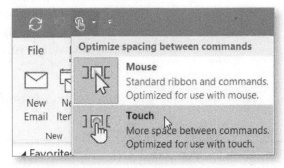

Figure 5-43 *Touch Mode*

Sort and Arrange Items

When mail items display in the *Content area*, they are typically sorted by date; the most recent item is listed first, and older items are listed below in sequential order. You can change the sort order by clicking one of the arrangement options in the *Arrangement* group on the *View* tab (Figure 5-45).

When an arrangement is selected, the items displayed in the *Content area* are sorted by that field. For example, if the *Date* arrangement is selected, items will be sorted by the date field. By clicking the *Reverse Sort* button in the *Arrangement* group, items can be sorted in ascending or descending order. The field by which the items are sorted is shaded and a small arrow to the right of the field name in the *Content area* indicates whether the sort is ascending or descending.

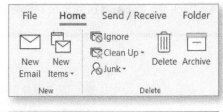

Figure 5-44 *Mouse Mode* on top and *Touch Mode* on bottom

Figure 5-45 Sort email by date

> **ANOTHER WAY**
>
> Items displayed in the *Content area* can also be sorted or arranged by clicking the **Filter** button below the *Search Current Mailbox* field (Figure 5-46).

Conversation arrangement (Figure 5-47) groups together related emails (same subject line). When *Conversation arrangement* is used, the related items are grouped together and collapsed so you don't see all the email. Each conversation includes a *Conversation header* that contains the number of unread messages and attachments. When you click the

Figure 5-46
Sort email in the *Content area*

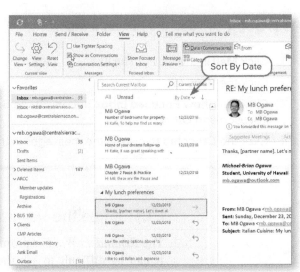

Figure 5-47 Email arranged as conversations

email icon in the *Content area*, the conversation group is expanded so you can view all the related emails in that conversation. When you receive a message that is part of a conversation, the entire conversation moves to the top of the Inbox. The *Conversation* view is available only when messages are arranged by date. The intent of this arrangement is to reduce the number of displayed emails in your Inbox.

▶ **HOW TO:** Use the Conversation Arrangement

1. Click **Mail** in the *Navigation* bar.
2. Click the **View** tab.
3. Click the **Show as Conversations** check box. Email displays as conversations.
4. Click the **Expand** button to display the messages in the conversation.

 MORE INFO

Sorting and arranging is not limited to just mail items. You can also sort or use arrangements for any contact, calendar, task, journal, or note views that display items in a list.

The *Clean Up Conversation* button in the *Delete* group on the *Home* tab will delete redundant emails from your Inbox, and the *Ignore* button will delete the selected emails in your Inbox and future emails related to the selected conversation.

Outlook includes a new feature called *Focused Inbox* to also help you to better manage your email. *Focused Inbox* filters low priority messages and moves them into a tab named *Other*. This helps you to quickly scan for important email messages rather than worry about the low priority messages in your Inbox. As you use *Focused* and *Other* inboxes by moving messages into each tab, *Focused Inbox* learns your habits and automatically moves messages for you. If *Focused Inbox* moves important messages into its *Other* tab, you can move messages back to your *Focused Inbox*. *Focused Inbox* is different from *Clean Up* and *Ignore* because it moves messages into the *Other* tab, as opposed to deleting messages.

▶ **HOW TO:** Use the Focused Inbox

1. Click **Mail** in the *Navigation* bar.
2. Click the **View** tab.
3. Click the **Show Focused Inbox** button (Figure 5-48). Email displays as *Focused* and *Other*.
4. Click the *Other* tab to display the messages in the *Other* group.

Figure 5-48 *Focused Inbox*

Customize the Reminders Window

The *Reminders Window* prompts you when appointments, events, and tasks are coming soon. It can be difficult to see these reminders if you are working in another program and the *Reminders Window* is not displayed over other windows. The *Reminders Window* can also include many appointments and events that are past due making it difficult to discern current appointments and past appointments. Outlook includes customization features to ensure the *Reminders Window* is visible and only includes upcoming items.

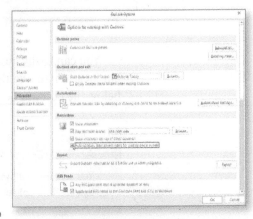

▶HOW TO: Customize the Reminders Window

1. Click the **File** tab. The *Backstage* view opens.
2. Click the **Options** button on the left. The *Outlook Options* dialog box opens (Figure 5-49).
3. Click the **Advanced** button. The advanced options display.
4. Click the **Show reminders on top of other windows** and **Automatically dismiss reminders for past events** check boxes.
5. Click **OK** to close the *Outlook Options* dialog box.

Figure 5-49 *Reminders Window* options

Add Columns and Use the Field Chooser

When viewing Outlook items in a list view (for example, *Phone* view in *Contacts*), you can add or remove columns or change the order of columns to display in the *Content area*. Suppose you want to display the *Category* column when viewing your contacts in *Phone* view. The ***Add Columns*** and ***Field Chooser*** features allow you to add fields to any list view in Outlook.

▶HOW TO: Add Columns to a View

1. Click **People** on the *Navigation* bar. Select *Phone* view.
2. Click the **View** tab and then the **Add Columns** button in the *Arrangement* group. The *Show Columns* dialog box opens (Figure 5-50).
3. In the *Available* columns area, select the column to be added and click the **Add** button. Columns can also be removed in this dialog box.
4. Arrange the display order of columns by clicking the column on the right and using the **Move Up** or **Move Down** button.
5. Click **OK** to close the *Show Columns* dialog box.

Figure 5-50 *Show Columns* dialog box

To display the *Field Chooser* dialog box, right-click any column heading in a list view and choose **Field Chooser**. The *Field Chooser* floating pane displays. Drag the selected field from the *Field Chooser* pane to the desired location in the *Content area* (Figure 5-51).

Figure 5-51 *Field Chooser*

You can easily move a field by dragging and dropping the field's column heading to a different location among the column headings, or remove a field by dragging and dropping the field below the column headings area in the *Content area*.

Show in Groups

When items display in a list in the *Content area*, Outlook can group the items by the field by which the items are sorted. For example, when items are sorted by date, Outlook will group them by *Today, Yesterday, Last Week, Two Weeks Ago, Three Weeks Ago, Last Month*, and *Older*.

▶ HOW TO: Show in Groups

1. Click the **Mail** button on the *Navigation* bar.
2. Click the **View** tab.
3. Click the **More** button in the *Arrangements* group or choose **Arrange By**.
4. Click **Show in Groups** (Figure 5-52). The items in the *Content area* display in groups (Figure 5-53).

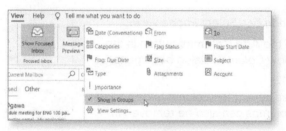

Figure 5-52 *Show in Groups* option

Figure 5-53 Email items grouped by *To* field

You can change the grouping by selecting a different field (column heading). Click a column heading to toggle it back and forth between ascending and descending sort order. Clicking the **Expand** button (small triangle) to the left of the group name expands or collapses the group. You have the option to turn off grouping by deselecting **Show in Groups**.

Expand or collapse groups by clicking the **View** tab and selecting **Expand/Collapse**. The options include *Collapse This Group, Expand This Group, Collapse All Groups*, and *Expand All Groups* (Figure 5-54).

Figure 5-54 *Collapse All Groups* option

Customize Views

Outlook also provides you with an ***Advanced View Settings*** dialog box (Figure 5-55) to further customize how your items display in the *Content area*. The *Advanced View Settings* dialog box allows you to customize the view. Click the **View Settings** button in the *Current View* group on the *View* tab to select the following view options:

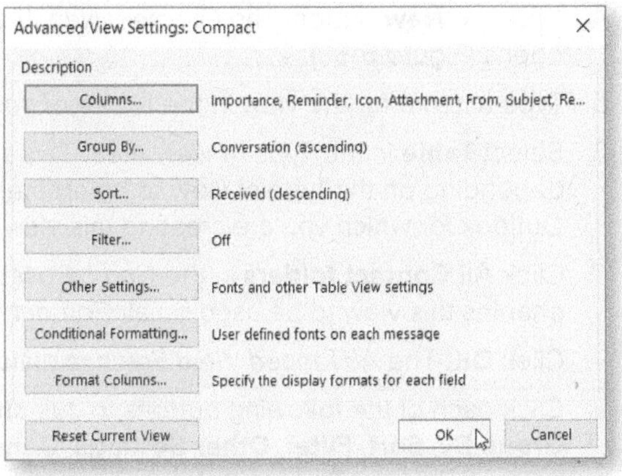

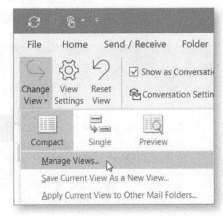

Figure 5-55 *Advanced View Settings* dialog box

- ***Columns***: Choose the fields to be displayed.
- ***Group By***: Group and sort by multiple fields.
- ***Sort***: Specify the fields and type of sort to be applied.
- ***Filter***: Create a filter so only certain items display.
- ***Other Settings***: Customize font, size, gridlines, *AutoPreview*, and *Reading* pane options.
- ***Conditional Formatting***: Customize how specific items display in the *Content area*. The options in this area vary depending on the type of Outlook items displayed in the *Content area*.
- ***Format Columns***: Customize the format, width, and alignment of the fields displayed.
- ***Reset Current View***: Reset the view to its original default settings.

> **ANOTHER WAY**
>
> The *Reset View* button in the *Current View* group on the *View* tab resets the selected view to its original settings.

> **MORE INFO**
>
> When you customize a view, the changes made will be saved and displayed whenever this view is used.

Create a Custom View

For each area of Outlook, you are provided with many different preset views. As discussed, you are able to modify any of these views to meet your individual needs. Use the ***Manage All Views*** dialog box to customize present views or to create a new custom view for that area of Outlook. Custom views can be saved and used on different folders in Outlook.

Figure 5-56 *Manage Views* option

> **HOW TO: Create a Custom View**
>
> 1. Click the **View** tab.
> 2. Click the **Change View** button.
> 3. Click **Manage Views** (Figure 5-56). The *Manage All Views* dialog box opens (Figure 5-57).

4. Click the **New** button. The *Create a New View* dialog box opens (Figure 5-58).

5. Type a name for the view in the *Name of new view* area.

6. Select **Table** in the *Type of view* area. This selection varies depending on the type of view to be created and the area of Outlook for which you are creating this view.

7. Click **All Contact folders** in the *Can be used on* area. This enables this view to be used on all *Contact* folders.

8. Click **OK**. The *Advanced View Settings* dialog box opens.

9. Click each of the following buttons to customize: **Columns**, **Group By**, **Sort**, **Filter**, **Other Settings**, **Conditional Formatting**, and **Format Columns**.

10. Click **OK** when all changes have been made to close the *Advanced View Settings* dialog box (Figure 5-59).

11. Click **Apply View** to apply the new view on the current folder.

12. Click **OK** to close the *Manage All Views* dialog box.

Figure 5-57 *Manage All View* dialog box

Figure 5-59 Advanced view settings for new view

Figure 5-58 *Create a New View* dialog box

This new view will now be available for use on all your contact folders (or whichever type of folders for which you created the new view). You can copy, modify, rename, or delete views from the *Manage All Views* dialog box.

PAUSE & PRACTICE: OUTLOOK 5-3

For this Pause & Practice project, you customize Outlook. Select *Outlook Today* for your default start screen, add your Inbox to *Favorites*, and add the print button to the *Quick Access* toolbar. If you prefer not to have these options, feel free to change them back to the default, since there are no submission items.

1. Customize *Outlook Today* and set it to display when you open Outlook.
   a. Click the **Mail** button on the *Navigation* bar.

    b. Click the email account in the *Folder* pane.
    c. Click the **Customize Outlook Today** button in the *Content area*. The *Customize Outlook Today* screen will be displayed in the *Content area*.
    d. Click the **When starting, go directly to Outlook today** check box.
    e. In the *Messages* area, choose the folders to be displayed in *Outlook Today*.
    f. In the *Calendar* area, select the number of days to display in *Outlook Today*.
    g. In the *Tasks* area, customize the tasks to be displayed.
    h. In the *Styles* area, choose the style of *Outlook Today*.
    i. Click **Save Changes**.

2. Add your Inbox to your *Favorites*.
    a. Right-click your Inbox.
    b. Select **Show in Favorites**.

3. Add the *Print* button to your *Quick Access* toolbar.
    a. Click the **Customize Quick Access Toolbar** button to the right of the toolbar.
    b. Select the **Print** option (Figure 5-60).

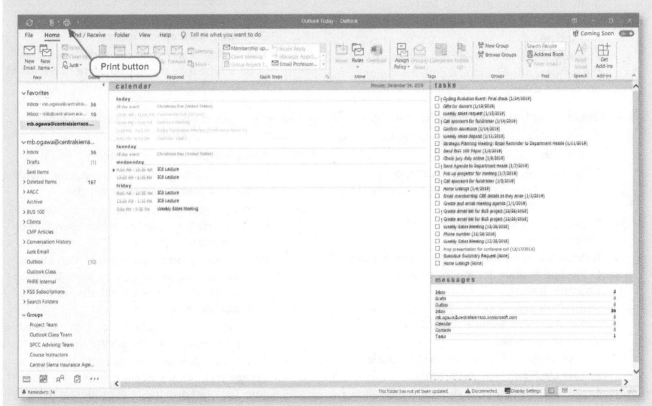

Figure 5-60 PP Outlook 5-3 completed

Chapter Summary

5.1 Distinguish between tasks and To-Do items (p. O5-174).

- *Tasks* are individual items in the *Tasks* area and also appear in the list of To-Do items.
- *To-Do items* include tasks, flagged email messages, and flagged contacts.
- Use tasks to create reminders.
- The *Task List* includes all of the tasks you created.
- Flagged items typically indicate that you need to follow up on a particular item. When you flag an item, it appears in the *To-Do List*.
- The *To-Do List* includes both task items and flagged items.
- The *To-Do bar* is located on the right side of the window and includes a date navigator, upcoming calendar items, and To-Do items.

5.2 Create and use tasks in Outlook (p. O5-175).

- Create a new task from the tasks folder or *New Task* button.
- Tasks include a subject, start date, due date, reminder, status, priority, reminder, percent complete, and a message.
- Tasks can include a *Status* to illustrate its progress.
- A *Priority* can be set for Tasks, which is similar to the *Importance* setting for email and Calendar items.
- *Reminders* can be set for Tasks, which will automatically give you a reminder in the *Reminder* window.
- Tasks can include tags such as *Categories*, *Follow Up Flags*, and *Importance*.
- Tasks can be marked as *Private*, which allows permissions for *Delegates* to access or not access *Private* appointments and *Events*.
- You can attach *Outlook items* and files to tasks.
- Tasks can be marked as completed, and the *Task List* displays completed items as strikethrough text.
- Tasks can be set to recur on a regular basis.
- You can drag-and-drop email messages and calendar items to the *Tasks* button on the *Navigation* bar to create tasks from different Outlook items.

5.3 Understand and customize the *Tasks* views and the *To-Do* bar (p. O5-184).

- Tasks and To-Do items can be viewed as *Detailed, Simple List, To-Do List, Prioritized, Active, Completed, Today, Next 7 Days, Overdue, Assigned*, or *Server Tasks*.
- Similarly to email, you can include the *Reading* pane for tasks.
- The *Daily Task List* is available in the *Day* and *Week* Calendar views.
- You can view tasks in the calendar view if you are viewing the calendar in *Day* or *Week* view.
- The *To-Do* bar can be customized to include *Calendar, People*, and *Tasks*.
- The originator of a task can receive a status update based on the *% Complete* or *Status* of a task.

5.4 Assign tasks to and accept tasks from other Outlook users (p. O5-186).

- Tasks can be assigned to others.
- When you receive a task request, you have the option to *Accept* or *Decline* the task.
- When accepting a task request, you have two options: *Edit the response before sending* or *Send the response now*.
- While working on a task request, send the original task requestor an update of the progress on the task. This can include the *Status*, *% Complete*, and a message.
- Using the details of a task, you can include the amount of hours worked on the task.
- When you mark an accepted task request as *Complete*, it automatically crosses the task off your *Task List* and the task requestor's list
- Outlook allows you to modify the default *Task Options* to meet your particular work style.

5.5 Customize the user interface in Outlook (p. O5-192).

- *Outlook Today* can be customized to include information that you want available as soon as you launch Outlook.
- Use the *Navigation Options* dialog box to select the number of visible items on the *Navigation bar*, to Compact Navigation, and to reorder the buttons on the *Navigation* bar.

- You can include folders that you use often in the *Favorites*.
- The **Quick Access toolbar** can be customized to include buttons you use most often.
- Sort email and tasks by using a variety of criteria including date received amongst other criteria.
- **Focused Inbox** helps you to quickly find important messages by separating messages into two categories, *Focused* and *Other*.
- The *Reminders Window* can be customized to appear above all other windows and to automatically dismiss past calendar items.
- Add additional fields to your tasks, which allow greater sort options.

- Email can be sorted to be viewed in groups, which includes weeks and days.
- The **Advanced View Settings** allows for deep customization of views based on many criteria.
- **Manage All Views** allows customization of views for different areas of Outlook.

Check for Understanding

The SIMbook for this text (within your SIMnet account) provides the following resources for concept review:

- Multiple-choice questions
- Short answer questions
- Matching exercises

Guided Project 5-1

For this project, you coordinate the Cycling Evolution Event for the American River Cycling Club (ARCC).
You create tasks that need to be completed in order to prepare for the event.
[Student Learning Outcomes 5.1, 5.2, 5.3]

Skills Covered in This Project

- Create a new task.
- Modify the task subject, start date, due date, reminder, priority, and message.
- Create a task from a calendar appointment.
- Create a recurring task.
- Email task items as attachments.

1. Create a new task.
   a. Click the **Tasks** button on the *Navigation* bar.
   b. Click the **Tasks** folder in the *My Tasks* area of the *Folder* pane.
   c. Click the **New Task** button in the *New* group on the *Home* tab.
   d. Enter the following information for the new task:

   Subject: Call city and county
   Start date: Today's date
   Due date: One week from today
   Reminder: Two days from today at 9:00 AM
   Priority: Normal
   Message: Make arrangements for road path

   e. Click the **Save & Close** button.

2. Create a new calendar appointment.
   a. Click the **Calendar** button on the *Navigation* bar.
   b. Click the **New Appointment** button [*Home* tab, *New* group].
   c. Enter the following information for the new appointment:

   Subject: Cycling Evolution Event
   Location: River City
   Start time: One month from today at 9:00 AM
   End time: One month from today at 12:00 PM
   Body: ARCC half-day event

   d. Click the **Save & Close** button.

3. Create a new task based on the appointment you created.
   a. Select the calendar item you created.
   b. Click and drag the calendar item to the *Tasks* button on the *Navigation* bar.
   c. Edit the task in the new task window as follows:

   Subject: Cycling Evolution Event: Final check
   Start date: None
   Due date: Two days before the event
   Reminder: Three days before the event at 10:00 AM

Priority: High
Message: Call city and county to double-check, set up road signs

    d. Click the **Save & Close** button.

4. Create a new task to email the membership each week to give additional details about the event.
    a. Click the **New Task** button in the *New* group on the *Home* tab.
    b. Enter the following information for the new task:

    Subject: Email membership CEE details as they arise
    Start date: None
    Due date: The upcoming Thursday
    Message: Include details such as course, maps, check-in areas, and registration

    c. Click the **Recurrence** button [*Task* tab, *Recurrence* group].
    d. Set the recurrence to be every Thursday with an end date of the Thursday before the event.
    e. Click the **OK** button.
    f. Click the **Save & Close** button.

5. Email the three tasks to your instructor as Outlook items.
    a. Click the **Mail** button on the *Navigation* bar.
    b. Click the **New Email** button [*Home* tab, *New* group].
    c. Enter the following information in your message:

    To: Instructor's email address
    Cc: Your email address
    Subject: Outlook Guided Project 5-1
    Body:
    Hi [instructor name],
    Attached are my Outlook items for the Guided Project 5-1 exercise.
    [your name]

    d. Click the **Attach Item** button [*Message* tab, *Include* group] and select **Outlook Item**.
    e. Select the **Tasks** option and locate the three tasks you created.
    f. Press the **Ctrl** key and select the three tasks and click **OK**.
    g. Click **Send** (Figure 5-61).

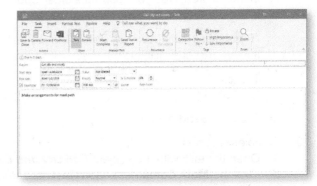

Figure 5-61 Guided Project 5-1 completed

Guided Project 5-2

For this project, you enlist the help of others because you found that the tasks to prepare for the Cycling Evolution Event for the ARCC are becoming overwhelming.
[Student Learning Outcomes 5.1, 5.3, 5.4]

Skills Covered in This Project

- Edit an existing task.
- Assign a task.

- Edit an assigned task message.
- Mark a task as complete.
- Email task items as attachments.

1. Assign the task with the subject *Email membership CEE details as they arise* to your partner.
   a. Click the **Tasks** button on the *Navigation* bar.
   b. Open the task with the subject **Email membership CEE details as they arise**.
   c. Click the **Assign Task** button [*Task* tab, *Manage Task* group].
   d. In the *To* area, type your partner's email address (or select it if it is in your contacts).
   e. In the message area, type:

   Hi [partner's name], I am a bit busy for the next few weeks. Would you be willing to write and send the CEE details to membership each week?

   Thanks,
   [your name]

   f. Click the **Send** button.

2. Assign the task with the subject *Cycling Evolution Event: Final check* to your partner.
   a. Open the task with the subject **Cycling Evolution Event: Final check**.
   b. Click the **Assign Task** button [*Task* tab, *Manage Task* group].
   c. In the *To* area, type your partner's email address (or select it if it is in your contacts).
   d. In the message area, type:

   Hi [partner's name], Are you available to perform the final check? My schedule is a bit tight, but I can do it if you are not available.

   Thanks,
   [your name]

   e. Click the **Send** button.

3. Complete the task.
   a. Open the task with the subject **Call city and county**.
   b. Click the **Mark Complete** button [*Task* tab, *Manage Task* group].

4. Email the two task request email messages and the completed task to your instructor as Outlook items.
   a. Click the **Mail** button on the *Navigation* bar.
   b. Click the **New Email** button [*Home* tab, *New* group].
   c. Enter the following information in your message:

   To: Instructor's email address
   Cc: Your email address
   Subject: Outlook Guided Project 5-2
   Body: Hi [instructor name],

   Attached are my Outlook items for the Guided Project 5-2 exercise.

   [your name]

d. Click the **Attach Item** button [*Message* tab, *Include* group] and select **Outlook Item**.
e. Select the **Sent Items** folder and locate the two task request email messages.
f. Select the **Tasks** option and locate the completed task you created.
g. Press the **Ctrl** key and select the two tasks and email message and click **OK**.
h. Click **Send** (Figure 5-62).

Figure 5-62 Guided Project 5-2 completed

Guided Project 5-3

For this project, you respond to task requests you received. Based on your schedule, you are able to accept one, accept one with a minor exception, and decline one.
[Student Learning Outcomes 5.1, 5.3, 5.4]

Skills Covered in This Project

- Accept a task request.
- Modify a reply to a task request.
- Decline a task request.
- Send a status update to a task request.

1. Accept the task request with the subject *Email membership CEE details as they arise*.
   a. Click the **Mail** button on the *Navigation* bar.
   b. Open the email message from your partner.
   c. Click the **Accept** button [*Task* tab, *Respond* group].
   d. Select the **Edit the response before sending** radio button and click **OK**.

e. In the message, type:

Hi [partner's name], OK. Will be sure to work on this every Thursday until the race!

[your name]

f. Click the **Send** button.

2. Send an update that the task is 25 percent complete.
    a. Click the **Tasks** button on the *Navigation* bar.
    b. Open the task that you accepted.
    c. Change the *% Complete* to **25%**.
    d. Click the **Send Status Report** button [*Task* tab, *Manage Task* group].
    e. Add the following text to the message in the email status report:

Hi [partner's name], Just wanted to let you know that I wrote the draft of the email for this coming Thursday's update.

[your name]

f. Click the **Send** button.
g. Click the **Save & Close** button.

3. Decline the task request with the subject *Cycling Evolution Event: Final check*.
    a. Click the **Mail** button on the *Navigation* bar.
    b. Open the email message from your partner.
    c. Click the **Decline** button [*Task* tab, *Respond* group].
    d. Select the **Edit the response before sending** radio button and click **OK**.
    e. In the message, type:

Hi [partner's name], Sorry, I have to drop my daughter off at her softball practice before going to the Cycling Evolution Event. Please take care of the final checks.

[your name]

f. Click the **Send** button.

4. Email the task request acceptance message, task decline message, and status update message to your instructor as Outlook items.
    a. Click the **Mail** button on the *Navigation* bar.
    b. Click the **New Email** button [*Home* tab, *New* group].
    c. Enter the following information in your message:

To: Instructor's email address
Cc: Your email address
Subject: Outlook Guided Project 5-3
Body: Hi [instructor name],

Attached are my Outlook items for the Guided Project 5-3 exercise.

[your name]

    d. Click the **Attach Item** button [*Message* tab, *Include* group] and select **Outlook Item**.
    e. Select the **Sent** option and locate the three messages you sent.
    f. Press the **Ctrl** key and select the three email messages and click **OK**.
    g. Click **Send** (Figure 5-63).

Figure 5-63 Guided Project 5-3 completed

Independent Project 5-4

For this project, you prepare for the Placer Hills Real Estate (PHRE) annual strategic planning meeting. You were chosen to lead the meeting and you create a *Tasks List* to keep yourself organized.
[Student Learning Outcomes 5.1, 5.2, 5.3]

Skills Covered in This Project

- Create a new task.
- Modify the task subject, start date, due date, reminder, priority, and message.

- Create a task from a calendar appointment.
- Create a recurring task.
- Email task items as attachments.

1. Create a new task with the following information:

   Subject: Reserve Board Room
   Start date: None
   Due date: One week from Monday
   Reminder: Two days from today at 9:00 AM
   Priority: Normal
   Message: Reserve conference room for two Mondays from today.

2. Create a new calendar appointment with the following information:

   Subject: Strategic Planning Meeting
   Location: Board Room
   Start time: Two Mondays from today
   Set the appointment to be an **Event**.
   Body: Planning for the upcoming fiscal year

3. Create a new task from the calendar appointment you created in step 2. Modify the appointment with the following details:

   Subject: Strategic Planning Meeting: Email Reminder to Department Heads
   Message: Send email to all department heads 3 days in advance
   Due Date: Three days before the strategic planning meeting
   Reminder: Three days before the strategic planning meeting at 9:30 AM

4. Create a new task with the following information.

   Subject: Send Agenda to Department Heads
   Start date: None
   Due date: One week from Monday
   Reminder: One week from today at 9:00 AM
   Priority: High
   Message: Develop agenda based on strategies discussed at the last board meeting.

5. Email the three tasks you created to your instructor as Outlook items. Enter the following information in your message:

   To: Instructor's email address
   Cc: Your email address
   Subject: Outlook Independent Project 5-4
   Body: Hi [instructor name],

   Attached are my Outlook items for the Independent Project 5-4 exercise.

   [student name]

   Attach the three tasks as Outlook Items (Figure 5-64).

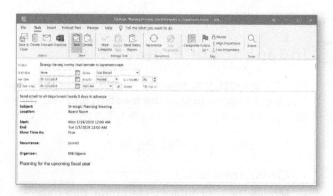

Figure 5-64 Independent Project 5-4 completed

Independent Project 5-5

For this project, you use your *Task List* and send out task requests to your peers to prepare for the PHRE strategic planning meeting.
[Student Learning Outcomes 5.1, 5.3, 5.4]

Skills Covered in This Project

- Edit an existing task.
- Assign a task.
- Edit an assigned task message.
- Mark a task as complete.
- Email task items as attachments.

1. Update the task *Reserve Board Room* to reflect the following:

   Subject: Reserve Conference Room A
   Message: Call Cammie for reservation.

2. Mark *Reserve Conference Room A* as complete.

3. Assign the task *Strategic Planning Meeting: Email Reminder to Department Heads* to a partner and include a message asking your partner to send the email reminder to the department heads.

4. Update the task *Send Agenda to Department Heads* to reflect the following:

   Status: **In Progress**
   % Complete: **50%**
   Message: Developed draft agenda.

5. Assign the task *Send Agenda to Department Heads* to a partner with a message that asks them to proofread the draft available in their shared folder.

6. Email the *Reserve Conference Room A* task and the two messages with assigned tasks to your instructor as Outlook items. Enter the following information in your message:

   To: Instructor's email address
   Cc: Your email address
   Subject: Outlook Independent Project 5-5
   Body: Hi [instructor name],

   Attached are my Outlook items for the Independent Project 5-5 exercise.

   [your name]

   Attach the three items as Outlook Items (Figure 5-65).

Figure 5-65 Independent Project 5-5 completed

Independent Project 5-6

For this project, you receive task requests from your peer to prepare for the PHRE strategic planning meeting. You send an update and complete a task.
[Student Learning Outcomes 5.1, 5.3, 5.4]

Skills Covered in This Project

- Accept a task request.
- Modify a reply to a task request.
- Decline a task request.
- Send a status update to a task request.

1. Accept the task request with the subject *Send Agenda to Department Heads*. Edit the response to indicate that you will review the agenda later today.

2. Open the *Send Agenda to Department Heads* task. Send a status report to your partner indicating the following:

   Message: Indicate that you reviewed the agenda and finalized it.
   % Complete: **75%**

3. Open the *Strategic Planning Meeting: Email Reminder to Department Heads* request.
   a. Decline the request.
   b. Edit the response to indicate that you reviewed the agenda but think that it would be better received if your partner sent it to the department heads.

4. Email the two task acceptance messages, status update message, and declined task message to your instructor as Outlook items. Enter the following information in your message:

   To: Instructor's email address
   Cc: Your email address
   Subject: Outlook Independent Project 5-6
   Body: Hi [instructor name],

   Attached are my Outlook items for the Independent Project 5-6 exercise.

   [your name]

   Attach the four items as Outlook Items (Figure 5-66).

Figure 5-66 Independent Project 5-6 completed

Challenge Project 5-7

Create a *Task List* for yourself based on your current school, work, and personal schedules for the current month. Be sure to include items such as homework, projects, activities, and preparation for events such as club activities.
[Student Learning Outcomes 5.1, 5.2, 5.3, 5.5]

- Include all tasks for the current month. Create at least 10 tasks.
- Use categories to organize tasks.
- Set appropriate start and end dates.
- Include details for tasks when necessary.
- Use recurrence for at least one task.
- Create at least one task from a calendar item or email message. You may use the calendar you created in the previous chapter.
- After a task is finished mark it as complete. At least one task should be completed.
- Customize your view.
- Email the tasks to your instructor as email attachments
- Attach each of the tasks to your email message (attach each task as an Outlook Item).
- Change the subject of your message to Outlook Challenge Project 5-7.

Challenge Project 5-8

Develop a *Task List* for an organization in which you currently belong. Be sure to assign tasks to different organization members and include progress for items that are currently being worked on but are not completed. The *Task List* should encompass at least one month of work for the organization.
[Student Learning Outcomes 5.1, 5.2, 5.3, 5.4, 5.5]

- Include all tasks for your organization for the current month. Create at least 10 tasks.
- Use categories to organize tasks.
- Set appropriate start and end dates.
- Include details for tasks when necessary.
- Include tags, such as priority when appropriate.
- At least one task is partially completed and should include the percentage.
- Assign tasks to different organization members. At least three tasks should be assigned.
- Customize your view.
- Email the tasks to your instructor as email attachments.
- Attach each of the tasks to your email message as an Outlook item.
- Change the subject of your message to Outlook Challenge Project 5-8.

Challenge Project 5-9

Work with a family member or friend to develop a *Task List*. The *Task List* can include items such as chores, homework, projects, and extracurricular activities. Be sure to include categories to organize the *Task List*.
[Student Learning Outcomes 5.1, 5.2, 5.3, 5.4, 5.5]

- Include all tasks for your friend or family member for an entire month. Create at least 10 tasks.
- Use categories to organize tasks.
- Set appropriate start and end dates.
- Include details for tasks that require them.
- Use recurrence for at least one task.
- After a task is finished mark it as complete. At least one task should be completed.
- Customize the view to meet his or her needs.
- Email the tasks to your instructor as email attachments.
- Attach each of the tasks to your email message as an Outlook item.
- Include a short message describing how your friend or family member used *Tasks Lists* in Outlook and how his/her method differs from yours.
- Change the subject of your message to Outlook Challenge Project 5-9.

CHAPTER 6	Folders, Rules, Quick Steps, and Search Folders

CHAPTER OVERVIEW

After completing the first half of this book, you now have a good understanding of the main components of Outlook—Email, Contacts, Calendar, and Tasks. Building on this essential foundation, we will delve into the numerous ways you can customize Outlook to best meet your needs. Outlook provides you with a range of features to help organize, categorize, and prioritize items within Outlook. Using folders, *Quick Steps*, rules, and search folders will help you to become a more efficient and effective Outlook user.

STUDENT LEARNING OUTCOMES (SLOs)

After completing this chapter, you will be able to:

SLO 6.1   Create, arrange, and modify Outlook folders (p. O6-216).
SLO 6.2   Create, apply, and change Outlook rules (p. O6-220).
SLO 6.3   Customize and use *Quick Steps* (p O6-230).
SLO 6.4   Utilize search folders to find email messages (p. O6-235).

CASE STUDY

For the Pause & Practice projects, you prepare for a group project and class by using folders, rules, Quick Steps, and search folders to help you more effectively and efficiently manage your email.

Pause & Practice 6-1: You create folders to organize your email messages. You begin by creating folders for your class, instructor, group project partners, and best friend. You delete the folder for your best friend.

Pause & Practice 6-2: You create two rules. The first rule is to move email from a specific instructor to the folder you created in the first Pause & Practice. The second rule moves all of your email messages from both of your group members into the folder you created in the first Pause & Practice.

Pause & Practice 6-3: You create two *Quick Steps* to help you be more efficient when working with email. For the first *Quick Step*, your instructor indicated that he or she wants you to email with a specific subject line. Rather than ensuring you type the right subject line for each message, you create a *Quick Step* for those messages. For the second *Quick Step*, you create tasks out of email messages for your group project to ensure you can view your work to complete in your tasks instead of searching through many email messages.

Pause & Practice 6-4: You utilize search folders to find information quickly. You create a search folder for email messages from your partners with attachments to allow you to easily locate files. You also want to use a search folder to quickly locate email messages from your instructor with the word "due" to quickly find messages with due dates or changes to due dates.

Using Folders

Most of you have a filing system in your home. You might have a filing cabinet with separate folders for monthly bills, insurance, income taxes, investments, and so forth. Can you imagine having just one drawer in your filing cabinet and throwing everything in that drawer? How big a mess would it be and how hard would it be to find an important paper?

In File Explorer, the *Documents* folder stores and organizes folders and files. Various types of files, such as, Word, Excel, PDF, and picture files are stored in folders within the *Documents* folder. For example, create a folder named *Travel* within the *Documents* folder. Within the *Travel* folder, you can create subfolders to store pictures and itineraries of recent trips.

In Outlook, use *folders* to organize and group your emails, contacts, calendar, tasks, notes, and journals. In contrast to the generic type of folders used in Windows, Outlook folders are specific to the type of Outlook items stored. For example, a *Mail* folder is used to store email and a *Task* folder is used to store tasks.

Create a Folder

Creating folders in Outlook is actually very simple. The most important aspect to remember is that each Outlook folder is created to store a specific type of Outlook item. When the *Create New Folder* dialog box opens, it is important to confirm the type of folder you are creating and the location of the file.

In Outlook, the following types of folders can be created:

- *Calendar Items*
- *Contact Items*
- *InfoPath Form Items*
- *Journal Items*
- *Mail and Post Items*
- *Note Items*
- *Task Items*

Follow these steps to create a new *Mail* folder. The steps are the same for creating any type of Outlook folder.

Figure 6-2 *Create New Folder* dialog box

▶ HOW TO: Create a Folder

1. Click the **Mail** button in the *Navigation* bar.
2. Click the **Folder** tab.
3. Click the **New Folder** button in the *New* group (Figure 6-1). The *Create New Folder* dialog box opens (Figure 6-2).

Figure 6-1 *New Folder* button

4. Type the name of the new folder to be created.
5. Confirm that the *Folder contains* drop-down list displays **Mail and Post Items**.
6. Specify the location of the new folder in the *Select where to place the folder* list.
7. Click **OK**.

> **ANOTHER WAY**
> You can create a new folder by right-clicking the folder inside which you would like to create a new folder and then selecting **New Folder**.

> **ANOTHER WAY**
> **Ctrl+Shift+E** opens the *Create New Folder* dialog box throughout Outlook.

Move a Folder

When you create a new folder in the wrong location or if you want to move a folder, you can use the *Ribbon* or the drag-and-drop method. The easiest way to move a folder to a new location is to click the folder to be moved in the *Folder* pane and drag and drop it to the new location. The folder and all its contents move to the new location.

Another way to move a folder is to use the *Move* feature.

▶ HOW TO: Move a Folder

1. Select the folder to be moved in the *Folder* pane.
2. Click the **Folder** tab.
3. Click the **Move Folder** button in the *Actions* group (Figure 6-3). The *Move Folder* dialog box opens (Figure 6-4).
4. Click the desired location to move the folder in the *Move the selected folder to the folder list* dialog box.
5. Click **OK**. The folder and all its contents will be moved to the new location.

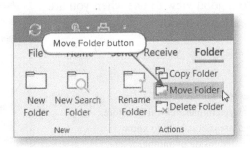

Figure 6-3 *Move Folder* button

Figure 6-4 *Move Folder* dialog box

> **ANOTHER WAY**
> You can right-click the folder to be moved and choose **Move Folder**, or simply drag and drop the folder to a new location in the *Folder* pane.

Delete a Folder

Folders are sometimes created to store information temporarily. Folders can be deleted when they are no longer needed. When you delete a folder, all the items in the folder are deleted as well. The deleted folder is moved to the *Deleted Items* folder.

▶HOW TO: Delete a Folder

1. Select the folder to be deleted in the *Folder* pane.
2. Click the **Delete Folder** button in the *Actions* group on the *Folder* tab (Figure 6-5).
   - A warning dialog box opens asking you if you are sure you want to move the folder to the *Deleted Items* folder.
3. Click **Yes** to delete the folder and all its contents.

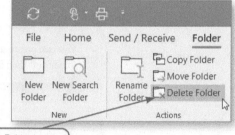

Delete Folder button

Figure 6-5 *Delete Folder* button

> ANOTHER WAY
>
> Right-click the folder to be deleted and choose **Delete Folder**.

> ANOTHER WAY
>
> **Ctrl+D** deletes the selected item. This shortcut will delete a folder or other selected Outlook items.

Use the Folders List

When you are in the Mail, Calendar, Contacts, Tasks, Notes, or Journal areas, only those folders associated with that part of Outlook display in the *Folder* pane. The ***Folders list*** (Figure 6-6) is a useful view to show all your Outlook folders in the *Folder* pane. This is also a good view to use when you are moving folders from one location to another.

> MORE INFO
>
> In all the areas of Outlook except Mail and the *Folders* list, your folders are not displayed in hierarchical structure. In other words, in these other areas, it is hard to know whether or not a folder is located inside of another folder.

Display the *Folders* list by clicking the **Options** button (. . .) in the *Navigation* bar and then clicking **Folders**.

> ANOTHER WAY
>
> **Ctrl+6** displays the *Folders* list in the *Folder* pane.

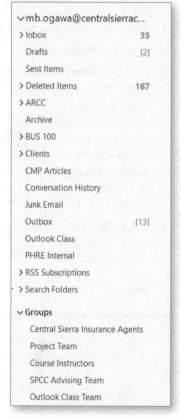

Figure 6-6 *Folders* list

For this Pause & Practice project, you create folders to help organize email messages. You begin by creating folders for your class, instructor, group project partners, and best friend. You delete the folder for your best friend.

1. Create a folder for your class.
   a. Click the **Mail** button in the *Navigation* bar.
   b. Click the **Folder** tab.
   c. Click the **New Folder** button in the *New* group. The *Create New Folder* dialog box opens.
   d. Type BUS 100 in the *Name* text area.
   e. Confirm that the folder type in the *Folder contains* menu is **Mail and Post Items**.
   f. Specify your main email account folder in the *Select where to place the folder section*.
   g. Click **OK**.

2. Create a folder for your instructor.
   a. Click the **Mail** button in the *Navigation* bar.
   b. Click the **Folder** tab.
   c. Click the **New Folder** button in the *New* group. The *Create New Folder* dialog box opens.
   d. Type your instructor's name in the *Name* text area.
   e. Confirm that the folder type in the *Folder contains* menu is **Mail and Post Items**.
   f. Specify your main email account folder in the *Select where to place the folder* section.
   g. Click **OK**.

3. Create a folder for your group project.
   a. Click the **Mail** button in the *Navigation* bar.
   b. Click the **Folder** tab.
   c. Click the **New Folder** button in the *New* group. The *Create New Folder* dialog box opens.
   d. Type Group Project in the *Name* text area.
   e. Confirm that the folder type in the *Folder contains* menu is **Mail and Post Items**.
   f. Specify your main email account folder in the *Select where to place the folder* section.
   g. Click **OK**.

4. Create a folder for your best friend.
   a. Click the **Mail** button in the *Navigation* bar.
   b. Click the **Folder** tab.
   c. Click the **New Folder** button in the *New* group. The *Create New Folder* dialog box opens.
   d. Type Nicole in the *Name* text area.
   e. Confirm that the folder type in the *Folder contains* menu is **Mail and Post Items**.
   f. Specify your main email account folder in the *Select where to place the folder* section.
   g. Click **OK**.

5. Move the *[instructor name]* and *Group Project* folders into the *[class name]* folder.
   a. Select **[instructor name]** folder in the *Folder* pane.
   b. Click the **Folder** tab.
   c. Click the **Move Folder** button in the *Actions* group. The *Move Folder* dialog box opens.
   d. Click the **BUS 100** folder in the *Move the selected folder to the folder* section.
   e. Click **OK**.

6. Move the *Group Project* folder into the *BUS 100* folder.
   a. Select **Group Project** folder in the *Folder* pane.
   b. Click the **Folder** tab.
   c. Click the **Move Folder** button in the *Actions* group. The *Move Folder* dialog box opens.
   d. Click the **[class name]** folder in the *Move the selected folder to the folder* section.
   e. Click **OK**.

7. Delete the *Nicole* folder.
   a. Select the **Nicole** folder in the *Folder* pane.
   b. Click the **Delete Folder** button in the *Actions* group on the *Folder* tab. A warning dialog box opens asking if you are sure you want to move the folder to the *Deleted Items* folder.
   c. Click **Yes** to delete the folder and all its contents. Figure 6-7 is a sample of your folder list at the end of Pause & Practice 6-1.

Figure 6-7 PP Outlook 6-1 completed

SLO 6.2

Creating and Using Rules

You may receive email messages from each of your instructors, family members, or coworkers. When all of these emails appear in your Inbox, it is difficult to distinguish routine email messages from messages with a higher priority. To help organize your email messages, create folders and rules to automatically move email messages to an appropriate folder.

Rules might be one of the most useful features in Outlook. Rules can be used to check incoming or outgoing emails and apply an action. If you have ever used the *IF* function in Microsoft Excel, rules operate similar to this if/then logical principle. Most rules have two basic parts: a *condition* and an *action*. An *exception* can also be added to the rule.

- *Condition*: The condition is what Outlook looks for when an email is received or sent. This could be an email that includes a specific word or words in the subject or body, sent from a specific person, received through a specific email account, or marked as high importance.
- *Action*: The action is what is done with the email when the condition is met. This could include moving the email to another folder, marking the email as high importance, categorizing the email with a specific category, deleting the email, or forwarding the email.
- *Exception*: An exception can be used to nullify an action. For example, a rule can be set up to look for the word "BUS 310" in the subject line and move it to the *BUS 310* folder, except if it comes from the *Dean of the CSIT* area. Exceptions are not commonly used in rules.

Quick Steps are similar to rules, but they do not include a condition. So rather than automatically applying an action to an email when it meets a condition, *Quick Steps* can be applied to email on an individual basis. For example, a *Quick Step* can be used to create a meeting request from a received email message.

Create a Rule

A rule can be created quickly based on an email in your Inbox. When you create a rule based on an email message, you have a limited number of options for the condition and action, and you cannot include an exception.

If you receive several email messages with the subject "Outlook," create a rule to manage the emails. The rule would automatically move all emails with the word "Outlook" in the subject line to an *Outlook* folder.

▶ HOW TO: Create a Rule Based on an Email in Your Inbox

1. Click the **Mail** button on the *Navigation* bar.
2. Open the email for which you would like to create a new rule.
3. Click the **Rules** button in the *Move* group on the *Message* tab.
4. Choose **Create Rule** (Figure 6-8). The *Create Rule* dialog box opens. Three conditions appear at the top of the dialog box, and three actions appear at the bottom of the dialog box (Figure 6-9).

Figure 6-8 *Create Rule*

5. In the conditions area (the top half of the dialog box), select the **Subject contains** check box and make sure the word in the subject is correct. If not, correct it.
6. In the actions area (the bottom half of the dialog box), select the **Move the item to folder** check box and click the **Select Folder** button.
7. Select the desired folder from the folder list and press **OK** (Figure 6-10). The *Create Rule* dialog box will still be open. Confirm that the correct folder was selected (see Figure 6-10). If not, click the **Select Folder** button and select the correct folder.

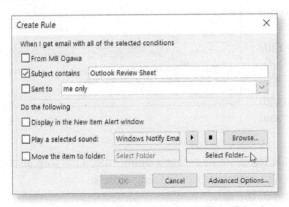

Figure 6-9 *Create Rule* dialog box

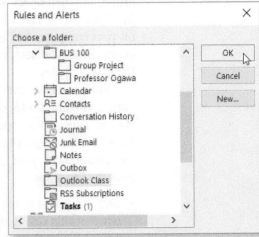

Figure 6-10 Select a folder for the rule

8. Click **OK**. A *Success* dialog box opens (Figure 6-11).

9. Select the **Run this rule now on messages already in the current folder** check box.

10. Click **OK**.

11. All the emails in your Inbox with a subject that matches the condition will be moved to the specified folder.

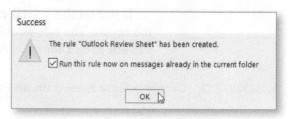

Figure 6-11 *Success dialog box*

> **MORE INFO**
>
> If you forget to create a folder before creating a rule, you can create a new folder in the *Rules and Alerts* dialog box by clicking the **New** button.

> **MORE INFO**
>
> When creating a rule that looks for a word in the subject, Outlook looks for *exactly* what you type. Common errors include misspellings and a space after the word. The word you type is not case sensitive.

> **ANOTHER WAY**
>
> Right-click an email message and choose **Rules** and then select **Create Rule**.

Create an Advanced Rule

Creating a rule based on an email in your Inbox is effective and efficient, but you are limited by the number of conditions and actions from which to select.

To have additional customization options for the rules you create, open the *Rules and Alerts* dialog box (click the **Home** tab, click the **Rules** button in the *Move* group, and then select **Manage Rules & Alerts** as shown in Figure 6-12). This dialog box lists the rules existing on your computer and is used to create, modify, delete, and order the existing rules.

Figure 6-12 *Manage Rules & Alerts*

When you click the *New Rule* button (Figure 6-13), the *Rules Wizard* dialog box opens. The *Rules Wizard* steps you through the creation of your rule and includes five steps.

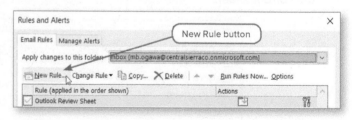

Figure 6-13 Create a new rule

- *Step 1*: Choose to use a rule template or create a blank rule. This step also determines whether this rule is applied to incoming or outgoing emails.
- *Step 2*: Select the condition of the rule.
- *Step 3*: Set the action Outlook is to perform if the condition is met.

- *Step 4*: Specify any exceptions to the rule.
- *Step 5*: Name and run the rule.

You can choose rule templates to create the most common types of rules. When you select a rule template, you move to the next step to specify the condition. You can also choose to start creating a rule from a blank rule.

▶ HOW TO: Create a New Rule

1. Click the **Mail** button in the *Navigation* bar.

2. Click the **Rules** button in the *Move* group on the *Home* tab and choose **Manage Rules & Alerts**. The *Rules and Alerts* dialog box opens.

3. Click the **New Rule** button. The *Rules Wizard* dialog box opens.

4. Select **Apply rule on messages I receive** in the *Start from a blank rule* section (Figure 6-14).

5. Click **Next**. You move to the next step to select a condition for the rule.

6. Select the **from people or public group** check box. The condition displays in the bottom section of the dialog box.

7. Click the **people or public group** link in the bottom section (Figure 6-15). The *Rule Address* dialog box opens.

8. Select the name of the individual for the condition of the rule (Figure 6-16).

9. Click **From** and **OK**.

   - The *Rule Address* dialog box closes and you return to the *Rules Wizard* dialog box.
   - Notice the person's name appears in the bottom section as the condition for which Outlook is looking.

Figure 6-14 Create a new blank rule

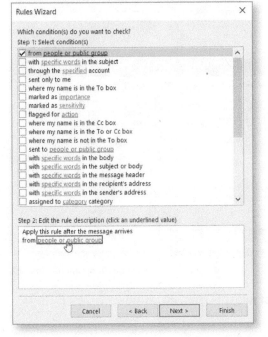

Figure 6-15 Click *the people or public group* link

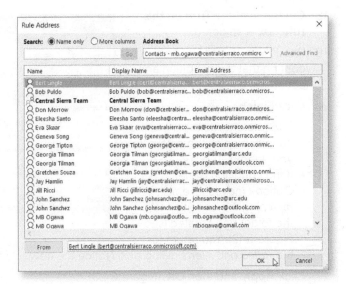

Figure 6-16 Select addresses

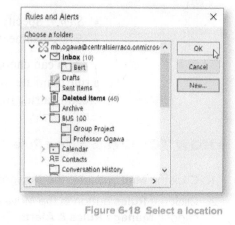

Figure 6-18 Select a location

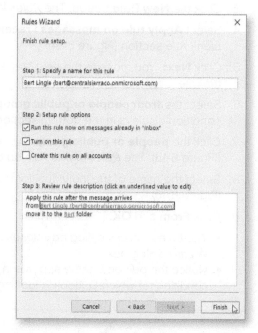

Figure 6-17 Select an action

10. Click **Next**. You move to the *action* step in the *Rules Wizard* dialog box.

11. Select the **move it to the specified folder** check box (Figure 6-17).

12. Click the **specified** folder link in the bottom section. The *Rules and Alerts* dialog box opens.

13. Click the desired folder and press **OK** (Figure 6-18). You return to the *Rules Wizard* dialog box. Always read the rule in the bottom section to make sure the condition and action are correct.

14. Click **Next**. You move to the *exceptions* step.

15. Click **Next**. No exceptions will be added to this rule. The *Finish rule setup* step appears.

16. Customize the name of the rule in the *Step 1* area.

17. Select the **Run this rule now on messages already in "Inbox"** check box (Figure 6-19).

18. Confirm that the **Turn on this rule** box is selected.

19. Read the rule one last time to confirm that the condition and action are correct.

20. Click **Finish**.

    • The rule checks the condition on all the emails in your Inbox.

    • If the condition is met, Outlook moves all emails matching the condition to the folder you created (see Figure 6-19). You return to the *Rules and Alerts* dialog box. Notice the new rule is in the list of rules.

21. Click **Apply** and then **OK**. (Figure 6-20).

Figure 6-19 Setup rule options

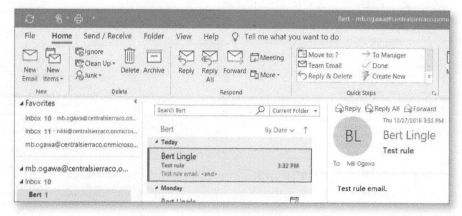

Figure 6-20 Email message automatically moved

Creating rules might seem like a daunting process, but once you have gone through the steps of creating a rule and understand the logical *condition, action, exception* sequence, you'll realize that creating rules is actually very simple. And not only are rules easy to create and use, but they are also very effective in helping you to organize and customize your Inbox.

> **MORE INFO**
>
> It is best to keep rules simple: a condition and one action (and an exception if necessary). The more conditions and actions you have in one rule, the greater the chance of either diluting the effectiveness of the rule or causing the rule to not function as intended.

> **MORE INFO**
>
> When using Outlook in a stand-alone environment, your rules are stored on your computer.
> If you are using Outlook in an Exchange environment, your rules are stored on the Exchange server.
> This means that most rules will run wherever you access Outlook, including Outlook web App.
> Some rules are client-only rules, which means they will run only on the computer on which they were created.

Modify a Rule

Once a rule is created, it is very easy to modify the condition, action, or exception. Rules can also be modified to run on different folders within your mailbox.

> **HOW TO: Modify a Rule**

1. Click the **Mail** button on the *Navigation* bar.

2. Click the **Rules** button and select the **Manage Rules & Alerts** option.

3. Select the rule to be modified, click the **Change Rule** button, and then choose **Edit Rule Settings** (Figure 6-21). The *Rules Wizard* dialog box opens. Alternatively, double-click the rule to open the *Rules Wizard* dialog box.

4. Change the condition, action, exception, name, or folder on which the rule is to run.

5. Select the **Run this rule now on messages already in "Inbox"** check box after you modify a rule.

6. Click **Finish** to apply the changes and run the rule.

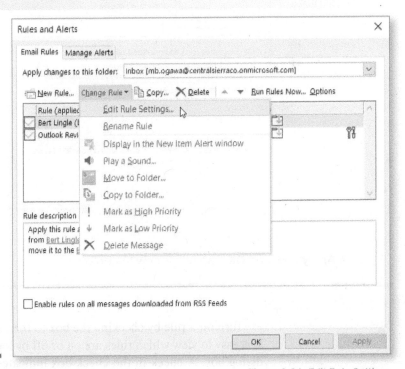

Figure 6-21 *Edit Rule Settings*

Delete or Turn On/Off a Rule

A rule can easily be deleted by selecting the rule in the *Rules and Alerts* dialog box and either pressing the **Delete** button or right-clicking the rule and choosing **Delete**.

One way to manage rules is to turn off a rule but not delete it. The rule can be turned on if you need to use it again.

▶HOW TO: Turn Off a Rule

1. Open the *Rules and Alerts* dialog box.
2. Deselect the check box to the left of the rule to turn it off (Figure 6-22).

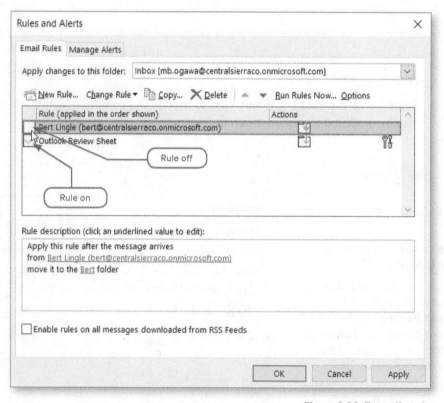

Figure 6-22 Turn off a rule

3. Click **Apply** and then **OK**. The rule is now turned off.

Turn on a rule by checking the box to the left of the rule in the *Rules and Alerts* dialog box. It is easy to view which rules are on or off by looking at your list of rules in the *Rules and Alerts* dialog box. A check in the check box indicates that a rule is turned on, and no check in the check box indicates that a rule is turned off.

> **MORE INFO**
>
> Outlook has a default rule (*Clear categories on mail*) that has been created for you. This rule clears any categories on incoming messages. It is important to keep this rule because you do not want others' categories conflicting with your categories.

Run a Rule

When a rule that was turned off is turned back on, it is important to run this rule on messages currently in the Inbox. Outlook provides you with a feature to run specific rules without having to step through the *Rules Wizard.*

Options include selecting the rules to be run, the folder on which to run each rule, and what type of messages on which to apply each rule (*All Messages*, *Unread Messages*, or *Read Messages*). A ***Rule Description*** displays in the middle of the dialog box for the selected rule.

HOW TO: Run a Rule

1. Click the **Rules** button [*Home* tab, *Move* group] and select **Manage Rules & Alerts**.
2. Select the *Rule* you want to run and click the **Run Rules Now** button. The *Run Rules Now* dialog box opens (Figure 6-23).
3. Check the rule to run. The *Rule Description* area displays the condition and action (and exception if applicable).
4. Specify the folder on which the rule is to run.
5. Specify the types of messages on which to apply the rule.
6. Click **Run Now**.
7. Click **Close** to close the *Run Rules Now* dialog box.

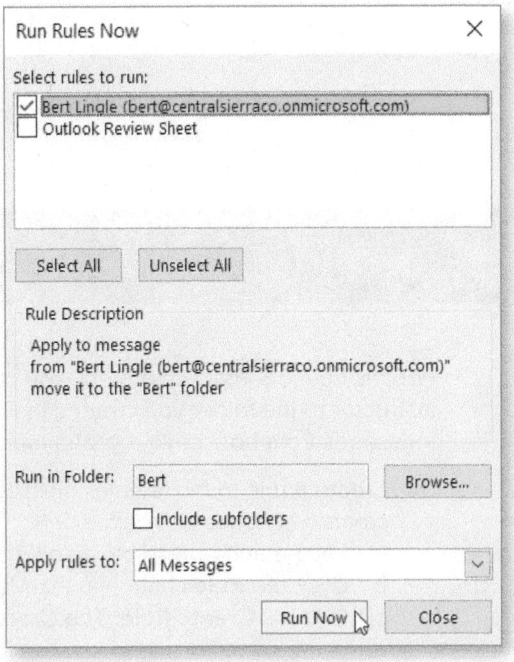

Figure 6-23 *Run Rules Now* dialog box

Rearrange Rules

As you begin using rules, you will find more and more uses for them. It will not be long before you have a long list of rules running in Outlook. The rules in Outlook are ***hierarchical***, which means that those at the top of the list are run before those at the bottom. It is important to order rules properly to prioritize the order in which the rules are run and minimize the potential for conflict. For example, if you have a rule to mark an email as important if it comes from a particular person and a rule to move all emails with attachments to an *Attachments* folder, you might have a conflict if you receive an email from that particular person and it has an attachment. If the attachment rule is above the mark as important rule, the email message will be moved to the *Attachments* folder but not marked as important.

You will need to determine which action is the most important and make sure the rule is above the other rules in the *Rules and Alerts* dialog box. Use the up and down buttons in the dialog box to move rules up or down in the rule hierarchy.

▶ HOW TO: Reorder Rules

1. Open the *Rules and Alerts* dialog box.

2. Select the rule to be moved up or down in priority.

3. Click the **Move Up** or **Move Down** button (Figure 6-24).

4. Click **Apply** and **OK**.

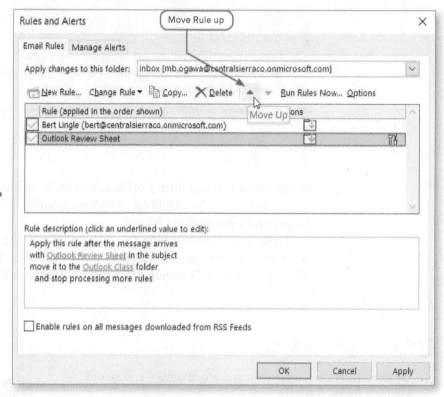

Figure 6-24 Move rules up or down

PAUSE & PRACTICE: OUTLOOK 6-2

For this Pause & Practice project, you create two rules. The first rule is to move email from a specific instructor to the folder you created in *Pause & Practice 6-1*. The second rule moves all of your email messages from both of your group members into the folder you created in *Pause & Practice 6-1*.

1. Create a rule to move email messages from your instructor into the *[instructor name]* folder you created in *Pause & Practice 6-1*.
   a. Locate and open a message from your instructor.
   b. Click the **Rules** button in the *Move* group on the *Message* tab.
   c. Choose **Create Rule**. The *Create Rule* dialog box opens.
   d. In the conditions area (the top half of the dialog box), check **From [instructor name]** (the name will vary based on your instructor's name).
   e. In the actions area (the bottom half of the dialog box), check **Move the item to folder** and click the **Select Folder** button.
   f. Select the **[instructor name]** folder from the folder list and press **OK**. The *Create Rule* dialog box remains open.
   g. Click **OK**.
   h. Select the **Run this rule now on messages already in "Inbox"** check box.
   i. Click **OK**.

2. Create an advanced rule to move emails from your two partners into the *Group Project* folder (Figure 6-25).
   a. Click the **Mail** button in the *Navigation* bar.
   b. Click the **Rules** button in the *Move* group on the *Home* tab and choose **Manage Rules & Alerts**. The *Rules and Alerts* dialog box opens.

c.	Click the **New Rule** button. The *Rules Wizard* dialog box opens.

d.	Select **Apply rule on messages I receive** in the *Start from a blank rule* section.

e.	Click **Next**. You will move to the next step to select a condition for the rule.

f.	Check the **from people or public group** box. The condition displays in the bottom section of the dialog box.

g.	Click the **people or public group** link in the bottom section. The *Rule Address* dialog box opens.

h.	Select the names of your group members if they are in your contacts list or type their email addresses with a semi colon (;) between their email addresses.

i.	Click **From** and **OK**.

j.	Click **Next**. You move to the *action* step in the *Rules Wizard* dialog box.

k.	Check the **move it to the specified folder** box.

l.	Click the **specified** folder link in the bottom section. The *Rules and Alerts* dialog box opens.

m.	Click the **Group Project** folder and press **OK**. You return to the *Rules Wizard* dialog box.

n.	Click **Next**. You return to the *exceptions* step.

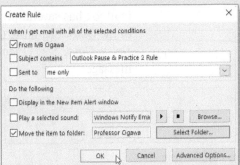

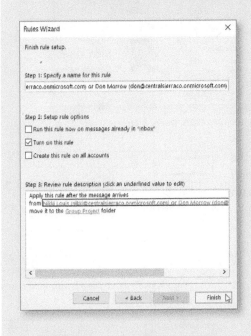

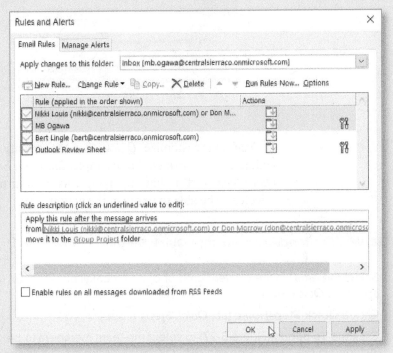

Figure 6-25 PP Outlook 6-2 completed

o.	Click **Next**. No exceptions are required for this rule. The *Finish rule setup* step appears.

p.	Type Class Name Group Project in the *Step 1* area.

q.	Confirm that the **Turn on this rule** box is selected.

r.	Read the rule one last time to confirm that the condition and action are correct.

s.	Click **Finish**.

t.	Click **Apply** and then **OK**.

Customize and Use Quick Steps

Quick Steps are a powerful tool in Outlook. Similar to a rule, a *Quick Step* performs an action on a selected email. The main difference between a *Quick Step* and a rule is that *Quick Steps* are not based on a condition, but rather they are applied to the selected emails.

Modify an Existing Quick Step

Outlook has several preset *Quick Steps*. When you select an email in your Inbox and click one of the *Quick Steps*, the *Quick Step* will automatically apply the action. For example, the *Reply & Delete Quick Step* (Figure 6-26) creates a reply message to the sender and deletes the original message.

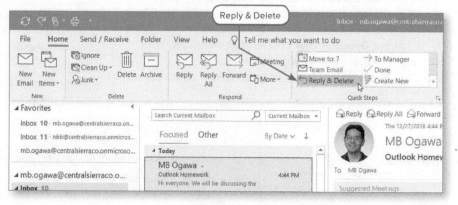

Figure 6-26 *Reply & Delete Quick Step*

You can customize *Quick Steps* to specify the action to be performed. For example, the *Team Email Quick Step* needs to have the recipients on your team selected to be able to perform the action.

Figure 6-27 *First Time Setup* dialog box

▶ HOW TO: Modify an Existing Quick Step

1. Select the email in the *Content area* or open an email on which to apply the *Quick Step*.

2. Click a **Quick Step** [*Home* tab, *Quick Steps* group].

3. Click the **To** button (Figure 6-27) to select the team members to be included in this *Quick Step* and click **OK**, or enter the email addresses followed by a semicolon.

4. Change the **Name** of the *Quick Step* as desired.

5. Click the **Options** button to open the *Edit [Quick Step's name]* dialog box (Figure 6-28). You can add additional actions to the *Quick Step* in this dialog box.

6. Click the **Show Options** link to display additional options available for this action. The **Hide Options** link will hide these available options.

7. Click **Save** to close this dialog box and return to the *Customize Quick Step* dialog box.

8. Click **Save** to save this *Quick Step* and apply it to the selected message.

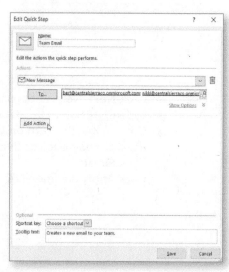

Figure 6-28 *Edit Quick Step* dialog box

Create a New Quick Step

As you begin using *Quick Steps*, you will find the need to create your own custom *Quick Steps*. These new custom *Quick Steps* will appear in the *Quick Steps* group on the *Home* and *Message* tabs. *Quick Steps* are not limited to one action but can include multiple actions to be performed on a selected email message. For example, you can create a *Quick Step* to mark an email as high importance, mark it as read, and move it to a folder.

▶**HOW TO:** Create a New Quick Step

1. Click the **Create New** *Quick Step* button [*Home* tab, *Quick Steps* group] (Figure 6-29). The *Edit Quick Step* dialog box opens (Figure 6-30).
2. Type a name for the *Quick Step*.
3. Click the **drop-down arrow** to display a list of actions. *Note: The list of actions in Figure 6-30 is not a complete list.*
4. Select the action to be performed (see Figure 6-30). If additional criteria are available, the *Show Options* link appears below the action.
5. Click the **Add Action** button to add another action (Figure 6-31). An action can be deleted by clicking the delete button to the right of the action (see Figure 6-31).

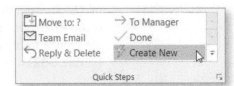

Figure 6-29 *Create New Quick Step* button

Figure 6-30 *Edit Quick Step* dialog box

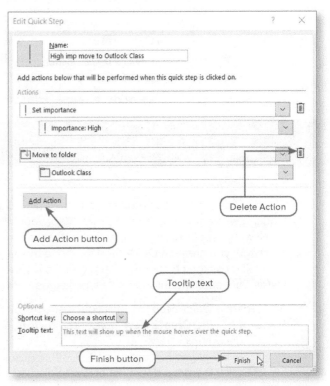

Figure 6-31 Completed *Quick Step*

6. In the *Tooltip text* area, type a description for this *Quick Step* (see Figure 6-31). This *Tooltip* appears when your pointer is placed over the *Quick Step.*

7. Click the **Finish** button when all the actions have been added (see Figure 6-31). The new *Quick Step* is included in the list of *Quick Steps.*

Manage Quick Steps

Like rules, *Quick Steps* can easily be managed. You can open the *Manage Quick Steps* dialog box by clicking the **Manage Quick Steps** option [*Home* tab, *Quick Steps* group, *More* button]. The *Manage Quick Steps* dialog box allows you to create new *Quick Steps* and modify, duplicate, or delete existing ones. Change the display order of *Quick Steps* by clicking the up or down arrows. You can also create groups to organize *Quick Steps* (Figure 6-32).

Figure 6-32 *Manage Quick Steps* dialog box

> **ANOTHER WAY**
>
> A shortcut can be added to a *Quick Step* by selecting a shortcut keystroke combination (**Ctrl+Shift+number**) when creating or editing a *Quick Step*.

> **MORE INFO**
>
> The *Restore Defaults* button in the *Manage Quick Steps* dialog box will restore the *Quick Steps* to their original settings.

PAUSE & PRACTICE: OUTLOOK 6-3

For this Pause & Practice project, you create two *Quick Steps* to help you be more efficient when working with email. For the first *Quick Step*, your instructor indicated that he or she wants you to send email with a specific subject line. Rather than checking that you typed the correct subject line for each message, you create a *Quick Step* for those messages. For the second *Quick Step*, you create tasks out of email messages for your group project to ensure you can view your work to complete in your tasks instead of searching through email messages.

1. Create a *Quick Step* to email your instructor with the subject *[class name]* (Figure 6-33).
   a. Click the **Create New** *Quick Step* button [*Home* tab, *Quick Steps* group]. The *Edit Quick Step* dialog box opens.
   b. In the *Name* text area type Email [instructor name].
   c. Click the **drop-down list arrow** to display a list of actions that can be performed.

    d. Select **New Message**.

    e. Click the **Show Options** link below the action.

    f. Click the **To** button. Select your instructor's email address and click the **To** button followed by **OK**. If your instructor's email address is not in your Contacts, type it into the *To* field in the *Edit Quick Step* dialog box.

    g. In the *Subject* field, type [class name].

    h. In the *Tooltip text* area, type Email to instructor for [class name].

    i. Click the **Finish** button to create the new *Quick Step*.

2. Create a *Quick Step* to create a task with an attachment (see Figure 6-33).

    a. Click the **Create New** *Quick Step* button [*Home* tab, *Quick Steps* group]. The *Edit Quick Step* dialog box opens.

    b. In the *Name* text area, type Group Project Task.

    c. Click the **drop-down list arrow** to display a list of actions that can be performed.

    d. Select **Create a task with attachment**.

    e. Click the **Add Action** button to add another action.

    f. Click the **drop-down list arrow** to display a list of actions that can be performed.

    g. Select **Delete message**.

    h. In the *Tooltip text* area, type Create task and delete message.

    i. Click the **Finish** button to create the new *Quick Step*.

3. Send an email message to one of your partners to request the draft of the executive summary.

    a. Click the **Mail** button in the *Navigation* bar.

    b. Click the **New Email** button [*Home* tab, *New* group].

    c. Enter the following information in your message:

        To: partner's email address
        Subject: Executive Summary Request
        Body: Hi [partner name],

        Please email me a draft of the executive summary when you finish it.

        Sincerely,
        [your name]

    d. Click **Send**.

4. Create a task from the message (see Figure 6-33).

    a. Locate the email your partner sent in the *Group Project* folder.

    b. Click the **Group Project Task** *Quick Step* [*Home* tab, *Quick Steps* group].

    c. Click the **Save & Close** button.

5. Email the task to your instructor as an Outlook item.

    a. Click the **Mail** button in the *Navigation* bar.

    b. Click the **New Email** button [*Home* tab, *New* group].

    c. Enter the following information in your message:

        To: instructor's email address
        Cc: your email address
        Subject: Outlook Pause & Practice 6-3
        Body: Hi [instructor name],

        Attached is the Outlook item for the Pause & Practice 6-3 exercise.

        Sincerely,
        [your name]

    d. Click the **Attach Item** button [*Message* tab, *Include* group] and select **Outlook Item**.

    e. Select the **Tasks** option and locate the task you created.

    f. Click **OK**.

    g. Click **Send**.

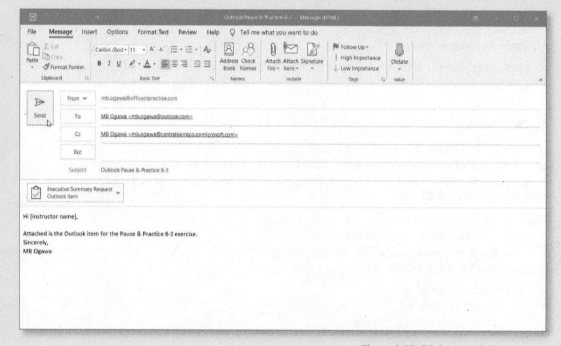

Figure 6-33 PP Outlook 6-3 completed

Using Search Folders

Search folders are related to rules in that they look for a specific condition or criterion in email messages, and if the condition is met, the message displays in the search folder. Search folders differ from rules in that the message is not physically moved to a different location.

Search folders are virtual folders; they don't actually contain any messages, but rather they display email items that are located in other folders that meet a certain condition. For example, you can create a search folder for ***Unread Mail***. Any email message in your mailbox that is unread will be displayed in the *Content area* when you click the *Unread Mail* search folder in the *Folder* pane (Figure 6-34).

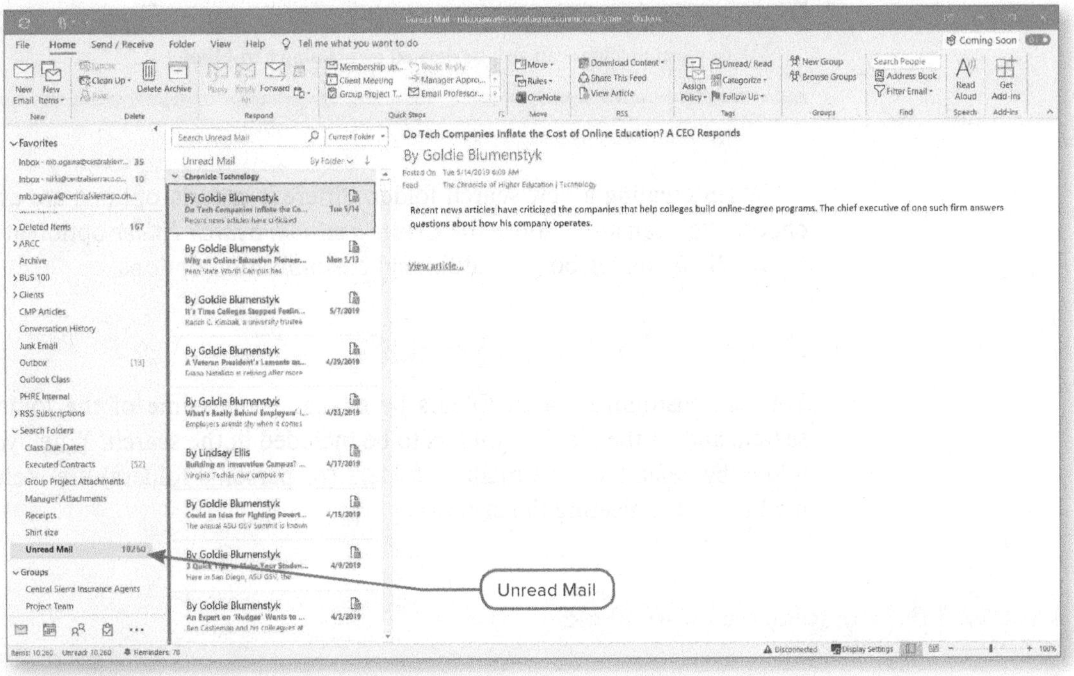

Figure 6-34 *Unread Mail* search folder

Create a New Search Folder

Suppose you want to create a search folder that looks for all the emails from your professor, but you do not want to create a rule to physically move these messages to a separate folder. A search folder can be created to find and display all the messages from your professor.

Search folders are very easy to create, customize, and delete.

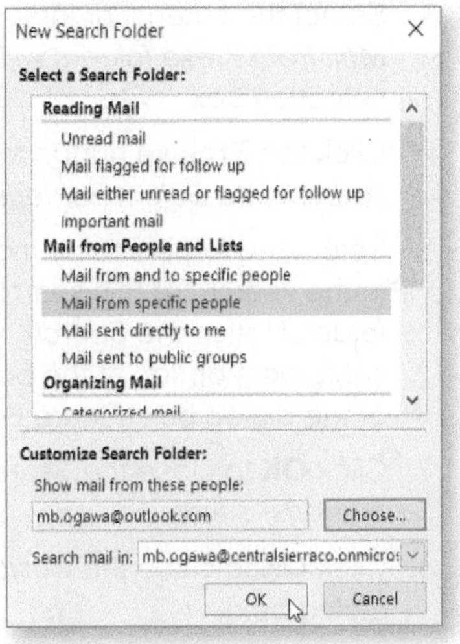

Figure 6-36 *New Search Folder* dialog box

HOW TO: Create a New Search Folder

1. Click the **Mail** button in the *Navigation* bar.
2. Click the **Folder** tab and then the **New Search Folder** button in the *New* group (Figure 6-35). The *New Search Folder* dialog box opens.
3. Select **Mail from specific people** as the condition (Figure 6-36).
4. Click **Choose** to select a contact. The *Select Names* dialog box opens.

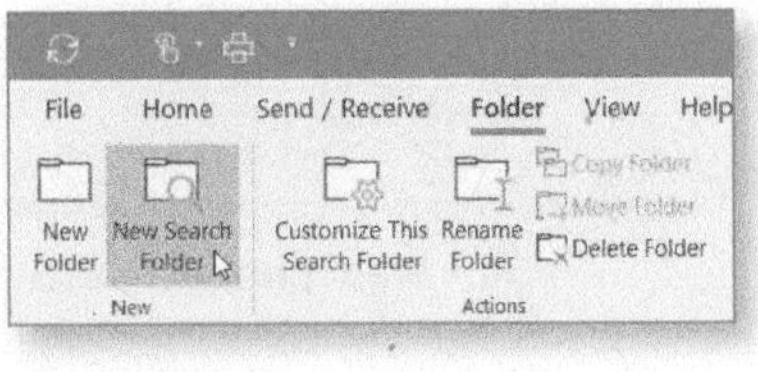

Figure 6-35 *New Search Folder* button

5. Select the name of the contact for the condition of the search folder.

6. Click the **From** button to add the contact or double-click the contact.

7. Click **OK** to close the *Select Names* dialog box.

8. Click **OK** to close the *New Search Folder* dialog box. The new search folder appears in your list of search folders in the *Folder* pane (Figure 6-37).

Figure 6-37 Search folder

> **ANOTHER WAY**
>
> A new search folder can also be created by pressing **Ctrl+Shift+P**.

When creating a new search folder, different criteria options are available from which to choose. You can also choose the *Create a custom Search Folder* option at the bottom of the *New Search Folder* dialog box for additional customization options.

Customize a Search Folder

You can customize search folders by changing the name of the folder, the criteria for the search, and/or the mailbox folders to be included in the search. When you create a new search folder, by default, all the mailbox folders (or personal folders) are included in the search for mail messages meeting the criterion.

▶HOW TO: Customize a Search Folder

1. Click the **Mail** button in the *Navigation* bar.

2. Select the search folder to be customized.

3. Click the **Folder** tab and then the **Customize This Search Folder** button in the *Actions* group (Figure 6-38). The *Customize* dialog box opens (Figure 6-39).

4. Select the criteria, or indicate which folders to include in the *Mail from these folders will be included in the Search Folder* selection box.

5. Click the **Browse** button to change the folders to be included in the search. The *Select Folder(s)* dialog box opens.

6. Select the folders to be included in the search for this search folder. Notice the *Search subfolders* option at the bottom of the dialog box (Figure 6-40).

7. Click **OK** to close the *Select Folder(s)* dialog box.

8. Click **OK** to close the *Customize* dialog box.

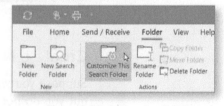

Figure 6-38 *Customize This Search Folder* button

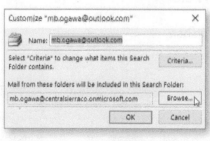

Figure 6-39 *Customize Search Folder* dialog box

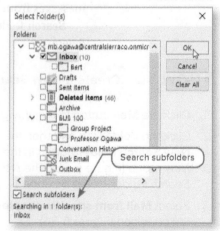

Figure 6-40 *Select Folder(s)* dialog box

Search folders can also be customized to show either the total number of items in the folder or the number of unread items in the folder.

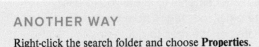

HOW TO: Customize the Number of Items Displayed in the Folder

1. Click a search folder.
2. Click the **Folder** tab.
3. Click the **Folder Properties** button in the *Properties* group. The *[Folder's Name] Properties* dialog box opens (Figure 6-41).
4. Click either **Show number of unread items** or **Show total number of items**.
5. Click **Apply** and then **OK**.

Figure 6-41 Search folder properties

Delete a Search Folder

Because search folders are virtual folders, they don't physically contain any email messages. When a search folder is deleted, none of the messages displayed in the search folder are deleted.

To delete a search folder, click the search folder in the *Folder* pane and click the **Delete Folder** button in the *Actions* group on the *Folder* tab or press **Delete** on your keyboard. You can also right-click the search folder and choose **Delete Folder**. When deleting a search folder, a dialog box opens asking if you want to delete the search folder and informing you that the items contained in the search folder will not be deleted (Figure 6-42). Press **Yes** to delete the search folder.

Microsoft Outlook   ✕

⚠ Are you sure you want to permanently delete this Search Folder? The items contained in this folder will not be deleted.

Yes   No

Figure 6-42 Delete search folder confirmation

> ### ANOTHER WAY
>
> **Ctrl+D** deletes a selected search folder throughout Outlook.

> ### MORE INFO
>
> Even though deleting a search folder will not delete the items contained in the search folder, email messages displayed in a search folder can be deleted by selecting the messages in the *Content area* and pressing **Delete**.

PAUSE & PRACTICE: OUTLOOK 6-4

For this Pause & Practice project, you utilize search folders to help you find information quickly. You create a search folder for email messages from your partners with attachments to allow you to easily locate files. You also want to use a search folder to quickly locate email messages from your instructor that contain the word "due" to quickly find messages with due dates or changes to due dates.

1. Create a new search folder to find messages from your partners with attachments.
   a. Click the **Mail** button in the *Navigation* bar.
   b. Click the **Folder** tab and then the **New Search Folder** button in the *New* group. The *New Search Folder* dialog box opens.
   c. Select **Create a custom Search Folder**.
   d. Click **Choose**. The *Custom Search Folder* dialog box opens.
   e. In the *Name* text area, type Group Project Attachments.
   f. Click the **Criteria** button. The *Search Folder Criteria* dialog box opens.
   g. In the *Messages* tab, type your partners' email addresses in the *From* text area or click the **From** button and select their contacts.
   h. Click the **More Choices** tab.
   i. Click the **Only items with** check box and ensure the option is set to **one or more attachments**.
   j. Click **OK** to close the *Search Folder Criteria* dialog box.
   k. Click **OK** to close the *Custom Search Folder* dialog box.
   l. Click **OK** to close the *New Search Folder* dialog box. The new search folder appears in your list of search folders in the *Folder* pane.

2. Customize the *Group Project Attachments* search folder to show the total number of items.
   a. Right-click the *Group Project Attachments* search folder and select **Properties**.
   b. Click the **Show total number of items** radio button.
   c. Click **OK**.

3. Create a new search folder to find messages from your instructor that contain the word "due" in the subject or body of the message.
   a. Click the **Mail** button in the *Navigation* bar.
   b. Click the **Folder** tab and then the **New Search Folder** button in the *New* group. The *New Search Folder* dialog box opens.
   c. Select **Create a custom Search Folder**.
   d. Click **Choose**. The *Custom Search Folder* dialog box opens.
   e. In the *Name* text area, type Class Due Dates.
   f. Click the **Criteria** button. The *Search Folder Criteria* dialog box opens.
   g. In the *Messages* tab, type your instructor's email address in the *From* text area or click the **From** button and select his or her contact.
   h. In the *Search for word(s)* text area, type Due. The search term is not case sensitive.
   i. Click the **In** drop-down arrow and select **subject field and message body**.
   j. Click **OK** to close the *Search Folder Criteria* dialog box.
   k. Click **OK** to close the *Custom Search Folder* dialog box.
   l. Click **OK** to close the *New Search Folder* dialog box. The new search folder will appear in your list of search folders in the *Folder* pane. See Figure 6-43 for completed *Pause & Practice 6-4*.

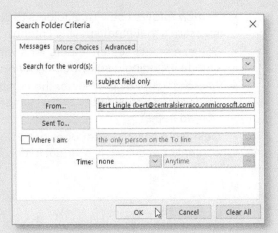
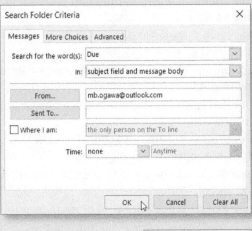

Figure 6-43 PP Outlook 6-4 completed

Chapter Summary

6.1 Create, arrange, and modify Outlook folders (p. O6-216).

- **Folders** in Outlook are similar to a physical filing cabinet with folders to organize email and other Outlook items.
- Outlook folders are specific to each type of Outlook item, such as a folder for tasks.
- Once folders are created, they can be moved.
- The **Folders list** displays all of your Outlook folders in the *Folder* pane.
- Deleting a folder also deletes its contents.

6.2 Create, apply, and change Outlook rules (p. O6-220).

- **Rules** check incoming or outgoing emails and apply an action.
- Rules have three main parts: a condition, an action, and an exception.
- A **condition** checks if an email message meets specific criteria.
- An **action** is what is done with the email when the condition is met.
- An **exception** nullifies an action if specific criteria are met.
- **Quick Steps** can be created to apply an action to an Outlook item.
- A rule can be created from an email message.
- The *Rules Wizard* guides you through the process of creating a rule from scratch.
- Rules can be edited after they are created.
- You can refer to the **Rule Description** in the *Run Rules Now* dialog box when manually running Rules.

- Rules run **hierarchically**; therefore, rules listed at the top run before those listed at the bottom.

6.3 Customize and use *Quick Steps* (p. O6-230).

- **Quick Steps** are similar to rules and can be applied to specific email messages.
- Outlook includes default *Quick Steps*, which are editable.
- New *Quick Steps* can be created for common tasks.

6.4 Utilize search folders to find email messages (p. O6-235).

- **Search folders** use virtual folders to display messages that meet specific criteria.
- You can create search folders for a variety of criteria including displaying only **Unread Mail**.
- Search folders display either the number of items in the virtual folder or the number of unread items.
- Deleting a search folder does not delete its contents because it is a virtual folder.

Check for Understanding

The SIMbook for this text (within your SIMnet account) provides the following resources for concept review:

- Multiple-choice questions
- Short answer questions
- Matching exercises

Guided Project 6-1

For this project, you are a real estate agent for Placer Hills Real Estate (PHRE). You just started working with two new clients, Nina Hu and Jim Cross, who are both looking for new homes. You use folders and rules to manage client and company email.

[Student Learning Outcomes 6.1, 6.2]

Skills Covered in This Project

- Create folders.
- Move folders.

- Delete a folder.
- Create a rule.
- Create an advanced rule.
- Run a rule.

1. Create a folder for clients.
   a. Click the **Mail** button in the *Navigation* bar.
   b. Click the **Folder** tab.
   c. Click the **New Folder** button in the *New* group. The *Create New Folder* dialog box opens.
   d. Type Clients in the *Name* text area.
   e. Confirm that the folder type is **Mail and Post Items** in the *Folder contains* menu.
   f. In the *Select where to place the folder* section, specify your main email account folder.
   g. Click **OK**.

2. Create a folder for Nina.
   a. Click the **Mail** button in the *Navigation* bar.
   b. Click the **Folder** tab.
   c. Click the **New Folder** button in the *New* group. The *Create New Folder* dialog box opens.
   d. Type Nina Hu in the *Name* text area.
   e. Confirm that the folder type is **Mail and Post Items** in the *Folder contains* menu.
   f. In the *Select where to place the folder* section, specify your main email account folder.
   g. Click **OK**.

3. Create a folder for PHRE internal messages.
   a. Click the **Mail** button in the *Navigation* bar.
   b. Click the **Folder** tab.
   c. Click the **New Folder** button in the *New* group. The *Create New Folder* dialog box opens.
   d. Type PHRE Internal in the *Name* text area.
   e. Confirm that the folder type is **Mail and Post Items** in the *Folder contains* menu.
   f. In the *Select where to place the folder* section, specify your main email account folder.
   g. Click **OK**.

4. Create a folder for Jim Cross.
   a. Click the **Mail** button in the *Navigation* bar.
   b. Click the **Folder** tab.
   c. Click the **New Folder** button in the *New* group. The *Create New Folder* dialog box opens.
   d. Type Jim Cross in the *Name* text area.
   e. Confirm that the folder type is **Mail and Post Items** in the *Folder contains* menu.
   f. In the *Select where to place the folder* section, specify your main email account folder.
   g. Click **OK**.

5. Move the *Nina Hu* folder into the *Clients* folder.
   a. In the *Folder* pane, select the **Nina Hu** folder.
   b. Click the **Folder** tab.
   c. Click the **Move Folder** button in the *Actions* group. The *Move Folder* dialog box opens.
   d. In the *Move the selected folder to the folder* section, click the **Clients** folder.
   e. Click **OK**.

6. Delete the *Jim Cross* folder since he decided to move to another state and will not need your services.
   a. Select the **Jim Cross** folder in the *Folder* pane.
   b. Click the **Delete Folder** button in the *Actions* group on the *Folder* tab. A warning dialog box opens asking you if you want to move the *Jim Cross* folder to the *Deleted Items* folder.
   c. Click **Yes** to delete the folder and all its contents.

7. Send an email message to a partner as Nina Hu.
   a. Click the **Mail** button in the *Navigation* bar.
   b. Click the **New Email** button [*Home* tab, *New* group].
   c. Enter the following information in your message:

      To: partner's email address
      Subject: Pre-approval from bank
      Body: Hi [partner's name]

      I just received my pre-approval letter from the bank. I am approved for a purchase up to $375,000 ($75,000 down payment and $300,000 loan).

      Sincerely,
      Nina

   d. Click **Send**.

8. Create a rule to move email messages from Nina into the *Nina Hu* folder.
   a. Locate and open a message from Nina.
   b. Click the **Rules** button in the *Move* group on the *Message* tab.
   c. Choose **Create Rule**. The *Create Rule* dialog box opens.
   d. In the conditions area (the top half of the dialog box), check **From Nina Hu** (the name may vary based on who sent you the message).
   e. In the actions area (the bottom half of the dialog box), check **Move the item to folder** and click the **Select Folder** button.
   f. Select the **Nina Hu** folder from the folder list and press **OK**. The *Create Rule* dialog box remains open.
   g. Click **OK**.
   h. Select the **Run this rule now on messages already in "Inbox"** check box.
   i. Click **OK**.

9. Create an advanced rule to move emails received from PHRE employees into the *PHRE Internal* folder.
   a. Click the **Mail** button in the *Navigation* bar.
   b. Click the **Rules** button in the *Move* group on the *Home* tab and choose **Manage Rules & Alerts**. The *Rules and Alerts* dialog box opens.
   c. Click the **New Rule** button. The *Rules Wizard* dialog box opens.
   d. Select **Apply rule on messages I receive** in the *Start from a blank rule* section.
   e. Click **Next**. You move to the next step to select a condition for the rule.
   f. Select the **with specific words in the sender's address** check box. In the bottom section of this dialog box, the condition displays.
   g. Click the **specific words** link in the bottom section. The *Search Text* dialog box opens.
   h. Type phre.com in the top text area and click **Add**.

i. Click the **OK** button.
  j. Click **Next**. You move to the *action* step in the *Rules Wizard* dialog box.
  k. Select the **move it to the specified folder** check box.
  l. In the bottom section, click the **specified** folder link. The *Rules and Alerts* dialog box opens.
  m. Click the **PHRE Internal** folder and press **OK**. You will return to the *Rules Wizard* dialog box.
  n. Click **Next**. You move to the *exceptions* step.
  o. Click **Next**. No exceptions will be added to the rule. The *Finish rule setup* step appears.
  p. Type PHRE Internal in the *Step 1* area.
  q. Confirm that the **Turn on this rule** check box is selected.
  r. Read the rule one last time to confirm that the condition and action are correct.
  s. Click **Finish**.
  t. Click **Apply** and then **OK** (Figure 6-44).

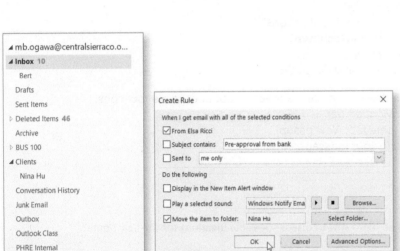

Figure 6-44 Guided Project 6-1 completed

Guided Project 6-2

As a real estate agent for PHRE, you send several emails on a regular basis. To improve your work efficiency, you create *Quick Steps*. You create a *Quick Step* to forward messages to your manager when you need approval and create an appointment when you meet with your clients.
[Student Learning Outcome 6.3]

Skills Covered in This Project

- Create a *Quick Step*.
- Use the *Forward* feature.

- Use options within actions.
- Add *Tooltips* to *Quick Steps*.
- Create an advanced *Quick Step*.
- Create appointments with a *Quick Step*.

1. Create a *Quick Step* to forward messages to your manager for approval.
   a. Click the **Create New** *Quick Step* button [*Home* tab, *Quick Steps* group]. The *Edit Quick Step* dialog box opens.
   b. In the *Name* text area, type Manager Approval.
   c. Click the **drop-down arrow** to display a list of actions.
   d. Select **Forward**.
   e. Click the **Show Options** link below the action.
   f. Click the **To** button. Select your partner's email address and click the **To** button or type it in the *To* text area. If your partner's email address is not in your Contacts, type it into the *To* field in the *Edit Quick Step* dialog box. Click **OK**.
   g. In the *Subject* field, type FW: Contract Approval.
   h. In the *Tooltip text* area, type Email to manager for approval.
   i. Click the **Finish** button to create the new *Quick Step*.

2. Create a *Quick Step* to create an appointment with an attachment.
   a. Click the **Create New** *Quick Step* button [*Home* tab, *Quick Steps* group]. The *Edit Quick Step* dialog box opens.
   b. In the *Name* text area, type Client Meeting.
   c. Click the **drop-down arrow** to display a list of actions.
   d. Select **Create an appointment with attachment**.
   e. In the *Tooltip text* area, type Set up client meetings.
   f. Click the **Finish** button to create the new *Quick Step*.

3. Send an email message to your partners to request a meeting about possible locations.
   a. Click the **Mail** button in the *Navigation* bar.
   b. Click the **New Email** button [*Home* tab, *New* group].
   c. Enter the following information in your message:

   To: partner's email address
   Subject: Possible locations?
   Body: Hi [partner name],

   Can we meet next week Monday at 10:00 AM to discuss possible locations for my new home?

   Thanks,
   [your name]

   d. Click **Send**.

4. Create an appointment from the message.
   a. Locate the email your partner sent. It is in the *Group Project* folder.
   b. Click the **Client Meeting** *Quick Step* [*Home* tab, *Quick Steps* group].
   c. Change the start time to be next week **Monday** at **10:00 AM**.
   d. Change the end time to be next week **Monday** at **12:00 PM**.
   e. Click the **Save & Close** button.

5. Email the task to your instructor as an Outlook item.
   a. Click the **Mail** button in the *Navigation* bar.
   b. Click the **New Email** button [*Home* tab, *New* group].
   c. Enter the following information in your message:

   To: instructor's email address
   Cc: your email address
   Subject: Outlook Guided Project 6-2
   Body: Hi [instructor name],

Attached is the Outlook item for the Guided Project 6-2 exercise.

Sincerely,
[student name]

d. Click the **Attach Item** button [*Message* tab, *Include* group] and select **Outlook Item**.
e. Select the **Calendar** option and locate the appointment you created.
f. Click **OK**.
g. Click **Send** (Figure 6-45).

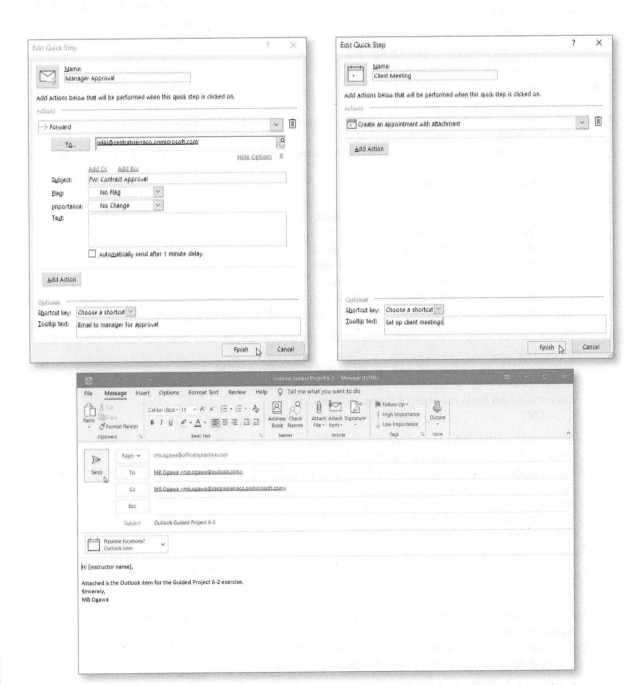

Figure 6-45 Guided Project 6-2 completed

Guided Project 6-3

While working with your coworkers and a variety of clients, you identified several email messages that you constantly reference. Therefore, you develop search folders to find messages that deal with executed contracts and messages from your manager with attachments.
[Student Learning Outcome 6.4]

Skills Covered in This Project

- Create a search folder.
- Search for specific words in search folders.
- Search for specific senders in search folders.
- Search for messages with attachments in search folders.
- Use multiple criteria for a search folder.
- Modify the messages shown in search folders
- Rename search folders.
- Modify a search folder.

1. Create a new search folder to find messages regarding executed contracts.
   a. Click the **Mail** button in the *Navigation* bar.
   b. Click the **Folder** tab and then click the **New Search Folder** button in the *New* group. The *New Search Folder* dialog box opens.
   c. Select **Mail with specific words**.
   d. Click **Choose**. The *Search Text* dialog box opens.
   e. In the first text area, type execute and click **Add**.
   f. In the first text area, type executed and click **Add**.
   g. In the first text area, type contract and click **Add**.
   h. In the first text area, type contracts and click **Add**.
   i. Click **OK** to close the *Search Text* dialog box.
   j. Click **OK** to close the *New Search Folder* dialog box.
   k. The new search folder appears in your list of search folders in the *Folder* pane.

2. Modify the search folder to be named *Executed Contracts* and show the total number of items in the search folder.
   a. Right-click the newly created search folder and select **Properties**.
   b. Replace the text in the first text area with Executed Contracts.
   c. Click the **Show total number of items** radio button.
   d. Click **OK**.

3. Create a new search folder to find messages from your manager with attachments.
   a. Click the **Mail** button in the *Navigation* bar.
   b. Click the **Folder** tab and then on the **New Search Folder** button in the *New* group. The *New Search Folder* dialog box opens.
   c. Select **Create a custom Search Folder**.
   d. Click **Choose**. The *Custom Search Folder* dialog box opens.
   e. In the *Name* text area, type Manager Attachments.
   f. Click the **Criteria** button. The *Search Folder Criteria* dialog box opens.
   g. Select the *Messages* tab and type your partner's email address into the *From* text area or click the **From** button and select their contact.
   h. Click the *More Choices* tab.
   i. Click the **Only items with** check box and ensure the option is set to **one or more attachments**.
   j. Click **OK** to close the *Search Folder Criteria* dialog box.
   k. Click **OK** to close the *Custom Search Folder* dialog box.

l. Click **OK** to close the *New Search Folder* dialog box. The new search folder appears in your list of search folders in the *Folder* pane (Figure 6-46).

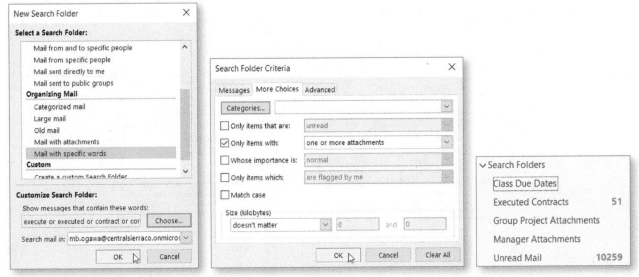

Figure 6-46 Guided Project 6-3 completed

Independent Project 6-4

For this project, you are coordinating the Cycling Evolution Event (CEE) for the American River Cycling Club (ARCC). This year, you take registrations via email. Therefore, you create folders and rules to automatically organize registration information. You also want to store email messages you send to the ARCC with updates in a specific folder to ensure you can quickly find the information.
[Student Learning Outcomes 6.1, 6.2]

Skills Covered in This Project

- Create a rule.
- Create an advanced rule.
- Create folders.
- Run a rule.
- Move folders.

1. Create a folder to organize ARCC email.
    a. Create a folder named *ARCC*.
    b. Create a folder named *Registrations*.
    c. Create a folder named *Member updates*.
    d. Move the *Registrations* and *Member updates* folders into the *ARCC* folder.

2. Create a rule to organize registration email messages using the following criteria:
    Condition: Messages received with the term "Registration" in the subject.
    Action: Moved into the *Registrations* folder.
    Exception: Unless there is a question mark (**?**) in the message.

3. Create a rule to organize membership update messages you send based on the following criteria:
   Condition: Messages sent with the term "Membership update" in the subject.
   Action: Copy to the *Member updates* folder (Figure 6-47).

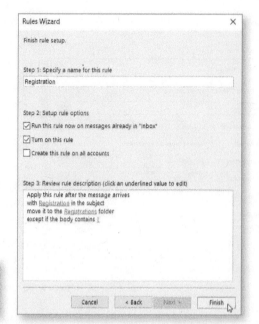

Figure 6-47 Independent Project 6-4 completed

Independent Project 6-5

After working on the registration last year, you remember that many of the ARCC members ask similar questions regarding the route. To make your work more efficient, you create a *Quick Step* to reply with the route information. You also create a *Quick Step* to quickly create messages to ARCC members.
[Student Learning Outcome 6.3]

Skills Covered in This Project

- Create a *Quick Step*.
- Use the reply feature.
- Use new mail feature.

- Use options within actions.
- Add *Tooltips* to a *Quick Step*.
- Create an advanced *Quick Step*.
- Create appointments with a *Quick Step*.

1. Create a *Quick Step* to reply to ARCC members with the following information.

   Name: Route Reply
   Action: Reply
   Options text: Please see the following URL for the most updated route information: http://www.arcc.org/ceeroute/.
   Tooltip text: Reply with up-to-date route information.

2. Create a *Quick Step* to send email messages to ARCC members with the following information.

> *Name*: *Membership update email*
> *Action*: *New Message*
> *To*: *members@arcc.org*
> *Options*:
> *Subject*: Membership update
> *Tooltip text*: Write membership update messages. (Figure 6-48).

Figure 6-48 Independent Project 6-5 completed

Independent Project 6-6

As the CEE coordinator, you recall members asking about receipts for their payments. Since you started giving digital receipts via email, you create a search folder to quickly find receipts to send to participants who accidentally lost the initial message. You also remember participants asking about their T-shirt size to ensure they receive the correct shirt when they finish the event. Therefore, you create a new search folder to find T-shirt sizes for all participants, which allows you to search within the search folder for a particular member's registration.

[Student Learning Outcome 6.4]

Skills Covered in This Project

- Create a search folder.
- Search for specific words in search folders.
- Search for specific senders.
- Search for messages with attachments in search folders.
- Use multiple criteria for a search folder.
- Modify the messages shown in search folders.
- Rename search folders.
- Modify a search folder.

1. Create a new search folder to find messages regarding receipt messages using the following criteria:

   Search folder name: Receipts
   From: [your email address]
   Search for the term "Receipt" in the subject field only.
   Search for items with attachments.
   Show the total number of items for the search folder.

2. Create a new search folder to find T-shirt sizes using the following criteria:

   Search folder name: Shirt size
   To: [your email address]
   Search for the term "size" in the subject field and message body.
   All messages were received in the last month.
   Show the total number of items for the search folder (Figure 6-49).

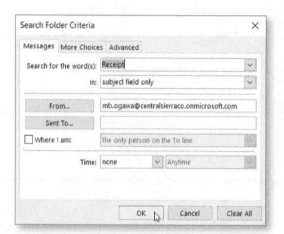

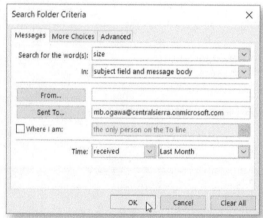

Figure 6-49 Independent Project 6-6 completed

Challenge Project 6-7

Consider the different types of email you send and receive for school, work, home, and other extracurricular activities. Identify at least two types of email you receive or send and how you can apply rules to manage your email. For example, you apply rules to emails received from specific people, words in the subject line, or flagged for action. After identifying the types of email you receive, create folders and rules to apply. Email a description of the folders created and rules applied to your instructor.
[Student Learning Outcomes 6.1, 6.2]

- Create at least two rules.
- Create folders for rules.
- Ensure you have a reason to justify each rule.
- Explain why the rule fits better than a *Quick Step* or search folder.
- Email your instructor using the following message format:

  Rule 1: [reason you are creating a rule for the type of message including why it works better than *Quick Steps* and search folders]
  Condition: [description of condition]
  Action: [description of action]
  Exception: [description of exceptions]
  Folder 1: [name and description of folder]

  Rule 2: [reason you are creating a rule for the type of message including why it works better than *Quick Steps* and search folders]
  Condition: [description of condition]
  Action: [description of action]
  Exception: [description of exceptions]
  Folder 2: [name and description of folder]

- Change the subject of your message to Outlook Challenge Project 6-7.

Challenge Project 6-8

Think about the different types of email messages you send and receive for school, work, home, and other extracurricular activities. Identify at least two types of email you receive and how you can apply *Quick Steps*. You can use *Quick Steps* for a variety of actions such as filing, changing status, creating categories, tasks, and flags, responding, creating new appointments, and managing conversations. After identifying possible *Quick Steps*, create folders for those that require a new folder. Email a description of the folders created and *Quick Steps* developed to your instructor.
[Student Learning Outcomes 6.1, 6.3]

- Create at least two *Quick Steps*.
- Create folders for *Quick Steps*.
- Ensure you have a reason to justify each *Quick Step*.
- Use at least two actions for each *Quick Step*.

- Explain why the *Quick Step* fits better than a rule or search folder.
- Email your instructor using the following message format:

  Quick Step 1: [reason you created a *Quick Step* for the type of message including why it works better than rules and search folders]
  Action: [description of action]
  Action: [description of action]
  Folder 1: [name and description of folder]

  Quick Step 2: [reason you created a *Quick Step* for the type of message including why it works better than rules and search folders]
  Action: [description of action]
  Action: [description of action]
  Folder 2: [name and description of folder]

- Change the subject of your message to be Outlook Challenge Project 6-8.

Challenge Project 6-9

You probably receive many email messages throughout the day for school, work, family, and extracurricular activities. Identify at least two types of email you send and receive and how you can apply search folders to help you find important messages. After identifying the types of email you send and receive, create search folders for those messages. Email a description of the search folders created to your instructor.
[Student Learning Outcome 6.4]

- Create at least two search folders.
- Ensure you have a reason to justify each search folder.
- Identify criteria for the search folder.
- One of the search folders should contain more than one criterion.
- Email your instructor using the following message format:

  Search Folder 1: [reason you created the search folder including why it works better than rules and *Quick Steps*]
  Criteria: [description of criteria]

  Search Folder 2: [reason you created the search folder including why it works better than rules and *Quick Steps*]
  Criteria: [description of criteria]
  Criteria: [description of criteria]

- Change the subject of your message to be Outlook Challenge Project 6-9.

Source of screenshots Microsoft Office 365 (2019): Word, Excel, Access, PowerPoint, Outlook.

Multiple Email Accounts, Advanced Email Options, RSS Feeds, and Search

CHAPTER OVERVIEW

As you begin to use and rely on Outlook to manage your emails and contacts and organize your calendar and tasks, you want to have the ability to customize Outlook to best meet your individual and professional needs. Outlook provides you with the opportunity to have multiple email accounts and to manage these accounts through the use of rules and folders. Outlook includes many "under the hood" default settings for email that can be used to tailor how Outlook works for you.

In addition to managing multiple email accounts, Outlook manages your RSS feeds. RSS is an acronym for "really simple syndication." Essentially, RSS feeds are a way of keeping track of the headlines on your favorite web sites, and Outlook manages your RSS feeds in a similar way to how it manages your email accounts.

STUDENT LEARNING OUTCOMES (SLOs)

After completing this chapter, you will be able to:

SLO 7.1   Connect and use multiple email accounts in Outlook (p. O7-254).

SLO 7.2   Manage multiple email accounts (p. O7-257).

SLO 7.3   Customize advanced email options (p. O7-262).

SLO 7.4   Integrate RSS feeds into Outlook (p. O7-270).

SLO 7.5   Utilize search features to find email and other Outlook items (p. O7-276).

CASE STUDY

For the Pause & Practice projects, you become more proficient with using Outlook with multiple accounts, RSS feeds, and searching for email and other Outlook items. You add accounts to Outlook to ensure you can work with both personal and school- or work-related email messages within the Outlook environment. You also add RSS feeds to enable you to receive news that is important to you and to share it with others. Lastly, you learn to search for information quickly and effectively.

Pause & Practice 7-1: You add an email account to Outlook. If you do not have a secondary email account, you can sign up for a free account at Gmail.com or Outlook.com. After adding the account, you will change the default account and send a message by selecting the account that is not set as default.

Pause & Practice 7-2: You subscribe to CNN RSS news feeds (available at http://www.cnn.com/services/rss/). You subscribe to an RSS feed, rename the feed folder, and share the feed with your instructor.

OUTLOOK

Pause & Practice 7-3: You search for the previous Pause & Practice email messages that you sent to your instructor because you did not receive a grade for the *Pause & Practice 7-2* assignment. After you find the message, you forward it to your instructor.

SLO 7.1   Connect and Use Multiple Email Accounts in Outlook

If you're like most people, you have multiple email accounts: one through your work (an Exchange account) and one through your ISP (internet service provider) at your home. You might also have a free email account such as Gmail, Outlook.com, or Yahoo Mail.

Outlook gives you the ability to set up multiple email accounts, including multiple Exchange accounts, and to send and receive emails through these accounts. Using Outlook to handle multiple email accounts saves you time because it consolidates your email accounts in one place so that you don't need to go to multiple web sites to check your different email accounts.

> **MORE INFO**
>
> Not all free email accounts can be set up through Outlook. Some types of accounts work seamlessly with Outlook, such as Gmail or Outlook.com. Others may require an annual fee to enable access through Outlook.

Auto Account Setup

You don't have to know much about your email account to set it up in Outlook. Outlook has simplified the process of adding an email account. It determines the type of account (Exchange, Exchange ActiveSync, POP, IMAP, or HTTP) and validates the account settings.

The two pieces of information you will need are your user name or email account and your password. Outlook will automatically detect your email account settings and set up your account in Outlook.

> **MORE INFO**
>
> The different types of email accounts were covered in chapter 1.

> **MORE INFO**
>
> For some online email accounts, you must enable POP or IMAP on the online account for your email to be delivered to Outlook. This is typically done by logging into your account on the internet and editing the settings to enable POP or IMAP. This will vary from account to account.

▶HOW TO: Add an Email Account to Outlook

1. Click the **File** tab. The *Backstage* view opens.
2. Click **Add Account** (Figure 7-1). The *Simplified Account Creation* dialog box opens (Figure 7-2).

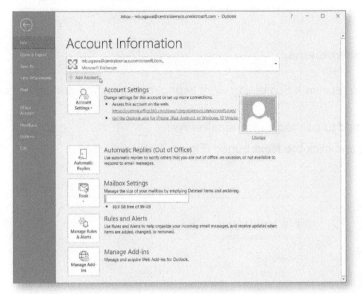

Figure 7-1 *Add Account* button

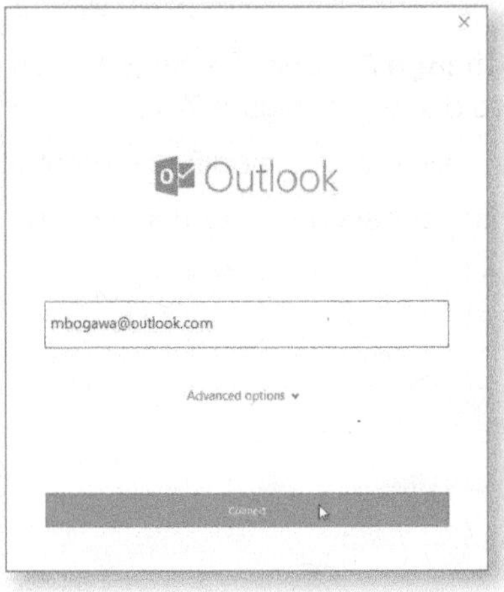

Figure 7-2 *Add Account* dialog box

3. Type your email address in the *Email address* field.
4. Click the **Connect** button
5. Type your password into the *Password* field.
6. Click the **Connect** button. Outlook will automatically detect your email account and validate it with your password. (Figure 7-3).
7. Click **Done** to close the dialog box.

> ### MORE INFO
> It is not a good idea to add your personal email accounts to your work computer, because most employers do not want you to be distracted by personal emails while at work.

Figure 7-3 Auto account setup completion

If you are using Outlook in an Exchange, Exchange ActiveSync, or IMAP environment, you will have folders for each of your accounts. Your email account through Exchange, Exchange ActiveSync, and IMAP will be handled in your *username@address.com* folders, and your personal email accounts will, by default, be handled in your *Personal Folders*.

> ### MORE INFO
> You will also have another set of folders called *Archive Folders*, which will be covered in chapter 10.

Troubleshoot Email Problems

Outlook may not be able to automatically detect the account settings for an email account that you are trying to set up. Outlook will try a couple of different options to configure your account.

If this process does not work, you can manually configure your account settings. You might have to go to the email account web site to find specific setup information to configure your account.

▶ **HOW TO:** Troubleshoot Email Connection Problems

1. Click the **Change Account Settings** button if you receive a *Something went wrong* message. The authentication settings are displayed (Figure 7-4).
2. Outlook will allow you to modify the protocols used to connect to the email server.
3. Confirm that your account information is correct and click the **Next** button (Figure 7-5).
4. Click **Done** to close the dialog box.

Figure 7-4 *Change Account Settings* button

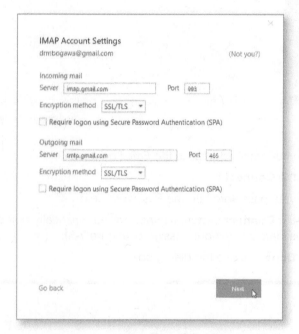

Figure 7-5 Account settings

> **MORE INFO**
>
> A setting change on the email server might cause an existing email account in Outlook to stop functioning properly. The *Repair* feature might be able to automatically adjust the account settings to restore this account.

> **MORE INFO**
>
> It is important to check with an email provider for the correct account settings if the *Simplified Account Creation* dialog box is unable to detect the account settings. Some require a specific application password based on multi-factor authentication.

Existing email accounts in Outlook may stop sending or receiving email messages for no apparent reason. If this email account was previously working and none of the account settings have been changed, you might try using the *Repair* feature provided in Outlook. This automated feature starts the *Simplified Account Creation* dialog box to automatically acquire all of the settings.

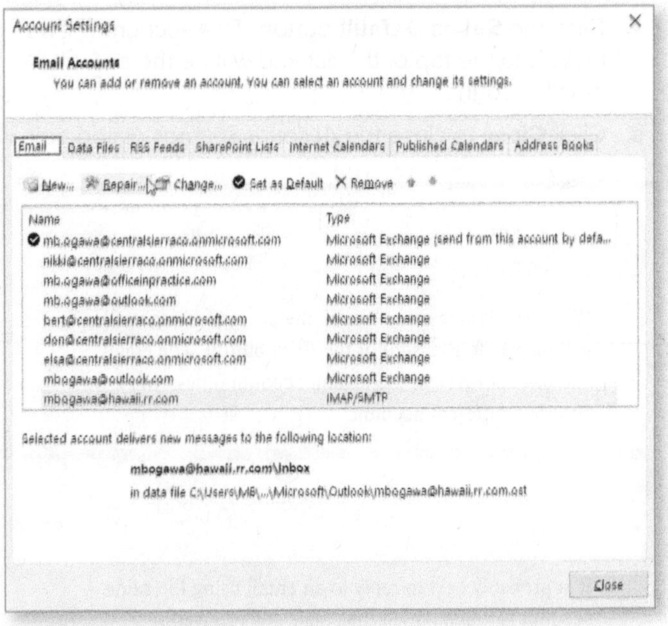

Figure 7-6 *Repair*

▶ **HOW TO:** Start the Repair Feature

1. Click the **File** tab. The *Backstage* view opens.
2. Click the **Account Settings** button and choose **Account Settings** to open the *Account Settings* dialog box.
3. Select the email address that is not working properly.
4. Click **Repair** to open the *Simplified Account Creation* dialog box (Figure 7-6).

SLO 7.2

Managing Multiple Email Accounts

One of the issues with having multiple email accounts in Outlook is keeping them separate in your mail folders. Managing multiple email accounts can become confusing if emails are all being delivered to the same Inbox. Another issue is choosing the account through which you create and send new emails and respond to or forward emails. Having multiple email accounts complicates this process. Being deliberate about setting your default email account and having emails delivered to different folders can help you to effectively manage multiple email accounts.

Set the Default Account

The default email account is the account that will be used to send new email messages. This should be the account used most often in Outlook. This will be the first email account you set up in Outlook unless you specify a different account. It is easy to change your default email account.

▶ **HOW TO:** Set an Account as Default

1. Click the **File** tab to open the *Backstage* view.
2. Click the **Account Settings** button and choose **Account Settings** to open the *Account Settings* dialog box (Figure 7-7). The default email account is noted with a check mark.
3. Click the email account you want as your default account.

4. Click the **Set as Default** button. This account will be moved to the top of the list and will be the default email account.

5. Click **Close** to close the *Account Settings* dialog box.

> ## MORE INFO
>
> When you create a new email, the account being used will display to the right of the *From* button. The email will be sent through the default account unless you choose a different account.

> ## MORE INFO
>
> It is probably best to reply to an email using the same account through which the email was received.

Figure 7-7 Set default account

Send Email through a Different Account

As mentioned earlier, when you create and send a new email, it will be sent through your default email account. But if you are replying to or forwarding an email, it will be sent through the account from which it was delivered. For example, if you received an email through your Gmail account (assuming this is not your default account), and you reply to or forward this email, it will be sent through your Gmail account unless you choose a different account through which to send this email.

When you have multiple email accounts set up in Outlook, you can decide from which account the email will be sent. This can be done on new emails, replies, or forwards. A *From* button appears to the right of the *Send* button on all your emails when you have multiple accounts set up in Outlook. Select the account from which to send an email using the *From* button (Figure 7-8).

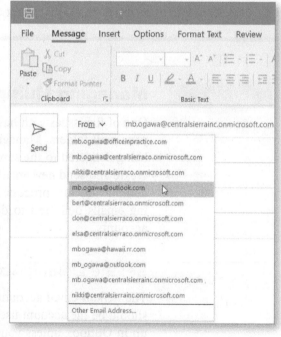

Figure 7-8 Set an account to send email

▶ HOW TO: Send Email through Another Account

1. Open an existing email.
2. Click the **Reply** or **Forward** button. To the right of the *From* button, the account that will be used to send the email displays.
3. Click the **From** button and choose a different account. Notice the account displayed on the right.
4. Click **Send** to send the email through the chosen account.

Change the Email Delivery Folder

If your personal email accounts use POP, you are able to change the folder to which your email is delivered. You do not have this option with an Exchange account. When managing multiple email accounts, it is probably best to have different accounts delivered to different folders. If your default account is being delivered to your Inbox, you might want to create a *Gmail* folder and have your Gmail always delivered to this folder. You can change the default delivery folder for an email account in the *Account Settings* dialog box.

> **HOW TO: Change the Email Delivery Folder**

1. Click the **File** tab to open the *Backstage* view.
2. Click the **Account Settings** button and choose **Account Settings** to open the *Account Settings* dialog box.
3. Click one of your account names that is not the default account. Notice the delivery folder to the right of the *Change Folder* button.
4. Click the **Change Folder** button (Figure 7-9). The *New Email Delivery Location* dialog box opens.
5. Select the new delivery folder (Figure 7-10). A new folder can also be created by clicking the **New Folder** button.

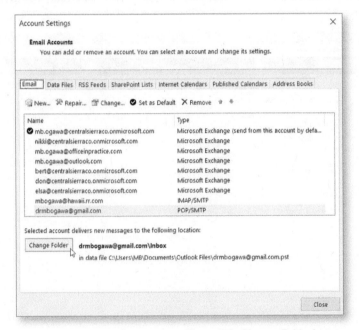

Figure 7-9 *Change Folder* button

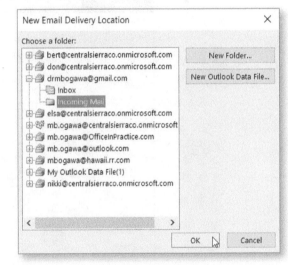

Figure 7-10 Select incoming mail folder

6. Click **OK** to close the *New Email Delivery Location* dialog box.
7. Click **Close** to close the *Account Settings* dialog box. All emails from the chosen account will now be delivered to the folder you chose.

> **MORE INFO**
>
> Changing the delivery folder is not available for IMAP email accounts. Rules can be used to deliver email received through these accounts to a different folder.

Create Folders and Use Rules

Rules can also be used to deliver emails from specific accounts to a different folder. The *condition* would be looking for emails received through a specified account (for example, a Gmail or Outlook.com account), and the *action* would be to move it to a specified folder. This rule is similar to changing the default delivery folder, but it could easily be turned off or on.

Outlook on the Web

One of the advantages of using email is the ability to access it from any computer that has internet access. If you have an email account through your internet service provider (ISP) or a free email account such as Gmail or

> **MORE INFO**
> Rules were covered in chapter 6.

Yahoo Mail, you can log on to the internet and access your email account through their web sites. You need to know your user name and password to have access to your online email account.

If you are using Outlook in an Exchange environment, most companies have their Exchange server connected to **Outlook on the web**. Outlook on the web allows you to access your Exchange account through the internet. You need to know the URL (web location) of your company's Outlook on the web and log on with your user name and password. Outlook on the web provides you not only with email access, but also access to your calendar, contacts, tasks, and notes (Figure 7-11).

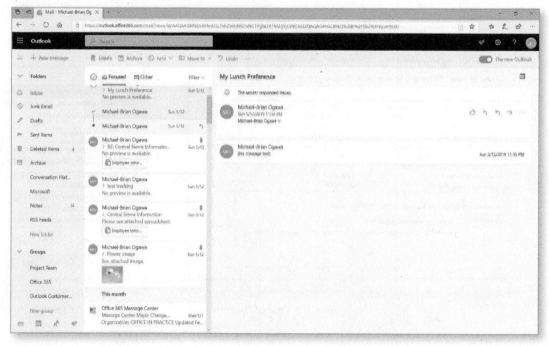

Figure 7-11 Outlook on the web App

Outlook on the web displays differently depending on the internet browser you're using (for example, Microsoft Edge, Google Chrome, or Mozilla Firefox). Outlook on the web will look different than Outlook on your computer, but you will still have most of the functionality of your Outlook account.

> **MORE INFO**
> Additional details about Outlook 365 online for business and personal accounts will be covered in chapter 10.

For this Pause & Practice project, you add an email account to Outlook. If you do not have a secondary email account, you can sign up for a free account at Gmail.com or Outlook.com. After adding the account, you will change the default account and send a message by selecting the account that is not set as default.

1. Add a new account to Outlook.
   a. Click the **File** tab. The *Backstage* view opens.
   b. Click **Add Account**. The *Simplified Account Creation* dialog box opens.
   c. Type your email address in the *Email address* field.
   d. Click the **Connect** button.
   e. Type your password in the *Password* field.
   f. Click the **Connect** button.
   g. Click **Finish**. The *Account Settings* dialog box appears. Notice your new email account is now included in your list of email accounts.
   h. Click **Close**.

2. Change the default email account.
   a. Click the **File** tab to open the *Backstage* view.
   b. Click the **Account Settings** button and choose **Account Settings** to open the *Account Settings* dialog box.
   c. Select the email account you added to Outlook in the first step.
   d. Click the **Set as Default** button.
   e. Click the **Close** button.

3. Send a message by selecting an account (Figure 7-12).
   a. Click the **Mail** button in the *Navigation* bar.
   b. Click the **New Email** button.
   c. Click the **From** button and select the email address that is not the default.

Figure 7-12 PP Outlook 7-1 completed

d. Enter the following information in the new message:
To: instructor's email address
Cc: your email address
Subject: Outlook Pause & Practice 7-1
Message: Hi [instructor's name],

I added a new address to my Outlook installation. For consistency, I want to be sure you are receiving messages from my school account.

Thanks,
[your name]

e. Click the **Send** button.

SLO 7.3

Customizing Email Options

After you use Outlook for a while and become familiar with the main tasks, you might want to change some of the default settings to customize Outlook. Within Outlook, many customization options are available. The ***Outlook Options*** dialog box (Figure 7-13) provides you with one location to change most of the default settings for email, calendar, contacts, tasks, notes, and other global Outlook settings. The *Outlook Options* dialog box can be accessed by clicking the **File** tab to open the *Backstage* view and choosing **Options**.

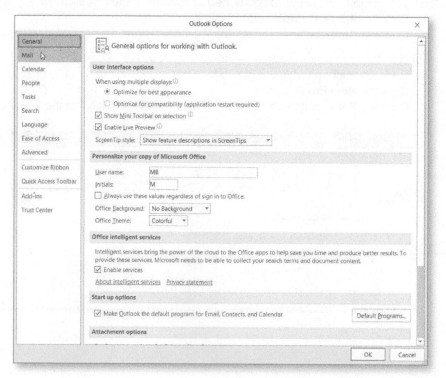

Figure 7-13 *Outlook Options* dialog box

> **MORE INFO**
>
> The email customization options covered in this section are global or default settings. These differ from message options, which allow you to customize individual email messages. Message options were covered in chapter 2.

Email Options

Customization options in the *Mail Options* dialog box are separated into sections. Several of these sections include buttons to open dialog boxes that include additional email options. Clicking the button to the right of the section opens the dialog box for more specific email options.

The following sections are available in *Mail* options:

- *Compose messages*
- *Outlook panes*
- *Message arrival*
- *Conversation Clean Up*
- *Replies and forwards*
- *Save messages*
- *Send messages*
- *MailTips (available on Exchange servers)*
- *Tracking*
- *Message format*
- *Other*

Compose Messages

The ***Compose messages*** section allows you to customize the format of email messages, spell checking, *AutoCorrect*, signatures, stationery, and themes. The button to the right of each of these areas opens a dialog box with additional features that you are able to customize.

The *Editor Options* and *Spelling and AutoCorrect* buttons open the *Editor Options* dialog box (Figure 7-14). In this dialog box, select and define *AutoCorrect* and spelling options. New to Outlook is the *Ease of Access* section, which improves accessibility options such as showing *ScreenTips* and automatically creating alt text. Alt text are descriptions for pictures to make them accessible for people with vision impairments.

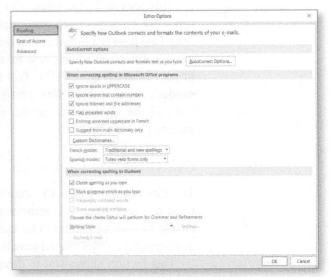

Figure 7-14 *Editor Options* dialog box

The *Signatures* and *Stationery and Themes* buttons open the *Signatures and Stationery* dialog box. In this dialog box, you create and edit signatures, while the *Personal Stationery* tab allows you to customize the theme and fonts for emails.

Outlook Panes

The ***Outlook panes*** section allows you to control how messages displayed in the *Reading Pane* interact with the *Content area*. Messages can be set to be marked as read when they display in the *Reading Pane* or marked as read when the selection in the

> **MORE INFO**
>
> *Signatures* and *Stationery* were covered in chapter 3.

Content area changes (Figure 7-15). Also, the spacebar can be set and used to move through the text of a message and move to the next message in the *Content area*. This is a handy feature to quickly preview and move through messages in the *Reading Pane*. If you use a computer that switches orientations between portrait and landscape, such as a tablet or portable computer like the Microsoft Surface, you can automatically enable full-screen reading when it enters portrait orientation.

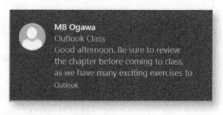

Figure 7-15 *Reading Pane* dialog box

Message Arrival

The *Message arrival* section (Figure 7-16) of *Mail Options* controls what happens in Outlook when a message arrives in your Inbox. By default, when a new email message arrives, a sound is played, the pointer briefly changes, an envelope displays in the notification area, and a desktop alert displays.

Figure 7-16 *Message arrival* options

This area will also allow you to control if a desktop alert displays when you receive a new message. A *desktop alert* is a message that briefly displays in a corner of your screen when a new email message is received in your Inbox (Figure 7-17). This message contains the sender's name, subject line, and part of the body of the message. Open the email message by clicking the alert.

> **MB Ogawa**
> Outlook Class
> Good afternoon. Be sure to review the chapter before coming to class, as we have many exciting exercises to Outlook

Figure 7-17 Desktop alert

Conversation Clean Up

The *Conversation Clean Up* section controls what happens when you remove redundant emails in a conversation. The conversation arrangement groups related emails together (Figure 7-18).

Figure 7-18 *Conversation Clean Up* options

This section allows you to designate the folder where cleaned-up messages will move (the default is in the *Deleted Items* folder) and the type of messages that Outlook will remove when using the *Clean Up* feature.

> ▶ MORE INFO
>
> It is good email etiquette to include the original message in the body when replying to or forwarding an email message. By doing this, you provide context for your response.

Replies and Forwards

Outlook allows you to tailor how your email message appears when you send a reply to or forward a message (Figure 7-19). By default, when you reply to or forward a message, the original message is included below the response in the body of the message.

Figure 7-19 *Replies and forwards* options

When replying to a message, you have the following options as a default setting (Figure 7-20):

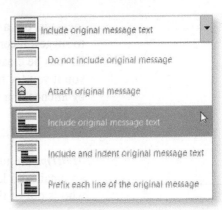

- *Do not include the original message*
- *Attach original message* (This option attaches the original message as an attachment and removes it from the body of the response.)
- *Include original message text* (This is the default setting in Outlook.)
- *Include and indent the original message text*
- *Prefix each line of the original message* (The default prefix is >.)

Figure 7-20 *Reply* options

When forwarding a message, you have the following options as a default setting (Figure 7-21):

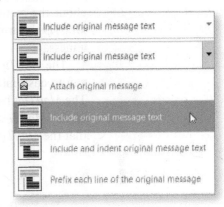

- *Attach original message* (This option attaches the original message as an attachment and removes it from the body of the response.)
- *Include original message text* (This is the default setting in Outlook.)
- *Include and indent the original message text*
- *Prefix each line of the original message* (The default prefix is >.)

Save Messages

Open messages that are either new, a reply, or a forward are, by default, saved every three minutes in the *Drafts* folder. The time duration and the folder can be customized. Also, by default, new messages, replies, and forwards are saved in the *Sent Items* folder (Figure 7-22).

Figure 7-21 *Forward* options

Figure 7-22 *Save messages* options

> **MORE INFO**
>
> It is not a good idea to have all emails marked with *High Importance*, a sensitivity tag, or an expiration date and time. Use these tags only as necessary so they do not lose their effectiveness on recipients.

Send Messages

When a new message is created, the default setting for importance and sensitivity is *Normal*. Normal means messages have no special tags or notifications. In the *Send messages* section (Figure 7-23), you can customize these default settings as well as set a default expiration.

Typically, a semicolon is used to separate recipients' email addresses in the *To* line of a

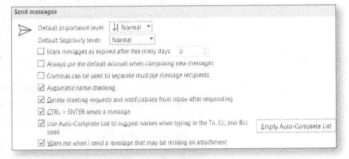

Figure 7-23 *Send messages* options

message, but a comma can also be used to separate recipients. The **Auto-Complete List** is used to suggest recently used names when typing names in the *To*, *Cc*, and *Bcc* lines of an email. This list can be cleared by clicking the *Empty Auto-Complete List* button. By default, Outlook warns you if you try to send a message that is missing an attachment. This feature can be turned off by unchecking the option.

MailTips (Available on Exchange Servers)

MailTips are used to inform you when you are sending an email to a large number of recipients, to a recipient who is out of the office, to recipients whose mailbox is full, or to an invalid email address and other email situations. *MailTips* provide you with real-time information about the status of an email message to be sent. The *MailTips* information bar appears in the *Info* bar area of a message.

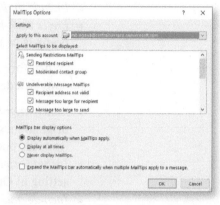

The *MailTips Options* dialog box (Figure 7-24) allows you to customize the settings for how *MailTips* appear. The *MailTips* bar, by default, displays when one or more of the *MailTips* apply. You can change the setting so that the *MailTips* bar will appear on all email messages.

Figure 7-24 *MailTips Options* dialog box

 MORE INFO

The *MailTips* section does not appear if *MailTips* are not available on your Exchange server.

Tracking Options

If you are using Outlook in an Exchange environment, Outlook automatically tracks responses when using voting buttons and meeting requests. Outlook will also track receipts received when a read receipt or delivery receipt has been used on an email. The **Tracking** options section (Figure 7-25) allows you to determine how Outlook tracks and responds to these items.

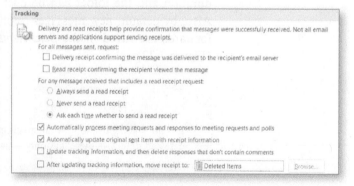

Figure 7-25 *Tracking* options

You are able to customize how voting button and meeting request responses are processed when they arrive in your Inbox. Also, you can change the default settings for read and delivery receipts for outgoing emails and how Outlook should handle read receipts on emails you receive.

 MORE INFO

Use read and delivery receipts sparingly. It can become very annoying to recipients to receive a read receipt on all emails they receive from you.

Also, if you receive an email that is requesting a read receipt, it is courteous to allow Outlook to send a read receipt.

Message Format and Other

The last two sections of the *Mail Options* dialog box (Figure 7-26) includes options for formatting your email messages. It is probably best to leave the default settings in these areas unless you have specific reasons to change them.

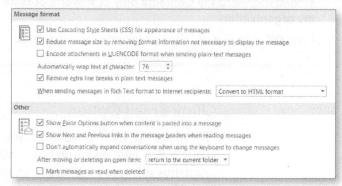

Figure 7-26 *Message format* and *Other* options

Out of Office Assistant

Most of us have instances when we are away from the office or home and are not able to respond to emails for an extended time. You might be on vacation or a business trip and don't want to totally ignore those who send you an email. The ***Out of Office Assistant*** is available if you are using an Exchange account and provides you the option of creating an automated response to reply to all emails you receive while you are not able to answer email.

You can set a specific date range for the *Out of Office Assistant*. If you don't specify a date range, the *Out of Office Assistant* will remain on until you turn it off. A message can be created to automatically respond to all those from whom you receive an email. These automated responses can be sent to those within your organization (those connected to your Exchange server), those outside of your organization, or both.

▶ **HOW TO:** Set Up an Out of Office Message

1. Click the **File** tab to open the *Backstage* view.
2. Click the **Automatic Replies** button (Figure 7-27). The *Automatic Replies* dialog box opens (Figure 7-28).

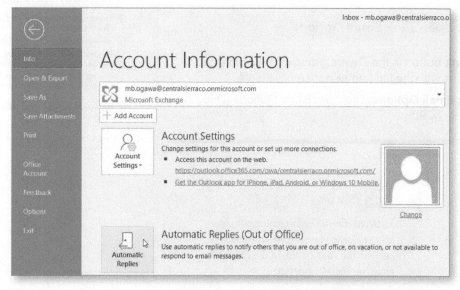

Figure 7-27 *Automatic Replies* button

3. Click **Send automatic replies** radio button. You can set a specific date range if you choose.

4. Compose a brief message in the body.

5. Click the **Outside My Organization** tab and type a brief message. You will have the option of sending the auto-response to **My Contacts only** or **Anyone outside my organization**.

6. Click **OK**. The *Out of Office Assistant* is now activated.

Figure 7-28 Set up automatic replies

Junk Email Options

If you are like most email users, you receive quite a few junk email messages each day. Antivirus software continues to improve and can identify and move potential junk email messages to a different folder. Even online email providers, like Gmail, Yahoo Mail, and Outlook.com, continue to enhance their efforts to identify spammers (those who send junk mail) and remove junk mail before it is delivered to your Inbox.

But even with these efforts, junk mail messages continue to make it to your Inbox. Email messages that are identified by Outlook as junk mail are moved to the *Junk Email* folder in your folder list.

Also, you may experience messages that should appear in your Inbox identified as junk and moved to the *Junk Email* folder.

The *Junk Email Options* dialog box allows you to control the level of junk email protection in Outlook.

Outlook allows you to customize your junk email settings, add safe senders, add safe recipients, and block senders or domain names.

▶**HOW TO: Open Junk Email Options**

1. Click the **Junk** button in the *Delete* group on the *Home* tab. A menu opens with the junk email options available.

2. Select **Junk Email Options**. The *Junk Email Options* dialog box opens (Figure 7-29).

> ▶ **ANOTHER WAY**
>
> The *Junk Email Options* dialog box can also be opened by opening an email and clicking the **Junk** button in the *Delete* group on the *Message* tab.

Figure 7-29 *Junk Email Options* dialog box

Safe and Blocked Senders and Recipients

Within the *Junk Email Options* dialog box, you are given the following options to control junk mail messages.

- *Safe Senders*: Senders' email addresses or domains (@mcgraw-hill.com) can be added to this list to ensure that emails received from these senders or domains are not treated as junk mail.
- *Safe Recipients*: Recipients' email addresses or domains can be added to this list to ensure that emails sent to these recipients or domains are not treated as junk mail.
- *Blocked Senders*: Senders' email addresses or senders' domains can be added to this list to ensure that emails received from these senders or domains will be treated as junk mail and moved to the *Junk Email* folder in your folder list.
- *International*: Outlook also allows you to block email messages received in different languages or from different country domains.

Email addresses or domain names can be manually added into these lists (with the exception of international ones) by selecting one of these lists in the *Junk Email Options* dialog box, clicking the *Add* button, and typing the email address or domain name.

An email message received in your Inbox can also be added to the *Safe Senders*, *Safe Recipients*, or *Blocked Senders* list.

▶ **HOW TO:** Add Senders or Groups to Block or Never Block Lists

1. Open the email to be added to one of these lists.
2. Click the **Junk** button in the *Delete* group.
3. Select **Block Sender, Never Block Sender, Never Block Sender's Domain,** or **Never Block this Group or Mailing List**.
   - If *Block Sender* is selected, the message will be moved to the *Junk Email* folder and the sender's email address is added to the *Blocked Senders* list. Outlook will always move email messages received from this sender to the *Junk Email* folder.
   - If *Never Block Sender, Never Block Sender's Domain,* or *Never Block this Group or Mailing List* is selected, the sender's email and/or domain name is added to the *Safe Senders* list.

Within the *Junk Email Options* dialog box, each of these lists can be edited. You can add or remove email addresses or domains from any of the lists, or edit entries included in the lists.

Retrieving Email That Is Marked as Junk

If an email is delivered to your *Junk Email* folder and it is not a junk email, it can be marked as *Not Junk*, and the sender's email address will be added to the *Safe Senders* list.

▶ HOW TO: Open the Junk Email Options Dialog Box

1. Select or open an email in the *Junk Email* folder.
2. Click the **Junk** button in the *Delete* group and select **Not Junk**. The *Mark as Not Junk* dialog box opens, and you are given the option to always trust email from this sender.
3. Click **OK**. The email will be moved to the *Inbox* folder, and the sender's email address will be added to the *Safe Senders* list.

▶ **ANOTHER WAY**

Ctrl+Alt+J marks an email message as *Not Junk*.

▶ **ANOTHER WAY**

You can also drag an email message from the *Junk Email* folder to your *Inbox* or another folder in your folder list.

▶ **MORE INFO**

It is important to check your *Junk Email* folder regularly to ensure that important emails that should be delivered to your Inbox do not get overlooked.

SLO 7.4

Using RSS Feeds

Most of you have watched the news on one of the cable television news shows and have seen the scrolling banner of news headlines at the bottom of the screen. This news feed is similar to an RSS (really simple syndication) feed from a web site. *RSS feeds* are headlines of new articles or information on web sites (Figure 7-30). After you subscribe to an RSS feed, new articles are automatically sent to your RSS feed reader. If you subscribe to news, sports, recipe, or entertainment web sites, each of the sites will send information to your RSS feed.

Figure 7-30 RSS article

Outlook manages your RSS feeds like it does your email accounts. When a new item is available on a web site, it is delivered to an RSS feed folder. You will receive RSS feeds like an email. These feeds will come with a subject line and a brief summary of the article. A link is usually provided to take you to the web site to read the full article if you're interested.

Subscribe to an RSS Feed

Outlook provides you with an *RSS Subscriptions* folder to store the RSS feeds to which you subscribe. On stand-alone installations, an *RSS Feed* folder is created instead of an *RSS Subscriptions* folder.

▶ **HOW TO:** Enable RSS Subscriptions

1. Click the **Mail** button in the *Navigation* bar.
2. Click the **File** button on the *Ribbon* and select **Options**.
3. Click the **Advanced** option.
4. Click the **Synchronize RSS Feeds to Common Feed List (CFL) in Windows** check box (Figure 7-31) and click **OK**.
5. Click the **RSS Subscriptions** folder in the *Mail Folders* list in the *Folder* pane. This folder is named **RSS Feeds** for stand-alone users.
6. Click the **RSS Subscriptions** folder drop-down arrow to view the available RSS feeds (Figure 7-32).

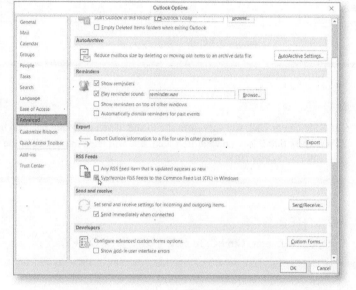

Figure 7-31 Subscribe to CFL list

Figure 7-32 *RSS Subscriptions* folder

Many commercial web sites provide you with RSS links that can be subscribed to in Outlook. Many web sites will also have the RSS feed icon or link to help you to subscribe to the RSS feed link (Figure 7-33).

Figure 7-33 RSS feed for CNN Top Stories

To subscribe to an RSS feed from a web site, you have to copy the web address (URL) of the RSS feed and paste it into the *New RSS Feed* dialog box.

▶ **HOW TO:** Subscribe to an RSS Feed from a Web Site

1. Go to the web page of your choice and locate the RSS feed icon or link. You may have to search to find the RSS feed icon or link. Not all web sites will have RSS feeds available.
2. Select the RSS URL.

3. Right-click the selected URL and choose **Copy** (Figure 7-34).

4. Return to Outlook and right-click the **RSS Subscriptions** folder in the *Folder* pane. This folder is named **RSS Feeds** for stand-alone users.

5. Choose **Add a New RSS Feed**. The *New RSS Feed* dialog box opens.

6. Click the **Enter the location of the RSS feed you want to add to Outlook** box.

7. Press **Ctrl+V** to paste the URL (Figure 7-35).

8. Click **Add**. A dialog box opens asking to *Add this RSS Feed to Outlook?*

9. Click **Yes** (Figure 7-36).

   • The RSS feed is subscribed to, and a new RSS feed folder is added to your *RSS Subscriptions* folder.

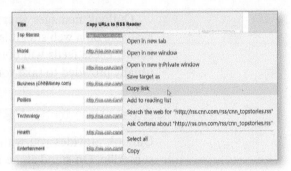

Figure 7-34 Copy the RSS address

Figure 7-35 *New RSS Feed* dialog box

Figure 7-36 *Add this RSS Feed* confirmation

MORE INFO

The RSS icon or URL will vary from site to site. If you copy and paste an incorrect URL, Outlook will let you know that it is not a valid **RSS** feed. You will need to go back to the web page and find the correct RSS feed link or URL.

ANOTHER WAY

To copy a URL, press **Ctrl+C**. To paste a URL, press **Ctrl+V**.

MORE INFO

Be careful when subscribing to RSS feeds; the volume of RSS feed emails can become overwhelming. You might get 10 to 30 feeds a day per **RSS** feed to which you are subscribed.

Manage RSS Feeds

After subscribing to RSS feeds, you will have a separate folder for each of your RSS feeds within the *RSS Feeds* folder. Inside of each of the RSS folders are the RSS feed emails.

Outlook manages RSS feeds in the *Account Settings* dialog box. Open the **Account Settings** dialog box and click the **RSS Feeds** tab. The RSS feeds to which you are subscribed display in a list (Figure 7-37). You have the option to rename a feed, change the delivery location, and change how information in the feed is downloaded.

Figure 7-37 *RSS Feeds* in account settings

You can also rename the RSS feed folder in the *Folder* pane.

▶ HOW TO: Rename RSS Feed Folders

1. Click the RSS feed folder to be renamed.
2. Click the **Folder** tab at the top of the window.
3. Click the **Rename Folder** button in the *Actions* group (Figure 7-38).
4. Type the new name for the RSS feed folder.
5. Press **Enter**. The folder will be renamed.

Figure 7-38 Rename an RSS feed folder

Share an RSS Feed

RSS feeds can easily be shared with other Outlook users. You might want to send them the URL of the RSS feed and have them add this link as a new RSS feed, but Outlook has provided a much easier way to share an RSS feed.

▶ HOW TO: Share an RSS Feed

1. Click one of the RSS feed folders in the *Folder* pane. All the RSS feed emails will be displayed in the *Content area*.
2. Open one of the RSS feed emails in the *Content area*.
3. Click the **Share This Feed** button (Figure 7-39) in the *RSS* group on the *RSS Article* tab. A new email opens (Figure 7-40).
4. Click the **To** button to select recipients and then press **Send**. This RSS feed email will be sent to recipients, and they will be given the option to add this RSS feed to their Outlook.

Figure 7-39 *Share This Feed* button

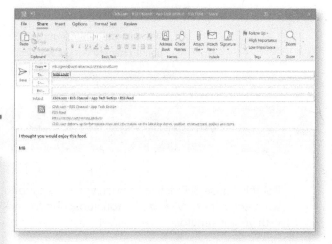

Figure 7-40 RSS share email message

When an RSS feed is shared with other Outlook users, they will receive an email in their Inbox. They can subscribe to this RSS feed by opening the email and clicking the **Add this RSS Feed** button in the upper-left corner of the email (Figure 7-41).

Figure 7-41 Add a shared RSS feed

Unsubscribe from an RSS Feed

You can unsubscribe from an RSS feed more than one way. If you want to unsubscribe from an RSS feed and remove the RSS feed folder and all the RSS feed emails, you can right-click the RSS feed folder and choose **Delete Folder**. A dialog box opens asking if you want to delete the folder and all its contents.

You can also unsubscribe from an RSS feed using the *RSS Feeds* tab in the *Account Settings* dialog box.

> **ANOTHER WAY**
>
> **Ctrl+D** deletes the selected folder.

▶ **HOW TO:** Unsubscribe from an RSS Feed

1. Open the *Account Settings* dialog box and click the **RSS Feeds** tab.
2. Select the RSS feed to be removed and click the **Remove** button.
3. Click **Yes** in the confirmation dialog box (Figure 7-42).
4. Click **Close** to close the *Account Settings* dialog box.

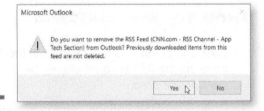

Figure 7-42 Remove an RSS feed

> **MORE INFO**
>
> When unsubscribing from an RSS feed using the *Account Settings* dialog box, the RSS feed subscription is removed but the RSS feed folder and previously received RSS feed emails are not deleted.

PAUSE & PRACTICE: OUTLOOK 7-2

For this Pause & Practice project, you subscribe to a *CNN Business* RSS news feed (available at http://www.cnn.com/services/rss/). You subscribe to an RSS feed, rename the feed folder, and share the feed with your instructor.

1. Add the *CNN Business* feed to your RSS feeds.
   a. Open a browser and go to the following URL: http://www.cnn.com/services/rss/.
   b. Locate the **Technology RSS URL**.
   c. Right-click the selected URL and choose **Copy link**.
   d. Return to Outlook and click the **Mail** button in the *Navigation* bar.
   e. Right-click the **RSS Subscriptions** folder in the *Folder* pane.
   f. Choose **Add a New RSS Feed**. The *New RSS Feed* dialog box opens.
   g. Click the **Enter the location of the RSS feed you want to add to Outlook** box.
   h. Press **Ctrl+V** to paste the URL.
   i. Click **Add**. A dialog box opens asking you *Add this RSS Feed to Outlook?*
   j. Click **Yes**.

2. Rename the RSS feed you added in the first step to *CNN Tech*.
   a. Right-click the RSS feed you added in the first step and select **Rename Folder**.
   b. Type CNN Tech and press **Enter**.

3. Share the feed with your instructor (Figure 7-43).
   a. Click the **CNN Tech** feed.
   b. Open the first message.
   c. Click the **Share This Feed** button [*RSS Article* tab, *RSS* group]. A new email opens.
   d. Type your instructor's email address in the *To* field.
   e. Type your email address in the *Cc* field.
   f. Modify the subject to include Outlook Pause & Practice 7-2 before the RSS feed title.
   g. Add the following message:

   Hi [instructor's name].

   I thought you would be interested in the CNN Tech feed!

   Thank you,
   [your name]

   h. Click the **Send** button.

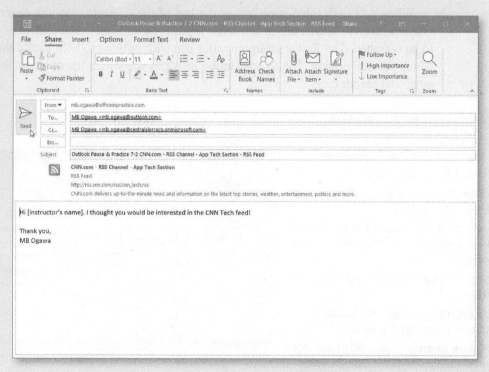

Figure 7-43 PP Outlook 7-2 completed

Searching for Outlook Items

SLO 7.5

Have you ever tried to find an email item that you sent or received months ago? You might have searched through many different folders looking for a specific email. You might not even remember who sent you the email, the subject of the email, or to whom the email was sent. Even if you don't remember all the specifics about the item for which you are looking, you can use the *Instant Search* feature to find Outlook items.

Instant Search

The *Instant Search* feature in Outlook quickly searches for Outlook items in a specific folder or all folders. It indexes all Outlook items in your folders and searches for items that match the specific criteria for which you are looking. For example, you can search all your mailbox folders for emails from your professor, for all emails with the word "Outlook" in the subject or body, or all contacts who work for "McGraw-Hill". Outlook displays all items that match your criteria in the *Content area*.

> **MORE INFO**
>
> If you are using Windows Vista, 7, 8, or 10, Outlook *Instant Search* is automatically turned on. If you are using a previous version of Windows, you will have to turn on or enable *Instant Search*.

> **ANOTHER WAY**
>
> **Ctrl+E** activates *Instant Search* on the selected folder.
> **Ctrl+Alt+A** activates *Instant Search* on *All Mail* items.

When you click the *Search* box at the top of the *Content area*, the *Search* tab displays in Outlook. On the *Search* tab in the *Scope* group, you can select the folders or areas of Outlook to be searched. The *Refine* group provides you with options to help locate the information for which you are looking. The *Options* group provides you with a list of recent searches and other advanced search tools.

▶ **HOW TO:** Search for Email Messages

1. Click the **Mail** button in the *Navigation* bar.
2. Click the folder to be searched.
3. Click the **Search** box at the top of the *Content area* (Figure 7-44).
4. Type the words to be searched in the *Search* box. Outlook displays matching emails in the *Content area*.
5. Additional criteria can be selected from the *Refine* group.
6. The *Scope* group allows you to specify where Outlook performs the search.
7. Click the **Close Search** button (**X**) to the right of the search field to clear the search and close the *Search* area and tab. You can also click one of your mailbox folders to close *Instant Search*.

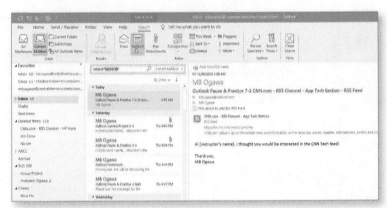

Figure 7-44 Search for email messages

When you use *Instant Search*, Outlook displays the matching items in the *Content area*, highlights the matching criteria, and lists the folder in which the item is located. Open a search result by double-clicking it in the *Content area*.

Figure 7-45 *Search Options*

Search Options

You can change the search options for *Instant Search* to customize which folders are indexed, how the results are displayed, whether or not the *Deleted Items* folder is included in the search, and the default folders to be searched.

Open the *Search Options* dialog box by clicking the **Search Tools** button in the *Options* group on the *Search* tab and selecting **Search Options** (Figure 7-45). The search section displays in the *Outlook Options* dialog box (Figure 7-46).

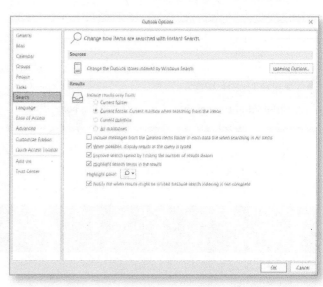

Figure 7-46 Search options in *Outlook Options*

> **ANOTHER WAY**
>
> The *Search Options* dialog box can be opened from the Outlook *Backstage* view. Click the **File** tab, choose **Options**, and click **Search**.

Advanced Find

When you use *Instant Search* in Mail, Outlook searches only for email items. Outlook also provides you with *Advanced Find* to search for any type of Outlook items rather than being limited to just one type of item. *Advanced Find* displays Outlook items that match your criteria in the *Advanced Find* dialog box.

▶ **HOW TO:** Perform an Advanced Search

1. Click the **Search** box at the top of the *Content area*.

2. Click the **Search Tools** button in the *Options* group on the *Search* tab, and select **Advanced Find** to open the *Advanced Find* dialog box.

3. Select the type of item to find in the *Look* area.

4. Select the location to search in the *In* area. Click the **Browse** button to select the folder to search.

5. Type the criteria for which to search.

   - You can click the *From* or *Sent To* buttons to select contacts.
   - Click either the *More Choices* or *Advanced* tabs for additional search options.

6. Click the **Find Now** button to search for items that match your criteria (Figure 7-47).

- The matching items will be displayed at the bottom of the dialog box.

7. Click **New Search** to clear the current search, or click the **X** in the upper-right corner to close the *Advanced Find* dialog box.

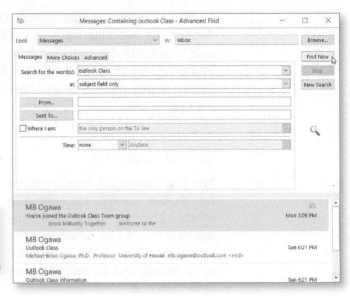

Figure 7-47 Search for any Outlook item

ANOTHER WAY

Ctrl+Shift+F opens the *Advanced Find* dialog box.

PAUSE & PRACTICE: OUTLOOK 7-3

For this Pause & Practice project, you search for the email messages from *Pause & Practice 7-2* that you sent to your instructor because you did not receive a grade for the *Pause & Practice 7-2* assignment. After you find the message, you forward it to your instructor.

1. Click the **Mail** button in the *Navigation* bar.

2. Click the **Sent Items** folder.

3. Click the **Search** box at the top of the *Content area*.

4. Click the **Current Mailbox** button [*Search* tab, *Scope* group].

5. Click the **Subject** button [*Search* tab, *Refine* group].

6. Type Pause Practice 7 as the keywords (Figure 7-48).

7. Locate and open the email message for **Outlook Pause & Practice 7-2**.

8. Forward the message to your instructor.
   a. Open the email message for **Outlook Pause & Practice 7-2**.
   b. Click the **Forward** button.
   c. Type your instructor's email address in the *To* field.
   d. Type your email address in the *Cc* field.
   e. Modify the subject to include Outlook Pause & Practice 7-3 before the RSS feed title.
   f. Add the following message:
      Hi [instructor's name].

      I am resending my Pause & Practice 7-2 assignment for you to check.

      Thank you,
      [student name]

Figure 7-48 Search criteria

g. Click the **Send** button (Figure 7-49).

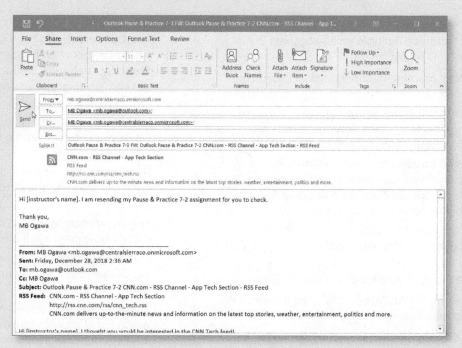

Figure 7-49 PP Outlook 7-3 completed

Chapter Summary

7.1 Connect and use multiple email accounts in Outlook (p. O7-254).

- You can manage multiple email accounts in Outlook.
- The *Auto Account Setup* automatically detects and validates account settings using your email account and password.
- You can troubleshoot your account by checking encryption and manually setting up your account if the *Auto Account Setup* is unable to detect the correct settings.
- Use the **Repair** feature to troubleshoot accounts that stop working.

7.2 Manage multiple email accounts (p. O7-257).

- The default email account is used to send new email messages.
- You can change the default email account.
- When you create a new message, you can select which account you would like to use to send the message from if multiple accounts are set available.
- If you have multiple POP email accounts, you can change the default folder that receives messages.
- Rules can be used to specify delivery folders for email messages.
- When using an Exchange account, you can use **Outlook on the web** to manage your email, tasks, calendar, and contacts from a web browser.

7.3 Customize advanced email options (p. O7-262).

- Many different options for email can be customized in the **Outlook Options** dialog box.
- The **Mail Options** dialog box includes email options.
- The **Compose messages** section allows you to customize the format of email messages and change spell checking, *AutoCorrect*, signatures, stationery, and theme options.
- The **Outlook panes** section allows you to control how messages displayed in the *Reading Pane* interact with the *Content area*.
- The **Message arrival** section of *Mail Options* controls what happens in Outlook when a message arrives in your Inbox.

- The **Conversation Clean Up** section allows you to control what happens when you use the *Clean Up* feature in Outlook to remove redundant emails in a conversation.
- The *Replies and forwards* section allows you to tailor how your email messages appear when you receive, send a reply to, or forward a message.
- New, reply, and forwarded messages are automatically saved to the **Drafts** folder every three minutes.
- The **Send messages** section allows you to modify how messages are sent.
- Outlook suggests recently used names in the *To, Cc,* and *Bcc* fields with an **Auto-Complete List**.
- The **MailTips** section allows you to modify which *MailTips* are shown. *MailTips* are applicable to Exchange environments.
- The **Tracking** section allows you to determine how Outlook tracks and responds to these items.
- The *Message Format* and *Other* sections include behind-the-scenes options for formatting your email messages.
- Use the **Out of Office Assistant** to create an automated reply message to people within and outside of your company. The *Out of Office Assistant* is applicable to Exchange environments.
- Outlook detects junk email and places it in the **Junk Email** folder.
- You can select *Safe Senders, Safe Recipients, Blocked Senders,* and *International* messages.

7.4 Integrate RSS feeds into Outlook (p. O7-270).

- Outlook allows you to receive RSS messages in your mailbox.
- You can add **RSS feeds** that you find on the internet.
- Manage RSS feeds from the *Account Settings* dialog box.
- Share RSS feeds via email.
- RSS feeds shared via email can be added to your account quickly.
- When unsubscribing from an RSS feed from the *Account Settings* dialog box, all feed messages received are not deleted. They must be deleted manually.

7.5 Utilize search features to find email and other Outlook items (p. O7-276).

- *Instant Search* allows you to quickly find Outlook items because it indexes them.
- Use the *Search* box at the top of the screen to quickly enter search criteria.
- The *Scope* of the search defines where you want to search for items, such as a specific folder.
- The *Refine* group in the *Search* tab allows you to set specific fields for your search (*From*, *Subject*, or *Has Attachments*).
- Search options can be customized to determine which folders are indexed, how the results display, whether or not the *Deleted Items* folder is included in the search, and the default folders to be searched.
- *Advanced Find* allows you to search for any type of Outlook item, as opposed to solely for email messages.

Check for Understanding

The SIMbook for this text (within your SIMnet account) provides the following resources for concept review:

- Multiple-choice questions
- Short answer questions
- Matching exercises

Guided Project 7-1

For this project, you are an academic advisor for Sierra Pacific Community College District (SPCCD). You started using your personal laptop for work because there are many tasks that you need to complete out of the office. Therefore, you have both your personal and work email accounts in Outlook. You decide to change your default email from your personal to work email, as you tend to send messages from your work account.

[Student Learning Outcomes 7.1, 7.2]

Skills Covered in This Project

- Set up an email account.
- Change the default email account.
- Select an account when creating a new message.

1. Add a new account to Outlook. (If you completed *Pause & Practice 7-1*, skip this step.)
   a. Click the **File** tab. The *Backstage* view opens.
   b. Click **Add Account**. The *Simplified Account Creation* dialog box opens.
   c. Type your email address in the *Email address* field.
   d. Click the **Connect** button.
   e. Type your password in the *Password* field.
   f. Click the **Connect** button.
   g. Click **Finish**. The *Account Settings* dialog box appears.
   h. Click **Close**.

2. Change the default email account to be your work account.
   a. Click the **File** tab to open the *Backstage* view.
   b. Click the **Account Settings** button and choose **Account Settings** to open the *Account Settings* dialog box.
   c. Select your school account (the first one you used to initially set up Outlook in chapter 1).
   d. Click the **Set as Default** button.
   e. Click the **Close** button.

3. Send a message ensuring the correct *From* address is selected.
   a. Click the **Mail** button in the *Navigation* bar.
   b. Click the **New Email** button.
   c. Click the **From** button and ensure your school account is selected.
   d. Enter the following information in the new message:
   To: your instructor's email address
   Cc: your email address
   Subject: Outlook Guided Project 7-1
   Message: Hi [instructor's name],

   I just added my work and personal accounts to my laptop. I wanted to be sure I am sending messages from the correct account. Could you please let me know if this message is coming from my work address?

   Thanks,
   [your name]

e. Click the **Send** button (Figure 7-50).

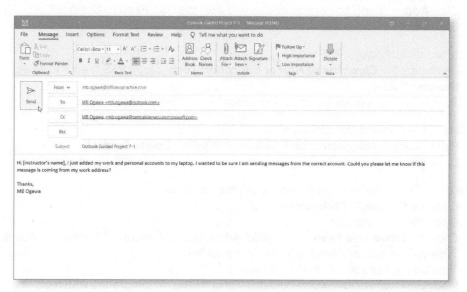

Figure 7-50 Guided Project 7-1 completed

Guided Project 7-2

For this project, you want to use Outlook as a central location for information. Therefore, you decide to stay up-to-date with higher education student services information by subscribing to RSS feeds from the Chronicle of Higher Education (the full RSS feed list is available at http://chronicle.com/sitemap). After reading a few articles, you determine which feed you want to keep and which feed you want to delete. You decide to share one of the RSS feeds with a colleague.
[Student Learning Outcome 7.4]

Skills Covered in This Project

- Add an RSS feed.
- Rename an RSS feed folder.
- Delete an RSS feed.
- Share an RSS feed.

1. Add the *Administration* RSS feed.
    a. Click the **Mail** button in the *Navigation* bar.
    b. Right-click the **RSS Subscriptions** folder in the *Folder* pane.
    c. Choose **Add a New RSS Feed**. The *New RSS Feed* dialog box opens.
    d. Click the **Enter the location of the RSS feed you want to add to Outlook** box.
    e. Type https://www.chronicle.com/section/Administration/16/rss.
    f. Click **Add**. A dialog box opens asking you *Add this RSS Feed to Outlook?*
    g. Click **Yes**.

2. Add the *Chronicle of Higher Education Technology* RSS feed.
    a. Click the **Mail** button in the *Navigation* bar.
    b. Right-click the **RSS Subscriptions** folder in the *Folder* pane.
    c. Choose **Add a New RSS Feed**. The *New RSS Feed* dialog box opens.

d. Click the **Enter the location of the RSS feed you want to add to Outlook** box.

e. Type http://chronicle.com/section/Technology/30/rss.

f. Click **Add**. A dialog box opens asking you *Add this RSS Feed to Outlook?*

g. Click **Yes**.

3. Rename the *Technology* RSS feed.

a. Right-click the **Chronicle of Higher Education Technology** RSS feed and select **Rename Folder**.

b. Type Chronicle-Technology and press **Enter**.

4. Delete the *Administration* RSS feed.

a. Right-click the **Administration** RSS feed and select **Delete Folder**.

b. Click **Yes**.

5. Share the *Chronicle-Technology* feed with your instructor.

a. Click the **Chronicle-Technology** feed.

b. Open the first message.

c. Click the **Share This Feed** button [*RSS Article* tab, *RSS* group]. A new email opens.

d. Type your instructor's email address in the *To* field.

e. Type your email address in the *Cc* field.

f. Modify the subject to include Outlook Guided Project 7-2 before the RSS feed title.

g. Add the following message:

Hi [instructor's name].

Wow, I just found this RSS feed with a lot of great technology information. Feel free to add it to your Outlook if you like the information. Let me know if you find any other great feeds, as I enjoy getting this information delivered to me in Outlook.

Thank you,
[your name]

h. Click the **Send** button (Figure 7-51).

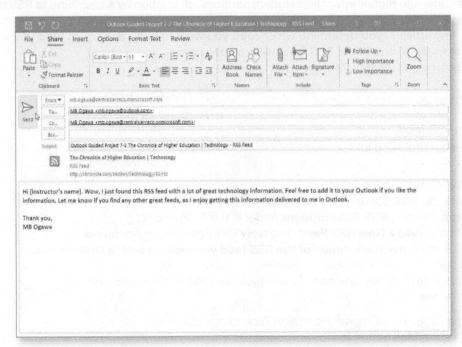

Figure 7-51 Guided Project 7-2 completed

Guided Project 7-3

You spoke with your colleague about the RSS feed that you shared. He said that he never received it. You were surprised, so for this project, you search for it and resend it when you get to a WiFi hotspot. [Student Learning Outcome 7.5]

Skills Covered in This Project

- Search using *Instant Search*.
- Use *Scope* to narrow search.
- Use *Refine* to narrow search.

---

1. Click the **Mail** button in the *Navigation* bar.

2. Click the **Sent Items** folder.

3. Click the **Search** box at the top of the *Content area*. The *Search* tab displays.

4. Click the **Current Folder** button [*Search* tab, *Scope* group].

5. Type RSS Feed as the keywords (Figure 7-52).

6. Click the **Sent To** button [*Search* tab, *Refine* group] and select **Sent to Another Recipient**.

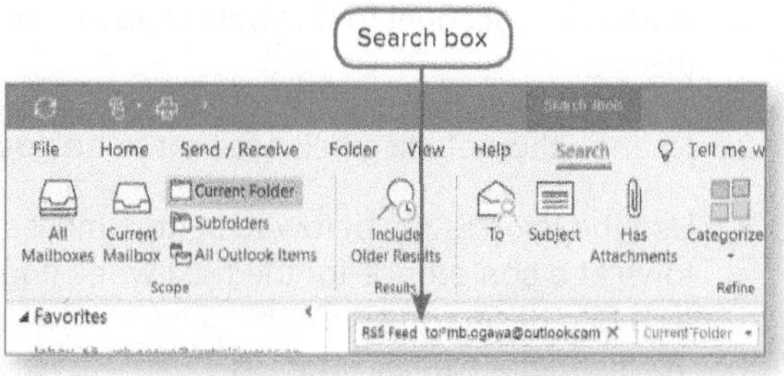

7. Type your instructor's email address as the keywords.

8. Locate and open the email message for ***Outlook Guided Project 7-2***.

9. Forward the message to your instructor.
   a. Open the email message for ***Outlook Guided Project 7-2***.
   b. Click the **Forward** button.
   c. Type your instructor's email address in the *To* field.
   d. Type your email address in the *Cc* field.
   e. Modify the subject to include Outlook Guided Project 7-3 before the RSS feed title.
   f. Add the following message:

      Hi [instructor's name].

      Here is the RSS feed we discussed today. Let me know if you receive it. The news really is awesome!

      Thank you,
      [your name]
   g. Click the **Send** button (Figure 7-53).

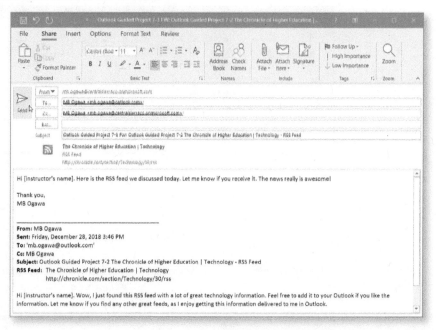

Figure 7-52 *Guided Project 7-3 search criteria*

Figure 7-53 Guided Project 7-3 completed

Independent Project 7-4

For this project, you are a doctor who works at Courtyard Medical Plaza (CMP). You recently joined the American Medical Association (AMA) using your professional email account. This account is different from your practice account, which you use specifically for email related to your medical practice. Since you use Outlook, you ensure both email accounts are available.
[Student Learning Outcomes 7.1, 7.2]

Skills Covered in This Project

- Set up an email account.
- Change the default email account.

- Select an account when creating a new message.

---

1. Add a new account to Outlook. (If you completed *Pause & Practice 7-1* or *Guided Project 7-1*, skip this step.)

2. Change the default email account to be your work account (school account).

3. Use the information below to send a message to your patient list indicating that you will be out of town at a conference for the next week (Figure 7-54). (In practice, you would likely send the message as a Bcc based on applicable laws.)
   To: instructor's email address
   Cc: your email address
   Subject: Outlook Independent Project 7-4
   Message: Hi everyone,

   I just wanted to let you know that I will be out of town at a conference next week. For emergencies, call 911; for office appointments, contact my assistant, Jane. She can set up appointments with my colleague, Dr. Goron.

   [your name]

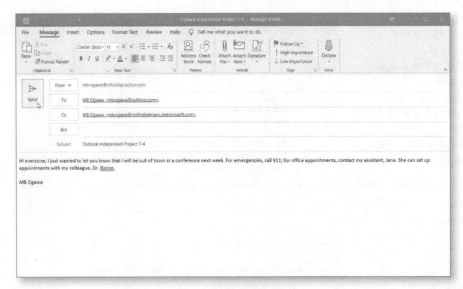

Figure 7-54 Independent Project 7-4 completed

Independent Project 7-5

You realize that as your practice grows, you have less time to keep up-to-date with health information. Therefore, for this project, you subscribe to RSS feeds to keep up-to-date with recent health news from MedlinePlus.

[Student Learning Outcome 7.4]

Skills Covered in This Project

- Add an RSS feed.
- Rename an RSS feed folder.
- Delete an RSS feed.
- Share an RSS feed.

---

1. Open a browser and navigate to https://medlineplus.gov/rss.html.

2. Locate the RSS feeds for **New Links on MedlinePlus**, **New NIH Links on MedlinePlus**, and **MedlinePlus on Twitter**. These RSS feeds are located in the *Wellness and Lifestyle* section of the page.

3. Add all three RSS feeds to your *RSS Feeds* folder.

4. Rename the **New Links on MedlinePlus** RSS feed MedlinePlus Links.

5. Rename the **New National Institutes of Health (NIH) Links on MedlinePlus** RSS feed NIH Links.

6. Delete the **MedlinePlus on Twitter - Recent Updates** RSS feed.

7. Share the **MedlinePlus Links** and **NIH Links** feeds with your instructor. They will be sent as two messages.
    a. Add the text Outlook Independent Project 7-5 in the subject line before the default subject.
    b. Add your email address to the *Cc* field.
    c. Add a short message to your instructor indicating that you are submitting your completed Independent Project (Figure 7-55).

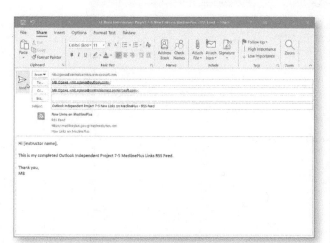
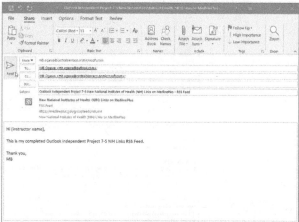

Figure 7-55 Independent Project 7-5 completed

Independent Project 7-6

Your email list for patients is not up-to-date. Therefore, a few patients do not know that you are away at a conference. For this project, you search for the email you initially sent to your patient list and forward it to the rest of the patients.
[Student Learning Outcome 7.5]

Skills Covered in This Project

- Search using *Instant Search*.
- Use *Scope* to narrow search.
- Use *Refine* to narrow search.
- Use *Advanced Find*.

1. Search for the message you sent using *Instant Search* or *Advanced Find*.

2. After locating the message, forward it to your instructor. (In practice, you would likely send the message as a Bcc based on applicable laws.)
   a. Be sure to add your address in the *Cc* field.
   b. Add Outlook Independent Project 7-6 in the subject line.
   c. Add a short message to your instructor with the following information:
   Message: Hi everyone.

   I am not sure if you received this message, so I am forwarding it to you to ensure you are aware that I will be away.

   Thanks,
   [your name]

   Below the message to your patients, include the following search information. Only include the features you utilized (Figure 7-56):

   Keywords: [keywords for search]
   Scope criteria: [criteria and reason for using it]
   Refine criteria: [criteria and reason for using it]
   Advanced Find criteria: [criteria and reason for using it]

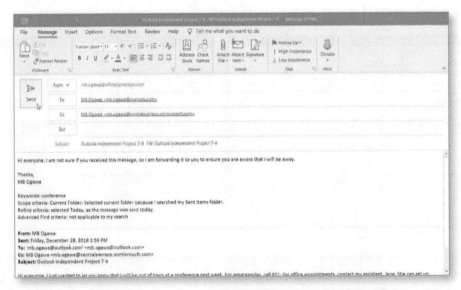

Figure 7-56 Independent Project 7-6 completed

Challenge Project 7-7

Most people have more than one email account. Working with multiple accounts and personalizing Outlook to meet your needs is definitely a challenge. For this project, you identify the different email accounts that you have. Determine if you will need additional accounts for different purposes, such as work, school, and personal. Send an email message to your instructor indicating which one would be set as default and why. Also indicate if and when you would use the web access counterpart, such as Outlook on the web. Lastly, you configure Outlook to better meet your needs and email your instructor which customizations you made to your installation and why. You should customize at least three advanced email options.
[Student Learning Outcomes 7.1, 7.2, 7.3]

- Identify the different email accounts that you have.
- Determine if you need additional accounts.
- Determine which account should be the default.
- Determine when the web mail counterpart, such as Outlook on the web, would be useful.
- Email your instructor using the following message format:

  Account 1: [purpose for the account]
  Default: [indicate if it is the default account or not and why]
  Web access: [indicate when the web access counterpart would be useful]

  Account 2: [purpose for the account]
  Default: [indicate if it is the default account or not and why]
  Web access: [indicate when the web access counterpart would be useful]

  Account 3: [purpose for the account]
  Default: [indicate if it is the default account or not and why]
  Web access: [indicate when the web access counterpart would be useful]

  Outlook Personalization: [list of features modified]
  Feature 1: [indicate modification and reason]
  Feature 2: [indicate modification and reason]
  Feature 3: [indicate modification and reason]

- Change the subject of your message to Outlook Challenge Project 7-7.

Challenge Project 7-8

Based on your interests, search the web to find at least two RSS feeds that interest you. Add the RSS feeds to your *RSS Feeds* folder and share them with your instructor.
[Student Learning Outcome 7.4]

- Search the web for at least two RSS feeds that interest you.
- Add the feeds to your *RSS Feeds* folder.
- Rename the feeds if you prefer a descriptive title.
- Share the feeds with your instructor (create two separate messages).

- In the email messages to your instructor, use the following message format:

  Feed Name: [reason you chose this feed]

- Change the subject of your first message to Outlook Challenge Project 7-8 Feed 1.
- Change the subject of your second message to Outlook Challenge Project 7-8 Feed 2.

Challenge Project 7-9

Identify one email message and one Outlook item that you created in the past year. Email your message and Outlook item as attachments to your instructor. Include your search criteria to find the message and Outlook item and why you would use the criteria for it.
[Student Learning Outcome 7.5]

- Identify an email message and Outlook item you created in the last year.
- Determine search criteria to find the message and Outlook item.
- You should include keywords in your search.
- For the email message, use one scope and one refine search criteria.
- For the Outlook item, use at least two criteria in addition to keywords.
- Include reasons for your search criteria.
- Email your instructor using the following message format:

  Email message: [Outlook attachment name]
  Keywords: [keywords for search]
  Scope criteria: [criteria and reason for using it]
  Refine criteria: [criteria and reason for using it]

  Outlook item: [Outlook attachment name]
  Keywords: [keywords for search]
  Criteria 1: [criteria and reason for using it]
  Criteria 2: [criteria and reason for using it]

- Change the subject of your message to Outlook Challenge Project 7-9.

Source of screenshots Microsoft Office 365 (2019): Word, Excel, Access, PowerPoint, Outlook.

Notes, Journal, Shortcuts, Archiving, and Security

CHAPTER OVERVIEW

This chapter will continue to explore organization features. Outlook Notes store information that does not qualify as a task or a calendar item. Use Outlook Journal to track the time spent on Outlook items and other Microsoft Office documents.

Shortcuts move quickly from one area of Outlook to another. Finally, you'll be introduced to the *Archive* feature. Archiving your Outlook data creates a different set of folders to store older information.

Security has become an increasingly important topic when dealing with digital information. Outlook provides many security features to protect your information from viruses and other potential threats.

STUDENT LEARNING OUTCOMES (SLOs)

After completing this chapter, you will be able to:

SLO 10.1   Create and use Notes in Outlook (p. O10-363).

SLO 10.2   Integrate the Outlook Journal with Outlook items and Microsoft Office documents (p. O10-365).

SLO 10.3   Incorporate shortcuts in Outlook (p. O10-368).

SLO 10.4   Store Outlook Items in archive folders (p. O10-371).

SLO 10.5   Customize security settings (p. O10-375).

SLO 10.6   Create deals with the Customer Manager (p. O10-383).

SLO 10.7   Understand the difference between Outlook on the Web and Outlook 365 Online (p. O10-386).

CASE STUDY

For the Pause & Practice projects, you continue to work with your BUS 100 group. You use the Outlook Notes feature to remember group discussions. You also use Journal to keep track of work completed and create a shortcut to Journal. You also decide that you want to use a digital signature with your email messages, so you import one and add it to your messages.

Pause & Practice 10-1: You continue working with your BUS 100 group. Your group decided to track each members' contribution,

so you write a note to remind yourself of the decision. Since your group decided to use the Journal feature in Outlook frequently, you create a shortcut to Journal. Lastly, you create a journal entry to keep track of time spent on your part of the group project.

Pause & Practice 10-2: You decide to set up a digital ID to ensure your recipients can verify that your messages are not tampered with. If your institution provides you with a digital ID, you can import it. Otherwise, you can use a free digital ID service, such as Comodo.

Pause & Practice 10-3: You realize that keeping track of email messages, calendar items, tasks, and contacts associated with a transaction is difficult. You decide to create deal based on a training request to keep asso ciated Outlook items in a single location.

SLO 10.1

Using Notes

Do you have sticky notes stuck to your computer monitor, bathroom mirror, or refrigerator? If you're like most people, you use these sticky notes to write down reminders or random pieces of information. Outlook provides you with a feature similar to paper sticky notes. *Notes* (Figure 10-1) can be used to store information that is not considered a task or calendar item. These items can be used to store a book wish list, a user name to a web site, a grocery list, a mileage rate for travel reimbursement, or other miscellaneous pieces of information.

Figure 10-1 Outlook Not

> **ANOTHER WAY**
>
> **Ctrl+5** opens Notes in Outlook.

> **MORE INFO**
>
> Be careful about storing sensitive information in Notes if you are using Outlook in a stand-alone environment where others have access to your Outlook account.

> **MORE INFO**
>
> If you prefer to have the *Notes* button visible in th *Navigation* bar, you can customize the *Navigation* bar to show more than four buttons. See chapter for details on customizing the *Navigation* bar.

Create a Note

The *Notes* button is located on the . . . (more button) in the *Navigation* bar. After you click the *No* button (Figure 10-1), the *Notes* folders display in the *My Notes* list in the *Folder* pane, and your not display in the *Content area*. Whenever the *Notes* button is mentioned, it is the *Notes* button from t *Navigation* bar being referenced; the . . . (more button) will not be included in each step.

▶ **HOW TO:** Create a Note

1. Click the **Notes** button in the *Navigation* bar.
2. Click the **New Note** button (Figure 10-2). A new note will be displayed.
3. Type the information to be included in the note.
4. Click the **X** in the upper-right corner to save and close the note. The first line of the note is the name of the note and displays in the *Content area*.

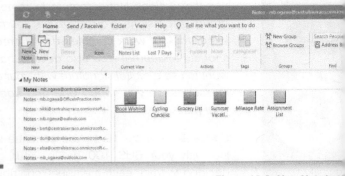

Figure 10-2 *New Note butt*

Edit a Note

Notes are very basic; you do not have as many formatting options available for notes that you have when customizing an email, task, signature, or calendar item. To edit a note, simply double-click the note to be edited in the *Content area*. The note opens, appearing similar to a sticky note on your computer screen, and you will be able to change the contents of the note. To save and close the note, click the **X** in the upper-right corner.

Categorize Notes

As with other Outlook items, notes can be assigned to a category. When a note is assigned to a category, the color of the note changes to the color of the category to which it is assigned.

HOW TO: Categorize Notes

. Select the notes to be categorized.
. Click the **Categorize** button [*Home* tab, *Tags* group] (Figure 10-3).
. Click the selected category. The notes change to the color of the assigned category.

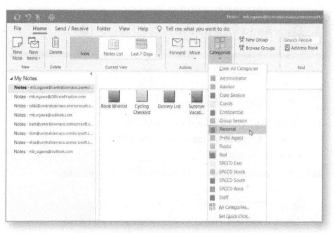

Figure 10-3 Categorize notes to organize them

Note Views

Notes can be displayed in a variety of ways. The different views are available in the *Current View* group. The default view is *Icon* (see Figure 10-3). Other note views include *Notes List* (Figure 10-4) and *Last 7 Days*. Both *Notes List* and *Last 7 Days* appear similarly with *Last 7 Days* showing only notes created or edited within the last week.

Notes can also display on your computer desktop (just like plac-

Figure 10-4 *Notes List* view

ing a sticky note on your computer screen). To display a note on your desktop, drag the note from the *Content area* and drop it on the desktop. A copy of the note is placed on the desktop.

Within the *Icon* view, the notes can be displayed as large icons, small icons, or as a list. Click the **View** tab to display the different options in the *Arrangement* group (Figure 10-5).

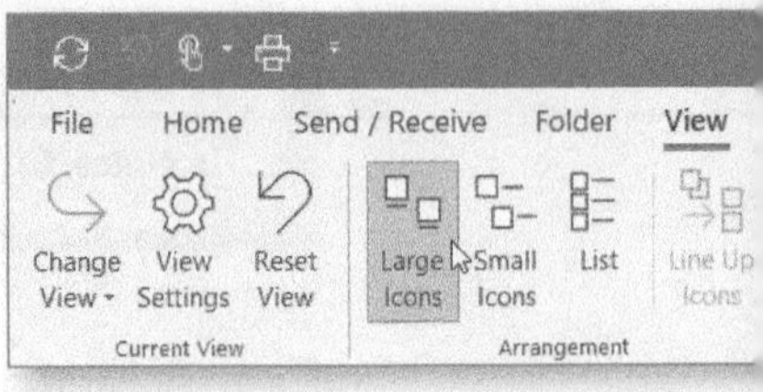

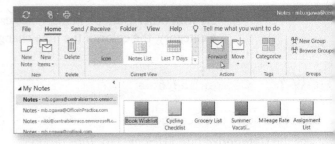

Figure 10-5 Arrangement options for notes view

Forward a Note

Notes can be forwarded as an attachment via email to other Outlook users. When a recipient receives a forwarded note, he or she can drag the attached note to the *Notes* button, and the note will be saved in his or her *Notes* folder.

> ▶ **HOW TO: Forward a Note**

1. Select the notes to be forwarded.
2. Click the **Forward** button in the [*Home* tab, *Actions* group] (Figure 10-6). A new email opens with the notes attached.
3. Select recipients, type a subject, and include necessary information in the body.
4. Click **Send** to send the notes (Figure 10-7).

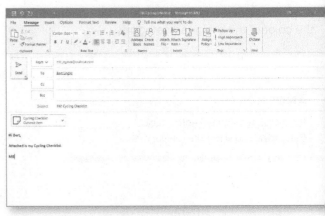

Figure 10-6 Forward a note

> **ANOTHER WAY**
>
> **Ctrl+F** can be used to forward selected notes. A new email message opens with the selected notes.

> **ANOTHER WAY**
>
> Right-click the selected notes and choose **Forward**.

Figure 10-7 Forwarded note email

Using the Journal

Outlook *Journal* (Figure 10-8) is a feature used to track the amount of time you have spent working on a particular document or task. You can also use a journal to track activities related to a particular contact. An Outlook journal can be particularly useful if you or your company charges customers based on the time spent working on activities

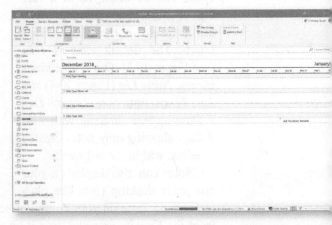

Figure 10-8 Outlook Journal

for them. A journal entry can be manually created and tracked, or you can have Outlook automatically create and track certain types of documents or specific contacts.

To access the Journal feature, click the more button (. . .) in the *Navigation* bar and select **Folders** (Figure 10-9). The *Journal* folder is available in the *Folders* list. The *Folder* button in the *Navigation* bar is similar to the *Notes* button, where they are hidden by default and can be made visible using the *Navigation Options*.

Figure 10-9 *Folders* option

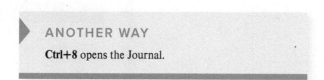
ANOTHER WAY

Ctrl+8 opens the Journal.

Record a Journal Entry

A journal entry can be created to track the amount of time spent on numerous Outlook and other activities. The different activities that can be tracked with a journal entry are:

- *Conversation*
- *Document*
- *Email message*
- *Fax*
- *Letter*
- *Meeting*
- *Meeting cancellation*
- *Meeting request*
- *Meeting response*
- *Microsoft Excel*
- *Microsoft Office Access*
- *Microsoft PowerPoint*
- *Microsoft Word*
- *Note*
- *Phone call*
- *Remote session*
- *Task*
- *Task request*
- *Task response*

When you manually create a journal entry, you record the *Subject, Entry type, Company, Start time*, and *Duration*. You can use the *Start Timer* button to automatically record the amount of time you spent on a journal entry, or you can manually enter the time into the journal.

HOW TO: Record a Journal Entry

Click the **Folders** button in the *Navigation* bar.

Click **Journal** in the *Folders* list.

3. Click the **Journal Entry** button (Figure 10-10). A new journal entry opens (Figure 10-11).

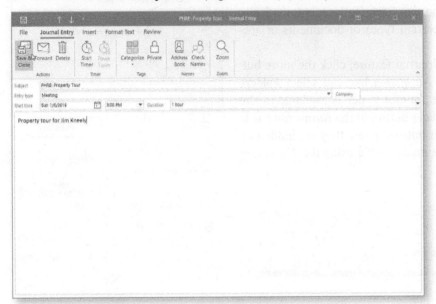

Figure 10-11 Sample journal entry

Figure 10-10 *Journal Entry* butt

4. Fill in the **Subject**.
5. Select the **Entry type**.
6. Select the **Start time** or click the **Start Timer** button. If not using the timer, select the **Duration** for the journal ent
7. Add any details to the body.
8. Click **Save & Close**.

> **ANOTHER WAY**
>
> When you are in Journal, **Ctrl+N** opens a new journal entry. **Ctrl+Shift+J** opens a new journal entry anywhere in Outlook.

Journal Views

Outlook has numerous preset views by which to see your journal entries in the *Content ar*
Some of the views display your journal entries in timeline format, while others display the
in list format. The preset journal views are:

- *Timeline* (timeline view)
- *Entry List* (list view)
- *Phone Calls* (list view)
- *Last 7 Days* (list view)

Journal entries in the time-line view display in a day, week, or month arrangement. These different arrangement options are provided in the *Arrangement* group on the *Home* tab (Figure 10-12).

Figure 10-12 View Journal by w

Using Shortcuts

In addition to *Mail, Calendar, Contacts, Tasks, Notes, Folder List,* and *Folder*, Outlook provides you with another module. The **Shortcuts** module (Figure 10-13) in the *Navigation* bar gives you the ability to create shortcut links to Outlook folders, other computer folders, programs on your computer, specific documents on your computer, or a web site. *Groups* can be created in the *Shortcuts* area to group related shortcuts. If the link in the *Shortcuts* area is to an Outlook folder, the Outlook folder displays in the *Content area* when the link is clicked. If the link in the *Shortcuts* area is to a program or file, the program or file opens in a new window when you click the shortcut.

Figure 10-13 Outlook Shortcuts

Create a New Shortcut

Shortcuts can be created to quickly move to a folder in Outlook. Over time, you typically build up a large folder repository. Therefore, you can create shortcuts to folders you frequently use.

   To access the *Shortcuts* area, click the more button (. . .) and select **Shortcuts** in the *Navigation* bar. The *Shortcuts* button is similar to the *Notes* and *Folder* buttons, as it is located within the . . . button and can be placed in the *Navigation* bar using *Navigation Options*.

▶ HOW TO: Create a Shortcut

1. Click the **Shortcuts** button in the *Navigation* bar.

2. Click the **Folder** tab.

3. Click the **New Shortcut** button in the *New* group (Figure 10-14). The *Add to Folder Pane* dialog box opens and displays all your Outlook folders (Figure 10-15).

4. Select an Outlook folder to be added as a shortcut.

5. Click **OK** to add the shortcut to the *Folder* pane. The shortcut appears in the *Folder* pane.

When you click a shortcut, the folder appears in the main document area.

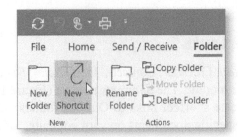

Figure 10-14 *New Shortcut* button

Figure 10-15 *Add to Folder Pa*
dialog b

▶ **ANOTHER WAY**

Right-click a shortcut group and choose **New Shortcut**.

Create a New Group

Groups can be created within the *Shortcuts* area to group related items. To create a new group, right-click the **Shortcuts** area in the *Folder* pane and select **New Shortcut Group** (Figure 10-16). A new group will be created in the *Folder* pane, and you will need to type the name of the new group.

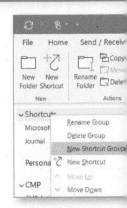

Figure 10-16 Creat
new shortcut gro

Edit a Shortcut or Group

Shortcuts and shortcut groups can be rearranged by dragging the shortcut to a new location in the list of shortcuts or right-clicking the shortcut and choosing *Move Up* or *Move Down* (Figure 10-17). Shortcuts can also be renamed by right-clicking the shortcut, choosing *Rename Shortcut*, and typing the new shortcut name. Groups can be rearranged or renamed similarly to how a shortcut link is rearranged or renamed.

You can delete shortcuts and groups by right-clicking the shortcut or group and choosing *Delete Shortcut* or *Delete Group*. If you remove a group, all the shortcuts within that group will be deleted.

Figure 10-17 Ed
shortcut or group us
the right-click optic

▶ **MORE INFO**

When you delete a shortcut, the actual item is not deleted; just the shortcut to the item is deleted.

For this Pause & Practice project, you continue working with your BUS 100 group. Your group decides to keep track of each member's contribution, so you write a note to remind yourself of the decision. Since your group decided to use the Journal feature in Outlook frequently, you decide to create a shortcut to the Journal feature. Lastly, you create a journal entry to keep track of time spent on your part of the group project.

1. Create a note indicating that your group will track work using the Journal feature.
   a. Click the **Notes** button in the *Navigation* bar.
   b. Click the **New Note** button. A new note displays.
   c. In the *Note* field, type BUS 100 group decided to track individual time spent using the Journal.
   d. Click the **X** in the upper-right corner to save and close the note.

2. Create a shortcut to the *Journal* folder.
   a. Click the **Shortcuts** button in the *Navigation* bar.
   b. Click the **Folder** tab.
   c. Click the **New Shortcut** button in the *New* group. The *Add to Folder Pane* dialog box opens and displays all your Outlook folders.
   d. Select the **Journal** folder.
   e. Click **OK** to add the shortcut to the *Folder* pane.

3. Create a journal entry indicating that you spent two hours on research.
   a. Click the **Shortcuts** button in the *Navigation* bar.
   b. Click the **Journal** shortcut.
   c. Click the **Journal Entry** button. A new journal entry opens.
   d. In the *Subject* field, type BUS 100 Library Research.
   e. In the *Entry type* field, select **Task**.
   f. In the *Start time* fields, select **yesterday's date** at **2:30 PM**.
   g. In the *Duration* field, select **2 hours**.
   h. Click **Save & Close**.

4. Send an email to your instructor with the note and journal entry as attachments.
   a. Click the **Mail** button in the *Navigation* bar.
   b. Click **New Mail** [*Home* tab, *New* group].
   c. In the *To* field, enter your instructor's email address.
   d. In the *Cc* field, enter your email address.
   e. In the *Subject* field, type Outlook Pause & Practice 10-1.
   f. In the message area, type:

      Dear [instructor name],

      Attached is my Outlook Pause & Practice 10-1.

      Thank you,
      [student name]

   g. Click the **Outlook Item** button [*Insert* tab, *Include* group].
   h. Select your note and click **OK**.
   i. Click the **Outlook Item** button [*Insert* tab, *Include* group].
   j. Select your journal entry and click **OK**.
   k. Click the **Send** button (Figure 10-18).

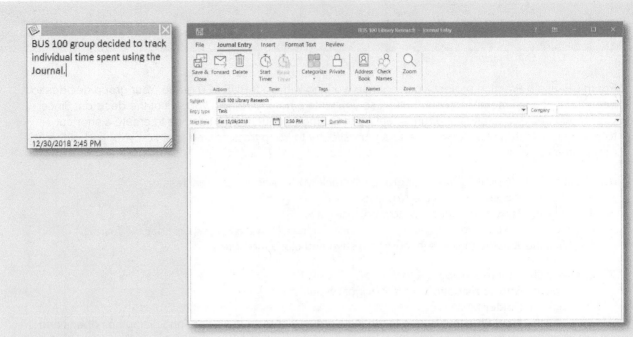

BUS 100 group decided to track individual time spent using the Journal.

12/30/2018 2:45 PM

Figure 10-18 Completed Pause & Practice 10-1

SLO 10.4

Storing Outlook Items in Archive Folders

After you have been using Outlook for some time, you will find that you have numerous o email and calendar items taking up storage space. If you are using Outlook in a stand-alo environment, space is typically not a problem, but if you are on an Exchange server, you ha only a limited amount of space on the server to store all your Outlook data. If you like to kee all your old email and calendar items, you might receive an email message warning you th you are close to or over your allotted space on the server.

Figure 10-19 Archi folde

Outlook provides you with a solution to this space limitation. *Archiving* is moving older Outlook items from their location (personal folders or mailbox folders) to a set of *archive folders* (Figure 10-19). When *AutoArchive* runs, a set of archive folders is created and stored locally on your computer rather than on the Exchange server. This set of folders mirrors the folders in your mailbox or personal folders and contains the older archived Outlook items. This helps to control the amount of space you are using on the Exchange server while still allowing you to save and have access to these older Outlook items.

AutoArchive can be set to run periodically and will automatically move older Outlook iter to your archive folders. You can customize the *AutoArchive* settings to move older mail, cale dar, tasks, notes, and journals to the archive folders. You can also customize the archive s tings for individual Outlook folders.

> **MORE INFO**
>
> Contacts are not archived because they are not time sensitive like emails, calendar items, tasks, notes, and journals.

AutoArchive Settings

AutoArchive is, by default, turned off in Outlook. The *AutoArchive* dialog box has many settings that you can customize. *AutoArchive* can be set to run automatically at a regular interval (every 14 days), and you can be prompted before *AutoArchive* runs. If you choose *Prompt before Auto-Archive runs*, a dialog box opens asking you if you want to run *AutoArchive*. If this option is not selected, *AutoArchive* will run automatically on the set schedule. In the *AutoArchive* dialog box, you have the option to either delete older Outlook items or move (archive) them to another set of folders. The default setting is to move older items to the archive folders, which are stored locally on your computer rather than on the Exchange server. In the *Clean out items older than* area, you can specify when you want your older items archived. This setting can be set from 1 day to 60 months. *AutoArchive* can also be set to delete expired email items. You can specify the location on your computer where you want archive folders saved. This set of folders is saved as an Outlook Data File (.pst).

The settings in the *AutoArchive* dialog box are global and can be applied to all Outlook folders by clicking the *Apply these settings to all folders now* button.

HOW TO: Modify AutoArchive Settings

. Click the **File** button on the *Ribbon* to open the *Backstage* view.

. Click **Options**. The *Outlook Options* dialog box opens.

. Select **Advanced** and click the **AutoArchive Settings** button (Figure 10-20). The *AutoArchive* dialog box opens (Figure 10-21).

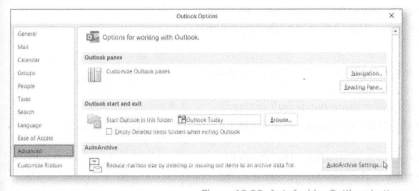

Figure 10-20 *AutoArchive Settings* button

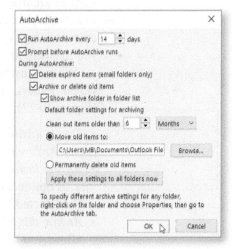

Figure 10-21 *AutoArchive* dialog box

. Make the desired changes to the *AutoArchive* settings. Here are a few general guidelines to follow:

- **Run AutoArchive every**: 14 days (2 weeks)
- Check **Prompt before AutoArchive runs**, as your computer may slow down a little depending on the speed during the archiving process.
- Check **Delete expired items (email folders only)** if you do not intend to revisit expired items.
- Check **Archive or delete old items**.
- Check **Show archive folder in folder list**.

- Clean out items older than **6 months** if you normally do not revisit items older than half a year,
- Select **Move old items to** and select an archive location on your computer that you will remember. This will allow you to revisit items archived if you need to and will help to keep your Outlook .pst file smaller to improve overall performance.

5. Click **OK** to close the *AutoArchive* dialog box.
6. Click **OK** to close the *Outlook Options* dialog box.

> **MORE INFO**
>
> Expired email was covered in chapter 2.
> Outlook Data Files (.pst) were covered in chapter 8.

> **MORE INFO**
>
> It is a good idea to archive rather than delete older items so that you have access to them if you need them in the future. If you delete older Outlook items, they will not be stored in the archive folders.

Custom AutoArchive Settings

You may have folders in Outlook that you do not want to archive, or you want to archive with different *AutoArchive* settings than the default ones. For example, you might not want to archive your Inbox and Tasks, but you might want to archive your calendar more or less frequently than your current default (global) *AutoArchive* settings. Outlook allows you to customize the archive settings on individual folders.

When customizing *AutoArchive* settings for individual folders, you have the following three options (Figure 10-22):

- *Do not archive items in the folder*: This option turns off *AutoArchive* on the selected folder.
- *Archive items in this folder using the default settings*: This option uses the default *AutoArchive* settings for the selected folder.
- *Archive this folder using these settings*: This option allows you to customize the *AutoArchive* settings for the selected folder.

Figure 10-22 *AutoArchive Inbo[x] folder settings*

Figure 10-23 *AutoArchive Calenda[r] folder settings*

▶ **HOW TO: Customize AutoArchive Settings**

1. Select the folder on which to customize *AutoArchive* settings.
2. Click the **Folder** tab and then on the **AutoArchive Settings** (or **Folder Properties**) button in the *Properties* group. The *[Folder name] Properties* dialog box opens. When using a stand-alone computer, select the **AutoArchive** tab in the *Properties* dialog box (Figure 10-23).

Select one of the three custom *AutoArchive* options and make any desired changes to the *AutoArchive* settings.

Click **Apply**.

Click **OK** to close the dialog box.

These custom settings will now be the *AutoArchive* settings for this folder and will override the default *AutoArchive* settings in Outlook. You can customize the *AutoArchive* settings on any of your folders that will be archived in Outlook.

> **ANOTHER WAY**
>
> You can right-click any Outlook folder and choose **Properties** to open the *Properties* dialog box. You will then need to click the **AutoArchive** tab.

Outlook allows further customization regarding the archiving of specific items. Individual Outlook items can be set so they are not archived even if they are in a folder that will be archived.

HOW TO: Mark an Outlook Item to NOT be Archived

Open the Outlook item you wish not to be archived.

Click the **File** tab to open the *Backstage* view.

Click the **Properties** button (Figure 10-24). The *Properties* dialog opens.

Check the **Do not AutoArchive this item** check box (Figure 10-25).

Figure 10-24 Properties for Outlook items

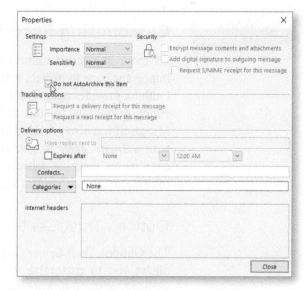

Figure 10-25 Ensure an Outlook item is NOT archived

Close the *Properties* dialog box.

Running AutoArchive and Archive

After you initially set up *AutoArchive*, it should run on its own for the first time based on t[...] criteria you defined. *AutoArchive* should also continue to run based on the schedule you s[...] However, you may want to archive your folders manually at times, such as seeing your quo[...] almost being filled.

> **HOW TO: Manually Archive Folders**

1. Select the folder you want to archive.
2. Click the **File** tab to open the *Backstage* view.
3. Select **Tools** and click **Clean Up Old Items** (Figure 10-26). The *Archive* dialog box opens (Figure 10-27).
4. Select **Archive all folders according to their AutoArchive settings** if you want to archive all folders.
5. Select **Archive this folder and all subfolders** and click a folder if you want to archive a specific folder.

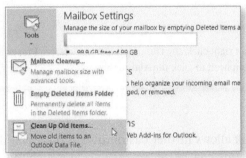

Figure 10-26 *Clean Up Old Items* button to manually archive folders

Figure 10-27 *Archive* dialog b[...]

6. Enter a date to determine the criteria in which to archive items.
7. Check **Include items with "Do not AutoArchive" checked** if you want to archive all items including the ones you indicated should not.
8. Click **Browse** and select a .pst file name and location. If you are archiving all folders, you may want to use the same .pst file you initially created.
9. Click **OK** to run the archive.

SLO 10.5   Customizing Security Settings

As more and more communication is being done through email, security has become [...] important issue to protect your computer and information from viruses and malicious attac[...] Outlook provides options for controlling which emails are treated as junk mail. Microsoft has also provided Office users with a *Trust Center* to give you control over many security aspects of online information in one central area.

Outlook Trust Center

The Outlook *Trust Center* (Figure 10-28) allows you to customize your Outlook security in the following areas: *Trusted Publishers*, *Privacy Options*, *Email Security*, *Attachment Handling*, *Automatic Download*, *Macro Security*, and *Programmatic Access*.

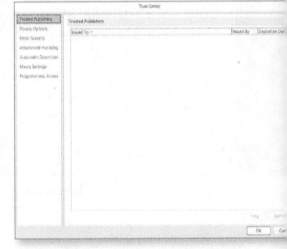

Figure 10-28 *Trusted Publishers* in the *Trust Cen[...]*

To open the *Outlook Trust Center*, click the **File** tab, select **Options**, and choose **Trust Center**.

Trusted Publishers

Trusted publishers (see Figure 10-28) are those organizations that are reputable and have a digital signature assigned to the macro or program that you allow to run on your computer.

The *Outlook Trust Center* stores this information to validate this publisher or developer. If a macro or other code attempts to run on your computer from a source that is not a trusted source, you will receive a warning message prompting you to allow or deny the action.

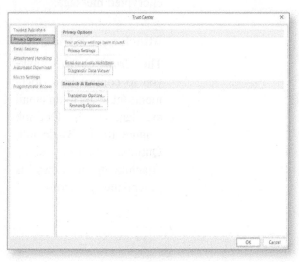

Privacy Options

The *Privacy Options* (Figure 10-29) area of the *Trust Center* controls what information is sent to and received from Microsoft. These options can provide additional functionality and resources in Outlook, as well as monitoring your Outlook usage to help with product improvement.

In this area, you can also control available translation and research options.

Figure 10-29 *Privacy Options*

Email Security

The *Email Security* area (Figure 10-30) allows you to control the use of encrypted emails and digital IDs.

Encrypting is a way to add another level of security to the messages and attachments you send. You can also choose to automatically include a digital signature to each message you send.

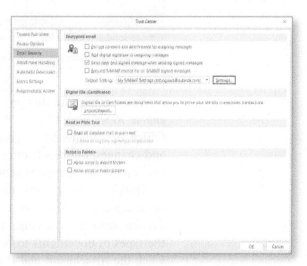

Figure 10-30 *Email Security*

MORE INFO

Digital signatures will be covered later in this chapter.

S/MIME (Secure/Multipurpose Internet Mail Extensions) can be used to confirm that an email was sent and received unaltered and provides details about when the email was opened and read.

Digital IDs (certificates) can be used to verify your identity and electronically sign documents of high importance. Digital IDs are used in conjunction with encryption to secure email messages and attachments. To encrypt a document, the sender must have a digital ID and use a *private key* to encrypt the data. The receiver of the encrypted message must have the *public key* that matches the private key of the sender to view the encrypted message.

Attachment Handling

The *Trust Center* allows you to control how documents attached to an email are handled in Outlook (Figure 10-31). By default, Outlook blocks some attachments it views as potentially dangerous.

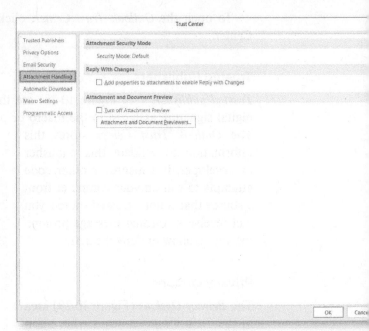

Figure 10-31 *Attachment Handli*

You can use the *Add properties to attachments to enable Reply with Changes* feature. Most Microsoft Office documents allow you to include comments and changes, but this feature provides this functionality on other documents sent as attachments.

Outlook allows you to preview many types of attachments. You can turn off the **Attachment Preview** feature or change the settings to control the types of documents to be previewed in Outlook. Click the **Attachment and Document Previewers** button to open the *File Previewing Options* dialog box (Figure 10-32).

Figure 10-32 *File Previewing Optic dialog b*

Automatic Download

Most of you have received an email message with embedded HTML content—pictures and te that look similar to a web page. By default, Outlook does not download pictures and graph embedded in these messages (Figure 10-33).

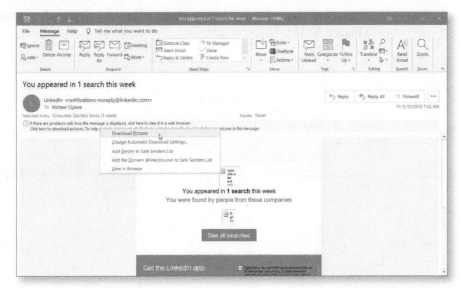

Figure 10-33 Pictures are not automatically downloaded in email messages

When you receive an email with HTML content, Outlook automatically blocks the content. The *Info* bar will give you the option of downloading the content of the email. When HTML content is downloaded from a server, the sender of the message knows that your email account is active and you might start receiving more unsolicited emails—junk mail. In the *Automatic Download* area (Figure 10-34), you can customize how Outlook handles this type of email.

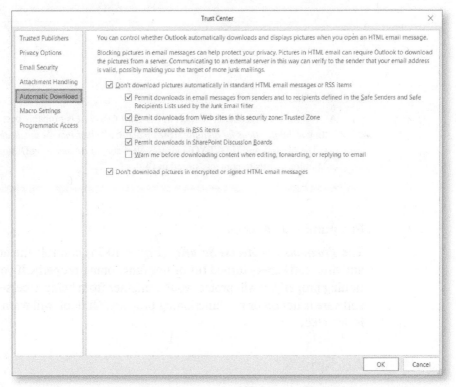

Figure 10-34 *Automatic Download* options

Macro Settings

Macros are simply a set of programming instructions. They are very common in electronic documents, and most perform some necessary actions in a document. But many viruses are spread by the use of macros, so Outlook tries to protect you from these malicious macros by proactively warning you about macros that are detected in email messages or attachmer (Figure 10-35).

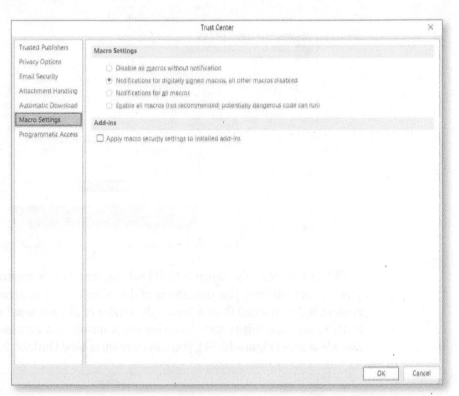

Figure 10-35 *Macro Settings*

Programmatic Access

The *Programmatic Access Security* (Figure 10-36) controls the actions in Outlook when yo antivirus software is turned off or not functioning properly. If your antivirus software is fur tioning properly, it will protect your computer from being accessed by a virus. If your antivir software is not on or not functioning properly, Outlook will warn you when suspicious activi is detected.

Add-Ins

Add-ins (Figure 10-37) are those programs that add functionality to your Outlook and c. be customized in the *Outlook Options* dialog box. This could include adding a button on t *Ribbon* such as *OneNote*. The add-ins are automatically listed in this area when a program application used in conjunction with Outlook is installed on your computer. This area of t *Trust Center* lists *Active*, *Inactive*, and *Disabled Application* add-ins. The area below the *Add-i* list gives you the publisher, location (on your computer), and description of the selected add-i

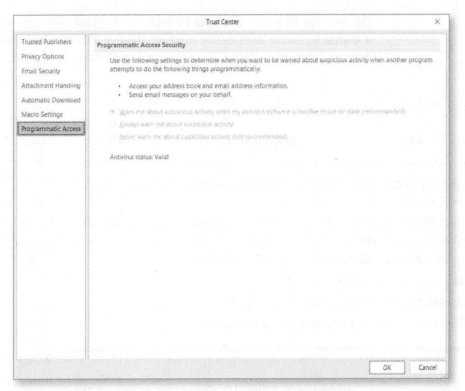

Figure 10-36 *Programmatic Access* options

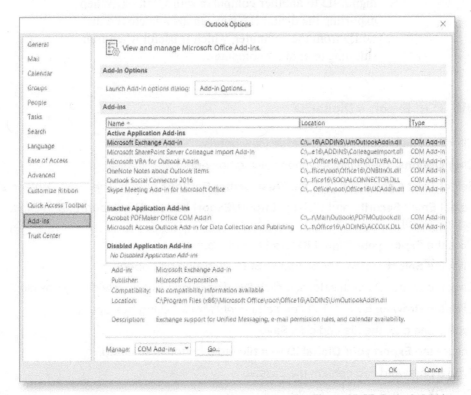

Figure 10-37 Outlook *Add-ins*

Digital Signatures

Digital signatures are used to verify the authenticity of the sender. Including a digital signature in a message is not the same as including a signature in a message. A digital signature uses a certificate to verify who you are and a public key that can be used by the receiver of the message to access encrypted information. Email messages with *Digital signatures* include a digital signature icon in the message. Digital IDs can be obtained through your Exchange administrator; most digital IDs are issued by third-party sources.

▶ HOW TO: Import a Digital ID

1. Click the **File** button. The *Backstage* view opens.
2. Click **Options**. The *Outlook Options* dialog box opens.
2. Select **Trust Center** and click the **Trust Center Settings** button. The *Trust Center* dialog box displays.
3. Select **Email Security** and click the **Import/Export** button. The *Import/Export Digital ID* dialog box displays (Figure 10-38).
4. Click the **Browse** button and locate your digital ID.
5. Enter your password and click **OK**.
6. Click **OK** to close the *Trust Center* dialog box.
7. Click **OK** to close the *Outlook Options* dialog box.

Figure 10-38 *Import/Export Digital ID dialog box*

Exporting a digital ID allows you to import the digital ID to another computer with Outlook. When exporting the digital ID, you can also delete the digital ID from the computer, which is useful when transitioning to another computer.

▶ HOW TO: Export a Digital ID

1. Click the **File** button. The *Backstage* view opens.
2. Click **Options**. The *Outlook Options* dialog box opens.
3. Select **Trust Center** and click the **Trust Center Settings** button. The *Trust Center* dialog box displays.
4. Select **Email Security** and click the **Import/Export** button. The *Import/Export Digital ID* dialog box displays (see Figure 10-38).
5. Click the **Export your Digital ID to a file** radio button.
6. Click the **Select** button. The *Windows Security* dialog box opens.
7. Click the digital ID (certificate) and click **OK**. The *Windows Security* dialog box closes.
8. Click the **Browser** button. The *Locate Security Profile* dialog box opens.
9. Type a name for the file and click **Save**.
10. Ensure the **Export your Digital ID to a file** radio button is selected.
11. Type a password and confirm the password.
12. Click **OK** to close the *Trust Center* dialog box.
13. Click the **Microsoft Internet Explorer 4.0 Compatible (low-security)** check box if desired (not recommended unless Microsoft Internet Explorer is still used).
14. Click the **Delete Digital ID from system** check box to remove the digital ID from the computer.
15. Click **OK**. The *Import/Export Digital ID* dialog box closes.

If you have a digital ID, you can include a digital signature on all outgoing email by changing the settings in the *Email Security* area of the *Trust Center* to *Add digital signature to outgoing messages* (Figure 10-39).

You can also add a digital signature individually to an email.

Figure 10-39 Add a digital signature to outgoing messages

HOW TO: Add a Digital Signature to an Email

Open a new email or an email to which you are going to reply.

Click the **Sign** button [*Options* tab, *Encrypt* group] (Figure 10-40).

Figure 10-40 *Sign* button

PAUSE & PRACTICE: OUTLOOK 10-2

For this Pause & Practice project, you decide to set up a digital ID to ensure your recipients can verify that your messages are not tampered with. If your institution provides you with a digital ID, you can import it. Otherwise, you can use a free digital ID service, such as Comodo. If you have a digital ID or received one from your institution, start at step 1. If you need to download one, start at step 2.

1. Import your digital ID.
    a. Click the **File** button and select **Options**.
    b. Select **Trust Center** and click the **Trust Center Settings** button. The *Trust Center* dialog box displays.
    c. Select **Email Security** and click the **Import/Export** button. The *Import/Export Digital ID* dialog box displays.
    d. Click the **Browse** button and locate your digital ID.
    e. Enter your password and click **OK**.
    f. Click **OK** to close the *Trust Center* dialog box.
    g. Click **OK** to close the *Outlook Options* dialog box.

2. Acquire a digital ID. Select a service, such as *Comodo*, and follow the on-screen instructions to install the ID. *Note: Read the web site installation instructions carefully, as some services require a specific browser to install digital IDs.*

3. Send an email to your instructor with a note.
   a. Click the **Mail** button in the *Navigation* bar.
   b. Click **New Mail** [*Home* tab, *New* group].
   c. Click the **Sign** button [Options tab, Encryptgroup].
   d. In the *To* field, enter your instructor's email address.
   e. In the *Cc* field, enter your email address.
   f. In the *Subject* field, type Outlook Pause & Practice 10-2.
   g. In the message area, type:

      Dear [instructor name],

      This is an email message with my digital ID.

      Thank you,
      [student name]

   h. Click **Send** (Figure 10-41).

Figure 10-41 Completed Pause & Practice 10-2

SLO 10.6

Creating Deals with the Customer Manager

The *Outlook Customer Manager* brings together all of the tools discussed in this text into single customer relationship management tool. You can quickly track your email messag with customers, create tasks, schedule meetings, start deals, and add additional files and no to each customer (Figure 10-42). You can track all information related to a specific person deal in a single location rather than searching for Outlook items in each tool to find an em message related to a task item, calendar item, or contact item, or note. This feature is availa on Exchange accounts with the feature enabled. Since you are familiar with most of the tools, this section will focus on its interface the *Deals* tool.

Figure 10-42 *Outlook Customer Manager* pane

Outlook Customer Manager Views

The Outlook Customer Manager has two main views. If you click the **Customer Manager** button on the *Home* tab, it will appear as a pane to the right of the *Reading* pane (see Figure 10-42). It will also appear as its own detailed view by clicking the more button (. . .) in the *Navigation* bar and selecting **Add-ons** (Figure 10-43).

Figure 10-43 *Outlook Customer Manager* view

The *Outlook Customer Manager* pane allows you to see your emails, deals, notes, tasks, files, meetings, and posts in a single location. You can create new Outlook items by clicking the **Add [item]** (email, deal, note, task, file, meeting, and post) link in each of the associated areas (Figure 10-44). You can view the details of each item by clicking the arrow to view the details such as an email conversation, task list, or a deal (Figure 10-45). Deals are the only item with additional details that were not covered in a previous chapter.

Figure 10-44 *Add deal* link   Figure 10-45 Email det

▶ **HOW TO:** Create a Deal

1. Click the **Customer Manager** button [*Home* tab]. The *Outlook Customer Manager* pane opens.
2. Click **Add Deal**. Type the name of the deal in the *New deal name* field and click **Save** (Figure 10-46).
3. Select the deal and click **View Details**.
4. Enter the *Deal Details* and click **Save** (Figure 10-47).
5. As a deal progresses, you can choose a state: *In-progress*, *Won*, *Loss*, or *Invalid*.
6. Click the **Share deal** button to enable sharing of the deal in your organization. This allows others to view its progress and contribute Outlook items.

Figure 10-46 Save a deal   Figure 10-47 Deal det

▶ MORE INFO

The detailed view is helpful in keeping track of multiple on-going deals (Figure 10-48).

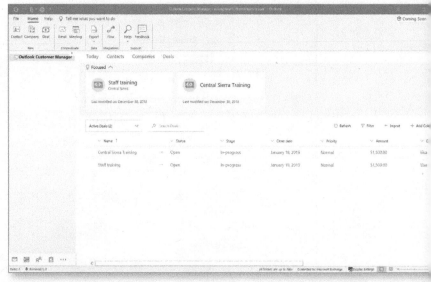

Figure 10-48 *Outlook Customer Manager* view with multiple de

Understanding the Difference between Outlook on the Web and Outlook 365 Online

Throughout the text, you became familiar with the features associated with Mail, Calendar, Contacts, Tasks, Notes, Journal, and the Customer Manager. Many of these features are available on any device through a web browser. If you are using an Exchange server, you can access your account using its web address. If you are using a personal account through Outlook.com, you can access these features through the web site. Even though both mirror the main features in Outlook, it is missing many of the detailed options available in Outlook. This concept was first presented in chapter 7. This section wll include additional detail about the differences between the web interface and Outlook interface. It will also discuss the differences between Exchange and Office 365 Online features.

Outlook on the Web

Users with an Exchange server will be able to access Outlook on the Web, which includes access to Mail, Calendar, People, and Tasks. After logging into the Exchange server with a browser, click the **App Launcher** button and select **Outlook** to open Outlook on the Web (Figure 10-49). The Outlook and Outlook on the Web interfaces are displayed in Figure 10-50.

Figure 10-49
App Launcher

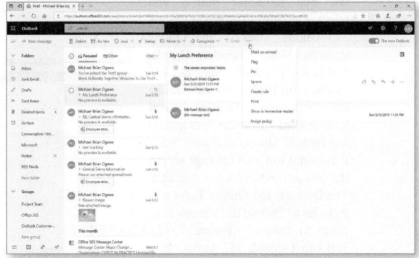

Figure 10-50 Outlook and Outlook on the Web Mail

Outlook includes the *Ribbon*, which has many functions grouped into tabs and group In Outlook on the Web, commonly used features such as *New*, *Delete*, *Junk*, *Sweep*, *Mo to*, and *Categories* are listed at the top of the interface. Outlook on the Web also include a more button (. . .) for additional features but does not include many options that are c the *Ribbon*. Features such as the *Address Book*, *Voting Options*, and viewing *To-Do* are not ava able from Mail directly. The Address Book can be accessed through the *People* link. You a able to respond to voting options but cannot create a message with voting options. The *To-L* bar is accessible from Tasks. Each of the functions work separately and are as integrated a Outlook. When creating a new email message, the Outlook interface includes more detaile options than Outlook on the Web (Figure 10-51).

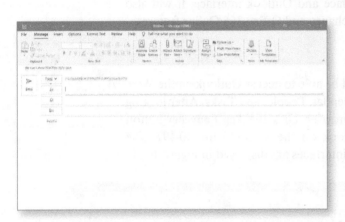

Figure 10-51 New message in Outlook and Outlook on the We

Similarly, the Calendar, People, and Tasks features in Outlook on the Web include le detailed options than Outlook. Outlook on the Web does not include access to features Outlook such as Notes, Shortcuts, Folders, and Journal.

Outlook 365 Online

Users with a personal account can access Outlook 365 Online at http://www.office.com or http://www.outlook.com. If you log in to http://www.outlook.com, click the **App Launcher** button and select **Outlook** to open Outlook 365 Online. Outlook 365 Online includes Mail, Calendar, People, and Tasks. The Mail, Calendar, and People tools in Outlook 365 Online are comparable to their equivalent tools in Outlook on the Web and do not include similar features. Since it does not use an Exchange server, the *Groups* function is not available. The Outlook 365 Online Tasks tool includes additional differences compared to Outlook (Figure 10-52). Tasks in Outlook 365 Online give you the ability to create a task with a

Figure 10-52 Tasks in Outlook and Outlook 365 Onli

reminder time, due date, repeat option, and notes. It does not include the ability to categorize, assign, or add attachments to tasks.

The online platform for Outlook 365 Online is consistently being updated by Microsoft, so it is important to note that some features that were not available may become available or vice versa at a later date. When considering Outlook on an Exchange server and Outlook 365 Online, it is important to understand the differences in the two environments. Exchange server specific features include:

- *Global Address List*
- *Tracking Voting Options*
- *Tracking Meeting Requests*
- *Task Requests*
- *Groups*
- *Delegation*
- *Customer Manager*

These features are vital to businesses automating tasks to improve productivity. The differences in these platforms are discussed in detail in appendix D.

PAUSE & PRACTICE: OUTLOOK 10-3

For this Pause & Practice project, you realize that it can be difficult to keep track of email messages, calendar items, tasks, and contacts associated with a deal. You decide to create a deal based on a training request to ensure all associated Outlook items are in a single location. *Note: This Pause & Practice works only for Exchange users with the Customer Manager enabled.*

1. Create a new email to a partner to request a training session.
   a. Click the **Mail** button in the *Navigation* bar.
   b. Click the **New Email** button.
   c. In the *Subject* field, type Training request for software.
   d. In the message area, type:

   Dear [partner name],

   I would like to request training for my company. We just upgraded our software to the latest version and many employees are having difficulty with it. Would it be possible to set up an appointment to discuss possible training options?

   Thank you,
   [student name]

   e. Click **Send**.

2. Create a deal for the training request
   a. Click the **Mail** button in the *Navigation* bar.
   b. Select the message from your partner with the subject *Training request for software*.
   c. Click the **Customer Manager** button. The *Outlook Customer Manager* pane opens.
   d. Click the **Add deal** link.
   e. Type the name Software Upgrade Training. Click the **Save** button.
   f. Click the **Software Upgrade Training** deal.
   g. Click **View Details**.
   h. Click **Amount** and type $3,000.00.
   i. Click **Priority** and select **High**.

j. Click **Close date** and select two weeks from today.

k. Click **Share deal** to change the option to **Yes** (Figure 10-53).

Figure 10-53 Completed Pause & Practice 10-3

Chapter Summary

10.1 Create and use Notes in Outlook (p. O10-363).

- Outlook **Notes** are digital versions of sticky notes.
- Information that cannot easily be classified into a task or calendar item can be created as a note.
- Like other Outlook items, notes can be categorized.
- Notes can be viewed as **Icons**, a **Notes List**, or notes created in the **Last 7 Days** depending on your preference.
- You can forward notes to others using email.

10.2 Integrate the Outlook Journal with Outlook items and Microsoft Office documents (p. O10-365).

- The **Journal** feature tracks the amount of time you spent on a particular activity.
- The Journal is located in the *Folders* list.
- You can manually input the duration of a journal entry or use the *Start Timer* and *Stop Timer* feature to keep track of time.
- Like other Outlook items, journals can be categorized.
- The journal can be viewed in a timeline or list view.

10.3 Incorporate shortcuts in Outlook (p. O10-368).

- The *Shortcuts* view allows you to create links to Outlook folders, items on your computer, and online.
- **Shortcuts** can be organized within a shortcut group.
- Shortcut **groups** and shortcuts can be reordered, renamed, or deleted using the context menu.

10.4 Store Outlook Items in archive folders (p. O10-371).

- **Archiving** moves older Outlook items such as email, calendar, tasks, notes, and journal items, from their current location to a set of **archive folders**.
- **AutoArchive** automatically runs an archive for you based on criteria you set.
- *AutoArchive* settings can be set globally or by folder.
- You can choose to omit specific Outlook folders and items from being archived.
- You can manually archive folders.

10.5 Customize security settings (p. O10-375).

- The **Trust Center** allows you to customize your Outlook security.
- **Trusted publishers** are organizations that are reputable and have a **digital signature** assigned to their macro or program.
- **Privacy Options** allow you to control information sent to and received from Microsoft.
- **Email Security** allows you to control the use of encrypted emails and **digital IDs**.
- **Encryption** is a way of adding security by scrambling a message.
- **S/MIME** can be used to confirm that an email was sent and received unaltered.
- **Digital IDs** are used to verify your identity as the sender.
- *Attachment Handling* allows you to control how attachments are handled, such as potentially dangerous file types.
- **Attachment Preview** can be turned on or off in the *File Previewing Options*.
- **Automatic Download** controls how emails are viewed such as emails in HTML format with embedded pictures.
- **Macros** are a set of programming instructions that Outlook tries to protect you from because the code may be malicious.
- **Programmatic Access Security** checks to ensure your antivirus software is functioning properly or not and warns you when suspicious activity is detected.
- **Add-ins** are programs that add functionality to Outlook.
- You can include a **Digital signature** in a message to verify your identity to the recipient.
- You can control which add-ins are enabled or disabled.

10.6 Create deals with the Customer Manager (p. O10-383).

- The **Outlook Customer Manager** is a customer relationship management tool that incorporates email, calendar items, tasks, and files into a single location.
- The Customer Manager can be viewed in a pane or as a view in Outlook.
- Deals integrate Outlook items with a transaction.

- Deals can be shared with others in your organization to allow multiple people to work on the integrated Outlook items.

10.7 Understand the difference between Outlook on the Web and Outlook 365 Online (p. O10-386).

- Outlook on the Web allows Exchange users to use Outlook via a web browser on any device.
- Outlook on the Web does not include the *Ribbon* and has less accessible features than Outlook.
- Outlook on the Web does not include full features for Notes, Shortcuts, Folders, and Journal.
- Outlook 365 Online is used with personal accounts.

- Outlook 365 Online does not include the *Ribbon* and includes less features than Outlook with a personal account.
- Exchange specific features include *Global Address List*, *Tracking Voting Options*, *Tracking Meeting Requests*, *Task Requests*, *Groups*, *Delegation*, and *Customer Manager*

Check for Understanding

The SIMbook for this text (within your SIMnet account) provides the following resources for concept review:

- Multiple-choice questions
- Short answer questions
- Matching exercises

Guided Project 10-1

For this project, you work as a receptionist at Courtyard Medical Plaza (CMP). You recently noticed that your desk and computer monitor were getting cluttered with Post-it notes, so you decided to start using Outlook Notes for messages. While sorting your messages in Outlook, you noticed that it became difficult to find frequently used folders, so you decide to create shortcuts and a shortcut group.
[Student Learning Outcomes 10.1, 10.3]

Skills Covered in This Project

- Create a note.
- Categorize a note.

- Create a shortcut group.
- Create a shortcut.
- Forward notes.

1. Create a new mail folder named CMP Articles.

2. Create a category named Business with a green color.

3. Create a category named Personal with an orange color.

4. Create a note for Dr. Saito.
    a. Click the **Notes** button in the *Navigation* bar.
    b. Click the **New Note** button. A new note will be displayed.
    c. In the *Note* field, type Dr. Saito: Dr. Callaway called at 2:00 regarding the article you are writing. (Figure 10-54).
    d. Click the **X** in the upper-right corner to save and close the note.

5. Categorize the note as *Business*.
    a. Select the note.
    b. Click the **Categorize** button and select **Business**.

6. Create a note for Dr. Sharuma.
    a. Click the **Notes** button in the *Navigation* bar.
    b. Click the **New Note** button. A new note will be displayed.
    c. In the *Note* field, type Dr. Sharuma: Your wife called and wants you to pick up the dry cleaning on the way home. (see Figure 10-54).
    d. Click the **X** in the upper-right corner to save and close the note.

7. Categorize the note as *Personal*.
    a. Select the note.
    b. Click the **Categorize** button and select **Personal**.

8. Create a shortcut group named *CMP*.
    a. Click the **Shortcuts** button in the *Navigation* bar.
    b. Click the **Folder** tab.
    c. Right-click the **Shortcuts** area in the *Folder* pane and select **New Shortcut Group**.
    d. Type CMP and press **Enter**.

9. Create a shortcut to the *CMP Articles* folder.
    a. Click the **Shortcuts** button in the *Navigation* bar.
    b. Click the **Folder** tab.

c. Click the **New Shortcut** button in the *New* group. The *Add to Folder Pane* dialog box opens and displays all your Outlook folders.
d. Select the **CMP Articles** folder.
e. Click **OK** to add the shortcut to the *Folder* pane (Figure 10-54).

10. Send an email to your instructor with the notes as attachments.
    a. Select the two notes you created (press the **Ctrl** key and click on each of the notes).
    b. Click the **Forward** button [*Home* tab, *Actions* group].
    c. In the *To* field, enter your instructor's email address.
    d. In the *Cc* field, enter your email address.
    e. In the *Subject* field, type Outlook Guided Project 10-1.
    f. In the message area, type:

        Dear [instructor name],

        Attached is my Outlook Guided Project 10-1.

        Thank you,
        [student name]

    g. Click the **Send** button.

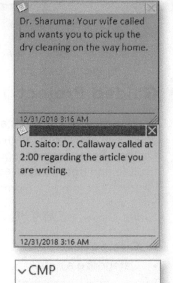

Figure 10-54 Completed Guided Project 10-1

Guided Project 10-2

For this project you work as a receptionist for CMP and recently learned that the office will undergo a reorganization. You have been asked to maintain daily journal logs.
[Student Learning Outcome 10.2]

Skills Covered in This Project

- Create a journal entry.
- Modify entry type.
- Modify duration.

---

1. Create a journal entry indicating that you spent one hour organizing files.
    a. Click the **Folders** button in the *Navigation* bar.
    b. Click **Journal**.
    c. Click the **Journal Entry** button. A new journal entry opens.
    d. In the *Subject* field, type Organizing files.
    e. In the *Entry type* field, select **Task**.
    f. In the *Start time* fields, select **today's date** at **1:00 PM**.
    g. In the *Duration* field, select **1 hour**.
    h. Click **Save & Close**.

2. Create a journal entry indicating that you spent 15 minutes on the phone with a pharmaceutical representative.
    a. Click the **Folders** button in the *Navigation* bar.
    b. Click **Journal**.
    c. Click the **Journal Entry** button. A new journal entry opens.

d. In the *Subject* field, type Conversation with pharmaceutical representative.

e. In the *Entry type* field, select **Phone call**.

f. In the *Start time* fields, select **today's date** at **4:00 PM**.

g. In the *Duration* field, select **15 minutes**.

h. Click **Save & Close**.

3. Send an email to your instructor with the journal entries as attachments (Figure 10-55).

a. Click the **Mail** button in the *Navigation* bar.

b. Click **New Mail** [*Home* tab, *New* group].

c. In the *To* field, enter your instructor's email address.

d. In the *Cc* field, enter your email address.

e. In the *Subject* field, type Outlook Guided Project 10-2.

f. In the message area, type:

Dear [instructor name],

Attached is my Outlook Guided Project 10-2.

Thank you,
[student name]

g. Click the **Outlook Item** button [*Insert* tab, *Include* group].

h. Press the **Ctrl** key and select your journal entries, and then click **OK**.

i. Click the **Send** button.

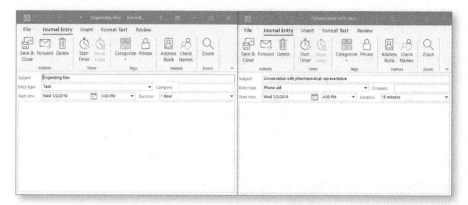

Figure 10-55 Completed Guided Project 10-2

Guided Project 10-3

For this project, you have been asked to email your journal entries as an archive to CMP management for review. You archive your journal entries and send them with a digital signature to ensure they are not modified in transit.
[Student Learning Outcomes 10.4, 10.5]

Skills Covered in This Project

- Mark an Outlook item to not be archived.
- Run a manual archive.
- Email using a digital signature.

1. Mark your *BUS 100 Library Research* journal entry to not be archived.
   a. Click the **Folders** button in the *Navigation* bar.
   b. Click **Journal**.
   c. Double-click the **BUS 100 Library Research** item.
   d. Click **File** and select the **Properties** button.
   e. Check **Do not AutoArchive** this item.
   f. Click **Close**.
   g. Click the **Save & Close** button.

2. Run a manual archive.
   a. Click **File** to open the *Backstage* view.
   b. Click the **Tools** button and select **Clean Up Old Items**.
   c. Select **Archive this folder and all subfolders**.
   d. Select your **Journal** folder.
   e. Change the date for **Archive items older than** to **tomorrow's date** to ensure you include the Journal items you created today.
   f. Click the **Browse** button and select a location on your computer. Change the *File name* to journal-CMP and click **OK**.
   g. Click **OK** to archive the *Journal* folder and close the *Archive* dialog box.

3. Send an email to your instructor with the journal entry an attachment.
   a. Click the **Mail** button in the *Navigation* bar.
   b. Click **New Mail** [*Home* tab, *New* group].
   c. Click the **Sign** button [*Options* tab, *Encrypt* group].
   d. In the *To* field, enter your instructor's email address.
   e. In the *Cc* field, enter your email address.
   f. In the *Subject* field, type Outlook Guided Project 10-3.
   g. In the message area, type:

   Dear [instructor name],

   Attached is my Outlook Guided Project 10-3.

   Thank you,
   [student name]

   h. Click the **Attach File** button [*Insert* tab, *Include* group].
   i. Select your **journal-CMP** file and click **OK**.
   j. Click the **Send** button.

Outlook may warn you about sending a potentially unsafe file. This is why you wanted to digitally sign the email to ensure it was not modified in transit. Outlook will also warn the recipient about the attachment (Figure 10-56).

> **MORE INFO**
> You will rarely, if ever, send a .pst file over email. This Guided Project should be used to help you understand how to archive folders. You should also be aware that sending and receiving .pst files can be dangerous.

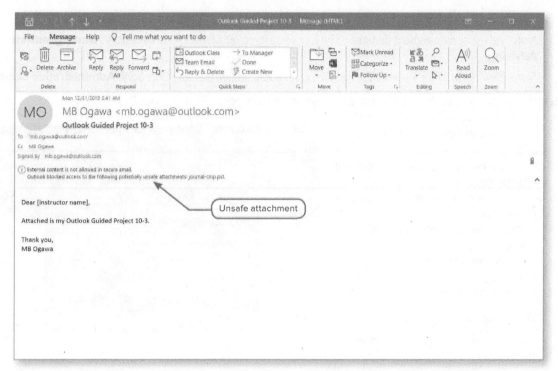

Figure 10-56 Completed Guided Project 10-3

Independent Project 10-4

For this project, you work as an academic advisor for the Sierra Pacific Community College District (SPCCD). You recently found yourself having trouble keeping your notes organized because they include sticky notes, note pads, and loose sheets of paper. You decide to take your laptop to meetings to take notes and to organize them.
[Student Learning Outcome 10.1]

Skills Covered in This Project

* Create notes.
* Categorize notes.
* Forward notes.

1. Create the following categories:

    Category: Undergraduate Advising; *Color*: **Blue**
    Category: Freshmen Retention; *Color*: **Red**
    Category: Administrative Duties; *Color*: **Purple**

2. Create and categorize the following notes:

    Note: New undergraduate core requirements available at campus web site; *Category*: **Undergraduate Advising**

    Note: Brainstorm campus engagement opportunities for freshmen; *Category*: **Freshmen Retention**

Note: Create 5 survey questions for incoming freshmen packet; *Category*: **Freshmen Retention**

Note: Advising requirement updated to be one session per academic year; *Category*: **Undergraduate Advising**

Note: New Form 27 for students applying for graduation, update records; *Category*: **Administrative Duties**

3. Send an email to your instructor with the notes as attachments (Figure 10-57).

   a. Select the five notes you created (hold the **Ctrl** key and click on each of the notes).
   b. Click the **Forward** button [*Home* tab, *Actions* group].
   c. In the *To* field, enter your instructor's email address.
   d. In the *Cc* field, enter your email address.
   e. In the *Subject* field, type Outlook Independent Project 10-4.
   f. In the message area, type:

      Dear [instructor name],

      Attached is my Outlook Independent Project 10-4.

      Thank you,
      [student name]

   g. Click the **Send** button.

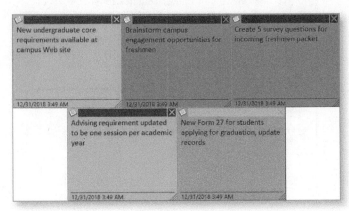

Figure 10-57 Completed Independent Project 10-4

Independent Project 10-5

For this project, you work as an academic advisor for the SPCCD. Recently, the dean asked all academic advisors to keep track of time spent advising undergraduate students to help the administration understand student needs. To help you keep track of advising sessions, you decide to use the Journal feature.
[Student Learning Outcome 10.2]

Skills Covered in This Project

- Create a journal entry.
- Modify entry type.
- Modify duration.

---

1. Create a journal entry for a face-to-face advising session using the following information:

   Subject: Randon Catallina (Freshman)
   Entry type: **Meeting**
   Start time: **tomorrow's date** at **9:00 AM**
   Duration: **1 hour**
   Message: Major exploration

2. Create a journal entry for a phone call advising session using the following information:

   Subject: Janelle Shin (Incoming Freshman)
   Entry type: **Phone Call**
   Start time: **tomorrow's date** at **10:30 AM**
   Duration: **30 minutes**
   Message: Registration inquiry

3. Create a journal entry for a face-to-face advising session using the following information:

   Subject: Shirley Santiago (Junior)
   Entry type: **Meeting**
   Start time: **tomorrow's date** at **2:00 PM**
   Duration: **1 hour**
   Message: Study skills assistance

4. Send an email to your instructor with the journal entries as attachments (Figure 10-58).
   a. In the *To* field, enter your instructor's email address.
   b. In the *Cc* field, enter your email address.
   c. In the *Subject* field, type Outlook Independent Project 10-5.
   d. In the message area, type:

      Dear [instructor name],

      Attached is my Outlook Independent Project 10-5.

      Thank you,
      [student name]

   e. Click the **Send** button.

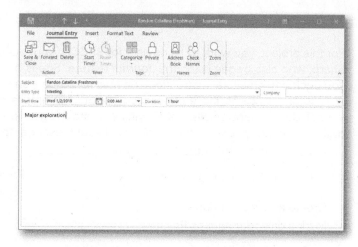

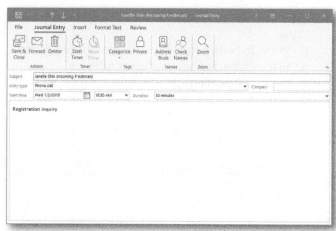

Figure 10-58 Completed Independent Project 10-5

Independent Project 10-6

For this project, you work as an advisor for SPCCD. You received an inquiry from another advisor, Megan Sharp, who also began using the *Journal* feature. She is having difficulty finding the Journal feature, so you decide to email her instructions on how to create a shortcut.

You also became more concerned about your emails being modified when sent to receivers, as your IT department emailed all faculty and staff regarding recent security issues. You begin using a digital signature to ensure the receivers of your message do not get a message that has been modified.
[Student Learning Outcomes 10.3, 10.5]

Skills Covered in This Project

- Create a new calendar.
- Mark a calendar item as *Private*.
- Forward a calendar item.
- Share a calendar.

1. Send an email to your instructor as Megan Sharp describing how to create a shortcut to the *Journal* folder.
   a. In the *To* field, enter your instructor's email address.
   b. In the *Cc* field, enter your email address.
   c. In the *Subject* field, type Outlook Independent Project 10-6.
   d. In the message area, describe to Megan how you can create a shortcut to the *Journal* folder.
   e. Add your digital signature (Figure 10-59).

Figure 10-59 Completed Independent Project 10-6

Challenge Project 10-7

Working in teams in school, clubs, organizations, and work can be challenging. Many topics, such as reasons for a group decision, come up that you need to write as notes. It can also be difficult to keep track of who did each task and how much time it took to complete to ensure work completed can be reported accurately. For this project, consider a team project in which you participated, whether it be for a class, club, work, or other organization. Write notes about discussions during the group project. Also, use the Journal feature to create a timeline of the tasks completed.
[Student Learning Outcomes 10.1, 10.3]

- Identify a team project.
- Create at least two notes for the group project.
- Categorize each note.
- Create at least two journal entries detailing work completed and duration.
- Categorize each journal entry.
- Create a secondary category for a journal entry with each team members' name.
- Apply each team members' name to each journal entry to make it easier to track work completed by person.
- Email your instructor using the following message format:

    Class/organization name: description of project
    Group: number of members in the group

- Attach your notes and journal entries to the message.
- Change the subject of your message to Outlook Challenge Project 10-7.

Challenge Project 10-8

Working at an organization that deals with many customers creates a lot of information in Outlook ranging from email messages, calendar items, contacts, tasks, and more. The Outlook Customer Manager allows you to create deals to quickly manage information around customer orders or service requests. For this project, work with a partner to create a deal that incorporates at least three different Outlook items. *Note: This Challenge Project works only for Exchange users with the Customer Manager enabled.*
[Student Learning Outcome 10.6]

- Identify a customer order or service request.
- Send an email to a partner to request the order or service.
- Create a deal from the email message.
- Modify the deal to include an amount, high priority, and closing date.
- Include a Task and Calendar item in the deal.
- Share the deal with your instructor.

Challenge Project 10-9

Although Outlook is available as an application on your computer and on the web, many differences in functionality exist that may impact you as a user. Compare Outlook on the Web or Outlook 365 Online to Outlook to identify at least three feature differences and indicate how they would impact your work.
[Student Learning Outcome 10.7]

- Identify differences in features in Outlook on the Web (or Outlook 365 Online) and your stand-alone Outlook.
- Describe how it would impact your work and if you could complete your work on the web.
- Email your instructor using the following message format:

   Feature Name 1: impact on work
   Feature Name 2: impact on work
   Feature Name 3: impact on work

- Change the subject of your message to Outlook Challenge Project 10-9.

Source of screenshots Microsoft Office 365 (2019): Word, Excel, Access, PowerPoint, Outlook.

Advanced Contacts

CHAPTER OVERVIEW

Contacts are an essential part of Outlook and are used when emailing, assigning tasks, and cr
ating meeting requests. The longer you use Outlook, the more you will find that your contacts l
will grow and that you are using this stored contact information on a regular basis. You will al:
realize how your stored contacts integrate with Outlook and other Microsoft Office programs.

As you become more familiar with the different features available in Outlook, you will want
customize how contacts appear, where they are stored, and how they are categorized. Outlo
also provides you with the ability to share contacts with other users or between different progran
Importing and exporting contacts and merging contacts with other programs can save you time

STUDENT LEARNING OUTCOMES (SLOs)

After completing this chapter, you will be able to:

SLO 8.1   Integrate Outlook contacts with folders and categories (p. O8-292).

SLO 8.2   Create and utilize electronic business cards (p. O8-297).

SLO 8.3   Share contact information by importing to and exporting from Outlook
(p. O8-302).

SLO 8.4   Use Outlook Contacts with other Microsoft Office programs (p. O8-308).

CASE STUDY

For the Pause & Practice projects, you use Outlook contacts to optimize your work by using folders and categories for your contacts. You also export folders to help you quickly build your contact directory.

As a developing professional, you use Outlook to create a business card that will express professionalism. For the final Pause & Practice project, you send postal mail thank you letters to your partners and instructor, because they prefer to receive physical letters. Use Outlook contacts to create mail merge address labels.

Pause & Practice 8-1: You work with two partners to create a contact folder and use

categories to organize your contacts. Af
creating and organizing your contacts, y
email them to your instructor.

Pause & Practice 8-2: Modify your busine
card and include an image of yourself.

Pause & Practice 8-3: You export the B
100 folder you created in *Pause & Practi*
8-1 to a .csv file format to make it easier
share with others.

Pause & Practice 8-4: Send physical tha
you letters to your partners and instructor. Y
use Outlook contacts and Word to help y
quickly create mailing labels.

OUTLOOK

Managing Contacts

As your list of contacts increases and you are using your contacts in Outlook on a more regular basis, you will want to customize your default address book, create folders in which to store contacts, and assign a category to a contact. Using folders and categories will help you to manage your list of contacts, and tracking contacts' activities will make you more effective in your use of Outlook.

> **MORE INFO**
>
> Contacts were covered in chapter 3. Creating and using folders and categories were covered in chapter 6.

Change the Default Address Book

When you create a new email, meeting, or task request and click the *To* button, your default address book opens allowing you to select recipients. If you are using Outlook as a stand-alone program, this address book will be your *Contacts folder*.

When you are using Outlook in an Exchange environment, your default address book will be the *Global Address List*. If you work for a medium or large company, this list of contacts could number in the hundreds or thousands. Your most frequently used contacts should be saved in your *Contacts* folder.

You can easily change the default address book so your contacts appear first when selecting recipients. This does not mean that you will not have access to your *Global Address List* or other contact folders, but it will prevent you from wasting time and being frustrated by not having to search through different address books to find your recipients.

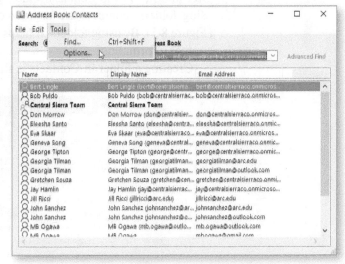

Figure 8-1 *Address Book* options

HOW TO: Change the Default Address Book

- Click the **People** button in the *Navigation* bar.
- Click the **Address Book** button in the *Find* group on the *Home* tab to open the *Address Book* dialog box.
- Click the **Tools** menu and choose **Options** (Figure 8-1) to open the *Addressing* dialog box.
- Choose the address book to be set as the default in the *When opening the address book, show this address list first* field (Figure 8-2).
- Click **OK** to close the *Addressing* dialog box.
- Close the *Address* dialog box.

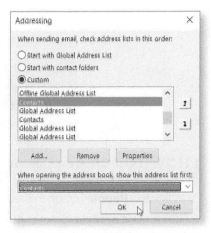

Figure 8-2 Select default address book

Create a Contacts Folder

If you use Outlook at both work and home and don't want all your contacts listed on after another in the *Contacts* folder, you can use folders to organize the contact records. B using folders, contacts are organized, and it is much easier to locate needed informatio (Figure 8-3). By using folders, it helps to keep contacts organized and it's much easier to loca contact information.

Creating a folder in Contacts is similar to creating an email folder.

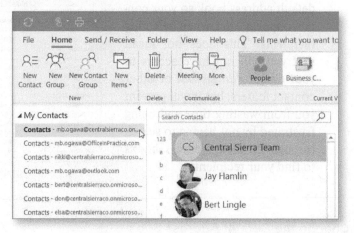

Figure 8-3 Contact folders

▶ HOW TO: Create a Contacts Folder

1. Click the **People** button in the *Navigation* bar.
2. Click the **Contacts** folder in the *My Contacts* area of the *Folder* pane.
3. Click the **Folder** tab.

Click the **New Folder** button in the *New* group to open the *Create New Folder* dialog box (Figure 8-4).

Type the name of the new folder. Confirm that **Contact Items** is selected in the *Folder contains* area and that the **Contacts** folder is selected in the *Select where to place the folder* area.

Click **OK**. The new folder appears in the list of contact folders (*My Contacts*).

Figure 8-4 *Create New Folder* dialog box

> **ANOTHER WAY**
>
> **Ctrl+Shift+E** opens the *Create New Folder* dialog box. Be sure the *Contacts* folder is selected before using this shortcut.

> **ANOTHER WAY**
>
> Right-click the **Contacts** folder and choose **New Folder**.

> **MORE INFO**
>
> Contact folders displayed in the *My Contacts* area are not displayed in a hierarchical format.

Once the new folder is created, you can drag and drop contacts from your *Contacts* folder or other contact folders to the new folder. When you click any of the contact folders, the contents of the folder display in the *Content area*.

Categorize Contacts

If you are working on a project and have a team of individuals with whom you're working, you might want to group these contacts together, but not necessarily move them to a different contact folder. Contacts can be viewed by category in the *List* view.

To assign a contact to a category, either use an existing category or create a new category.

> **MORE INFO**
>
> Creating categories were covered in chapter 7.
>
> A contact record can be assigned to more than one category. When viewed with *By Category*, this contact will appear in the list in each of the assigned categories.

HOW TO: Categorize Contacts

Click the **People** button in the *Navigation* bar.

Click **Contacts** in the *My Contacts* area.

3. Select the contacts to be categorized.

4. Click the **Categorize** button in the *Tags* group on the *Home* tab, and select the desired category (Figure 8-5).

5. Click **List** in the *Current View* group [*Home* tab]. Your contacts display in list format and grouped *By Category* in the *Content area* (Figure 8-6).

Figure 8-5 Apply a category to a cont

> **ANOTHER WAY**
>
> Assign a category to an open contact by clicking the **Categorize** button in the *Tags* group on the *Contact* tab.

When a contact record is open and if it has been assigned to a category, the category displays in the *Info* bar of the contact record. To clear this category or add another category, right-click the *Info* bar for the different category options available.

⌄ Central Sierra A Items				
ᴿᵉ	Jay Hamlin	Manager	Central Sierra	Hamlin, Jay
ᴿᵉ	Bert Lingle	Insurance Au...	Central Sierra	Lingle, Bert
ᴿᵉ	Don Morrow	Associate	Central Sierra	Morrow, De
ᴿᵉ	Bob Pulido	Associate	Central Sierra	Pulido, Bob
ᴿᵉ	Eleesha Santo	Vice Presid...	Central Sierra	Santo, Elee
ᴿᵉ	Eva Skaar	Agent	Central Sierra	Skaar, Eva
ᴿᵉ	Gretchen Souza	Associate	Central Sierra	Souza, Gre
ᴿᵉ	George Tipton	Associate	Central Sierra	Tipton, Ge

Figure 8-6 View contacts by category List vi

> **MORE INFO**
>
> The *Info* bar is available on most Outlook items that have been flagged, categorized, or answered. Clicking or right-clicking the *Info* bar provides you with a menu of actions from which to choose.

Update Contacts

Outlook can automatically *update* information on your contact records using information from your company's *Global Address List* when using Outlook in conjunction with an Exchange server.

To update a contact, click the **Update** button (Figure 8-7) in the *Update* group on the *Contact* tab. Any changes made to the contact displays in the *Notes* area of the contact record.

Figure 8-7 Update contact from the *Global Address*

Customize Contact Options

In chapter 7, you learned how to customize many of the different options available for ema Outlook also allows you to customize options in Contacts.

The Contacts customization options are available by opening the *Outlook Options* dialog box [*File* tab, *Options*] and selecting the **People** button on the left (Figure 8-8).

You can customize the order you want Outlook to use for new names and the setting for how Outlook saves new contacts. Outlook can even check for duplicate contacts for you.

The *Show an additional index* feature allows you to display an additional language when scrolling through your contact list (Figure 8-9). This feature is especially useful when you are more comfortable with another language.

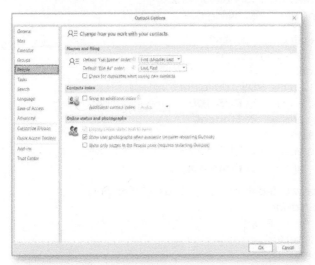

Figure 8-8 Outlook options for *People*

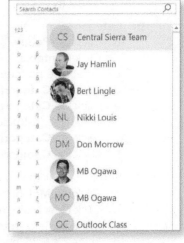

Figure 8-9 Additional Greek contact index

The *Online status and photographs* feature allows you to view your contacts' status and photographs. You can also choose to display only names, as opposed to contact information and photographs. Use the *People Peek* search tool when searching for contacts by right-clicking the **People** button on the *Navigation* bar.

PAUSE & PRACTICE: OUTLOOK 8-1

For this Pause & Practice project, you work with two partners to create a contact folder and use categories to organize your contacts. After creating and organizing your contacts, you email them to your instructor.

1. Click the **People** button in the *Navigation* bar.

2. Create three new contacts, a new contact for each of your partners and instructor. Include a first name, last name, email address, and mailing address (you can use the school's address for everyone). You may skip this step if you already have these contacts.

3. Create a folder for your group project.
    a. Click the **Contacts** folder in the *My Contacts* area of the *Folder* pane.
    b. Click the **Folder** tab.
    c. Click the **New Folder** button in the *New* group to open the *Create New Folder* dialog box.
    d. Type BUS 100 for the name of the folder.
    e. Click **OK**.

4. Add your two partners and instructor to the *BUS 100* folder.
    a. Click the **People** button in the *Navigation* bar.
    b. Click and drag both of your partners' contacts into the *BUS 100* folder. You may hold the **Ctrl** key while clicking and dragging the contacts to create a copy in the *BUS 100* folder.
    c. Click and drag your professor's contact into the *BUS 100* folder.

5. Create categories for *BUS 100* (blue category), *Student* (green category), and *Professor* (yellow category).
   a. Click the **Categorize** button [*Home* tab, *Tags* group] and select **All Categories**. The *Color Categories* dialog box opens.
   b. Click **New** to open the *Add New Category* dialog box.
   c. Type the name of the category in the *Name* field.
   d. Click the **Color** drop-down arrow and select a color.
   e. Click **OK** to close the *Add New Category* dialog box.
   f. Click **OK** to close the *Color Categories* dialog box.

6. Categorize your partners' and instructor's contacts.
   a. Click the **People** button in the *Navigation* bar.
   b. Click **Contacts** in the *My Contacts* area.
   c. Select the partners' contacts in the *BUS 100* folder.
   d. Click the **Categorize** button and select **BUS 100**.
   e. Click the **Categorize** button and select **Student**.
   f. Select the instructor's contact.
   g. Click the **Categorize** button and select **BUS 100**.
   h. Click the **Categorize** button and select **Professor**.

7. Send an email to your instructor with the three contacts as attachments.
   a. Click the **Mail** button in the *Navigation* bar.
   b. Click **New Mail** [*Home* tab, *New* group].
   c. In the *To* field, enter your instructor's email address.
   d. In the *Cc* field, enter your email address.
   e. In the *Subject* field, enter Outlook Pause & Practice 8-1.
      In the message area, type:

      Dear [instructor's name],

      Attached is my Outlook Pause & Practice 8-1.

      Thank you,
      [student name]

   f. Click the **Business Card** option [*Message* tab, *Include* group, *Attach Item*] and select **Other Business Cards**.
   g. Select the three cards you created and click **OK**.
   h. Click the **Send** button (Figure 8-10).

Figure 8-10 PP Outlook 8-1 completed

Using Business Cards

Have you ever been asked to send your contact information to someone via email? This is a very common request, and many times can be done by inserting an existing signature containing this information. But if you are sending this information to other Outlook users, they will still have to type this information into a new contact record.

Outlook allows you to send a contact record (or more than one) as an attachment to an email. You can also add an electronic **business card** to a signature or customize your business card.

Send an Electronic Business Card

Sending electronic business cards in an email is similar to attaching a file to an email. The difference is you will be attaching an Outlook item rather than a different type of file, such as a Word document or picture.

HOW TO: Email an Electronic Business Card as an Attachment

Open a new email.

Select recipients, include a subject, and type a brief message.

Click the **Attach Item** button in the *Include* group on the *Message* tab, choose **Business Card**, and then choose **Other Business Cards** (Figure 8-11). The *Insert Business Card* dialog box opens.

Select the **Contacts** folder in the *Look in* area.

Select the contacts to be attached (Figure 8-12).

Click **OK** to close the *Insert Business Card* dialog box. The selected contacts will be attached to the email, and a graphic of the business card will be inserted in the body of the message.

Click the **Send** button to send the email.

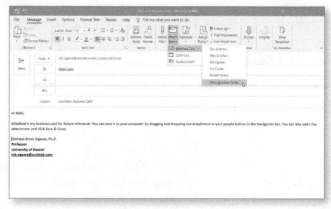

Figure 8-11 Attach a business card

Figure 8-12 *Insert Business Card* dialog box

You can also send a contact as a business card from the *Contacts* area.

▶ HOW TO: Forward a Business Card

1. Click the **People** button in the *Navigation* bar.
2. Select the **Contacts** folder in *My Contacts*.
3. Select the contacts to whom you want to send a business card.
4. Right-click the contact, choose **Forward Contact**, and select **As a Business Card** (Figure 8-13). A new email opens with the business card attached and a graphic of the business card in the body of the message.
5. Select recipients, include a subject, and type a brief message (Figure 8-14).

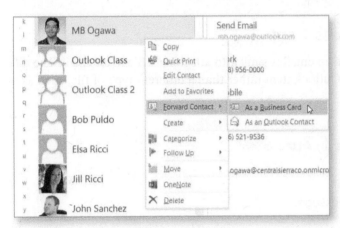

Figure 8-13 Forward contact as a business card   Figure 8-14 Contact attached in an email message

6. Click **Send**.

> **MORE INFO**
>
> The graphic of the business card, which is inserted into the body of the message, can be deleted. This graphic is not the attachment and might confuse the recipient if he or she tries to drag this graphic to the *Contacts* button.

Include Your Business Card in a Signature

Another way to include your business card in an email message is to attach it to your signature. You can set up multiple signatures in Outlook, and you might want to create a signature that includes your business card. This will save you from having to manually attach or forward your business card.

> **MORE INFO**
>
> Signatures were covered in chapter 2.

> **MORE INFO**
>
> When using multiple email accounts in Outlook, you can have a different default signature for each email account.

When you insert a signature that has a business card attached, the business card will automatically be included as an attachment to the email.

HOW TO: Include a Business Card in a Signature

1. Open the *Signatures and Stationery* dialog box [*File* tab, *Options*, *Mail*, *Signatures* button].

2. Click the *E-mail Signature* tab.

3. Click **New**. A *New Signature* dialog box opens.

4. Type the name of the signature and click **OK**.

5. Type the information to be included in the signature in the *Edit signature* area.

6. Click the **Business Card** button (Figure 8-15). The *Insert Business Card* dialog box opens.

7. Select the contact to be included as a business card.

8. Click **OK**. The business card graphic will be included with your signature (Figure 8-16).

9. Click **Save** to save your signature.

10. Click **OK** to close the *Signatures and Stationery* dialog box.

11. Click **OK** to close the *Outlook Options* dialog box.

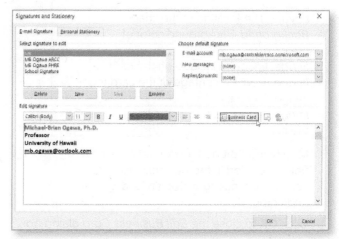

Figure 8-15 *Business Card* button

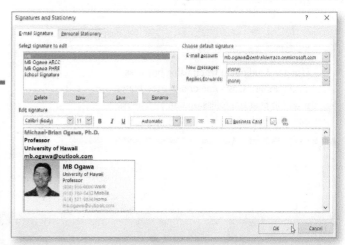

When you insert this signature into an email, the signature and graphic of the business card will be inserted into the body of the email. The graphic of the business card can be deleted without removing the attachment.

Figure 8-16 Business card in a signature

> **MORE INFO**
>
> The size of the business card graphic in the signature can be changed. This is done in the *Signatures and Stationery* dialog box.

> **MORE INFO**
>
> It is not necessary to include a signature on every email you send. This is especially true if your business card is attached to the signature.

Customize Your Business Card

When you create a contact record, a business card is automatically generated. Outlook provides flexibility in customizing the layout, colors, styles, and information of a business card.

HOW TO: Edit a Business Card

Open a business card and click the **Business Card** button (Figure 8-17) in the *Options* group on the *Contact* tab. The *Edit Business Card* dialog box opens (Figure 8-18).

2. Modify the *Card Design* options to change the format and layout.

> *Layout*: The location of the image
> *Background*: Background color of the card
> *Image*: Image to include on the card
> *Image Area*: Percentage of the card the image occupies
> *Image Align*: Location of the image on the card

3. Modify the **Edit** options to add or remove fields included in the business card. You can also change font size, style, alignment, and color.

4. Click **OK** to close the *Edit Business Card* dialog box.

Figure 8-17 *Business Card* options butt

> **MORE INFO**
>
> Use good judgment when using business card templates, as some creative templates might appear unprofessional in a business environment.

Figure 8-18 *Edit Business Card* dialog be

PAUSE & PRACTICE: OUTLOOK 8-2

For this Pause & Practice project, you modify your business card to improve its format and layout. If possible, you should include an image of yourself.

File Needed: Your image

1. Click the **People** button in the *Navigation* bar.

2. Click the **Business Card** view [*Home* tab, *Current View* group].

3. Double-click your business card.

4. Click the **Business Card** button in the *Options* group on the *Contact* tab. The *Edit Business Card* dialog box opens.

5. Modify the *Card Design* options to change the format and layout using the following options:

> *Layout*: **Image Right**
> *Background*: **Blue**
> *Image*: Include an image of yourself
> *Image Area*: **30%**
> *Image Align*: **Top right**

Select each of the text fields that are available on your business card and change the text color to **White**.

6. Click **OK** to close the *Edit Business Card* dialog box.

7. Click the **Save & Close** button [*Contact* group, *Actions* tab].

8. Email the business card to your instructor as an attachment.

   a. Click the **People** button in the *Navigation* bar.
   b. Select the **BUS 100** folder in *My Contacts*.
   c. Select your business card.
   d. Right-click the contact, choose **Forward Contact**, and select **As a Business Card**. A new email opens with the business card attached and a graphic of the business card in the body of the message.
   e. Select your instructor as the recipient.
   f. Add your email address in the *Cc* field.
   g. Change the subject to Outlook Pause & Practice 8-2.
   h. Type a short message to your instructor indicating that the completed *Pause and Practice 8-2* project is attached to the message.
   i. Click **Send** (Figure 8-19).

Tilman, Georgia

Georgia Tilman
American River College
Student

georgiatilman@arc.edu
georgiatilman@outlook.com

4700 College Oak Drive
Sacramento, CA 95841

Figure 8-19 PP Outlook 8-2 completed

SLO 8.3

Importing and Exporting Contact Information

By now you have created new contacts in Outlook. Create contacts in Outlook from scratch, from a received email, from a contact from the same company, and from a contact record sent to you as a business card. What if you had to enter 30, 50, 100, or 1,000 new contacts from a database or spreadsheet? This would take hours of time to complete.

Outlook provides *Import* and *Export* features that enable you to both import and export records without spending a long time manually creating them in Outlook. Outlook can import and export comma separated values and Outlook Data Files (.pst).

The importing and exporting process is one of the more complex tasks in Outlook, but Outlook walks you through it with a step-by-step wizard. After going through the importing and exporting process a couple of times, you'll be amazed at the time saved by using this feature.

> **MORE INFO**
>
> Remember a *field* is one piece of information about a contact such as *First Name*, *Last Name*, *Phone*, or *Email*. A *record* (contact record) is a group of related fields. It is important to make this distinction when working with database information.

Import Contacts

Outlook imports contacts from a variety of file types. The following is an overview of the steps you will take to import contact records. Prior to importing, it is important to first create a contact folder that serves as the location for the imported contact records. Select the **Import** process and select the appropriate file type. Select a location for the import records and map the fields.

▶HOW TO: Import Contacts

1. Click the **Contacts** button in the *Navigation* bar.
2. Create a new contact folder in which to save the new contacts (the folder is named *Placer Hills* in this example).
3. Click the **File** tab to open the *Backstage* view.
4. Click **Open and Export** and choose **Import/Export** (Figure 8-20) to open the *Import and Export Wizard* dialog box.
5. Click **Import from another program or file** and then click **Next** (Figure 8-21) to open the *Import a File* dialog box.
6. Click **Comma Separated Values** as the type of file to import from and click **Next**. The next *Import a File* dialog box opens.
7. Click the **Browse** button to locate the file on your computer to import, select the file to import, and click **OK** (Figure 8-22). The path to the file appears in the *File to Import* text box.
8. The *Options* area gives you choices about what action Outlook should perform if duplicate contact records are detected. Click **Next**.
   - Because you are importing into a new folder with no contact records, these options are irrelevant.
   - If you are importing to a folder containing existing contacts, select from one of the options.
9. Choose your newly created folder (*Placer Hills* in this example) as the *destination folder*, the folder into which the new contact records will be imported, and click **Next**.
10. Click the **Map Custom Fields** button. The *Map Custom Fields* dialog box opens.
    - The fields from the .csv file (*Placer Hills Real Estate* in this example) are listed on the left, and the fields available in the Outlook contact record are listed on the right.
    - The fields on the *left* (from .csv) need to be mapped to the fields on the *right* (to Outlook contact record).
    - Outlook compares fields that are similar; this does not ensure that they are correct.
11. Click the **Clear Map** button. This clears the *Mapped from* fields on the right.

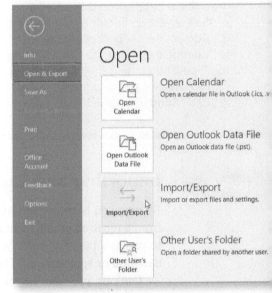

Figure 8-20 *Import/Export* files and settings

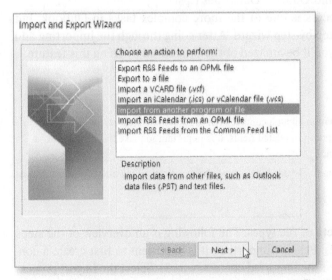

Figure 8-21 Import from another program or file

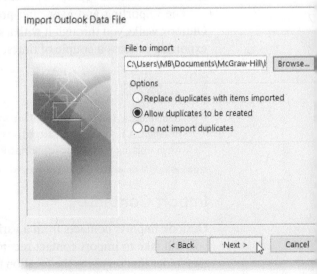

Figure 8-22 Select a file to import

2. Drag each field from the left (.csv) to the corresponding field on the right (Outlook contact) (Figure 8-23). Use the following table to map fields. *(Hint: Don't drag a field from the left to a field on the right with a plus sign by it (First Name)).* Open this field category (click the **plus sign**) to see the individual fields.

3. Click the **Next** button once you have mapped all of the fields. The first record displays on both the left and right. The actual field contents will be displayed next to their corresponding Outlook contact fields.

From Comma Separated Values (CSV)	To Outlook Contact
First	First Name
Last	Last Name
Company	Company
Department	Department
Job	Job Title
Street	Business Street
City	Business City
State	Business State
Zip Code	Business Postal
Country	Business Country
Email	Email Address
Phone	Business Phone

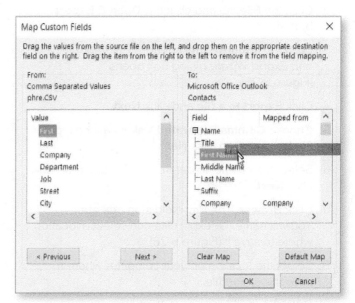

Figure 8-23 Match each field from the .csv file to the Outlook contact

4. Click **OK** when you have confirmed that all the fields are mapped correctly.

5. Click **Finish** to import the records from the .csv file.

6. Display the Contacts in *List* view to display all of the contacts from *Placer Hills Real Estate* (Figure 8-24). You can optionally create a contact folder for an organization to add all of the imported contacts.

Figure 8-24 Imported Placer Hills Real Estate contacts

Once you go through this process a couple of times, you'll be able to perform an import in about the time it would take to type a contact record.

 MORE INFO

Usually, if a mistake is made, it is in mapping fields. If you find a mistake, it is usually quicker to delete the contact records from the contact folder and redo the import.

Export Contacts

Exporting is a similar process to importing, but it is a little easier. Rather than mapping the fields, you just have to drag over the fields from the contact that you want included in the export. Not all of the Outlook contact fields will be exported because many of the fields in a contact record are blank.

▶ HOW TO: Export Contacts

1. Click the folder to be exported in the *My Contacts* area in the *Folder* pane.

2. Click the **File** tab and click the **Open & Export** button.

3. Click the **Import/Export** button. The *Import and Export Wizard* dialog box opens (Figure 8-25).

4. Click **Export to a file** and click **Next**.

5. Choose **Comma Separated Values** as the type of file to create and click **Next**.

6. Select the contact folder from which to export and click **Next**.

7. Click **Browse**. The *Browse* dialog box opens. You will name the export file and select a location where to save it (Figure 8-26).

8. Select the location on your computer where to save the export file.

9. In the *File name* box, type the name of the file. Confirm that you are saving as a **Comma Separated Values** file in the *Save as type* box.

10. Click **OK** and then click **Next**.

11. Click the **Map Custom Fields** button. The *Map Custom Fields* dialog box opens.

    - The fields from the Outlook contact are listed on the left, and the fields to be exported to a comma separated values file are listed on the right.
    - You don't want all the fields to be exported because you will have many blank fields in the exported spreadsheet if you do.
    - By default, Outlook removed most unused fields. You can clear the map and select specific fields to be exported.

12. Click **Clear Map** to clear the fields to be exported.

13. Drag fields from the *left* side (Outlook contact) to the *right* side (Excel export): Example: **First Name**, **Last Name**, **Company**, **Job Title**, and **Email Address** (Figure 8-27).

14. Click **OK** to close the *Map Custom Fields* dialog box.

15. Click **Finish**. The Excel file is now created with the exported contacts.

16. Open the new .csv file to confirm that the records were exported correctly.

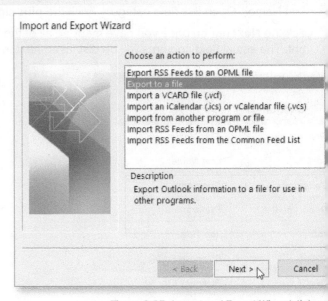

Figure 8-25 *Import and Export Wizard dialog*

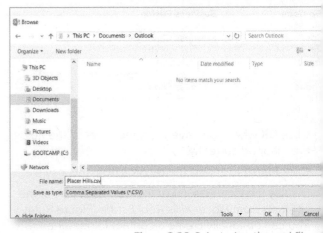

Figure 8-26 Select a location and file na

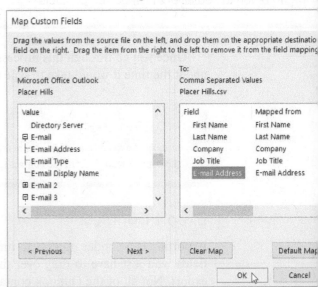

Figure 8-27 Select fields to ex

After a contact has been exported, the exported file can now be sent to others as an attachment and can be used to import contact records into Outlook or to use with other programs.

 MORE INFO

A .csv file can be edited in Microsoft Excel, which makes it easy to add or remove contacts quickly.

Export an Outlook Data File

When you get a new computer, you may dread the amount of time it is going to take to set up all the software and copy all the files. You might wonder how you are going to get all your information from Outlook on your existing computer to the new computer.

If you're working in an Exchange environment, all this information is stored on the Exchange server, so setting up Outlook and retrieving all your information is done when you set up your Exchange account in Outlook on the new computer. But what if you are getting a new home computer and want to transfer all your existing Outlook information to the new computer? Or what if your computer crashes?

Outlook has provided you with a way to transfer and backup your files with ease. Outlook stores all your information in an *Outlook Data File*, which is a *.pst* file. This file resides on your computer and contains all your Outlook information.

If you are changing from one computer to another, Outlook helps you export the *Outlook Data File*. Then this file, which contains all your Outlook information, can be imported into Outlook on the new computer.

HOW TO: Export an Outlook Data File

Click the **Import/Export** button [*File* tab, *Open & Export*]. The *Import and Export Wizard* opens.

Choose **Export to a File** and click **Next** (Figure 8-28).

Select **Outlook Data File (.pst)** and click **Next**.

Choose the folder to export and click **Next** (Figure 8-29). It is a good idea to export your entire *Personal Folders* (or Mailbox) including subfolders.

Figure 8-28 Export to a file

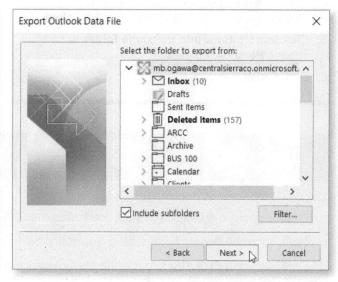

Figure 8-29 Select folder to export

5. Browse to the location to save the file, name the export file, and click **OK**.

6. Click **Finish**. The *Create Outlook Data File* dialog box opens.

7. Type a password and verify it as desired.

8. Click **OK** to close the *Create Outlook Data File* dialog box.

> **MORE INFO**
> If you are using Outlook in a stand-alone environment, it is a good idea to occasionally back up (export) your *Outlook Data File* and save this file in a location other than your computer.

> **MORE INFO**
> Passwords help to keep your *Outlook Data File* from being accessed.

Import an Outlook Data File

The process to import an *Outlook Data File* is similar to the importing and exporting proce described previously. Importing your *Outlook Data File* is a much more streamlined proce than importing contacts from a different file format.

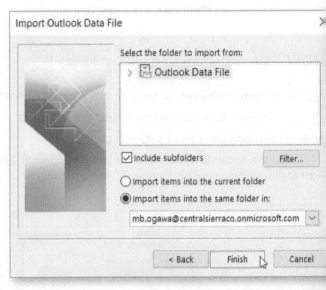

> ▶ **HOW TO:** Import an Outlook Data File
>
> 1. Click the **Import/Export** button. The *Import and Export Wizard* dialog box opens.
> 2. Choose **Import from another program or file** and click **Next**.
> 3. Choose **Outlook Data File (.pst)** and click **Next**.
> 4. Use the **Browse** button to locate and select the *Outlook Data File* to import and then click **Next**.
> 5. Click **Import items into the same folder in** and choose **Personal Folders**.
> 6. Click **Finish** (Figure 8-30).

Figure 8-30 Import folder locat

PAUSE & PRACTICE: OUTLOOK 8-3

For this Pause & Practice project, you export the *BUS 100* folder you created in *Pause & Practice 8-1*.

1. Click the **People** button in the *Navigation* bar.

2. Click the **BUS 100** folder in the *My Contacts* area in the *Folder* pane.

3. Click the **File** tab and click the **Open & Export** button.

4. Click the **Import/Export** button. The *Import and Export Wizard* dialog box opens.

5. Click **Export to a file** and click **Next**.

6. Choose **Comma Separated Values** as the type of file to create and click **Next**.

7. Select the **BUS 100** folder as the contact folder from which to export and click **Next**.

8. Click **Browse**. The *Browse* dialog box opens.

9. Select the location on your computer where to save the export file.

10. In the *File name* box, type BUS 100 [your initials] as the name of the file. Confirm that you are saving as a **Comma Separated Values** file in the *Save as type* box.

11. Click **OK** and then click **Next**.

12. Click the **Map Custom Fields** button. The *Map Custom Fields* dialog box opens.

13. Click **Clear Map** to clear the fields to be exported.

14. Drag the following fields from the *left* side (Outlook contact) to the *right* side (Excel export): **First Name**, **Last Name**, **Email Address**, **Business Street**, **Business City**, **Business State**, and **Business Postal Code**.

15. Click **OK** to close the *Map Custom Fields* dialog box.

16. Click **Finish**.

17. Send an email to your instructor with the .csv file you exported as an attachment.
    a. Click the **Mail** button in the *Navigation* bar.
    b. Click **New Mail** [*Home* tab, *New* group].
    c. In the *To* field, enter your instructor's email address.
    d. In the *Cc* field, enter your email address.
    e. In the *Subject* field, enter Outlook Pause & Practice 8-3.
    f. In the message area, type:

    Dear [instructor's name],

    Attached is my Outlook Pause & Practice 8-3.

    Thank you,
    [student name]

    g. Click the **Attach File** button [*Message* tab, *Include* group] and select the exported Excel file.
    h. Click the **Send** button (Figure 8-31).

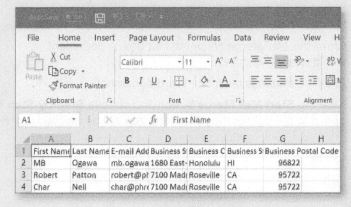

Figure 8-31 PP Outlook 8-3 completed

Using Contacts with Other Office Programs

An advantage of using Microsoft Office products is the ability to share information between programs. You can easily use your Outlook Contacts to create mailing labels, envelopes, and business letters. Contacts can also be used in conjunction with Excel and Access. Comma separated value files are easy to import and manage.

Use Contacts to Create Mailing Labels in Word

Outlook has streamlined the process of using information in your contact records in a *Mail Merge*. Outlook works in conjunction with Microsoft Word to create labels, envelopes, or form letters. You can use all the contacts in a folder or choose the contacts to be included in the merge. You don't have to be an expert in Word to create mailing labels; the *Mail Merge* feature will walk you through this process.

The following example will walk you through the process of creating mailing labels from all the contacts you imported into the *Placer Hills* contacts folder.

▶ HOW TO: Use Mail Merge with Outlook Contacts

1. Select the contacts folder to be used in the merge in the *Folder* pane.

2. Click the **Mail Merge** button in the *Actions* group on the *Home* tab. The *Mail Merge Contacts* dialog box opens (Figure 8-32).

3. Select the **All contacts in current view** option in the *Contacts* area, and select **New document** in the *Document file* area.

4. Select **Mailing Labels** in the *Document type* list box, and select **New Document** in the *Merge to* list box.

5. Click **OK**.
   - Microsoft Word opens, and a dialog box opens informing you to set up your mailing labels.

6. Click **OK**. The *Mail Merge Helper* dialog box opens.

7. Click **Setup** (Figure 8-33). The *Label Options* dialog box opens.

8. Select your label brand and type (Avery 5160 is a standard label type) and click **OK** (Figure 8-34).

9. Close the *Mail Merge Helper* dialog box. A document with the labels displays.

10. Click the **Mailings** tab in the Word document.

11. Click the **Start Mail Merge** button and choose **Step-by-Step Mail Merge Wizard**. The *Mail Merge Wizard* opens to the right of the document. You will be on *Step 3 of 6*.

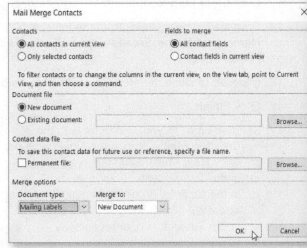

Figure 8-32 *Mail Merge Contacts* dialog box

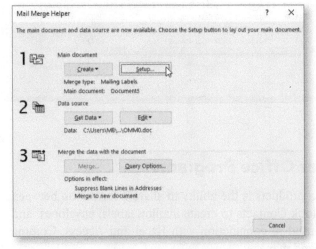

Figure 8-33 *Mail Merge Helper* dialog box

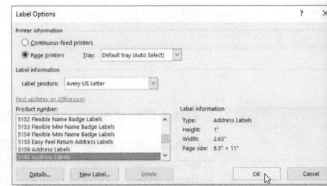

Figure 8-34 Select your label brand and type

Click **Next: Arrange your labels**.

Click the **Address Block** link. The *Insert Address Block* dialog box opens.

Select how you want your address block to appear and click **OK** (Figure 8-35).

Click the **Update all labels** button and click **Next: Preview your labels** (Figure 8-36). Labels appear for preview.

Click **Next: Complete the merge**. Figure 8-37 includes the completed mail merge.

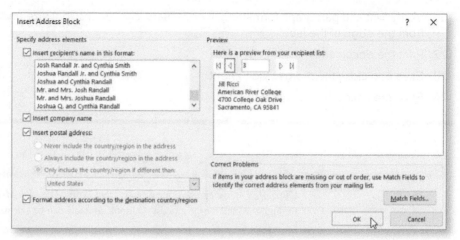

Figure 8-35 Select your address block appearance

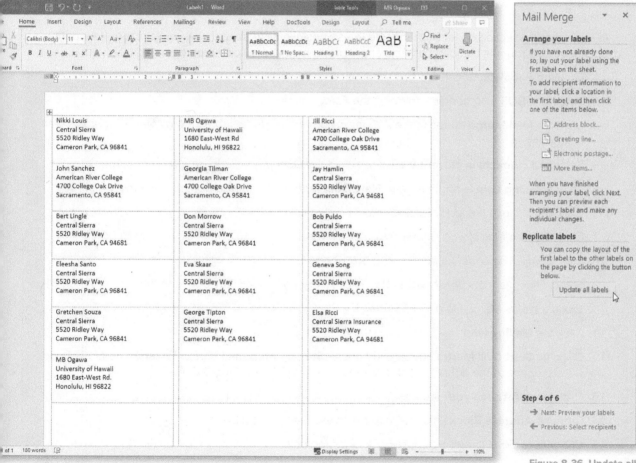

Figure 8-37 Completed mail merge

Figure 8-36 Update all labels

Select the entire document (**Ctrl+A**) and click the **Home** tab.

Click the **Paragraph launcher** and change the spacing before to **0 pt**, and change the spacing after to **0 pt**.

Click **Edit individual labels** to open the *Merge to a New Document* dialog box.

Select **All**, and click **OK**. A new document displays for final review and printing.

21. Verify font and paragraph formatting. If necessary, change the font size and set a left indent to move text awa[y] from the edge of the label.
22. Print the document.
23. Save and close the merged document.
24. Save the main label document.

> **ANOTHER WAY**
> Using *Mail Merge* can be done directly from Word. The *Mail Merge Wizard* in Word will walk you through the mail merge process. Outlook contacts can be selected as a data source.

PAUSE & PRACTICE: OUTLOOK 8-4

In this Pause & Practice project, you decide to use postal mail to send thank you letters to your partners and instructor. You use Outlook contacts and Word to help you quickly create mailing labels.

1. Click the **People** button in the *Navigation* bar.
2. Select the **BUS 100** contacts folder in the *Folder* pane.
3. Click the **Mail Merge** button in the *Actions* group on the *Home* tab. The *Mail Merge Contacts* dialog box opens.
4. Select **All contacts in current view** and select the *Document file* to be a **New document**.
5. Select **Mailing Labels** and merge to **New Document** in the *Merge options* section.
6. Click **OK** to close the *Mail Merge Contacts* dialog box.
7. Click **OK**. The *Mail Merge Helper* dialog box opens.
8. Click **Setup**. The *Label Options* dialog box opens.
9. Select Label vendors, **Avery US Letter**, click **Avery 5160** (half way down on the list), and click **OK**.
10. Close the *Mail Merge Helper* dialog box.
11. Click the **Mailings** tab.
12. Click the **Start Mail Merge** button and choose **Step by Step Mail Merge Wizard**. The *Mail Merge Wizard* opens to the right of the document and you will be on *Step 3 of 6*.
13. Click **Next: Arrange your labels**.
14. Click the **Address Block** link. The *Insert Address Block* dialog box opens.
15. Click **OK** to close the *Insert Address Block* dialog box.
16. Click the **Update all labels** button and click **Next: Preview your labels**. The labels display in the Word document (Figure 8-38).
17. Click **Next: Complete the merge**.
18. Select the entire document (**Ctrl+A**), change the paragraph spacing to **0 pt before** and **after**, and change the line spacing to **Single**.

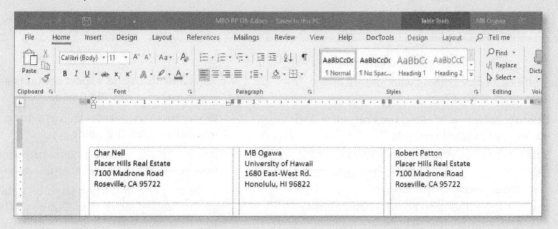

Figure 8-38 PP Outlook 8-4 completed

19. Select **Edit individual labels** and click **OK** to close the *Merge to New Document* dialog box.

20. Click the **File** button and select **Save As**. Save the file as [your initials]PP O8-4.

21. Close the saved merge document and close without saving the main merge document.

22. Send an email to your instructor with the completed mail merge as an attachment.
    a. Click the **Mail** button in the *Navigation* bar.
    b. Click **New Mail** [*Home* tab, *New* group].
    c. In the *To* field, enter your instructor's email address.
    d. In the *Cc* field, enter your email address.
    e. In the *Subject* field, enter Outlook Pause & Practice 8-4.
    f. In the message area, type:

       Dear [instructor name],

       Attached is my Outlook Pause & Practice 8-4.

       Thank you,
       [student name]

    g. Click the **Attach File** button [*Message* tab, *Include* group] and select the completed mail merge file.
    h. Click the **Send** button.

Chapter Summary

8.1 Integrate Outlook contacts with folders and categories (p. O8-292).

- **Contact folders** and categories organize and manage your list of contacts.
- You can change your default address book.
- Use folders to organize contacts similar to the way folders work in Windows.
- You can drag and drop contacts into folders.
- Categories label contacts without moving them into folders.
- You can **update** contacts using the **Global Address List** if your company uses an Exchange server.
- Use the *People* button in the **Outlook Options** dialog box to customize how you view and work with contacts.

8.2 Create and utilize electronic business cards (p. O8-297).

- Sending your **business card** allows other Outlook users to quickly add you as a contact.
- Business cards are attached to email messages as Outlook items.
- Business cards can be included in signatures.
- Outlook allows you to customize the appearance of your business card.

8.3 Share contact information by importing to and exporting from Outlook (p. O8-302).

- Outlook allows you to **import** and **export** content.
- Outlook stores all of your information in a **.pst** file known as an **Outlook Data File**.

- You can import and export contacts and folders in **.pst** and .csv file types.
- When importing contacts, it is a good idea to manually match the fields.
- It is important to export contacts based on how you want to import them.
- Exporting and importing Outlook data can h you to quickly move your Outlook informatio to a new computer.
- If you are using an Exchange environment, your Outlook data is saved on the server.

8.4 Use Outlook Contacts with other Microsoft Offi programs (p. O8-308).

- Outlook contacts can be used with other Microsoft Office products such as Word, Exc and Access.
- You can quickly create a **Mail Merges** includ ing mailing labels, envelopes, and business letters in Word.
- Contact data exported in .csv format can ea be imported into Excel or Access.

Check for Understanding

The SIMbook for this text (within your SIMnet accoun provides the following resources for concept review:

- Multiple-choice questions
- Short answer questions
- Matching exercises

Guided Project 8-1

For this project, you are a real estate agent for Placer Hills Real Estate (PHRE). You decide to set up your home computer to include your contacts from work. Therefore, you exported your contacts in your office computer to a .csv file. For this project, you are looking to import your contacts from work and organize them using folders and categories.
[Student Learning Outcomes 8.1, 8.2, 8.3]

File Needed: ***phre.csv***

Skills Covered in This Project

- Create a contacts folder.
- Import contacts from a .csv file.
- Map fields.
- Select an account when creating a new message.
- Assign categories to contacts.
- Email business cards as attachments.

1. Click the **People** button in the *Navigation* bar.

2. Create a new **Contacts** folder in which to save new contacts, and name this folder *Placer Hills*.
   a. Click the **Contacts** folder in the *My Contacts* area of the *Folder* pane.
   b. Click the **Folder** tab.
   c. Click the **New Folder** button in the *New* group to open the *Create New Folder* dialog box.
   d. Type Placer Hills for the name of the folder.
   e. Click **OK**.

3. Click the **File** tab to open the *BackStage* view.

4. Click **Open and Export** and choose **Import/Export** to open the *Import and Export Wizard* dialog box.

5. Click **Import from another program or file** and click **Next** to open the *Import a File* dialog box.

6. Click **Comma Separated Values** as the type of file to import from and click **Next**. The next *Import a File* dialog box opens.

7. Click the **Browse** button to locate and select the ***phre.csv*** file on your computer and click **OK**.

8. Select **replace duplicates with items imported** in the *Options* area and click **Next**.

9. Choose **Placer Hills** as the *destination folder*, the folder into which the new contact records will be imported, and click **Next**.

10. Click the **Map Custom Fields** button. The *Map Custom Fields* dialog box opens.

11. Click the **Clear Map** button.

12. Drag each field from the left (.csv) to the corresponding field on the right (Outlook contact). Use the following table to map fields.

From Access	To Outlook Contact
First	First Name
Last	Last Name
Company	Company
Department	Department
Job	Job Title
Street	Business Street
City	Business City
State	Business State
Zip Code	Business Postal Code
Country	Business Country
Email	Email Address
Phone	Business Phone

13. Click the **Next** button to see the first record displayed at both the left and right. The actual field contents will be displayed next to their corresponding Outlook contact fields.

14. Click **OK** when you have confirmed that all the fields are mapped correctly.

15. Click **Finish** to import the records from the .csv file.

16. Click the **Placer Hills** folder in the *My Contacts* area of the *Folder* pane. The contents of this folder display in the *Content area*.

17. Create a category named **PHRE Agent** with the color **blue**.

18. Select the contacts for **Char Nell**, **Robert Patton**, and **Elisa Richards**. Click the **Categorize** button [*Home* tab, *Tags* group] and select **PHRE Agent** (Figure 8-39).

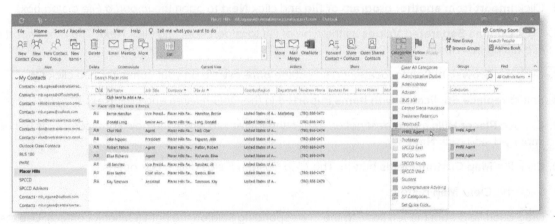

Figure 8-39 Guided Project 8-1 completed

19. Email **Char Nell**, **Robert Patton**, and **Elisa Richards'** business cards to your instructor as an attachment.

   a. Click the **Mail** button on the *Navigation* bar.
   b. Click the **New Mail** button [*Home* tab, *New* group].
   c. In the *To* field, enter your instructor's email address.
   d. In the *Cc* field, enter your email address.
   e. In the *Subject* field, enter Outlook Guided Project 8-1.
   f. In the message area, type:

   Dear [instructor's name],

   Attached is my Outlook Guided Project 8-1.

   Thank you,
   [your name]

   g. Click the **Business Card** option [*Message* tab, *Include* group, *Attach Item*] and select **Other Business Cards**.
   h. Select the three cards you categorized as **PHRE Agent** and click **OK**.
   i. Click the **Send** button.

Guided Project 8-2

For this project, you are Robert Patton, an agent for PHRE. You recently realized that the appearance of your Outlook business card is very important because it is viewed both internally by members of the PHRE team and externally by clients. Therefore, you decide to modify it to improve its appearance. [Student Learning Outcome 8.2]

File Needed: *card.png*

Skills Covered in This Project

- Edit the contents of a contact template.
- Modify the appearance of a contact template.

1. Click the **People** button in the *Navigation* bar.

2. Select the **Place Hills** contact folder.

3. Click **Business Card View** [*Home* tab, *Current View* group].

4. Double-click **Robert Patton**'s business card.

5. Click the **Business Card** button [*Contact* tab, *Options* group].

6. Modify the **Card Design** options for Robert Patton to change the appearance using the following options.
   a. Click the **Background Color** button and select a **dark blue**.
   b. Select each of the text fields that are available on your business card and change the text color to **White**.
   c. Select the **Full Name** field and click the **Center Align** button.

d. Click the **Change** button. Locate and select the file ***card.png*** (available in the student files). Modify the *Image Area* to be **30%**.

e. Set the *Image Align* to be **Fit to Edge**.

7. Click **OK** to close the *Edit Business Card* dialog box.

8. Click the **Save & Close** button.

9. Email the business card to your instructor as an attachment.

a. Click the **People** button in the *Navigation* bar.

b. Select the **Placer Hill** contact folder in *My Contacts*.

c. Right-click the **Robert Patton** contact, choose **Forward Contact**, and select **As a Business Card**. A new email opens with the business card attached and a graphic of the business card in the body of the message.

d. Select your instructor as the recipient.

e. Add your email address in the *Cc* field.

f. Change the subject to Outlook Guided Project 8-2.

g. In the message field, type:

Dear [instructor's name],

Attached is my Outlook Guided Project 8-2.

Thank you,
[your name]

h. Click **Send** (Figure 8-40).

Figure 8-40 Guided Project 8-2 completed

Guided Project 8-3

For this project, you are Jake Nguyen, President of PHRE. You decide to have a surprise Christmas party for your staff. Since it is a surprise, you decide to send the invitation to each individual employee via postal mail. You decide to use *Mail Merge* to help you create shipping labels for each of your employees. [Student Learning Outcome 8.4]

Skills Covered in This Project

- Create a mail merge from Outlook contacts.
- Create mail merge mailing labels.

1. Click the **People** button in the *Navigation* bar.

2. Select the **Placer Hills** contacts folder in the *Folder* pane.

3. Click the **Mail Merge** button in the *Actions* group on the *Home* tab. The *Mail Merge Contacts* dialog box opens.

4. Select **All contacts in current view** and select the *Document file* to be a **New document**.

5. Select **Mailing Labels** and merge to **New Document** in the *Merge options* section.

6. Click **OK** to close the *Mail Merge Contacts* dialog box.

7. Click **OK**. The *Mail Merge Helper* dialog box opens.

8. Click **Setup**. The *Label Options* dialog box opens.

9. Select Label vendors, **Avery US Letter**, click **Avery 5160**, and click **OK**.

10. Close the **Mail Merge Helper** dialog box.

11. Click the **Mailings** tab in the Word document.

12. Click the **Start Mail Merge** button and choose **Step by Step Mail Merge Wizard**. The *Mail Merge Wizard* opens to the right of the document and you will be on *Step 3 of 6*.

13. Click **Next: Arrange your labels**.

14. Click the **Address Block** link. The *Insert Address Block* dialog box opens.

15. Click **OK** to close the *Insert Address Block* dialog box.

16. Click the **Update all labels** button and click **Next: Preview your labels**. Your labels will appear in the document.

17. Click **Next: Complete the merge**.

18. Select the entire document (**Ctrl+A**), change the paragraph spacing to **0 pt before** and **after**, and change the line spacing to **Single**.

19. Select **Edit individual labels** and click **OK** to close the *Merge to New Document* dialog box (Figure 8-41).

20. Click the **File** button and select **Save As**. Save the file as [your initials] GP O 8-3.

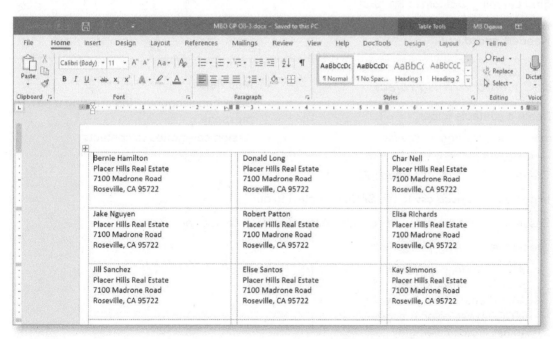

Figure 8-41 Guided Project 8-3 completed

21. Send an email to your instructor with the completed mail merge as an attachment.
    a. Click the **Mail** button in the *Navigation* bar.
    b. Click **New Mail** [*Home* tab, *New* group].
    c. In the *To* field, enter your instructor's email address.
    d. In the *Cc* field, enter your email address.
    e. In the *Subject* field, enter Outlook Guided Project 8-3.
    f. In the message area, type:

    Dear [instructor's name],

    Attached is my Outlook Guided Project 8-3.

    Thank you,
    [your name]

    g. Click the **Attach File** button [*Message* tab, *Include* group] and select the completed mail merge file.
    h. Click the **Send** button.

Independent Project 8-4

For this project, you are an academic advisor for Sierra Pacific Community College District (SPCCD). After looking through your contact list, you noticed that you had contacts that were administrative or academic advisors from a variety of campuses. You decide to organize your contacts using categories to help you find people by position or institution.
[Student Learning Outcomes 8.1, 8.3]

File Needed: ***spccd.csv***

Skills Covered in This Project

- Create a contacts folder.
- Import contacts from a .csv file.
- Map fields.
- Select an account when creating a new message.
- Assign categories to contacts.

1. Create a contact folder named SPCCD.

2. Import the file ***spccd.csv*** to the **SPCCD** contact folder.

3. Ensure the fields are mapped correctly. Allow duplicate items to be created.

4. Create the following categories:

   SPCCD North, color: green
   SPCCD South, color: red
   SPCCD East, color: yellow
   SPCCD West, color: orange
   Administrator, color: gray
   Advisor, color: blue

5. Apply *Categories* to the contacts in the *SPCCD* contact folder (Figure 8-42) using the following table:

First	Last	Category 1	Category 2
Jim	Cooke	SPCCD North	Advisor
Jake	Duane	SPCCD North	Advisor
Denise	Fong	SPCCD West	Advisor
Debbie	Huan	SPCCD East	Advisor
Nellie	Nelson	SPCCD West	Administrator
Virginia	Pulson	SPCCD South	Advisor
Marcie	Ritt	SPCCD South	Administrator
Melissa	Somora	SPCCD East	Administrator
Joey	Tomlin	SPCCD North	Administrator

Figure 8-42 Independent Project 8-4 completed

6. Export the *SPCCD* folder as a .pst file named spccd-contacts. Do not add a password.

7. Email the .pst file to your instructor as an attachment based on the information below.
   a. In the *To* field, enter your instructor's email address.
   b. In the *Cc* field, enter your email address.
   c. In the *Subject* field, enter Outlook Independent Project 8-4.
   d. In the message area, type:

   Dear [instructor's name],

   Attached is my Outlook Independent Project 8-4.

   Thank you,
   [your name]

Independent Project 8-5

For this project, you are Jim Cooke, an academic advisor for Sierra Pacific Community College District (SPCCD). You will edit the Outlook business card for Jim Cooke to improve its appearance.
[Student Learning Outcome 8.2]

File Needed: *jim.jpg*

Skills Covered in This Project

- Edit the contents of a contact template.
- Modify the appearance of a contact.

1. Add Jim Cooke's picture to his business card. The image, **jim.jpg**, is available in the student data folder.

2. Modify the *Card Design* options to ensure the following:
   a. Position Jim's picture on the **left** side of the card.
   b. The image area is **50%**.
   c. Align Jim's image to the **Center Left** of the card.

3. Modify the text fields in the following ways:
   a. Italicize the *Company*.
   b. Change the *E-mail* to have a **green** font color.

4. Email the business card to your instructor as an attachment.
   a. Change the subject to Outlook Independent Project 8-5.
   b. Type a short message to your instructor indicating that the completed *Independent Project 8-5* is attached to the message (Figure 8-43).

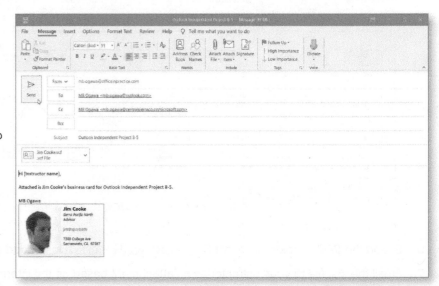

Figure 8-43 Independent Project 8-5 completed

Independent Project 8-6

For this project, you are Melissa Somora, provost for SPCCD. It is that time of the year to send student reminders about registration. Since SPCCD uses postal mail to send official reminder letters to each advisor to remind them about registration, you decide to use the mail merge feature to create mailing labels. [Student Learning Outcomes 8.1, 8.4]

Skills Covered in This Project

- Create a mail merge from Outlook contacts.
- Create mail merge mailing labels.

1. Create a new contact folder named SPCCD Advisors and copy all of the advisors to it.

2. Create a mail merge for all academic advisors.

3. Create mailing labels using **Avery 5160** as the template.

4. Apply formatting changes to ensure text is viewable on all labels (Figure 8-44).

5. Save the completed Word file as [your initials] IP 8-6.

6. Send an email to your instructor with the completed mail merge as an attachment.
   a. Click the **Mail** button in the *Navigation* bar.
   b. Click **New Mail** [*Home* tab, *New* group].
   c. In the *To* field, enter your instructor's email address.
   d. In the *Cc* field, enter your email address.
   e. In the *Subject* field, enter Outlook Independent Project 8-6.
   f. In the message area, type:

   Dear [instructor name],

   Attached is my Outlook Independent Project 8-6.

   Thank you,
   [student name]

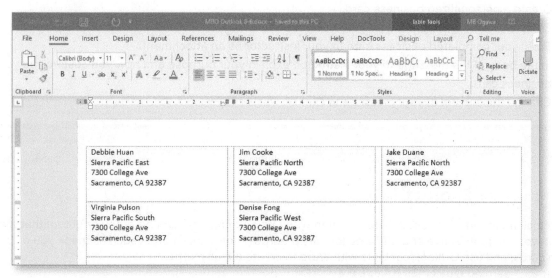

Figure 8-44 Independent Project 8-6 completed

Challenge Project 8-7

Most people have their own way of organizing information. For this project, you will organize your contacts using folders and categories. Even though this sounds like a simple task, you will need to explain how they are organized to your instructor. To submit the assignment, you will export the contacts from Outlook and share them with your instructor as an email attachment.
[Student Learning Outcomes 8.1, 8.3]

- Create at least 10 contacts.
- Identify how you will organize your contacts.
- Both folders and categories should be implemented.

- Email your instructor using the following message format:

  Folder list: [include the name of each folder and why it was created]

  Category list: [include the name of each category and indicate why it was created]
- Change the subject of your message to Outlook Challenge Project 8-7.
- Export your contacts and include them as an attachment to your instructor.

Challenge Project 8-8

Outlook business cards include more information than your contact information. The way a business card appears can also be seen as an extension of how you represent yourself. For this project, you will create a business card for yourself and send it to your instructor.
[Student Learning Outcome 8.2]

- Create a personalized business card.
- Be sure to identify a purpose for your business card.
- Email your completed business card to your instructor as an attachment.
- In the body of the message to your instructor, explain your purpose and how you customized your business card.
- Change the subject of your message to Outlook Challenge Project 8-8.

Challenge Project 8-9

The mail merge in Word used in conjunction with Outlook contacts can be a powerful tool that makes your work more effective and efficient. Identify a purpose for a mail merge, such as thank you or invitation cards, and use Outlook contacts with Word to create a mail merge.
[Student Learning Outcomes 8.1,8.3, 8.4]

- Identify a purpose for a mail merge.
- Create a contact group with at least eight contacts for the merge.
- Create a mail merge using the contact group.
- Export your contact group as a .csv file.
- Email your completed mail merge and contact group to your instructor as attachments.
- Change the subject of your message to Outlook Challenge Project 8-9.

Source of screenshots Microsoft Office 365 (2019): Word, Excel, Access, PowerPoint, Outlook.

Advanced Calendars and Sharing

OUTLOOK

CHAPTER OVERVIEW

Now that you are comfortable using an electronic calendar to help organize your daily life, you are ready to incorporate some of the additional Outlook calendar features. In this chapter, you will learn how to create and use multiple calendars, incorporate advanced calendar features, customize the default calendar options, and print and share calendars.

   A distinct advantage of Outlook in an Exchange environment is its ability to share your information with others. Many of you collaborate with others on work projects. The *Delegates* feature in Outlook enables you to give access to certain areas of Outlook to others with whom you work.

> **MORE INFO**
>
> If you need to review the basics of the Outlook calendar, they were covered in chapter 5.

STUDENT LEARNING OUTCOMES (SLOs)

After completing this chapter, you will be able to:

SLO 9.1   Create and use multiple Outlook calendars (p. O9-325).

SLO 9.2   Customize your Outlook calendar using calendar options (p. O9-327).

SLO 9.3   Incorporate printing and sharing with your Outlook calendar (p. O9-330).

SLO 9.4   Utilize advanced calendar features (p. O9-337).

SLO 9.5   Collaborate with other Outlook users' delegates (p. O9-344).

CASE STUDY

For the Pause & Practice projects, you create a new calendar for your BUS 100 class. Since you are working with a new calendar, you will need to create appointments and categorize them to improve the overall organization. You attach your homework to the recitation session for class to ensure it is easy for you to find. Lastly, you realize that you will be out of town and have minimal access to the internet. Therefore, you ask a partner to serve as a delegate for your calendar.

Pause & Practice 9-1: Create a new calendar for your BUS 100 class. Add three appointments and share your calendar with your instructor. You also forward your group meeting appointment to your instructor so that he/she knows when you are meeting for your project.

Pause & Practice 9-2: Improve the organization of your BUS 100 calendar by using categories. Attach a homework file to the *BUS 100*

Recitation appointment. Since your lecture occurs weekly, you set the calendar item to recur weekly till the end of the semester (10 weeks).

Pause & Practice 9-3: You will be out of town with minimal internet access. Therefore, you

ask one of your partners to be a delegat while you are away. Since you are concerne about the calendar, you give your partne *Author* permissions so that he can add grou meeting dates while you are away.

Using Multiple Calendars

Up to this point, you probably have been recording calendar items on the default Outloo calendar. But what if you wanted to keep all your personal calendar items on one cale dar and all your business-related calendar items on a separate calendar? Or you might b involved in a professional organization, club, or charity organization and would like to hav a separate calendar for each of these activities. Outlook provides you with the option of hav ing multiple calendars.

Create a New Calendar

Creating a new calendar is similar to creating a new Inbox or *Contacts* folder. When you creat a new calendar, it appears in the *My Calendars* list in the *Folder* pane.

▶ HOW TO: Create a New Calendar

1. Click the **Calendar** button in the *Navigation* bar.

2. Click the **Folder** tab and then on the **New Calendar** button in the *New* group (Figure 9-1). The *Create New Folder* dialog box opens.

Figure 9-1 *New Calendar* button

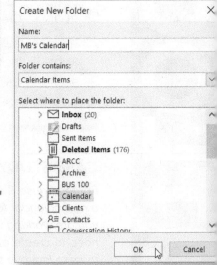

3. Type the **Name** of the new calendar (Figure 9-2). Confirm that the folder contains **Calendar Items**, and the new calendar will be placed in the **Calendar** folder.

4. Click **OK**. The new calendar is created and appears in the *My Calendars* area in the *Folder* pane.

▶ ANOTHER WAY

Right-click **Calendar** in the *My Calendar* list and choose **New Calendar**.

Figure 9-2 *Create New Folder* dialog b

You can also create new calendars from shared resources such as meeting rooms and othe resources. This feature is set up by the Exchange administrator, where meeting rooms incluc their own calendar that Outlook users can view to determine if a resource is available for duration of time.

Click the **Calendar** button in the *Navigation* bar.

Click the **Folder** tab and then on the **Add Calendar** button [*Share* group] and select **From Room List** (Figure 9-3). The *Select Name: All Rooms* dialog box opens.

Select a room from the list and click the **Rooms** button (Figure 9-4).

Click **OK**. The new calendar is created and appears in the *Rooms* area in the *Folder* pane.

Figure 9-3 Add a calendar From Room List

Figure 9-4 *Select Name: All Rooms* dialog box

> **MORE INFO**
>
> The **Add Calendar** button also allows you to create calendars for people in your *Address Book* and from the internet.

You can delete a calendar by selecting the calendar and clicking the **Delete Calendar** button in the *Actions* group on the *Folder* tab. The default Outlook calendar cannot be deleted.

> **ANOTHER WAY**
>
> **Ctrl+D** deletes the selected calendar.

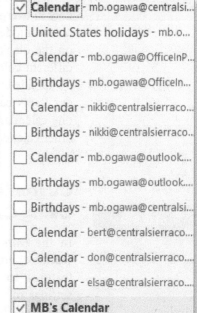

Figure 9-5 Select multiple calendars

View Multiple Calendars

By default, your main calendar (Calendar) will be displayed in the *Content area*. The check box to the left of the calendars listed in the *My Calendars* area indicates which calendars will be displayed in the *Content area* (Figure 9-5).

An additional or different calendar displays in the *Content area* by checking the box to the left of the calendar name in the calendars area indicates which calendars display in the *Content area*.

> **MORE INFO**
>
> At least one calendar must be selected at all times; Outlook will not allow you to deselect all the calendars in the calendars lists.

When multiple calendars display in the *Content area*, they can be viewed in **side-by-side mode** or in **overlay mode**. When calendars are viewed in side-by-side mode (Figure 9-6), the items on each of the calendars are smaller and more difficult to read. The overlay mode allows you to easily switch between calendars in the *Content area*. Each calendar appears in a different color.

The tab at the top of each calendar displays the name of the calendar. When you are in overlay mode (Figure 9-7), click a tab to display the selected calendar. Click the small arrows to the left of each of the calendar names to switch the display mode.

When you view your calendars in overlay mode, the items on the hidden calendar appear on the displayed calendar in a different color.

In side-by-side mode, calendar items can be copied from one calendar to another by selecting a calendar item and dragging and dropping it onto other calendar.

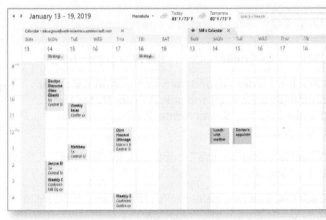

Figure 9-6 Multiple calendars in side-by-side me

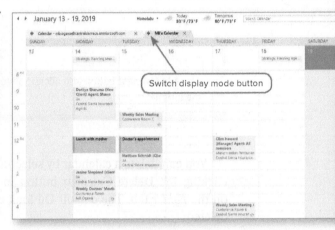

Figure 9-7 Multiple calendars in overlay me

Customizing the Calendar Using Calendar Options

SLO 9.2

In the *Outlook Options* dialog box, Outlook provides you with many features to customize the default settings of your calendar, including changing the work week options, changing the calendar color, adding holidays, changing the default reminder setting, adding time zones, and customizing the *Scheduling Assistant*. You can access calendar options by clicking the **File** tab to open the *Backstage* view, selecting **Options**, and choosing **Calendar** in the *Outlook Options* dialog box (Figure 9-8).

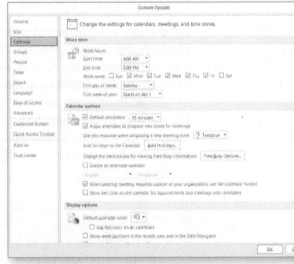

Figure 9-8 Calendar Opti

Work Time Options

By default, Outlook is set up like a regular calendar with Sunday as the first day of the week. What if you don't work a standard Monday–Friday work week? You can customize your Outlook calendar to begin on whichever day you choose by changing the settings in the *Work time* area of the *Calendar Options* dialog box.

When a calendar displays in *Week* view, you have the options of *Show work week* or *Show full week*. If you work a Wednesday–Sunday work week, you can change the settings to reflect your work week on your Outlook calendar.

Calendar Options

The default setting for a reminder on an appointment is 15 minutes, which means an electronic reminder opens on your computer 15 minutes before a scheduled appointment. The default reminder can be changed, or reminders can be changed when you create or edit an appointment.

The *Calendar Options* area also allows you to control whether or not attendees of a meeting can propose new times and the default response when proposing a new time for a meeting. When you set up a

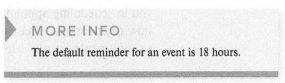

MORE INFO

The default reminder for an event is 18 hours.

meeting request, attendees will have the option to propose a new time for the meeting. If you do not want this option to be available, you can deselect this option in the *Calendar Options* dialog box.

Free/Busy Options are used in conjunction with an Exchange server to allow the meeting organizer to see free and busy time on your calendar. Outlook allows you to set up an alternate calendar to accommodate different types of calendars used throughout the world. Also, by default, when you send a meeting request outside your organization, Outlook uses an *iCalendar* format, which enables other email users to view the meeting information.

Outlook can automatically add *holidays* to your Outlook calendar, and you can choose the country or countries from which to add holidays.

HOW TO: Add Holidays to Your Calendar

Click the **File** tab and choose **Options**. The *Outlook Options* dialog box opens.

Click the **Calendar** button. The *Calendar Options* dialog box opens.

Click the **Add Holidays** button. The *Add Holidays to Calendar* dialog box opens (Figure 9-9).

Select the country or countries of your choice.

Click **OK**. The holidays will be added to your calendar.

Click **OK** to close the *Outlook Options* dialog box.

Figure 9-9 Add holidays to your calendar

MORE INFO

Most countries have many holidays. Be careful not to add too many countries' holidays, so as not to clutter your calendar.

Display Options

The color of the default Out-look calendar can be changed (Figure 9-10). When you view multiple calendars in the *Content area*, Outlook will automatically select a different color for each calendar displayed in the

Figure 9-10 Display optio

Content area. You have the option of changing the displayed calendars to the same color checking the *Use this color on all calendars* box. It is probably best to have each calendar be different color to help you distinguish between calendar items.

 Week numbers (1–52) can be added so they will be displayed in *Month* view and in the *D Navigator*. By default, Outlook does not display week numbers.

 Schedule view displays a single calendar or multiple calendars in the timeline view to ass you in scheduling appointments and meetings. The last two check boxes allow you to cont how calendars and free appointments are viewed when using *Schedule* view. By default, fr appointments are not displayed in *Schedule* view.

Time Zones

What if you regularly do business with a company or individual from a different time zone? Outlook will allow you to change the time zone on your calendar or add an additional time zone to your calendar (Figure 9-11). If you add an additional time zone to your calendar, up to

Figure 9-11 Select multiple time zor

three time zones will be displayed when you view your calendar in *Day* or *Week* view. You c also add labels to each of the time zones, which display on the calendar in *Day* and *Week* view

Scheduling Assistant

The *Scheduling Assistant* (Figure 9-12) can be used when creating meetings, appointments, events on your calendar. It displays your calendar in timeline view in the body of a new cal dar item to assist you in selecting a day and time for the calendar item. By default, calendar details display in both *ScreenTips* and the scheduling grid.

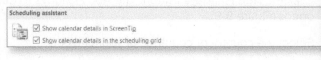

Figure 9-12 Scheduling assistant optie

Automatic Accept or Decline

Outlook also includes the option of automatically accepting meeting requests and removi canceled meetings (Figure 9-13). You can also change the default settings to control how O look handles meeting requests that conflict with other calendar items and how Outlook handles recurring meeting requests.

Figure 9-13 Automatic accept or decline optie

Weather

You can view the weather in the Outlook calendar. The Outlook options (Figure 9-14) allow you to choose the temperature based on Celsius or Fahrenheit based on your preference. You can also remove it if you prefer not to see the weather when viewing the calendar.

Figure 9-14 Weather options

If you want to add a weather location, you can click the drop-down arrow next to the *City/State* and type a location. Outlook will search and you can select a location.

> **MORE INFO**
>
> Recurring meeting requests will be covered later in this chapter.

SLO 9.3

Printing and Sharing an Outlook Calendar

It's great being able to manage all your appointments and events on your calendar, but you may need a hard copy of your calendar, or you may want to share your calendar with others. Outlook provides a variety of ways to both print and share your Outlook calendar.

Print an Outlook Calendar

There are times when you might be away from your computer, but you would like to have your calendar available. Outlook prints a calendar in several formats. You can print your calendar in the following styles:

- *Daily Style*
- *Weekly Style*
- *Monthly Style*
- *Tri-fold Style*
- *Calendar Details Style*

HOW TO: Print a Calendar

Click the **File** tab to open *Backstage* view.

Click the **Print** button to display the print options on the *Backstage* view (Figure 9-15). Options include:

- *Printer*: Output printer
- *Print options*: Additional options including *Page range*, *Copies*, and *Print range*
- *Settings*: Print style

Select the style of calendar to print in the *Settings* area.

Click the **Print Options** button to open the *Print* dialog box.

Click **Print** to print the calendar.

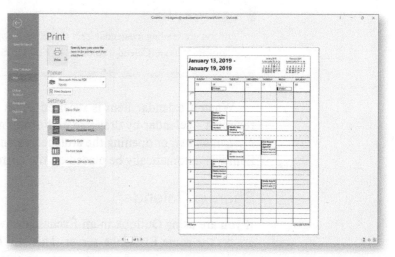

Figure 9-15 *Print* options

Forward an Appointment

When you create and send a meeting request, the meeting is automatically placed on the recipient's Outlook calendar. When a meeting request is not needed or not appropriate, you can send a calendar item to another Outlook user by forwarding the calendar item as an attachment.

▶ **HOW TO:** Forward an Appointment

1. Open an item on your calendar.
2. Click the **Forward** button in the *Actions* group on the *Appointment* (or *Event*) tab (Figure 9-16). A new email opens with the calendar item as an attachment (Figure 9-17).
3. Select the recipients and include any necessary information in the body.
4. Click **Send**.

Figure 9-16 Forward an appointment

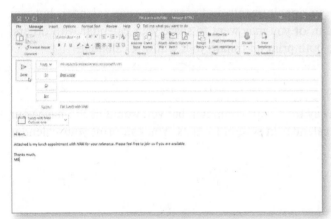

Figure 9-17 Forwarded appointment email

▶ **ANOTHER WAY**

You can also right-click a calendar item and choose **Forward**. A new email opens with the calendar item attached.

▶ **ANOTHER WAY**

Ctrl+F will forward a calendar item when the item is selected on your calendar.

▶ **MORE INFO**

If you are sending a calendar item to recipients who are not using Outlook, it is probably best to forward it as an iCalendar so they can view the details of the calendar item.

When a calendar item is received as an attachment to an email, it can be added to the recipient's calendar by dragging and dropping the attachment on the *Calendar* button in the *Navigation* bar, or opening the attached calendar item and clicking *Save & Close*. The calendar item will automatically be placed on the correct date on the calendar.

Share a Calendar

If you are using Outlook in an Exchange environment, you can share your calendar with others on the same Exchange server. This will enable them to view your calendar and use it to facilitate scheduling of events, appointments, and/or meetings. Later in this chapter you will see how sharing an Outlook calendar works in conjunction with planning a meeting and using *AutoPick* to select a meeting time.

When you share your calendar with other Outlook users on the same Exchange server, an email will be sent informing them that you have shared your calendar with them. You can request that they share their calendar with you also. Those with whom you share your calendar will have *Reviewer* (read-only) permission when viewing your calendar.

HOW TO: Share a Calendar

. Click the **Calendar** button in the *Navigation* bar.

. Click the **Share Calendar** button in the *Manage Calendars* group on the *Home* tab and select your calendar. The *Calendar Properties* dialog box opens (Figure 9-18).

. Click the **Add** button. The *Add Users* dialog box opens.

. Select the person you would like to share your calendar with and click the **Add** button. Click **OK** to close the *Add Users* dialog box (Figure 9-19).

. Select the person you added and click the permission you would like to give for the user (Figure 9-20). Select one of the following options:

- *Can view when I'm busy*: Times are listed as busy when appointments, events, and meetings are scheduled.
- *Can view titles and locations*: Includes titles and locations for appointments, events, and meetings.
- *Can view all details*: Includes titles, locations, and full details of calendar items.
- *Can edit*: Includes titles, locations, full details, and the ability to edit calendar items.
- *Delegate*: Includes full access to calendar including the creation of new calendar items.

. Click **Apply**.

. Click **OK** to close the *Calendar Properties* dialog box. An email message indicating that the calendar is being shared is sent to the recipient.

Figure 9-18 *Calendar Properties*

Figure 9-19 *Add Users dialog box*

Figure 9-20 *Select Permissions*

> **MORE INFO**
>
> By default, Outlook will share your main calendar. To share other calendars, right-click the calendar, choose **Sharing**, and select **Share Calendar**.

When your calendar has been shared with others, they will receive an email message informing them they now have access to your calendar (Figure 9-21). The *Accept* button will share the recipient's

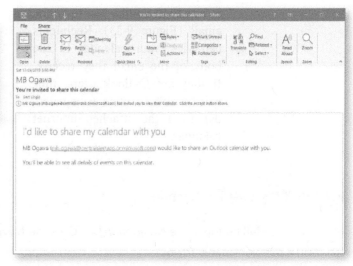

Figure 9-21 Accept a shared calendar

calendar with the sender (as requested). Shared calendars will appear in the *Shared Calendar* area in the *Folder* pane.

Figure 9-22 Sharing a calendar with those outside of your Exchange system

Send a Calendar via Email

What if you want to send your calendar to someone who does not even use Outlook? Outlook allows you to send a calendar via email. You can specify the calendar to send, the date range

to send, the details to be included, and the layout of the email.

This feature creates a type of ***internet calendar*** to be attached to the email and a ***Calendar Snapshot***, which displays the calendar information in the body of the email (Figure 9-23). Recipients can view your calendar in the body of the email they receive. If they are Outlook users, they will be able to open your calendar from the attached internet calendar.

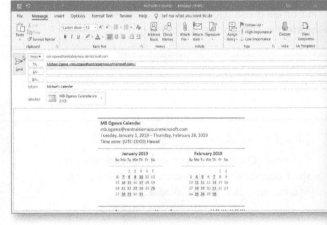

Figure 9-23 Share calendar via email message

▶ **HOW TO: Email a Calendar**

1. Click the **Mail** button in the *Navigation* bar. Click the **New Email** button [*Home* tab, *New* group].
2. Add a recipient in the *To* field.
3. Add a subject to the *Subject* field.

Click the **Attach Item** button [*Message* tab, *Include* group] and select **Calendar**. The *Send a Calendar via Email* dialog box opens (Figure 9-24).

Choose the **Calendar** to send.

Choose a **Date Range**.

Choose a **Detail**.

Click the **Show** button in the *Advanced* area to display other detail options. Options include: *Include details of items marked private* or *Include attachments with calendar item*.

Choose an **Email Layout**. Your options are *Daily schedule* or *List of events*.

Click **OK** to close the *Send a Calendar via Email* dialog box.

Click **Send**.

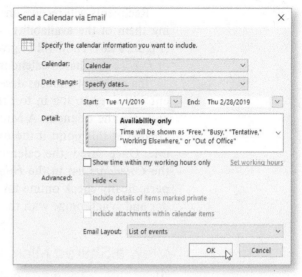

Figure 9-24 *Send a Calendar via Email* dialog box

Share a Microsoft Account Calendar

Suppose you belong to a cycling club and keep a separate Outlook calendar for all the club rides, events, and activities. If you are using a Microsoft account and update it regularly, you don't want to send a new internet calendar through email each time an update occurs. A more effective method would be to share your calendar online.

An Outlook calendar using a *Microsoft account* is automatically synced with the *Microsoft Calendar*. This service allows you to invite others to view or edit your calendar. A shared calendar is synchronized on a regular basis so that those viewing the calendar see current calendar information. To share your Outlook calendar, you must have a Microsoft account.

HOW TO: Share a Calendar

Click the **Calendar** button in the *Navigation* bar.

Click the **Share Calendar** button in the *Share* group on the *Folder* tab and select your *Microsoft Account* calendar. The *Calendar Properties* dialog box opens.

Click the **Add** button. The *Add Users* dialog box opens.

Select the person you would like to share your calendar with and click the **Add** button. Click **OK** to close the *Add Users* dialog box.

Select the person you added and click the permission you would like to give for the user (Figure 9-25). Select one of the following options:

- *Can view*: Includes access to view the calendar.
- *Can edit*: Includes access to view and edit calendar items.

Click **Apply**.

- Click **OK** to close the *Calendar Properties* dialog box. An email message indicating that the calendar is being shared is sent to the recipient.

Figure 9-25 Microsoft account calendar permissions

Recipients will receive an email message informing them of the availability of this online calendar (Figure 9-26). They will be given the option to *Accept* or *Decline* the shared calendar.

If a recipient chooses *Accept and view*, the recipient will need to log in to their Microsoft account and save the calendar. A Microsoft account can be created at this point if the recipient does not have one. Once saved, the calendar will be available in the *Calendars* list in the *Folder* pane. Outlook will periodically check online for updates to this calendar and synchronize with the shared calendar.

Figure 9-26 Microsoft account shared calendar email

View a Shared Microsoft Account Calendar

When others have shared their Outlook calendar with you, these calendars will appear in the *Shared Calendars* area in the *Folder* pane (Figure 9-27). When you save calendars, these calendars will appear in the *Other Calendars* area of the *Folder* pane.

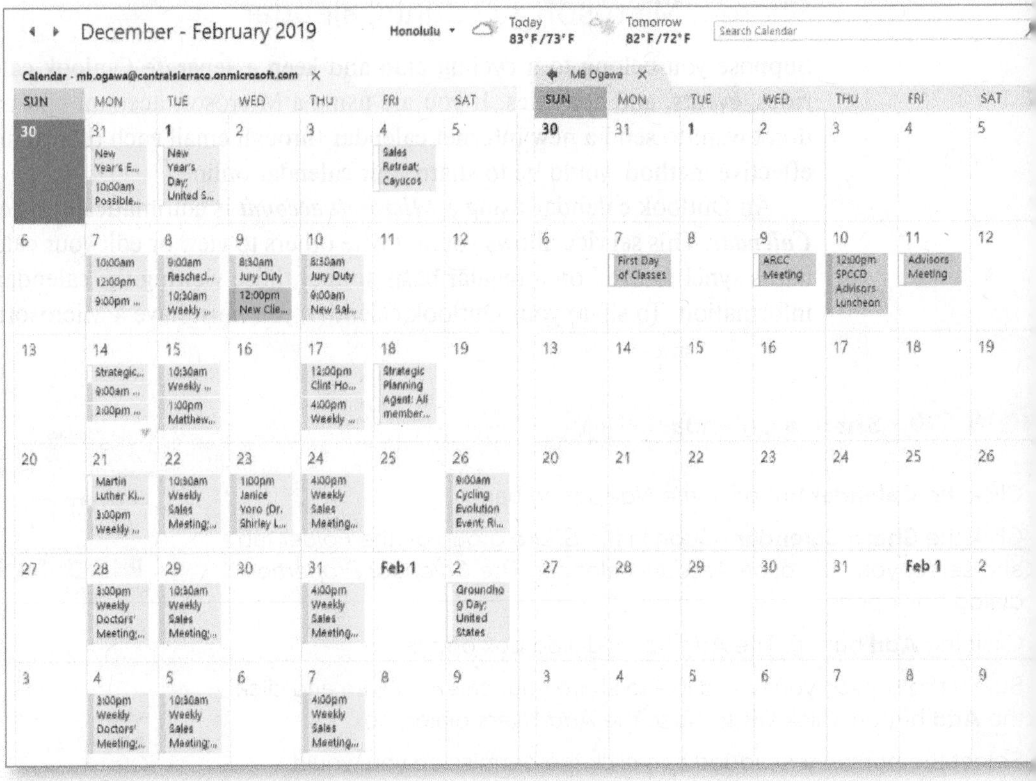

Figure 9-27 Shared calendar

To view a shared calendar or one you have subscribed to, check the box to the left of the calendar name. The calendar displays in the *Content area*. When you deselect the calendar check box, the calendar no longer displays in the *Content area*.

To remove any of the calendars from the *Shared Calendars* list, right-click the calendar and choose **Delete Calendar**. This will remove the calendar from the *Shared Calendars* list, but it will not remove your permission to view this calendar. Only the owner of the calendar can change the permission settings.

PAUSE & PRACTICE: OUTLOOK 9-1

For this Pause & Practice project, you create a new calendar for your BUS 100 class. You create three appointments and share your calendar with your instructor. You also forward your group meeting appointment to your instructor so that he knows when you are meeting for your project.

1. Click the **Calendar** button in the *Navigation* bar.
2. Create a new calendar for your BUS 100 class.
   a. Click the **Folder** tab and then on the **New Calendar** button in the *New* group. The *Create New Folder* dialog box opens.
   b. Type BUS 100 as the **Name** of the new calendar. Confirm that the folder contains **Calendar Items**, and the new calendar will be placed in the **Calendar** folder.
   c. Click **OK**.
3. Select the **BUS 100** calendar.
4. Create an appointment with the following information:
   a. *Subject*: BUS 100 Lecture
      Location: HH132
      Start time: Next week Tuesday at 9:00 AM
      End time: Next week Tuesday at 10:30 AM
5. Create another appointment with the following information:
   a. *Subject*: BUS 100 Recitation
      Location: Online
      Start time: Next week Friday at 4:30 PM
      End time: Next week Friday at 6:00 PM
6. Create a third appointment with the following information:
   a. *Subject*: BUS 100 Group Meeting
      Location: Cafe
      Start time: Next week Wednesday at 10:30 AM
      End time: Next week Wednesday at 11:30 AM
7. Forward the **BUS 100 Group Meeting** appointment to your instructor.
   a. Double-click the **BUS 100 Group Meeting** appointment.
   b. Click the **Forward** button [*Appointment* (or *Event*) tab, *Actions* group]. A new email opens with the calendar item as an attachment.
   c. Select your instructor as the recipient.
   d. Add your email address to the *Cc* field.
   e. Change the subject to Outlook Pause & Practice 9-1.
   f. In the message area, type:

      Dear [instructor name],

      Attached is my Outlook Pause & Practice 9-1.

      Thank you,
      [student name]

   g. Click **Send**.

8. Share your calendar with your instructor. *Note: The permission settings are different for Exchange and Microsoft Account users.*
    a. Click the **Share Calendar** button in the *Manage Calendars* group on the *Home* tab. The *BUS 100 Properties* dialog box opens.
    b. Click the **Add** button.
    c. Select your instructor and click the **Add** button in the *Add Users* dialog box. Click **OK**.
    d. Select **Can view titles and locations** as the *Permissions*. If you are on a Microsoft account, select **Can View**.
    e. Click **Apply**.
    f. Click **OK** to close the *BUS 100 Properties* dialog box (Figure 9-28).

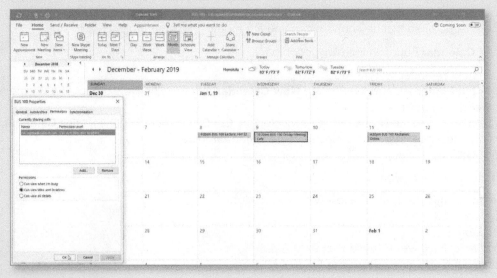

Figure 9-28 Completed Pause & Practice 9-1

Using Advanced Calendar Features

Outlook provides you with many advanced calendar features to help you organize your calendar items and schedule meetings. Calendar items can be assigned to a category. Files and other Outlook items, such as an email or contact, can be attached to a calendar item. Calendar items can be marked as private so others with whom your calendar is shared cannot see the details of an event or appointment. Outlook can also work in conjunction with shared calendars to assist you in scheduling meetings.

Categorize Calendar Items

Just as with emails, contacts, and tasks, *categories* can be used to group calendar items. A category can be assigned to a calendar item by selecting the calendar item, clicking the **Categorize** button in the *Tags* group (Figure 9-29), and selecting the category. Also, with a calendar item open, you can assign it to a category by clicking the **Categorize** button in the *Tags* group on the *Event* or *Appointment* tab.

Figure 9-29 *Categorize butt*

To view calendar items by category, you will need to be in a list view. Click the **View** tab, click the **Change View** button, and select **List**. Next, click the **Categories** button in the *Arrangement* group on the *View* tab. Choose **Calendar** view in the *Change View* menu to return to the default calendar view.

> **MORE INFO**
>
> Creating, editing, and assigning categories were covered in chapter 2.

> **MORE INFO**
>
> Using one of the calendar list views is an easy way to find, edit, and/or delete calendar items.

Attach Items to a Calendar Item

Suppose you have created a vacation event on your calendar. You might want to attach the email confirmation you received from the hotel or airline to the calendar item. You might also want to attach a Word document that contains your itinerary and/or a contact record of a friend with whom you are planning on visiting during your vacation. Well, you can do this in Outlook.

HOW TO: Attach Items to a Calendar Item

Open the calendar item.

Click the **Outlook Item** button [*Insert* tab, *Include* group] (Figure 9-30). The *Insert Item* dialog box opens (Figure 9-31) to select the type of Outlook item to attach.

Figure 9-30 *Attach Outlook Item button*

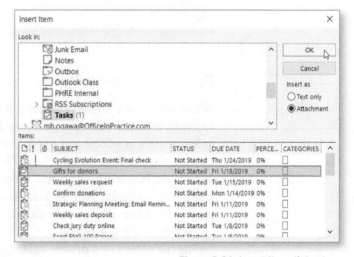

Figure 9-31 *Insert Item dialog box*

Select the Outlook items to attach to the calendar item and click **OK**.

Click the **Attach File** button in the *Include* group to attach a file such as a Word or Excel document. The *Insert File* dialog box opens.

Browse to find the file(s) on your computer, select the file(s), and click **Insert**.

Click **Business Card** and choose **Other Business Cards**. The *Insert Business Card* dialog box opens.

Select the business cards to attach and click **OK**.

8. Click **Save & Close**. Figure 9-32 is a calendar item with attachments.

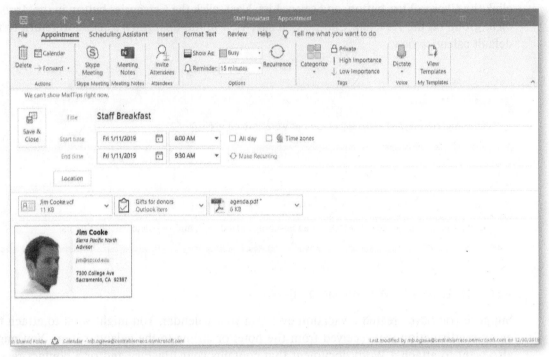

Figure 9-32 Calendar item with attachments

> **MORE INFO**
>
> When you forward a calendar item with attachments, those attachments will be included with the calendar item.

Private Calendar Items

When you have a shared calendar, it is good practice to mark selected calendar items as *Private*. When a calendar item is selected or open, the *Private* button is available in the *Tags* group (Figure 9-33). When a calendar item is marked as private, those with whom you share your calendar will be able to see the calendar item but not the details of the calendar item.

Figure 9-33 Mark a calendar item as *Priva*

When printing a calendar, you have the option of hiding the details of a private calendar item.

▶**HOW TO:** Print a Calendar without Private Appointments

1. Click the **File** tab to open the *Backstage* view.
2. Click the **Print** button.
3. Click the **Print Options** button. The *Print* dialog box opens.

4. Check the **Hide details of private appointments** check box in the *Print Range* area (Figure 9-34).

5. Click **Print**.

Figure 9-34 Hide private appointments when printing

Recurring Meetings

If you have a weekly brainstorming meeting, create a meeting request that recurs on a scheduled interval. Creating a recurring meeting request is similar to creating a recurring appointment or event. This recurring meeting appears on your calendar for each date and time it recurs.

> **MORE INFO**
>
> Creating recurring appointments and events were covered in chapter 4.
> Creating meeting requests was covered in chapter 4.

Figure 9-35 *Recurrence* button

HOW TO: Create a Recurring Appointment

1. Create a new appointment.

2. Enter **Subject**, **Location**, **Start time**, and **End time**.

3. Click **Invite Attendees** in the *Attendees* group.

4. Click the **To** button, select attendees, and click **OK**.

5. Click the **Recurrence** button in the *Options* group (Figure 9-35). The *Appointment Recurrence* dialog box opens (Figure 9-36). Confirm the appointment start and end times and duration.

6. Set a **Recurrence pattern**. This determines the frequency of the recurring meeting.

7. Set the **Range of recurrence**. This determines the date range of the recurring meeting.

8. Click **OK** to close the *Appointment Recurrence* dialog box.

9. Click **Save & Close**.

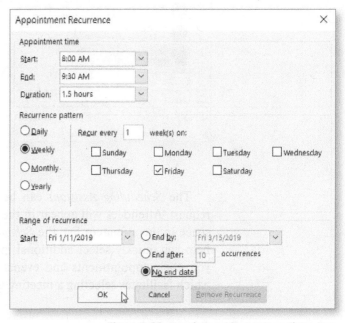

Figure 9-36 *Appointment Recurrence* dialog box

When a recipient accepts a meeting request, the recurring meeting request will be saved on his or her calendar.

> **ANOTHER WAY**
>
> **Ctrl+G** opens the *Appointment Recurrence* dialog box.

Scheduling Assistant

When creating an appointment or meeting request, you will sometimes have to check you[r] calendar for other calendar items on that date. Rather than having to switch between Outloo[k] windows, use the *Scheduling Assistant* to show existing appointments, events, or meetings cu[rrently] on your calendar.

To use the *Scheduling Assistant*, click the **Scheduling Assistant** button in the *Show* grou[p.] The *Scheduling Assistant* displays your calendar items in timeline format in the body section o[f] the new appointment (Figure 9-37). You can adjust the date and/or time of the appointmen[t] based on your other calendar items.

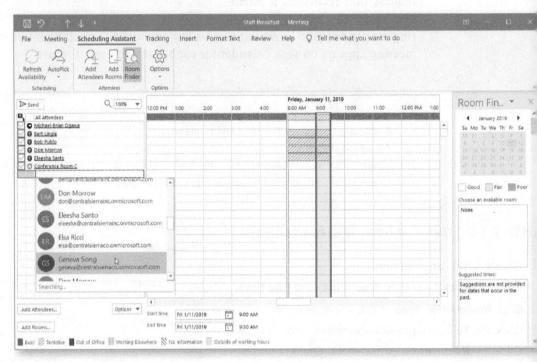

Figure 9-37 *Scheduling Assista[nt]*

The *Scheduling Assistant* can be particularly helpful when you are creating a meetin[g] request. Attendees will appear in the list at the left of the body. If you click on the first ope[n] space in the attendees list, the *Scheduling Assistant* will display a list of possible attendees t[o] help you quickly select additional invitees. If the attendees have shared their calendar wit[h] you, their appointments and events display in timeline format below your calendar item[s,] which facilitates selecting a meeting date and time.

> ### MORE INFO
>
> The *Scheduling Assistant* is available when using Outlook in both an Exchange and stand-alone environment. But displaying others' calendars is available only when using Outlook on an Exchange server.

AutoPick a Meeting Time

Occasionally, a scheduled meeting needs to be changed. If you have already sent out a mee[t-] ing request and others have responded to it, you can make changes to the meeting request an[d] send an update to attendees.

Outlook has an *AutoPick* feature that can automatically pick a new time for the meeting based upon the shared calendars of others. To use this feature, you must be working on an Exchange server and the attendees must also be on the same Exchange server. Clicking the **AutoPick** option in the *Scheduling Assistant* (Figure 9-38) will pick the next time available for those to whom the meeting request was sent.

Figure 9-38 *AutoPick* options

HOW TO: AutoPick a Meeting Time

Open the meeting to be rescheduled from your calendar.

Click the **Scheduling Assistant** button in the *Show* group.

- The list of attendees appears on the left.
- If attendees shared their calendar with you, they will appear in timeline view in the body of the meeting request.

Click the **Options** button and select one of the *AutoPick* options (Figure 9-39):

- *All People and Resources*
- *All People and One Resource*
- *Required People*
- *Required People and One Resource*
- *Earlier Time*

Figure 9-39 *AutoPick* based on *Required People's* schedules

Click the **Appointment** button to return to the meeting request.

Click **Send Update**. An update will be sent to all the recipients of the original meeting request.

For this Pause & Practice project, you decide to improve the organization of your BUS 100 calendar by using categories. You also attach your homework file to the *BUS 100 Recitation* appointment. Since your lecture occurs weekly, you set the calendar item to recur weekly till the end of the semester (10 weeks).

File Needed: **sales.xlsx**

1. Click the **Calendar** button in the *Navigation* bar.

2. Select the **BUS 100** calendar.

3. Create the following categories:

    Name: Class Session, *Color*: **Red**
    Name: Group Session, *Color*: **Blue**

4. Apply categories to the three appointments you created in *Pause & Practice 9-1*.
    a. Select the **BUS 100 Lecture** appointment.
    b. Click the **Categorize** button [*Appointment* tab, *Tags* group].
    c. Click **Class Session**.
    d. Select the **BUS 100 Recitation** appointment.
    e. Click the **Categorize** button [*Appointment* tab, *Tags* group].
    f. Click **Class Session**.
    g. Select the **BUS 100 Group Meeting** appointment.
    h. Click the **Categorize** button [*Appointment* tab, *Tags* group].
    i. Click **Group Session**.

5. Attach the file **sales.xlsx** to the *BUS 100 Recitation* appointment.
    a. Open the **BUS 100 Recitation** appointment.
    b. Click the **Attach File** button [*Insert* tab, *Include* group]. The *Insert File* dialog box opens.
    c. Browse to find the file **sales.xlsx** on your computer, select the file(s), and click **Insert**.
    d. Click **Save & Close**.

6. Mark the *BUS 100 Recitation* appointment as *Private*.
    a. Open the **BUS 100 Recitation** appointment.
    b. Click the **Private** button [*Appointment* or *Event* tab, *Tags* group].
    c. Click **Save & Close**.

7. Forward the *BUS 100 Recitation* appointment to your instructor.
    a. Double-click the **BUS 100 Recitation** appointment.
    b. Click the **Forward** button [*Appointment* (or *Event*) tab, *Actions* group]. A new email opens with the calendar item as an attachment.
    c. Select your instructor as the recipient.
    d. Add your email address in the *Cc* field.
    e. Change the subject to Outlook Pause & Practice 9-2.
    f. In the message area, type:

        Dear [instructor name],

        Attached is my Outlook Pause & Practice 9-2.

        Thank you,
        [student name]

    g. Click **Send**.

8. Set the *BUS 100 Lecture* appointment to recur weekly for the next 10 weeks.
   a. Open the **BUS 100 Lecture** appointment.
   b. Click the **Recurrence** button [*Appointment* or *Event* tab, *Options* group]. The *Appointment Recurrence* dialog box opens.
   c. Select **Weekly, Recur every 1 week**, on **Tuesday** in the *Recurrence pattern* section.
   d. Select **End after 10 occurrences** in the *Recurrence pattern* section.
   e. Click **OK** to close the *Appointment Recurrence* dialog box.
   f. Click **Save & Close** (Figure 9-40).

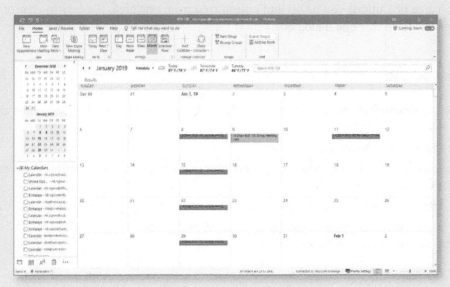

Figure 9-40 Completed Pause & Practice 9-2

Sharing Your Outlook with Others

Earlier in this text we discussed sharing your Outlook calendar with others. Outlook also allows you to share other areas of Outlook with coworkers who are on the same Exchange server. The *Delegate* feature gives you control over who has access to your Outlook information and how much access they have. This feature will work with those who are on the same Exchange server.

Delegates and Permissions

A *delegate* is someone to whom you have given access to certain folders of your Outlook. This feature is commonly used with administrative assistants and members of a work team so they have access to the emails, calendars, contacts, tasks, notes, and/or journals of others.

The delegate feature gives you more flexibility than simply sharing a calendar. Not only can you specify what areas of Outlook to share, but also the *permissions* of the delegate. The permission is the level of access granted to a delegate. For example, when sharing a calendar with another Outlook user, the default permission they have is a *Reviewer*, which means they can see your calendar but cannot create, delete, or edit an appointment.

The permission settings for a delegate can be customized for each area of Outlook. Four different permissions can be granted.

- *None*: Delegate does not have access to this area of Outlook.
- *Reviewer*: Can read items, but does not have access to create, delete, or edit items.
- *Author*: Can read and create items, but does not have access to delete or edit items.
- *Editor*: Can read, create, delete, or edit items.

Assign a Delegate

The advantage of using the *Delegate* feature rather than the sharing feature is that the role [f]
each area of Outlook can be set and customized from one area. It's easy to view or change p[
missions from this one dialog box.

▶ **HOW TO:** Assign a Delegate

1. Click the **File** tab, click the **Account Settings** button, and choose **Delegate Access**. The *Delegates* dialog box opens (Figure 9-41).
2. Click the **Add** button. The *Add Users* dialog box opens.
3. Select the name of the delegate to be added and click **Add**. You can select multiple delegates and customize the permission level for each delegate.
4. Click **OK** to close the *Add Users* dialog box. The *Delegate Permissions* dialog box opens (Figure 9-42).
   - You can set the permission level for this delegate for each area of Outlook.
   - Different roles can be set for different areas of Outlook.

Figure 9-41 Add delegate

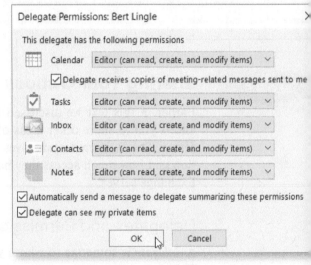

Figure 9-42 *Delegate Permissio[*

5. Check the **Automatically send a message to delegate summarizing these permissions** check box. This will automatically generate and send an email message to the delegate informing him or her of the permissions granted.
6. Check the **Delegate can see my private items** box if you want the delegate to see your private items.
7. Click **OK** to close the *Delegate Permissions* dialog box.
8. Click **OK** to close the *Delegates* dialog box.
9. Click the **Back** button to return to Outlook.

Open Another Outlook User's Folders

When an Outlook user on your Exchange server assigns you as a delegate, you will most likely receive an email summarizing your permission levels for the different areas of Outlook.

Once you have been granted permission, you can open that user's folders in your Outlook. For example, you can open the user's calendar and view it in your Outlook.

HOW TO: Open Outlook Folders as a Delegate

Click the **Calendar** button in the *Navigation* bar.

Click the **Add Calendar** button [*Home* tab, *Manage Calendars* group] and choose **Open a Shared Calendar**. The *Open a Shared Calendar* dialog box opens (Figure 9-43).

Click the **Name** button to open the *Select Name* dialog box.

Select the name of the contact, and click **OK**. The calendar appears in the *Shared Calendars* list in the *Folder* pane.

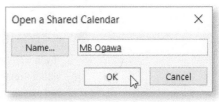

Figure 9-43 *Open a Shared Calendar* dialog box

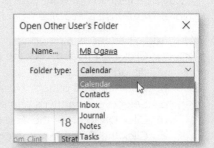

Figure 9-44 Select a shared folder from the *Open Other User's Folder* dialog box

Create Outlook Items as a Delegate

If you are assigned the role of *Author* or *Editor*, you can create emails, calendar items, contac[...] tasks, notes, or journal items for those to whom you are a delegate.

For example, to create a task for another user, you must first open his or her *Tasks* folder[...] you can view it in your Outlook.

When his or her *Tasks* folder is selected from the *Shared Tasks* area in the *Folder* pane[...] displays in the *Content area*. You can create a task in his or her *Tasks* folder in the same w[...] you would create a task in your folder. The task that you create as a delegate will appear in [...] or her Outlook task list.

Remove a Delegate

When working with delegates, it is important to remove access when their access is no longer needed. In the *Delegates* dialog box, you can change the permission settings for a delegate by clicking the **Permissions** button and making the desired changes.

To delete a delegate, select the delegate to be removed and click the **Remove** button (Figure 9-45). The delegate will be removed from the delegate list and will no longer have access to your Outlook.

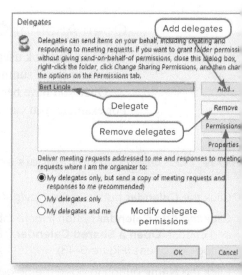

> ### ANOTHER WAY
>
> If you want to restrict access of a delegate without removing him or her as a delegate, you can change the permission settings to *None* in any of the areas you want to restrict.

Figure 9-45 Edit or remove delegates from t[...]
Delegates dialog b[...]

PAUSE & PRACTICE: OUTLOOK 9-3

For this Pause & Practice project, you will be out of town with minimal internet access. Therefore, you decide to assign one of your partners to be a delegate while you are away. Since you are concerned about the calendar, you give your partner *Author* permissions to add group meeting dates while you are away. You also do not want your partner to accidentally delete any of your current calendar items. *Note: This Pause & Practice works only for Exchange users*.

1. Add a partner as a delegate.
   a. Click the **File** tab, click the **Account Settings** button, and choose **Delegate Access**. The *Delegates* dialog box opens.
   b. Click the **Add** button. The *Add Users* dialog box opens.
   c. Select your partner's name and click **Add**.
   d. Click **OK** to close the *Add Users* dialog box. The *Delegate Permissions* dialog box opens.
   e. Click the **Calendar** drop-down arrow and select **Author**.
   f. Click the **Tasks, Inbox, Contacts**, and **Notes** drop-down menu and change the permissions to **None**.

g. Check the **Automatically send a message to delegate summarizing these permissions** check box.

h. Uncheck the **Delegate can see my private items** box.

i. Click **OK** to close the *Delegate Permissions* dialog box.

j. Click **OK** to close the *Delegates* dialog box.

k. Click the **File** tab to return to Outlook.

2. Open your partner's calendar.

   a. Click the **Calendar** button in the *Navigation* bar.

   b. Click the **Open Calendar** button [*Home* tab, *Manage Calendars* group] and choose **Open a Shared Calendar**. The *Open a Shared Calendar* dialog box opens.

   c. Click the **Name** button to open the *Select Name* dialog box.

   d. Select your partner's name and click **OK**. The calendar appears in the *Shared Calendars* list in the *Folder* pane.

3. Create a new appointment for a group meeting using the following information.

   Subject: BUS 100 Group Meeting

   Location: Cafe

   Start time: One week after your first meeting on Wednesday at 10:30 AM

   End time: One week after your first meeting on Wednesday at 11:30 AM

   Categorize the appointment as a **Group Session**.

4. Remove your partner as a delegate.

   a. Click the **File** tab, click the **Account Settings** button, and choose **Delegate Access**. The *Delegates* dialog box opens.

   b. Select your partner and click **Remove**.

   c. Click **OK** to close the *Delegates* dialog box.

5. Forward the *Delegate* designation message to your instructor.

   a. Click the **Mail** button in the *Navigation* bar.

   b. Select the *Delegate* message. It should have the subject **You have been designated as a delegate for [name]**.

   c. Click the **Forward** button.

   d. Select your instructor as the recipient.

   e. Add your email address in the *Cc* field.

   f. Change the subject to Outlook Pause & Practice 9-3.

   g. In the message area, type:

   Dear [instructor name],

   Listed below is my Outlook Pause & Practice Project 9-3.

   Thank you,
   [student name]

   h. Click **Send** (Figure 9-46).

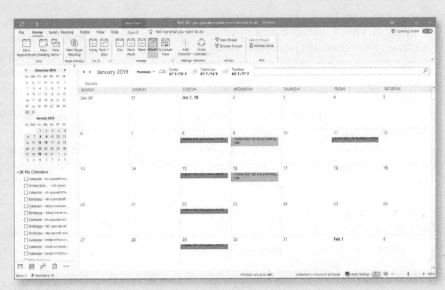

Figure 9-46 Completed Pause & Practice 9-3

9.1 Create and use multiple Outlook calendars (p. O9-325).

- You can create multiple calendars in Outlook.
- You can view multiple calendars simultaneously.
- Calendars can be viewed in *side-by-side* or *overlay mode*.
- Specifying your *Work time* modifies Outlook's default calendar to fit your work schedule.
- *Free/Busy Options* allow meeting organizers to see when you are free or busy.
- Outlook uses the *iCalendar* format when sending meeting requests to people outside your organization.

9.2 Customize your Outlook calendar using calendar options (p. O9-327).

- The *Outlook Options* dialog box includes calendar-specific options.
- You can specify your work week if it is not Monday–Friday.
- On Exchange servers, you can control whether or not recipients of meeting requests can propose new times.
- Outlook can automatically add *holidays* based on region to your calendar.
- Display options can be modified to change calendar color, include *week numbers*, and view by *Schedule view*.
- You can select multiple time zones for your calendar which is useful when you work with others from different regions.
- The *Scheduling Assistant* options allow you to view details in *ScreenTips* and a scheduling grid.
- Automatic *Accept* or *Decline* can be used in conjunction with an Exchange server to automatically respond to meeting requests.
- Select weather options to view weather information for a specific area.

9.3 Incorporate printing and sharing with your Outlook calendar (p. O9-330).

- Print calendars in *Daily, Weekly, Monthly, Tri-fold*, or *Calendar Details* style.
- You can forward an appointment if you want to let the recipient know about a meeting without it automatically being added to his/her calendar.
- When using an Exchange server, you can share your calendar with other Exchange users. Sharing options include *Can view when I'm busy, Can view titles and locations, Can view all details, Can edit*, and *Delegate*.
- You can share your calendar with others via email as an *internet calendar* Outlook attachment.
- A *Calendar Snapshot* is included within the body of an email message when sharing an *internet calendar*.
- If you are using a *Microsoft account*, your calendar is synced with *Microsoft Calendar*.
- You can share your *Microsoft account* calendar and allow others to view or make edits.

9.4 Utilize advanced calendar features (p. O9-337).

- Calendar items can include *categories*.
- Calendar items can include file attachments and Outlook items.
- Marking a calendar item as *Private* sets permissions to not allow others who share your calendar to see those items.
- You have the option to print calendars without private items.
- Recurrence can be used when calendar items occur on a regular basis.
- The *Scheduling Assistant* allows you to see others' schedules and helps you to select a meeting time.
- The *AutoPick* option in the *Scheduling Assistant* automatically picks a new time for a meeting based on other attendants' calendars.

9.5 Collaborate with other Outlook users' delegates (p. O9-344).

- The *Delegate* feature allows others to have control and access over specific parts of your Outlook information when using an Exchange server.
- The *Delegate* feature includes the following permission levels:
  - *None*: Delegate does not have access to this area of Outlook.
  - *Reviewer*: Can read items, but does not have access to create, delete, or edit items

- *Author*: Can read and create items, but does not have access to delete or edit items.
- *Editor*: Can read, create, delete, or edit items.

- You can change **permissions** for *Delegates* based on each aspect of Outlook.
- You can add, remove, or modify permissions for **delegates** at any time.

Check for Understanding

The SIMbook for this text (within your SIMnet account) provides the following resources for concept review:

- Multiple-choice questions
- Short answer questions
- Matching exercises

Guided Project 9-1

For this project, you work as an insurance agent for Central Sierra Insurance (CSI). Your Outlook calendar became too cluttered, as you initially used your default Outlook calendar to host both your home and work calendars. You decide to create a new calendar specifically for work. You add a few appointments and share your new calendar with a colleague.
[Student Learning Outcomes 9.1, 9.3, 9.4]

Skills Covered in This Project

- Create a new calendar.
- Mark a calendar item as *Private*.
- Forward a calendar item.
- Share a calendar.

1. Click the **Calendar** button in the *Navigation* bar.
   a. Click the **Folder** tab and then click the **New Calendar** button in the *New* group. The *Create New Folder* dialog box opens.
   b. Type Central Sierra as the **Name** of the new calendar. Confirm that the folder contains **Calendar Items**, and the new calendar will be placed in the **Calendar** folder.
   c. Click **OK**.

2. Select the *Central Sierra* calendar.

3. Create an appointment with the following information:

   Subject: Staff Breakfast
   Location: Conference Room A
   Start time: Next week Monday at 8:00 AM
   End time: Next week Monday at 9:30 AM

4. Create another appointment with the following information:

   Subject: New Client: Jim Santiago
   Location: My office
   Start time: Next week Wednesday at 2:30 PM
   End time: Next week Wednesday at 3:30 PM

5. Mark the **New Client: Jim Santiago** appointment as *Private*.
   a. Open the **New Client: Jim Santiago** appointment.
   b. Click the **Private** button [*Appointment* or *Event* tab, *Tags* group].
   c. Click **Save & Close**.

6. Create a third appointment with the following information:

   Subject: Agents Meeting
   Location: Beach Cafe
   Start time: Next week Thursday at 12:00 PM
   End time: Next week Tuesday at 1:30 PM

7. Forward the **New Client: Jim Santiago** appointment to your instructor.
   a. Double-click the **New Client: Jim Santiago** appointment.
   b. Click the **Forward** button [*Appointment* (or *Event*) tab, *Actions* group]. A new email opens with the calendar item as an attachment.
   c. Select your instructor as the recipient.
   d. Add your email address in the *Cc* field.
   e. Change the subject to Outlook Guided Project 9-1.
   f. In the message area, type:

   Dear [instructor name],

   Attached is my Outlook Guided Project 9-1.

   Thank you,
   [student name]

   g. Click **Send**.

8. Share your calendar with your instructor. *Note: The permission settings are different for Exchange and Microsoft Account users.*
   a. Click the **Share Calendar** button in the *Manage Calendars* group on the *Home* tab. The *Central Sierra Properties* dialog box opens.
   b. Click the **Add** button.
   c. Select your instructor and click the **Add** button in the *Add Users* dialog box. Click **OK**.
   d. Select **Can view titles and locations** as the *Permissions*. If you are on a Microsoft account, select **Can View**.
   e. Click **Apply**.
   f. Click **OK** to close the *Central Sierra Properties* dialog box (Figure 9-47).

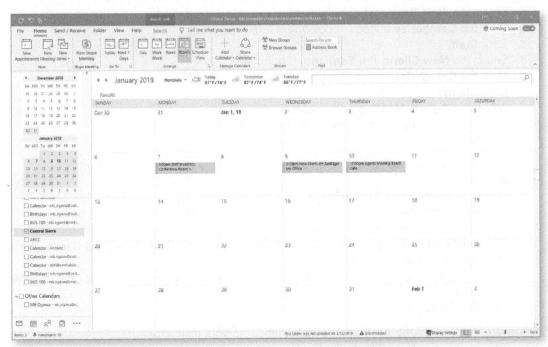

Figure 9-47 Completed Guided Project 9-1

Guided Project 9-2

For this project, you work as an insurance agent for CSI. You notice that your new calendar is a little unorganized, as you created appointments without categorizing them. Therefore, you decide to categorize appointments so each one is easy to recognize at glance. You also decide to attach a preparation file and business card for your new client meeting. Your supervisor informed you that the agent's meeting will occur every other week.

[Student Learning Outcomes 9.3, 9.4]

File Needed: ***insurance.xlsx***

Skills Covered in This Project

- Create categories.
- Apply categories to calendar items.
- Attach a file to a calendar item.
- Attach an Outlook item to a calendar item.
- Forward a calendar item.
- Set recurrence for a calendar item.

---

1. Click the **Calendar** button in the *Navigation* bar.

2. Select the **Central Sierra** calendar.

3. Create the following Categories [*Appointment* tab, *Tags* group, *Categorize* button]:

    Name: Staff, *Color*: **Red**
    Name: Clients, *Color*: **Yellow**

4. Apply categories to the three appointments you created in *Guided Project 9-1*.
    a. Select the **Staff Breakfast** appointment.
    b. Click the **Categorize** button [*Appointment* tab, *Tags* group].
    c. Click **Staff**.
    d. Select the **New Client: Jim Santiago** appointment.
    e. Click the **Categorize** button [*Appointment* tab, *Tags* group].
    f. Click **Clients**.
    g. Select the **Agents Meeting** appointment.
    h. Click the **Categorize** button [*Appointment* tab, *Tags* group].
    i. Click **Staff**.

5. Attach the ***insurance.xlsx*** file and your business card to the *New Client: Jim Santiago* appointment.
    a. Open the **New Client: Jim Santiago** appointment.
    b. Click the **Attach File** button [*Insert* tab, *Include* group]. The *Insert File* dialog box opens.
    c. Browse to find the file ***insurance.xlsx*** on your computer, select the file(s), and click **Insert**.
    d. Click **Business Card** [*Insert* tab, *Include* group], and choose **Other Business Cards**. The *Insert Business Card* dialog box opens.
    e. Select your business card and click **OK** (it is okay if your business card is the one you created in a previous project).
    f. Click **Save & Close**.

6. Forward the *New Client: Jim Santiago* appointment to your instructor.
    a. Double-click the **New Client: Jim Santiago** appointment.
    b. Click the **Forward** button [*Appointment* (or *Event*) tab, *Actions* group]. A new email opens with the calendar item as an attachment.
    c. Select your instructor as the recipient.
    d. Add your email address in the *Cc* field.
    e. Change the subject to Outlook Guided Project 9-2.

f. In the message area, type:

  Dear [instructor name],

  Attached is my Outlook Guided Project 9-2.

  Thank you,
  [student name]

  g. Click **Send**.

7. Set the *Agents Meeting* appointment to recur every other week without an end date.
    a. Open the **Agents Meeting** appointment.
    b. Click the **Recurrence** button [*Appointment* or *Event* tab, *Options* group]. The *Appointment Recurrence* dialog box opens.
    c. Select **Weekly**, **Recur every 2 weeks**, on **Thursday** in the *Recurrence pattern* section.
    d. Select **No end date** in the *Range of recurrence* section.
    e. Click **OK** to close the *Appointment Recurrence* dialog box.
    f. Click **Save & Close** (Figure 9-48).

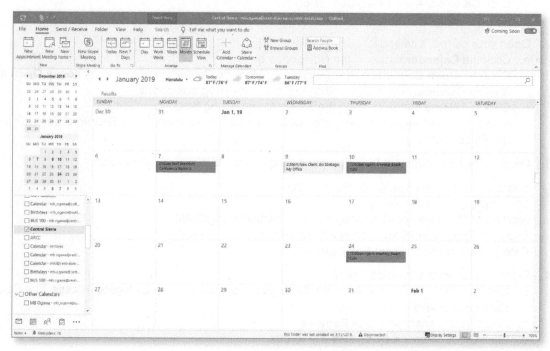

Figure 9-48 Completed Guided Project 9-2

Guided Project 9-3

For this project, you work as an insurance agent for CSI and plan to vacation in two weeks. Even though you are on vacation, work does not stop. You decide to assign your assistant as a delegate. You decide that your assistant needs access to your Calendar and Tasks with *Author* permission. While you are away, your assistant sets up a follow-up meeting with Jim. *Note: This Guided Project works only for Exchange users.*

[Student Learning Outcome 9.5]

Skills Covered in This Project
- Add a delegate.
- Set permissions for a delegate.
- Open a calendar as a delegate.
- Create a calendar item as a delegate.
- Remove a delegate.

1. Add a partner as a delegate.
   a. Click the **File** tab, click the **Account Settings** button, and choose **Delegate Access**. The *Delegates* dialog box opens.
   b. Click the **Add** button. The *Add Users* dialog box opens.
   c. Select the name of the delegate (your partner) to be added and click **Add**.
   d. Click **OK** to close the *Add Users* dialog box. The *Delegate Permissions* dialog box opens.
   e. Click the **Calendar and Tasks** drop-down arrow and select **Author**.
   f. Click the **Inbox, Contacts, and Notes** drop-down arrow and change the permissions to **None**.
   g. Check the **Automatically send a message to delegate summarizing these permissions** check box.
   h. Uncheck the **Delegate can see my private items** box.
   i. Click **OK** to close the *Delegate Permissions* dialog box.
   j. Click **OK** to close the *Delegates* dialog box.
   k. Click the **Back** button to return to Outlook.

2. Open your partner's calendar.
   a. Click the **Calendar** button in the *Navigation* bar.
   b. Click the **Open Calendar** button [*Home* tab, *Manage Calendars* group] and choose **Open a Shared Calendar**. The *Open a Shared Calendar* dialog box opens.
   c. Click the **Name** button to open the *Select Name* dialog box.
   d. Select your partner's name, and click **OK**. The calendar appears in the *Shared Calendars* list in the *Folder* pane.

3. Create a new appointment for a group meeting using the following information.

   Subject: Jim: Follow-up on life insurance policy
   Location: Conference Room A
   Start time: Three weeks from today on Wednesday at 10:30 AM
   End time: Three weeks from today on Wednesday at 11:30 AM
   Categorize the appointment as **Clients**.

4. Remove your partner as a delegate.
   a. Click the **File** tab, click the **Account Settings** button, and choose **Delegate Access**. The *Delegates* dialog box opens.
   b. Select your partner and click **Remove**.
   c. Click **OK** to close the *Delegates* dialog box.

5. Forward the *Delegate* designation message to your instructor.
   a. Click the **Mail** button in the *Navigation* bar.
   b. Select the *Delegate* message. It should have the subject You have been designated as a delegate for [name].
   c. Click the **Forward** button.
   d. Select your instructor as the recipient.
   e. Add your email address in the *Cc* field.
   f. Change the subject to Outlook Guided Project 9-3.
   g. In the message area, type:

   Dear [instructor name],

   Listed below is my Outlook Guided Project 9-3.

   Thank you,
   [student name]

h. Click **Send** (Figure 9-49).

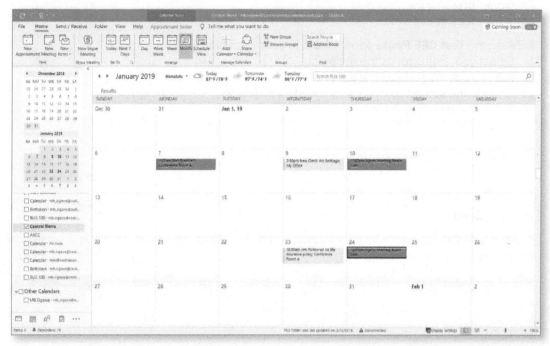

Independent Project 9-4

For this project, you are a coordinator for the American River Cycling Club (ARCC). Since you are new to the position, you decide to use Outlook to help you organize the events for ARCC. So, you create a new calendar in Outlook and enter calendar items for the event. You also share the calendar with a co-coordinator, so you can both view the calendar.

[Student Learning Outcomes 9.1, 9.3, 9.4]

Skills Covered in This Project

- Create a new calendar.
- Mark a calendar item as *Private*.
- Forward a calendar item.
- Share a calendar.

---

1. Create a new calendar named ARCC.

2. Create an appointment with the following information:

   Subject: ARCC Membership Meeting
   Location: American River Coffee House
   Start time: Next week Wednesday at 7:00 AM
   End time: Next week Wednesday at 8:00 AM

3. Create another appointment with the following information:

   Subject: Test CEE Route
   Location: ARC Stadium
   Start time: Next week Thursday at 5:00 PM

End time: Next week Thursday at 7:00 PM
Message: Executive members only
Mark the meeting as *Private*.

4. Forward the **Test CEE Route** appointment to your instructor.
   a. Select your instructor as the recipient.
   b. Add your email address in the *Cc* field.
   c. Change the subject to Outlook Independent Project 9-4.
   d. In the message area, type:

      Dear [instructor name],

      Attached is my Outlook Independent Project 9-4.

      Thank you,
      [student name]

   e. Click **Send**.

5. Share the **ARCC** calendar with your instructor with permission to view all details in the calendar and not ability to edit (Figure 9-50).

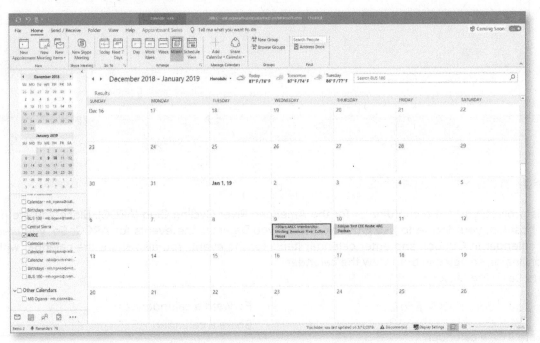

Figure 9-50 Completed Independent Project 9-4

Independent Project 9-5

For this project, you are a coordinator for ARCC. Since you created the calendar, you notice it is difficult to differentiate items listed in the calendar. You decide to assign categories to help identify each item in the calendar. You also attach a file to the appointment.
[Student Learning Outcomes 9.3, 9.4]

File Needed: *ceeroute.pdf*

Skills Covered in This Project

- Create categories.
- Apply categories to calendar items.
- Attach a file to a calendar item.
- Forward a calendar item.
- Set recurrence for a calendar item.

1. Click the **Calendar** button in the *Navigation* bar.

2. Select the **ARCC** calendar.

3. Create the following categories:

   Name: Confidential, *Color*: **Red**
   Name: Public, *Color*: **Green**

4. Apply categories to the two appointments you created in *Independent Project 9-4*.
   a. Categorize **ARCC Membership Meeting** as **Public**.
   b. Categorize **Test CEE Route** as **Confidential**.

5. Attach the file **ceeroute.pdf** to the **Test CEE Route** appointment.

6. Forward the **Test CEE Route** appointment to your instructor.
   a. Select your instructor as the recipient.
   b. Add your email address in the *Cc* field.
   c. Change the subject to Outlook Independent Project 9-5.
   d. In the message area, type:

      Dear [instructor name],

      Attached is my Outlook Independent Project 9-5.

      Thank you,
      [student name]

   e. Click **Send**.

7. Set the **ARCC Membership Meeting** appointment to recur monthly on the second Wednesday of each month without an end date (Figure 9-51).

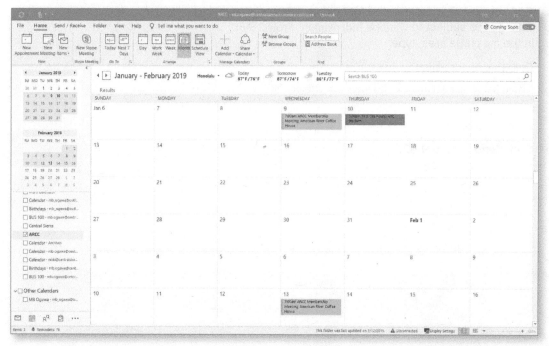

Figure 9-51 Completed Independent Project 9-5

Independent Project 9-6

For this project, you are a coordinator for ARCC. Your work load has increased so you enlisted the help of one of your co-coordinators to serve as a delegate for you until your work slows down. You decide to assign your co-coordinator *Author* privilege for your Tasks, Calendar, and Notes. *Note: This Independent Project works only for Exchange users.*
[Student Learning Outcome 9.5]

Skills Covered in This Project

- Add a delegate.
- Set permissions for a delegate.
- Open a calendar as a delegate.
- Create a calendar item as a delegate.
- Remove a delegate.

1. Add a partner as a delegate with the following permissions:

   Author: Tasks, Calendar, and Notes
   None: Inbox and Contacts
   a. Check the **Automatically send a message to delegate summarizing these permissions** check box.
   b. Uncheck the **Delegate can see my private items** box.

2. Open your partner's calendar and create a new appointment for a coordinators meeting using the following information:

   Subject: CEE Coordinators Meeting
   Location: American River Coffee Bar
   Start time: Two weeks from today on Tuesday at 7:00 AM
   End time: Two weeks from today on Tuesday at 8:00 AM
   Categorize the appointment as **Public**.

3. Remove your partner as a delegate.

4. Forward the *Delegate* designation message to your instructor.
   a. Select your instructor as the recipient.
   b. Add your email address in the *Cc* field.
   c. Change the subject to Outlook Independent Project 9-6.
   d. In the message area, type:

      Dear [instructor name],

      Listed below is my Outlook Independent Project 9-6.

      Thank you,
      [student name]

   e. Click **Send** (Figure 9-52).

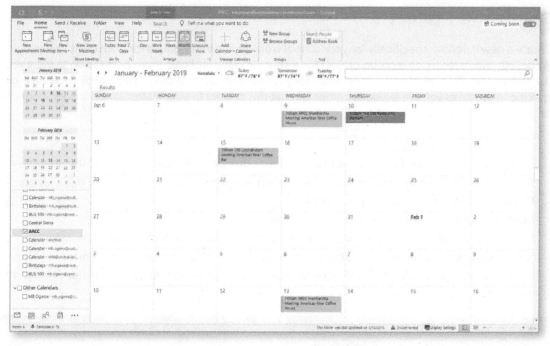

Figure 9-52 Completed Independent Project 9-6

Challenge Project 9-7

Create a new calendar in Outlook for a club or association that you are involved with. Be sure to include activities for the organization and categorize the items. To submit the assignment, you will print the calendar and share it with your instructor.

[Student Learning Outcomes 9.1, 9.2, 9.3, 9.4]

- Create a new calendar.
- Include at least 10 appointments or events for an organization you are involved in.
- Attach items to each appointment or event when necessary.
- Create at least three categories and apply them appropriately to each calendar item.
- The calendar should include activities for two months.
- Share your calendar with your instructor via Outlook.com or an Exchange server.
- Print a physical copy of the calendar in *Weekly Style* and submit it.

Challenge Project 9-8

Create a new calendar specifically for your school work. Include categories for each class that you are taking. Work with two partners on a group project for a specific class and give them permission to view your calendar with details. Mark all of your school work for your other classes as private so that they can see only items specific to the class you are taking together. Submit this project to your instructor by sharing your calendar.
[Student Learning Outcomes 9.1, 9.2, 9.3, 9.4]

- Create a new calendar.
- Include your class meeting times and assignment due dates for two months of the semester.
- Attach items to each appointment or event when necessary.
- Create categories for each of your classes.
- Mark appointments for other classes as *Private*.
- Share the calendar with two of your classmates giving them *Limited details* permission.
- Share your calendar with your instructor giving him or her *Full details* permission.
- Print a copy of your calendar in *Weekly* format including calendar items marked as *Private* and submit it to your instructor.

Challenge Project 9-9

Consider a future career in which you are interested. Think about how you could use delegates in the workplace and the types of permissions you would give to different users, such as a personal assistant. Email at least two uses of delegates for the position you are considering to your instructor.
[Student Learning Outcome 9.5]

- Identify a job that you are interested in
- Determine how you could use delegates in the position
- Include at least two delegates for your position. If you do not have two delegates, you can use two different possible jobs.
- Email your instructor using the following message format:

   Job title: [responsibilities]

   Delegate 1: [position in relation to your future job]
   Calendar: [permission level: reason for permission]
   Tasks: [permission level: reason for permission]
   Inbox: [permission level: reason for permission]
   Contacts: [permission level: reason for permission]

   Delegate 2: [position in relation to your future job]
   Calendar: [permission level: reason for permission]
   Tasks: [permission level: reason for permission]
   Inbox: [permission level: reason for permission]
   Contacts: [permission level: reason for permission]

- Change the subject of your message to Outlook Challenge Project 9-9.

Source of screenshots Microsoft Office 365 (2019): Word, Excel, Access, PowerPoint, Outlook.

appendices

Setting Up Outlook for an On-Site or Online Classroom Environment

Ideally, the course using this text will be taught as an on-site course. In an on-site course, students will be able to experience all the benefits of using Outlook in an Exchange environment and practice using the features of Outlook with classmates in a computer lab environment. But many Outlook courses are taught in an online environment. In this appendix, you'll be provided with some tips to help you set up your Outlook course whether it is an online or on-site course.

On-Site Course

If you're teaching this course on-site, you should create a set of student accounts on an Exchange server. These accounts can be generic accounts that get recycled from semester to semester. It is probably best to have a separate domain for the classroom Exchange server so it does not conflict with your campus or district Exchange server. Using a separate server also helps prevent students from having access to the entire Global Address List of your school, district, or company.

Creating User Accounts

These accounts can easily be managed through *Active Directory* and *Exchange System Manager*. The student accounts are given a generic name (for example, D01, D02, D03, etc.), and a generic password is used (for example, student). Once one account is created in Active Directory, it can be copied so that only the user name and password need to be reentered. Here is the process that can be used to create the generic student accounts.

▶**HOW TO:** Create User Accounts

1. Open **Active Directory** and create a container to store the user accounts.

2. Create a **New User** (Figure A-1). The name information and user name can be generic rather than a specific student's name.

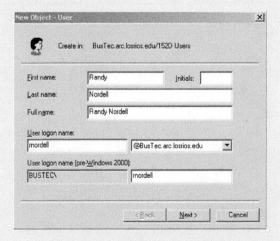

Figure A-1 Create a new user

3. Type in the password and confirm password.

4. You can set the password options to your preference. It is best to use the same password for all students and set the account to **User cannot change password** and **Password never expires** (Figure A-2).

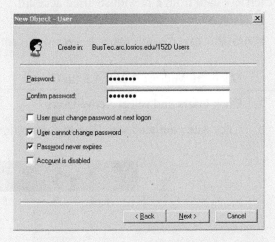

Figure A-2 Password options

5. Check the box to **Create an Exchange mailbox**. This will automatically create an *Exchange* email account with this user's information when the account is created in Active Directory.

6. Confirm the Exchange server and mailbox storage of the user.

7. Confirm the new user information and click **Finish** (Figure A-3). The new user account will be created both in Active Directory and on the Exchange server.

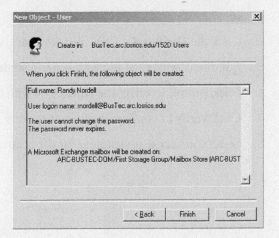

Figure A-3 Confirm new user information

8. You can create additional accounts by copying the new account and entering in the new user name and password. All the other settings will remain the same.

> **MORE INFO**
>
> Active Directory and Exchange System Manager might look a little different than the figures displayed depending on the operating system and version of the software being used.

If you are using a Business Exchange account which has access to the Microsoft 365 Admin center, you can add users with a .csv file upload. This will automate the task of creating and deleting accounts with the start of each class. However, the default setting saves data for 30 days after deletion, so it may be helpful to have two sets of accounts in case you need to retrieve data from a previously used account.

▶ **HOW TO:** Create User Accounts in Microsoft 365 Admin Center

1. Open the Microsoft 365 Admin Center.

2. Click **Users** and select **Active Users**.

3. Click **Add multiple users**. The *Import multiple users* section opens (Figure A-4).

Figure A-4 Import multiple users

4. Click the **Download a CSV file with headers and sample user information**.

5. Edit the downloaded file with generic student account information.

6. Click **Browse** to select the edited .csv with student account information.

7. Click **Verify** to confirm the format of your .csv.

8. Select the license assignment for the accounts (Figure A-5).

Figure A-5 Assign licenses to users

9. Click **Next** to create all of the accounts.

10. Click **Download results** to download a .csv file with the user names and passwords (Figure A-6).

Figure A-6 Download results

Recycling User Accounts

At the end of each semester, these Exchange email accounts can be recycled so they can be used again for subsequent semesters. The recycling process consists of deleting the accounts from Active Directory, purging the deleted accounts from Exchange System Manager, and re-creating the accounts.

▶ **HOW TO:** **Recycle User Accounts Microsoft 365 Admin Center**

1. Click the **Home** button.
2. Select the accounts to be deleted and delete them. This will not delete the Exchange accounts, but it will mark these accounts for deletion.
3. Open the Exchange System Manager and navigate to the *Mailboxes* folder in the proper server folder.
4. Right-click on the **Mailboxes** folder and choose **Run Cleanup Agent** (Figure A-7). This will mark with a red **X** all the accounts that were deleted in Active Directory. You can scroll through to see the disabled accounts.

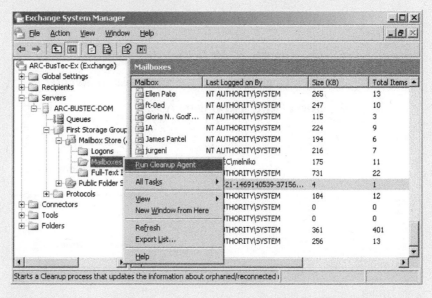

Figure A-7 *Run Cleanup Agent*

5. Right-click on each account to be deleted and choose **Purge**. This step has to be done individually on each account to be deleted (Figure A-8).

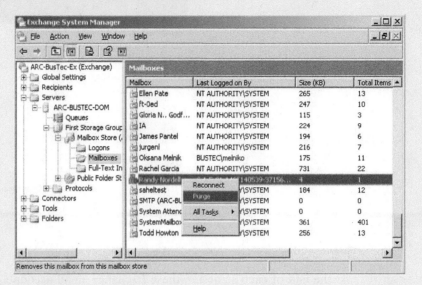

Figure A-8 Purge each account individually

6. Once the accounts have been purged, they are no longer on the Exchange server or in Active Directory.

7. Follow the steps previously outlined in the *Creating User Accounts* section to re-create the new set of user accounts.

Although this might seem like a daunting process, it actually takes only about 15 minutes. Most likely this process will be done by the person who manages the Exchange server at your institution. This person can easily set up a separate domain in the forest for the class Exchange server.

When working with the Microsoft 365 Admin Center, you can delete all of the accounts and import them again. Since data is kept for 30 days, you may want to have a second set of accounts by modifying the .csv with student account information to have a second set. For example, you may label accounts with FA for fall, SP for spring, and SU for summer or another naming convention.

▶**HOW TO: Recycle User Accounts**

1. Open the Microsoft 365 Admin Center.

2. Click **Home** and select the **arrow** next to *Edit user*.

3. Select **Delete user** (Figure A-9).

Figure A-9 Select *Delete user*

4. Click the **check box** next to each user.

5. Click **Select** (Figure A-10).

Figure A-10 Select users to delete

6. Click **Delete**. The selected users are deleted. Their accounts are retrievable within 30 days (Figure A-11).

Figure A-11 Delete selected users

7. Follow the instructions to import a new group of students with the .csv template file.

Online Course

When teaching an Outlook course in an online environment, there will be some decisions that need to be made by the instructor, and it's important to think through some of these issues prior to setting up your class. The following are some issues to think about before setting up your course and some suggestions to help make your online course as effective as possible.

Email

One of the major issues of teaching a course such as this online is email accounts. Do students use their personal email account, school account, or a new email account? Also, how do students get the contact information for other students in the course?

There are a couple of reasons why it is probably not a good idea to have students use their personal email accounts for a course such as this. Students will be interacting via email with others in the course. They do not necessarily want all students in the class to have their personal email accounts. Also, there will be a large volume of emails being sent and received in this class. It will be much better if class emails are not intermingled with personal emails.

Below are a couple of suggestions:

- *Generic email accounts*: You can set up generic email accounts for your class using one of the free email services such as Gmail or Microsoft Outlook Mail. You could use a generic format such as ARC-Student1@outlook.com, ARC-Student2@outlook.com, and so forth. At the end of the semester, you could recycle these accounts by deleting all emails and changing passwords.

  At the beginning of the semester, each student would be given an email account and a list of the email addresses for other students and the professor in the class. Students would type in the email addresses of other students and the professor until contacts are covered in chapter 3.

- *Student-created email accounts*: Students could create a new email account to be used specifically for this course. These email addresses could then be sent to the professor. A list of email addresses could then be created and distributed to all students in the class.

- *School-created email accounts*: Many schools provide email accounts for students. Depending on the type of account, it is possible that these accounts can be set up and used in Outlook. If these school-created accounts are either POP3 or IMAP accounts, they can be set up in Outlook.

  It would still be a good idea to have your email administrator set up a unique set of student accounts that can be used specifically for this course. These accounts could then be recycled each semester.

  In chapter 7, students will be adding an additional account. At this point they will create a new account and share their email addresses with other classmates. They will have enough knowledge of email and contacts to easily get this new information to others in the class without the professor having to handle this administrative task.

Using SimNet

One of the difficulties of teaching an Outlook course in an online environment is that students are not on a common Exchange server. Also, students will not be able to experience all the benefits of using Outlook in conjunction with an Exchange server.

For an online course, I would highly suggest using this text in conjunction with SimNet, which will allow you to create lessons and tests that can be used with the students. The features that are unique to using Outlook in an Exchange environment can be covered in SimNet. Appendix D lists many of the features that are unique to Outlook in an Exchange environment.

Source of screenshots Microsoft Office 365 (2019): Word, Excel, Access, PowerPoint, Outlook.

Outlook Shortcuts

Global Outlook Commands

Activity	Shortcut
Go to Mail	**Ctrl+1**
Go to Calendar	**Ctrl+2**
Go to Contacts	**Ctrl+3**
Go to Tasks	**Ctrl+4**
Go to Notes	**Ctrl+5**
Go to Folder List	**Ctrl+6**
Go to Shortcuts	**Ctrl+7**
Go to Journal	**Ctrl+8**
New item	**Ctrl+N**
New email message	**Ctrl+Shift+M**
New calendar appointment	**Ctrl+Shift+A**
New meeting request	**Ctrl+Shift+Q**
New contact	**Ctrl+Shift+C**
New contact group	**Ctrl+Shift+L**
New task	**Ctrl+Shift+K**
New task request	**Ctrl+Alt+Shift+U**
New note	**Ctrl+Shift+N**
New folder	**Ctrl+Shift+E**
Save	**Ctrl+S**
Save as	**F12**
Move item	**Ctrl+Shift+V**
Print	**Ctrl+P**
Open	**Ctrl+O**
Close an open Outlook item or dialog box	**Esc** or **Alt+F4**
Copy	**Ctrl+C**
Cut	**Ctrl+X**
Paste	**Ctrl+V**
Undo	**Ctrl+Z**
Bold	**Ctrl+B**
Italicize	**Ctrl+I**
Underline	**Ctrl+U**
Select all	**Ctrl+A**
Select range of items	**Shift+click** on first and last item in range
Select nonadjacent items	**Ctrl+click**
Help	**F1**
Search	**F3** or **Ctrl+E**
Advanced find	**Ctrl+Shift+F**
Open Address Book	**Ctrl+Shift+B**

(continued)

Activity	Shortcut
Switch between panes	F6
Activate *Ribbon*/menu	F10
Send/receive all folders	F9
Move forward one field	Tab
Move back one field	Shift+Tab
Repeat command or typing	Ctrl+Y
Forward selected item	Ctrl+F
Delete selected item	Ctrl+D

Mail

Activity	Shortcut
Go to Mail	Ctrl+1
New email message	Ctrl+N
New email message (anywhere in Outlook)	Ctrl+Shift+M
Open selected email	Ctrl+O
Close an open email	Esc or Alt+F4
Reply	Ctrl+R
Reply all	Ctrl+Shift+R
Reply with meeting	Ctrl+Alt+R
Forward	Ctrl+F
Forward email as an attachment	Ctrl+Alt+F
Send	Alt+S
Mark as read	Ctrl+Q
Mark as unread	Ctrl+U
New mail folder	Ctrl+Shift+E
Delete selected email or folder	Ctrl+D
Ignore conversation	Ctrl+Del
Clean up conversation	Alt+Del
Display Address Book	Ctrl+Shift+B

Calendar

Activity	Shortcut
Go to Calendar	Ctrl+2
New appointment	Ctrl+N
New appointment (anywhere in Outlook)	Ctrl+Shift+A
New meeting request	Ctrl+Shift+Q
Open selected calendar item	Ctrl+O
Close an open calendar item	Esc or Alt+F4
Forward calendar item	Ctrl+F
Open *Recurrence* dialog box	Ctrl+G
Create new calendar	Ctrl+Shift+E
Delete selected calendar item or calendar	Ctrl+D

(continued)

Activity	Shortcut
Display calendar in *Day* view	**Ctrl+Alt+1**
Display calendar in *Work Week* view	**Ctrl+Alt+2**
Display calendar in *Week* view	**Ctrl+Alt+3**
Display calendar in *Month* view	**Ctrl+Alt+4**
Display calendar in *Schedule* view	**Ctrl+Alt+5**

Contacts

Activity	Shortcut
Go to Contacts	**Ctrl+3**
New contact	**Ctrl+N**
New contact (anywhere in Outlook)	**Ctrl+Shift+C**
New contact group	**Ctrl+Shift+L**
Open selected contact	**Ctrl+O**
Close an open contact	**Esc** or **Alt+F4**
Open Address Book	**Ctrl+Shift+B**
New contact folder	**Ctrl+Shift+E**
Forward contact as a business card	**Ctrl+F**
Delete selected contact or folder	**Ctrl+D**

Tasks

Activity	Shortcut
Go to Tasks	**Ctrl+4**
New task	**Ctrl+N**
New task (anywhere in Outlook)	**Ctrl+Shift+K**
New task request	**Ctrl+Alt+Shift+U**
Open selected task	**Ctrl+O**
Close an open task	**Esc** or **Alt+F4**
Open *Recurrence* dialog box	**Ctrl+G**
New task folder	**Ctrl+Shift+E**
Delete selected contact or folder	**Ctrl+D**

Notes

Activity	Shortcut
Go to Notes	**Ctrl+5**
New note	**Ctrl+N**
New note (anywhere in Outlook)	**Ctrl+Shift+N**
Open selected note	**Ctrl+O**
Close an open note	**Esc** or **Alt+F4**
Forward note	**Ctrl+F**
New note folder	**Ctrl+Shift+E**
Delete selected note or folder	**Ctrl+D**

Journal

Activity	Shortcut
Go to Journal	**Ctrl+8**
New journal entry	**Ctrl+N**
Open selected journal	**Ctrl+O**
Close an open journal	**Esc** or **Alt+F4**
Forward journal	**Ctrl+F**
Open Address Book	**Ctrl+Shift+B**
New journal folder	**Ctrl+Shift+E**
Delete selected journal or folder	**Ctrl+D**

Customer Manager

Activity	Shortcut
Go to Customer Manager	**Ctrl+9**

Formatting

Activity	Shortcut
Copy	**Ctrl+C**
Cut	**Ctrl+X**
Paste	**Ctrl+V**
Undo	**Ctrl+Z**
Select all	**Ctrl+A**
Bold	**Ctrl+B**
Italicize	**Ctrl+I**
Underline	**Ctrl+U**
Align left	**Ctrl+L**
Align center	**Ctrl+E**
Align right	**Ctrl+R**
Align justified	**Ctrl+J**
Add bullet	**Ctrl+Shift+L**
Insert hyperlink	**Ctrl+K**
Increase indent	**Ctrl+M**
Decrease indent	**Ctrl+Shift+M**
Increase font size	**Ctrl+>(Ctrl+Shift+.)**
Decrease font size	**Ctrl+<(Ctrl+Shift+,)**
Clear all formatting	**Ctrl+spacebar**

Outlook Quick Reference Guide

Global Outlook Features

Task	Action	Alternative Method	Keyboard Shortcut
Advanced Find	Click in the *Search* box above the *Folder* pane • *Search* tab • *Options* group • *Search Tools* button • *Advanced Find*		**Ctrl+Shift+F**
Archive—folder settings	Select folder • *Folder* tab • *Properties* group • *AutoArchive Settings*	Right-click on folder • *Properties* • *AutoArchive* tab	
Archive—global settings	*File* tab • *Options* • *Advanced* • *AutoArchive Settings*		
Categories—assign	With Outlook item open • *Tags* group • *Categorize* button • select category	In list view, right-click on the *Category* column • select category	
Categories—create new	*Home* tab • *Tags* group • *Categorize* button • *All Categories*	Open Outlook item • *Tags* group • *Categorize* button • *All Categories*	
Categories—set *Quick Click*	*Home* tab • *Tags* group • *Categorize* button • Set *Quick Click*	*File* tab • *Options* • *Advanced* • *Other* section • *Quick Click*	
Delegate—assign	*File* tab • *Account Settings* • *Delegate Access* • *Add*		
Delegate—edit permissions	*File* tab • *Account Settings* • *Delegate Settings* • select delegate • *Permissions*		
Delegate—remove	*File* tab • *Account Access* • *Delegate Access* • *Remove*		
Email account—create new	File tab • Add account	*File* tab • *Account Settings* • *Account Settings* • *New*	
Email account—edit	*File* tab • *Account Settings* • *Account Settings* • *Change*		
Empty Deleted Items upon exiting—default setting	*File* tab • *Options* • *Advanced* • *Empty Deleted Items* folder when exiting Outlook		
Empty Deleted Items—manually	Click on *Deleted Items* folder in the *Navigation* pane • *Folder* tab • *Clean Up* group • *Empty Folder* button	Right-click on *Deleted Items* folder • *Empty Folder*	
Export Outlook data file	*File* tab • *Options* • *Advanced* • *Export* • *Export to a file* • Outlook data file (.pst)		
Folder—create new	*Folder* tab • *New* group • *New Folder* button	In the *Navigation* pane, right-click on folder in which the new folder will be created • *New Folder*	**Ctrl+Shift+E**

(continued)

Task	Action	Alternative Method	Keyboard Shortcut
Folder—delete	*Folder* tab • *Actions* group • *Delete Folder* button	In the *Navigation* pane, right-click on folder to be deleted • *Delete Folder*	**Ctrl+D**
Folder—move	*Folder* tab • *Actions* group • Move Folder button	In the *Navigation* pane, drag the folder to the desired location in the list of folders	
Folder—rename	*Folder* tab • *Actions* group • *Rename Folder* button	In the *Navigation* pane, right-click on folder to be renamed • *Rename Folder*	
Import Outlook data file	*File* tab • *Open* • *Import* • Import from another program or file • Outlook data file (.pst)		
Instant Search	Click in the *Search* box above the *Folder* pane		**Ctrl+E**
Modifying views	*View* tab • *Current View* group • *Change View* button • *Manage Views*		
Navigation buttons	*More* (...) button • *Navigation Pane Options*		
Navigation pane options	*Configure Buttons* • *Navigation Pane Options*	*File* tab • *Options* • *Advanced* • *Outlook Panes* section • *Navigation* pane	
Outlook Today—customize	Click on *Mailbox* folder • *Customize Outlook Today*		
Outlook Today— default start window	*File* tab • Options • *Advanced* • Start Outlook in this folder	Click on *Mailbox* folder • *Customize Outlook Today* • Check *When starting, go directly to Outlook Today*	
Quick Access toolbar—customize	Click on *Customize Quick Access Toolbar* button • *More Commands*	*File* tab • *Options* • *Quick Access Toolbar*	
Reading pane	*View* tab • *Layout* group • *Reading Pane* button		
Ribbon—customize	*File* tab • *Options* • *Customize Ribbon*	Right-click on the *Ribbon* or a tab • *Customize the Ribbon*	
Security settings	*File* tab • *Options* • *Trust Center* • *Trust Center Settings*		
Shortcut group— create new	Right-click on *Shortcuts* • *New Shortcut Group*		
Shortcut group—delete	Right-click on *Shortcuts* • *Delete Group*		
Shortcut—create new	Click on *Shortcuts* button in *Navigation* pane • *Folder* tab • *New* group • *New Shortcut*	Click on *Shortcuts* button in *Navigation* pane • Right-click on *Shortcuts* • *New Shortcut*	
Shortcut—delete	Right-click on shortcut • *Delete Shortcut*		
View—add columns (in list views only)	*View* tab • *Arrangement* group • *Add Columns* button	Right-click on column heading in the *Folder* pane • *Field Chooser*	

(continued)

Task	Action	Alternative Method	Keyboard Shortcut
View—custom view	*View* tab • *Current View* group • *Change View* button • *Manage Views* • *New*		
View—modify	*View* tab • *Current View* group • *View Settings* button	*View* tab • *Current View* group • *Change View* button • *Manage Views* • *Modify*	
View—show in groups	*View* tab • *Arrangement* group • *More* button • *Show in Groups*	*View* tab • *View* group • *View Settings* button • *Group By*	
View—sorting	Click on column header to sort by column • Click to toggle between ascending and descending sort	*View* tab • *Current View* group • *View Settings* button • *Sort*	

Mail

The context of most of these commands is with a new email open, or replying to or forwarding an email.

Task	Action	Alternative Method	Keyboard Shortcut
Attach—file	*Message* tab • *Include* group • *Attach File* button	*Insert* tab • *Include* group • *Attach File* button	
Attach—Outlook item	*Message* tab • *Include* group • *Attach Item* button • *Other Outlook item*	*Insert* tab • *Include* group • *Outlook Item* button	
Attachment—preview	Click on attachment • Attachment will be displayed in body of message		
Attachment—print	Click on attachment • *Attachment* tab • *Actions* group • *Quick Print*	Right-click on attachment • *Quick Print*	
Attachment—save	Click on attachment • *Attachment* tab • *Actions* group • *Save As*	Right-click on attachment • *Save As*	
Bcc	*Options* tab • *Show Fields* group • *Bcc*	To button • *Bcc*	
Category	Select email in *Folder* pane • *Home* tab • *Tags* group • *Categorize*	Right-click on email in *Folder* pane • *Categorize*	
Change email format—default setting	*File* tab • *Options* • *Mail* • Compose message in this format		
Change email format—individual email	*Format* tab • *Format Text* group • select format		

(continued)

Task	Action	Alternative Method	Keyboard Shortcut
Delay delivery	*Options* tab • *More Options* group • *Delay Deliver* button		
Delete email	*Home* or *Message* tab • *Delete* group • *Delete* button	Right-click on email in *Folder* pane • *Delete*	**Ctrl+D**
Delivery receipt	*Options* tab • *Tracking* group • *Request a delivery receipt*	*Message* tab • *Tags* group • *Expand* button • *Request a delivery receipt for this message*	
Desktop alert settings	*File* tab • *Options* • *Mail* • *Message arrival* area • *Desktop Alert* settings		
Direct Replies To	*Options* tab • *More Options* group • *Direct Replies To*	*Message* tab • *Tags* group • *Expand* button • *Have replies sent to*	
Email—change default delivery folder	*File* tab • *Account Settings* button • *Account Settings* • select account • *Change Folder*		
Email—options	*File* tab • *Options* • *Mail*		
Email—send through different account	Create new email or choose *Reply, Reply All,* or *Forward* on existing email • *From* button • Select account		
Email account—set default	*File* tab • *Account Settings* button • *Account Settings* • Select account • *Set as Default*		
Expiration date/time on email	*Message* tab • *Tags* group • *Expand* button • *Expires after*	*Options* tab • *More Options* group • *Expand* button • *Expires* after	
Favorites—add folder	Select folder to add to *Favorites* • *Folder* tab • *Favorites* group • *Show in Favorites*	Right-click folder to add to *Favorites* • *Show in Favorites*	
Favorites—remove folder	Select folder to remove from *Favorites* • *Folder* tab • *Favorites* group • *Show in Favorites*	Right-click folder to remove from *Favorites* • *Show in Favorites*	
Flag for Recipients	*Message* tab • *Tags* group • *Follow Up* button • *Custom* • *Flag for Recipients*		
Follow Up flag	*Message* tab • *Tags* group • *Follow Up*		
Font—default	*File* tab • *Options* • *Mail* • *Stationery and Fonts* • *Personal Stationery* tab		
Format text	*Message* tab • *Basic Text* group	*Format Text* tab	
Forward email as attachment	*Home* or *Message* tab • *Respond* group • *More* button • *Forward as Attachment*		**Ctrl+Alt+F**
Importance	*Message* tab • *Tags* group • *High Importance*	Click on *Expand* button in *Tags* group • *Importance*	

(continued)

Task	Action	Alternative Method	Keyboard Shortcut
Junk email—block sender	Select email to be blocked • *Home* tab • *Delete* group • *Junk* button • *Block Sender*	Open email to be blocked • *Message* tab • *Delete* group • *Junk* button • *Block Sender*	
Junk email—manage lists	*Home* tab • *Delete* group • *Junk* button • *Junk Email Options* • Choose list to manage	Open email • *Message* tab • *Delete* group • *Junk* button • *Junk Email Options* • Choose list to manage	
Junk email—never block sender or sender's domain	Select email • *Home* tab • *Delete* group • *Junk* button • *Never Block Sender* or *Never Block Sender's Domain*	Open email • *Message* tab • *Delete* group • *Junk* button • *Never Block Sender* or *Never Block Sender's Domain*	
Junk email—options	*Home* tab • *Delete* group • *Junk* button • *Junk Email Options*		
Mark email as read/unread	Click on email in *Folder* pane • *Home* tab • *Tags* group • *Read/Unread* button	Right-click on email in *Folder* pane • *Mark as Read/Unread*	**Ctrl+Q** (mark as read) **Ctrl+U** (mark as unread)
Out of Office Assistant	*File* tab • *Automatic replies (Out of Office)*		
Print email	*File* tab • *Print*	*Quick Print* button on *Quick Access* toolbar	**Ctrl+P**
Quick Steps—create new	*Home* tab • *Quick Steps* group • *Create New*	*Home* tab • *Quick Steps* group • *More* button • *New Quick* Step	
Quick Steps—manage	*Home* tab • *Quick Steps* group • *More* button • *Manage Quick Step*		
Quick Steps—use existing	*Home* tab • *Quick Steps* group • Select *Quick Step* to use		
Read receipt	*Options* tab • *Tracking* group • *Request a Read Receipt*	*Message* tab • *Tags* group • *Expand* button • Request a read receipt for this message	
Recall sent message	*Sent Items* folder • *Open* email to be recalled • *Message* tab • *Move* group • *Actions* button • *Recall This Message*	*Sent Items* folder • Open email to be recalled • *File* tab • *Recall* or *Resend* button • *Recall This Message*	
Reminder	*Message* tab • *Tags* group • *Follow Up* • *Add Reminder*	Right-click on email in *Folder* pane • *Follow Up* • *Add Reminder*	
Resend sent message	*Sent Items* folder • Open email to be recalled • *Message* tab • *Move* group • *Actions* button • *Resend This Message*	*Sent Items* folder • Open email to be recalled • *File* tab • *Recall* or *Resend* button • *Resend This Message*	
RSS feed—delete	*File* tab • *Account Settings* button • *Account Settings* • *RSS Feed* tab • select RSS feed • *Remove*	Right-click on RSS Feed folder to delete • *Delete Folder*	Select RSS feed folder to delete • **Ctrl+D**
RSS feed—share	Open an existing RSS feed email • *RSS Article* tab • *RSS* group • *Share This Feed*	Right-click on an RSS feed email • *Share This Feed*	

(continued)

Task	Action	Alternative Method	Keyboard Shortcut
RSS feed—subscribe	*File* tab • *Account Settings* button • *Account Settings* • *RSS Feeds* tab • *New*	In the *Navigation* pane, right-click on the *RSS Feeds* folder • *Add a New RSS Feed*	
Rules—create	*Home* tab • *Move* group • *Rules* button • *Manage Rules & Alerts* • *New Rule*	Right-click on email message • *Rules* • *Create Rule*	
Rules—delete	*Home* tab • *Move* group • *Rules* button • *Manage Rules & Alerts* • Select rule • *Delete*		
Rules—edit	*Home* tab • *Move* group • *Rules* button • *Manage Rules & Alerts* • Select rule • *Change Rule* • *Edit Rule Settings*	*Home* tab • *Move* group • *Rules* button • *Manage Rules & Alerts* • Double-click on rule	
Rules—order	*Home* tab • *Move* group • *Rules* button • *Manage Rules & Alerts* • Select rule • *Move Up* or *Move Down* button		
Rules—run rules now	*Folder* tab • *Clean Up* group • *Run Rules Now* button • Select rules to run • *Run Now*	*Home* tab • *Actions* group • *Rules* button • *Manage Rules & Alerts* • *Run Rules Now* button • Select rules to run • *Run Now*	
Rules—turn on/off	*Home* tab • *Move* group • *Rules* button • *Manage Rules & Alerts* • Select rule • Select or deselect check box		
Save email—draft	*Save* button on *Quick Access* toolbar	*File* tab • *Save*	**Ctrl+S**
Save email—outside of Outlook	*File* tab • *Save As*		**F12**
Save Sent Item To	*Options* tab • *More Option* group • *Save Sent Items To* button • *Other Folder*		
Search folder—create new	*Folder* tab • *New* group • *New Search Folder*	Right-click on *Search Folders* • *New Search Folder*	**Ctrl+Shift+P**
Search folder—customize	Select search folder • *Folder* tab • *Actions* group • *Customize This Search Folder*		
Search folder—delete	Select search folder • *Folder* tab • *Actions* group • *Delete Folder*	Right-click on search folder • *Delete Folder*	**Ctrl+D**
Security	*Message* tab • *Tags* group • *Expand* button • *Security Settings*		
Sensitivity	*Message* tab • *Tags* group • *Expand* button • *Sensitivity*	*Options* tab • *More Options* group • *Expand* button • *Sensitivity*	
Signature—create	*File* tab • *Options* • *Mail* • *Signatures* • *New*	*Message* tab • *Include* group • *Signature* button • *Signatures*	

(continued)

Task	Action	Alternative Method	Keyboard Shortcut
Signature—default	*File* tab • *Options* • *Mail* • *Signatures* • Set default signature account and type	Open email • *Message* tab • *Include* group • *Signatures* button • *Signatures* • Set default signature account and type	
Signature—insert	*Message* tab • *Include* group • *Signatures* button • Select signature	*Insert* tab • *Include* group • *Signatures* button • Select signature	
Theme—individual email	*Options* tab • *Themes* group • *Themes* button		
Theme—set default	*File* tab • *Options* • *Mail* • *Stationery and Fonts* • *Theme*		
Voting buttons—custom	*Options* tab • *Tracking* group • *Use Voting Buttons* button • *Custom*	*Message* tab • *Tags* group • *Expand* button • *Use Voting Buttons* • Type voting buttons separated by a semicolon	
Voting buttons—preset	*Options* tab • *Tracking* group • *Use Voting Buttons* button • Select preset voting buttons	*Message* tab • *Tags* group • *Expand* button • *Use Voting Buttons*	
Voting buttons—track responses	Open email with voting response • Click on *InfoBar* • View voting responses	Open original email with voting buttons from *Sent Items* folder • *Message* tab • *Show* button • *Tracking*	
Voting buttons—vote	Open email with voting button • *Respond* group • *Vote* button • Select response		

Calendar

Task	Action	Alternative Method	Keyboard Shortcut
Add holidays	*File* tab • *Options* • *Calendar* • *Calendar options* area • *Add Holidays*		
Appointment	*Home* tab • *New* group • *New Appointment* button	Type appointment on calendar in *Day* or *Week* view	**Ctrl+N** (when in Calendar) **Ctrl+Shift+A** (anywhere in Outlook)
Attach business card to calendar item	Open new or existing calendar item • *Insert* tab • *Include* group • *Business Card* • *Other Business Cards*		
Attach file to calendar item	Open new or existing calendar item • *Insert* tab • *Include* group • *Attach File*		
Attach Outlook item to calendar item	Open new or existing calendar item • *Insert* tab • *Include* group • Outlook item		
AutoPick meeting times	Open new or existing meeting request • *Meeting* tab • *Show* group • *Scheduling Assistant* button • *Options* button • *AutoPick Next*		

(continued)

Task	Action	Alternative Method	Keyboard Shortcut
Calendar—create new calendar folder	*Folder* tab • *New* group • *New Calendar* button	Right-click on the *Calendar* folder in the *Navigation* pane • *New Calendar*	**Ctrl+Shift+E**
Calendar item—copy	Select calendar item • Hold down **Ctrl** key • Drag to new location		**Ctrl+C** (copy) **Ctrl+V** (paste)
Calendar item—delete	Select calendar item • *Actions* group • *Delete* button	Open existing calendar item • *Appointment, Event,* or *Meeting* tab • *Actions* group • *Delete*	**Ctrl+D**
Calendar item—move	Open calendar item • Change date/time • *Save & Close*	Drag the calendar item to new location on the calendar	**Ctrl+X** (cut) **Ctrl+V** (paste)
Calendar view—*Day*	*Home* tab • *Arrangement* group • *Day View* button	*View* tab • *Arrangement* group • *Day View* button	**Ctrl+Alt+1**
Calendar view—*Month*	*Home* tab • *Arrangement* group • *Month View* button	*View* tab • *Arrangement* group • *Month View* button	**Ctrl+Alt+4**
Calendar view—other views	*View* tab • *Current View* group • *Change View* button • Select view		
Calendar view—*Schedule*	*Home* tab • *Arrange* group • *Schedule View* button	*View* tab • *Arrangement* group • *Schedule View* button	
Calendar view—*Week*	*Home* tab • *Arrange* group • *Week View* button	*View* tab • *Arrangement* group • *Week View* button	**Ctrl+Alt+3**
Calendar view—*Work Week*	*Home* tab • *Arrange* group • *Work Week View* button	*View* tab • *Arrangement* group • *Work Week View* button	**Ctrl+Alt+2**
Convert email to calendar item	Select email • *Home* tab • *Quick Steps* • *Create Appointment*	Drag email to *Calendar* button	
Event	*Home* tab • *New* group • *New Appointment* button • All day event	Type event on calendar in *Event* area of *Day, Week,* or *Month* view	
Forward calendar item	Select calendar item • *Appointment* tab • *Actions* group • *Forward* button	Open calendar item • *Appointment, Event,* or *Meeting* tab • *Actions* group • *Forward* button	**Ctrl+F**
Forward calendar item—as iCalendar	Select calendar item • *Appointment* tab • *Actions* group • Small arrow below the *Forward* button • *Forward as iCalendar*	Open calendar item • *Appointment, Event,* or *Meeting* tab • *Actions* group • Small arrow to the right of the *Forward* button • *Forward as iCalendar*	
Meeting—create	*Home* tab • *New* group • *New Meeting* button	Open existing appointment or create new appointment • *Appointment* tab • *Attendees* group • *Invite Attendees* button	**Ctrl+Shift+Q**
Meeting—respond	Open meeting request email • *Meeting* tab • *Respond* group • Select response		
Meeting—tracking	From your calendar, open the meeting request you created • *Meeting* tab • *Show* group • *Tracking* button	From your calendar, open the meeting request you created • *Tracking* summary in the *InfoBar*	

(continued)

Task	Action	Alternative Method	Keyboard Shortcut
Meeting—updating	From your calendar, open the meeting request you created • *Meeting* tab • Make desired changes • *Send Update*		
Print calendar	*File* tab • *Print* • Select settings • *Print*	*Print* button on *Quick Access* toolbar	**Ctrl+P**
Private calendar item	Open new or existing calendar item • *Appointment*, *Event*, or *Meeting* tab • *Tags* group • *Private* button	Right-click on calendar item • *Private*	
Recurring calendar item	Open new or existing calendar item • *Appointment*, *Event*, or *Meeting* tab • *Options* group • *Recurrence* button	Select calendar item • *Appointment* tab • *Recurrence* button	**Ctrl+G**
Reminder—default settings	*File* tab • *Options* • *Calendar* • *Calendar options* area • *Default reminders*		
Reminder—set reminder	Open calendar item • *Appointment*, *Event*, or *Meeting* tab • *Options* group • *Reminder*		
Scheduling Assistant—default settings	*File* tab • *Options* • *Calendar* • *Scheduling Assistant* area		
Scheduling Assistant—use	Open existing or new calendar item • *Appointment*, *Event*, or *Meeting* tab • *Show* group • *Scheduling Assistant* button		
Send calendar via email	*Home* tab • *Share* group • *Email Calendar*	Right-click on calendar • *Share* • *Email Calendar*	
Share calendar	*Home* tab • *Share* group • *Share Calendar*	Right-click on calendar • *Share* • *Share Calendar*	
Time zones	*File* tab • *Options* • *Calendar* • *Time zones* area		
Weather bar location	*Location* • *Add Location*		
Work time options	*File* tab • *Options* • *Calendar* • *Work time* area		

Contacts

Task	Action	Alternative Method	Keyboard Shortcut
Add multiple email addresses	Open new or existing contact record • Click on arrow next to *Email* button • Select *Email 2* or *Email 3*		
Change default address book	*Home* tab • *Find* group • *Address Book* • *Tools* menu • *Options*		

(continued)

Task	Action	Alternative Method	Keyboard Shortcut
Change field name	Open new or existing contact record • Click on arrow next to field name • Select new field name		
Contact—add from Global Address List	Open Global Address List • Right-click on contact to be added • Add to Contacts	Open Global Address List • Select contact to be added • File menu • Add to Contacts	
Contact—create new	Home tab • New group • New Contact button		**Ctrl+N** (when in Contacts) **Ctrl+Shift+C** (anywhere in Outlook)
Contact—from received email	With email open or in Reading pane, right-click on name or email address • Add to Outlook Contacts	With email open or in Reading pane, move pointer on name or email address • Click on+button • Add to Outlook Contacts	
Contact—new from same company	Keep existing contact open • Contact tab • Actions group • Small arrow next to the Save & New button • Contact from the Same Company		
Contact folder—new	Folder tab • New group • New Folder button	Right-click on Contacts • New Folder	**Ctrl+Shift+E**
Contact group—add members	Open new or existing contact group • Contact Group tab • Members group • Add Members button		
Contact group—create new	Home tab • New group • New Contact Group		**Ctrl+Shift+L**
Contact group—delete	Select contact group • Home tab • Delete group • Delete button	Right-click on contact group • Delete	**Ctrl+D**
Contact group—remove members	Open new or existing contact group • Select members to be removed • Contact Group tab • Members group • Remove Member button	Open new or existing contact group • Select members to be removed • Press Delete	
Contact options	File tab • Options • Contacts		
Create mailing labels using Contacts	Home tab • Actions group • Mail Merge button		
Customize business card	Open existing contact • Contact tab • Options group • Business Card button		
Delete contact	Select contact • Home tab • Delete group • Delete button	Right-click on contact • Delete	**Ctrl+D**
Export contacts	File tab • Options • Advanced • Export • Export to a file		
Forward business card	Select contact • Home tab • Share group • Forward Contact • As a Business Card	Right-click on contact • Forward Contact • As a Business Card	**Ctrl+F**

(continued)

Task	Action	Alternative Method	Keyboard Shortcut
Import contacts	*File* tab • *Open* • *Import* • Import from another program or file		
Include business card in signature	*File* tab • *Options* • *Mail* • *Signatures* • *Business Card*		
Map contact address	Open existing contact with address • *Map It* button	Open existing contact with address • *Contact* tab • *Communicate* group • *More* button • *Map It*	
Picture—add	Open new or existing contact • Click on *Add Contact Picture* button	Open new or existing contact • *Contacts* tab • *Options* group • *Picture* button • *Add Picture*	
Picture—remove	Open new or existing contact • *Contacts* tab • *Options* group • *Picture* button • *Remove Picture*		
Send email to contact	Select contact • *Contact* tab • *Communicate* group • *Email*	Right-click on contact • *Create* • *Email*	

Tasks

Task	Action	Alternative Method	Keyboard Shortcut
Attach file to task	Open new or existing task • *Insert* tab • *Include* group • *Attach File* button		
Attach Outlook item to task	Open new or existing task • *Insert* tab • *Include* group • *Outlook Item* button		
Mark task as complete	*Select* task • *Home* tab • *Manage Task* group • *Mark Complete*	Right-click on task • *Mark Complete*	
Private	Select task • *Home* tab • *Tags* group • *Private* button	Open new or existing task • *Task* tab • *Tags* group • *Private* button	
Recurring task	Open new or existing task • *Task* tab • *Recurrence* group • *Recurrence* button		**Ctrl+G**
Reminder	Open new or existing task • Check *Reminder* • Set reminder date and time	Select task • *Home* tab • *Follow Up* group • *Custom* button • *Reminder*	
Task—create new	*Home* tab • *New* group • *New Task* button		**Ctrl+N** (when in Tasks) **Ctrl+Shift+K** (anywhere in Outlook)
Task—delete	*Select* task • *Home* tab • *Delete* group • *Delete* button	Right-click on task • *Delete*	**Ctrl+D**
Task—new from email	Drag email to *Tasks* button	Select email • *Home* tab • *Move* group • *Move* button • *Copy to Folder* • *Tasks*	
Task options	*File* tab • *Options* • *Tasks*		

(continued)

Task	Action	Alternative Method	Keyboard Shortcut
Task request—accept	Open task request email • *Task* tab • *Respond* group • *Accept*		
Task request—assign	Open new or existing task • *Task* tab • *Manage Task* group • *Assign Task* button	Right-click on task • *Assign Task*	
Task request—create new	*Home* tab • *New* group • *New Items* button • *Task Request*	Open new task • *Task* tab • *Manage Task* group • *Assign Task* button	**Ctrl+Alt+Shift+U**
Task request—mark complete	Select an accepted task • *Home* tab • *Manage Task* group • *Mark Complete*	Right-click on accepted task • *Mark Complete*	
Task request—send status report	Open an accepted task • *Task* tab • *Manage Task* group • *Send Status Report*		
To-Do bar—view	*View* tab • *Layout* group • *To-Do bar* button • Select options	Click the **X** next to each option to remove it from the *To-Do* bar	

Notes and Journal

Task	Action	Alternative Method	Keyboard Shortcut
Journal—manually record	*Home* tab • *New* group • *Journal Entry*		**Ctrl+N** (when in Journal) **Ctrl+Shift+J** (anywhere in Outlook)
Note—create new	*Home* tab • *New* group • *New Note*		**Ctrl+N** (when in Notes) **Ctrl+Shift+N** (anywhere in Outlook)
Note—delete	Select note to be deleted • *Home* tab • *Delete* group • *Delete* button	Right-click on note to be deleted • *Delete*	**Ctrl+D**
Note—edit	Double-click on note • Make editing changes		**Ctrl+O**
Note—forward	Select note • *Home* tab • *Actions* group • *Forward* button	Right-click on note • *Forward*	**Ctrl+F**

Customer Manager

Task	Action	Alternative Method	Keyboard Shortcut
Deal	*Home* tab • *Deal*		
Deal—add contact	*Home* tab • *Deal name* • +		
Deal—delete contact	*Home* tab • *Deal name* • **X**		
Deal—files	*Home* tab • *Deal name* • *Note* • +		
Deal—meeting	*Home* tab • *Deal name* • *Schedule a meeting*		
Deal—note	*Home* tab • *Deal name* • *Note*		
Deal—task	*Home* tab • *Deal name* • *New Task*		
Deal—task completion	*Home* tab • *Deal name* • check box		

Exchange Server versus Stand-Alone Usage

Outlook Features Available When on an Exchange Server

Some features of Outlook are available only when it is operating within an Exchange environment. Microsoft Exchange on a business network handles all the incoming and outgoing mail. Each individual user of Exchange is actually a client of this Exchange network, and the network administrator sets up an account for each individual user. In addition to handling email, Exchange also stores all the data associated with calendars, contacts, tasks, notes, and journals. All this information is stored on the Exchange server.

Outlook in an Exchange environment has the same user interface as in a stand-alone environment, but Outlook with an Exchange server does allow you more functionality.

Global Address List

The Global Address List (Figure D-1) is the list of Outlook contact records of all the employees in an organization. If an organization is using an Exchange server, each individual in the organization has a unique email address. This email address, as well as other contact information such as title, department, and phone, is stored in the Global Address List. It usually includes contact groups as well. The Global Address List is maintained by the person who is responsible for maintaining the Exchange server.

Contact records that you use frequently can be added from the Global Address List to your *Contacts* folder.

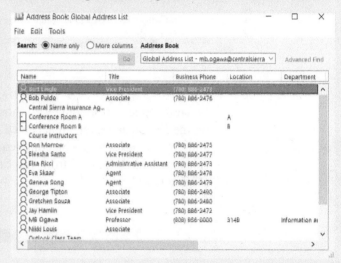

Figure D-1 Global Address List

> **MORE INFO**
> The Global Address List is covered in chapters 3 and 8.

Tracking

Outlook can track the responses to meeting requests, task requests, and emails with voting buttons (Figure D-2). When you recall an email message, Outlook will also track whether or not the recall succeeded or failed. When you use one of these tasks in Outlook, you will be provided with a summary of responses to voting buttons, meeting requests, task requests, or success and failures of email recalls. Tracking is a very powerful tool and is unique to using Outlook on an Exchange server.

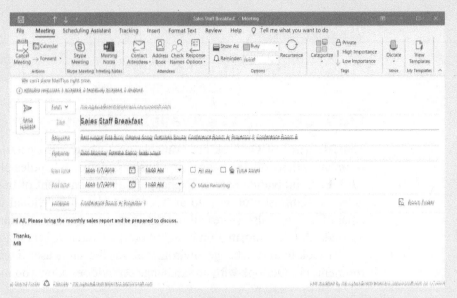

Figure D-2 Track responses

▶ MORE INFO
Tracking is discussed in chapters 2, 4, and 7.

Meeting Requests, Scheduling Assistant, and AutoPick

Meeting requests work only with those on your Exchange server. Because calendars are stored on the Exchange server, an accepted meeting request is automatically saved on your calendar, and the responses to the meeting request are available on this calendar item. When a meeting calendar item is opened from the calendar, you can view the attendees and their responses (Figure D-3).

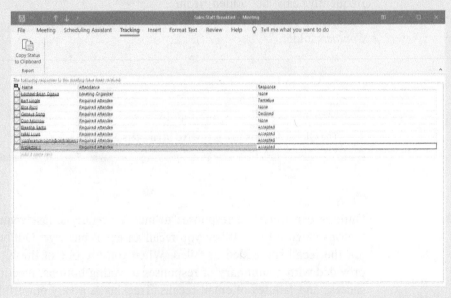

Figure D-3 Track meeting responses

Also, the *Scheduling Assistant* and *AutoPick* meeting times are available when using Exchange. These features gather information from other calendars stored on the Exchange server. These features will work only if others have shared their calendar with you.

MORE INFO

Meeting requests are covered in chapter 4, and sharing calendars, the *Scheduling Assistant*, and *AutoPick* are discussed in chapter 9.

Task Requests

When a task request is sent to another user on your Exchange system and that task is accepted, it is recorded in Tasks. You will see a different task icon displayed in the *Task* list to indicate that a task has been assigned and accepted. When an assigned task has been completed, the originator of the task will receive a message and the task will automatically be marked as complete (Figure D-4).

Figure D-4 Track tasks

MORE INFO

Task requests are covered in chapter 5.

Voting Buttons

Using voting buttons on an email is a great way to get information from others. If you wanted to find out the restaurant preference for the members of your team, you could set up voting buttons with three choices of restaurants from which they could choose. The benefit of using voting buttons as opposed to having recipients just type their selection is the body of the message is that Outlook will consolidate the voting results for you (see Figure D-2). For voting buttons to work properly, the recipients must be using Outlook on an Exchange server.

MORE INFO

Voting buttons are covered in chapter 2.

Groups

Groups allow folks who work together regularly on a project to have a shared conversation history and meeting calendar (Figure D-5). It can be used with both small and large groups.

Groups are especially useful when you want to quickly access conversation history in a shared location, as opposed to searching through your email for a specific message. Groups can also be set to be public (visible) so anyone in your organization can view group content. Groups can be used only when all members of your team are using an Exchange server.

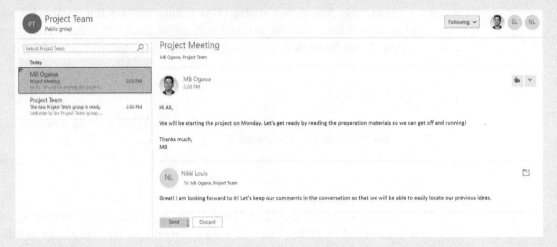

Figure D-5 Group conversation

> MORE INFO
> Groups are covered in chapters 3 and 4.

Sharing and Delegates

One of the advantages of using Outlook in conjunction with an Exchange server is the ability to share different parts of your Outlook (Mail, Calendar, Contacts, Tasks, etc.) with others on your Exchange system (Figure D-6). Since your Outlook information is stored on an Exchange server, you can allow others to access your Outlook information and control the amount of access they have by setting the permission level. This feature is particularly helpful for scheduling meetings and appointments. When you have access to view others' calendars, you can open a shared calendar in your Outlook to view available times and dates. Sharing and delegate permissions work in all areas of Outlook.

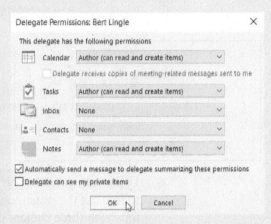

Figure D-6 *Delegate Permissions*

> MORE INFO
> Sharing calendars and delegates are covered in chapter 9.

Outlook on the Web

If you have an email account at work, most likely it is set up on an Exchange server. If so, then you most likely have access to your email and other Outlook information through the internet on Outlook on the web.

If you are on a business trip, working from home, or away from your office computer, you can still access your Exchange mailbox by using Outlook on the web (Figure D-7). You can connect to Outlook on the Web through the internet and a web browser. You can log into your Outlook on the web account with your user name and password. The information stored on the Exchange server is available to you in Outlook on the web.

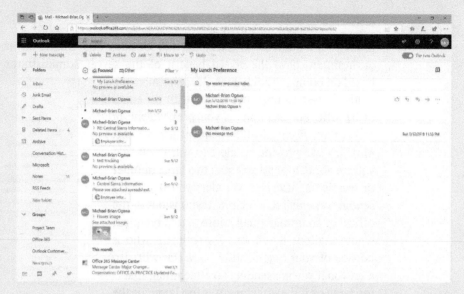

Figure D-7 Outlook on the Web

> MORE INFO
>
> Outlook on the Web has different capabilities compared to Outlook 365 Online, which does not include Exchange services.

> MORE INFO
>
> Outlook on the web access is discussed in chapter 7.

Out of Office Assistant

The *Out of Office Assistant* is available when using Outlook in a stand-alone environment (Figure D-8), but you are given additional *Out of Office* options when using Outlook in an Exchange environment. You can set up your out of office replies to those inside of your organization (on the same Exchange server) and those outside of your organization. You can set up a different message and different criteria for these two groups.

Figure D-8 *Automatic Replies*

> MORE INFO
>
> The *Out of Office Assistant* is covered in chapter 7.

MailTips

MailTips are available in Exchange and Outlook 365 Online environments. Those in Exchange environment have the added benefit of the server administrator adding additional *MailTips* based on company guidelines. *MailTips* alert the Outlook user to potential issues with an email to be sent. For example, if you press *Reply All* rather than *Reply* and the recipient list is large, *MailTips* will provide an alert to warn you that you are about to send an email to a large number of recipients. *MailTips* will alert you if you are sending an email to a recipient who is out of the office, to an invalid email address, to a recipient whose mailbox is full, or to a recipient who is outside of your organization. *MailTips* will also alert you if you are sending an attachment that is too large or if the attachment is too large for the recipient. *MailTips* will work only in conjunction with Microsoft Exchange Server (Figure D-9).

Figure D-9 *MailTips Options*

 MORE INFO

MailTips are covered in chapter 7.

Customer Manager

The Customer Manager is used to centralize Outlook items around deals, people, and businesses. It allows you to create a deal and link associated contacts, tasks, calendar items, files, and notes in a centralized location. It makes searching for information around a deal a streamlined process. The Customer Manager is available both as a pane and as its own view (Figure D-10).

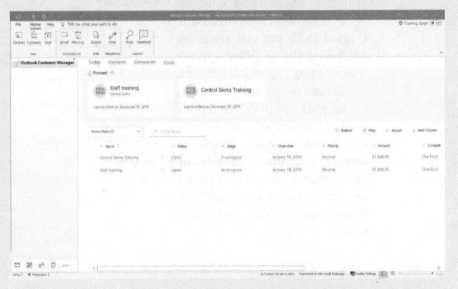

Figure D-10 Customer Manager

Source of screenshots Microsoft Office 365 (2019): Word, Excel, Access, PowerPoint, Outlook.

Quick Tips and Troubleshooting

Email Accounts: Outlook provides you with an email account *Setup Wizard* to help you easily set up email accounts. The following are some troubleshooting tips if your email account is not working properly. (Email accounts are discussed in chapters 1, 2, and 7.)

- **User name and password**. Make sure your user name and password are correct. Typically, user names are not case sensitive while passwords are case sensitive.

- *Repair* **feature**. If your account is not working properly, you might try using the *Repair* feature. In the *Accounts Settings* dialog box, there is a *Repair* button, and Outlook will automatically make account setting changes in an attempt to repair an existing email account.

- **Default account**. If you have multiple email accounts, the first account you create will be your default account. The default account is the account by which new email will be sent. On each email message, you can change the account through which the email is sent. You can also change your default email account in the *Account Settings* dialog box.

- **Primary Exchange account**. If you are using multiple Exchange accounts, the first one added will be your primary account. You can remove a primary Exchange account from Outlook only if there are no other Exchange accounts.

Address Books: A common error is confusing or not distinguishing between the Global Address List and Contacts. (Contacts, Global Address List, and address books are covered in chapters 4 and 9.)

- **Global Address List**. The Global Address List is available only when you are using Outlook in an Exchange environment. You cannot add to or make changes to the Global Address List because this list is maintained by your Exchange server administrator.

- *Contacts* **folder**. Whether you are using Outlook as a stand-alone program or in an Exchange environment, you will have a *Contacts* folder. The *Contacts* folder is by default the folder in which new contacts are saved. You can add, edit, or delete contacts from this folder.

- **Default address book**. When using Outlook in an Exchange environment, the Global Address List is the default address book. You can change the settings to make your *Contacts* folder the default address book (see chapter 8).

- *Address Book*. When the *Address Book* dialog box is open, you can select the address book to use from the *Address Book* pull-down list.

- **Save contact to a different folder**. By default, new contacts will be saved to your *Contacts* folder. You can save to a different folder by clicking on the **File** tab to open the *Backstage*, clicking on the **Move to Folder** button, and selecting the desired folder.

- **Contacts folder not displayed in** *Address Book*. If you have multiple contacts folders, these folders can be made available in your address book by changing the properties of the folders. Right-click on the contacts folder to add to the address book, choose **Properties**, click on the **Outlook Address Book** tab, check **Show the folder as an email Address Book**, and press **OK** to close the dialog box.

Rules—Troubleshooting: See the following for some common errors pertaining to rules and some troubleshooting tips. (Rules are covered in chapter 6.)

- **Incorrect folder**. Be sure to specify the folder on which the rule is to run. Normally this should be the Inbox, but a common error is having the rule running on a different folder. This will cause the rule to not function as intended.

- **Misspellings and extra spaces**. If the rule is looking for a word or group of words, a misspelled word or an extra space after the last word will cause the rule to not function properly.

- **Deleted folder**. If a *Mail* folder that is referenced in a rule is deleted, Outlook will recognize the error in the rule and the rule will not function properly. An error message will appear when you open the *Rules and Alerts* dialog box, and the rule will be marked as having an error.

- **Run rules after modifying**. After modifying a rule, you must select **Run Rules Now** in order for the rule to run on those items in your Inbox or the folder on which the rule is to run.

Rules—Effectiveness: It is important to create rules that are effective and efficient. See the following tips to increase the effectiveness of your rules. (Rules are covered in chapter 6.)

- **Keep rules simple**. Rules are most effective when they are simple. The effectiveness of a rule can be diluted if there are too many conditions, actions, and exceptions.

- **Break up a complex rule**. If a rule has multiple conditions, actions, and/or exceptions, try breaking the rule into two or more rules.

- **Ordering rules**. Rules run in the order in which they are listed in the *Rules and Alerts* dialog box. When creating, editing, and managing rules, you must think about the order in which they appear and the conflicts that might occur.

Quick Steps: These can be used and customized to perform one-click actions on email messages. (*Quick Steps* are covered in chapter 6.)

- **Using default *Quick Steps***. Outlook provides a number of preset *Quick Steps*. On some of these *Quick Steps*, you will need to set the criteria of the action. Once the criteria are defined, Outlook will remember and perform the action.

- **Modifying *Quick Steps***. *Quick Steps* can be modified by clicking on the **More** button in the *Quick Steps* group and choosing **Manage Quick Steps**. You can customize an existing *Quick Step* or reset a *Quick Step* to its original default setting. A *Quick Step* can also be modified to perform multiple actions.

- **Creating *Quick Steps***. A new *Quick Step* can be created, or an existing *Quick Step* can be duplicated and modified.

Voting Buttons: This feature in Outlook is an excellent way to gather and track responses to a question via email. Voting buttons are unique to working with Outlook in an Exchange environment. (Voting buttons are covered in chapter 2.)

- **Custom voting buttons**. When creating custom voting buttons, be sure to separate each choice with a semicolon.

- **Tracking responses**. You can track voting responses in two ways. After responses have been received, you can open the original email (from the *Sent Items* folder) and click on the **Tracking** button to view the responses. You can also open a voting response received in your Inbox and click on the *InfoBar* to view responses.

- **Voting buttons not working**. Voting buttons will only work consistently within your Exchange server system. If you are sending an email to recipients outside of your Exchange system, the voting buttons will not track properly.

Signatures: Information can be saved as a signature and inserted into an email. Signatures are not limited to name and company information but can include other commonly used information such as a paragraph or multiple paragraphs of text. Signatures can be inserted individually in an email message, or default signatures can be set. (Signatures are covered in chapter 2.)

- **Default signature**. A signature can be set to automatically appear on all new email messages and/or replies and forwards. Default signatures are set in the *Signatures and Stationery* dialog box. Signatures can also be inserted individually in an email message.

- **Different default signatures for different email accounts**. If you are using multiple email accounts in Outlook, you can set up different default signatures for different email accounts. This can be done in the *Signatures and Stationery* dialog box by selecting the email account and then choosing the default signature.

- **Multiple signatures in an email message**. Only one signature can be used in an email message. If you insert a second signature, it will replace the previous signature.

- **Signature appears different**. When a signature is inserted into an email to which you are replying, it might appear different than you created. If the message is a Plain Text message, the signature will appear as plain text without any styles or colors. Also, if the original message to which you are replying has a theme applied, your signature might appear different.

Search Folders: These folders are virtual folders that display email items that meet the criteria of the folder. These folders don't actually contain any email messages but rather just display them from other folders. Outlook comes with some preset search folders. (Search folders are covered in chapter 6.)

- **Customizing a search folder**. You can customize search folders by specifying which folders are to be searched to locate items matching the criteria.

- **Too many items displayed**. A common error is having the search folder look in all your *Mailbox* folders rather than specifying just the Inbox and subordinate folders. It is probably not a good idea to have your search folders look in the *Deleted Items* and *Sent Items* folders.

- **Deleting search folders**. When you delete a search folder, none of the emails displayed in that folder will be deleted because these items being displayed are actually located in a different folder.

- **Deleting email in a search folder**. When you delete an email from within a search folder, the email will be deleted.

HTML Content in Email Messages: Email messages with embedded HTML (Hypertext Markup Language) are becoming more common. Outlook, by default, will block the images in these messages. (HTML content is covered in chapter 10.)

- **Displaying HTML content**. When an email message with HTML content is received, the images are blocked by Outlook. You can display these images by clicking on the *InfoBar* and choosing **Download Pictures**.

- **Add to *Safe Sender List***. If a sender is added to your *Safe Sender List* (*Junk Email Options*), the HTML content will automatically be displayed when you receive an email from this sender.

Tasks and *To-Do* Lists: The *Tasks List* and the *To-Do List* can be confusing at first glance. Each of these lists has a unique purpose in Outlook. (The *Tasks List*, *To-Do List*, and *To-Do* bar are covered in chapter 5.)

- **To-Do List**. The *To-Do List* is more inclusive than the *Tasks List*. Any Outlook item marked with a flag is included in the *To-Do List*. This list can include email messages, tasks, and contacts.

- **Tasks List**. The *Tasks List* includes only tasks. When a task is created, it is automatically marked with a *Follow Up* flag and is included in both the *Tasks* and *To-Do* lists.

- **To-Do bar**. The *To-Do* bar provides you with a list of the items in the *To-Do List*. The *To-Do* bar also includes a date navigator and upcoming calendar items.

glossary

A

action What Outlook does when a condition to a rule is met.

add-ins Third party software programs that add functionality to Outlook.

address book The collection of names and email addresses from a *Contacts* folder or Global Address List. An address book can be used to populate an email message, meeting request, or task request.

Advanced Find An Outlook feature to refine searches for Outlook items.

appointment A calendar item that is less than 24 hours in duration.

arrangement The way Outlook items are grouped or sorted for display in the *Content area*.

attachment A file or other Outlook item attached to an email message, contact, calendar item, task, or journal.

Auto Account Setup An Outlook feature to automatically detect email account settings and use these settings to create an account in Outlook.

AutoArchive The automatic process of removing older Outlook items and storing them in a separate set of folders in Outlook.

AutoPick An Outlook calendar feature that will pick available meeting times.

B

backstage The window displayed when the *Office* button is clicked.

Bcc Acronym for blind carbon copy and can be used to hide a recipient's name and email address from other recipients of an email message.

business card (or electronic business card) An Outlook item created from a contact record that can be sent to other Outlook users.

C

Calendar An electronic calendar used to create appointments or events, edit these items, replicate calendar items, set electronic reminders, create meeting requests, and share calendar items with other Outlook users or other devices.

Calendar Snapshot Displays calendar details in the body of an email message.

category A grouping tool that can be used on all Outlook items. Categories can be customized by name and color.

Cc Acronym for carbon copy and is used when someone is not the main recipient of the email message.

Clean Up A feature that will delete redundant items related to an email conversation.

condition The part of an Outlook rule for which Outlook is looking when an email is received or sent.

contact A group of related pieces of information (fields) about an individual or company.

contact group A selected set of contacts that are saved together in a group.

context sensitive Groups and buttons will change based on the context of the selection. For example, the *Home Ribbon* will display different groups and buttons depending on whether *Mail* or *Calendar* is selected.

conversation An Outlook arrangement that groups together messages with the same subject.

Customer Manager An Outlook feature that centralizes information and Outlook items around specific contacts or deals.

D

Daily Task List A list of current tasks that appears at the bottom of the calendar in the *Content area* when viewing the calendar in *Day, Week,* or *Work Week* views.

database A file consisting of related groups of information (records), and each record consists of individual pieces of information (fields).

Date Navigator A calendar thumbnail that appears in the *To-Do* bar. Clicking on a date on the date navigator will display that day in the *Content area*.

default settings Those settings that come preset in Outlook. Many default settings can be changed in the *Options* dialog box.

Delay Delivery A feature used to delay the sending of an email message.

delegate An Outlook user who has access to Outlook folders of another Outlook user on an Exchange server.

Delivery Receipt An Outlook feature that can be used to send a receipt to the sender of a message when the recipient(s) receive the email message.

desktop alert A notification that appears when you receive an email message.

dialog box A separate window that opens and provides additional selection options.

Dictate A mail feature that allows you to use speech to text for hands free typing.

digital ID A certificate that can be used to verify your identity with electronically signed documents.

digital signature A method of authenticating an email message.

draft An email message that has been created and saved but not yet sent. A draft message is stored in the *Drafts* folder.

E

email The commonly used term for an electronic message.

Encrypt An email message option that scrambles the message and/or attachment to add security to a message.

event A calendar item that is a full day or more in duration.

exception An optional part of the rule that would cause an action to not be performed when a condition is met.

Exchange ActiveSync A method that allows users to set up a Microsoft account in Outlook.

expand button At the bottom-right corner of some groups is an expand button that will open a dialog box with additional selections.

export The process of sending Outlook data to another file format.

F

Favorites The area of Outlook in the *Navigation* pane that contains links to commonly used mail folders.

field An individual piece of information.

Field Chooser The dialog box that allows users to choose fields to be displayed in the *Content area*.

File **button** The button or tab to the left of the *Home* tab that opens the Outlook *Backstage*.

Flag for Recipient A flag and *InfoBar* message added to an email that recipients receive.

Focused Inbox A feature that automatically learns the user's habits and keeps important messages in the focused inbox moves low priority messages to the *Other* folder.

folder Similar to a physical filing cabinet with folders to organize email and other Outlook items.

Folder List The selection that displays all of the Outlook folders in the *Navigation* pane.

Folder **pane** The section of Outlook at the left-hand side of the window used to navigate between the different Outlook folders.

Follow Up **flag** A flag that can be added to Outlook items that serves as a reminder for the user. When an Outlook item is marked with a follow up flag, that item will also be included in the *To-Do List*.

G

Global Address List The collection of contact records available when using Outlook in conjunction with an Exchange server.

Group A feature on Exchange servers that allows users to manage members, includes a shared location for conversation history, meetings, files, and a notebook.

groups Each *Ribbon* has buttons and options categorized by groups. Some groups can be expanded to open a dialog box with additional options. Groups can also refer to how items are grouped and displayed in the *Content area*.

H

HTML (Hypertext Markup Language) A message format that is the standard format for email messages. This format supports the use of different fonts, styles, colors, and HTML content.

HTTP (Hypertext Transfer Protocol) A type of email account that uses hypertext transfer protocol for sending and receiving email.

I

iCalendar A calendar format that can be sent via email and is compatible with many other software programs.

Ignore An Outlook feature that will move current and future email messages related to a particular conversation to the *Deleted Items* folder.

IMAP (Internet Message Access Protocol) A standard internet protocol for sending and receiving email.

import The process of bringing data from another file into Outlook.

importance A tag that can be added to Outlook items. Importance can be set at high, normal, or low.

InfoBar An informational bar that appears above the *From* line in an email message and provides additional information for the recipient(s).

Instant Search An Outlook feature to quickly search for Outlook items in a specific folder or all folders.

internet service provider (ISP) A company that offers access to the internet and provides email accounts for users.

J

journal An Outlook item to record the amount of time spent working on a document or other task.

junk email An email message that is identified by Outlook as potentially dangerous or from a disreputable source.

L

launcher A button that opens a dialog box with additional options associated with a group of items in a tab.

M

macro A set of programming instructions.

MailTip Alert that warns the user of potential email issues.

Map It A tool that launches a Bing map linked to a Contact address.

meeting (or meeting request) A calendar item that can be used to invite other Outlook users to an appointment or event.

member A contact who is part of a contact group.

Microsoft Exchange Server A file server used to manage Outlook accounts and data within a company.

N

Navigation **bar** The section of Outlook at the bottom left-hand side of the window used to navigate between the different Outlook features and provide access to the folders in each of these areas.

notes Electronic sticky notes that are an excellent way of storing information such as a user name and password to log into a web site, gift ideas for family and friends, or a list of books you'd like to read.

O

Out of Office Assistant An Outlook feature that will allow the user to create an automated response to reply to email received.

Outlook 365 Online The online environment to access your Outlook personal account.

Outlook Data File Outlook stores user data in a .pst file.

Outlook on the Web The online environment to access your Outlook Exchange account.

Outlook Today The opening window that is displayed in the content area when Outlook is started.

P

panes Separate areas within the Outlook window, which include the *Navigation* pane and *Reading* pane.

People Card A new way of viewing contacts in Outlook 2013. The *People Card* includes contact information in a single place and allows you to schedule meetings, send email, or call from a single location.

People pane Displays Outlook items associated with the individual. The *People* pane appears below the *Reading* pane in the main Outlook interface and at the bottom of received email messages, contacts, meetings, and task requests.

permission The amount of access a delegate has to an area of Outlook.

Plain Text A message format that supports only basic text.

POP3 (Post Office Protocol) A standard internet protocol for sending and receiving email.

Priority A tag that can be added to tasks. Priority can be set at high, normal, or low.

Private A tag that can be used on calendar items, contacts, tasks, and journal entries that hides details of these items from delegates or other users with whom areas of Outlook are shared.

Private Key A tool used by the message sender to encrypt an email message.

Programmatic Access Security A feature that controls actions in Outlook when antivirus software is turned off or not functioning properly.

Public Key An authentication tool used by the receiver of a message to unencrypt and view an encrypted message.

Q

Quick Access toolbar The toolbar at the top left of the Outlook window that contains buttons for commonly used features. The *Quick Access* toolbar is available on all Microsoft Office products.

Quick Steps Provide one-click access to email actions.

R

Read Aloud A mail feature that uses text-to-speech to play back messages as spoken words.

Read Receipt An Outlook feature that can be used to send a receipt to the sender of a message when the recipient(s) open the email message.

Reading pane The *Reading* pane can appear below or to the right of the content area. The *Reading* pane displays the Outlook item selected in the content area. The *Reading* pane can also be turned off.

Recall An Outlook feature used to recall a previously sent message.

record A group of related fields about an individual or company.

recurrence A calendar item or task can be set to recur at a specified interval.

reminder A reminder can be set on Outlook items and a reminder dialog box will open to alert the user.

Repair An Outlook feature used to troubleshoot accounts that stop working.

Resend An Outlook feature used to resend a previously sent message.

Ribbon Each Outlook *Ribbon* provides users with groups and buttons for easy access to Outlook features and commands. Each *Ribbon* is accessed by clicking on its tab.

Rich Text Format (RTF) A message format that is unique to Outlook and supports the use of different fonts, styles, colors, and HTML content.

RSS feed Acronym for Really Simple Syndication and can be retrieved by Outlook to allow easy access to headlines of new articles or information from a web site similar to an email message.

rule An Outlook feature that controls the handling of email messages. Rules operate on a logical condition(s), action(s), and exception(s) sequence.

S

Schedule view A calendar view that displays calendar(s) in timeline format.

Scheduling Assistant An Outlook calendar feature that displays multiple calendars in timeline format to help facilitate meeting, appointment, and event scheduling.

ScreenTip A small label that appears when the pointer is placed on a button or area of a *Ribbon*.

search folder A virtual folder that will display email items from other folders that match specified criteria.

sensitivity A tag on an email message that provides a handling message to the recipient.

shortcut A link to a section or item in Outlook.

signature A stored group of text that can be automatically or manually inserted into an email, meeting request, or task request.

S/MIME (Secure/Multipurpose Internet Mail Extensions) A security feature that can be used to confirm that an email was sent and received unaltered and provides details about when the email was opened and read.

stand-alone Refers to Outlook being used without being connected to a Microsoft Exchange server.

T

tab Each *Ribbon* in Outlook has a tab that has the name of that *Ribbon*.

task An electronic notepad used to write down your to-do items and then cross them off as they are completed.

Task List A list of all of the tasks in Outlook.

Task Request A task that is assigned to another Outlook user.

Tell me what you want to do The help feature. Allows you to type what you want to accomplish and gives recommendations and links to additional help online.

Template Customizable predefined email responses.

theme A set of fonts, colors, background, and fill effects in the body of an email message.

To-Do bar The area at the right of the Outlook window that displays a date navigator, upcoming calendar items, and the To-Do items.

To-Do items All Outlook items marked with a follow up flag.

To-Do List A list of Outlook items that have been marked with a follow up flag. This list is available in Tasks.

Tracking A Microsoft Exchange feature that provides the sender with a summary of responses to meeting requests, voting buttons, and read and delivery receipts.

Trust Center The area of Outlook that allows users to customize the security settings.

trusted publisher Reputable organizations that have a digital signature assigned to a macro or program to be run on a user's computer.

V

view How items are displayed in the *Content area*.

voting buttons These preset or custom buttons can be used on an email message to gather responses from recipients.

W

weather bar Displays the weather in the calendar.

index

Symbols

A